Simon Sebag Montefiore is a prizewinning historian whose bestselling books have been published in over forty-five languages. *Catherine the Great and Potemkin* was shortlisted for the Samuel Johnson Prize; *Stalin: The Court of the Red Tsar* won the History Book of the Year Prize at the British Book Awards; *Young Stalin* won the Costa Biography Award, *LA Times* Biography Prize and Le Grand Prix de Biographie; *Jerusalem: The Biography* was a number one bestseller and won the Jewish Book Council's Book of the Year prize; *The Romanovs: 1613–1918* was an international bestseller and won the Lupicaia del Terriccio Book Prize. Montefiore is also the author of the acclaimed Moscow Trilogy of novels *Sashenka*, *Red Sky at Noon* and *One Night in Winter*. He read history at Cambridge University where he received his PhD, and now lives in London with his wife, the novelist Santa Montefiore, and their two children.

www.simonsebagmontefiore.com
@simonmontefiore

Also by Simon Sebag Montefiore

Non-fiction
Catherine the Great and Potemkin
Stalin: The Court of the Red Tsar
Young Stalin
Jerusalem
The Romanovs: 1613–1918

Fiction
Sashenka
One Night in Winter
Red Sky at Noon

Children's fiction (with Santa Montefiore)
The Royal Rabbits of London
The Royal Rabbits of London: Escape from the Tower

John Bew is Professor of History and Foreign Policy at the War Studies Department at King's College London. He is the author of five books, including *Citizen Clem: A Life of Attlee* (2016).

Martyn Frampton is Senior Lecturer in Modern History at Queen Mary, University of London. His publications include *The Long March* (2009) and *Legion of the Rearguard* (2010).

Dan Jones is a journalist, broadcaster and historian. His publications include *The Plantagenets* (2012), *The Hollow Crown* (2015) and *The Templars* (2017).

Claudia Renton, previously an actress in both television and theatre, is a practicing barrister and author of *Those Wild Wyndhams* (2014).

TITANS OF HISTORY

The Giants Who Made Our World

SIMON SEBAG MONTEFIORE

WEIDENFELD & NICOLSON

First published in 2012 by Quercus,
with additional material provided from two volumes,
Heroes (2008) and *Monsters* (2009), also by Quercus.

This updated edition, including new material,
published in 2017 by Weidenfeld & Nicolson
an imprint of The Orion Publishing Group Ltd
Carmelite House, 50 Victoria Embankment
London EC4Y 0DZ

An Hachette UK Company

1 3 5 7 9 10 8 6 4 2

A CIP catalogue record for this book is
available from the British Library.

ISBN 978 1 4746 0646 2

Typeset by Input Data Services Ltd, Somerset

Printed and bound by CPI Group (UK) Ltd, Croydon, CR0 4YY

www.orionbooks.co.uk

TO MY CHILDREN LILY AND SASHA

Contents

ACKNOWLEDGEMENTS

Thank you to David North, Mark Smith, Patrick Carpenter and Josh Ireland; to my fellow contributors Dan Jones, Claudia Renton, John Bew and Martyn Frampton, all gifted historians; my agent Georgina Capel, Anthony Cheetham, Slav Todorov, Richard Milbank, Mark Hawkins-Dady; Professor F. M. Eloischari; Robert Hardman; Jonathan Foreman; and my publisher at Orion, Holly Harley. And, above all, my darling children Lily and Sasha and my wife Santa.

INTRODUCTION

When I was a child, I read a short article – like one of those contained in this book – about the sinister world of Josef Stalin. It fascinated me enough to make me read more on the subject. Many years later, I found myself working in the Russian archives to research my first book on Stalin. My aim is that these short biographies will encourage and inspire readers to find out more about these extraordinary individuals – the men and women who created the world we live in today.

But history is not just the drama of the terrible and thrilling events of times gone by: we must understand our past to understand our present and future. 'Who controls the past controls the future,' wrote George Orwell, author of *1984*, and, 'Who controls the present controls the past.' Karl Marx joked about Napoleon and his nephew Napoleon III that 'all historical facts and personages appear twice – the first time as a tragedy, the second time as farce.' Marx was wrong about this – as he was about much else: history does not repeat itself but it contains many warnings and lessons. Great men and women have rightly studied history to help them steer the present. For example three of the 20th century's most homicidal monsters, Hitler, Stalin and Mao – all of whom appear in this book – were history buffs who spent much of both their misspent youths and their years in power reading about their own historical heroes.

At the time that Hitler came to order the slaughter of European Jewry in the Holocaust, he was encouraged by the Ottoman massacres of the Armenians during the First World War: 'Who now remembers the Armenians?' he mused. The Armenian massacres feature in this book. When Stalin ordered the Great Terror, he looked back to the atrocities of his hero, Ivan the Terrible: 'Who now remembers the nobles killed by Ivan the Terrible?' he asked his henchmen. Ivan the Terrible too is in this book. And Mao Zedong, as he unleashed waves of mass killings on China, was inspired by the First Emperor, another character who can be found in this book's pages.

This is a collection of biographies of individuals who have each somehow changed the course of world events. This list can never be either complete or quite satisfactory: I have chosen the names; thus the list is totally subjective. There may be names you think are missing and others whose very inclusion you question: that is the fun and frustration of lists. You will find familiar names here – Elvis Presley, Jack Kennedy, Jesus Christ, Mozart, Tchaikovsky, Byron, Picasso and Churchill for example – but also many you may not know.

When I started this project, I tried to divide these characters into good and bad, but I realized that this was futile because many of the greatest – Napoleon, Cromwell, Genghis Khan, Peter the Great, to name just a few – combined the heroic with the monstrous. In this book, I leave it to you to make such judgements. It is certainly true, as Voltaire quipped, that 'it is forbidden to kill. Therefore all murderers are punished – unless they kill in large numbers and to the sound of trumpets.' Success often justifies terrible deeds, but in the past, before human rights became essential, crimes were overlooked if they formed a part of great achievements, hence the presence in this book of the likes of Alexander the Great, Tamerlane, Rameses II and Julius Caesar. As Winston Churchill reflected, 'history is written by the victors', and one might add that the cleverest of the tyrants died in their beds, revered by posterity.

The political and artistic genius of even the most admirable of these characters requires ambition, insensitivity, egocentricity, ruthlessness, even madness, as much it demands decency and heroism. 'Reasonable people,' said George Bernard Shaw, 'adapt themselves to the world. Unreasonable people adapt the world to themselves. Therefore change is only possible through unreasonable people.' Greatness needs courage (above all) and willpower, charisma, intelligence and creativity but it also demands characteristics that we often associate with the least admirable people: reckless risk-taking, brutal determination, sexual thrill-seeking, brazen showmanship, obsession close to fixation and something approaching insanity. In other words, the gap between evil and goodness is a thin one: the qualities required for greatness and wickedness, for heroism and monstrosity, for brilliant, decent philanthropy and brutal dystopian murderousness are not too far distant from each other. The Norwegians alone have a word for this: *stormannsgalskap* – the madness of great men.

In the last half-century, many history teachers seemed to enjoy making history as boring as possible, reducing it to the dreariness of mortality rates, tons of coal consumed per household and other economic statistics, but the study of any period in detail shows that the influence of character on events is paramount, whether we are looking at the autocrats of the ancient world or the modern democratic politicians of our own day. In the 21st century, no one who looks at world history after 9/11 would now claim that the character of US President George W. Bush was not decisive in its contribution to the decision to order the catastrophic invasion of Iraq. The erratic presidency of Donald J. Trump and the imperial autocracies of Russia or China demonstrate that even today, personalities have the ability to create and to warp their nations and the wider world. Therefore, we must study them. Plutarch, the inventor of biographical history, puts this best in his introduction to his portraits of Alexander and Caesar: 'It is not histories I am writing, but lives; and in the most glorious deeds, there is not always an indication of virtue, of vice; indeed a small thing like a phrase or a jest often makes a greater revelation of a character than battles where thousands die.'

SIMON SEBAG MONTEFIORE

RAMESES THE GREAT

*c.*1302–1213 BC

*His majesty slaughtered them all; they fell before his horse, and
his majesty was alone, none with him.*

Inscription on the temple walls of Luxor

Rameses II was the most magnificent of the Egyptian pharaohs,
whose long reign – over sixty years – saw both military successes
and some of the most impressive building projects of the ancient
world. He subdued the Hittites and the Libyans, and led Egypt into
a period of creative prosperity but he was probably the villain of
the Exodus.

Some of the greatest wonders of the ancient world owe their
existence to Rameses: he typifies the old-fashioned hero-king,
admired for his conquests and monumental works, often won
and built at a terrible human cost. His reign marks the high point
of the Egypt of the pharaohs, in terms of both imperial power
and artistic output.

During the reign of Rameses' father, Seti I, Egypt had been
involved in struggles for control over Palestine and Syria with
the Hittites of Anatolia (in modern Turkey). Despite some initial
success, when Rameses inherited the throne in 1279 BC Hittite
power extended as far south as Kadesh in Syria.

Having been a ranking military officer, in title at least, since the
age of ten, Rameses was keen to begin his reign with a victory.
However, his first engagement with the Hittites, at the Battle of
Kadesh in 1274, was a strategic failure. Despite winning the battle,

1

Rameses could not consolidate his position and capture the actual city of Kadesh. In the eighth or ninth year of his reign he captured towns in Galilee and Amor, and shortly afterwards he broke through the Hittite defences, taking the Syrian towns of Katna and Tunip. No Egyptian ruler had been in Tunip for at least 120 years.

Despite these successes, Rameses found his advances against the Hittite empire unsustainable, so in 1258 the two sides met at Kadesh and agreed the first recorded peace treaty in history. With typical ostentation, the treaty was inscribed not on lowly papyrus but on silver, in both Egyptian and Hittite. It went further than merely agreeing to end hostilities; it also established an alliance by which both sides agreed to help the other in the event of an attack from a third party. Refugees from the long years of conflict were given protection and the right to return to their homelands.

The treaty ushered in a period of prosperity that lasted until the later years of Rameses' reign. During that time the pharaoh indulged his ruling passion: building gargantuan monuments, many of which can still be seen in various parts of Egypt. The Ramesseum was a vast temple complex built near Kurna, which incorporated a school for scribes. It was decorated with pillars recording victories, such as the Battle of Kadesh, and featured statues of Rameses that stood 56ft (17m) tall and weighed more than 1000 tons. On an even bigger scale were the monuments built at the temple of Abu Simbel. Four colossal statues of Rameses, each more than 65ft (20m) high, dominate the vast façade of the temple, which also includes friezes and depictions of other Egyptian gods and pharaohs, and statues of Rameses' favourites and family. Among these was his favourite wife Nefertari, who had her own, smaller temple built to the northeast. Her tomb in the Valley of the Queens features some of the most magnificent art of the entire ancient Egyptian period.

These works are only a few of the vast architectural projects of Rameses' reign. He completed the buildings of his father, finishing the hall at Karnak and the temple at Abydos, and in the east built the frontier city of Per-Atum. He inscribed his name and records of all his deeds on many of the monuments built by his predecessors. There is little of the surviving architecture of ancient Egypt that does not bear his mark.

It is possible that Rameses was the pharaoh of the biblical book of Exodus, the ruler who cruelly enslaved the Israelites until God sent the ten plagues that persuaded the pharaoh to release the Chosen People: this miraculous escape is celebrated in the Jewish festival of Passover. They were led to freedom by an Israelite boy discovered abandoned in Nile bulrushes and raised as an Egyptian prince with the name Moses. As they wandered through Sinai, God granted Moses the Ten Commandments. If the Israelites obeyed them, God promised them the land of Canaan. When Moses asked the nature of this God, the answer came: 'I am that I am.' But Moses died before he reached Canaan. It is highly likely that Rameses's monuments were built by slave labour. Many Semites did settle in Egypt and Moses' name is Egyptian, which suggests that he at least originated there. There is no reason to doubt that Moses, the first charismatic leader of the monotheistic religions, did receive a divine revelation after such an escape from slavery. Overall, the tradition of a Semitic people escaping captivity is plausible but defies dating.

Rameses was idolized by later Egyptian kings, and his reign was a high-water mark in the military, cultural and imperial achievements of ancient Egypt. He died in 1213, when he was in his early nineties.

DAVID & SOLOMON

*c.*1040–970 BC   *c.*1000–928 BC

Blessed be the Lord thy God, which delighted in thee, to set thee on the throne of Israel: because the Lord loved Israel for ever, therefore made he thee king, to do judgment and justice.

The Queen of Sheba to Solomon, 1 Kings 10:8–9

David and Solomon were rulers of the Israelite kingdom in the 10th century BC at the apex of its splendour, power and wealth. David united the Israelite tribes and made Jerusalem their capital while his son Solomon was the founder of Jerusalem's Temple, the king whose myth transcended the bare bones of biblical history to embrace astonishing abilities as a sage, poet, lover and tamer of nature.

Yet the main source for both is the Bible, probably written centuries later. David was portrayed by the Bible as firstly a holy, ideal king but also as a superb warrior, a poet and harpist, a flawed warlord and adventurer, a collaborator with the Philistines, an adulterer, even a murderer. As an ailing king, he was responsible for the execution of his own rebellious son. The portrait of David is thus a surprisingly rounded and human one.

Born in Bethlehem the son of Jesse, during the reign of King Saul, first monarch of Israel, David was selected by the Prophet Samuel and anointed. Called to court to calm the increasingly demented Saul, he played his harp and won royal favour. When the Philistines invaded, fronted by a giant champion Goliath, David volunteered to fight and though still a boy, killed the champion with a shot from his sling. Now a hero, best friends with Saul's

4

son Jonathan, he married Saul's daughter but, faced with the murderous jealousy of the king, he was forced to flee. He even crossed the lines to the Philistines, accepting a generalship and city from their king. When the Philistines again invaded and fought the Israelites at Mount Gilboa, Saul and Jonathan were both killed. David mourned for them in his famous poetical lament. He became King of Judah, ruling from Hebron while one of Saul's sons ruled the northern tribes of Israel until David united both into his Kingdom of Israel. He attacked the Jebusite city of Jerusalem, which became the new neutral capital of his united kingdom and brought the famed Ark of the Covenant to the city. One day he saw there – bathing on the roof – the beautiful Bathsheba, who was married to one of his generals Uriah the Hittite. David seduced her and had her husband put on the front line in the wars – he was killed. David married Bathsheba. Buying land on the Temple Mount, he planned to build a house of God there, a temple – but God intervened: David was a man of blood and the building of the Temple must wait for his untainted son. In old age, the weakening warlord found it hard to control his seething court with its struggles for the succession. His main problem was his favourite son Absolom, the darling of the crowd, who rebelled against his father, expelling him from Jerusalem. David suppressed the rebellion but Absolom was killed, provoking another heartbreaking lament. According to the biblical account, Solomon was the surviving son of David and Bathsheba, and was anointed king while his father was still alive in order to thwart the conspiratorial aspirations of a half-brother.

After inheriting the kingdom, Solomon soon defeated his foes and built a booming commercial empire, exploiting the strategic location of Palestine – bridging the Mediterranean and Red Sea, Asia and Africa. With armies and merchants, he established a vast network of ports and overland trading routes.

The Bible describes a reign of unparalleled magnificence, in which Solomon reputedly fielded an army of 12,000 cavalarymen and 1400 chariots, and for his pleasure and prestige had a harem of 700 wives and 300 concubines. Such biblical calculations are undoubtedly exaggerations, but possibly not by much. (In Megiddo alone, the remains have been discovered of stalls said to be for 450 horses.) Using marriage to strengthen alliances, Solomon wed the daughters and sisters of kings. His marriage to the daughter of the Egyptian pharaoh, for example, secured him the Canaanite city of Gezer. The biblical report that Solomon granted the visiting Queen of Sheba 'all that she desired, whatever she asked' has prompted three thousand years' worth of rumours that this included a child. Since Sheba was probably a prosperous kingdom that included modern Ethiopia and Yemen, this was another example of Solomon's shrewd realpolitik.

The biblical pinnacle of Solomon's achievement was the Temple he built to house the Ark of the Covenant. Described as a building of stone and cedar, with a magnificently carved interior and an exterior covered in gold, it was a wondrous testament to the greatness of God. After seven years' labour, Solomon was able to dedicate it, and it became the holiest place in the Jewish world, the memory of it cherished for thousands of years at the heart of the Jewish faith: this was the first temple built on Jerusalem's Temple Mount, which is also known by Muslims as the Haram-al-Sharif.

Solomon continued to build, and on a colossal scale, with cities and forts springing up throughout the empire. He constructed breathtaking palaces for his wives, a city wall for Jerusalem, and facilities to encourage foreign traders, including pagan shrines to make them feel at home.

Solomon's 1005 songs and his sayings, collected in the Book of Proverbs, bear witness to his genius and wisdom. Confronted in his court by two women each claiming to be the mother of the same child, Solomon proposed dividing the infant in half, correctly judging that the real mother would abandon her claim rather than see the death of her beloved.

God was said to have granted Solomon power over all living creatures and mastery of the elements. The Jewish Bible, the Tanakh, and the Islamic sacred scripture, the Koran, both cite his miraculous ability to speak the language of the birds and ants, and to control the winds. He was said to have a magic carpet and a magic ring, the Seal of Solomon, which gave him power over demons. In the Persian and Arabic stories that, in a later millennium, made up The Arabian Nights, Solomon is the wizard who imprisoned the djinn (genies) in jars and cast them into the sea.

There was, though, a price to pay: Solomon suffered 'imperial over-stretch': exorbitant taxes oppressed the Hebrews. When the king died, his united realm fragmented into two rival kingdoms, Israel and Judah – this was, the Bible has it, God's punishment for Solomon's breaking of his covenant.

The main sources for David and Solomon are the biblical Books of Samuel, Kings and Chronicles. There is archaeological proof that David existed, though it is doubtful whether Jerusalem was the glorious capital described in the Bible and whether the Davidic kingdom was an empire extending from the Egyptian border to Damascus. Archaeologists now believe the city was small and the kingdom was more of a tribal federation. On the other hand, 10th century traces have been found in the City of David in Jerusalem, which, thanks to its recently discovered Canaanite remains, was clearly a substantial stronghold. The lack of traces in itself is not decisive – after all the Maccabean kingdom a thousand years later, which covered similar territory to that of David, also left remarkably few traces. The court history of David in the Bible does read like a realistic first-hand account of a king in decline. And the Tel

Dan stele, discovered in 1993/4, proves that David was a historical character, using the name 'House of David' to describe the Kingdom of Judah ruled by David's royal descendants.

As for Solomon, there is no archaeological proof of his personal existence. Unlike the rounded portrait of his father, Solomon appears as the legend of an ideal Oriental emperor. There is certainly wishful thinking and perhaps projection in the splendour of his court and brilliance of his life, and it is likely the biblical writers, forming their text four hundred years later, were describing their own Jerusalem, their own Temple, ambitions and nostalgia, in their Solomonic portrait. Little has been found of his Temple in Jerusalem but its biblical description is totally plausible in size and style – typical of temples discovered all over the Middle East. His gold and ivory wealth is credible too – artefacts have been discovered in other Israelite palaces such as those at Samaria. His famous mines resemble ancient 10th century mines recently discovered in Jordan. The size of his army is feasible – a king of Israel fielded 2000 chariots a century later. As for his fortress cities of Megiddo, Gezer and Hazor, the ruins there were initially assigned to Solomon's period but there is now debate as to whether they actually belong to the Kings of Israel a century later. However, new analysis of the stables there suggest that they may be his after all. As for the Temple, it certainly existed within a few years of his death, because Egyptian inscriptions confirm that the Pharoah Sheshonq invaded Judaea and was paid off with the gold of the Jerusalem Temple. If Solomon's magnificence is exaggerated, it is likely he did build the Temple.

NEBUCHADNEZZAR II

c.630–562 BC

Then was Nebuchadnezzar full of fury . . . And he commanded the most mighty men that were in his army to bind Shadrach, Meshach and Abednego, and to cast them into the burning fiery furnace.

Daniel 3:19–20

Nebuchadnezzar was the Lion of Babylon and the Destroyer of Nations. Ruler of the great neo-Babylonian empire from 605 until 562 BC, he was the embodiment of the warrior-king. The Bible records that Nebuchadnezzar was the instrument of God's vengeance on the errant people of Judaea – a destiny he appears to have embraced with relish.

Born some time after 630 BC, Nebuchadnezzar was the eldest son of King Nabopolassar (ruled 626–605 BC), the founder of the Chaldean dynasty in Babylon. Nabopolassar had successfully thrown off the yoke of the Assyrian empire to the north, and had even sacked the great city of Nineveh. Boasting of his triumphs, he had spoken of how he had 'slaughtered the land of Assyria' and 'turned the hostile land into heaps of ruin'.

The young Nebuchadnezzar was involved in his father's military conquests from an early age, and in 605 he oversaw the defeat of Egyptian forces at Carchemish, a victory that helped make the Babylonians the masters of Syria. Nabopolassar died later that year, and Nebuchadnezzar mounted the throne but immediately faced rebellions around his entire empire – which he crushed with remarkable energy and acumen.

Nebuchadnezzar set about expanding his dominions westwards; a marriage alliance with the Median empire to the east had ensured there would be no trouble from that quarter. Between 604 and 601 various local states – including the Jewish kingdom of Judah – submitted to his authority, and Nebuchadnezzar declared his determination to have 'no opponent from horizon to sky'. Buoyed by his success, in 601 Nebuchadnezzar decided to take on his greatest rivals, sending his armies into Egypt. But they were repulsed, and this defeat provoked a series of rebellions amongst Nebuchadnezzar's previously quiescent vassals – most notably Judah.

Nebuchadnezzar returned to his Babylonian homeland, plotting his revenge. After a brief hiatus, he stormed westwards once again, carrying almost all before him. In 597 the kingdom of Judah submitted. Nebuchadnezzar had the king, Jehoiachin, deported to Babylon. In 588, Judah, under the king's uncle Zedekiah, revolted. In 587–586 Nebuchadnezzar marched on defiant Jerusalem, besieged it for months, and finally stormed it, wreaking total destruction. Nebuchadnezzar ordered the city levelled, the people slaughtered, the Jewish Temple razed and Prince Zedekiah was made to witness his sons' executions before his own eyes were gouged out. The Jews were then deported east, where they mourned Zion 'by the rivers of Babylon'.

Nebuchadnezzar's achievements on the battlefield were accompanied by a surge of domestic construction. Drawing on the slave labour of the various peoples he had subjugated, Nebuchadnezzar had numerous temples and public buildings erected or renovated. The extravagant new royal palace, begun by his father, was completed. And, most famously, the king commissioned the Hanging Gardens of Babylon – one of the wonders of the ancient world – as a present for his wife.

In his chronicles and inscriptions, he stressed above all his devotion to the god of Babylon, Marduk, and his love and promotion of justice for his people: he was a reformer who rebuilt the law courts, banned bribery, prosecuted officials for corruption, and stressed that he would not tolerate anyone who persecuted the poor and powerless. Furthermore, the biblical story of his madness is in fact a historical mistake, made deliberately to taint his reputation by the Bible's Jewish writers, who hated him. It was actually the last King of Babylon, Nabonidus (556–539 BC) – who left the city for ten years to live in Arabia – who was said to have gone mad before losing his empire to Persia. Nebuchadnezzar died in 562; his son and heir was a failure, assassinated after two years – and his empire scarcely outlived him by twenty years. Cyrus the Great of Persia conquered Babylon in 539.

Despite his many benevolent achievements, Nebuchadnezzar is indelibly associated with unbridled conquest and the brutal treatment of subject peoples – the Destroyer of Nations who fulfilled the vision of the Jewish prophet Jeremiah: 'He has gone out from his place, to make your land a waste. Your cities will be ruins, without inhabitant.'

SAPPHO

c.630/610–c.570 BC

Dark Sappho! Could not verse immortal save
That breast imbued with such immortal fire?
Could she not live who life immortal gave?
Lord Byron, Childe Harold's Pilgrimage (1819–24),
Canto 2, stanza 39

Sappho was the first and greatest female poet of antiquity. For two and a half millennia she has been an iconic figure, as a creator of ravishing lyrical poetry, the first female literary star and as the original lesbian – a word that derives from her native island of Lesbos.

Though little more than fragments of her work survive today, Sappho was greatly admired and imitated by both Greek and Roman poets in the centuries following her death. A sense of vanished beauty, combined with the mystery of her passionate relationships with young women, have combined to make her the source of numerous legends and the subject of many works of art, from paintings to poems and plays, right up to the present.

Many myths may have sprung up throughout the ages, but the hard facts of Sappho's life are tantalizingly elusive. She was born some time in the late 7th century BC, probably between 630 and 610. Her family seems to have belonged to the aristocratic class on Lesbos, a large Greek island in the Aegean Sea, close to the Turkish mainland. She had at least two brothers, named Larichus and Charaxus, and devoted a poem to the latter. The family probably lived in Mytilene, a significant city on the island. Sappho was said to be small and dark, and her friend the poet Alcaeus called her 'violet-haired, pure, honey-smiling'. Tradition holds that she married a wealthy man called Cercylas who came from the island of Andros. If this is true, then Sappho's famous poem mentioning a young girl called Cleïs probably referred to her daughter.

Whatever the case, Sappho lived a privileged life in the aristocratic circles of Lesbos. Her poems refer to ladies of the court, and to great social occasions such as festivals, parades and military ceremonies. She was probably exiled with the rest of her family to Syracuse in Sicily some time around 600, as a consequence of the turbulent politics of the time. Among the many legends surrounding her is one that tells how she ended her life by throwing herself off the Leucadian Rock out of love for a young sailor called Phaon.

Sappho had a great influence on the young women who surrounded her. She was the leader of a thiasos, a female community that met under her tutelage to develop religious knowledge and social skills. In Victorian times Sappho was portrayed as the head of a girls' finishing school, but the group was not as formal as that. It was more of a close community that prepared its young mem- bers for the demands of marriage and travel away from the island. Membership of Sappho's thiasos was an intensely personal and emo- tional experience. Aphrodite, the Greek goddess of love, sexual desire and beauty, was their guiding deity. Much of Sappho's poetry is dedicated to, or written about, the goddess. Clearly the choice of Aphrodite was related to the goal of marriage, but there were also passionate homoerotic bonds between the members, mirroring the close, sexually charged male bonds that existed in the societies of ancient Athens and Sparta. The atmosphere was certainly not one of sexual abandon, but homoeroticism was without doubt an accepted part of the initiation and bonding of the thiasos. This, together with the highly charged passion that runs through Sappho's poetry, have made her a symbol and heroine of female homosexuality – Sapphic love or lesbianism – throughout the ages.

Sappho created a huge body of work. She turned away from the epic, male tradition of telling tales of the gods and of great heroes, and instead developed a more intimate lyric style, in which the exploration of the poet's own feelings was of supreme importance. Sappho's poems, written in her native Aeolian dialect, were intended to be sung, usually by more than one voice, and accompanied by an instrument. She wrote erotic poems to and about her female friends but also explored every aspect of love, both male and female, including all of love's attendant emotions, from hate and jealousy to frenzied lust and trembling passion:

My flesh runs with soft fire,
My eyes lose sight,
My ears hear nothing but the roar of the wind.
All is black.

Sweat streams off me,
Trembling seizes me,
The colour drains from me like grass in autumn.
I almost die.

In the 3rd century BC, long after her death, Sappho's verse was arranged into nine books, and she continued to enjoy great fame throughout the classical period. The philosopher Plato is said to have considered Sappho the tenth muse. Five centuries after her death the Roman erotic poet Catullus used Sappho's great poem 'To me he appears like a god' as a model for his own work.

Many of Sappho's poems were lost as the classical world began to dim into the Dark Ages, and for many centuries her reputation suffered at the hands of those who found her frankly expressed female eroticism both dangerous and offensive to their concept of femininity. The little of her work that does survive permits us a mere glimpse of her genius.

CYRUS THE GREAT

590/580–530 BC

I am Cyrus, the Great, the King.

Inscription from Pasargadae

Cyrus the Great, king of Persia, was the founder of a powerful empire that dominated western Asia and the eastern Mediterranean for two centuries. He was a peerless ruler: a bold soldier and conqueror but also a tolerant monarch who recognized the human rights of his subjects, permitted religious freedom and liberated the Jews from slavery. In the ancient world he was lauded as the model of the ideal king, even by the Greeks, and was something of a role model for Alexander the Great. Cyrus' realm stretched from modern Israel, Armenia and Turkey in the west to Kazakhstan, Kyrgyzstan and the fringes of the Indian subcontinent in the east.

Cyrus – Kourosh – was born in Persis, in modern-day Iran. His mother was the daughter of Astyages, king of the Medes in western Iran. As with other great heroes, such as Moses or Romulus and Remus, a legend was passed down about Cyrus' birth (recorded by Greek historian Herodotus amongst others). Astyages had a dream that he interpreted as a sign that Cyrus would grow up to overthrow him: his daughter urinated a golden stream that squirted out his entire kingdom. Then he dreamed that a vine was growing out from between his daughter's thighs. Clearly his grandson was a threat so he ordered that the infant be put to death. But Astyages' adviser Harpagus could not bring himself to murder a newborn child, so he gave the baby to a shepherd. By the time Cyrus was ten, his precocious gifts had brought him to the court of Astyages, where his identity was discovered. Astyages allowed the child to live, but had his brutal revenge on Harpagus by tricking him into eating his own son.

Whether true or not, the legend shows that from the start Cyrus was seen as the anointed redeemer of his people. In 559 BC he succeeded his father Cambyses I as head of the Achaemenid dynasty that ruled Persia, which was then restricted to an area of southwest Iran and subject to the Medes. In 554 Cyrus allied himself with Harpagus and led a rebellion against his cruel grandfather Astyages. The revolt gathered momentum during the next four years, and when Cyrus marched against Astyages in 550, the Median soldiers defected. Cyrus captured the land of the Medes and made its capital, Ecbatana, his own.

In 547 he conquered the kingdom of Lydia, (in today's Turkey) deposing the fabulously wealthy king, Croesus. This extended his domain throughout all Asia Minor, and drew in the Greek cities along the coast of the Aegean Sea. Having secured the western frontiers of his empire, Cyrus turned his attention to Babylonia.

Babylon was the most splendid of the ancient cities, but it was governed by a tyrannical and unpopular king, Nabonidus. Cyrus was welcomed as a liberator when, in 539, he dug a canal to divert the River Euphrates and marched his army into the thousand-year-old capital. With Babylon came vast territories including Syria and Palestine, which gave Cyrus control over most of the Near East.

Within twenty years Cyrus had assembled the greatest empire the world had ever seen. He realized that keeping his vast new domain together would require peaceful diplomacy, rather than oppression and violence. So instead of forcing Persian customs and laws on the newly conquered peoples, he set about creating a new concept of world empire, selecting the best elements from different areas to create a better whole. He employed Median advisers, mimicked the dress and cultural influence of the Elamites, and tolerated religious freedom everywhere in return for total political submission. He governed from three capitals: Ecbatana, the Persian capital Pasargadae, and Babylon.

In Babylon he freed the Jews who had been held there in slavery since the 586 BC Babylonian destruction of Jerusalem. Cyrus returned them to Jerusalem; paid for their return, and funded the rebuilding of their temple. As a result, he is the only Gentile to be regarded by some Jews as possessing messianic qualities. His reputation was further enhanced by the discovery in the 19th century of the 'Cyrus Cylinder', an artefact inscribed with details of Cyrus' conquests and his overthrow of tyranny, and declaring his belief in religious toleration and his opposition to slavery. It is recognized by the United Nations as the first charter of human rights. He was no liberal – brutally repressing any political revolts – but he did grant religions tolerance.

Cyrus died on campaign in 530 BC, fighting Tomyris, queen of the Massagetai, who was intent on exacting bloody revenge for the death of her son, who had been held captive by Cyrus. The inscription on Cyrus' tomb in Pasargadae, which still stands, was: 'O man, whoever you are and wherever you come from, for I know you will come, I am Cyrus, who won the Persians their empire. Do not therefore grudge me this little earth that covers my body.' Cyrus was succeeded by his son, Cambyses II, whose short reign resulted in the capture of the only territory in the Near East that Cyrus had not added to his empire: Egypt. The Achaemenid Empire almost fell apart but was refounded by a second Persian empire builder, only distantly related to Cyrus: Darius the Great conquered all of Cyrus's realms, confirmed Cyrus's tolerant policies, invaded Ukraine, India and Europe and organised the first imperial postal service and world currency: he was the Augustus of the Persian empire. But he pushed into Greece, where, before his death in 490 BC and was defeated by the Greeks at Marathon. Darius' successor, his son, Xerxes, failed to crush the Greeks – but his legacy ensured that Cyrus' empire lasted two centuries.

THE BUDDHA

c.563–483 BC

'Are you a god?' – 'No,' he replied.
'Are you a reincarnation of god?' – 'No,' he replied.
'Are you a wizard then?' – 'No.'
'Well, are you a man?' – 'No.'
'So what are you?' they asked in confusion.
'I am awake.'

Siddhartha Gautama, the Buddha,
questioned on the road after his enlightenment

The Buddha's teachings of benevolence, toleration and compassion have a universal appeal that extends far beyond those who expressly follow him. His quest for enlightenment gave rise to a movement that is as much a code of ethics as a religion. It provides each of his followers with the ability and the desire to live a life of contentment and spiritual fulfilment.

According to legend, the Buddha was conceived when Mahamaya, the queen consort to the king of the Sakyas, dreamed that a white elephant had entered her womb. Born in a curtained enclosure in a great park in Nepal, the prince was originally called Siddhartha Gautama (the title Buddha – 'enlightened one' – was conferred on him later). His forename, meaning 'one whose aim is accomplished', was an allusion to priestly predictions that he would achieve greatness either as a ruler or as a religious teacher. Some scholars have suggested his birth was later than tradition holds, around 485 BC.

Seven days after his birth, Gautama's mother died. Eager that his son should follow the former, worldly path, his father had Gautama 'exceedingly delicately nurtured', shielding him from any sight of hardship. He seldom left his palaces (he had one for each season of the year), and on the rare occasions that he did, the king ensured that the streets were filled with young, healthy and cheerful people. Only when he was twenty-nine did chance encounters, first with an old man, then with a sick man and finally with a corpse, alert Gautama to the existence of age, infirmity and death. This realization inspired a fundamental aspect of his doctrine – that human existence is one of suffering.

Subsequently catching sight of a peaceful wanderer with shaven head and yellow robe, Gautama made the 'Great Renunciation', abandoning princely luxury in the hope that an austere religious life might bring greater spiritual fulfilment. Taking one final look at his sleeping wife and newborn son, he stole out of the palace in the dead of night to embrace the life of a wandering ascetic.

Gautama's search for spiritual enlightenment took him first to two renowned sages, but when his abilities outstripped his tutors', he refused their offer to become his disciples. Instead, accompanied by five ascetics, he retreated to the village of Uruvela, where he spent six years trying to attain his ultimate goal of nirvana – an end to suffering. Fasting and denial, however, proved unrewarding. With limbs 'like withered creepers' and 'buttocks like a buffalo's hoof', Gautama framed another of his fundamental tenets: the path to enlightenment lies in a life of moderation – the 'Middle Way'. It was a decision that so disgusted his ascetic companions that they deserted him. Left alone, the thirty-five-year-old Gautama finally reached nirvana while meditating cross-legged under the Bodhi tree. As the watches of the night passed, he fought and triumphed over the devil, saw all his past lives and all the past and future lives of all the world, and with his soul purified emerged as the Buddha: 'my mind was emancipated . . . darkness was dispelled, light arose'.

The Buddha promptly converted the five ascetics and spent the rest of his life teaching the path to enlightenment. He trained his followers to convert others, and his community of monks (the title by which the Buddha addressed his disciples) flourished. Pressed by eager followers, he later instituted an order of nuns. A teacher beyond compare, the Buddha instinctively understood the capacity of each student. When, before his death, he asked his disciples if they had any doubts they wanted clarified, none of them did. Those who came determined to oppose him left converted. When even a famously murderous outlaw became a monk, the Buddha's opponents accused him of being some sort of magician who possessed an 'enticing trick'.

At the age of eighty the Buddha announced his intention to die and did so shortly afterwards, having eaten a pork dish prepared by a lay follower. Despite the pleas of his closest disciple, Ananda, he refused to appoint a successor. Undogmatic to the end, the Buddha held that his teachings should be treated as a set of rational principles that each person should apply for themselves. Resting on a couch – soon to be his deathbed – placed between two trees in a park, he instructed his disciples to let the truth that is dharma (natural order) 'be your Master when I am gone'.

CONFUCIUS

551–479 BC

A man who has regard to the old in order to discover the new is best qualified to teach others.

Confucius, *Analects* 2, 11

Confucius was a Chinese philosopher and teacher whose influence was felt – and continues to be felt – not only in his native China but throughout east Asia. He regarded learning as the true path towards individual self-improvement, but, in a manner that was to leave an indelible mark on all subsequent Eastern thinking, he also took an eminently practical view of his role. He saw culture and refinement, based firmly on tradition and correct ritual observance, as the keys to good governance and sought to put his ideas into practice by taking an active role in the administration of his country.

The son of impoverished aristocrats, Confucius was born and grew up in the state of Lu (the modern-day Shandong province). 'Confucius' is a Latinized version of his name; in the East he is known as Kongzi or Kongfuzi (meaning 'Master Kong' – his family name). Though his exact birthday is not certain, it is celebrated according to east Asian tradition on 28 September.

By the age of fifteen Confucius had become an avid and dedicated learner, with a prodigious appetite for the six disciplines of calligraphy, arithmetic, archery, charioteering, ritual and music. He was particularly noted for his incessant questioning of his teachers at the Grand Temple. As a young man he took various jobs, working as a cowherd, shepherd, stable manager and book-keeper.

He married when he was nineteen and dutifully followed tradition in mourning his mother for three years after she died when he was twenty-three. Confucius spent most of his twenties combining his working life with a devotion to education.

His knowledge of the six disciplines was bolstered by extensive study of history and poetry, and in his thirties he was ready to start on a brilliant teaching career. Before his day, teaching was usually carried out by private tutors to the children of the wealthy, or else it was essentially vocational training in administrative posts. Confucius took a radical new approach, advocating learning for all as a means of benefiting both pupil and society alike. He started a programme of study designed for potential leaders, reasoning that an educated ruler would be able to disseminate his learning to his subjects and so improve society as a whole.

Unlike many other wise men of the time, who shunned human interaction and were detached from society, Confucius engaged wholeheartedly with the government of his state. He served as a magistrate, rising to become assistant minister of public works, and then was promoted to the position of minister of justice. When he was fifty-three, he became chief minister to the king of Lu, accompanying him on diplomatic missions.

But Confucius' influence on the king and his strict moral principles alienated him from the rest of the court, who conspired to obstruct him. Realizing that his message was going unheeded, Confucius left the court and went into self-imposed exile. During the twelve years of his absence, Confucius toured the states of Wei, Song, Chen and Cai, teaching and developing his philosophy. His reputation as the 'wooden tongue in the bell of the age' began to spread.

Confucius' thinking was partly a reaction to the extreme lawlessness of his age, a time of unrest in which neighbouring warlords were constantly in conflict with one another. His position was essentially conservative, emphasizing the importance of tradition, proper ritual observance and respect for elders and ancestors. He saw himself as a conduit of learning, who invented nothing but simply passed on received wisdom and encouraged self-inquiry and the personal quest for knowledge. He believed that rulers, chosen on merit rather than according to lineage, should not impose rules and govern by means of threats of punishment, but rather should develop their own virtues and so earn the devotion of their subjects.

Confucius' sayings were collected after his death in the Analects, which form the basis of what Westerners now call Confucianism (the term does not translate meaningfully into Chinese). His most famous precept, the so-called 'golden rule', is mirrored in countless later moral systems (including Christianity). It is well captured in the following exchange:

Adept Kung asked: Is there one word that can guide a person in life?
The master replied: How about shu? Never impose on others what you would not choose for yourself.

The idea of *shu* (roughly, reciprocity) runs through Confucius' ethics, which are also underpinned by the notions of *li, yi* and *ren*. The concept of *li* equates approximately with ritual, *yi* with righteousness, and *ren* with kindness or empathy.

Confucius ended his exile aged sixty-seven, returning to the state of Lu to write and teach. Burdened by the loss of his son, he died at the age of seventy-three.

SUN TZU

*c.*544BC–496 BC

> *Be extremely subtle, even to the point of formlessness. Be extremely*
> *mysterious, even to the point of soundlessness. Thereby you can*
> *be the director of the opponent's fate.*

Sun Tzu (or Sunzi), was the author of a treatise on war that is still hugely important in military thought, business, politics and the psychology of human relationships.

Little is known about Sun Tzu's life but he was a contemporary of Confucius. He is believed to have been a general for the state of Wu towards the end of the Spring and Autumn Period (770–476 BC). In *The Art of War* he distilled his military genius into an organized series of instructions and axioms that covered every aspect of waging a successful war.

One of the most striking things about this work is Sun Tzu's insistence that although 'the art of war is of vital importance to the state', it is often better to avoid battle, which he views as costly, disruptive and damaging to the population at large:

> *To fight and conquer in all your battles is not supreme excellence;*
> *supreme excellence consists in breaking the enemy's resistance*
> *without fighting.*

Where fighting cannot be avoided, preparation and knowledge of the enemy are all:

If you know the enemy and know yourself, you need not fear the result of a hundred battles. If you know yourself but not the enemy, for every victory gained you will also suffer a defeat. If you know neither the enemy nor yourself, you will succumb in every battle.

To forsake this advice because it necessitates going to the expense of gathering intelligence is simply wrong:

To remain in ignorance of the enemy's condition simply because one begrudges the outlay of a hundred ounces of silver . . . is the height of inhumanity.

As Sun Tzu makes clear in many passages, attention to detail can win the battle before it begins: 'making no mistakes is what establishes the certainty of victory, for it means conquering an enemy that is already defeated'. And this, in theory, ought to minimize the damage done by battle:

The best thing of all is to take the enemy's country whole and intact; to shatter and destroy it is not so good. So, too, it is better to capture an army entire than to destroy it, to capture a regiment, a detachment or a company entire than to destroy them.

Though he could be dispassionate and ruthless about war, Sun Tzu stresses the need for violence and bloodshed only as far as is absolutely necessary. Enemy soldiers should be kindly treated and lengthy, destructive campaigns avoided in favour of swift victory. It is Sun Tzu's mixture of brilliant strategy and tactical analysis with a concern for human welfare that makes him relevant even to this day.

LEONIDAS

d. 480 BC

*In the course of that fight Leonidas fell, having fought like a man
indeed. Many distinguished Spartans were killed at his side – their
names, like the names of all the three hundred . . . deserve to be
remembered.*

Herodotus, *The Histories*, Book VII

The last stand of Leonidas and his 300 against the might of Persia
spread the legend of Spartan bravery across the world. A peerless
fighter, Leonidas sacrificed himself for Greek freedom. His intrepid defence at Thermopylae gave the Greeks the time and the
inspiration to defeat the massively superior Persian force that sought
to overwhelm them.

For over a decade the Greeks had been fighting the Persians, who
were determined to absorb them into their empire. Faced with Greek
intransigence, the Persian Great King Xerxes assembled the greatest
army the ancient world had ever seen. In 480 BC it crossed the Dardanelles on a bridge of boats, then swarmed along the coast towards
the Greek heartlands. Xerxes' progress seemed inexorable, Greece's
subjugation inevitable.

Ten years or so earlier, Leonidas had succeeded to the throne
of Sparta, a city-state in the area of the southeastern Peloponnese
known as Lacedaemonia. The latter name gives us the word 'laconic',
for the Spartans were renowned for their terseness of speech – as
exemplified by the Spartan discipline, toughness and endurance
that Leonidas and his fellows were to display.

There was only one career for a male Spartan: as a fighting machine. In an education system as ruthless as it was effective, Sparta raised men who belonged, as the Roman historian Plutarch said, 'entirely to their country and not to themselves'.

Sparta was frozen into an ancient constitution laid down in the 7th century BC by the semi-legendary King Lycurgus. Innovation was a mortal offence, individualism mercilessly eradicated. Foreigners were discouraged, money was replaced by iron bars, meals were taken in common. Nothing was allowed to divide the brotherhood of Sparta.

Sparta began selecting its warriors at birth. Inspecting all male infants, the council of elders weeded out the sickly and malformed, abandoning them on the mountainside to die. The sturdy, destined to protect rather than burden the state, were sent back to their fathers to be reared by nurses.

At the age of seven boys were taken into the care of the state, which set about transforming them into some of the toughest warriors the world has ever seen. The balletic grace of Sparta's soldiers was honed by years of gymnastics and athletics, all undertaken in the nude. So endlessly did Spartans indulge in such exercises that the Athenians gave them the nickname *phaenomerides*, the 'displayers of thighs'.

Boys were taught only the skills needed in war. Literacy was of no importance, and music only valued insofar as it encouraged heroic thoughts. Cunning, endurance, stamina and boldness were all prized. The boys slept on pallets made of rushes they gathered themselves. They were kept hungry to encourage them to take the initiative and steal food and were only punished if they were caught.

Flogging competitions tested their mental and physical stamina. Some boys died, but as long as they had betrayed no flicker of emotion they were commemorated with a statue. Pitched into battles against each other, the boys went at it with unremitting savagery. They spent long periods fending for themselves in the wild. As the twenty-year-old soldier-citizens approached the end of their training, the elite were sent out to live a guerrilla existence, using *helots* (slaves) as target practice.

All young men had to live in barracks until they were thirty. They were encouraged to marry, but they could only visit their wives by stealth. 'Some of them,' reports Plutarch, 'became fathers before they looked upon their own wives by daylight.' It mattered little: their education had produced an unbreakable bond. 'They neither would nor could live alone,' Plutarch continues, 'but were in manner as men incorporated one with another.'

'A city will be well fortified which is surrounded by brave men and not by bricks,' declared Lycurgus. Sparta's citizens did not work – that was for the *helots*, who outnumbered them twenty-five to one. They were rather born and bred to fight, so in this respect the heroism of the 300 at Thermopylae should not surprise us.

It was said that the Delphic Oracle had prophesied to Leonidas that only the sacrifice of a king descended from Hercules could save his city from destruction. Leonidas, the seventeenth king of the Agiad dynasty, knew that his family claimed descent from Hercules and thus from Zeus. When representatives of the terrified Greek city-states met to confer at Corinth to discuss Xerxes' advance, Leonidas volunteered to lead his men to head off the Persians at the only choke-point left: the narrow pass of Thermopylae.

It seemed an unwinnable battle from the start. With the Athenians setting sail to fight the Persians at sea and the other city-states apparently resigned to their fate and focusing instead on securing victory at the Olympics, Leonidas was given a force of no more than 7000 Greeks to combat the vast Persian army. Even Sparta – occupied by its own ceremonial games and wanting to re-serve the mass of its troops to defend the Isthmus of Corinth, the gateway to the Peloponnese – allowed its king just 300 soldiers.

Leonidas, who chose only men with sons old enough to assume their fathers' role, seemed in no doubt that he was going to his death, telling his wife: 'Marry a good man and have good children.'

The laconic wit of the Lacedaemonians spread the legend of Spartan intrepidity across the world. Asked by Xerxes' envoy to order his army to lay down its arms, Leonidas replied, 'Come and get them.' His men were no less defiant. When the Persians threatened to let loose so many arrows that the light of the sun would be blotted out, one Spartan commented, 'So much the better. We will fight in the shade.'

Xerxes was confident of victory after his scout reported that the Spartans appeared to be preparing for battle by performing stretching exercises and combing their long hair. But as wave upon wave of Persians tried to force their way through the pass the next day, they were cut down in their thousands. The oncoming Persians were forced to scale a wall of their fallen comrades, and then they found themselves in a death trap. After three days of hurling tens of thousands of men at the small band of Greeks, Xerxes withdrew to rethink.

Had it not been for the actions of one man, the Delphic Oracle might have been proved false. But when a Greek traitor called Ephialtes showed the Persians a hidden path that led behind Greek lines, the fate of Leonidas was sealed. Leonidas sent away the bulk of his army. With 700 Thespians who chose to stay, and 400 Thebans who deserted almost immediately, Leonidas and his 300 Spartans set themselves up as a rearguard to delay the Persian advance and protect the retreating Greeks. They knew they would die fighting.

They fought with spears. When their spears shattered they fought with swords. Once those were broken, they fought with teeth and hands until they fell. The historian Herodotus estimated that this tiny band inflicted losses of 20,000 on the Persians. When Leonidas' body was recovered, Xerxes, raging impotently at his ignominious victory, ordered that the dead king be decapitated and his body crucified. Forty years later Leonidas' remains were finally returned to the Spartans, to be buried with the honour they were due.

Leonidas' last stand inspired the Greeks to rally and fight for their freedom. Their subsequent victories over the Persians at sea (Salamis) and on land (Plataea) ensured that Xerxes was the first, and last, Persian sovereign to set foot on Greek soil. The suicidal bravery of the Spartans, so gloriously victorious in defeat, is commemorated in a famous epitaph inscribed on a stone marking the place where they fell at Thermopylae:

> Go tell it in Sparta, stranger passing by,
> That here, obedient to their laws, we lie.

HERODOTUS

c.484–430/420 BC

[I write] in the hope of thereby preserving from decay the remembrance of what men have done.

Herodotus, *The Histories*, Book I

Herodotus was the West's 'Father of History'. An adventurous traveller, he used his gift for storytelling to recount the upheavals affecting the lands where Europe, Asia and Africa meet. He is best known as a hawk-eyed observer of the epic wars between Greece and Persia in the 5th century BC, but he also charted the growing rivalry between Athens and Sparta.

Herodotus was the first to employ many of the techniques of

modern historical writing, and although his credibility has sometimes been called into question, modern research has often proved
him right.

He was probably born in Halicarnassus, then under Persian
rule, but he lived for much of his life in Athens, where he met
the Greek dramatist Sophocles. Herodotus left Athens for Thurii,
a colony in southern Italy that was sponsored by Athens. The last
event recorded by Herodotus took place in 430 BC, although it is
not certain when he died.

If our knowledge of his life is sketchy, our understanding of
Herodotus' times is exceptional, thanks to the work he undertook.
He travelled extensively through Egypt, Libya, Syria, Babylonia,
Lydia and Phrygia. He sailed up the Hellespont to Byzantium, vis-
ited Thrace and Macedonia, and journeyed north to the Danube,
then travelled east along the northern coast of the Black Sea.

Herodotus' masterpiece was his *Histories*, divided into nine
books, each named after one of the Greek muses. The first five
books concern the background to the Graeco-Persian Wars of
499–479 BC. The final four comprise a history of the wars themselves, culminating in the invasion of Greece by the Persian king
Xerxes at the head of a vast army.

The books setting up the background to the wars are subtle
works that give a wealth of geographical and political information
about the Persian empire and its rulers. They also chart the fundamental differences between Persian and Greek society, with a level
of comparison that was unmatched by the city chroniclers who had
been the writers of history before Herodotus. Herodotus notes how
the Persian empire, although made up of diverse peoples divided by
religion, geography and language, nevertheless acts with a remarkable unity. The Greeks, by contrast, drawn from a relatively small
pool of culturally homogeneous city-states, are prone to faction
and infighting.

Such astute general observations help to provide an explanation for the events contemporary with Herodotus' own life, when the political rivalries and disputes within Athens affected the course of the bloody contests between the Athenians and the Spartans. This grand, thematic approach was something quite new in historical writing.

The Histories is a detailed account of four generations of Persian kings and their conquests. Herodotus first describes Cyrus the Great's expedition to Lydia, followed by Cambyses' conquest of Egypt and his stalled expedition to Ethiopia. After Cambyses' madness and death comes the reorganization and further expansion of the empire under Darius the Great, and finally Herodotus recounts the campaigns led by Xerxes against the Greeks.

Herodotus tends to attach importance to the actions, personalities and squabbles of individual protagonists. Xerxes is portrayed as arrogant, petulant, savage and cruel, and Herodotus suggests that it was these defects of character that caused his invasion to fail.

For Herodotus, pride always comes before a fall, but he emphasizes that such failures are not the punishment of the gods, but rather result from human mistakes. This rational approach, in which the gods did not intervene in the affairs of men, was a major innovation and formed the basis for the tradition of Western history.

The 'Father of History', has also been called the 'Father of Lies'. It is true that some of his tales, such as that of the giant man-eating ants, are fables. But his methods were those of a true historian: he compared his sources wherever possible. He was also a consummate storyteller; the first historian, and arguably one of the greatest ever.

ALCIBIADES

c.450–404 BC

It is wiser not to rear a lion's whelp, but if you do, you must accept its ways.

> The dramatist Aeschylus' verdict on Alcibiades
> (as represented by Aristophanes in his play *The Frogs*)

Alcibiades was the gilded youth in the golden age of classical Greece, who took centre stage in the life-and-death struggle that enveloped Athens in the second half of the 5th century BC. A dazzling politician and brilliant military leader, he was uniquely blessed: well-born, charming, beautiful, charismatic, quick-witted, eloquent. But his virtues were matched by deep flaws: vanity, unscrupulousness and egotism. Hamstrung by his political enemies and by his own short-comings, in the end he was unable to harness his talents to save his city from destruction.

At the time of Alcibiades' birth in or just before 450 BC, the city of Athens was at the height of its power and wealth. Less than thirty years earlier, the Athenians had led an alliance of Greek states to turn back the armies of Persian invaders rolling in from the east. But what had started as a voluntary league of equals had gradually been transformed into an Athenian maritime empire. Throughout Alcibiades' adolescence there had been growing tension and eventually, in 431, Sparta, a conservative state increasingly alarmed at the expansive imperial ambitions of Athens, could take no more and attacked, so precipitating the Peloponnesian War. This was to engulf the Greek world for the next twenty-seven years and finally led to the total defeat of Athens.

Alcibiades' father had died in battle in 447, leaving the boy to be raised in the household of Pericles, the greatest Athenian statesman and heroic leader of the day. Alcibiades was a follower of the philosopher Socrates and his superb oratorical skills must in part have been due to the excellent grounding in rhetoric he received at the hands of Socrates and Pericles.

In 421, after ten years of indecisive fighting, Athens and Sparta negotiated the precarious Peace of Nicias. Piqued at being considered too young to take part in the peace talks, Alcibiades instead set about undermining them, first holding private discussions with the Spartan ambassadors and then attempting to ridicule them before the Athenian assembly. He was elected general in 420 and orchestrated a new alliance against Sparta, but his aggressive ambitions were thwarted two years later when the new allies were heavily defeated by the Spartans at Mantinea.

The defining moment of Alcibiades' career came in 415, when he once again took up the cause of the war party by championing an ambitious plan to send a major expeditionary force to attack the city of Syracuse in Sicily. His view prevailed and he was appointed one of the three generals to lead the expedition. However, as he was about to set sail, his enemies managed to embroil him (perhaps unjustly) in scandal when the hermoi – sacred boundary posts positioned all around Athens – were mysteriously mutilated. The outrage was considered a bad omen for the mission, which nevertheless set sail with the charges unresolved.

Recalled to face trial, Alcibiades fled and was sentenced to death in his absence. Now revealing the full depths of his vengeance, he defected to Sparta and persuaded them to send forces to re-inforce Syracuse, which contributed to the catastrophic defeat of the Athenians two years later. Then he encouraged Sparta to build a fortified outpost at Decelea, in sight of the city of Athens. This cut off the Athenians from their homes, crops and silver mines, forcing them to live inside the city walls all year round.

Having caused trouble for Athens at home, Alcibiades moved east to Ionia (Asia Minor), fomenting revolts among Athens' subject allies. However, his scheming with Sparta came to an abrupt end when he was suspected of having an affair with the Spartan king's wife. In mortal danger, he defected once again, this time to Persia. Now in negotiation with the Persians, Alcibiades was involved in stirring up political unrest in Athens, where in 411 a new (albeit short-lived) oligarchic regime was set up.

Believing (unrealistic) promises of Persian assistance, the Athenian fleet reinstated Alcibiades as general. Between 411 and 408 he redeemed himself by leading the Athenians to a spectacular recovery with a series of military successes. Most notably, he inflicted a crushing defeat on the Spartan fleet at Cyzicus in 410 and helped Athens regain control over the supply route through the Black Sea.

Invited back to Athens and cleared of any impropriety, Alcibiades was given complete command of the war on land and at sea. But following a naval setback at Notium in 406 (due to the disobedience of one of his subordinates – Alcibiades himself was absent), he lost his position. In 405, following a catastrophic naval defeat at Aegospotami – which occurred despite Alcibiades' warnings to the Athenian commanders – he returned to Persia, where he was murdered, probably at the instigation of Sparta, in 404.

Alcibiades was a mass of contradictions, a fascinating, duplicitous meteor capable of brilliance one moment and dark recklessness the next. At its times of greatest need, Athens could not trust him enough to make use of his colossal talents, leading finally to his own destruction and that of his city.

PLATO

*c.*428–347 BC

Courage is knowing what not to fear.

Plato

Pupil of Socrates and teacher of Aristotle, Plato showed such vision and originality in his thinking that he stands as the second and central figure in the great triumvirate that laid the foundations of Western thought.

Born to a noble Athenian family, Plato could trace his ancestry back to the last kings of Athens. He was a disciple and fervent admirer of the plebeian Socrates, whose refusal to toe the line and temper his ideas brought about his enforced suicide for impiety and corruption of youth in 399 BC.

Disappointed by the demagogic democracy of Athens, Plato travelled abroad, to Italy and to Syracuse. On his return to Athens he founded the Academy in 387 BC, an institution that trained the greatest thinkers of the next generation, of which Aristotle was the brightest star. Teaching at the Academy until his death forty years later, Plato wrote his greatest works, including the many Socratic dialogues featuring his inspirational tutor and the monumental *Republic*, in which he outlines the ideal state.

It has been said that Western philosophy exists as footnotes to Plato. An extreme rationalist, Plato was a proponent of the philosopher-ruler of the *Republic*, who would reign only according to reason. But as experience suggested that no man was capable of such restraint, he proposed that laws must rigidly circumscribe a

36

ruler's actions. He adopted the ideas of Socrates in arguing that the good is an immutable and fundamental concept or 'form'. While opinion may shift, Plato argued, knowledge is eternal and unchanging; goodness is objective, inextricably linked to justice and personal well-being.

Plato was the first major thinker to express the idea that the higher functions of the mind (*psyche*) are, or should be, in control of the base passions and appetites of the body. His belief that the soul is a prisoner inside the body was countered by Aristotle's view that it is an inherent part of the body. However despite these differences in their philosophy, his disciple Aristotle so esteemed Plato that he considered it 'blasphemy in the extreme even to praise' such a genius.

ARISTOTLE

384–322 BC

Aristotle was, and still is, the sovereign lord of the understanding.
Samuel Taylor Coleridge

Aristotle was the philosophical giant who, along with Plato and Socrates, laid the principal foundations of Western thought. He was the ultimate polymath: ethicist, physicist, biologist, psychologist, metaphysicist, logician, literary and political theorist. Being tutor to Alexander the Great ensured that his feet stayed firmly on the ground.

The son of Macedonia's court physician, Aristotle spent twenty years studying under Plato at his Academy in Athens. His unquench-able thirst for knowledge prompted his tutor to comment that he needed 'a bridle', and Aristotle's enthusiasm shines through in his scientific works. His *History of Animals*, begun in the decade he spent travelling after Plato's death, is a complete record of every species of animal known to the Greek world; he charts innumerable organisms, using his minute observations to explain their structure. There are of course some errors (a bison, for instance, is unlikely to defend itself by projectile excretion), but this work of genius and tireless energy nevertheless paved the way for the science of zoology.

A willingness to refine or contradict previous doctrines and opinions; to pose questions to which he did not know the answers; to wrestle with his own ideas – in all these ways, Aristotle transformed the methodology of thought. His surviving works do not make easy reading. They are mostly fragments, used as notes when he lectured at the academies he established on his travels and at the Lyceum, the covered garden in which he taught on his return to Athens. The school of philosophy that Aristotle founded – the Peripatetic school – is believed to have been named after the Lyceum's walkway (*peripatos*), where he delivered his lectures with lucidity and wit. Greece's brightest youth flocked to learn from him.

This wealthy dandy, who sported jewellery and a fashionable haircut, championed the mind above all else. Aristotle's philosophy insisted on thought as man's greatest attribute. Philosophical speculation implied civilization: only when a person had secured everything else could he afford the luxury of pure, untrammelled thought. In his works on ethics Aristotle came to the conclusion that human goodness derives from rational thought – that 'the good of man is the active exercise of his soul's faculties in conformity with excellence'; it is an assertion of the uniqueness of mankind that has influenced our understanding of civilization ever since.

The reputedly lisping logician established a new vocabulary of thought. Aristotle made logic an independent branch of philosophy. Struggling to express his meaning more precisely, he coined new terms for his concepts: substance, essence, potential, energy.

He argued that as language is a distinctively human trait, it is therefore an expression of the soul. He developed the idea that analysis of our words is the key to understanding our thought. His system of syllogistic logic (e.g. 'All men are mortal; Greeks are men; therefore Greeks are mortal') was the cornerstone of logical analysis for over 2000 years.

At the age of forty-two, Aristotle returned to his homeland to tutor the Macedonian king's thirteen-year-old son Alexander. Aristotle tried to instil in his charge two of Greece's greatest contributions to civilization: epic heroism and philosophy. How much of Aristotle's political theory he absorbed is open to debate. Aristotle's ideas were based on the belief that Greeks were superior to other races. While he recognized that governments must be chosen in accordance with their citizens' needs and capacities, he favoured the city-state ruled by an enlightened oligarchy as the best form of government. Such ideas may not have had much impact on Alexander as that autocratic ruler forged his empire. Nevertheless, Aristotle's beliefs were a vast advance on contemporary political concepts and they fundamentally influenced the development of Greek civilization.

In his *Poetics* Aristotle established the fundamentals of tragedy that would long be observed in drama: unity of action and a central character whose tragic flaw, such as *hubris* (excess of pride), brings about his downfall. Aristotle also identified a process of cleansing or purification (*catharsis*) in which the audience's feelings of pity and fear are purged by experiencing them vicariously through the actions played out on stage.

The death of Alexander in 323 BC released a wave of anti-Macedonian sentiment in Athens, forcing Aristotle to flee the city. Referring to the death of that other great thinker Socrates, Aristotle reportedly said he feared the Athenians would sin twice against philosophy. He withdrew to his mother's estates on the island of Euboea but died of a stomach complaint just one year later.

Aristotle was reputedly kind and affectionate and his will was generous both to his children and servants. It makes reference (as his philosophy implies) to a happy family life. He described man as 'a monument of frailty', but the ultimate conclusion of his philosophy is optimistic. According to Plato, the soul is trapped in the body, desperate to escape the world of change and illusion. Aristotle argued instead that the soul is an inherent part of the body and that life is desirable for its own sake.

Aristotle's world view, like so much of his thought, delighted in man and celebrated his potential. He believed that 'All men by nature desire to know', a statement which offers a fitting testimony to the enduring thirst for knowledge that drove him throughout his life.

ALEXANDER THE GREAT

356–323 BC

He would not have remained content with any of his conquests, not even if he had added the British Isles to Europe; he would always have reached beyond for something unknown, and if there had been no other competition, he would have competed against himself.

Arrian, *The Anabasis* (c.AD 150),
translated as *Alexander's Expedition*, 7.1

Alexander III of Macedon stretched the limits of the possible. In little more than a decade of brilliant military campaigning, he forged the most extensive empire the world had seen, stretching from Greece and Egypt in the west to India in the east and taking in all or part of seventeen modern states. It is said that he wept that there were no more worlds to conquer. With some justification, the statue erected to him after his death bore the legend 'I hold the Earth'.

Alexander was one of the greatest military commanders who has ever lived. Julius Caesar, a superb general in his own right, was plunged into deep despair whenever he pondered Alexander's achievements. Probably short with red-blonde hair, Alexander was distinguished by his personal beauty, grace and courage and above all for his tolerance and chivalry, but he was also ruthless in battle and in court politics, and a hard drinker who personally murdered one of his top commanders.

Within two years of inheriting the Macedonian throne on the assassination of his remarkable warrior-king father, Philip II of Macedon, who had conquered much of Greece, the small and tough twenty-two-year-old had united Greece's disparate city-states under his leadership in order to wage war on the mighty Persian empire. It was the Hellenic world's most prized dream, and a goal Philip had spent his life working towards.

Alexander set out on his mission in 334 BC. Within two years the Persians had been totally defeated in victories such as that at Issus, which showed Alexander's military genius and tactical virtuosity. He went on to establish himself at the head of his own empire, one that included not only Greece and Macedonia but also the entire Middle East, from Egypt and Asia Minor to Mesopotamia, Persia and beyond, into Afghanistan, parts of central Asia and, on the far side of the Hindu Kush mountains, the rich valley of the Indus. Only the final, stubborn refusal of his Macedonian army to breach the limits of the known world prevented him from going further. When he died in Babylon, aged just thirty-two, he was planning the conquest of Arabia and may have had designs on the western Mediterranean.

Alexander's rule united East and West for the first time. Perhaps influenced by his boyhood tutor, Aristotle, Alexander was determined to govern well. He ordered his ministers to 'break up the oligarchies everywhere and set up democracies instead'. He forbade his armies to plunder conquered lands, and he founded new cities galore – usually named Alexandria. The greatest of these, at the mouth of the Nile Delta, became for many centuries the intellectual and commercial centre of the Mediterranean world. Alexander wanted to create an empire fusing the best of both Greek and Eastern cultures. He recruited Persians into his armies and assigned Persian wives to his generals, sending back to Europe any Macedonians who resisted this enforced equality. He himself married the daughter of the dethroned Persian king.

Alexander was revered as a god in his own lifetime. He was reputedly a descendant of Achilles on his mother's side, and rumours of Alexander's supernatural abilities abounded, reinforced by his unnatural speed and apparent personal invincibility in battle. Described by a friend as 'the only philosopher whom I have ever seen in arms', he loved poetry and music. As a boy he declared that if he could only save one possession it would be Homer's *Iliad*. He was always alert to symbolism. On first setting foot on the shores of the Persian empire, in Asia Minor, his first act was to make a pilgrimage to Troy to honour his ancestor Achilles. He named Bucephala, a town on the Indus, after his beloved horse Bucephalus, which had died in battle.

'Sex and sleep alone make me conscious that I am mortal,' he reportedly declared. He had several wives and mistresses, including two Persian princesses and the Bactrian beauty Roxana, with whom he had a son, Alexander IV. But his great love was his boyhood friend Hephaistion, who became one of his generals and top advisors. Alexander was heartbroken by his early death – although later he enjoyed relationships with others, including Bagoas, a Persian eunuch.

Alexander could be merciless. On succeeding to the throne after his father's assassination, he executed all rival claimants, including his infant half-brother. He executed one of his greatest friends for treason, and also the friend's blameless father, his veteran general, Parmenion: Alexander refused to run the risk of paternal vengeance. He murdered one of his oldest comrades, Cleitus the Black, who had once saved his life, during a drunken row at a royal banquet. Alexander ran him though with a javelin – a crime he deeply regretted, which revealed the vicious rivalries of his court. He enslaved or crucified all the Tyrians after they resisted his siege of their city and razed Thebes to the ground, a warning to the restless Greek city-states of what they could expect from rebellion. Towards the end of his life he became increasingly despotic.

Alexander's treatment of his enemies, however, often demonstrated his nobility of spirit. When an Indian king demanded to face him in battle, Alexander fought and defeated him, but rewarded him with the restoration of his kingdom and that of a less fortunate neighbour as well. He treated the wives of Darius, the defeated Persian king, with 'the utmost delicacy and respect' and allowed the Jews, Persians and others to worship as they wished.

Alexander changed the face of the world by making Hellenism – the Greek way of life – into the global culture, but he increasingly adopted Perisan customs of kingship. In June 323, Alexander fell ill with a fever, possibly caused by bad water, an excess of strong wine, or poison. Most likely it was typhoid, malaria or pancreatitis. Unable to speak, his weeping soliders filed past him – but there had been much tension between the king and his advisors about his pro-Persian culture and plans for further conquests. He died on 10 or 11 June, aged just thirty-two. There was no heir (although Roxana was pregnant with the future Alexander IV), and a war between Alexander's generals started quickly, dividing the empire into powerful kingdoms dominated by new dynasties ruling Egypt and Syria/Iraq, founded by his commanders Ptolemy and Selecus. His son Alexander IV was murdered at fourteen and Alexander's body, lain in a gold sarcophagus, was seized by Ptolemy and taken to his capital, Alexandria, in Egypt, where it was later admired by Caesar and then by Augustus, who clumsily knocked its nose off. Later it vanished, its fate unknown.

QIN SHI HUANGDI

*c.*259–210 BC

If you govern the people by punishment, the people will fear. Being fearful, they will not commit villainies.

Lord Shang's legalism, adopted by Qin Shi Huangdi
as the basis for his rule

Qin Shi Huangdi created the first unified Chinese empire, which emerged from the Warring States Period. By 221 BC he had successfully destroyed the last remaining rival kingdoms within China and made himself supreme ruler: the First Emperor. A ruthless statesman and conqueror of manic gifts, haunted by madness, sadism and paranoia, Qin Shi Huangdi's reign quickly degenerated into a brutal and bloody tyranny. His reputation in China had always been that of a tyrant until Chairman Mao Zedong, another monstrous dictator, associated himself with the First Emperor and promoted him as his glorious precursor.

Born a prince of the royal family of the Kingdom of Qin, Zheng, as the future emperor was named, was raised in honourable captivity. His father, Prince Zichu of Qin, was then serving as a hostage

44

to the enemy state of Zhaou, under a peace agreement between the two kingdoms. Subsequently released, Zichu returned to Qin and assumed the crown, with his son Zheng as his heir.

In 245 BC, Zichu died and the thirteen-year-old Zheng acceded to the throne. For the next seven years he ruled with a regent, until in 238 BC he seized full control in a palace coup. From the beginning, Zheng showed a new ruthlessness: he regularly executed prisoners of war, contrary to the established etiquette of the time.

Zheng now vied for power with the other Chinese kingdoms, creating a powerful army. When he had come to the throne, Qin had been a vassal state of the Kingdom of Zhaou. In a sequence of military victories, six kingdoms fell to Zheng's forces: the Han (230), Zhaou (228), Wei (228), Chu (223), Yan (222) and Qi, the last independent Chinese kingdom, in 221 BC. A superb commander, Zheng was also a skilled diplomat, especially in exploiting divisions among his enemies. He now stood unchallenged within a unified China. To commemorate this feat he took a new name that reflected his unparalleled status: Qin Shi Huangdi, 'The First August Emperor of Qin'.

Qin Shi Huangdi now created a strong centralized state across his territories. In an extension of existing practice in the Kingdom of Qin, the old feudal laws and structures that had remained in much of China were abolished, to be replaced by centrally appointed officials and a new administrative apparatus. Standardization of the Chinese script, currency, weights and measures changed the spheres of economics, law and language, with a unified system of new roads and canals, to weld China together as a cohesive national unit.

There was, however, a price to be paid – borne by the ordinary people of China. A million men were put to work as forced labour to build some 4700 miles of roads. Qin Shi Huangdi would have his edicts carved in vast letters on mountain rock faces. As his projects of national unity became ever more ambitious, so too did the human toll they exacted. One such project was to link up the numerous independent frontier walls that barricaded northern China from the threat of hostile tribes. This effectively created a forerunner to the Great Wall of China, but it cost hundreds of thousands of lives.

At the same time, Qin Shi Huangdi was unwilling to accept any limits on his own power – in contradiction to the Confucian belief that a ruler should follow traditional rites. So he outlawed Confucianism and persecuted its adherents brutally. Confucian scholars were buried alive or beheaded; a similar fate befell the follower of any creed that might challenge the emperor's authority. All books not specifically approved by the emperor were banned and burned; intellectual curiosity of any kind was to be replaced by unswerving obedience.

As he grew older, Qin Shi Huangdi became obsessed with his own death. He regularly dispatched expeditions in search of an 'elixir of life' that might make him immortal. He grew ever more fearful of challenges to his position, and with good reason, as he was the target of several assassination plots. The emperor's efforts to counter such a fate became ever more paranoid and bizarre. At random, servants in the imperial household would be ordered to carry him in the middle of the night to an alternative room to sleep. Numerous doubles were deployed to confuse any would-be assassins. A close watch was kept, and anyone suspected of disloyalty was instantly removed.

Ultimately, it was Qin's pursuit of immortality that was his downfall. It was widely believed that a man might live longer by drinking precious metals, gaining some of their durability. The emperor died in 210 BC, on tour in eastern China, having swallowed mercury tablets, created by his court physician in an effort to confer immortality.

Even in death, Qin Shi Huangdi seemed afraid that he might be vulnerable to attack. Long before he died he had ordered a gigantic three-mile-wide mausoleum to be built, guarded by a full-scale 'terracotta army' of over 6000 full-sized clay models of soldiers. Qin Shi Huangdi's aim was to ensure that in death, as in life, his every whim and desire would be catered for in his huge subterranean palace. Again, the epic scale of the building project exacted a monumental cost in terms of lives lost. Some 700,000 conscripts were required, a substantial proportion of whom did not survive its completion.

The terracotta army was rediscovered in March 1974 by a group of Chinese peasants sinking a well near the city of Xian. Digging down, they stumbled upon a vast chamber containing the figures. Upon further exploration, it became clear that the individually sculpted infantrymen, cavalry, charioteers, archers and cross-bowmen were guarding the entrance to the enormous tomb of the First Emperor, Qin Shi Huangdi.

So far, only the soldiers that guard the path to the door of the tomb have been uncovered. Each is fashioned in precise detail, and each has unique facial characteristics. All of the figures face east, from where it was assumed the enemies of the eternally sleeping emperor would come. In total, the entire funerary compound fills a whole mountain, covering a site of over twenty square miles.

The scale of what remains to be uncovered is indicated by the words of ancient Chinese historian Sima Qian (Ssu-ma Ch'ien; c.145–c.85 BC), who describes the tomb thus:

The labourers . . . built models of palaces, pavilions, and offices, and filled the tomb with fine vessels, precious stones and rarities. Artisans were ordered to install mechanically triggered crossbows set to shoot any intruder. With quicksilver the various waterways of the empire, the Yangtze and Yellow rivers, and even the great ocean itself, were created and made to flow and circulate mechanically. With shining pearls the heavenly constellations were depicted above, and with figures of birds in gold and silver and of pine trees carved of jade the earth was laid out below.

Qin Shi Huangdi's immediate legacy did not last long. He had declared that the empire he had built would last for a thousand years, but it collapsed only four years after his death, as China entered a fresh period of civil war. Yet Qin Shi Huangdi created the reality and the idea of a Chinese empire, a similar territory to today's People's Republic of China.

HANNIBAL

247–*c.*183 BC

Let no love or treaty be between our nations. Arise, unknown avenger, from my ashes to pursue with fire and sword . . . may they have war, they and their children's children!
The suicidal Dido, queen of Carthage, to her lover Aeneas, who has abandoned her to found Rome – in the words of Virgil's *Aeneid*

The Carthaginian general Hannibal was the man who came closest to bringing Rome to its knees. A commander of determination and resourcefulness, he devised novel strategies and tactics that are still studied today. He achieved the seemingly impossible in leading an army and more than thirty war elephants over the Alps into Italy, where he inflicted a series of crushing defeats on the Romans. To them he was their nemesis, a terrifying and ruthless figure, his very name evoking fear and dread and inspiring the phrase 'Hannibal is at the gates!'

Carthage, near modern-day Tunis, had been settled by Phoenicians from Tyre in the 9th century BC, and their descendants, the Carthaginians, proceeded to build up their own trading empire in the region. It was in Sicily that Carthage first came up against its rival for power in the western Mediterranean: Rome. The consequence was the First Punic War, from which Rome emerged victorious in 241 BC.

Hannibal's father, the general and statesman Hamilcar Barca, had fought in this war, and it is said that he made his young son swear eternal hatred for the Romans. Hannibal fought alongside him as he conquered a new Carthaginian empire in Spain that was, at least partly, a family fiefdom. In 221 BC, some years after his father's death in battle, Hannibal was appointed commander in Spain, and here, three years later, seeking revenge for his father's defeat by the Romans, he deliberately provoked the Second Punic War by capturing the city of Saguntum, an ally of Rome.

Determined on the complete destruction of his sworn enemy, Hannibal assembled 40,000 infantry, 12,000 cavalry and a contingent of war elephants. With this mighty force he crossed the Pyrenees and traversed southern Gaul and the waters of the Rhône to the foothills of the Alps. Historians argue about Hannibal's precise route, but whichever sequence of passes he used would have presented formidable obstacles. Not only did he have to contend with narrow icy paths, landslides and starvation, but he also had to fight off hostile local tribes. Eventually, after a five-month ordeal, Hannibal and the surviving half of his army arrived on the plains of northern Italy, ready to march on Rome.

The Alpine crossing had been made possible by the immense loyalty Hannibal commanded. Even Hannibal's staunchest enemies recognized his remarkable rapport with his men, who were drawn from many different peoples. As the historian Polybius remarked, his enterprises were 'desperate and extraordinary', but Hannibal never asked his men to do what he would not do himself. He had been only twenty-six when the army in Spain had elected him their commander, and in all his long career there is no record of mutiny or even a desertion among his forces.

Sometimes known as the 'Father of Strategy', Hannibal pioneered the idea that war could be won beyond the set-piece battle. A master of the ambush, he attacked the enemy's communications and seized cities and supplies behind its back. The Romans accused him of duplicity, but he was also masterly in open battle, as his overwhelming victories over the Romans at Lake Trasimene (217) and the bloodbath that was Cannae attest. His deployment of encirclement at Cannae (216), resulting in a reported 50,000 Roman deaths, was admired by Napoleon and Wellington and is still discussed by military tacticians. After this humiliation of Roman military prestige, some of Rome's allies in Italy deserted to the Carthaginian side.

Receiving negligible support from Carthage, Hannibal had to levy troops on the spot and provision his men himself. Eventually the Romans deployed guerrilla tactics too, wearing their enemy down. Hannibal continued to campaign, largely in southern Italy, with little help from his Italian allies. Despite winning some further victories, his army was never strong enough to attack Rome itself. In 207 his younger brother, Hasdrubal Barca, led another Carthaginian army into Italy to join with Hannibal in a march on Rome, but Hasdrubal was killed and his army defeated at the River Metaurus.

When, in 203, the Roman general Scipio Africanus mounted a counter-invasion of North Africa, Hannibal was recalled to Carthage, and the following year was defeated decisively by Scipio at the Battle of Zama. Charged by Carthage's senate with misconduct of the war, Hannibal entered politics, where his admirable administrative and constitutional reforms alienated Carthage's old elite; before long they denounced him to the Romans. Hannibal fled.

Hannibal spent his last years waging war against Rome for any prince who would have him. He served Antiochus III of Syria and then was heard of in Crete and Armenia. He ended up at the court of King Prusias of Bithynia, but the Romans had long memories and were set on revenge. Eventually they pressured Prusias to give Hannibal up, but the general chose death over captivity. In the Bithynian village of Libyssa he drank the poison that he had long carried with him in his ring, and so evaded his old enemy one final time.

JUDAH THE MACCABEE AND HIS BROTHERS

2nd century BC

God forbid that we should forsake the law and our ordinances. We will not hearken to the king's words to go from our religion

1 Maccabees 2:19

The Maccabees, so named for their hammer-like military force, were five brothers – and their elderly father – who, against all odds, rebelled against and defeated the oppressive Greek empire of the Seleucid dynasty to win religious and political freedom – and establish their own Jewish kingdom.

The Greek kings of Asia who then dominated the Near East were descended from Seleucus, one of Alexander the Great's generals who, after his patron's death, had seized a vast empire. Now, thanks to the conquests of Antiochus III the Great, they ruled a Middle Eastern empire that included Judaea, where the Jews worshipped their one god. The dynasty practised religious tolerance, but after the early death of Antiochus III his beautiful but unhinged son changed all that.

Antiochus IV tried to add Egypt to his empire. He successfully conquered Egypt but the Romans foiled his plan – and the Jews of Judaea rebelled at his rear. The furious Antiochus, who took for himself the name Epiphanes (meaning the manifestation of a divine being), decided to crush the Jewish religion. He issued a series of decrees banning Judaism in all its manifestations. Observance of the Torah, the laws of keeping kosher, the practice of circumcision – all were forbidden on pain of death. In 168 BC the Jewish Temple, the holiest place in Jerusalem, was forcibly converted to a shrine to Zeus, while troops patrolled the streets and the countryside to make sure the Judeans were now worshipping Hellenic gods. Antiochus himself entered the Temple and sacrificed pigs on its altar.

Many Judaeans did comply with the new laws, while a minority fled. It was old Mattathias, a priest at the hill town of Modin, who initiated active resistance by lashing out at a Jew complying with the new orthodoxies and killing a soldier of the evil empire. With his five sons, Mattathias retreated to Jordan to marshal his Jewish forces into a formidable guerrilla army. People flocked to join them from across Judaea, rightly sensing that in these men they had found the champions of their faith.

The events of 168–164 BC are testimony to their bravery and leadership. Having dispensed with the essentially suicidal refusal to fight on the Sabbath (a prick of conscience that had ensured early defeats for them), the rebels achieved dazzling victories against the Seleucids and the Jewish 'collaborators' ranged against them. Much of this success was thanks to the inspired leadership of the eldest son Judah, dubbed Maccabeus ('The Hammer') before the name was applied to the family as a whole. The Maccabeans inflicted a series of crushing defeats on better-equipped troops who vastly outnumbered them.

Within three years the Maccabees had taken Jerusalem, and in 164 BC the now more accommodating Antiochus died and his successor sued for peace (albeit a temporary one). Vitally, Jewish freedom of worship was restored. The Temple was cleansed and rededicated in December 164 BC. Even though the oil for the Temple lamp had run out, the lamp remained alight for eight days, a miracle that inspired the joyful Hanukkah Festival of Lights, in which Jews still celebrate religious freedom from tyranny.

Having won the right to practise their religion, the Maccabees fought on for the political freedom that would protect it. The result was the creation of an independent Jewish state, with Mattathias' descendants at its head. Fighting to drive the Syrian empire out of Judaea, Judah was killed in battle. His successor, Jonathan 'the cunning', secured his brother's military achievements with diplomacy. As dynastic struggle and civil war consumed the Seleucid empire, Jonathan's astute appraisal of the political balance, and judicious offers of support, secured him substantial territorial gains. But the Seleucids tried to re-conquer Judaea: Jonathan was tricked, captured and killed. In 142 BC Simon the Great, the youngest and by now the only surviving son of Mattathias, negotiated the political independence of Judaea. It was the culmination of all his family had fought for. A year later, by popular decree, he was invested as hereditary leader and high priest of the state. This marked the establishment of the Hasmonean dynasty, which took its title from Mattathias' family name. For the next century and a half, the Maccabees ruled an independent Jewish kingdom as kings and high priests, conquering an empire that soon extended to much of today's Israel, Jordan and Lebanon. Gradually the family's gifts weakened and they became Hellenic tyrants – until Rome imposed its will on the Middle East.

The Maccabees represent nobility, courage and freedom, as well as the audacity to resist an empire and the right of all to worship as they wish. In a David-and-Goliath struggle, the first recorded holy war, a small band of warriors succeeded in defeating the mighty phalanxes of an arrogant despot.

SULLA

138–78 BC

'His unparalleled good fortune – up to his triumph in the civil war – was well matched by his energy ... Of his subsequent conduct I could not speak without feelings of shame and disgust.'
Sallust, The Jugurthine War (c.41–40 BC)

Grey-eyed with red-gold hair, Sulla was the general and dictator whose murderous rule sounded the death knell of the Roman Republic. A gifted but ruthless military commander and conservative politician, he annihilated his rivals, winning a reputation as half-fox, half-lion. Though he styled himself the 'guardian of the constitution', Sulla's reckless ambition was ultimately to prove its undoing.

Lucius Cornelius Sulla was a latecomer to the rough-and-tumble world of Roman politics. Although of noble birth, he was left all but penniless by the death of his father. In his late teens and twenties, according to the Roman historian Plutarch, 'He spent much time with actors and buffoons and shared their dissolute life.' One thing these experiences gave Sulla was the common touch – essential for any ambitious populist.

Sulla furthered his ambition by establishing himself as the lover of a wealthy widow, who bequeathed him her fortune when she died. On the back of this windfall, Sulla was able to embark on the cursus honorum – the process by which budding politicians rose through the ranks of public life under the Roman Republic. By this time, though, he was already 30. And with many of his rivals having started their careers in their early twenties, Sulla was, from the start, a man in a hurry.

In 107 BC Sulla became quaestor, and distinguished himself in a successful military campaign against the Numidian king, Jugurtha, serving under the consul Gaius Marius. Some twenty years Sulla's senior, Marius would go from being the younger man's mentor to his fiercest rival. Between 104 and 101 BC Sulla again served with distinction under Marius, and returned to Rome with a triumphant reputation and bright prospects.

At this point, however, Sulla's career entered something of a lull. It was not until the Social War of 91–88 BC, in which Rome faced a massive revolt from its hitherto loyal Italian allies, that Sulla returned to frontline service and won a reputation as a brilliant general in his own right. In helping to defeat the insurgency he displayed the combination of military flair and savage brutality that was to become his hallmark.

Returning to Rome in triumph, Sulla became consul for the year 88 BC – the pinnacle of elected office under the Republic. He also secured an enormously lucrative post-consular military command, campaigning in the east against King Mithridates of Pontus. Marius, though ageing, remained supremely ambitious and believed that Sulla's command in the east should have been his. Thus, when Sulla was absent from Rome, Marius took the opportunity to have his political allies transfer Sulla's position to him.

But Marius had badly misjudged his rival. The possibility that Sulla might now lose everything for which he had worked so long and so hard made him fiercely determined to defeat his enemies by any means necessary. Sulla had at his command six legions – almost 30,000 men. He now took the scandalous and unprecedented step of marching against Rome – the First Civil War.

Marius was defeated and fled to Africa. Sulla had his foes branded 'enemies of the state', and had his original offices restored. Apart from this, his retribution was surprisingly moderate. He introduced various reforms, and then, in 87 BC, departed for the east, where he achieved significant victories over Mithridates and crushed a rebellion in Greece. During the siege of Athens, he ordered the destruction of the groves where Plato and Aristotle had reflected on the human condition. When the city itself finally fell, Sulla gave his troops free rein to pillage and murder as they saw fit.

But Sulla was again being challenged back in Rome. Taking advantage once more of his rival's absence, Marius had returned and become consul – for the seventh time. He declared all of Sulla's laws invalid and exiled him from Rome. In 82 BC Sulla returned to the capital – once more at the head of an army – and this time there was to be no limit to his vengeance.

Marius himself had died during his last consulship in 86 BC, but his political allies and family were hunted down mercilessly. Having destroyed his rivals, early in 81 BC Sulla was appointed dic- tator by a fearful Senate, and soon lists of 'proscribed' individuals began appearing in Rome's central forum. All proscribed individ- uals were condemned to be executed and their property plundered.

In the space of a few months, as many as 10,000 people may have been killed. On one notorious occasion Sulla addressed the timorous Senate even as the cries of prisoners being tortured and killed rang out from a neighbouring building. The banks of the

Tiber were littered with bodies, and the public buildings filled with severed heads.

In the midst of the carnage, Sulla attempted to rebuild the integrity of the Roman Republic that he himself had helped shatter. Portraying himself as the 'guardian of the constitution', he introduced new laws to restore the power of the Senate and elected officials. In 79 BC, having vanquished his foes and completed his constitutional reforms, he ostentatiously retired from public life.

Far from saving the Republic, Sulla had paved the way for its eventual collapse. Power, he had made clear, lay not with the politicians, but with the generals. And ultimate power resided with whichever man could wield military force with the most merciless brutality. It was Sulla, with his unbridled savagery, who opened the door through which the emperors would march.

CICERO

106–43 BC

There was a humanity in Cicero, a something almost of Christianity, a stepping forward out of the dead intellectualities of Roman life into moral perceptions, into natural affections, into domesticity, philanthropy, and conscious discharge of duty . . .

Anthony Trollope,
in the introduction to his *Life of Cicero* (1880)

Cicero was a supreme master of the spoken word whose stirring calls in defence of the Roman republic finally cost him his life. In his own day he was uncontested as Rome's finest orator, a statesman whose devotion and loyalty to the republic was unquestioned. He was also a man of exceptional intellect and refinement who has exerted an enduring influence on Western civilization.

In spite of being a *novus homo* ('new man') – none of his ancestors had attained the highest offices of state – Marcus Tullius Cicero went on to become one of Rome's leading statesmen. A brilliant youth who studied under the best minds of the day, he entered the law as a route to politics. He rose swiftly and was renowned for the brilliance of his mind and his dazzling oratorical skills.

Cicero was never troubled by false modesty, but the Roman people generally shared his high opinion of himself. An outsider to the patrician-dominated political system, he won election to the highest offices of state, in each case at the earliest permitted age. In 63 BC, after reaching the pinnacle of political preferment, the consulship, he quickly established himself as a national hero. Discovering the Catiline conspiracy, a patrician plot to overthrow the republic, Cicero successfully swayed the senate into decreeing the death penalty for the conspirators, trouncing Julius Caesar in debate in the process. When he announced their execution to the crowds with just one word, *vixerunt* ('their lives are done'), Cicero was hailed with tumultuous rapture as *pater patriae* – 'father of the country'.

In the space of a few sentences he could move juries and crowds from laughter to tears, anger or pity. Using simple words he could expose the heart of a complex matter, but if required he could befuddle his audience with rhetoric, winning cases by, as he put it, 'throwing dust in the jurymen's eyes'. His renowned declaration '*Civis romanus sum*' ('I am a Roman citizen') has come to encapsulate the defence of a citizen's rights against the overbearing power of the state. Cicero's highly distinctive speaking style transformed the written language. His ability to layer clause upon clause while maintaining his argument's clear line became the model for formal Latin.

A century after Cicero's death, Plutarch eulogized him as the republic's last true friend. In a time of civil unrest Cicero harked back to a golden age of political decorum. Idealistic yet consistent, he was convinced that virtue in public life would restore the republic to health. Refusing to be involved in political intrigue that might undermine the system, he rejected Caesar's offer to join him in the so-called First Triumvirate of 60 BC. Cicero played no part in Caesar's assassination in 44 BC, but he seized on the end of his dictatorship to vigorously re-enter politics. Over the following months, taking his lead from the renowned Athenian orator Demosthenes, Cicero delivered the *Philippics*, a series of fourteen coruscating orations against the tyranny of Caesar and against his faithful henchman Mark Antony. It was a magnificent, if ultimately forlorn, cry for political freedom.

After Caesar as dictator had encouraged the staunch republican to refrain from politics, Cicero turned to philosophy to keep himself amused. As a youth he had been tutored by the famous Greek philosophers of the day. His knowledge, as broad as it was deep, was unmatched in Rome. Cicero's treatise on the value of philosophy, *Hortensius*, was practically required reading in late antiquity. St Augustine credited it as instrumental in his conversion. The early Catholic Church deemed Cicero a 'righteous pagan'.

Cicero introduced to Rome the Greek ideas that formed the basis of Western thought for the next 2000 years. His works have sometimes been criticized as derivative, but he laid little claim to originality in his treatises. 'They are transcripts,' he wrote to a friend. 'I simply supply words and I've plenty of those.' It is a remarkably humble statement for a man who made such an extraordinary contribution to Western philosophy: he translated Greek works, invented Latin words to explain hitherto untranslatable concepts, and elucidated the main philosophical schools. His vast discourse amounted to an encyclopedia of Greek thought.

In the end, Cicero's inability to hold his tongue proved his undoing. When Octavian, Caesar's adopted son and the future Augustus, learned of Cicero's remark about him – 'the young man should be given praise, distinctions, and then disposed of' – it spelled doom for the orator. Octavian, Mark Antony and Lepidus formed the Second Triumvirate shortly afterwards, and Cicero was declared an enemy of the state. Pursued by soldiers as he half-heartedly fled Italy, Cicero was brutally murdered, his head hacked off, and the hand with which he had written the offending speeches displayed in the Roman forum.

'There is nothing proper about what you are doing, soldier,' Cicero reportedly said to his assassin, 'but do try to kill me properly.'

CAESAR

100–44 BC

I had rather be first in a village than second at Rome.

Gaius Julius Caesar, possessed of all the talents of war, politics and literature, was born of a noble but no longer rich family. Ruthless, cold and irrepressibly energetic, (yet an epilectic), he climbed the *cursus honorum* of Roman republican politics with astonishing speed, a rise made possible by the brutal civil war between Marius and Sulla. Aged nineteen and keeping his distance from Sulla, he first distinguished himself in the wars of the east (where he was accused of a gay affair with the king of Bithynia). Caesar was captured by pirates, who ransomed him. Typically, once he was freed, he put together a flotilla and returned to hunt them down, killing all of them. Caesar was a keen practitioner of the adventurous school of politics and a serial seducer of married women – a sexual adventurer, nicknamed the bald adulterer who slept with the wives of his rivals Crassus and Pompey as well as the mother of his future assassin, Brutus. And then there was Cleopatra.

As a nephew of Marius, Caesar was almost murdered by Sulla – and was only able to begin his career after the dictator's death. His rise was initially limited by the supremacy of Pompey the Great, the conqueror of Syria and Rome's greatest soldier and wealthiest statesman, who had been awarded an exceptional three triumphs. Elected consul in 61 BC, Caesar managed to form the First Triumvirate with Pompey and Crassus to rule Rome peacefully. But he really made his name with his astounding nine-year conquest of Gaul and the west for Rome, a campaign he later recounted (in the third person) in his *Commentaries*, revealing his expertise as a historian. He personally fought fifty battles. It was in Gaul that Caesar made his reputation – and his fortune.

Caesar was forty-one. It was late in life for a conqueror – Alexander was dead at thirty-three, Hannibal fought his last battle at forty-five, Napoleon and Wellington both fought their last battle, Waterloo, at forty-six.

In 54 and 55 BC he invaded, but did not occupy, Britain. In 53 the Triumvirate fell apart; Pompey dominated Rome and the Senate ordered Caesar to resign his command. Caesar refused. Caesar's crossing of the Rubicon, the river that separated his own Gallic provinces from Italy itself, marked his bid for power. Pompey retreated to rally his forces in Greece, and Caesar took Rome, where he was appointed dictator. Caesar defeated his enemies at Pharsalus in 48 BC. Pompey was afterwards murdered in Egypt, where Caesar fell in love with the young queen Cleopatra and fought to establish her rule. They celebrated and rested on a luxurious cruise down the Nile. On the way home, he stopped in Asia to defeat King Pharnaces of Bosporus at the Battle of Zela, his quickest victory, which he celebrated with the laconic 'Veni, vidi, vici' – 'I came, I saw, I conquered.' Caesar fought and defeated the Pompeyans not only in Greece but in Italy, Spain and then in Africa. He finally returned to Rome in 46 BC to celebrate a record four triumphs. In 44 BC he planned new campaigns in the Balkans and against Parthia. In Rome, he was politically supreme, his power absolute and nearly monarchical, but though his supremacy was feared and resented, he did not rule by terror and was forgiving and clement, using his power for the greater good. Caesar turned down the throne but received the titles Father of the Country, *imperator*, dictator for life and consul for ten years, and he was declared to be sacred.

Caesar's monarchical powers led to an assassination plot under his erstwhile supporters Brutus and Cassius. Caesar was warned that he might be assassinated on the Ides of March, but he ignored the warnings. On the Ides of March 44 BC, sixty senators attacked and stabbed Caesar as he received petitioners at a Senate meeting. When he lay dead, he was found to have 23 wounds. After the conspirators were defeated in a civil war, the empire was divided uneasily between Caesar's commander Mark Antony and his heir, great-nephew and adopted son, Octavian. In 31 BC, however, Octavian defeated Antony at Actium, thereby uniting the Roman empire and emerging as its first emperor: Caesar became a title synonymous with 'emperor' or his heir. 'Caesar' came to signify legitimate power, the German 'Kaiser' and Russian 'Tsar' being its derivatives.

HEROD THE GREAT

c.73–4 BC

Then Herod, when he saw that he was mocked of the wise men, was exceeding wroth, and sent forth, and slew all the children that were in Bethlehem, and in all the coasts thereof, from two years old and under.

Matthew 2:16

Herod the Great was the half-Jewish, half-Arab King of Judaea and Roman ally, whose thirty-two-year reign saw colossal achievements and terrible crimes. Famously handsome in his youth, he was a talented, energetic and intelligent self-made monarch who combined Hellenistic and Jewish culture, presiding over the rebuilding of the Jewish Temple, the embellishment and restoration of Jerusalem, and the building of great cities and impressive fortresses. He created a large, rich and powerful kingdom with a special status at the heart of Rome's eastern empire. Yet in his lust for power, women and glory, he became the bloodthirsty villain of the Christian Gospels and the despot of Josephus' *Histories of the Jews*. Even though he did not actually order the Massacre of the Innocents, as told in the Gospels, he killed three of his own sons, as well as his wife and many of his rivals, and used terror and murder to hold on to power right up until his death.

Born around 73 BC, Herod was the second son of Antipater, an Idumean convert to Judaism and chief minister of the Jewish king Hyrcanus II, great-grandson of Simon the Maccabee, who had established Judaea in 142 BC as an independent Jewish state. The Maccabees had ruled Judaea as both kings and high priests ever since, but to win back his throne in 63 BC, after his brother Aristobulus had wrested it from him, the ineffectual Hyrcanus was forced to ally himself with the Roman strongman Pompey the Great, ceding control of Judaea to Rome. Herod and his father Antipater were shrewd students of politics in Rome, always supporting the winner in the civil wars, from Pompey to Augustus, in order to keep power. When Julius Caesar subsequently appointed Antipater as governor of Judaea in 47 BC, Hyrcanus continued as king in name only, and though he survived a revolt in 43 BC led by his popular nephew Antigonus – a revolt in which Antipater was poisoned – he was exiled three years later. The Parthians, Rome's rival empire, invaded and overran the Middle East, and Antigonus became king under their patronage. Herod escaped to the protection of Queen Cleopatra of Egypt and thence to Rome, where the two dominant strongmen, Mark Antony and Octavian (the future Emperor Augustus) appointed him king of Judaea. It took him three years to conquer his kingdom. When he took Jerusalem, he slaughtered forty-six of the Jewish ruling council.

Already hated by his people, Herod attempted to legitimize his position by discarding his first wife Doris and marrying the Maccabee princess Mariamme, the teenage granddaughter of Hyrcanus. In all, he was to marry ten times and produce fourteen children, three of whom he murdered while another three eventually succeeded him.

Herod ordered a series of grandiose construction projects, which included aqueducts, amphitheatres, the stunning trading port of Caesarea (considered by many to be one of the great wonders of the world), and the fortresses of Masada, Antonia and Herodium. Most ambitious of all was the rebuilding of the Second Temple in Jerusalem – a massive project that took years to complete.

Over 10,000 men spent ten years constructing the Temple Mount alone, and work on the Temple courts and outbuildings continued long after Herod's death. The last supporting wall remains today the holiest site of Judaism: the Western Wall.

He ruled by terror, having the high priest – his wife's brother Aristobulus, whom he feared as a potential rival – drowned in 36 BC. Old King Hyrcanus was also killed. Herod's marriage to the gorgeous, proud Maccabean princess Mariamme was passionate and destructive. They both loved and hated each other, but had two sons together. In 29 BC, he ordered the execution of Mariamme following suggestions she was plotting against him. Later, in 7 BC, he ordered the execution of Aristobulus and Alexander – his sons by Mariamme – after being persuaded by Antipater (his son by Doris) that the two were scheming against him. Augustus joked that he would rather be Herod's pig than his son since Jews do not eat pigs.

Close friends with Emperor Augustus and his powerful deputy Marcus Agrippa, Herod's sons were educated at the imperial court in Rome; and his mercantile empire of mines, wine and luxury goods made him probably the richest man in the empire after the imperial family. But by the end the poisonous intrigues of his decadent Jewish–Greek court began to destroy both his family and his reputation as a reliable ruler of the turbulent Middle East. Old age and debilitating health problems (Herod suffered from a horrifying condition that entailed a decay of the genitals, described by the Jewish historian Josephus as 'a putrification of his privy member, that produced worms') brought no respite from the killing. Stung by criticism from the Essenes – a rigid Jewish community – Herod had their monastery at Qumran burned down in 8 BC. Then, when a group of students tore down the imperial Roman eagle from the entrance to the Temple in 4 BC, he had them burned alive. Days before his death, he ordered the execution of his son Antipater, whom he suspected of plotting to take the throne, and his last act was to gather the foremost men of the nation to approve his last will, dividing the kingdom between three of his sons.

CLEOPATRA

69–30 BC

Fool! Don't you see now that I could have poisoned you a hundred times had I been able to live without you.

Cleopatra VII was the last pharaoh-queen of Egypt but she was Greek, not Egyptian, and using the prestige of her royal dynasty, her own political acumen and her sexual charisma, she tried to regain her family's lost empire – and nearly succeeded. She was descended from Ptolemy, one of Alexander the Great's generals, who conquered his own Mediterranean empire, based on Egypt.

The Ptolemies had fused the Egyptian pantheon of gods with that of the Greeks while adopting the ancient pharaonic practice of sibling marriage. In 51BC, the teenage Cleopatra VII co-inherited the throne with her brother-husband Ptolemy XIII, but the ambitious, cunning queen, aged eighteen, made clear her intention to rule alone. Forced into exile by her brother, she sought the support of Julius Caesar.

In 48 BC, Caesar arrived in Egypt in pursuit of his defeated rival for supremacy in the Roman empire, Pompey, who was killed by the Egyptians. But Caesar, now dictator of Rome, was drawn into the Egyptian civil war by Cleopatra. He was fifty-two, she was twenty-one, the heir of the oldest dynasty of the Western world.

She was probably not beautiful – her nose was aquiline, her chin pointed – but she possessed a ruthless aura like Caesar himself and shared a taste for sexual theatre and adventurous politics.

Cleopatra smuggled herself into Caesar's presence rolled up in a laundry bag (not a carpet). As soon as the highly intelligent and seductive queen tumbled out at his feet, Caesar was bewitched. Often in danger of defeat and hampered by meagre forces, Caesar managed to rout her enemies and restore Cleopatra. As he fled the lovers' combined army, Ptolemy XIII drowned in the Nile. Cleopatra's youngest brother became Ptolemy XIV and her new husband.

Bearing a son by Caesar called Caesarion, the Egyptian queen lived openly as Caesar's consort in Rome, causing a scandal. It was rumoured that Caesar intended to become king of Rome and make Cleopatra his queen. On the Ides of March in 44 BC Caesar was murdered by his political enemies, and Cleopatra fled.

Back in Egypt, Cleopatra set about re-establishing her influence. The swashbuckling general Mark Antony, one of the Triumvirate who now ruled the republic, summoned Cleopatra to his presence. Her breathtaking entrance – reclining, dressed as Venus on a gold-burnished barge – captivated Antony as effectively as she had hooked Caesar. Mark Antony was assigned the *imperium* of the east, while Caesar's adopted heir Octavian ruled the west. But Antony soon embraced a Hellenistic eastern vision of kingship, encouraged by Cleopatra, which was very different from the Roman tradition of austere dignity. She was determined to use Roman backing to re-establish the Ptolemaic empire.

Antony treated Cleopatra not as a protected sovereign but as an independent monarch. He gave her vast tracts of Syria, Lebanon and Cyprus, and appointed their children the monarchs of half a dozen countries. Antony saw Cleopatra as the co-founder of his eastern dynasty, and her new Egyptian territories as a key cornerstone to support his Roman empire in his wars against the Parthians. But Rome could not allow the re-emergence of an independent Ptolemaic empire. Pressed by Octavian, half-brother to Antony's abandoned Roman wife, the Senate in Rome declared war on Egypt.

The lovers who had designated themselves gods were vanquished by Octavian at the Battle of Actium in 31 BC. Antony committed suicide, and Cleopatra, rather than facing the shame of being paraded in chains through Rome, had a venomous snake smuggled to her in a basket of figs. When Octavian's soldiers came for her, they found the queen laid out on her golden bed, the pinpricks of an asp's deadly fangs on her arm. Cleopatra had wanted to be the greatest of her dynasty, but she turned out to be its memorable last. She gambled her bid for empire on her relationship with a general who rarely won a battle – and she lost everything.

AUGUSTUS & LIVIA

63 BC–AD 14   58 BC–AD 29

He found Rome in brick and left it in marble.

Rome's first and greatest emperor, Augustus, was the heir of Julius Caesar and founder of the Julio-Claudian imperial dynasty, which ruled until the fall of Nero.

Born in genteel obscurity as Octavius, he was the great-nephew of the dictator of Rome, Julius Caesar, who adopted the boy as his son. Caesar's assassination in 44 BC – when Octavius was only nineteen – made him the great man's heir, politically and in terms of his vast fortune. Now calling himself Caesar Octavian, he was initially mocked or ignored as a young novice but showed his mettle, first challenging the swashbuckling cavalry general Mark Antony, then joining him in alliance against Caesar's assassins. The First Triumvirate – Antony, Octavian and Lepidus – defeated the assassins Brutus and Cassius at Philippi in 42 BC and then divided the Roman empire – with Octavian getting Rome and the west and Antony the east, where he went into political and romantic partnership with Cleopatra of Egypt. As Antony and Cleopatra's ambitions alienated the Romans, the two sides went to war: Octavian – who was no soldier but whose forces were commanded by the talented general Marcus Agrippa – defeated his nemesis at Actium in 31 BC, leaving him master of the empire. Antony and Cleopatra commited suicide.

Octavian now combined various different roles in the Roman republic into a new position – princeps, emperor, which he held until his death. At first, the position was not meant to be hereditary. Still only thirty-three, Augustus ('Revered One') as he now called himself, was slim and cold, a punctilious manager, delicate, unemotional, censorious, adulterous, a master of men and politics. He reformed government, provincial administration and justice, regulated taxation, patronized writers such as Horace, Virgil and Livy, embellished Rome, and tried not to expand the empire beyond its already vast borders, campaigning mostly against the Germans. In 9 AD, he was heartbroken by the loss of a legion under Varus in Germany. His last years were dominated by his wife Livia and the issue of succession. But however demented and murderous some of his successors, he had created a system of sometimes hereditary, sometimes elective autocrats – the emperors – that lasted until the end of the Roman empire. As it turned out, the dynastic future belonged to his wife and her family.

Livia was born in 58 BC into the family of Marcus Livius Drusus Claudianus, a magistrate from an Italian town whose blood lines carried a proud heritage. She was betrothed to her cousin Tiberius Claudius Nero in 42 BC and gave birth to her first son also named Tiberius Claudius Nero – the future emperor.

It was a tumultuous time, however, to be starting a family. In the civil wars that followed the murder of Julius Caesar in 44 BC, both Livia's husband and her father supported the assassins of Caesar against Caesar's heir, the young Octavian. When Octavian and his ally Mark Antony defeated Caesar's murderers at Philippi in 42 BC, Livia's father committed suicide. Then her husband joined the new anti-Octavian forces that gathered around Mark Antony, whose alliance with Caesar's heir had proved short-lived. As a result, the family was forced to abandon Italy in 40 BC to escape Octavian's proscription of his enemies.

After a brief time in Sicily and then Greece, Tiberius Claudius Nero and his wife were persuaded to return to Rome in 39 BC, when Octavian offered an amnesty to supporters of Mark Antony. Back in the capital, Livia was introduced to Octavian for the first time, and by all accounts he immediately became besotted with her. By this stage, she was pregnant with a second son, Drusus, but despite this, her husband was persuaded to divorce her and present her as a political gift to Octavian.

From the moment of her marriage to Octavian, Livia carried herself in public as a reserved, dutiful and loyal wife. As her husband's political strength grew, so her status gained recognition. In 35 BC she was made *sacrosanctas*, which gave her inviolability equal to that of a tribune.

But it was behind the scenes that she wielded her greatest, often supposedly malign, influence. She was a powerful woman and the sources are very prejudicial against her. There is no doubt she was ruthless and shrewd but equally there is no evidence she actually commited any of the poisonings for which she is infamous.

Augustus's only child was Julia, a daughter from a previous

marriage; so it was not clear who might succeed him. It was quite clear, though, to Livia: her own sons should inherit the throne.

The emperor's first choice was his nephew Marcus Claudius Marcellus. However, in 23 BC, Marcellus died, in strange circumstances. Livia, who cultivated various experts on poison, was suspected of murder.

Next, Augustus favoured Marcus Vipsanius Agrippa, his closest friend and his chief military commander, the victor of Actium. In 17 BC Augustus adopted Agrippa's two youngest sons, Gaius and Lucius Caesar, and the line of succession seemed to be secure.

Agrippa died in 12 BC, however, and the question of who would succeed Augustus was thrown into further doubt when, in AD 2 and 4 respectively, Lucius and Gaius died. The circumstances of the young princes' deaths were mysterious, and again Livia was widely blamed. At last, Augustus was forced to embrace the option pushed by Livia: her son Tiberius, diffident but able, was adopted as the ailing emperor's son in AD 4 – thereby establishing him as one of the heirs to the throne.

Livia was forced into one final intervention. In AD 4, during the final rearrangement of his succession plans, Augustus also adopted Agrippa Postumus – Agrippa's sole surviving son. Within two years, Postumus was exiled from Rome, possibly because of allegations that he had been involved in a coup plot against Augustus, though again Livia's hand in events should not be discounted. Nevertheless, by AD 14 there were signs that Augustus was looking to rehabilitate his last adoptive son. Unwilling to countenance a possible late challenger to Tiberius, Livia is said to have poisoned her own husband, the aged emperor.

After Augustus' death, Agrippa Postumus was quickly murdered, and Tiberius became emperor. Livia continued to be a figure of major importance – not least because her husband had bequeathed her one third of his estate (a highly unusual move).

She now became known by the title Julia Augusta. Tiberius had always been appalled by her intrigues, even though they were in his favour; now he resented her interference.

When she died in AD 29 he did not attend the funeral. He also forbade her deification. Livia's most fitting eulogy was delivered by Augustus's great-grandson, whom she had helped to bring up in her own household. Caligula described her as a 'Ulysses in a matron's dress' – his praise perhaps the surest damnation that Livia could ever have received.

Though Tiberius was a competent administrator and talented general, he was all too aware that he was not his adopted father's first choice – nor, indeed, his second or third preference, which perhaps explains why he never seemed comfortable as a ruler. Much of his reign was plagued by internal unrest and political intrigue. In AD 26, tiring of affairs of state, he moved to a palace on the island of Capri and spent the last decade of his rule in semi-retirement, leaving the Praetorian prefect, Lucius Aelius Sejanus, as *de facto* day-to-day ruler.

The ambitious Sejanus viewed his new role as a stepping-stone towards absolute power. From AD 29 he unleashed a terror. His enemies among the senatorial and equestrian classes were falsely accused of treason, tried and executed, making him the most powerful man in Rome. Sejanus also contrived to sideline Tiberius' heirs. On becoming heir to Emperor Augustus in AD 4, Tiberius had adopted his nephew Germanicus, who became a popular general and later governed the eastern part of the empire. In AD 19, however, Germanicus died in Syria in mysterious circumstances. Tiberius' own son Drusus died in AD 23 – possibly poisoned by Sejanus, who was looking to further his political ambitions by marrying Drusus' widow Livilla. Tiberius, however, refused him permission to marry her. When two of Germanicus' sons were removed from the scene in AD 30, the succession looked as though it must fall to Germanicus' surviving son Caligula or to Drusus' son Tiberius Gemellus. In AD 31 Sejanus, determined to seize power for himself, hatched a plot to eliminate the emperor and the surviving male members of the imperial house. Tiberius had the Praetorian prefect arrested, then strangled and torn to pieces by a mob.

Meanwhile in Capri, Tiberius had devoted himself to more sensual pleasures since moving from Rome. The sensationalist historian Suetonius offers a flavour of what this entailed in his shocking *Life of Tiberius*:

> *On retiring to Capri he devised a pleasance for his secret orgies: teams of wantons of both sexes, selected as experts in deviant intercourse and dubbed analists, copulated before him in triple unions to excite his flagging passions. Some rooms were furnished with pornography and sex manuals from Egypt – which let the people there know what was expected of them. Tiberius also created lechery nooks in the woods and had girls and boys dressed as nymphs and Pans prostitute themselves in the open ... He acquired a reputation for still grosser depravities that one can hardly bear to tell or be told, let alone believe. He had little boys trained as 'minnows' to chase him when he went swimming and to get between his legs and nibble him. He also had babies not weaned from their mother's breast suck at his chest and groin.*

On Tiberius's death in 37 AD, he was succeeded by Caligula.

JESUS

c. 4 BC–*c.* AD 30

Blessed are the poor in spirit, for theirs is the kingdom of heaven.
Blessed are those who mourn, for they shall be comforted.
Blessed are the meek, for they shall inherit the earth.

The first three of the nine beatitudes (blessings)
delivered by Jesus in his Sermon on the Mount

Jesus of Nazareth was the founder of Christianity, whose followers believe that he was the son and earthly manifestation of God. He lived in Judaea and Gallilee under the Romans and the princes of the Herodian dynasty. After working as a carpenter his ministry was short – perhaps one year, no more than three. He preached the coming of the kingdom of God and exhorted his followers to live lives of humility and compassion. He is also reported to have healed the sick and performed miracles. As a result of his activities, he was crucified, after which Christians believe he rose from the dead and ascended to heaven. His legacy, in the form of the Christian Church, not only underpins much of Western society and culture but also provides spiritual inspiration and guidance to millions of people worldwide.

The story of Jesus' birth is well known, but little is recorded of the rest of his early years. His parents were Joseph, a carpenter, and Mary, who is known as the Virgin, though the Gospels of the New Testament differ over whether Jesus was immaculately conceived and there is much debate as to whether Jesus had brothers and a sister. Competing views of the exact nature and composition of his family continue to proliferate. He was born in the town of Bethlehem during a census that took place at the end of the reign of the Judaean king Herod the Great, who died in 4 BC. Various groups of pilgrims, including shepherds and 'wise men' from the east, visited him at the time of his birth. Like all Jews, he was circumcised in the Temple of Jerusalem and had a dove sacrificed for his blessing.

Jesus was apparently a precociously intelligent child. As a young man he went to be baptized by his cousin, John the Baptist, a prophet who had predicted his arrival. Some time after this, Jesus became an itinerant preacher and healer, travelling the Jewish areas of Palestine and spreading his message.

The Gospels report that Jesus was able, usually by the laying-on of hands, to cure men and women of blindness, paralysis, leprosy, deafness, dumbness and bleeding. He was also famed for his powers of exorcism – he visited synagogues to cast out demons, thereby apparently curing both mental and physical ailments. It is said that he conferred this ability on his disciples.

Further attention and bigger crowds were attracted by Jesus' ability to perform miracles. Some of his most famous miracles included the ability to walk on water; to multiply small numbers of fishes and loaves to feed large groups of people; and to turn water into wine. When he cursed a fig tree, it withered, to the amazement of his disciples.

As well as performing miracles, Jesus preached and his main message was the imminence of the kingdom of God, the Apocalypse and Judgement Day in which eternal life awaited those who repented and believed in him. He approved of poverty as a state of grace and chose to surround himself with sinners and the deprived, asserting that he was sent to preach not to the righteous but to those who had strayed. Jesus also taught the forgiveness of enemies and the observance of a humble and pious moral code.

According to some of the Gospels, he saw himself as the Messiah (or Christ), others claimed he used instead the vaguer 'Son of Man'. A student of the Jewish prophets, his every act was a consious fulfilment of the prophecies of Isaiah, Ezekiel and others. But he mocked the Temple's priestly aristocracy and Herodian princelings and that, coupled with his apocalyptic message, made him a threat to the Romans too. Judaea was disturbed by a constant succession of Jewish 'pseudo-prophets' and self-declared Messiahs, all of whom were ruthlessly suppressed by the Romans. Jesus remained a practising Jew and as such he knew that a Jewish prophet had to live and die in Jerusalem. So when, around AD 30, Jesus went to Jerusalem for Passover, he was a source of considerable concern to the city's governors.

Roman troops were usually stationed in Jerusalem for Passover, as the crowds present spelled trouble. Soldiers would have watched Jesus' triumphant entry into the city, mounted on a donkey. But he created far greater concern when he entered the city's Temple, turning over tables as people convened to pay the temple tax and buy sacrificial pigeons.

The Jewish authorities were understandably aggrieved at the disruption, but the Roman prefect Pontius Pilate had already crushed a Galilean rebellion in the city. Pilate – notorious for his clumsy violence, tactless blunders and brutal repressions – would not tolerate any Jewish threats, particularly one connected to messianic expectations. Pilate encouraged the high priest to ensure Jesus was silenced. The high priest suborned one of Jesus' disciples, Judas Iscariot, to betray him. After a final meal with his disciples – the Last Supper – at which they shared bread and wine, Jesus led his disciples to the Mount of Olives for prayer. Here, in the garden of Gethsemane, Jesus was identified by Judas, arrested and taken before Caiaphas, the Jewish high priest, who adjudged him guilty of blasphemy. Brought before Pontius Pilate, Jesus was sentenced to death. He was flogged, forced to drag a cross through the streets of Jerusalem, and crucified outside the city in the company of two thieves. It was clear from his crucifixion that his trial and execution were the acts of the Romans: had it been the act of the Jewish high priests, he would have been stoned.

Three days after Jesus' death, sightings of him began to be reported. He did not reappear as a ghost, nor as a reanimated corpse, but was transformed in some mysterious way. After visiting a number of his acquaintances and friends, Jesus ascended to heaven, leaving his followers the task of establishing the Christian Church.

After centuries of persecution, the Christian Church eventually became the dominant religious force in the Western world. While Catholics, Protestants and others have at times been responsible for appalling excesses in the name of their particular denomination or viewpoint, Jesus' philosophy of pacifism, humility, charity and kindness has endured through the ages. Judaeo-Christian ideas provide the inspiration for, and foundation of, much of Western political thought, government and law, morals, art, architecture, music and literature.

Yet there is an irony in the story of Christianity: Jesus left no writings; the Gospels were mostly written forty years later, after the destruction of the Jewish Temple by the Romans in AD 70. Until then, the Christians, led by members of Jesus's family, had prayed as Jews in the Temple. The destruction of Jerusalem and the fall of the Jews led to the final separation of Christianity from the mother-religion. However it is clear that Jesus saw himself as a Jew and not the founder of a new religion, but certainly a prophet, a reformer and the Son of Man, if not the actual Messiah. It was the dynamic visionary Saul of Tarsus, a Jew converted on the road to Damascus, who as Saint Paul forged Christianity as a universal religion based not so much on Jesus's teachings, but on his sacrificial crucifixion and resurrection and the achievement of grace through faith in Jesus the saviour of all mankind. It was Paul – keen to convert Gentiles, not just Jews – who made Christianity a world religion.

CALIGULA

AD 12–41

Make him feel that he is dying.
Caligula's order when any of his victims was being executed,
according to Suetonius

Caligula ascended the imperial throne as the young darling of the Romans – and ended his four-year reign with a reputation as an insanely cruel tyrant. Capricious, politically inept and militarily incompetent, sexually ambiguous and perversely incestuous, he went from beloved prince to butchered psychopath in a reign that quickly slid into humiliation, murder and madness.

Caligula – properly Gaius Caesar – was the great-grandson of Augustus, the first emperor of Rome. His nickname Caligula – meaning 'little boots' – derives from the miniature army sandals he was dressed in as a boy when he accompanied his father Germanicus on campaign. This made Caligula the favourite mascot of the army. Germanicus died suddenly in AD 19, followed by Caligula's two elder brothers and his mother Agrippina. Many suspected that Caligula's great-uncle the emperor Tiberius had poisoned the much-loved Germanicus as a threat to his throne. In AD 31 Caligula went to live with Tiberius at his villa on the island of Capri. It was during this time that the dark side of Caligula's character began to emerge. As the Roman historian Suetonius (albeit not an objective source) later reported, 'He could not control his natural cruelty and viciousness, but he was a most eager witness of the tortures and executions of those who suffered punishment, revelling at night in gluttony and adultery, disguised in a wig and a long robe.' Rumours also began to circulate that Caligula was conducting an incestuous relationship with his sister Drusilla.

When Tiberius died in March AD 37 some said that Caligula had smothered the old man with a pillow. Tiberius had willed that after his death Caligula and his cousin Tiberius Gemellus should rule jointly, but within months of his accession, Caligula had Gemellus murdered. Caligula's lack of political experience, combined with his spoilt arrogance and lust for absolute power, would prove disastrous.

There are many examples of Caligula's megalomania. To repudiate a prophecy that he had as much chance of becoming emperor as he did of riding a horse across the Gulf of Naples, he had a bridge of ships built across the water, over which he rode in triumph, wearing the breastplate of Alexander the Great. It was also said that he elevated his favourite horse, Incitatus, to the consulship. On another occasion, while in Gaul, he ordered his troops to defeat Neptune by gathering seashells from the shore, as 'spoils of the sea'.

Caligula became deeply paranoid, and made it an offence for anyone to even look at him, so sensitive was he about his increasing baldness and luxuriant body hair. Those suspected of disloyalty – often on the flimsiest of pretexts – were, prior to their execution, subjected to a variety of ingenious torments devised by the emperor, such as being covered in honey and then exposed to a swarm of angry bees.

Anyone was a potential victim. As Suetonius records, 'Many

men of honourable rank were first disfigured with the marks of branding irons and then condemned to the mines, to work at building roads, or to be thrown to the wild beasts; or else he shut them up in cages on all fours, like animals, or had them sawn asunder. Not all these punishments were for serious offences, but merely for criticizing one of his shows, or for never having sworn by his Genius.'

Caligula began to believe himself to be divine. He had the heads of statues of the Olympian gods replaced with likenesses of himself, and almost provoked a Jewish revolt by ordering his godhead to be worshipped in the Temple in Jerusalem. Suetonius reports that he regularly talked to the other deities as if they stood beside him. On one occasion he asked an actor who was greater, himself or Jupiter. When the man failed to respond with sufficient alacrity, the emperor had him mercilessly flogged. His cries, Caligula claimed, were music to his ears. On another occasion, when dining with the two consuls, he started laughing manically. When asked why, he retorted, 'What do you expect, when with a single nod of my head both of you could have your throats cut on the spot?' Similarly, he used to kiss his wife's neck whilst whispering, 'Off comes this beautiful head whenever I give the word. If only Rome had one neck.' The most repugnant story of the emperor's depravity tells how, after he had made his sister Drusilla pregnant, he was so impatient to see his child that he ripped it from her womb. Whether this story is true or not, Drusilla is known to have died in AD 38, probably of a fever, whereupon Caligula declared her to be a goddess.

Caligula's unbridled narcissism and ever greater appetite for brutality alienated every section of society. The Praetorian Guard resolved that his rule must be brought to an end, and in January AD 41 two of its number killed the emperor by ambushing him as he left the stadium in Rome. They went on to kill his wife and baby daughter, smashing the latter's head against a wall.

The life of Caligula demonstrated how much the imperial system created by Augustus, whilst preserving the trappings of the republic, had actually concentrated absolute power in the hands of one man. Caligula stripped away the veneer of constitutional restraint and flaunted his total authority over his subjects in the most capriciously horrific manner. Caligula personifies the immorality, bloodlust and insanity of absolute power.

NERO

AD 37–68

He showed neither discrimination nor moderation in putting to death whomsoever he pleased.

Suetonius

The emperor who 'fiddled while Rome burned', Nero was the last of the Julio-Claudian dynasty that took Rome from republic to one-man rule. Raised amidst violence and tyranny, he ruled with ludicrous vanity, demented whimsy and inept despotism. Few mourned his abdication and death amidst the chaos that he himself had created.

Lucius Domitius Ahenobarbus was born in AD 37 in the town of Antium, not far from Rome, while the Emperor Caligula – Nero's uncle – was on the throne. Like so many, he was to suffer at Caligula's hands – forced with his mother Agrippina into exile when she lost favour with the emperor. Agrippina was Caligula's sister. Their incestuous relationship supposedly ended when she plotted to overthrow him: Agrippina ranks as one of the most poisonous women in Roman history. Mother and son were allowed to return by Caligula's successor, Claudius, who had recently executed his nymphomaniacal empress, Messalina. In AD 49 Agrippina became the emperor's fourth wife. Claudius not only adopted Nero as his son but made him joint heir to the throne with his own son by Messalina, Britannicus.

Agrippina, however, was unwilling to allow nature to take its course and in AD 54 she supposedly poisoned Claudius. Relations between mother and son were also flawed, and when, in the following year, Agrippina realized her hold over Nero was slipping, she conspired in a plot to replace him with Britannicus. On discovering the conspiracy, Nero promptly had his rival poisoned and banished Agrippina from the imperial palace on the pretext of having insulted his young wife, Octavia.

Despite such intrigues, the early years of Nero's reign were marked by wise governance, largely because much state business was handled by shrewd advisers such as the philosopher Seneca, the Praetorian prefect Burrus and reliable Greek freedmen. This relative calm was not destined to last. Increasingly assured, Nero sought to free himself from the control of others and exercise power in his own right.

The first to feel the consequences of his new assertiveness was his mother, who had continued plotting behind his back. Tired of her machinations, Nero resolved to do away with her in AD 59. When an initial attempt to drown her in the Bay of Naples proved unsuccessful, the emperor sent an assassin to complete the job. Legend has it that, realizing what was about to happen as the killer approached, Agrippina drew back her clothes and cried, in one final act of scorn for her matricidal son, 'Here, smite my womb!'

With his mother out of the way, Nero's reign quickly sank into petty despotism. Burrus and Seneca were both brought to trial on trumped-up charges, and though eventually acquitted lost much of their influence. Yet, even as he gained greater control over the levers of power, so the emperor appeared increasingly to lose touch with reality. He became infatuated with Poppaea Sabina, wife of one of his friends, and resolved to marry her. According to the historian Suetonius, Poppaea's husband was 'persuaded' to grant her a divorce, while Nero's wife Octavia was first exiled and then murdered on the emperor's orders – paving the way for the Nero–Poppaea union.

In AD 64, a huge fire swept through Rome which the emperor observed with indifference, supposedly playing his lyre. Indeed, according to the Roman chronicler Tacitus, Nero himself was behind the inferno, which was started to make room for his new palace. In fact he probably helped extinguish the fire and gave shelter to the homeless in his gardens. But his reputation for being frivolous, feckless and inept was established. In an effort to divert attention, Nero sought a scapegoat, thus beginning his persecution of the Christians. Tacitus recounts the atrocities committed: 'Mockery of every sort was added to their deaths. Covered with the skins of beasts, they were torn by dogs and perished, or were nailed to crosses, or were doomed to the flames and burnt, to serve as a nightly illumination, when daylight had expired.'

Increasingly convinced that rivals were plotting against him, Nero had any potential critics executed, including, in AD 62–3, Marcus Antonius Pallas, Rubellius Plautus and Faustus Sulla. Then, in AD 65, a conspiracy led by Gaius Calpurnius Piso to oust the emperor and restore the republic was uncovered. Nearly half of the forty-one accused were either executed or forced to commit suicide, Seneca among them. Taking himself increasingly seriously as an actor and neglecting his duties as the Roman economy faltered and disorder spread, Nero began to sing and act on the public stage, spending more time in the theatre than running the empire. He also fancied himself as a sportsman, even taking part in the Olympic Games of AD 67 – ostensibly to improve relations with Greece, but more likely to milk the obsequious praise that invariably greeted his efforts. He won various awards – mostly secured in advance by hefty bribes from the imperial exchequer.

By AD 68, elements within the army – which the dilettante emperor had largely ignored – decided that things could not continue. The governor of one of the provinces in Gaul rebelled and persuaded a fellow governor, Galba, to join him. Galba emerged as a popular focus for opposition to Nero and, crucially, the Praetorian Guard now declared their support for him. Faced with the desertion of the army, Nero was forced to flee Rome and went into hiding; a short time later, he committed suicide with the words 'What an artist the world is losing in me.' His legacy was one of unrest across the empire, as Rome suffered the Year of the Four Emperors, during which civil war broke out between competing claimants to the throne. Hostilities ended only with the emergence of Vespasian and the founding of the Flavian dynasty.

MARCUS AURELIUS

121–180

Every instant of time is a pinprick of eternity. All things are petty, easily changed, vanishing away.

Marcus Aurelius, *Meditations* 6.36

Marcus Aurelius was the philosopher-king of the Roman empire, who exemplified the qualities he praised in his philosophical writings in a reign marked by principled and reforming rule over a vast and turbulent domain. He had an unselfish and pragmatic approach to governing his empire and did not shirk from sharing supreme power for the greater political good. His major written work, the Meditations, is an urbane and civilized commentary on life, expressing in a tender and personal voice a Stoic view of life, death and the vicissitudes of fortune.

Marcus Aurelius, born Marcus Annius Verus in AD 121, came from a family well acquainted with high office. His paternal grandfather was a consul and the prefect of Rome. An aunt was married to Titus Aurelius Antoninus, who would later become the emperor Antoninus Pius. And his maternal grandmother stood to inherit one of the largest fortunes in the Roman empire. He also came from liberal stock: the emperors of the 1st and 2nd centuries were more sober, munificent and inclined towards good deeds than the flamboyant urban emperors of the previous, Julio-Claudian dynasty founded by Augustus.

Marcus was handpicked for great things. In AD 138 the emperor Hadrian had arranged for Marcus to be adopted by his appointed heir, Antoninus, which marked out the seventeen-year-old as a future joint emperor, along with another young man, who would become the emperor Lucius Verus.

Marcus received his education in Greek and Latin from the best tutors, including Herodes Atticus and Fronto, one of the principal popular literary figures of the day. But practice in rhetoric and linguistic exercises did not fully satisfy such a bright young man, and he keenly embraced the *Discourses* of Epictetus. Epictetus was a former slave who had become an important moral philosopher of the Stoic school, which taught that it was through fortitude and self-control that one could attain spiritual well-being and a clear and unbiased outlook on life. Philosophy in general, and Stoicism in particular, would be the intellectual touchstones of Marcus' life.

When his adoptive father died in AD 161, Marcus was already prepared to take over the imperial duties. But in accordance with his sense of honour and political intelligence, he insisted that Lucius Verus be made joint emperor with him. Although Marcus could easily have eliminated his rival, he realized that with such a diverse empire to govern it made sense to have a partner with the political authority to rule when required but without the seniority to be a threat to stable government. It was Marcus who carried out the serious work of government.

As emperor, Marcus continued the benign policies of his predecessors. He made various legal reforms and provided relief to the less favoured in society – slaves, widows and minors all felt the benefits of his rule. Although there was some concern over the gap between the legal rights and privileges enjoyed by *honestiores* and those enjoyed by *humiliores* (the better-off and worse-off in society), Marcus was generally committed to building a fairer, more prosperous empire for his subjects.

One thing that Marcus could not control was the caprice of fate in sending disease and war. While fighting the Parthians between 162 and 166, many soldiers contracted the plague, which spread throughout the empire. From 168 until around 172, Marcus (with Verus until his death in 169) was preoccupied with subduing the German tribes along the Danube, who were intent on marauding into the Roman Empire.

In spite of such engrossing problems, Marcus Aurelius remained a keen scholar of Stoicism, and in the last ten years of his life, in breaks between his campaigning and administrative duties, he wrote his *Meditations*. Written in Greek and randomly arranged just as they came to him, these are an eclectic selection of diary entries, fragments and epigrams in which he addresses the challenges of life at war, the fear of death, and the cares and injustices of everyday life.

The general sentiment of the *Meditations* is that overreaction and lingering bitterness are the most damaging responses to life's iniquities. 'If you are pained by any external thing, it is not this that disturbs you, but your own judgement of it,' he writes. 'And it is in your power to wipe out this judgement now.' Another typical injunction reads: 'A cucumber is bitter; throw it away. There are briars in the road; turn aside from them. This is enough. Do not add "And why were such things made in the world?"'

As the *Meditations* were written against the backdrop of war, mortality naturally features prominently in them. Marcus' position is clear: 'Do not act as if you were going to live ten thousand years. Death hangs over you. While you live, while it is in your power, be good.'

It is advice that Marcus followed throughout his life but he did not succeed as a father. Before he died on campaign in 180, he appointed as his successor his son Commodus, whose diabolical and demented tyranny ended in assassination. But in spite of all, Marcus Aurelius managed to articulate with greater compassion than any of his contemporaries a timeless vision of fortitude in the face of human injustice and mortality.

CONSTANTINE THE GREAT

c.285–337

In hoc signo vinces – *'In this sign shalt thou conquer'*
The words accompanying the divinely inspired vision
that appeared to Constantine before the Battle of
Milvian Bridge, AD 312

Constantine was a bundle of contradictions – he was no saint but a brutal, bull-necked, flamboyant soldier who murdered his friends and allies and even his closest family. He owed his supremacy to the sword. Nonetheless, his embrace of Christianity was a decisive act in Western history.

When Constantine was born in the middle or late 280s, the Roman empire had recently been divided by the emperor Diocletian into eastern and western halves. Constantine was the son of Constantius, a general who later, in 305, was to be proclaimed emperor of the western empire. As a child, Constantine was sent to Nicomedia (modern Izmit in Turkey) to be raised at the court of Diocletian, who had taken for himself the eastern portion of the empire. Under Diocletian's rule, Constantine witnessed fierce persecution of Christians, which intensified after 303.

In 305 a complex power struggle for control of both the eastern and the western parts of the empire began. Constantius died at York, in Britain, in 306, whereupon Constantine was proclaimed emperor by his troops. A capable soldier, Constantine set about consolidating his power, which was initially centred on Gaul. In 312 he crossed the Alps with an army, attacking and defeating the western emperor Maxentius at the Battle of Milvian Bridge, and becoming the sole western emperor himself. Following a dream in which God appeared to him, he made his soldiers paint a Christian monogram on their shields. 'By this sign you will conquer,' said the dream. His vision of Christ coincided in his belief in the one divinity of the Unconquered Sun. His victory made Jesus his god of victory – he believed he owed his power to Christianity. But his embrace of Christianity was also political: the idea of a single empire under one emperor, one god.

In 313 Constantine met the eastern emperor Licinius, and the two men agreed the Edict of Milan, a historic proclamation that extended to all people the freedom to worship whatever deity they chose. For Christians, this meant that they were granted legal rights for the first time and were able to organize their forms of worship as they chose. The edict also restored all property that had been confiscated under the recent persecutions.

After the Edict of Milan, relations between Constantine and Licinius deteriorated, and in 320 the latter once again began to persecute Christians in his portion of the empire. By 324 the rivalry had spilled over into civil war.

Emerging victorious, Constantine reunited the whole of the Roman empire under the banner of Christianity. At this high point in his fortunes he wrote that he had come as God's chosen instrument for the suppression of impiety, calling himself 'The Equal of the Apostles', and he told the Persian king that through God's divine power he had come to bring peace and prosperity to all lands. Crucifixion, sexual immorality, prostitution, pagan sacrifice and gladiatorial shows were all abolished; Sunday – the day of Constantine's favoured pagan deity – became the Sabbath. This was no age of tolerance: on the contrary, the persecution of the Jews, the 'Christ killers', started immediately and intensified.

Constantine rededicated the town of Byzantium, which from 330 was known as Constantinople, the eastern Rome (today's Istanbul).

The church of the Holy Apostles in Byzantium was built on the site of a temple to Aphrodite. In Jerusalem Constantine ordered the church of the Holy Sepulchre to be built; in Rome, the church of St Peter was handsomely endowed with plate and property. The intellectual credentials of the Church were reinforced when Constantine summoned the Council of Nicaea in 325 to deal with the violent debates on the nature of Christ, as man or god.

Constantine used Christianity to unify the state, but he was as ruthless as he was practical. In 326 he executed his son Crispus and his own wife Fausta for treason and possibly adultery together, thereby joining Herod the Great of Judaea, Emperor Claudius,

Ivan the Terrible, Suleiman the Magnificent, the Iranian Shah, Abbas the Great and Peter the Great of Russia, and England's Henry VIII as royal killers of their own wives or sons – though only Herod and Constantine managed to kill both categories.

Constantine himself was baptized on his deathbed – perhaps prompted by the realization that his position had often necessitated unchristian acts.

ATTILA THE HUN

406–453

He was a man born into the world to shake the nations, the scourge of all lands, who in some way terrified all mankind by the dreadful rumours noised abroad concerning him.

> Jordanes, *The Origin and Deeds of the Goths*,
> 6th-century Goth historian

Attila, king of the Huns from 434 to 453, had a voracious appetite for gold, land and power. Defeated only once, he was the most powerful of the barbarian rulers who fed off the last vestiges of the crumbling Roman empire. According to legend, he carried the Sword of Mars, bestowed on him by the gods as a sign he would rule the world.

The Huns were a collection of tribes from the Eurasian steppes with a fearsome reputation (the Great Wall of China was built to keep them at bay). Basing themselves in what is now Hungary, they took advantage of the decline of the Roman empire during the 4th and 5th centuries to expand their territories, until, at its peak under Attila, their empire stretched from the River Danube to the Baltic Sea, encompassing large swathes of Germany, Austria and the Balkans.

Attila was said to be as ugly as he was successful: short, squat and swarthy with a large head, deep-set eyes, squashed nose and sparse beard. Aggressive and short-tempered, he was every inch a soldier, eating meat served on wooden dishes while his lieutenants ate assorted delicacies off silver plates. In the Hun tradition, he would often eat and negotiate on horseback, while at camp he was entertained by a fool, dwarf or one of his many young wives.

In 434, Attila's uncle King Ruglia died, leaving Attila and his older brother Bleda in joint charge of the kingdom. The Roman empire had long since been divided into two, the eastern (also known as the Byzantine) empire being ruled in Attila's time by Theodosius II. To avoid attack from the Huns, Theodosius had agreed to pay an annual tribute, but when he defaulted on payments, Attila invaded Byzantine territory, capturing and destroying several important cities, including Singidunum (Belgrade).

Following an uneasy truce negotiated in 442, Attila attacked again the following year, destroying numerous towns and cities along the Danube and massacring their inhabitants. The slaughter in the city of Naissus (in what is present-day Serbia) was so great that, several years later, when Roman ambassadors arrived there for negotiations with Attila, they had to camp outside the city to escape the stench of rotting flesh. Countless other cities endured a similar fate. According to one contemporary account: 'There was so much killing and bloodletting that no one could number the dead. The Huns pillaged the churches and monasteries, and slew the monks and virgins ... They so devastated Thrace that it will never rise again and be as it was before.' Constantinople was only spared because Attila's forces were unable to penetrate the capital's walls, so he turned instead on the Byzantine army, inflicting a crushing and bloody defeat. Peace came at the cost of repaying the tribute owed and tripling future payments. Then, around 445, Bleda was murdered, surely on his brother's orders, leaving Attila in sole command of the kingdom. Another assault on the eastern empire followed in 447, as the Huns struck further east, burning down churches and monasteries as they went, and using battering rams and siege towers to smash their way into cities, which they again razed to the ground, butchering the inhabitants.

Attila's only defeat came when he invaded Gaul in 451. His initial intention had been to attack the Visigothic kingdom of Toulouse rather than to overtly challenge Roman interests in the area. In 450, however, Honoria – the sister of Valentinian III, the western emperor – appealed to Attila to rescue her from an arranged marriage to a Roman senator. Having received her engagement ring, Attila took this as a proposal of marriage and demanded half of Rome's western empire as a dowry. When the Romans refused, Attila invaded Gaul with a massive army. In response, the Roman general Flavius Aetius combined his forces with the Visigoths to resist the Hun invasion. The rival armies clashed at Orléans, and in the ensuing Battle of Châlons (in modern Champagne), in which thousands of men from both sides were killed, the Huns were forced to retreat. It was one of the last great victories for the western empire but a pyrrhic one, for their forces were spent.

When the Huns invaded Italy in 452, Aetius was powerless to stop them. Mobile and rapacious, Attila's armies sacked and burned yet more towns and cities, including Aquileia, Patavium (Padua), Verona, Brixia (Brescia), Bergomum (Bergamo) and Mediolanum (Milan). Only an outbreak of illness among Attila's troops slowed his campaign, but by the spring he was on the verge of taking Rome itself, in which the western Roman emperor, Valentinian III, had taken refuge. It took a direct appeal from

Pope Leo I to dissuade him from sacking the city, Attila agreeing to go no further south.

Attila's death came in 453 after a night of heavy drinking following his marriage to another young bride. He suffocated in a pool of blood after suffering a heavy nosebleed while asleep. The soldiers who buried him were killed afterwards, so that none of his enemies would ever be able to find and desecrate his grave.

JUSTINIAN I & THEODORA

482–565   c.497–548

Escape is not the right choice . . . Better to die. I agree with the saying: 'Royal purple is the noblest death shroud'.

Theodora during the Nika Riots

Justinian, one of the greatest of the Eastern Roman – or Byzantine – emperors, managed to restore Roman control of much of the western Mediterranean, codify Byzantine law and, in his Great Church of St Sophia, still dominates the city of Istanbul over a millennium after his death. It was an astonishing performance – but for much of his reign he ruled in partnership with his wife, Theodora, who was clearly intelligent, ruthless, domineering and extraordinary. A life-force. She certainly contributed to his great achievements but, even if we discount some of the scandal and despotism attached to her name, she was clearly feared, hated and respected in equal measure. Justinian owes much of his achievements to her will and determination.

Justinian was born in Macedonia of Thracian peasant origin but he was also the last of the Eastern Roman emperors to speak

Latin – and to think like a Roman rather than a Greek-speaking, eastern-orientated Byzantine. He was brought to Constantinople by his uncle Justin, an illiterate ex-swineherd who had risen to commander of the imperial guard, the Excubitors. Justin adopted his nephew under the new name of Justinian. When Justin was raised to the throne in 518 AD, the well-educated and brilliant Justinian probably made most of his decisions, especially once his uncle became senile and he was raised to associate emperor.

If Justinian was no soldier he seemed in all other respects the perfectly qualified emperor – except for his taste in mistress. He fell in love with a much younger girl named Theodora, whose origins could hardly have been less imperial and more sordid. She was the daughter of one of the bear trainer in the Hippodrome, where she was brought up amidst the sweaty charioteers, the horses and the menagerie. Our main sources for her and Justinian's lives is one of their court historians, Procopius, who initially produced respectful histories of their wars and building projects but must have secretly hated both of them, especially Theodora, because he privately wrote *The Secret History*. One has to read it as one might a 21st century tabloid newspaper – half of it may be just tittle-tattle – but much of it must have been true. Theodora, encouraged by her debauched mother it seems, started as a teenage burlesque strip artist and sexual showgirl. She was startlingly beautiful but was soon notorious, even in these circles, for her extreme shows and the relish she took in the most outrageous acts of promiscuity. As Procopius noted, 'No role was too scandalous for her to accept without a blush.' In one particularly striking sketch, she would lie naked on her back, while grain was scattered across her entire body. Geese (representing the god-king Zeus) would then peck up the food with their bills – to the gratification of the prostrate Theodora.

Her insatiable sexual appetite became the stuff of legend. 'Often she would go picnicking with ten young men or more, in the flower of their strength and virility, and dallied with them all, the whole night through,' writes Procopius, adding that she preferred to leave none of her three orifices unfilled. She would go to dinner parties and take on all the guests and soon became the mistress of older men. At one point, she fell out with a patron with whom she was travelling around the east and instead embarked on a sex tour of the eastern cities, earning her way home on her back.

She fell pregnant and gave birth to her only child, a son. But this all changed when she met Justinian, who was dazzled by her. Theodora must have experienced some sort of Christian revelation, an almost Damascene conversion. For while Justinian was already religious, like most Byzantines, henceforth Theodora became an extremely pious and serious devotee of the Christological debates that divided and obsessed everyone in Constantinople.

When he succeeded to the throne in 527 Justinian officially made Theodora his Augusta, having previously, on the death of his first wife, repealed the law that prohibited marrying actresses so he could wed his mistress. But the two of them were soon hated by the mob of Constantinople – especially the chariot-racing teams.

The only place to be on a public holiday was the Hippodrome, rebuilt by Constantine the Great; it was the vibrant, seething and seamy centre of public life. There, thousands of supporters would cram in to watch their sporting icons – the charioteers compete for honours. There were four main teams, each with their own set of fans and each defined by the colours they wore: whites, reds, greens and blues, later consolidated into two teams, the Blues and Greens. Justinian himself was a known supporter of the Blues. In the absence of any other avenue for popular political expression, the factions served as an outlet for all grievances – sporting, social or political – while their adherents would often indulge in hooliganish thuggery that ended in murder and rapine. Often spectators would harangue emperors with political demands between races.

In early 532, Justinian ordered the arrest of two gangs of Blues and Greens for murder. In the process he unwisely united both the factions against him. When Justinian arrived at the Hippodrome in January 532, after months of popular discontent, the stage was set for a week-long rebellion that nearly brought about his downfall. By the end of the first day's competition, the Blues and Greens had united to chant 'Nika' ('win') in an expression of their unhappiness with the emperor's policies.

As the baying mob at the Hippodrome declared their allegiance to an alternative emperor, riots broke out and Constantinople slipped out of Justinian's control. The entire imperial district around the palace was burned to the ground. The Hippodrome became the rebel headquarters, the imperial palace was besieged and Justinian lost his nerve and prepared to flee. But Theodora stiffened his resolve, saying she would prefer to die in the imperial purple than to live without it. She then devised a plan to crush the opposition forces. She and Justinian sent an emissary to the Hippodrome to buy off half the assembled crowd so that only the diehard rebels remained. They also summoned their top young general, Belisarius, whose wife was Theodora's best friend and had also begun as a showgirl. Belisarius and his men burst into the crowded Hippodrome and massacred the entire crowd of 30,000, whose bodies were buried under the grass and sand of the stadium itself in mass graves. No wonder Justinian treated Theodora as his partner in power, and many regarded her as dangerously over-mighty in her malice and intrigues. But the partnership worked.

Justinian codified Roman law in a project that he worked on personally and whose legacy and influence would last for many centuries, but he and his wife also believed that the Roman emperor was the rightful and sacred ruler of all Christendom and all the lands once ruled by the Roman empire. It was their mission to unite the empire under one emperor, one god, one capital. Justinian first made an Eternal Peace with his only rival, the shah of Sassanid Persia. Then he dispatched a series of military expeditions, initially led by his favourite commander Belisarius, to conquer North Africa from the Vandals, and Rome, Italy and southern Spain from the Goths. North Africa fell to Belisarius; southern Spain fell to one of his subordinates and finally, in two hard fought wars commanded by Belisarius and competently by the eunuch Narses, the Byzantines retook Dalmatia, Italy and Sicily. Justinian now riled the entire Mediterranean and the two greatest imperial capitals – Rome and Constantinople.

The emperor and empress embarked upon a vast building programme to assert Justinian as the Roman emperor of all Christendom, the universal autocrat, and Constantinople as the sacred capital. Out of the ashes of the Nika Riots, he raised a first a small domed church, the Aya Irene, which still stands in the grounds of the Topkapi Palace, and then his greatest achievement of all: the vast, magnificent and unique St Sophia, a building so ambitious and so majestic that Justinian supposedly gasped 'Solomon, I have surpassed thee!'. The Great Church, with its colossal spaces and gargantuan dome, was unique and became the temple of the city, completing the city's sacralisation as imperial-sacred capital of the Roman empire and Christendom itself. It was to be the Great Church for 900 years, a mosque for 500 years after that under the Ottomans, and then a secular museum for over eighty. Still awesome, it may become a mosque again. Certainly it is one of the finest buildings of history – its grace and glory far outstrips the gigantic St Peter's in Rome.

Everything Justinian did, he did with style: even his basilica cistern under Constantinople looks more like a subterranean palace than a water system. As a monarch who compared himself to Solomon and thought of himself as emperor of the three Christian holy cities, he built the huge Nea Church in Jerusalem that clearly rivalled the Church of the Holy Sepulchre and probably the fallen Jewish Temple itself in scale and ambition. But he had probably overreached himself.

Plague ravaged the empire in the 540s and Justinian fell ill himself. Theodora was now notorious not just for her origins, but for her intolerance of any opposition, thin-skinned sensitivity and humourless sanctimony. The empress was utterly ruthless in maintaining her own position. Political opponents were seized by unknown assailants, flogged and castrated and left to die. Others who earned her displeasure found themselves confined to the warren of private dungeons beneath her palace; among those she kept there, it was said, was her own son, whom she feared would cause her embarrassment. Those who might emerge as rivals for her husband's affections – such as the Gothic queen Amalasuntha – were murdered. All official appointments had to be approved by Theodora, as did all the marriages amongst imperial courtiers. 'No other tyrant since mankind began ever inspired such fear, since not a word could be spoken against her without her hearing of it: her multitude of spies brought her the news of whatever was said and done in public or in private,' reports Procopius. 'When this female was enraged, no church offered sanctuary, no law gave protection, no intercession of the people brought mercy to her victim; nor could anything else in the world stop her.'

Justinian and his wife were nervous of Belisarius's brilliant military successes and glamour and constantly recalled, undermined and humiliated him, even when this brought about the failure of their own enterprises. Shah Chosroes of Persia invaded the east and sacked its most important city, Antioch, a terrible humiliation

SIMON SEBAG MONTEFIORE

for Justinian, who belatedly dispatched Belisarius, and finally had
to make a costly peace.

When Theodora died, probably of cancer, aged about fifty,
Justinian never recovered – and he lived too long. The last fifteen
years of his reign were a disaster. The empire was overstretched,
it armies decayed, its borders exposed, its treasury increasingly
empty, and its old emperor was hated. Soon after his death,
Rome and much of Italy were lost, most of his conquests fell
away (though the Byzantine presence in Italy lasted well into the
Middle Ages). Nonetheless Justinian and Theodora rank as one of
the most successful political-romantic partnerships in history, and
amongst the greatest Roman rulers.

MUHAMMAD

570–632

*I have perfected your religion for you, and I have completed My
blessing upon you and I have approved Islam for your religion.*

Koran, sura 5

Muhammad was the founder of the Islamic faith. Muslims believe
that he was the messenger of God and the last of his prophets and
that he transmitted the word of God to his people in the form of
the Koran. For Muslims, the Koran and the Hadith, collections
of Muhammad's deeds and sayings, together provide complete
guidance on how to live a good and devout life.

While he founded Islam against a background of turbulent
tribal feuding, Muhammad encouraged his followers to serve God
with decency, humility and piety. But he was also clearly a gifted

and ruthless soldier-statesman, founding a successful and expanding state by diplomacy and warfare – as well as a new world religion.

Muhammed ibn Abdullah was born in Mecca in AD 570. He spent his early years in the Arabian desert in the care of a Bedouin wet-nurse. Both his parents and his grandfather were dead by the time he was eight, and he grew up under the guardianship of his uncle Abu Talib. Muhammad grew into a handsome young man with a generous character and great skill at arbitrating in disputes.

This inspirational visionary was renowned as a devout and spiritual man. He would regularly retreat to the desert to meditate and pray. It was on one such retreat in 610 that he first claimed to have experienced the presence of the archangel Gabriel, who appeared to him with a command to begin his revelation of the word of God. Terrified, he told his first wife, Khadijah, of his experience. She and her blind Christian cousin Waraqah interpreted Muhammad's experience as a sign that he was God's prophet.

Over the next few years, Muhammad continued to receive the revelations that would become the Koran and which Muslims believe are the direct word of God. Soon he began to preach to the people of Mecca, converting small groups of his friends and family and various prominent Meccans. He taught them that there was one God, deserving of their complete submission (the meaning of the word Islam), and that he, Muhammad, was God's true prophet. This was seen as disruptive by many of the polytheistic tribesmen of Mecca, and Muhammad's supporters were threatened and persecuted. Muhammad sent one group of his followers to Abyssinia (modern-day Ethiopia) to seek refuge.

In 619, the 'year of sorrows', Khadijah and Abu Talib died. It was around this time that Muhammad experienced the most intense religious experience of his life. He felt the angel Gabriel transport him from Mecca to Jerusalem, and from the Temple

Mount ascended to heaven. Witnessing the divine throne of God and meeting prophets such as Moses and Jesus, he learned of his own supreme state among them. The form of daily prayer was also revealed to him. This two-part journey is known as *Isra* (Night Journey) and Mi'raj (Ascension).

Still persecuted in Mecca, in 622 Muhammad led his supporters out of the city in the Hijra, a great flight to the city of Yathrib, now known as Medina. There he was recognized as the judge and arbiter, and his following grew. There he created a new state of tolerance under a constitution. But the Jewish tribes of Medina resisted his claim to be the last prophet with the final revelation. At first he had made Jerusalem the direction of prayer – *qibla* – but now he turned it back to Mecca. Nevertheless, tensions remained between Muhammad and the Meccans, and between 624 and 627 there was a series of battles between the two groups. In the first of these, the Battle of Badr, 313 Muslims defeated a force of 1000 Meccans. In 627 a truce was concluded following a great victory for the Muslims at the Battle of the Ditch. Muhammad was both religions visionary and military-political statesman. When some Jewish tribes backed the Meccans, Muhammad broke with them and had them judged. The result was the execution of male Jews. His Koran promised both tolerance to all those who recognised Islamic supremacy and paid a tax of submission, but also jihad, holy war, against those who resisted. As a spiritual guide and military-political leader of a state, he was both prophet and pragmatist – and his legacy contains both these themes.

In 629 Muhammad carried out the first haj (pilgrimage) to Mecca, a tradition still followed by hundreds of thousands of Muslims each year. In 630, when the Meccans broke the truce, Muhammad led a force of 10,000 of his followers to the city, capturing it and destroying the idols of the polytheistic tribes. By the following year he had extended his influence to most of

Arabia, so bringing to an end what he called the 'age of ignorance'. After preaching his final sermon to 200,000 pilgrims in 632, Muhammad died, leaving Arabia stronger and united under the banner of Islam.

Muhammad's promulgation and interpretation of God's word were based on the virtues of humility, magnanimity, justice, meritocracy, nobility, dignity and sincerity. The concept of internal jihad – the inner struggle to live a better, more pious life – was as important to him as taking up arms against enemies – the jihad of holy war. Both ideas are powerful components of Islam. He enhanced the rights of women – compulsion to wear the veil did not arise until well after his death – and slaves. He condemned Arab practices such as female infanticide; reformed tribal custom in favour of a unifying divine law; and denounced corrupt hierarchies and privilege. His name is the inspiration for countless beautiful calligraphic works and much exquisite Islamic poetry. Christian contemporaries confirm that he existed but most of the details of his biography derive from histories written in Iraq and Iran, one or two centuries later. His life and words are indispensable to the Muslim world. Despite the excesses carried out in his name by extremists, he continues to provide spiritual direction to millions of ordinary people. On the basis of Muhammad's achievements, it is little wonder that Muslims believe that he was the 'perfect man' – not divine but 'a ruby among stones'.

MUAWIYA & ABD AL-MALIK: THE CALIPHS

Abd al-Malik ibn Marwan is one of the greatest Arab and Muslim Caliphs. He followed in the footsteps of Umar ibn al-Khattab, the Commander of the Believers, in regulating state affairs.

Ibn Khaldun, 14th century

After the death of the Prophet Muhammad, his new theocratic realm almost fell apart, but his successors, known as the Caliphs or the Commanders of the Believers, not only restored Islamic rule in Arabia but then embarked on an astonishing military campaign that, in a matter of a few decades, conquered a new empire that stretched from Spain in the west to the borders of India in the east. The first four of the successors were known as the Righteous Caliphs, but this epoch of triumphant success ended in two bursts of civil war, fought for political control of the new empire and religion. These wars remain relevant today because they created the schism in Islam between the Sunni and Shia. But in each case, the scars were healed by two remarkable rulers from the Ummayad dynasty.

After the Prophet's death, he was succeeded by his old support-er Abu Bakr, who sent probing expeditions into the Byzantine provinces of the Middle East. But on Abu Bakr's death, the next Caliph Omar the Just – an austere and severe giant – dispatched Arab armies that conquered the great cities of Damascus and Jerusalem and ultimately Syria, Palestine, Iraq and Egypt. Then the Arabs conquered Persia – and this was only the beginning.

In 644 Omar was assassinated, succeeded by Othman, who con-tinued the conquests but whose nepotism and bad management led to his murder. For those who believed the succession should lie with the family of Muhammad, the ideal successor was his first cousin Ali, married to his daughter Fatima – but others felt Ali was implicated somehow in the murder of Othman and so they named as their leader Muawiya, who became one of the greatest Arab rulers.

Muawiya was a Meccan aristocrat, son of Abu Sufyan, who had led the opposition to Muhammad. When Mecca surrendered to Islam, Muhammad welcomed the family into the fold, Muawiya became his secretary, and he married his sister. Caliph Omar appointed Muawiya as governor of Syria, describing him as the 'Arab Caesar' – a backhanded compliment that has some truth in it. Muawiya ruled Syria and Palestine for twenty years for his cousin Caliph Othman but on his assassination he defied the new Caliph Ali. In the civil war ensuing in Iraq, Ali was killed – the last of the Righteous Caliphs – and in 661 Muawiya became the Caliph of the vast empire that included Egypt, Syria, Palestine, Iraq, Persia and Arabia.

He was handsome, shrewd, well bred and prided himself on his prowess both as a general and a lover of women. He built an Islamic fleet that conquered Rhodes and Cyprus and almost took Constantinople in his annual attacks on the Byzantines. He treated Jerusalem as his spiritual capital but ruled from Damascus, creating a new ideal of imperial monarchy, the Islamic-Arab king-ruler, that has lasted to the present era. He ruled through Christian bureaucrats and tolerated Christians and Jews alike, seeing himself as something between Arab sheikh, Islamic caliph and Roman emperor. He was tolerant and pragmatic, following an early, looser version of Islam, happy to worship at Christian and Jewish sites, and share their shrines. Later he expanded the empire into eastern Persia, central Asia, the Sahara and into today's Libya and Algeria.

Muawiya was famed for his good sense and witty decency at a time when he was probably the most powerful ruler on earth. He prided himself on his patience and forbearance: no one has ever so cleverly stated the essence of politics as Muawiya, who said: 'I apply not my sword when my lash suffices nor my lash when my tongue suffices. And even if but one hair is binding me to my fellow men, I don't let it break. When they pull, I loosen, if they loosen, I pull.'

On his death in 680, his son Yazid failed to grasp the succession, facing rebellions in Arabia and Iraq. Muhammad's grandson Hussein rebelled to avenge his father Ali's death but was brutally murdered at Karbala in Iraq, his martyrdom creating the Shia, 'the party', a division that still splits Islam today. However, after Yazid's early death, Muawiya's old kinsman Marwan started to reconquer the empire, dying in 685 and leaving this troubled inheritance to his son Abd al-Malik, the second of the titanic Ummayad Caliphs. Abd al-Malik was less humane and flexible but more ruthless and visionary than Muawiya. He first mercilessly crushed the rebellions, retaking Iraq and Arabia; in Jerusalem he built the Dome of the Rock on the Temple Mount, a triumph of religious expression and imperial grandeur, the oldest Islamic shrine, and ordered the building of the Aqsa Mosque.

Abd al-Malik was severe, thin, hook-nosed, curly-haired and, his enemies claimed, in what can probably be dismissed as hostile propaganda, that he had breath so noxious he was nicknamed the Flykiller. Abd al-Malik saw himself as God's shadow on earth: if Muawiya was Caesar of the Arabs, he was a mixture of St Paul and Constantine the Great – he believed in the marriage of empire, state and god. As such it was Abd al-Malik who collated the book of Islam – the Koran – into its final form (the inscriptions in Jerusalem's Dome of the Rock are the first examples of the final Koran text), who defined Islamic rituals and who unified Islam into a single religion recognizable today with the emphasis on Koran and Muhammad, expressed in the double *shahada*: 'There is no God but God and Muhammad is the apostle of God.' Abd al-Malik and his son Caliph Walid expanded their empire to the borders of India and the coasts of Spain. Yet their dynasty remained part Islamic theocrats, part Roman emperors, often living in a distinctly unIslamic decadence. This led to the family's downfall in the revolution of 750, when they were replaced by the Abbasid caliphs who ruled from Iraq and blackened the reputation of the Ummayads. To the Shia, they remained heretics and sinners because the Shia believed the real Caliphs were the twelve descendants from Ali and Fatima: indeed the Shia of Iran still await the return of the Twelfth.

ZHAO WU

625–705

Wu is a treacherous monster! May it be that I be reincarnated as a cat and she be reincarnated as a mouse, so that I can, for ever and ever, grab her throat.

Consort Xiao, one of Empress Wu's many victims

The only woman in Chinese history to rule in her own right, the empress Wu was both depraved megalomaniac and intelligent puppeteer. Beginning life as the emperor's concubine, she dominated the imperial court for over half a century, eventually achieving absolute power as the self-styled 'Heavenly Empress'.

Wu Zhao, as she was then known, was only thirteen when in 638 she entered the imperial palace as a concubine of the emperor

Taizong. From an early age she was aware of the power that flowed from her good looks and intelligence, and by the time Taizong died a decade or so later, she had already ingratiated herself with his son and heir, Gaozong.

As was customary for concubines following the death of their master, Wu Zhao spent a brief period in retreat at a Buddhist convent. But within a couple of years she was back at the centre of imperial court life, her return being partly driven by the empress Wang, Gaozong's wife: jealous of one of her husband's other concubines, Consort Xiao, Wang had hoped that Wu might divert his attention. It was to be a fatal move.

As Wang had anticipated, Wu quickly displaced Xiao as the new emperor's favourite concubine, and went on to bear him four sons. But Wu now wanted power for herself, and sought ways of eliminating the influence of the empress Wang. When in 654 Wu gave birth to a daughter who died shortly afterwards, Wu ensured that Wang emerged as prime suspect in the baby's death. Gaozong believed his concubine over his wife and duly had both Wang and Consort Xiao removed from their positions. In their place, Wu became empress.

Increasingly, Gaozong suffered from debilitating bouts of ill health, giving the empress Wu greater opportunities to exert her power. She used her agents to spy on and eliminate potential rivals and officials whose loyalty she doubted – including members of her own family. Some were demoted, some exiled – and many put to death. Among the hundreds who were strangled, poisoned or butchered were the former empress Wang and Consort Xiao, whose murders Wu ordered after it emerged that Gaozong might consider pardoning them. An atmosphere of general terror spread through the imperial court, with servile obedience the only guarantor of survival.

In 675, with Gaozong's health deteriorating still further, the empress Wu manoeuvred for the succession. The emperor's aunt Princess Zhao, whom he had appeared increasingly to favour, was placed under house arrest and starved to death. Then Wu's son Crown Prince Li Hong died suddenly – poisoned by an 'unknown' hand. He was replaced by his brother – Wu's second son – Li Xian. Wu's relationship with him also quickly broke down, and in 680 Wu had him charged with treason and exiled. He was later forced to commit suicide. The line of succession now passed to a third son, Li Zhe.

When Gaozong finally died in 684, it was Li Zhe who became emperor, taking the new name Zhongzong. Needless to say, real authority still lay with Wu, now empress dowager. When Zhongzong looked as if he was about to challenge her power, she had him deposed and replaced him with another of her sons, who became Emperor Ruizong.

Wu now exercised even greater control, preventing Ruizong from meeting any officials or conducting any government business. Anyone who questioned this state of affairs was summarily removed and, frequently, executed. In 686 she offered to return imperial powers to Ruizong, but he had the good sense to decline.

Ever on the lookout for possible threats to her position, Wu encouraged her secret police to infiltrate official circles and identify would-be conspirators. In 688 a putative plot against the empress dowager was smashed, and this sparked a particularly ferocious round of political killings. False accusations, torture and forced suicides became almost routine. Then, in 690, following a series of 'spontaneous' petitions demanding that the empress dowager take the throne herself, she acceded to the request. Ruizong was demoted to crown prince and Wu became emperor.

For the next fifteen years Wu ruled using the same ruthless methods that had guaranteed her elevation, and politically motivated denunciations and state-sanctioned killings remained commonplace. In 693 the wife of her son Ruizong (the former emperor and now heir again) was accused of witchcraft and executed. Ruizong was too afraid of his mother to object.

Eventually, in 705, with her own health now failing, Wu was prevailed upon by Ruizong to surrender the throne. Unlike so many of her own victims, she died peacefully in her bed that same year, at the age of 80. Whilst she was in power, imperial politics had been reduced to little more than a deadly game, in which many ended up losers. An old Chinese proverb has it that the rule of a woman is like having a 'hen crow like a rooster at daybreak'. Given the country's experience with Empress Wu, it is scarcely surprising that she has been the only person to put that maxim to the test.

THE VENERABLE BEDE

673–735

The candle of the church, lit by the Holy Spirit, is extinguished.
St Boniface, on hearing the news of Bede's death

The 'Venerable' Bede was the outstanding English writer of the early Middle Ages, a master whose works were read by virtually every literate person for 1000 years after his death. He provided us with much of what we know about the early English Church and almost single-handedly invented the modern way of writing history. His dedication to knowledge and devout study made him famous in his own day, while his extraordinary skill in describing the world of the first millennium has ensured that he has kept his place in the literary pantheon ever since.

Plenty of medieval priests were called 'venerable', but fittingly it is with Bede that history has associated the description. It is an indication of the extraordinary piety and learning of the man who was England's proudest representative in a tradition of Christian thinkers. Bede wrote more than 30 works, ranging from collections of hymns and saints' lives to translations of the Gospels and Latin textbooks that educated generations of scholars well into the second millennium. We still rely on Bede's most famous work, his *Ecclesiastical History of the English People*, to tell us about the formative years of the English nation.

Bede was born to well-off parents in Northumbria and lived his whole adult life in the Monastery of St Paul at Jarrow, where he became a deacon at nineteen and a priest by the age of thirty. For the rest of his life he devoted himself to mastering all the learning of his day. 'I spent all my life in this monastery,' he wrote, 'applying myself entirely to the study of Scriptures.' The library at Jarrow was one of the finest in England, containing between 300 and 500 books – an impressive collection at a time when books were extremely valuable property. Bede studied all the Greek and Roman authors available, and from his late twenties he was applying himself to the important intellectual matters of the day.

Bede was a pioneer in medieval science, influencing thinking in the field with works such as *On the Nature of Things* and *The Reckoning of Time*. The latter, a treatise on chronology, made an important contribution to one of the burning questions of Bede's day: the age of the world. Traditionally the earth was supposed to be 5000 years old at the time of Christ's birth, but Bede calculated a new figure of 3952 years. He also applied his powerful intellect to the important and politically sensitive matter of working out the correct date of Easter.

Bede is rightly known as the 'father of English history'. He wrote numerous early saints' lives, including three full accounts of the lives of the early martyrs Felix, Anastasius and Cuthbert, and short accounts of 116 others. Rather than relating stories uncritically, Bede sought out original sources and records of his subjects. It was a technique which came to glorious fruition in the *Ecclesiastical History of the English People*, an 85,000-word account of the church in England which runs from Julius Caesar's arrival in Britain to the date of the book's completion (*c*.731). Bede went to great lengths to establish accurate dates, to include original documents and to cite his sources – methods that were centuries ahead of his time. Still working even in the final hours before his death, Bede managed to complete the first ever English translation of the Gospel of St John.

After his death in 735, Bede came rapidly to be regarded as a saint, and his writings were in huge and constant demand. Much of his work contained important truths on how Christian kings and bishops should act, and King Alfred used an English trans-lation of the *Ecclesiastical History* (originally written in Latin) as part of his educational programme when he was attempting to unite the English people in one kingdom. Bede had always regarded the individual kingdoms of early England as having an Anglo-Saxon unity, and as the country became more politically united, his works grew ever more relevant. Indeed, a new type of script had to be developed at Jarrow as the monks worked franti-cally to meet the demand for copies of Bede's work. His fame even spread to the continent, and in the 14th century he was granted a place in paradise by the great Italian poet Dante in his *Divine Comedy*.

Some of Bede's forthright thinking about the traditions of the church led to his being accused of heresy in his lifetime, but this was soon forgotten in what was generally recognized as a blame-less career. His celebrated contemporary Boniface said that Bede shone like a candle of the church by virtue of his knowledge of the Scriptures, and it was not long after his death before miracles began to be attributed to his relics.

The cult of Bede was adopted by his medieval fellows. His Latin style influenced his successors at the monastery at Jarrow. And his striving both for accuracy and intellectual truth in the writing of history has been passed down from generation to generation.

CHARLEMAGNE

768–814

Let peace, concord and unanimity reign among all Christian people . . . for without peace we cannot please God.

Charlemagne, *The Admonitio* (789)

Charlemagne – literally 'Charles the Great' – transformed his Frankish kingdom into a Christian empire that extended from France's western coast eastward into Germany, northward into the Low Countries, and southward into Italy. Charlemagne was not only a conqueror; he also presided over a court renowned for its artistic and scholarly achievements, especially in the preservation of classical learning.

The grandson of Charles Martel – the Hammer – who defeated the Islamic invasion of France, Charlemagne succeeded to the Frankish throne jointly with his brother, but the latter's death three years later left him in sole possession of the crown. His will for power driven by a sense of divine purpose, Charlemagne set about building a Christian realm during a reign of forty-six years and fifty-three military operations. In eighteen campaigns he subdued and converted the pagan Saxons. A decade later he conquered Bavaria, uniting the west Germanic tribes into one political entity for the first time. His influence extended still further. Campaigning from his Bavarian base, Charlemagne turned the Avar principalities (in modern-day Hungary and Austria) and the Slavic states along the Danube into dependants of the greatest empire since that of the Romans. In 773 Pope Adrian summoned him to help against the Lombards. By 778, he was master of Italy. Only once, when he made an unsuccessful incursion into Spain, was Charlemagne's effort to dominate Europe thwarted.

Pope Leo III's coronation of Charlemagne as emperor was one of history's most extraordinary Christmas presents. On Christmas Day AD 800, Charlemagne was attending mass in St Peter's Basilica in Rome for the consecration of his son, the future Louis the Pious, as king of Aquitaine. As Charlemagne rose from prayer, the pope slipped an imperial crown on his head. While the Romans present acclaimed him as 'Augustus and Emperor', the astonished Charlemagne, who a minute before had been kneeling at the tomb of the first pope, found himself with the current incumbent at his feet, 'adoring' him 'after the manner of emperors of old'.

According to the chronicler Einhard, Charlemagne's imperial coronation caught him completely off guard. Had he known what was going to happen, the emperor reportedly said, he would never have gone to the basilica that day. Charlemagne's outrage was surely feigned: the smoothness of the operation suggests that there was meticulous planning and negotiation beforehand.

The Byzantines did eventually deign to acknowledge him as 'emperor' (although they refused to automatically recognize his successors). For his part, Charlemagne laid no claim to their throne.

The so-called Carolingian Renaissance – named after

Charlemagne himself – transformed western Europe's spiritual and cultural life, as Charlemagne strove to fulfil what he saw as his divinely sanctioned purpose: the creation of a truly Christian empire. From the early years of his reign, Charlemagne sent out appeals for copies of remarkable or rare texts, whether Christian or classical. Libraries and schools flourished in monasteries and cathedrals across his realms. At his court at Aix-la-Chapelle (Aachen) Charlemagne gathered together Europe's most eminent scholars to instruct a new generation of the clergy, seeking to set up a chain of learning that would ultimately disseminate this Christian culture to the people. Greek was revived, and the intensive learning of Latin became compulsory in all educational establishments.

Charlemagne's single-minded drive for empire did breed a certain ruthlessness. He had few qualms about dealing with rivals, even among his own family. His nephews mysteriously disappeared when they fell into his hands; he deposed his cousin in order to conquer Bavaria; and when his hunchback son Pepin rebelled in 792, he put down the revolt with brutal force. Having secured the pope's approval for his conquest of Italy by promising to increase papal territory, Charlemagne reneged on the deal, keeping Lombardy for himself. When the Saxons rebelled, after accepting his sovereignty and converting to Christianity, Charlemagne was merciless. He considered their rebellion apostasy as well as treason, and he put it down with a level of violence rare even in his own violent era: on one occasion he executed 4000 Saxons in a single day. Yet in general he respected the rights and traditions of the lands he conquered.

Finally, Charlemange became a man of mystical myth: he corresponded with the caliph of the Abbasid empire, Haroun, who allowed him to protect the Christians of Jerusalem, where he built a small Christian quarter. The rumour spread that the emperor had secretly visited Jerusalem, inspiring the crusaders and French leaders up into the 20th century. Indeed Christians came to believe Charlemange might be the last emperor before the Last Judgement.

When Charlemagne felt the shadow of death upon him in 813, he crowned his son Louis, king of Aquitaine, as emperor. He died a few months later. Louis succeeded his father – but on his own death he divided his territories between his sons. Charlemagne's empire did not last long.

HAROUN AL-RASHID AND THE ABBASID CALIPHS

763/6–809

A goodly place, a goodly time,
For it was in the golden prime
Of good Haroun Alraschid
Alfred, Lord Tennyson,
'Recollections of the Arabian Nights' (1830)

Renowned for his luxury, hedonism, generosity and piety, Haroun al-Rashid was the remarkable caliph who reigned over the Abbasid Arab empire during its golden age. A lover of poetry, music and learning, Haroun's fabulous court has been immortalized, and fictionalized, in The Arabian Nights.

Haroun appears in many of *The Arabian Nights'* tales as a man devoted to pleasure and sensuality, a ruler who only abandons his magnificent court when he sneaks out incognito into the city at night for amorous encounters. The real Haroun was actually a capable military commander and autocrat. His piety was of the rational sort. He encouraged singing, believing the Koran's ban on music did not extend to the human voice. A keen horseman, he built race courses and is said to have introduced polo to the Arabs. Feast days and hunting expeditions became occasions of unparalleled splendour.

Haroun's empire extended from the borders of India to Spain, affording him the pursuit of pleasure on a scale that no other kingdom could match. Occasionally he checked himself, murmuring: 'I ask pardon of God, I have spent too much money.' But his largesse was widely distributed: every morning Haroun donated at least 1000 dirhams to the poor, setting an example that his wealthy subjects emulated, and giving rise to rumours that Baghdad's streets were paved with gold.

The Abbasids had seized the throne of the Islamic empire in 750, moving their court from Damascus to a new capital called Baghdad in Iraq. The court of the Abbasid caliphs was the marvel of the world. Ambassadors from other lands rubbed their eyes as they were shown elephants and lions decked out in brocade and satin, and gasped as they stood under the shade of a tree made of gold and silver, festooned with jewelled fruits. Proceeding through scores of courtyards, miles of marble arcades, innumerable chambers dripping with almost unimaginable wealth, they finally reached the caliph's presence. Here they were dazzled by the ebony throne and jewels so bright they seemed to eclipse the sun.

The caliphs embraced excess with abandon. When Haroun's son Mam'un married, the bride was showered with a thousand pearls. Haroun's 2000 singing and servant girls, twenty-four concubines and five wives seem moderate compared with the 4000 concubines of one of his descendants, who, in a reign lasting only a thousand nights, managed to sleep with every single one of them. Less successful was Mam'un's wedding night: the newly married couple found the scent of the precious ambergris candles irritating and ordered them to be removed from the bedroom. Mam'un himself subsequently withdrew when it became apparent that the bride's menstruation precluded consummation.

Legends of the harem abounded, and death awaited any man other than the caliph who gained entry to this shadowy, voluptuous kingdom. Fragranced with saffron and rosewater, each of the seven slave girls who attended Haroun at his daily siesta knew that sensuality could garner unimaginable rewards – Haroun's mother Khaizuran herself had risen from slave girl to powerful wife of the caliph.

Poets and musicians flocked to the court, which became the cultural centre of the Islamic world. Praising their ruler in language as lavish as his surroundings, the poets earned themselves considerable rewards. Musicians, hidden behind velvet curtains, provided the backdrop to long evenings of drinking and feasting. But death could come suddenly amid the hedonism, for intrigues abounded in the shadows.

Haroun made Baghdad the hub of civilization, earning it the name 'Bride of the World'. Believing that 'It is a disgrace for a ruler not to be learned,' he was on a constant quest for knowledge, and also promoted learning and the arts among his own people. He endowed scholarships, invited wise men from every kingdom to visit Baghdad and encouraged his formerly introspective scholars to profit from their knowledge. Haroun initiated an age of translation of Greek and other Christian classics of philosophy, and mathematics, medicine, astronomy and engineering all flourished.

Haroun's great love was poetry. No mean poet himself, his knowledge of verse was unparalleled even by learned men – he frequently corrected them on a slipped word. Poets filled his courts and were handsomely rewarded. Poetry was such a consuming passion for Haroun that he gave it up when on pilgrimage as an act of self-denial.

Haroun's strength as a ruler lay in the personal loyalty he commanded. When he became the fifth Abbasid caliph in 786 at the age of twenty-two, Baghdad's populace spontaneously crowded the streets to rejoice. He has been criticized for leaving a clan of administrators, the Barmakids, to govern in the early years of his reign, and for being too influenced by his redoubtable mother, Khaizuran. Open and instinctively trusting, Haroun was content to accept the advice of his viziers and theologians. Leaving his administration in capable hands, Haroun preferred instead to undertake extensive tours of inspection across his vast territories, making himself personally known to his subjects. His forays through the streets of Baghdad were in fact more paternalistic than amorous; he was said to roam his capital in disguise to check on his people's welfare.

Haroun was hot-tempered but quick to feel remorse and rarely vengeful. His most ruthless act was his removal of the Barmakids from power. Yahya al-Barmaki had been Haroun's boyhood tutor, his first vizier, and the man he called father. After seventeen years of service in which Yahya and his family established a monopoly over the government of the caliphate, Haroun, in a lightning *coup d'état*, executed or imprisoned the entire clan and its clients. Romance has it that this was revenge for an affair between his vizier at that time, Jafar al-Barmaki, and Haroun's sister. When Haroun eventually decided to move against the Barmakid clan, he ordered his grand vizier Jafar to spend the night feasting; while thus occupied he received a stream of gifts from the caliph until the arrival of a messenger bearing Haroun's only request: the head of Jafar. More characteristic of Haroun was his subsequent pilgrimage to Mecca. The last of nine, this time he made the thousand-mile journey barefoot as penance for his acts against a family to whom he owed so much.

Haroun was one of the most respected rulers of his age, acknowledged by both of Europe's emperors. Charlemagne reportedly sent him gifts, receiving an elephant and the keys of the Christian quarter of Jersusalem in return. The tribute of Byzantium's emperors, however, was secured by military force rather than goodwill: Haroun defeated the Byzantines several times. After Nicephorus I became Byzantine emperor, he tried to renege on the tribute owed to the caliphs and furthermore demanded reimbursement for the tributes made by his predecessor, Empress Irene. Haroun's response was simple: 'You will hear my reply before you read it.' The former civil servant Nicephorus was no match for the military skill of the caliph. After Haroun and his 135,000-strong army laid waste to Asia Minor and a parallel naval force overwhelmed Cyprus, the emperor capitulated and agreed to pay a yearly tribute of 30,000 gold pieces, each stamped with the head of the caliph and his three sons.

Haroun's death at the age of forty-seven cut short the reign of one of the most admired of the caliphs.

MAROZIA AND THE
PAPAL PORNOCRACY

c.890–932

... this monster without one single virtue to atone for his many vices.

> The verdict of the bishops convened by Otto
> to try Pope John XII, 963

Beautiful, sinister and canny, Marozia was a political harlot and powerful noblewoman who became senatrix and patrician of Rome, queen of Italy and the mistress, murderess, mother and grandmother of popes. Hers was an astonishing career of depravity, greed, murder and ruthlessness that dominated the papacy for decades.

Marozia was born in 890, the daughter of Count Theophylact of Tusculum and his courtesan, Theodora, called a 'shameless whore' and 'sole monarch of Rome' by her enemies. Indeed both mother and her two daughters Marozia and another Theodora were infamous. As the English historian Edward Gibbon wrote:

The influence of two prostitutes Marozia and Theodora was founded on their wealth and beauty, their political and amorous intrigues: the most strenuous of their lovers were rewarded with the Roman mitre and their reign may have suggested to darker ages the fable of a female pope. The bastard son, the grand-son and great-grandson of Marozia, a rare genealogy, were seated in the Chair of St Peter.

At fifteen Marozia became Pope Sergius III's mistress, producing a bastard son, later Pope John XI. In 909 she married Alberic, marquess of Spoleto, producing another son, Alberic II. The senatrix of Rome was now the most powerful of a dominant aristocracy. After Alberic I was killed, she became mistress of the reigning Pope John X, a tough and intelligent man, who resisted her control. (He had been a lover of her mother's too.) He defeated the Saracens but Marozia came to hate him: she turned against him, marrying his enemy Guy of Tuscany. Together they conquered Rome, imprisoning the pope. Marozia had John X (914–928) strangled in the Castel Sant'Angelo and then seized power for herself, ruling through her puppet popes Leo VI and Stephen VIII before raising her own papal bastard to the throne of St Peter as John XI, aged twenty-one, in 931. Widowed again, Marozia married Hugh of Arles, king of Italy, with whom she ruled. (Hugh was already married; his wife conveniently died, another victim of Marozia no doubt.) The couple were overthrown by her son Duke Alberic II, who imprisoned his mother until her death. Alberic ruled Rome through four popes. When the fourth resisted him, he was tortured to death. Alberic, on his own deathbed, demanded that his bastard son Octavian be made pope.

Reigning 955–964, Octavian, known as Pope John XII, grandson of Marozia, was the most shameful pontiff to lead the Christian Church, the antithesis of Christian virtues. He lived a private life of brazen immorality, turning the Vatican into a brothel. His behaviour was duplicitous, cruel and foolish – he and his grandmother personified the papal 'pornocracy' of the first half of the tenth century. Fittingly, he finally brought about his own downfall through his insatiable depravity.

On 16 December 955, Octavian became the highest authority in the Christian Church, both the spiritual and temporal ruler of

Rome at only eighteen years old, renaming himself John XII.

Through his mother Alda of Vienne he was a descendant of Charlemagne, but he showed none of the virtues expected of a pope. His private life was a litany of sin. Disdaining the celibacy his position required, he was a rampant adulterer, fornicating with literally hundreds of women, including his father's concubine Stephna. The sacred Lateran Palace, once the abode of saints, became a whorehouse, in which lounged hundreds of prostitutes, ready to serve his sexual whims. John had incestuous relations with two of his sisters.

Throughout his reign, John's fortunes were interwoven with those of the German King Otto I the Great, a friend of the Church to whom John appealed for help after suffering defeat in a war against Duke Pandulf of Capua, and then losing the Papal States to King Berengarius of Italy. Otto arrived in Italy with his powerful army, forcing Berengarius to back down. On reaching Rome in late January 962, Otto took an oath of allegiance to recognize John's authority, and on 2 February 962 John crowned Otto Holy Roman Emperor, along with his wife, Queen Adelaide, whom he made empress.

This powerful alliance was of benefit to both John and Otto but each immediately set about struggling to dominate the other. Shortly after Otto was crowned emperor, he issued his 'Ottonian Privilege', a treaty that promised to recognize the Pope's claim to the bulk of central Italy in exchange for a pledge that all future popes would only be consecrated after they had sworn allegiance to the holy Roman emperor. However, when Otto left Rome on 14 February 962 to continue his war against King Berengarius, John – fearful of Otto's strength – began secret negotiations with Berengarius' son Adalbert to rise up against him, and sent letters to other European rulers, encouraging them to do the same. However German troops intercepted these letters, the plot was laid bare, and if John had any hopes of placating the furious Otto, these soon ended. After John received Adalbert in Rome with great ceremony, bishops and nobles sympathetic to the German king rebelled. On 2 November 963, John was forced to flee Rome as Otto re-entered the city.

Whilst John hid in the mountains of Campania, Otto convened a panel of fifty bishops in St Peter's Basilica, who compiled a list of political and personal charges against him. These ranged from sacrilege (swearing oaths and toasting the devil with wine) to adultery, perjury and even murder (he was accused of blinding his confessor, Benedict, leading to his death, and of castrating and murdering his cardinal subdeacon). The excesses of his private life had also led him into flagrant abuses of his office, including simony – bestowing bishoprics and other ecclesiastical titles in return for payments – in order to pay his extensive gambling debts.

On 4 December 963, the synod found John guilty and deposed him, replacing him with Pope Leo VIII. However, the new appointment was made without following proper canonical procedure and few regarded Leo as a legitimate replacement. As Otto and Adalbert clashed on the battlefield again, a new revolt broke out in Rome, restoring John to the papacy, while Leo fled. Those who had betrayed John now suffered horrible vengeance. Cardinal Deacon John had his right hand cut off by the merciless pope while Bishop Otgar of Speyer was scourged; another official lost his nose and ears, many more were excommunicated. On 26 February 964, John repealed Otto's decrees in a special synod and re-established his own authority as pope.

John's position was still precarious and when Otto finally defeated Berengarius on the battlefield and started back for Rome, it seemed highly likely he would be deposed again. However, on 16 May 964, lustful to the last, John collapsed and died eight days after being caught in the act of adultery. Some say he was beaten up by the jealous husband; others that he was murdered; others again that the devil had claimed him as his own. Most believed he had been struck down by divine intervention or carnal exhaustion.

Pope John XII was a stain on the name of the Christian Church. It is said that monks prayed day and night for his death. 'You are charged with such obscenities as would make us blush if you were a stage player,' was Emperor Otto's verdict, writing to him after convening a council of bishops to depose him, 'It would require a whole day to enumerate them all.'

BASIL THE BULGAR SLAYER

957/8–1025

The emperor did not relent, but every year marched into Bulgaria and laid waste and ravaged all before him . . . The emperor blinded the Bulgarian captives – around 15,000 they say – and he ordered every hundred to be led back . . . by a one-eyed man.

John Skylitzes, late 11th-century Byzantine historian

Basil II was one of the most powerful, effective and brilliant – if merciless – rulers of the Byzantine empire, the ultimate hero-monster. A remarkably successful statesman and soldier, perennially engaged in warfare, Basil – who never married or fathered children – reigned for fifty years, expanding his empire to its greatest extent. He converted the Russians to Christianity, defeated the Bulgars, conquered the Caucasus and patronized the arts.

Accounts of Basil's appearance tally well with his brutal persona. Athletic in build, with a round face, bushy moustache and piercing blue eyes, he had a habit of twirling his whiskers between his fingers whenever he was angry or agitated – a frequent occurrence given his explosive temper. Reportedly he chose his words sparingly, barking rather than speaking them, in accordance with his generally abrupt manner. Never one to relax, he was always on guard for enemies, his right hand invariably poised to reach for his sword. He scorned jewellery, dressing in armour and eating the same rations as his troops, promising to look after their children if they died in battle for him.

Basil was the grandson of Constantine VII and the son of Romanos II. But Byzantine power politics were treacherous and the early years of Basil's life were marked by intrigue and rebellion. Romanos II had died in 963, leaving five-year-old Basil and his younger brother Constantine as the joint emperors; although Constantine would succeed Basil in 1025 and rule in his own right for three years, he did not play an active part in Basil's reign, accepting his brother's supremacy and preferring to watch the chariot racing at the Constantinople Hippodrome.

In 963, however, Basil was too young to rule the empire himself so his mother Theophano married a general in the army, who became Emperor Nikephoros II in 963. In 969, Theophano had Nikephoros murdered by her next lover, John Tzimisces, who also became emperor until his death in 976. Basil, now eighteen, finally acceded to the throne, but he soon faced open rebellion led by two ambitious landowners: first, Bardas Skleros, whose armies were swiftly destroyed in 979, and second, Bardas Phakos, whose forces were defeated in battle in April 989 after two years of fighting. Legend has it that Basil sat patiently on his horse, with his sword in one hand and a picture of the Virgin Mary in the other, preparing to face Phakos in one-to-one combat, before the latter suddenly died of a stroke.

Still a young man, Basil – who had demanded Phakos' severed head as a trophy – had shown himself to be a brave and ruthless combatant, not afraid to lead his armies into battle. Nonetheless, government of the empire remained largely in the hands of his uncle, the eunuch Basil Lekanpenos, the grand chamberlain of the imperial palace, so Basil accused him of secretly sympathizing with the rebel cause, and exiled him from Byzantium in 985. Distrustful of the established elite, Basil preferred to offer patronage and protection to small farmers in return for providing military service and regular taxes. He systematically toppled any other potential rivals, confiscating their lands and money to help fund his relentless military campaigns.

In 995, angered by Arab incursions into Byzantine territory, he gathered 40,000 men and attacked Syria – securing it for the Empire for the next 75 years. In the process, he sacked Tripoli and nearly reached Palestine and Jerusalem. His mortal enemy, however, was the equally ambitious and self-styled Tsar Samuel of Bulgaria, who had used the distractions of the Byzantine civil wars to extend his own empire from the Adriatic to the Black Sea, swallowing up swathes of Byzantine territory. Basil's early forays against the Bulgarians, such as the siege of Sofia in 986, had been costly and unsuccessful, leading to the disastrous ambush at the Gates of Trajan, in which thousands of his soldiers were lost and he barely escaped alive. From 1001, however, having eradicated his domestic enemies, Basil began to eat back into the territory conquered by Samuel, soon regaining Macedonia. Success was steady rather than spectacular until a massive victory at the Battle of Kleidon, on 29 July 1014, Basil's forces taking Samuel's capital.

As a brutal denouement to the campaign, Basil lined up the defeated prisoners and had them blinded. In a macabre gesture, he left one eye for every hundred men so that the hapless troops could find their way back to their homes. A reported 15,000 shuffled away in pathetic columns, wounded, blinded and utterly terrorized. According to the 11th-century historian John Skylitzes, the tsar fainted after seeing his soldiers return and died of a stroke. In this single horrifying moment, Basil earned his epithet Bulgar Slayer.

MELISENDE

1105–1161

AND THE CRUSADER KINGS OF JERUSALEM

. . . if you had been there you would have seen our feet coloured to our ankles with the blood of the slain. But what more shall I relate? None of them were left alive; neither women nor children were spared.

Fulcher of Chartres, medieval chronicler and chaplain
to the armies of Godfrey of Bouillon and his brothers,
describing the siege of Jerusalem in 1099

The idea of the crusade belonged to one visionary: in 1095, Pope Urban II announced a new theological concept – Christian holy war. In Clermont on 27 November, Urban addressed a crowd to declare that all who took the Cross and fought to liberate and cleanse the Holy Sepulchre of Jerusalem, to liquidate the infidel, would be granted remission of sins. As many as 80,000 people – from princes to peasants – answered the call and set off for Jerusalem, raising money any way they could, often with massacres and looting of Jewish communities. Some were adventurers who hoped to make their fortunes but this was an age of faith and the great majority were believers who risked their lives (and most died on the way) to reach Jerusalem. Godfrey of Bouillon, along with his brothers Eustace and Baldwin, were among the princes who answered the call.

Godfrey was born in 1060, probably in Boulogne-sur-Mer, to Eustace II, count of Boulogne (who had fought on the side of the Normans at the Battle of Hastings in 1066), and Ida 'the Blessed' of Boulogne (a pious and saintly figure who founded a number of monasteries). Godfrey was an athletic and fair-haired boy of 'pleasing' features, who, in the words of William of Tyre, was 'tall of stature . . . strong beyond compare, with solidly built limbs and a stalwart chest'. As the second son of the family, Godfrey did not stand to inherit much from his father, but in 1076 his childless hunchback uncle bequeathed him the duchy of Lower Lorraine.

In August 1096, Godfrey's army – estimated at 40,000 – began the long march through Hungary towards Constantinople. When they arrived in November, it soon became apparent that the crusaders and the Byzantine Emperor Alexius I had very different priorities. Alexius wanted to concentrate on winning back the lands he had lost to the Turks, whereas the crusaders were eager to conquer Jerusalem and capture the Holy Land. After a period of political tension throughout 1097 – in which Godfrey's troops pillaged the neighbourhood of Salabria – Godfrey tentatively agreed that his army would submit to Alexius's orders for a time before marching southwards towards Jerusalem.

From the summer of 1098, Godfrey's force – which had now joined up with other crusading armies – began to make inroads into Muslim lands, his reputation growing as he did so. In October, he reportedly killed 150 Turks with only twelve knights in a battle outside Antioch and the following month he cut a Turk in half with a single, downward swipe of his sword. Eventually, in February 1099, the various crusading armies conquered the major cities of Antioch and Edessa, founding new Christian principalities, and began their advance on Jerusalem, fighting through Tripoli and Beirut before arriving to besiege the city in June. Only about 12,000 crusaders had survived to reach the Holy City, under the command of five princes, Raymond the count of Toulouse, Robert the count of Flanders and Robert the duke of Normandy (son of William the Conqueror), plus the princely Norman adventurer Tancred de Hauteville and Godfrey of Bouillon. On the morning of Friday 15 July, Godfrey was among the first crusaders to breach the city's weak spot in its northern wall, after his men had built and scaled a movable tower which they had placed against the defences. Ferocious fighting took place on the parapets as Godfrey bravely held his position and directed his men into the city so that they could open the gates.

Thousands of crusaders flooded into the streets, as the Muslim citizens fled to al-Aqsa mosque. The Fatimid governor of the city made his last stand in the Tower of David. He and some of his soldiers were allowed to escape, but over the next forty-eight hours, those left in the city – combatant and civilian, Muslim and Jew – were put to the sword and murdered in the streets. The crusaders pillaged Muslim holy sites such as the Dome of the Rock and either burned their victims to death or cut open their stomachs, believing that Muslims swallowed their gold. The city's Jews had fled to a synagogue, which the crusaders simply burned to the ground. Raymond of Aguilers reported that he saw 'piles of heads, hands and feet' scattered across the city, while Fulcher of Chartres, a military chaplain, wrote approvingly that 'this place, so long contaminated by the superstition of the pagan inhabitants' had been 'cleansed from their contagion'. Six months later, it still stank of putrefaction.

At the height of the systematic massacre, Godfrey and the other 'pilgrims' stripped to their undergarments and walked solemnly, reeking of gore, barefoot through the blood, to pray at the Holy Sepulchre, site of Jesus' crucifixion. On 22 July, his fellow crusaders chose him to be the first Christian ruler of Jerusalem, although he refused to take the name of king in the city in which Christ had died, preferring instead the title 'duke and advocate of the Holy Sepulchre'. It was there that he was buried after dying of plague on 18 July 1100, his mission complete.

The massacre of Jews and Muslims in Jerusalem was a terrible crime (although its scale was exaggerated: Muslim historians claimed that 70,000 or even 100,000 died in the slaughter but it is likely there were no more than 30,000 inside the city and the latest research from contemporary Arab source el-Arabi suggests the number may be closer to between 3,000 and 10,000). Crusader brutality demonstrates an era dominated by intolerance: when the crusader cities of Edessa and Acre later fell, Muslim conquerors slaughtered all the inhabitants of these much larger cities.

As for Godfrey, his short reign founded a kingdom and a dynasty, built by gifted and remarkable warlords: most significantly his much more dynamic, talented (and bigamous) brother, Baldwin, count of Edessa who succeeded him as king of Jerusalem. Baldwin I conquered a substantial kingdom in what is today's Israel, Syria, Jordan and Lebanon. He was known as 'the arm of his people, the terror of his enemies': relentless war was his duty and his passion – he died on one of his frequent raids on Islamic Egypt. His heir was his cousin Baldwin II, who continued to build the kingdom, succeeded by his half-French, half-Armenian daughter, the shrewd Queen Melisende, one of the great female rulers. While married to the competent but charmless Fulk, Count of Anjou, it was she who held the power. Slim, dark and clever, she notoriously flirted with a handsome cousin – but under her the Jerusalem kingdom reached its golden age: it was Melisende who built not only today's church of the Holy Sepulchre but also the Tomb of the Virgin Mary and the markets of Jerusalem that survive today. Finally, after a near civil war, she ceded the throne to her dashing warrior son Baldwin III. But his early death in 1162 was a grave misfortune for Outremer, 'across the sea', as the Crusader kingdoms were known. His fat brother Amaury, both intellectual and soldier, repeatedly raided Egypt, almost conquering it – but he died at thirty-eight. His son Baldwin IV seemed promising, but he was already doomed. The tragedy of Baldwin IV– a brave teenage prince who was slowly dying of leprosy – symbolized the crisis of the kingdom, beset by corruption, ineptitude and intrigue. The leper-king fought Jerusalem's increasingly organized enemies, now led by the formidable Saladin, until blind and decaying, he perished. His heir, the feckless and vain Guy of Lusignan, married to the king's sister, was no match for Saladin, who defeated the crusaders at the Battle of Hattin on 4 July 1187. Jerusalem fell a few months later but a rump kingdom based along the coast around Acre survived until 1291.

SALADIN

c.1138–1193

He was a man wise in counsel, valiant in war and generous beyond measure.

William of Tyre, *A History of Deeds Done Beyond the Sea*
(1170)

The Kurdish-born sultan Saladin became the ideal of the warrior-king, he was an efficient commander and a tolerant ruler devoid of fanaticism. Ruling an empire stretching from Libya to Iraq, Saladin drew together disparate elements of the Arab and Turkish world in the struggle between Islam and Christendom for control of the Holy Land. A merciless warlord in his rise to power, and never quite the liberal gentleman of Victorian romance, he nevertheless embraced the code of chivalry and was respected by his enemies. By the standards of medieval empire-builders, he was indeed an attractive character.

Yusuf ibn Ayyub, who later adopted the name Salah-al-Din, the Goodness of the Faith, was born to a Kurdish family in Tikrit, now in northern Iraq (and much later the birthplace of the tyrant Saddam Hussein), son of the local governor and nephew of a lieutenant of Nur ad-Din, ruler of Syria. At twenty-six, Saladin set off with his mace-wielding and very fat uncle Shirkuh to defeat the crusaders in a war to win control of Fatmid Egypt. They succeeded but Shirkuh died of a heart attack. In 1171, Saladin seized Egypt on his master's behalf after massacring 5000 Sudanese guards. Three years later Nur ad-Din died, and Saladin took control of Syria as well.

Ruling from Damascus, Saladin built an empire based on a combination of political cunning, ruthless order, military prowess and Islamic justice. After a lifetime killing his fellow Muslims in his quest for a personal empire, he now devoted himself to the jihad to liberate Jersualem from the crusaders of the Christian Kingdom of Jerusalem. By 1177 Saladin had built up an army capable of opposing the Christian occupiers of the Holy Land – as holy to Muslims as to Christians. Yet at the Battle of Montgisard his army of 26,000 was surprised and routed by a far smaller crusader force under the 'Leper King' of Jerusalem, Baldwin IV.

This was the last major reverse in Saladin's struggle against the Christian interlopers. Though a truce was called in 1178, the following year Saladin resumed his jihad against the crusaders, besieging and capturing the castle the crusaders were building at Jacob's Ford, which presented a strategic threat to Damascus. Saladin razed the castle to the ground.

During the 1180s Saladin was dragged into increasingly serious skirmishes with the crusaders, in particular Prince Raynald of Chatillon. Unrestrained by weak kings in Jerusalem, Raynald intensified the conflict when the crusaders could ill-afford the risk, harassing Muslim pilgrims on haj, showing a total disregard for the sanctity of the Muslim holy sites of Mecca and Medina. All this only served to fire Saladin's determination to win his holy war.

By 1187 he had raised sufficient forces to invade the Kingdom of Jerusalem, which had been weakened by the long illness of Baldwin IV, the infighting of its barons and the weak ineptitude of the new King Guy. The crusaders were annihilated at the Battle of Hattin, only a few thousand escaping the field. Saladin took King Guy of Jerusalem and Prince Raynald as prisoners. He gave King Guy iced water later – but personally beheaded Raynald. In October Jerusalem itself fell, ending eighty-eight years of crusader occupation.

The fall of Jerusalem opened a new chapter in the history of the crusades: Saladin's rivalry with Richard I of England, known as Richard the Lionheart. Richard arrived in the Holy Land in June 1191, and the following month Acre fell to the crusaders. In September Richard defeated Saladin at Arsuf but not decisively. With both sides' resources depleted, the Lionheart could not take Jerusalem so they agreed a truce in autumn 1192. Richard won a partition of Palestine: the crusaders got a rump along the coast centred on Acre but he had lost the great game because Saladin kept Jerusalem and his empire of Egypt, Syria and Iraq. Saladin demonstrated his tolerance by agreeing to allow unarmed Christian pilgrims into Jerusalem. Richard left the Holy Land shortly afterwards. Though the two never met again, and Saladin died the following year, the relationship between the two men passed into legend. Richard seems to have been genuinely struck by Saladin's skill, tolerance and magnanimity as a ruler and battlefield commander.

There is no denying that Saladin could be merciless towards prisoners of war. Like Richard, he thought little of massacring them if the conditions of war demanded it. After Hattin, he slaughtered all the Knights Templar in cold blood. Such were the standards of medieval religious warfare. But chroniclers on both sides sang the praises of Saladin the lawgiver, just ruler and great prince. He could inspire men to take to the battlefield despite daunting odds, and he was usually courteous and chivalrous towards his Christian enemies.

After Saladin's death, the Muslim chronicler Baha al-Din called him 'one of the most courageous of men; brave, gallant, firm, intrepid in any circumstance'. Saladin, sultan of Egypt and Syria, left an Ayyubid empire to his brother Safadin and the family dominated until 1250. The pre-eminent Kurd in history, he became a symbol of Arab pride in the 20th century, with revolutionary Egypt, Iraq and Palestinian groups adopting his eagle symbol.

RICHARD THE LIONHEART & JOHN SOFTSWORD

1157–1199 & 1167–1216

Richard was a bad son, a bad husband and a bad king, but a gallant and splendid soldier.

Steven Runciman

Richard I was one of the most capable and glamorous of English kings; his youngest brother John was one of the most inept and unattractive. They were the sons of King Henry II and his wife Eleanor of Aquitaine, who together ruled England and half of France – the Angevin empire. Henry was to spend much of his reign repelling attacks by the ambitious Philip II of France, who was determined to extend his own borders.

Henry had four legitimate sons. The first – also Henry – was known as Young King after Henry II had him crowned while he himself was still alive, and who died in his twenties. The second was Richard, who ultimately succeeded to the throne as RichardI; Geoffrey became duke of Brittany and earl of Richmond; John was the fourth. The rivalry between the old king and his greedy, jealous and violent sons was so vicious that they were known as the Devil's Brood. However, the overbearing and dominating Henry II, a swashbuckling royal titan, often favoured John, perhaps because he was the weakest and least able – and therefore the lesser threat to his own power.

More legends have accrued around Richard I than any other English king. His chivalrous rivalry with Saladin during the Third Crusade was the subject of famous ballads and tales across Europe, as was his long, Odysseus-like journey home. Richard was the archetypal Angevin king. Like the rest of his family, he had a furious temper and could be irresponsible and impulsive. And, being an Angevin with huge European interests, he simply regarded England as another fiefdom to defend and a resource to fund his conquests.

Brash, tall, with red-golden hair, he adopted scarlet as his colour, and wielded a sword he called Excalibur. Highly intelligent, energetic and flexible, he was capable of gruesome cruelty and ruthlessness. He massacred thousands of Muslim prisoners in cold blood outside Acre and, on another occasion, arranged the heads of executed Muslims around his tent – yet he also once stripped naked and whipped himself in church for his sins. He was not interested in women except as political pawns, though he did father at least one bastard (it is unlikely he was gay as claimed by some scholars). War was his ruling passion and outstanding talent.

Richard was invested with land and power from the age of eleven, when he was raised to duke of Aquitaine. He became duke of Poitou four years later and immediately allied with his brothers and his mother in a failed rebellion against their father Henry II in 1173–4. A harsh lord, Richard himself provoked rebellion among his subjects in Gascony in 1183, and a few years later was rebelling again against his father, this time in alliance with Louis, the king of France and his mother's former husband.

In 1188, Henry finally lost patience and declared he no longer saw Richard as his heir, which propelled the future Lionheart once more to come out in open rebellion. Initially, John fought alongside Henry, but, in what was to become a familiar pattern, he switched sides when it was clear Richard was set to triumph. King Henry died shortly afterwards, heartbroken at the betrayal by his sons: in 1189 Richard succeeded as king of England and ruler of the Angevin empire. But his focus was on Jerusalem, which Saladin had conquered in 1187. After mortgaging as much of his kingdom as he could and taxing England with the so-called Saladin tithe, Richard sailed for the Holy Land via Sicily in 1190. 'I'd have sold London if there had been a buyer,' he said.

He ravaged Sicily then conquered Cyprus on the way. On arrival he fought hard and bloody battles against Saladin's forces, besieging and capturing Acre, butchering 3,000 Muslim prisoners to counter Saladin's delaying negotiations and winning the Battle of Arsuf with a cavalry charge, but he failed to take the main prize of Jerusalem. Despite their violent struggle, Richard and Saladin held for each other a chivalrous respect. Each thought and spoke with the highest regard of the other. When Richard was sick and thirsty,

Saladin sent him fresh fruit and water, and when he was in need of a horse, Saladin sent him one of his finest.

During their peace negotiations, Saladin was dazzled by Richard's scarlet-clad exploits – especially his last-minute rescue of Jaffa, wading into the sea right under Saladin's nose. The sultan is said to have called Richard 'so pleasant, upright, magnanimous and excellent that, if the land [Jerusalem] were to be lost in my time, he would rather have it taken into Richard's mighty power than to have it go into the hands of any other prince whom he had ever seen'. When both sides had fought themselves to exhaustion, Richard offered Saladin a unique and imaginative deal: his brother Safadin would marry Richard's sister and rule Palestine together from Jerusalem. It did not work of course but it shows Richard's dynamic flexibility.

In his absence, John, now raised to count of Mortain and granted huge estates to assuage his greed – in return for agreeing not to visit England at all – was plotting to seize power and meddling in English politics, breaking his ban. Richard had to settle things in the Holy Land and rush home. But on his way back his enemies Emperor Henry VI and Duke Leopold of Austria captured him and held him to ransom, giving John the opportunity, in January 1193, to control England. John, however, failed in an attempt to invade England with the assistance of King Philip II of France, and then unsuccessfully attempted to bribe Richard's captors to hand him over to his custody. As Richard once put it, 'my brother John is not the man to win lands by force if there is anyone at all to oppose him'.

On his return (after the astonishing sum of 150,000 marks had been raised for his release), Richard showed incredible leniency to his wayward brother and officially declared him his successor before leaving the country to make war against Philip of France. So, when Richard was killed in 1199 by crossbow bolt at a siege in

France, John became king of England and duke of Normandy and Aquitaine.

King John lost most of his empire, broke every promise he ever made, dropped his royal seal in the sea, impoverished England, murdered his nephew, seduced the wives of his friends, betrayed his father, brothers and country, foamed at the mouth when angry, starved and tortured his enemies to death, lost virtually every battle he fought, fled any responsibility whenever possible and died of eating too many peaches. Treacherous, lecherous, malicious, avaricious, cruel and murderous, he earned his nicknames Softsword for military cowardice and incompetence, and Lackland for losing most of his inheritance.

On his succession, his nephew, Arthur, duke of Brittany, the son of Geoffrey II and Constance, was a serious rival to the throne, considered by many as the rightful king, so John quickly arrested the boy, aged fifteen, and – in a crime not unlike that of Richard III and the Princes in the Tower – had him murdered the following year. Arthur's murder provoked a rebellion in Brittany and a humiliating retreat for John's armies, who were forced to withdraw from the region in 1204. By 1206, Softsword had lost nearly all of England's territorial possessions in France, putting up only limp resistance. In fact, when Normandy – England's last possession on the continent – was seized by the French, John reportedly stayed in bed with his wife, as his soldiers fell in the rout.

Richard, for all his faults, had been admired for his chivalry, unlike the priapic John, who had countless mistresses and illegitimate children, often trying to force himself on the wives and daughters of important noblemen. His treatment of prisoners was particularly odious; he starved to death the wife and son of one of his enemies.

Stranded on English soil and short of funds, John imposed large increases in taxation and mercilessly exploited his feudal prerogatives, giving rise to the popular legend of Robin Hood holding out in Sherwood Forest against royal extortion. Between 1209 and 1213, when John was excommunicated by Pope Innocent III, he shamelessly plundered the revenues of the Church.

From 1212, John faced increasing opposition from the nobility, who began to plot against him. After another thoroughly disastrous military campaign in France in 1214, rebellion finally broke out in England. At a famous meeting in a meadow by the Thames at Runnymede on 15 June 1215, the barons forced John to seal Magna Carta, the foundation of modern English liberties, guaranteeing them rights against the arbitrary rule of the king. John had no intention of keeping his word, and quickly betrayed his promise to abide by the charter, prompting a return to civil war. As he tried his rally his forces, his entourage – with his treasure and bags – was almost lost as he crossed the Wash. The tides rose unexpectedly, and in his frantic efforts to save his possessions he lost the Great Seal of England. As the king betrayed his promises of Magna Carta, he faced a French invasion and a general baronial revolt: his power was slipping away when he fell ill. His death too became him: the king succumbing to dysentery after an excessively voracious meal of peaches and ale.

GENGHIS KHAN

c.1163–1227

The greatest happiness is to scatter your enemy, to drive him before you, to see his cities reduced to ashes, to see those who love him shrouded in tears, and to gather into your bosom his wives and daughters.

Genghis Khan

Charismatic, dynamic, ferocious, violent and ambitious, Genghis Khan was a military genius, brilliant statesman and world conqueror who united the nomadic tribes of the Asian steppes to create the Mongol empire, the largest land empire in history. But the triumphs of this heroic monster had a terrible price – a reign of terror and mass killing across Eurasia on a scale never before seen.

Genghis Khan was born between 1163 and 1167 in the mountainous terrain of Khentii province in Mongolia, reportedly clutching a blood clot – a supposed portent of his future greatness as a warrior. He was named Temujin, after a tribesman recently captured by his father. The third son of Yesukhei – a local chieftain – and Hoelun, Temujin was soon to experience at first hand the dangerous world of Mongolian tribal politics. When Temujin was aged just nine, his father arranged for him to marry Börte, a girl from a neighbouring tribe. He was sent to live with Börte's family, but, shortly afterwards, Yesukhei was poisoned by vengeful tribesmen, and Temujin was obliged to return home. Deprived of their protector, Temujin's family was forced out into the wilderness, where they survived by eating berries, nuts, mice and other small animals. At thirteen, Temujin murdered his own half-brother.

Several years of wandering followed, marked by intertribal kidnapping and feuds, during which time Temujin – who soon became known and feared for his leadership, intelligence and military ability – built up a sizeable following. A tall, strong and hardened young man, with piercing green eyes and a long reddish beard, he finally married Börte at the age of sixteen and was taken under the wing of Toghril Ong-Khan, ruler of the Kerait tribe (and his father's blood brother). When Börte was later kidnapped by the Merkit tribe, Temujin and Toghril joined forces with Jamuka, a childhood friend of Temujin and now a Mongol chieftan, sending a large army to rescue her. (Börte turned out to be pregnant, and Temujin brought up the child, Jochi, as his own son.) The three-way alliance enabled the Mongols and Keraits to force other tribes into submission.

Following this success, in 1200 Toghril declared Temujin his adoptive son and heir – a fateful decision that enraged both Toghril's natural son, Senggum, and the ambitious Jamuka, leading ultimately to a war in which Temujin defeated first Jamuka and then Toghril to establish his dominance over the Mongol tribes. In 1206, a council of leading Mongolian tribesmen – called the Kurultai – met and recognized Temujin's authority, giving him the name Genghis Khan, meaning Oceanic Khan or Ruler of the Universe.

Before 1200, the Mongols had been a scattered people, but Genghis – claiming a mandate from heaven – was swiftly to transform them into a powerful and unified nation. 'My strength,' he declared, 'was fortified by Heaven and Earth. Foreordained by Mighty Heaven, I was brought here by Mother Earth.' His soldiers were mainly nomadic warriors, including deadly archers who travelled on small but sturdy Mongolian-bred ponies capable of covering great distances. Genghis turned them into a disciplined and brilliantly coordinated war machine that swept all before them.

In 1207 – having secured an alliance with the Uighurs and subjugated the Mongols' old rivals, the Merkit tribe – Genghis immediately began expansionist operations, eating into the Xi Xia territory in northwest China, as well as parts of Tibet. His target was the Silk Road – a key trade route between east and west and the gateway to wealth. In 1211, after refusing to pay tribute to the Jin dynasty in northern China, he went to war again, besieging and destroying the Jin capital, Yanjing, now Beijing, and securing instead tribute for himself. He returned to Mongolia in triumph, taking with him booty, artisans and, above all, guaranteed trade with China.

In 1219, Genghis turned his attentions west after an attack on a caravan of traders he had sent to establish trading links with the Khwarazm empire – a realm including most of Uzbekistan, Iran and Afghanistan under the rule of the sultan Muhammad Khwarazmshah. Genghis showed restraint, but when members of a second Mongolian delegation were beheaded, he raised 200,000 troops and marched into central Asia, with his four sons, Jochi, Ogodei, Chaghatai and Touli serving as commanders. Over the next three years, he subjected the Khwarazm people to a terrifying campaign of shock and awe, taking the cities of Bokhara, Samarkand, Herat, Nishapar and Merv – his troops lining up the civilians of the latter and, in a cold-blooded killing spree, slitting their throats.

A peerless strategist, Genghis recognized the value of fear in building an empire, often sending out envoys to cow enemies into submission through tales of his exploits: civilians slaughtered, money and booty stolen, women raped, molten silver poured into people's ears. For all this brutality, however, Genghis did not indulge in killing for the sake of it. He was loyal to his friends and generous to supporters, a shrewd manager of men, who promoted an elite of top generals, giving them enormous powers. He spared those who surrendered, reserving wholesale slaughter to make an example of those who resisted. Nor did the Mongols wantonly maim, mutilate or torture – their chief interest was in booty rather than barbarism. Indeed, in some ways Genghis showed himself to be an enlightened ruler, combining political acumen with economic shrewdness. He used divide-and-rule tactics to weaken enemies and promote loyalty. He recognized the importance of good administration, fostering the spread of a unified official language across his empire and a written legal system called Jasagti. He was also tolerant of religions and gave priests an exemption from taxation. Believing in the importance of providing a safe passage of trade between the east and the west, he forbade troops and officials to abuse merchants or citizens, his reign becoming a period of cultural interaction and advancement for the Mongolian people. He was also a patron of artists, craftsmen and literature.

After his early triumphs over the Khwarazm empire, Genghis pressed on, eager to consolidate his gains. He pushed into Russia, Georgia and the Crimea, defeating the forces of Prince Mstitslav of Kiev at the Battle of Kalka River in 1223, in which, after a feigned retreat, his forces turned on their pursuers and routed them. He now ruled a vast empire stretching from the Black Sea to the Pacific, his people enjoying ever-increasing wealth. In 1226, however, he died after he fell from his horse hurrying back to Xi Xia, where a rebellion had erupted in his absence.

The Great Khan left his empire to his son Ogodei, though it was soon divided amongst the descendants of his sons, who founded their own khanates which ruled the Near East, Russia and China (where his grandson Kublai Khan founded his own dynasty). The

Mongol empire thus expanded even further, until it stretched from the Pacific coast of Asia in the east to Hungary and the Balkans in the west. The Crimean khanate, longest-lasting of the successor states of the Mongol empire, would survive up until 1783.

A Y chromosomal lineage in an astounding 8 per cent of men in Asia is descended from one source. Most likely this was Genghis himself.

FREDERICK II OF HOHENSTAUFEN: WONDER OF THE WORLD

1194–1250

He was an adroit man, cunning, greedy, wanton, malicious, bad-tempered, but at times when he wished to reveal his good and courtly qualities, consoling, witty, delightful, hard working.

Salimbene di Adam, *Chronicle* (1282–90)

The author of a book on falconry called *The Art of Hunting with Birds*, Frederick was the most powerful ruler in Europe – Holy Roman Emperor, king of Sicily, later king of Jerusalem and heir to vast German-Italian lands. Green-eyed, ginger-haired, son of the German Emperor Henry IV and the Norman heiress of Sicily, Constance, he was raised in Sicily, a court that blended Christian and Islamic, Arab and Norman culture. If his upbringing – speaking Arabic and at home with Jews and Muslims – made him seem exotic, his eccentricity was his own. He travelled with Arab bodyguards, a Scottish magician, Jewish and Arab scholars, fifty falconers, a zoo and a sultanic harem of odalisques. He was said to be an atheistic scientist who joked that Jesus, Muhammad and Moses were frauds and was portrayed as a proto-Dr Frankenstein who sealed a dying man in a barrel to see if his soul would escape.

Yet he was actually an effective and ruthless politician with a clear vision of his own role as universal Christian emperor. In 1225, he married Yolande, fifteen, heiress to Jerusalem, making him king of the Holy City. He seduced one of her ladies at the wedding and she died at sixteen. But, after many false starts Frederick set off in 1227 on crusade, even though already ex-communicated by Pope Gregory IX for his delays. Backed by his Teutonic Knights, Frederick offended the crusader barons with his imperial air, seduced local ladies and marched down the coast – all the time, negotiating with Saladin's nephew, Sultan Kamil of Egypt, who, faced with his own rebellions as well as this new crusader threat, agreed a most unconventional peace deal.

The sultan agreed to share Jerusalem with the emperor. Like a modern peace deal in the Middle East, the Muslims kept the Temple Mount (Haram al-Sharif), the Christians got the rest of Jerusalem. Frederick arrived in Jerusalem to reclaim the Holy City, where he showed his unusual respect for Islam. In the church of the Holy Sepulchre, he held a crown-wearing ceremony to promote his vision of himself as Christian emperor. But he then had to flee – pursued by the papal ban. He ruled Jerusalem from afar for ten years – but the majority of his life was devoted to his war against the papacy.

Papal policy had dictated his upbringing. His father, Emperor Henry VI, had challenged the popes for leadership of Christendom. After Henry's sudden death, the curia ensured the division of his lands: two other candidates were installed in the German kingdom, while the infant Frederick was left with Sicily. His mother died shortly afterwards, and the four-year-old king of Sicily became a ward of the papacy. After his German replacements had proved too territorially ambitious, Frederick was reinstalled as a teenager in his northern titles, but not before his erstwhile guardian, Pope Innocent III, had extracted from him promises of extensive papal privileges and numerous vows never to reunite Germany and Sicily under one ruler.

Frederick, however, refused to be a puppet. He saw the Holy Roman Empire as sacred and universal. His conception of imperial sovereignty drove him to extend his authority into the Italian states that lay between his northern and southern lands.

Frederick's conflict with his former guardians overshadowed European politics for half a century. On one level the gigantic struggle was simply a personality clash between the piously intellectual Pope Gregory IX, elected in 1227, and the witty and worldly Frederick. When Gregory IX excommunicated Frederick in 1227 for apparently malingering rather than going on crusade, Frederick's decision to go anyway, and in the process crown himself king of Jerusalem, did little to improve relations.

At the heart of this bitter conflict lay the question of who would dominate Christendom: pope or emperor. With each side buoyed up by a messianic belief in his cause, Italy became the battleground of papal troops and imperial forces. Missives, manifestos, papal bulls and insults flew across Europe. Frederick was again excommunicated. If he was the Wonder of the World to his admirers, he was henceforth Beast of the Apocalypse to his enemies. Two different popes, Gregory IX and Innocent IV, fled Rome, the former dying in exile. In 1245 Innocent IV fired the papacy's ultimate salvo: he announced the emperor was deposed. For the next five years it was all-out war. In the end it was death, not the papacy, that defeated Frederick. Fighting on against the almost insurmountable twin obstacles of excommunication and deposition, Frederick was regaining ground in both Italy and Germany when he died suddenly in 1250.

EDWARD III & THE BLACK PRINCE

1312–1377   1330–1376

> *The greatest soldier of his age.*
> Jean Froissart, *Chronicles* (late 14th century)
> on the Black Prince

Edward III and the Black Prince were the father and son who personified the glory, energy and triumph of English chivalry at its medieval apogee. Edward III was the most successful and heroic of English kings; the Black Prince – formally Edward, Prince of Wales – was the most chivalrous and celebrated knight in Europe. Along with King Henry V, they are the greatest princes in British history.

Edward III displayed, throughout his extraordinary long reign, remarkable energy, daring and ambition, often distinguishing himself in the thick of the fighting. He grew up under the shadow of his disastrously weak father Edward II, who was deposed and murdered in 1327 by his mother, Queen Isabella, and her lover Roger Mortimer. The two then ruled despotically until the side-lined king, aged just seventeen, arranged a successful *coup d'état*, personally leading the posse of his close friends to seize Mortimer, an act of characteristic derring-do.

Dynamic, talented and athletic, Edward first waged war against the Scots, leading the conquest of much of the Lowlands and achieving a glorious victory at Halidon Hill in 1333. Like his grandfather Edward I, he tried to impose his own candidate, in this instance Edward Balliol, on the Scottish throne. In 1346, the king's army won an even greater victory at Neville's Cross, capturing

King David II of Scotland, who was destined to spend many years as a hostage at the court in London.

In 1338, Edward launched his new policy aimed at reasserting the English claim to the crown of France and the Angevin territories lost by King John. By 1340, he was acclaimed king of France and then won a naval battle at Sluys against the French, though he had to return to London to face a political and financial crisis which ended with his dismissal of his minister, John Stratford, Archbishop of Canterbury. He returned to France in 1346, conquering territory including Calais and winning the ultimate of his many victories at the Battle of Crécy, the achievement of his skill in command and his English archers. After Crécy, Halidon Hill and Sluys, and the conquest of Calais, Edward's prestige as king and warrior were enormous. In 1350, hearing that Calais was about to be betrayed, Edward, at great risk to himself, secretly rushed there with an armed group, saved the town in a brief skirmish and destroyed the traitors – a virtuoso performance.

When his eldest son and heir, Edward of Woodstock, was thirteen, the king allowed him to start campaigning abroad. As the English faced the French at Crécy in 1346, the king placed Edward's company in the thick of the fighting. The French fell upon the prince and his men, and it took every ounce of strength to batter them back. Although later stories tell of the king refusing to help until the prince had 'won his spurs', in fact Edward III realized that his son was in grave danger and sent reinforcements of twenty senior knights. But when they arrived, they found the prince and his companions catching their breath, having already repulsed the French.

The legend of the Black Prince – named for his black armour – was born at Crécy, and it was one that the prince was keen to maintain. One of the allies of the French, King John of Bohemia, had demanded to be brought into battle despite being totally blind. Not surprisingly, he did not survive long. But the prince was impressed with his chivalry and adopted the Bohemian ostrich feathers as his own heraldic device in the dead king's honour. The ostrich feathers still form the crest of the Prince of Wales today.

Edward appointed his son as prince of Aquitaine. Ten years later, in 1356, with a decade's experience of command behind him, the Black Prince commanded another division of English troops to an even greater victory. Without his father to back him up, the prince was not particularly enthused by the idea of engaging the French king, John II; yet on 19 September he led his men into battle about five miles from Poitiers. The prince used his tactical nous to outflank his enemies, charging down-hill at them and engaging them in hand-to-hand combat. The French king was captured, and a victory even greater than Crécy was won.

Stories of the Black Prince's chivalrous deeds spread across Europe: he famously deferred to the superior rank of his captive, King John, refusing to eat with him but rather serving him at table.

Poitiers marked the high point of the prince's career. As governor of Aquitaine he was hated for his harsh rule, and he also ill-advisedly became involved with Spanish politics in Castile. With his beautiful wife Joan, 'The Fair Maid of Kent', he gained a reputation for lavish indulgence and a lack of political finesse.

Edward III now revelled in his chivalric glory as he held two kings – of France and Scotland – to ransom in London and earned vast sums from both. He celebrated his success by founding the Order of the Garter, playing up to his legend as a latter-day King Arthur. Yet despite these astonishing victories, Edward now found it hard to dominate Scotland and hold on to his conquests in France – signing an unsatisfactory treaty with the latter in 1360.

Edward had been happily married to Queen Philippa, with

whom he had many children. But he now embarked on an affair with Alice Perrers, who was soon notorious for her greed and corruption in partnership with the unscrupulous Lord Latimer. The court was now in decline. Edward suffered strokes and the Black Prince returned from Aquitaine and his unsuccessful Castilian enterprises incapacitated by illness. John of Gaunt, duke of Lancaster, who also became entangled in the Castilian intrigues – hoping to become king of Castile – took control of government as Edward III's next ranking son. After Queen Philippa died, Alice Perrers became more brazen and wealthy.

By 1376, the glorious reign, blessed with so many victories, had turned sour. The Black Prince died – the most famous knight in Europe. Edward was sick and John of Gaunt's attempts to defend his father and the crown were clumsy. In 1376 and 1377 the 'Good Parliament' effectively demanded the dismissal of Alice Perrers and the trial of Lord Latimer. Edward III and John of Gaunt were tainted with scandal and humiliation.

In 1377, Edward finally died after a reign of fifty years, succeeded by his ill-starred grandson Richard II, son of the Black Prince. Nonetheless, Edward had proved a brilliant monarch and military commander, with a winning personal charm and glamour, remarkable courage, luck in war and politics and a feel for theatre and pageantry. The Black Prince was less politically astute – but no less glamorous. The English rarely dub their kings great, but if any deserve this soubriquet, it is Edward the Great.

TAMERLANE

1336–1405

He loved bold and valiant soldiers, by whose aid he opened the locks
of terror, tore men to pieces like lions, and overturned mountains.
Arab writer Ahmad ibn Arabshah, describing Tamerlane

Tamerlane was a statesman and military commander of astonishing brilliance and brutal ferocity who built an empire stretching from India to Russia and the Mediterranean Sea. Never defeated in battle, he ranks alongside Genghis Khan and Alexander the Great as one of the great conquerors of all time, leaving in his wake both pyramids of human skulls and the aesthetic beauty of his capital Samarkand.

Timur – meaning iron in Turkic – was born in Kesh, south of Samarkand, in 1336. His father was a minor chief of the Barlas tribe, settled in Transoxiana (roughly present-day Uzbekistan), at the heart of the crumbling Mongol empire, which was breaking apart into warring factions ruled by descendants of Genghis Khan, chief among them the Jagatai, the il-Khanid dynasty and the so-called Golden Horde. The situation within the Jagatai khanate – of which the Barlas were a part – was further complicated by tensions between predominantly nomadic tribes and those wanting a settled life of peace and trade. Tribal infighting was consequently common, and participating in a raid as a young man, Timur – described by contemporaries as strong, with a large head and long beard of a reddish hue – sustained wounds that left him partially paralyzed down one side and with a distinctive limp, hence the nickname Timur the lame, later abbreviated to

Tamerlane. He nonetheless became a skilled horseman and superior soldier, quickly building up a substantial following. According to the Arab writer Arabshah, he was 'steadfast in mind and robust in body, brave and fearless, firm as rock ... faultless in strategy'. Intellectually he was equally adept, speaking at least two languages, Persian and Turkic, and having a keen interest in history, philosophy, religion and architecture, as well as being an enthusiastic chess player.

In 1361, Timur was put in charge of the area round Samarkand, having sworn allegiance to Tughluq, who had taken over the Jagatai khanate. When Tughluq died soon afterwards, Timur cemented his position by forming a coalition with Hussein, another tribal chief, whose power base was in Balkh. The two carved up much of the surrounding area as their armies swept aside rival tribes, but simmering tensions in their relationship – previously kept in check by family ties – erupted after the death of Timur's first wife, Hussein's sister. Timur – who had won popular support by generously rewarding loyalty – turned on and defeated his former ally, only to release him shortly afterwards, overwhelmed at the sight of his old friend in shackles. Such leniency, however, was short-lived. Timur subsequently had two of Hussein's sons executed, taking four of his wives for his own, and hunting down his prominent supporters throughout the region, beheading them and sharing their wives and children among his men like gifts.

By 1370, as the undisputed leader of an ever-expanding domain centred on Samarkand – where he had opulent temples and beautiful gardens constructed behind new defensive walls and a moat – Tamerlane began to dream of greatness. Claiming descent from Genghis Khan (though he was probably Turkic), he announced his goal of re-establishing the Mongol empire. First, though, he had to bring stability to his new regime, so he married Hussein's widow, Sarai Khanum, and used only the title emir – commander, ruling through Genghizid puppets. He re-established and monop-olized the Silk Road, by which trade had once passed from China to Europe. Through this strategy of war abroad and peace at home, he could satisfy those who longed for new conquests as well as those who wanted prosperous stability.

Tamerlane presided over a highly efficient war machine, divided into *tumen*, units of 10,000 men, a skilled cavalry – including, even-tually, an elephant corps from India – equipped with supplies for lengthy campaigns and heavily armed with bows and swords, as well as catapults and battering rams for siege warfare. His soldiers – whose livelihoods depended on conquest – were composed of an eclectic ethnic mix, including Turks, Georgians, Arabs and Indians. Between 1380 and 1389 Timur embarked on a series of campaigns in which he conquered a colossal empire, embracing Persia, Iraq, Armenia, Georgia and Azerbaijan, Anatolia, Syria, all of central Asia, northern India, the approaches to China and much of southern Russia: his longest struggle was against Tokhtamysh, khan of the Golden Horde, whom he finally defeated and destroyed in 1391.

Terror was a key weapon in Tamerlane's armoury. He sent secret agents ahead of his troops to spread rumours about the atrocities he had committed – such as the vast pyramids of decapitated heads constructed by his soldiers to celebrate victories in battle or the mass killing of around 70,000 citizens in Ifshahan, 20,000 at Aleppo, the beheading of 70,000 in Tikrit and 90,000 in Baghdad, the in-cineration of a mosque full of people in Damascus and wholesale destruction of cities in Persia following a revolt there in 1392. Fear alone was often sufficient to ensure compliance – though many millions were killed in his campaigns. Yet he beautified Samarkand, created the game of Tamerlane chess, practised religious tolerance and engaged scholars in learned debates on philosophy and faith. He was altogether an extraordinary man, contradictory, a force of nature.

In 1398 – extending his empire further than either Alexander the Great or Genghis Khan had achieved – Tamerlane invaded India and captured Delhi. A hundred thousand civilians were massacred there, and a similar number of Indian soldiers murdered in cold blood after their surrender following the Battle of Panipat. Still Tamerlane pressed on. In 1401, his men conquered Syria, rampaging through Damascus; in July 1402, after a huge and bloody battle near Ankara, Tamerlane defeated the Ottoman sultan Bayezid I, looting, among other treasures, the famous gates from the Ottoman palace of Brusa; and later the same year he annihilated the Christian city of Smyrna, floating the severed heads of his victims out to sea on candlelit dishes. By 1404, even the Byzantine emperor John I was paying him tribute in return for a guarantee of safety.

In his late sixties, Tamerlane embarked on his final adventure – an attempted invasion of China – but he became ill on the march and died in January 1405. His body was returned to Samarkand, where a mausoleum was erected to him. After his death, his sons and grandsons fought for control of the empire, before his younger son, Shahrukh, finally assumed power in 1420 as the sole survivor of the family. His most illustrious descendant was Babur, founder of the Timurid dynasty that ruled India as the Mughals until 1857. A ruthless killer, whose armies were responsible for unrivalled pillage and brutality, Tamerlane was equally a shrewd statesman, brilliant general and sophisticated patron of the arts. Revered in Uzbekistan to this day – his monument in Tashkent standing where Marx's statue once presided – Tamerlane was buried in a beautiful simple tomb in Samarkand. Legend said that the disturber of his tomb would be cursed: in June 1941, a Soviet historian opened the tomb. Days later, Hitler attacked Soviet Russia.

FILIPPO BRUNELLESCHI

1377–1446

*It may be said that he was given by Heaven to invest architecture
with new forms.*

Giorgio Vasari, Lives of the Artists (1568)

The magnificent dome on the Cathedral of Santa Maria del Fiore,
in Florence, is testament to the genius of one of the world's finest
architects, Filippo Brunelleschi, who preceded other geniuses of
the Renaissance such as Michelangelo and Leonardo da Vinci.
As did many of his fellow and later artists, Brunelleschi sought to
revive the forms of Greek and Roman antiquity, and in so doing he
pioneered a dazzling new style of design.

In developing the tools to realize his vision, Brunelleschi
achieved some remarkable feats of engineering. His inquisitive
and unorthodox mind could solve puzzles that stumped the finest
talents in Europe, and his legacy, the great dome that dominates
the Florentine sky- line, is still one of the most beautiful and iconic
buildings in the world.

Born in Florence in 1377, Brunelleschi was a bright child,
whose natural instinct for draughtsmanship led his father to place
him as an apprentice to the master goldsmith Benincasa Lotti.
He formed a close friendship with a fellow trainee, the sculptor
Donatello, and learned the intricacies of the goldsmith's trade.
As well as perfecting such skills as engraving and embossing,
this also involved a study of mechanics, and by his early twenties
Brunelleschi was a talented artist with a solid grasp of cogs, gears,
wheels and weights.

In 1401 a competition was held to design the doors of the city's Baptistery. Although Brunelleschi entered a magnificent design, the competition was won by his rival Lorenzo Ghiberti. Piqued by the slight, Brunelleschi left Florence for Rome, where he and Donatello spent the next decade.

Rome's classical remains fascinated Brunelleschi. He spent his time observing, measuring and sketching the city's ancient buildings. He was intrigued by Roman engineering, especially as embodied in the Pantheon, where the Romans had poured concrete over a timber frame to create a great dome. When word reached him that the authorities in Florence were looking for an architect to build a dome on the city's new cathedral, Brunelleschi began at once to plan his return.

Arriving back in Florence, Brunelleschi won a commission from the silk merchants' guild to build a state orphanage – the elegant Ospedale degli Innocenti, which was the first building in Florence to show classical influences. The powerful Medici family then employed him to remodel the Basilica of San Lorenzo.

Most doubted that doming the huge cathedral could be achieved – the recipe for concrete was long forgotten, and creating an elaborate interior scaffold seemed impossible. Yet Brunelleschi had been secretly working on plans, designs and technical ideas for the dome for years, and managed to convince the cathedral authorities that he had the technical expertise to match the task. To demonstrate his prowess he recommended a Europe-wide contest, which attracted master-architects from across the continent.

Brunelleschi's original and daring ideas for constructing a double- vaulted, self-supporting dome were far better than any other sug- gestions advanced, which included such bizarre schemes as filling the cathedral with a mixture of earth and coins to support the roof as it was built, then inviting the ordinary citizens to remove the semiprecious mud when work was completed.

Having been granted the commission, Brunelleschi set about the mammoth task. There was no way that an internal scaffold could be erected in the cathedral, so he invented a lifting machine that could be driven by an ox to hoist and lower brick and sandstone supports hundreds of feet up to the roof. To keep his workers safe and satisfied, he controlled the food and wine on site, building inns within the structure to cut down on the time spent travelling for refreshments in the baking heat of the Tuscan summer. A safety net allowed the builders to work at dizzying heights, and when there was a strike among the native craftsmen, he drafted in labourers from Lombardy to keep production going.

The dome took 16 years to build. In 1434 a visitor from Rome described it as 'a structure so great, rising above the skies, large enough to shelter all the people of Tuscany in its shadow, built without the help of any centring or of much woodwork, of a craftsmanship perhaps not even the ancients knew or understood'.

It was a unique achievement – two vaults weighing 37,000 tons, with more than four million interlocking bricks that kept the struc- ture from collapsing under its own weight and holes to accom- modate expansion and contraction with the change of seasons. The 66-ft (20-m) lantern on the very top shone a thin shaft of sun- light on to the cathedral floor, providing a means of checking that the roof was not moving.

When the pope consecrated the cathedral on Easter Sunday 1436, it was Brunelleschi's moment of triumph. The greatest architect of an age famous for producing brilliance in every field of the arts was eventually buried beneath his supreme achievement, where a statue of him still stands.

HENRY V

1387–1422

Too famous to live long.
Duke of Bedford

On 31 August 1422, at Bois de Vincennes outside Paris, Henry V of England succumbed to the grim fate of so many of his soldiers and died of 'camp fever' – most likely dysentery. Shakespeare's Young Prince Hal was just thirty-four years old and had succeeded his father to the English throne only nine years earlier. Yet Henry was young in years, not in experience. Indeed, such were the accomplishments of his brief life that he has been described by one modern historian as 'the greatest man that ever ruled England'.

When Henry came to the throne in 1413, the country had been riven for decades by dynastic warfare: his father Henry IV – Henry Bolingbroke, son of John of Gaunt – had seized the throne in 1399 from his cousin, Richard II. Henry IV spent the early years of his reign at war and on the defensive, suppressing rebellions by the Percy family and the Welsh. His son was given independent commands in these campaigns and soon distinguished himself. In one battle, the young prince was grievously wounded with an arrow that penetrated and broke off deep in his face. He was miraculously saved by an ingenious surgeon who invented a contraption that pulled the arrow out, not through its entry wound but through the neck. Henry recovered.

During the last years of his father's reign, king and prince competed for power and almost came to conflict. On succeeding in

1413 it became clear how exceptional the new young king was: he was profoundly pious and religious, believing in his sacred mission, but also generous-spirited, energetic, highly intelligent, brave and gifted as a military planner as well as a general. Young Henry V, offering hope of a clean break with the past, rapidly set about doing his all to unite the country. A 'very English Englishman' himself, he aimed to nurture a sense of nationhood and national identity, abandoning the usual practices of his predecessors and reading and writing in English rather than in French. Like his predecessors in the Hundred Year War, he believed himself to be the rightful king of France.

Just before he set off for France, he uncovered an aristocratic conspiracy against himself: he ruthlessly crushed the so-called Southampton Plot, executing Henry, Baron Scrope and his cousin the earl of Cambridge. Nothing could interfere with Henry's solemn war.

Henry set sail for France in August 1415 with a plan to capture a number of strategically placed towns in northern France that could be garrisoned and used as footholds for further conquests. By the end of September he had succeeded in taking the port of Harfleur, but as his army had already been severely depleted by disease, he decided to return to England to regroup. On 25 October the English army of around 6000 found its path to Calais blocked near Agincourt by a far superior French force. Outnumbered by at least three to one, the thin English line was drawn up in a strong defensive position, forming a funnel with trees on either flank and several large groups of archers positioned along the line. When the French knights, on horseback and wearing heavy armour, finally advanced, they found themselves increasingly constricted and caught in a deadly hail of arrows. Laying down their bows after the initial volleys, the English longbowmen then piled into the French, now hopelessly crushed together and in total confusion, and inflicted horrendous casualties. Henry's great victory was thus also the triumph of the powerful longbow of the English archers (many of them from Cheshire), whose sustained barrage of arrows was, in its terrifying and murderous way, the medieval equivalent of the machine gun.

Over the next few years, inspired by the leadership of their charismatic and dynamic young king, the English army rampaged through northern France, inflicting one devastating blow after another on the disorganized and divided French. Buoyed up by his successes, by 1420 Henry was in a position to impose a severe settlement on his adversaries, and according to the terms of the Treaty of Troyes the ailing French king Charles VI accepted Henry as his regent and future heir. Early death prevented Henry from fully exploiting his victories, but he was already guaranteed immortality as one of the greatest heroes that England has produced.

Henry's victory brought France to its knees, and much of it under English control, but he wanted not just the restoration of the old Angevin empire but the throne of France itself. In 1417, he captured Rouen. The murder of the duke of Burgundy by its powerful Armagnac faction at the French court pushed the Burgundians into alliance with Henry and this, along with his military success, was decisive. The French signed the Treaty of Troyes in 1420: Henry became regent of France with the right of succession to the French throne and he married the French princess Catherine, with whom he had a an heir, the future Henry VI. The Dauphin of France fought on against Henry, killing his brother the duke of Clarence in battle in 1421, but the next year, Henry captured Meaux. It seemed likely that Henry V would indeed add the crown of France to that of England and establish an Anglo-French empire with his Anglo-French baby son as heir. Instead he died young and unexpectedly, leaving a baby heir and his brothers in control. Of these, the duke of Bedford won remarkable victories in

France – though Orleans was saved with the help of the Maid of Orleans, Joan of Arc.

The child-king Henry VI was crowned king of France in Paris but there was a deep problem on the English side: Henry VI lacked any of the characteristics necessary for medieval kingship, suffering long periods of mental illness. Henry V's French conquests were lost – and ultimately England was lost too in the dynastic civil conflict the War of the Roses. Henry VI was murdered in the tower of London in 1471.

JOAN OF ARC

c.1412–1431

I have been sent here by God, the King of Heaven, to drive you, an eye for an eye, from the whole of France.
Joan of Arc, in a letter to the English forces besieging Orléans
(22 March 1429)

France's national heroine, Joan of Arc, was a simple peasant girl who became a soldier, a martyr, and finally a saint. Convinced that God had told her to free France, she showed remarkable moral and military leadership and inspired the French to fight on against the English in the Hundred Years' War. Dressed in men's clothes, Joan defied convention, and the objections of both statesmen and churchmen, and in the end embraced death in her pursuit of salvation.

Joan was just fourteeen when she first heard the 'voices' of Saints Michael, Catherine and Margaret calling her to save France from the English. After half a century of war, the French seemed on the verge of losing the contest for their crown. Five years after the death of the Valois king Charles VI, his son, the Dauphin Charles, had still not been crowned, and the city of Orléans, the key to central France, seemed about to fall to the English.

Joan travelled across war-torn enemy territory to seek an audience with Charles, driven on by the persistent voices of the saints. Her quiet unbending determination gained her access to the Dauphin and persuaded him that he must reinvigorate the campaign against the English, and that it was God's will that he should be crowned at Rheims. She never disclosed what she had whispered to him that day, but Charles and the French leadership were either convinced that she had divine guidance or that this peasant girl would be useful to the French cause, probably a little of both.

Clad in white armour and wielding a battleaxe, Joan rode at the head of Charles's army to relieve the besieged city of Orléans. The English were routed, and other victories followed – as Joan was somehow sure they would. Hailed by the French as their saviour, and accused by the English of being a witch, it seemed that the Maid of Orléans must have some supernatural power, as the myth of English invincibility that had sprung up since Agincourt was conclusively shattered. In July 1429 the Dauphin was crowned as Charles VII at Rheims, with Joan in attendance.

Indefatigable, Joan urged the vacillating Charles on to push his advantage and press on to Paris. When Valois forces finally attacked the capital, Joan stood high on the earthworks, calling to the city's inhabitants to surrender to their rightful king. Undaunted by wounds received in the fight, she refused to leave the field – although the attempt to take Paris was not successful.

Captured by the English allies, the Burgundians, as she rushed to help the besieged town of Compiègne, Joan was sold to the English and tried as a heretic in Rouen, the seat of English power in France. Charles, eager for a truce with Burgundy and reluctant to be associated with a witch, was nowhere to be seen. At her trial the peasant girl faced up to France's leading theologians, confident of her divine mission, while avoiding being tricked into criticizing the Church. Joan was so impervious to the threat of torture that her interrogators decided that it would be useless to try.

But when the Church threatened to hand her over to the secular courts, Joan – petrified and ill – confessed to heresy and agreed to put on women's clothes, choosing life imprisonment over a painful death. Within days of recanting, however, Joan changed back into men's clothes, saying the voices had censured her treacherous abjuration. Handed over to the secular authorities, the young woman barely out of her teens – who had always had a premonition of an early death – was burnt at the stake as a witch.

Joan's conviction was unwavering. Allowed to make her confession and receive communion, she died gazing at a cross held up by a priest, who, acceding to her request, shouted out assurances of salvation so that she could hear him over the fire's roar. So anxious were the English that no relic of her should remain to keep her legend alive, they burnt her body three times, then scattered her dust in the River Seine.

Twenty years later, safely installed on his throne, Charles VII ordered an inquiry into the trial. Joan's conviction was overturned. Five hundred years later, on 16 May 1920, she was made a saint by the Roman Catholic Church.

TORQUEMADA AND THE SPANISH INQUISITION

1420–98

If anyone possesses a certain amount of learning, he is found to be full of heresies, errors, traces of Judaism. Thus they have imposed silence on men of letters; those who have pursued learning have come to feel, as you say, a great terror.

> Don Rodrigo Manrique, son of the inquisitor general,
> letter to Luis Vives, 1533

The very name of Tomás de Torquemada, the first inquisitor general in Spain, was enough to induce a tremor of fear among even the most hardened of his contemporaries. Since then, Torquemada – the persecutor of Jews, Moors and other supposed heretics under the intolerant and repressive rule of Ferdinand and Isabella – has become a byword for religious fanaticism and persecuting zeal.

Little is known of his early life, other than the fact that the man who would become the bane of Spain's Jews was himself of Jewish descent: his grandmother was a converso – a Jewish convert to Catholicism. During his youth Torquemada joined the Dominican religious order, and in 1452 he was appointed prior of a monastery in Santa Cruz. Though he continued to occupy that post for the next two decades, he also became a confessor and adviser to King Ferdinand II of Aragon and Queen Isabella I of Castile, whose marriage in 1479 effectively united the two principal Spanish kingdoms. Under their dual monarchy, a renewed effort was made to complete the Reconquista (the re-conquest of Spain from Muslim rule) that had stalled some two centuries earlier. This endeavour ended in success in 1492 with the fall of Granada, the last Muslim outpost in Spain.

In the meantime, Torquemada had convinced the government that the continued presence in Spain of Jews, Muslims and even recent converts to Christianity from those faiths represented a dangerous corruption of the true Catholic faith. As a result of Torquemada's urging, repressive laws had been passed aimed at forcing the expulsion of Spain's non-Christian minorities.

The Spanish Inquisition was established on 1 November 1478 by Pope Sixtus IV. Its job was to root out deviance and heresy from within the Church, and every girl over the age of twelve and every boy over the age of fourteen was subject to its power. It was not the first time such an entity had been created – an inquisition had temporarily existed in 13th-century France, to deal with the remnants of the Cathar heretics in the aftermath of the Albigensian Crusade. This new Inquisition, however, was to be far more enduring and methodical in its operation.

The first two inquisitors were appointed in 1480, and the first burnings followed a few months later, in February 1481, when six people were executed as heretics. Thereafter the pace of killing picked up, and in February 1482, to cope with the increasing workload, a further seven inquisitors – including Torquemada – were appointed by the pope. Within a decade, the hearings of the Inquisition were operating in eight major cities across Spain.

Inquisitors would arrive in a town and convene a special Mass, which all were obliged to attend. There they would preach a sermon before calling on those guilty of heresy to come forward and confess. Suspected transgressors were given a period of thirty to forty days to turn themselves in. Those who complied were liable to be 'rewarded' with a less severe penalty than those who proved recalcitrant. Nevertheless, all who did confess were also required to identify other heretics who had not complied. Denunciation was thus as integral to the working of the inquisition as confession. In consequence, the inquisition quickly became an opportunity to settle old scores.

The accused were arrested and thrown into prison, and their property, and that of their family, was confiscated. Interrogation then followed, the inquisitors being instructed to apply torture according to their 'conscience and will'. A suspect could have water forced down his throat, be stretched on the rack, or hung with his hands tied behind his back – whatever was deemed necessary to extract a confession. Many were maimed in the process; countless others died. And for those who broke under the pressure, there was only one outcome: death by burning. Before being burnt alive at the euphemistically named *auto da fé* (act of faith), the victim had two choices. They could repent and kiss the cross, or remain defiant. In the former case they were granted the mercy of being garrotted prior to the flames being lit; otherwise, a protracted and hideously painful death was sure to follow.

In 1482 Torquemada was appointed as one of the inquisitors, and shortly afterwards he became inquisitor general, the most senior position in the entire organization.

Torquemada was now almost as powerful as Ferdinand and Isabella themselves; certainly, he was more feared than the temporal authorities. Under his guiding hand the inquisition hit new heights of activity. In 1484 he oversaw the proclamation of twenty-eight articles, listing the sins that the inquisition was attempting to expose and purge. They ranged from apostasy and blasphemy to sodomy and sorcery – though many were focused on identifying and exposing Jews. During the course of their investigations, inquisitors were empowered to use all means necessary to discover the truth – a ruling that de facto legitimized torture in pursuit of a forced confession.

The result was a policy of violent persecution. In the month of February 1484 alone, thirty people in the city of Ciudad Real were found guilty of an assortment of 'crimes' and burnt alive. Between 1485 and 1501, 250 were burnt in Toledo; and on one occasion in 1492, in Torquemada's home town of Valladolid, thirty-two people were burnt in one inferno.

Arguing that the soul of Spain was in jeopardy, Torquemada declared that the Jews, in particular, were a mortal threat, and in 1492 Ferdinand and Isabella decreed that all Jews who had not accepted the truth of the Christian revelation were to be expelled from Spain. Some 30–80,000 left the country – many of them rescued and given sanctuary by the tolerant Islamic Ottomans in Istanbul, Izmir and Salonika (modern Thessaloniki in Greece).

Torquemada still did not deem his work done, and even refused the bishopric of Seville to continue in his role. In so doing, he found that the rewards of his exertions were not solely spiritual; indeed, he amassed a large personal fortune from the confiscated wealth of those whom the Inquisition had found guilty of heresy. Wherever he travelled, he was accompanied by fifty mounted men and 250 foot soldiers, a force that reflected his growing unpopularity, but which also added to the terror and awe inspired when he arrived in a new town to root out its heretics.

Ultimately, only death removed Torquemada from office. Over the previous two decades his relentless zeal had led to as many as two thousand people meeting a hideous end in the flames. Torquemada will forever be remembered as religious bigotry personified – the living incarnation of Fyodor Dostoyevsky's Grand Inquisitor who seeks to burn Jesus Christ himself for the sake of his beloved Catholic Church, but who ends up in a spiritual abyss.

VLAD THE IMPALER

1431–76

His way of life was as evil as his name.
Late-15th-century Russian manuscript

Vlad III, *hospodar* (prince) of Wallachia, claimed he was saving his Christian people from the Muslim Ottomans, but he was more interested in wielding his personal power in the treacherous intrigues of local dynastic and imperial politics. He was a degenerate, murderous sadist who displayed a cruelty so savage that he inspired the legend of Dracula. Yet the story of Dracula is tame compared with the reality. Murdering tens of thousands of people – from crippled peasants and vagrants to nobles and foreign ambassadors – he became known as the Impaler Prince: his favourite method of execution was to impale his victims on sharpened wooden stakes, oiled at the tip and inserted into their intestines. Vlad was most likely born in a military fortress, the citadel of Sighisoara, Transylvania (part of today's Romania) in 1431. His family name was Dracul, meaning dragon, handed down through his father, who had been a member of the Order of the Dragon – which Vlad also joined at the age of five – a secret organization created by the holy Roman emperor to uphold Christianity and resist Muslim Ottoman incursions into Europe. His mother was a Moldavian princess and his father Vlad II, a former prince of Wallachia, exiled in Transylvania.

When Vlad was a child, his father, under threat of attack from the Ottoman sultan, had been forced to reassure the Turks of his obedience by sending two of his sons, including Vlad, into Ottoman custody in 1444. The experience, lasting four years, in which he was beaten and whipped for his insolence and fiery character, left Vlad with a hatred of the Turks.

Wallachia (also in modern-day Romania) was not a traditional hereditary monarchy and although Vlad had a claim to the throne, his father's exile put him in a weak position. His elder brother, Mircea II, ruled briefly in 1442, but was forced into hiding the following year and eventually captured by his enemies in 1447, who burned out his eyes and buried him alive. Wallachian politics were duplicitous and brutal: Vlad's young brother, Radu the Handsome, later enlisted the help of the Ottoman sultan Mehmet II to oust his brother.

In 1447, the same year Mircea was killed, boyars (regional noble families) loyal to John Hunyadi, the White Knight of Hungary, also captured and murdered Vlad's father, claiming he was too dependent on the Ottomans. The Ottomans invaded shortly afterwards to assert their control in the region and installed the seventeen-year-old Vlad as a puppet prince in 1448, only for Hunyadi to intervene again and force him to flee to Moldavia. Vlad subsequently took the bold step of travelling to Hungary – with which Wallachia had repeatedly been at war. Impressing Hunyadi with his anti-Ottoman credentials, he eventually became Hungary's preferred candidate for the Wallachian throne.

In 1456, as the Hungarians attacked the Ottomans in Serbia, Vlad used the opportunity to invade and take control of Wallachia, killing his rival Vladislav II from the Danesti clan, and taking the throne back for the Draculs. On Easter Sunday, he invited the leading boyars to a banquet, killing the oldest and enslaving those who were still young enough to work. Many died working on new fortifications for Vlad's castles in conditions so severe that their noble finery disintegrated, leaving them naked.

Establishing Tirgoviste as his capital, Vlad was determined to make Wallachia a great kingdom, with a prosperous and healthy people. To him, however, that meant eradicating the nobility, as well as anyone else perceived as a drain on the country's resources. Among his targets were the poorest and most vulnerable – vagrants, the disabled and the mentally ill – thousands of whom he invited to a feast in Tirgoviste, only to lock them in the hall and burn them alive as soon as they had finished eating. (It was dangerous to accept an invitation from Vlad, but even more dangerous to refuse.) Vlad also persecuted women accused of immoral acts such as adultery – their breasts were cut off, and they were then skinned or boiled alive, and their bodies put on public display. German merchants living in Transylvania, whom he regarded as foreign parasites, were also the object of the wrath of Vlad. On St Bartholomew's Day, 1459 he ordered the execution of 30,000 merchants and boyars from the city of Brasov – 10,000 more followed in Sibiu the following year.

Usually his victims were impaled. Death was excruciating and could take hours, as the stake eventually made its way through the guts and out of the mouth. Executing thousands at the same time, he would organize the stakes in concentric circles round his castles, and forbid anyone to remove the victim, often dining in the presence of rotting flesh – the higher the rank, the longer the stake reserved for them. Other methods of execution included skinning and boiling, and he once hammered nails into the heads of foreign ambassadors who refused to remove their hats at his court. Such was his bloodthirstiness that it was also rumoured he drank the blood of his victims and feasted on their flesh.

In the winter of 1461–2, he crossed the Danube and pillaged the Ottoman-controlled area between Serbia and the Black Sea, killing 20,000 people. As Sultan Mehmet II gathered tens of thousands of troops for a revenge mission, they arrived on the banks of the Danube to see 20,000 Turkish prisoners whom Vlad's armies had impaled, creating a forest of bodies on stakes.

Despite a daring attempt to infiltrate the enemy camp in disguise and kill the sultan, Vlad was overwhelmed by the scale of the Ottoman onslaught. As the Turks surrounded his castle in 1462, his wife jumped from the window, while Vlad fled, and the Ottomans installed his younger brother Radu on the throne. Captured by the Hungarians, Vlad spent the next ten years in custody, dreaming of regaining his throne while impaling mice and birds on miniature stakes. Somehow, he secured the backing of the Hungarians again, remarrying into the Hungarian royal family and winning support for his invasion of Wallachia in 1476, when he briefly deposed the new ruler, Basarab the Elder of the Danesti. Once again, however, he was no match for the invading Ottomans, and he was killed near Bucharest, perhaps even by his own men, his head removed and sent back to Constantinople, where it was displayed on a stick.

MEHMET THE CONQUEROR

1432–81

'Glory is to build a beautiful city'

Mehmet II was the Ottoman sultan who conquered Constantinople, ending a thousand-year Christan-Roman civilization, and who built and restored the city as Istanbul, the scared-imperial capital of his growing cosmopolitan empire that stretched from the Balkans to the eastern borderlands of Anatolia. He was open-minded and erudite, ruthless and imperious. A student of Greek philosophy and science, Sufism, the Koran and Christian theology; he spoke Turkish, Greek and Arabic as well as possessing a passing knowledge of Hebrew and the ability to write poetry in courtly Persian. Above all, he was ambitious enough to want to convert his Ottoman inheritance, the mainly European, overwhelmingly Christian Balkan empire ruled from the Ottoman capital Edirne, into a new world empire: he wanted to be Roman emperor and Caesar as well as sultan.

As a boy Mehmet grew up amidst the vicious intrigues of the Ottoman court: his father Murad II abdicated in 1444 and Mehmet reluctantly succeeded the throne aged twelve. Faced with Hungarian attacks on his fluid central European borders, the boy forced his father to return and defeat their Christian enemies. When he succeeded to the throne again in 1451, he was twenty-one and immediately, single-mindedly set about preparing to take Constantinople. The seat of the Byzantine eastern Roman empire was so diminished that the city was almost empty and its dominion did not extend much beyond the walls of settlement itself and the waters of the Bosphorus and the Golden Horn. But it was still the thousand-year-old sear of the Caesars and the most famous city on earth.

Mehmet first supervised the creation of an Ottoman navy, then built Rumeli Hisari, 'the Roman fortress', opposite the Andolu Hisari, the Anatolian stronghold constructed by his great-grandfather. With this, he dominated the Bosphorus strait, but no one took him particularly seriously until a Venetian ship refused to stop and pay his tax; the ship was sunk and its captain impaeled on the shore.

In April 1453, Mehmet deployed a vast army of between 80,000 and 200,000 men, over 300 ships and the biggest cannon in Europe, constructed by his engineer Orban. He besieged Constantinople on three sides but was unable to complete the encirclements because the Byzantines had a huge chain across the mouth of the Golden Horn. After several failed assaults and minor naval setbacks, Mehmet was infuriated and considered executing his admirals, riding his horse into the sea in frustration. He did execute his grand vizier for some sort of contact with the Byzantines – perhaps for receiving bribes from them. The sultan realized that the city, even if only defended by a tiny force commanded by the Roman Emperor Constantine XI in addition to 5,000 quixotic daredevil adventurers, sailors and knights from Italy and across Europe, was not going to fall until he controlled the Golden Horn. He ordered an amazing *coup de main*: Overnight, his engineers laid wooden rails across the land from the Bosphorus to the Golden Horn. When darkness fell, slaves and oxen hauled the entire Ottoman fleet overland before floating it on the Golden Horn. A terrifying and doom-laden vision then greeted the Byzantine defenders when they awoke – their ultimate nightmare. On 29 April, Mehmet launched the final assault, breaking into the city from two directions. The last Roman emperor perished in the heat of the fray, his body never found. Mehmet allowed his army the traditional three days of plunder and rapine, but he stopped them after one, perhaps because his men had looted everything there was: they found a city that was broken down into little poverty-stricken villages with a population of barely 50,000 in a metropolis that once held 500,000. The tents of the Ottomans were filled with slaves from the sacking of the celebrated city. The sultan entered the city as conqueror, sprinkled earth on his turban outside the Great Church of St Sophia, built by Justinian, and then went in. One of his soldiers was trying to loot the paving stones but Mehmet struck him: 'The buildings are mine,' he said, and declared the greatest church in Christendom would henceforth be the Great Mosque of Aya Sofia. He promised to respect all the other Christian churched but this student of philosophy was moved by the ruined glory of the place: when he inspected the imperial palaces, he adapted the poetry of Saadi and declaimed:

The spider weaves the curtains in the palace of the Caesars
The owl calls the watches in the towers of Afrasiab

Now he called himself Kaiser-i-Rum – Caesar of Rome – and he set to work restoring the city, which was henceforth often called Istanbul as well as Constantinople. It was Mehmet who truly created the city of Istanbul as we see it today: where the palace of the Caesars had stood, he created the Topkapi Palace. He built the Mosque of Eyyup Sultan on the reputed site of the grave of Ayyub al-Ansari, a companion of the Prophet Muhammad, which was discovered in a timely manner: the companion had died during the Arab siege of Constantinople ordered by the caliph Muawiya in 674. The new mosque would become the holiest site for Turkish Muslims beyond Mecca, Medina and Jerusalem. Mehmet was making Istanbul into a holy city of Islam. On the site of the Church of Holy Apostles, burial place of the Caesars, he built his own Conqueror, or Fatih, Mosque and his tomb, crested with the gargantuan turban of a world-conqueror descended from chieftains of the horse-archers of the steppes, would be there too, staking his claim to be the heir of Constantine the Great and the other emperors.

Mehmet ordered the raising of a fortress for the city and a market bazaar too, and settled thousands of people, many of them Jews and Christians as well as Turks; for unlike the narrowly, fanatically Christian Byzantines, he saw himself as emperor of a multinational empire. Indeed, he restored the Patriarchate and invited back the Genoese and the Greeks. By 1478, there were 80,000 people in the city, 20 per cent of whom were Christian and 10 per cent Jewish. All had freedom of worship and tolerance, provided they paid a minority tax and recognized the absolute supremacy of Islam and the Ottoman emperor. By his death, Istanbul was expanding so rapidly it would soon again be the biggest city in the world, and a world-city too.

Mehmet himself was a remarkable mixture of scholar and warrior: he constantly studied astronomy in Greek and Arabic texts, wrote poetry under the pseudonym Avni (The Helper), invited Italian artists and Greek scholars to court, and flirted with Greek philosophy and Latin literature. He embraced Sufism, which appalled some more orthodox Muslims. There were even rumours that he would convert to Christianity, but he was actually always a devout Muslim. He was painted by the Italian artist Gentile Bellini, whose outstanding portrait catches the intelligence, ruthlessness and cunning of his acute eyes and hawkish nose. Yet this extraordinary ruler was still only in his early twenties – he went on to attack the defiant Serbs and besiege Belgrade, finally wiping out Serbian independence and swallowing Bosnia. Then he conquered the last vestiges of Byzantine power, the despotate of Morea in Greece and the empire of Trebizond, as well as suppressing Wallachia, modern Romania, where the resistance was led by the psychotic Voevode, Vlad the Impaler. Meanwhile the pope called a Crusade to stop Mehmet's advance, but he defeated both the Hungarians and Venetians. In 1466, he tried to break the resistance of the Albanians, led by their legendary Prince Skanderbeg, who would prove to be one of the few to successfully outfight Mehmet.

The Ottoman empire may have been advancing into central and southern Europe, but swathes of Anatolia in Asia Minor were still ruled by other Turkish princes who had taken advantage of the Ottoman defeat seventy years previously at the hands of Tamerlane. Now, in the early 1470s, Mehmet reconquered Anatolia, giving him the chance to return to Albania: after the death of Skanderbeg, he was finally able to add that country to his empire

– and he started to probe Italy itself. Many feared he would add Rome to Constantinople, but Mehmet the Conqueror, probably the most successful and exceptional of all the talented Ottoman warrior-sultans, died in May 1481. Aged forty-nine, he was most probably poisoned at the instigation of his son. His conquests and policies had helped make the Ottoman realm a tolerant world empire, Istanbul an imperial holy city, and the Ottoman sultans into Islamic Caesars. In Turkey he is known simply as Fatih – the Conqueror.

RICHARD III

1452–85

And thus I clothe my naked villainy
With old odd ends stolen out of holy writ,
And seem a saint when most I play the devil.
Richard III in William Shakespeare,
Richard III, Act 1, scene 3

Richard III was the hunchbacked usurper whose infamous murder of his own two nephews, one of them the rightful king of England, brought about his own destruction. Since he lost his throne to the Tudors, it was they who wrote the history of Richard III to assert the claim of their own dynasty, probably exaggerating his pitiless ambition and physical deformities.

Richard was the second son of Richard, 3rd duke of York, and Cecily Neville, daughter of Ralph Neville, 1st earl of Westmorland and granddaughter of John of Gaunt. An ugly child with protruding teeth, he grew up during the War of the Roses, fought between the rival dynastic houses of Lancaster and York. After the triumph of the Yorkists in March 1461, in a struggle that saw his father killed in battle, Richard's eldest brother became King Edward IV.

From 1465 Richard was raised in the house of his cousin Richard Neville, later known as the Kingmaker, although there is no reason to believe that young Richard set his sights on the throne at this stage. He gave every sign of loyalty to his brother Edward, for which he was duly rewarded, gaining land and positions of influence. After the Lancastrians had briefly reinstated Henry VI as king in 1470, forcing the York brothers into exile in The Hague, Richard joined Edward on his campaign of 1471, in which Henry VI was deposed for a second time.

An able general and skilled administrator, Richard was entrusted with control of the north of England during Edward's reign, and earned a reputation for fairness and justice. He acquired a string of castles in Yorkshire, Durham and Cumbria during the Yorkist campaigns, but his loyalty – shown for example in a successful campaign that Richard waged on Edward's behalf against the Scots in 1481 – meant that the king tolerated his brother's growing influence.

In 1478, Richard may have allowed himself to dream of the crown for the first time when George, the middle York brother, was executed for treason, possibly at Richard's behest, thus removing another potential obstacle to the throne. But it was when Edward IV died unexpectedly on 9 April 1483 that his ambitions were truly laid bare. Next in line to the throne was the twelve-year-old Edward V, followed by his nine-year-old brother, Richard of Shrewsbury, the two sons of the king's beautiful wife, Elizabeth Woodville. As the lord protector of the late king's will, Richard swore allegiance to his young nephew, but less than a month later he seized first Edward, then his younger brother, and imprisoned them both in the Tower of London.

Richard initially claimed he had seized the two boys for their own protection, and, on specious charges of treason, ordered the execution of those previously entrusted with their care. Just two months later, however, he had an announcement made outside St Paul's Cathedral declaring Edward IV's marriage to Elizabeth Woodville illegitimate since, according to the testimony of an unnamed bishop, Edward was already secretly married at the time to his mistress, Lady Eleanor Butler. Richard forced an act through Parliament to annul the marriage posthumously, simultaneously bastardizing his nephews and clearing his own way to the throne. After quashing a brief uprising against him, he was crowned Richard III at Westminster Abbey on 6 July 1483.

To secure his position, Richard seized and brutally murdered several barons who might oppose his accession. He was acutely aware, however, that, as long as they lived, his two nephews would pose a serious threat to his rule, so it must have surprised no one when, in the summer of 1483, both boys were declared missing. By autumn, it was widely assumed they were dead and nobody doubted their uncle was responsible. According to Sir Thomas More, writing some years afterwards, the two boys were smothered on the king's orders as they slept. It was not until 1647, when the skeletons of two children were discovered under a staircase in the Tower, that they were finally buried in Westminster Abbey.

That Richard had murdered the princes was accepted as true during his reign and regarded with horror even in those brutal times. For contemporary chroniclers, deformity was sign of an evil character and Richard's actions in 1483 evoked the image of the startlingly ugly creature they described: buck teeth, excessive body hair from birth, a crooked back, withered arm and haggard face. According to one chronicler, he was tight-lipped and fidgety, 'ever with his right hand pulling out of the sheath to the middle, and putting in again, the dagger which he did always wear'.

Tudor propagandists certainly exaggerated Richard's grotesque cruelties and physical deformities. The nervy and sinister hunchback portrayed in William Shakespeare's *Richard III*, 'so lamely and unfashionable/That dogs bark at me as I halt by them', formed his image for future generations. His chief Lancastrian rival, Henry Tudor – who later launched an organized campaign to blacken Richard's name and present him as a monster – collected an army on the continent and invaded England in a campaign that reached a climax at the Battle of Bosworth Field on 22 August 1485. The turning point of the encounter came when Henry Percy, the earl of Northumberland, refused to throw his reserves into the battle, while Richard's ostensible allies, Thomas Stanley, afterwards the earl of Derby, and his brother, Sir William – who had been waiting to see which way the battle turned – intervened on the side of Henry. Though Richard continued to fight on bravely, hacking his way through the opposing army and very nearly reaching Henry himself, he was eventually encircled and killed by the poleaxe of a Welshman. The last Plantagenet king of England, Richard had reigned for just two years. Henry Tudor became Henry VII, his dynasty ruling until the death of Elizabeth I in 1603.

Richard remains a tyrannical, homicidal villain for many while the Richard III Society still fights to rehabilitate him. After he was killed his body, slung naked over a horse, was taken into nearby Leicester and quietly buried. It was lost for 500 years until 2012, when archaeologists found his remains, miraculously intact and identified by DNA, under a car park. The skeleton proved that Richard did suffer from scoliosis which would have caused one shoulder to be higher than the other – and revealed he died in battle from multiple wounds to his skull, with a halberd jab proving fatal. In total he had ten wounds, suggesting a brave death in the fray. A pelvic wound, probably inflicted post-mortem, implied he was stabbed in the bottom while his corpse was being taken into Leicester on horseback. He was reburied in Leicester Cathedral in 2015.

SAVONAROLA

1452–98

The first city to be renewed will be Florence . . . as God elected the people of Israel to be led by Moses through tribulation to felicity . . . so now the people of Florence have been called to a similar role led by a prophetic man, their new Moses [Savonarola himself] . . . In the Sabbath Age men will rejoice in the New Church and there will be one flock and one shepherd.

Girolamo Savonarola's 'Sermon on the New Age', 1490s

The Italian Dominican friar Girolamo Savonarola was a reactionary zealot and bigoted theocrat who vehemently opposed the humanism of the Florentine Renaissance. His 'Bonfire of the Vanities' burned books and art he deemed immoral. Savonarola's 'Christian and religious republic' was an intolerant, sanctimonius and murderous reign of terror.

Born and raised in the city of Ferrara (then the capital of an independent duchy), Savonarola received his first education from his paternal grandfather, Michele Savonarola, before moving on to university. His earliest writings already exhibited the mixture of pessimism and moralizing for which he would become notorious; the poems 'De Ruina Mundi' ('On the Downfall of the World') and 'De Ruina Ecclesiae' ('On the Downfall of the Church') are exemplary in this regard.

In 1475 Savonarola entered the Dominican order at the convent of San Domenico in Bologna. Four years later he transferred back to the convent of Santa Maria degli Angeli in his native Ferrara, before finally becoming the prior of the convent at San Marco in Florence. It was here that he would earn his place in history.

From the outset, Savonarola denounced the political and religious corruption he believed to have permeated society. His Lent sermons of 1485–6 were especially vehement, and it was during those addresses that he began to call for the cleansing of the Church as a prelude to its reform.

In 1487 Savonarola left Florence for a time to return to Bologna as 'master of studies', but in 1490 he returned on the encouragement of the humanist philosopher Count Pico della Mirandola and with the patronage of Lorenzo de Medici, the ruler of Florence. Once back in Florence, Savonarola soon set about excoriating the very government that had made his return possible. In florid language, Savonarola heralded the approaching 'end of days' and claimed to be in direct contact with God and the saints. He condemned the alleged tyranny of the Medicis, and prophesied the impending doom of Florence, unless the city changed its ways.

Such predictions seemed altogether vindicated when the French king, Charles VIII, invaded Florence in 1494. Lorenzo de Medici's son and successor, Piero, was driven out of a city, which was by then in the grip of Savonarola's demagoguery. With French support, a democratic republic was now established in Florence, with Savonarola as its leading figure. In his new role, combining political and religious power, he was determined to create a 'Christian and religious republic'. One of the first acts of this new, wholesome republic was to make homosexuality punishable by death.

Savonarola intensified his criticism of the Roman curia – its corruption personified by the notorious Borgias – and he even went so far as to attack Pope Alexander VI's disreputable private life. At the same time, he urged the people of Florence to live ever more ascetic lives. The result of the latter exhortations was the act for which the priest became most famous – the Bonfire of the Vanities, in which personal effects, books and works of art, including some by Botticelli and Michelangelo, were destroyed in a conflagration in Florence's Piazza della Signoria.

Even as Savonarola reached the height of his power and influence, domestic opposition to his rule was beginning to form. Pointing to his pronouncements against the papacy, these domestic opponents were able to secure the excommunication of Savonarola in May 1497. Beyond Florence, Savonarola was opposed not only by the corrupt Borgia pope, Alexander VI, but also by the duke of Milan – both of whom sought to overturn the king of France's regional ambitions.

When French forces withdrew from the Italian peninsula in 1497, Savonarola suddenly found himself isolated. His final undoing came in 1498, in a bizarre episode that reflected the zealous atmosphere he had done so much to create. A Franciscan monk had challenged anyone who refused to accept the pope's excommunication of Savonarola to an ordeal by fire. One of Savonarola's most committed followers had duly accepted the contest, the outcome of which would be decided by he who withdrew first (that person being the loser). In the event, the Franciscan failed to appear for the trial – formally handing Savonarola the victory. Yet many felt that Savonarola had somehow dodged the test. A riot ensued, in the course of which Savonarola was dragged from his convent and placed in front of a commission of inquiry, packed with his opponents.

Effectively placed on trial by papal commissioners, Savonarola was tortured into making an admission of guilt. He was then handed over to the secular authorities to be crucified and burnt at the stake. The sentence was carried out on 23 May 1498, at the very spot on which the Bonfire of the Vanities had been lit, and where

Savonarola had himself overseen the execution of various 'criminals'. As his own pyre was lit, the executioner was reputed to have declared, 'The one who wanted to burn me is now himself put to the flames.'

ISABELLA & FERDINAND

1451–1504   1452–1516

The King of France complains that I have twice deceived him.
He lies, the fool; I have deceived him ten times and more.

Ferdinand

They were probably the most successful royal partnership of their era. Isabella was the pious, solemn, red-haired, and blue-eyed queen of Castile, one of the kingdoms that made up Christian Spain, while Ferdinand was the shrewd, crafty, ambitious king of Aragon, another Spanish kingdom, and the ideal Machiavellian monarch. Their marriage in 1469 effectively created the kingdom of Spain by uniting Aragon and Castile (though actually the kingdoms remained separate units). The formation of Spain was just one of the couples' achievements. Spain, once almost completely ruled by the Muslims, who had created a blossoming Arab-Jewish culture, had been largely reconquered by crusading Spanish monarchs in what was known as *La Reconquista*. As the Christians gradually reconquered Spain, many of its Jews – known as the Sepharad, the Sephardis – and indeed Muslims, had converted to Christianity, or at least pretended to do so: these converts were called *conversos*. Clearly some remained Jews in secret but in all likelihood many converted wholeheartedly. Yet gradually the Christian powers in Spain became suspicious of these Jews as a taint in the blood of the Christians – were they really loyal? Were they traitors? The belief that they might represent a taint in the Christian bloodstream was one of the first examples of the racial anti-Semitism that resurfaced in the late nineteenth century. The Inquisition, led by Torqemarda and backed by Ferdinand and Isabella, began its investigations and tortures.

In 1492, they completed this process when they conquered the last Islamic principality, the Emirate of Granada, a triumphant moment for the couple because they were completing the last crusade. Both regarded themselves as crusaders and indeed Isabella was accustomed to rule from a military camp. The last emir of Granada surrendered on the understanding that Muslims would have freedom of worship. The monarchs would soon go back on this promise, forcing Muslims to convert to Christianity. Then, literally days later, the two Catholic Monarchs – a title awarded them by the Pope – issued their Alhambra Decree, which ordered the Jews of Iberia to either convert to Christianity or face expulsion. Already under sustained persecution, many Jews probably did now convert, but the vast majority – somewhere between 30,000 and 80,000 – had to leave Spain, beginning one of the most traumatic experiences in Jewish life between the fall of the Jerusalem Temple in AD 70 and the Holocaust of the 20th century. It seems that Ferdinand had calculated that the Jews would simply convert and was surprised by Jewish loyalty to their faith. Either way, Ferdinand and Isabella set off a tumultuous movement of people: they also expelled the Jews from their other kingdoms – Ferdinand ruled swathes of Italy – and other monarchs in Europe followed suit, expelling their Jews too. The Jews moved gradually eastwards, thousands of them ending up in Poland – then one of the most tolerant kingdoms of Europe – in Holland, and the eastern Mediterranean, where many were welcomed by the Ottoman sultans, who settled them in cities from the capital Istanbul to Salonika. These Jews added to the growing Jewish populations of Poland and Ukraine but also became the Jewish Sephardic communities of the Arab world: they often spoke Turkish, Arabic and their own special language – Ladino, a patois of Spanish and Hebrew.

That was not the last key decision of 1492 – the Catholic Monarchs next agreed to fund the expedition of Christopher Columbus that discovered the New World and began the Spanish conquest of a new continent. Thus in many ways, the couple played a key role in the creation of the modern world.

Ferdinand was also king of Sicily and Naples and spent many of his later years campaigning in Italy, but he never gave up his crusading credentials. His ultimate aim was to liberate Jerusalem and indeed he claimed the title of king of Jerusalem, one still used by the king of Spain. He launched a series of attacks along the coast of Muslim North Africa, even conquering Tripoli in today's Libya.

The couple married their daughter Catherine of Aragon to Prince Arthur, son of King Henry VII of England and after the prince's death, she married his son and heir, Henry VIII, becoming the mother of Queen Mary I. When Isabella died in 1508, she was succeeded on the Castilian throne by their daughter Juana. Juana was married to Philip the Handsome, Habsburg duke of Burgundy and son of the Emperor Maximilian and they had a son, Charles of Ghent. But Juana the Mad was unbalanced; Philip the Handsome died young and so Ferdinand ruled Castile as regent until his death when the Spanish kingdoms along with vast Habsburg lands in Germany and the Low Countries as well as the new territories of America, were inherited by Ferdinand and Isabella's grandson, Charles V, Holy Roman Emperor and king of Spain, who in his day was the most powerful monarch in the world.

COLUMBUS

1451–1506

*For the execution of the voyage to the Indies, I did not make use
of intelligence, mathematics or maps.*

Christopher Columbus

Cristobal Colon – better known as Christopher Columbus – was
the maverick son of a Genoese weaver who for years had dreamed
of sailing across the Atlantic to open up a new path to India, but
instead discovered America. An extraordinary sailor, adventurer,
dreamer, and obsessional eccentric of remarkable drive and will,
he had petitioned the Portuguese court in vain for many years to
fund this voyage. He then turned his attentions to the Catholic
Monarchs of Spain, Ferdinand and Isabella who, on finally
conquering the last Islamic principality of Iberia agreed to fund
the voyage. Bizarrely, part of his dream was to find the spices and
gold that would pay for a crusade to liberate Jerusalem, to rebuild
the Temple for Catholicism and even to attack the Holy City from
the other side. In return for royal backing, he demanded and received the title of Grand Admiral of the Ocean Sea, Viceroy and
Governor of any new lands plus a generous share of the income
from them.

On 3 August 1492, Columbus set off on his first expedition
with three ships and on 12 October he spotted land, one of the
islands of the Bahamas – the first sight of the Americas. He went
on to explore the coast of Cuba and Hispaniola before returning
to Spain, convinced that he had simply discovered a new route

to the Indies. Indeed he called the indigenous people Indians. A year later he set off again with a much larger expedition of settlers, soldiers, priests.

In all there were four voyages around the Caribbean, via Jamaica and Hispaniola, during which Columbus landed on mainland Central and South America, establishing the Spanish presence on the new continent. But Columbus, now Grand Admiral and Governor of the Indies, accompanied by his brothers and children, found it hard adapting to his new role, particularly when he came into confrontation with the newly appointed governors sent by the court in Spain.

Ultimately he was arrested and sent back to Spain, though on his return he was freed by the Catholic Monarchs and reconfirmed in his titles. He was allowed to take one more voyage, his fourth, but his career as an actual governor was over.

He spent his last years frustrated by his great achievements and limitations and his bad health, writing books of plans for his new Jerusalem Temple and other dreams. His eldest son Diego, who married the niece of the duke of Alba, was confirmed in 1509 in his father's titles as Grand Admiral and Viceroy and spent many years governing parts of the Indies from his residence in San Domingue in today's Dominican Republic. On his death, his son Luis Colon was awarded the title of Admiral of the Indies and a dukedom. But there ended the three generations of the dynasty of Columbus. Others would conquer and govern the new empire of Spain. To Christopher Columbus himself, the new lands were always the Indies. It was the Florentine navigator Amerigo Vespucci after whom the Americas were to be named. Vespucci was the one who called them 'The New World'.

SELIM THE GRIM

1470–1520

*A carpet is large enough to accommodate two sufis, but the world is
not large enough for two Kings.*

Selim the Grim

Sultan Selim I defeated Persia (Iran) and the Mamluks, and
conquered the entire Middle East, including Mecca, Medina and
Jerusalem for his Ottoman empire, in a reign that was short, bloody
and extremely successful. Having eliminated all internal challeng-
ers, he established the Ottomans as the pre-eminent power in the
Islamic world. One of the cruellest sultans, he was also one of the
greatest.

Selim was born in 1470, the son and heir apparent of Sultan
Bayezid II, whose reign had been undermined by royal infighting
as the sultan found himself challenged by his brother Cem. The
latter had sought assistance from various European allies – notably
the military order of the Knights of St John and the papacy – but
ultimately wound up dead in a Neapolitan jail. This family feud,
however, was nothing compared with what was to follow.

Tall and strong, the young Selim stood out for his bravery and
his keen intelligence. Many looked to him as a model ruler in
waiting. One who was not so convinced, however, was his brother
Ahmed, who desired the throne for himself. The rivalry between
the two became increasingly bitter. In 1511, after Ahmed had pac-
ified a rebellious Ottoman province in Asia Minor, he made as if
to march on the capital, Istanbul. Selim fled.

In semi-exile as governor of Trabizon (a region of northern Anatolia, next to the Black Sea), Selim honed his military skills, leading a succession of military campaigns against Georgia and succeeding in bringing the towns of Kars, Erzurum and Artvin under Ottoman control. Selim returned from his provincial assignment in 1512, and, with the support of the Janissary militias, defeated and killed Ahmed in battle. He then forced his father to abdicate.

Bayezid died soon afterwards, and there ensued an extraordinary bout of intra-familial bloodletting. Selim understood the problems that could flow from sibling rivalry, having witnessed the clash between his father and uncle, not to mention his own experiences with his brother Ahmed. He came up with a simple but ferocious solution: the elimination of all possible rivals to the throne. He not only had his two surviving brothers and his nephews murdered, but even his own sons – with the sole exception of Suleiman, the son he had designated as his one true heir.

Selim then set about adding to his dominions. Hitherto, the focus for Ottoman expansion had been westwards into Europe – particularly the Balkans. Selim adopted a different policy. Signing a peace treaty with the European powers, he turned his attention east, to the Safavids of Persia, whose Shi'ite empire posed a direct ideological challenge to the Ottoman sultans, upholders of the Sunni tradition. In addition, the Safavids had been stirring up unrest among the Kizilbash (Turkmen tribes in eastern Anatolia). In 1514 Selim moved decisively against his Safavid neighbours, and defeated them at the Battle of Chaldiran on the River Euphrates.

With his immediate rivals thus neutralized, Selim then prepared to take on the empire of the Mamluks to the south, whose rule extended from Egypt through Palestine to Syria, and who had provoked Selim's anger by their apparent interference in Ottoman affairs. Marching his army south, Selim destroyed successive

Mamluk armies at Marj Dabiq (north of Aleppo) in 1516 and at al-Raydaniyyah (near Cairo) in 1517. In so doing, he brought Syria, Palestine and Egypt under Ottoman sway. Selim now proclaimed himself caliph, and was declared guardian of the Islamic holy cities of Mecca and Medina. His triumph was to be short-lived. In September 1520 he died after a short illness, probably a form of cancer, leaving his empire to his son, Suleiman.

THE CONQUISTADORS: CORTÉS & PIZARRO

1485–1547　　　　c.1475–1541

> He came dancing across the water
> With his galleons and guns
> Looking for the new world
> In that palace in the sun . . .
> He came dancing across the water
> Cortéz, Cortéz
> What a killer.
>> Neil Young, 'Cortez the Killer'

Hernán Cortés was like Pizarro the personification of the triumphant conquistador whose deeds – both blood-spattered and heroic – brought so much of the New World under the harsh rule of Spain. Arriving in Mexico at the head of a tiny mercenary army, he slaughtered the innocent and pillaged the land, destroying the civilization of the Aztecs and enriching himself beyond his wildest dreams. But the evidence suggests he was not himself cruel and rarely initiated atrocities. He was however a wholy remarkable leader – probably with Pizarro (a distant relative) the outstanding Spaniard of his time, who literally conquered a new empire.

Cortés was born of a noble Castilian family in Medellín, Spain, in 1485. After a sickly childhood, his parents sent him to the prestigious University of Salamanca in the hope that the rarefied intellectual environment might be the making of their son. It was not to be, however, and Cortés soon returned home. Small-town provincial life proved no more satisfactory to young Cortés (except where women were concerned), and in 1502 he decided to move to the New World. Arriving in Hispaniola (modern-day Haiti and the Dominican Republic) in 1503, he soon established himself as a capable man with an eye for an opportunity.

In 1510, at the age of twenty-six, Cortés managed to obtain a place on an expedition to conquer Cuba. The expedition was led by Diego Velázquez de Cuéllar, who went on to become the governor of the newly seized territory; having impressed Velázquez, Cortés was appointed as his secretary. The cordial relationship between the two men did not last, however – in part because of Cortés' continual philandering, even as he secured the hand in marriage of Velázquez's sister-in-law, Catalina.

Cortés grew increasingly restless with his life in Cuba, and in 1518 he persuaded Velázquez to give him command over an expedition that was to explore and colonize the mainland (modern-day Mexico). At the last minute the governor changed his mind and attempted to have Cortés removed from his command. But it was too late: Cortés ignored the countermand and proceeded as originally planned.

In March 1519 Cortés and a force of some 600 men landed on the Yucatán Peninsula, and a month later he formally claimed the land for the Spanish crown. To create a reality to match the rhetoric, Cortés marched first north and then west, achieving a series of victories over hostile native tribes and proving himself a skilled exponent of divide and conquer.

In October 1519 Cortés and his troops arrived at Cholula, then the second largest city in the region. Many of the city's nobility had gathered in the town's central square in the hope of parleying with the approaching Spaniard, but he was in no mood to listen to them. In an act of calculated terror, he ordered his troops to raze the city. Thousands of unarmed citizens were butchered in the process.

In the wake of this massacre, Cortés and his men were received peacefully by the Aztec emperor, Moctezuma II, in the city of Tenochtitlán (Mexico City). The Aztec empire, which emerged in the 14th and 15th centuries from an alliance of three rapidly growing cities – Tenochtitlán, Texcoco and Tlacopan, had been fashioned by Moctezuma I (c.1398–1469) into a cohesive political and cultural unit, with Tenochtitlán at its capital, and reached its zenith under Ahuitzotl (c.1486–1502), who more than doubled the territory under Aztec control. He was succeeded on his death by his nephew, Moctezuma II – the man on the throne when Cortés and his mercenaries arrived seventeen years later. The Aztecs practised human sacrifice of men, women and children – sometimes on a vast scale. On one occasion in the 1480s, it was said that they sacrificed 84,000 prisoners at the Great Pyramid of Tenochtitlan.

Moctezuma believed Cortés to be the incarnation of the Aztec god Quetzalcoatl (the Feathered Serpent), and, having heard of the military superiority of the intruders, was anxious to avoid direct confrontation. For his part, Cortés was determined to receive the submission of the Aztec emperor to the Spanish king, and to this end he took Moctezuma prisoner.

Back in Cuba, meanwhile, Velázquez had grown jealous of Cortés' success, and in 1520 he sent a force under Pánfilo de

Narváez to retrieve the insubordinate conquistador. Despite the numerical inferority of his troops compared to those of Narváez, Cortés defeated the challenge. However, during his absence from Tenochtitlán, the man he had left in charge had slaughtered many of the city's leading figures and provoked an uprising, during which Moctezuma was killed. After attempting to re-enter Tenochtitlán, Cortés was forced to abandon it and only just avoided defeat at the hands of pursuing Aztec forces.

Having regrouped in the lands of his allies, the Tlaxcala, he returned in late 1520, intent on recapturing the city. In the war that followed, the Spaniard sought to break the Aztec resistance through a strategy of attrition. Tenochtitlán was isolated, and resistance eventually crushed. The fall of the city effectively marked the end of the Aztec empire. Cortés was now the undisputed master of the territory, which he renamed the New Spain of the Ocean Sea.

As governor of the new colony from 1521 to 1524, Cortés oversaw the destruction of many artefacts of Aztec culture. The indigenous people were forced into a system of forced labour, under which they were ruthlessly exploited for centuries to come. All the while, the principal concern of the Spanish conqueror was personal aggrandisement. Those who suffered under Cortés' yoke were finally relieved of their burden when he was dismissed from his post by the Spanish king, who had received various reports of his viceroy's misrule. In 1528 Cortés returned to Spain to plead his case, but despite being made marques del Valle de Oaxaca, Cortés was not convinced he had won the king's support. Charles V never forgave him for his insubordination to royal officials and would never let him command in Europe.

The final two decades of Cortés' life saw the increasingly embittered conquistador journeying back and forth between Spain and his estates in the New World, and attempting to counter what he felt were the lies of his 'various and powerful rivals and enemies'.

Vastly rich, perhaps the most titanic European of his time, the marquis of the Valley died in 1547, en route to South America.

Like Cortés, Pizarro's place in history is that of the man who destroyed the Incan empire and delivered the riches of Peru into Spanish hands. One of the greatest Europeans of his age, Pizarro was lean, tall, fit and a superb, kindly, quiet-spoken leader, beloved by his men. He was illiterate, old-fashioned and usually wore a black cassock, white hat and sword and dagger. But he was enormously experienced in the warfare of the conquest of the Indies and prepared to be utterly ruthless and brutal to his enemies. He displayed the same qualities against the Indians to achieve the psychological dominance needed to compensate for his massive numerical inferiority. His achievements – the conquest of an empire with a preposterously small band of men – remain astonishing and Pizarro is still regarded as a hero in his home town of Trujillo in Spain.

Like many other young Europeans of the time, he was lured by the promise of the New World. He was accompanied and assisted by his brothers and by 1502 Pizarro had arrived in the Caribbean island of Hispaniola. By 1513 he was fighting alongside the masterful explorer and conquistador Vasco Núñez de Balboa who had founded the first town, Dariena, on mainland America and reached the Pacific Ocean. However the following year Balboa was removed from his position as governor of Veragua. Pizarro immediately professed his loyalty to Balboa's replacement, Pedrarias Dávila. Five years later, on the orders of Dávila, Pizarro arrested Balboa, who was subsequently executed for insubordination. As a reward for his allegiance to Dávila, Pizarro was made mayor of the recently founded Panama City.

Although Pizarro used his new role to accumulate significant riches, these did not satisfy his ambitions. Rumours of a fabulously wealthy country to the south – Piru – had reached Panama by this time. Inspired by such stories, Pizarro formed a partnership with a soldier-adventurer, Diego de Almagro: they agreed to lead an expedition in search of 'Piru', with all the lands they conquered to be divided equally between them.

An unsuccessful attempt in 1524 was followed by a far more promising expedition in 1526, in which the existence of a wealthy empire to the south was confirmed. With their appetites whetted, the conquistadors resolved on a third trip. However, the governor of Panama had grown impatient with Pizarro's failure to deliver immediate results and ordered the venture to be abandoned.

When news reached Pizarro of the governor's decision, he drew a line in the sand with his sword and declared, 'There lies Peru with its riches; here, Panama and its poverty. Choose, each man, what best becomes a brave Castilian.' Of those present, just thirteen men committed to stay with him. Accompanied by Almagro and Luque, Pizarro now continued on his journey, and in 1528 he first entered the territories of the Inca empire. Originating in the Peruvian highlands in the twelfth century, the Inca by the mid-1500s had grown into a mighty empire encompassing much of the west coast of South America. Under three particularly successful rulers (Pachacuti, r. c.1438–c.1471; Topa Inca, r. c.1471–c.1493; and Huayna Capac, r. c.1493–1525) they came to dominate much of what is modern-day Ecuador, Peru, parts of Argentina, and Chile. Shortly before the Spaniards arrived in 1532, however, the empire was fractured by civil war that broke out during the rule of Huayna Capac's son, Atahualpa, leaving the empire a sitting target, especially given the technical superiority of the Incas' European assailants.

Pizarro encountered human sacrifice among the Inca people. They practised it less than their Aztec counterparts in Mexico, but would respond to momentous events (such as a natural disaster, or the death of an emperor – who was worshipped as a god) by engaging in the tradition of capacocha – the sacrifice of children – in an attempt to ensure the gods' continued blessing.

Anxious to build on this promising initial encounter with a vulnerable and wealthy empire, but short on resources, Pizarro returned briefly to Europe to appeal in person to Charles V, king of Spain and Holy Roman Emperor, who now agreed to assist him.

Returning to the New World, Pizarro sent emissaries to meet the representatives of the Inca emperor, Atahualpa. It was agreed that Pizarro would meet the emperor at the town of Cajamarca in November 1532. Advancing with his army of 80,000 men, Atahualpa believed he had little to fear from Pizarro's force of 106 infantry soldiers and 62 cavalry. On arrival at Cajamarca, Atahualpa decided to leave most of his troops outside the city and entered with a far smaller retinue – not realizing he was walking into a carefully laid trap. In a brief exchange, the emperor contemptuously rejected the suggestion that he should become a Spanish supplicant. Pizarro immediately ordered his men to open fire on the astonished Incas. Almost all of Atahualpa's escort party – perhaps 3000 or 4000 men – were slaughtered, and the massacre continued outside the city. In total some 7000 Incas perished in a hail of gunfire; the Spanish took fewer than ten casualties in reply. The emperor himself was taken hostage. Pizarro took as his mistress Atahualpa's teenage sister with whom he would go on to have children.

Pizarro demanded a vast ransom be paid for Atahualpa's release: the room where the emperor was being held was to be filled from floor to ceiling with gold and silver. Amazingly, Atahualpa's people delivered as requested. But rather than release his enemy, Pizarro now went back on his word and had the emperor executed.

Rewarded by Charles V with the title Marquis of the Conquest, Pizarro sealed the conquest of Peru by taking Cuzco in 1533, and in 1535 he founded the city of Lima as its capital. He then set about accumulating an astonishing fortune. Power and wealth bred jealousy, however, and Pizarro soon fell out with his partner, Almagro, over the spoils. In 1538 the dispute between them came to war. Pizarro defeated Almagro at the Battle of Las Salinas, and had his former comrade executed. The dead man's son vowed revenge, and in 1541 his supporters attacked Pizarro's palace and murdered him within its walls.

This was not the end of the Pizarro story. His brother Hernando returned to Spain to answer the case against the family and was imprisoned for decades. When he was finally released, he married Pizarro's super-rich half-Inca daughter and built the Palace of Conquest in Trujillo. Meanwhile another brother Gonzalo seized Peru, rebelled against the royal authorities and considered making himself king – but he was ultimately defeated and killed by the royal viceroy.

The Spanish would rule most of the continent for 300 years. Over that time, the Spanish interbred with the indigenous people, known as Indians, and the black slaves imported as labour from Africa, to form the complicated peoples of today's continent. It was ruled by royal viceroys, and the silver mined there funded the Spanish empire. All power remained with the Spaniards and the creoles, Hispanics born in the colonies, while those of mixed race, the so-called mestizos and mulattos, were discriminated against. From the very start up to the 21st century, the continent has suffered from its cult of the caudillos, almighty military strongmen, and its racial prejudices – both the legacies of the conquistadors.

MICHELANGELO

1475–1564

Michelangelo was regarded even during his lifetime as the greatest artist in the world, but the centuries since have not dimmed the brilliance of his versatile genius. He was a sculptor, painter, architect and poet – the very personification of the High Renaissance – and even today it is simply impossible not to wonder at his creativity, admire his astonishing dynamism and bow before the indefatigable energy that earned the nickname of Il Divino, the Divine One, and the tempestuous and awesome grandeur that also made him Il Terribile, the Terrible One. He was agonized by his own private life, tormented by his faith, tortured by the stress of accepting and delivering colossal commissions from popes and kings, irritated by the greed of his own family, consumed by the process of creation, even the choosing and moving of vast blocks of marble, he was both tyrannical in his work and demands and yet he was also a loving and loyal friend.

Born on 6 March 1475 in Caprese, Tuscany, Michelangelo di Lodovico Buonarroti Simoni was the son of a Florentine civil servant from a minor but old noble family, obsessed with its diminished grandeur. When his mother died young, he spent time with a nanny and her stonecutter husband who taught him about the glories of marble and early on, he found he had the gift of chiselling figures from the stones. As a boy he was sent to be educated in Florence, the city-state that was already the capital of the Renaissance, the rebirth of classical creativity, then ruled effectively but always tenuously by the Medici family in the person of Lorenzo the Magnificent. The Medicis, originally international bankers, prided themselves on their reputation as patrons and connoisseurs of the arts. At thirteen, Michelangelo was apprenticed to the atelier of one of the doyens of the Florentine Renaissance, Domenico Ghirlandaio, and it was he who sent the talented boy to the household of Medici himself, where he was introduced to the great court of Italian power as well enjoying a playful and rather decadent life amongst painters and poets in the great city, probably also enjoying love affairs with older and younger men as was traditional at that time.

Michelangelo lived at the court of Medici for five years, favoured by The Magnificent himself. But the death of Lorenzo the Magnificent in 1492 and the rise of a terrifyingly puritanical priest Savronola, who raised the people against the debauchery and artistry of Medici dominion in what he called the 'Bonfire of the Vanities', ended Michelangelo's princely idyll and he returned to his father. But he still received commissions from the Medici family and was constantly sculpting and developing his style – until the violent overthrow of the Medicis meant that he had to leave Florence. Finally, aged twenty-one, he was invited to Rome by a patron, Cardinal Raffaele Riario, and he started to receive commissions including one to sculpt a Pietà, a sculpture of the Virgin Mary holding the body of Christ. The result was Michelangelo's first masterpiece. His Pietà is now in St Peter's Basilica in Rome, and it is so exquisite that the stone seems to assume the quality of skin itself. He was just twenty-four and suddenly he was famous. In 1498, the grotesque Savronola was overthrown and executed, allowing Michelangelo to return home. There the Florentine potentates commissioned a statue of King David. When he finished it in 1504, its sheer virtuosity, boldness of vision and technical accomplishment astounded everyone. Soon afterwards the city council asked him to paint the Battle of Anghiari at the same time as his rival Leonardo da Vinci. But Michelangelo's first masterpiece of painting was that of the Holy Family, now known as the *Doni Tondo*, which is today in the Uffizi Gallery.

In 1505, he met his match in terms of grandeur and temperament when he was invited back to Rome by the tyrannical, aggressive and fearsome pope, Julius II, a warrior-pontiff who was known as '*il papa terribile*' both for his furious temper and his determination to restore papal power, often leading his own armies himself and frequently beating his servants with his cane. Neither Michelangelo nor Julius would accept the mastery of anyone and they sparked off each other. Offering a vast payment, Julius ordered the artist to build his future tomb, a grandiose conception with forty statues. It took forty years, a commission that tormented Michelangelo with its twists and turns and negotiations and it was never quite finished – the unfinished and much smaller tomb is now in the Church of San Pietro in Vincoli, including the peerless statue of Moses. Simultaneously the capricious Julius bombarded his artist with highly paid but urgent commissions that often outraged Michelangelo. The greatest of them was, in 1508, to paint the ceiling of the Sistine Chapel. The artist at first tried to refuse this overwhelming duty and when the pope insisted, he demanded freedom of vision and Julius agreed to his idea of rendering stories from Genesis, including the Creation and the Fall of Man. Michelangelo had to construct a scaffold and lie on his back, high above the chapel, to paint over 5000 square feet of frescoes. In the process, he damaged his neck, his back and his eyes, cursing the work, yet knowing that this was both sacred work and his masterpiece. This furiously witty sonnet by Michelangelo reveals the peppery energy, passionate earthiness and the authentic voice of the artist embroiled in the physical battle to create the Sistine ceiling:

I've already grown a goiter from this toil
as water swells the cats in Lombardy
or any other country they might be,
forcing my belly to hang under my chin.
My beard to heaven, and my memory
I feel above its coffer. My chest a harp.
And ever above my face, the brush dripping,
making a rich pavement out of me.
My loins have been shoved into my guts,
my arse serves to counterweigh my rump,
Eyelessly I walk in the void.
Ahead of me my skin lies outstretched,
and to bend, I must knot my shoulders taut,
holding myself like a Syrian bow.

The fresco of God creating Man is probably the most famous painting in human history. After its completion in 1512, Julius II died but was succeeded as pope by one of the Medici, an old friend of Michelangelo and fellow Florentine, Leo X, a son of Lorenzo the Magnificent. A much easier master than Julius, he was demanding nonetheless: ordered back to Florence, the artist worked on the Medicis' Basilica of San Lorenzo, combining architectural design with sculpture, creating the tomb of the Medici family, including statues of Lorenzo the Magnificent and also allegorical sculptures of Night and Day, Dusk and Dawn, all typically sensual and lifelike and bold in vision. Later he designed the Laurentian Library for the Medicis but his time in Florence was interrupted by political instability – first the fall and then the restoration of the Medicis. Michelangelo privately disapproved of the royal ascendancy of the Medicis and his dissidence attracted the hostility of the new ruthless, decadent young duke, Alessandro, known as Il Moro, the Moor, whose mother may have been a black slave-girl. Though

Alessandro would soon be assassinated, Michelangelo had to leave the city in 1534 and return to Rome, where he found favour with another of the Medici family, Giulio, now Pope Clement VII, who commissioned him to paint the altar wall of the Sistine Chapel. The resulting Last Judgement took over six years to complete and is striking in its human passion and muscular physicality, showing the artist's view that the beauty of the human body is a manifestation of God's greatness. Jesus appears muscular and naked while Michelangelo included a mocking vision himself in the frayed skin of St Bartholomew. It is in some ways a dark and terrifying vision of astonishing power as Jesus comes again and the souls of the dead are judged – some believe it was inspired partly by the vicious depredations of the sack of Rome by an imperial army in 1527. But the nakedness of sacred figures shocked and horrified the puritanical Cardinal Gian Carafa who denounced Michelangelo. Carafa much later became the oppressive, malicious and fierce Pope Paul IV who absurdly ordered trousers to be drawn onto some of Michelangelo's naked bodies.

Michelangelo earned huge sums of money in his lifetime, which he tried to save in order to enrich his nephews, constantly buying land to restore his noble family to ancient glories. He was irascible and tempestuous to both his family and his assistants, writing them furious, plain-spoken and often cursing letters and frequently complaining about the strain of finding the right marble, and how to juggle the demands of his papal and royal patrons. He was a most affectionate friend to his inner circle of painters and poets and was himself a brilliant poet. He enjoyed a passionate but platonic friendship with the aristocrat Vittoria Colonna, widow of the Marchese of Pescara, who was herself a famous poetess and patroness. She and Michelangelo exchanged poetry. Despite his huge wealth, Michelangelo lived with rough-hewn austerity, accompanied by a crew of his assistants and apprentices, mainly young men. He was an admirer of male beauty, as his sculptures show, and his 300 love poems are often highly homoerotic. There is much argument as to whether this highly pious Catholic had physical relationships, but it seems from the sensuality of his poetry that it is highly probable he did. In 1532 he fell passionately in love with Tommaso dei Cavalieri, a twenty-three-year-old nobleman of beauty and taste, and for a while he returned the love of the fifty-seven-year-old Michelangelo, who wrote many love poems and dedicated drawings to him. They were lifelong friends. He fell in love with others, some of them outrageous grifters who exploited him.

In 1536, Michelangelo was asked by Paul III to design the piazza of the ancient Capitoline Hill in preparation for a visit by Emperor Charles V and for the new design for the pope's family palazzo, the Farnese. In 1546, Michelangelo was given another gigantic job. It was Pope Julius II who had decided in 1506 to demolish the ancient basilica of St Peter, which dated partly from the reign of Constantine the Great, to build a colossal new cathedral. The work was still unfinished when Michelangelo was appointed its architect – it was a commission that lasted for the rest of his life. In old age he became more curmudgeonly and austere in his habits, dying at eighty-eight, perhaps the greatest artist who has ever lived. What joy for mankind that so many of his works survive and can still be admired.

BARBAROSSA & SILVER ARM

*c.*1478–1546   *c.*1474–1518

*They came upon a ship from Genoa laden with grain and seized it
on the spot. Then they saw a fortress-like galleon, a merchant ship
laden with cloth, and took that without any difficulty. Returning to
Tunis, they handed over the fifth of booty [due to the ruler], divided
the rest, and set out again with three ships for the infidel coasts.*

Katib Chelebi, in his *History of the Maritime Wars of the
Turks* (*c.*1650), describing an early episode in the life of
Barbarossa and his older brother Oruc

Barbarossa – a brilliant Ottoman admiral, canny politician
and founder of his own dynastic kingdom – was one of the
four freebooting Muslim corsair brothers who dominated the
Mediterranean and slaughtered and enslaved innocent Christians
with audacious enthusiasm in the early 16th century.

Barbarossa Hayreddin Pasha was born on the Aegean island
of Lesbos around 1478 as Yakupoglu Hizir – one of four sons and
two daughters – to a Turkish Muslim father, Yakup Aga, and his
Christian Greek wife, Katerina. Hizir was an intelligent youngster,
blessed with charisma and the ability to lead others. Dark in
complexion, he later boasted a luxuriant beard with a reddish hue
– hence his European nickname Barbarossa, meaning 'red beard'
(a corruption of Baba Oruc, an honorific title later inherited from
his gifted brother Oruc, who earned it in 1510 after helping large
numbers of Spanish Muslims flee persecution).

As young men, the four brothers – Ishak, Oruc, Hizir and

Ilyas – bought a boat to transport their father's pottery products, but with Ottoman vessels subject at the time to repeated raids at the hands of the hated Knights of St John, based on the island of Rhodes, Oruc, Ilyas and Hizir soon turned to privateering, while Ishak helped oversee the family business at home. Hizir worked the Aegean Sea, and Oruc and Ilyas the coast of the Levant until their boat was intercepted by the Knights. Ilyas was killed and Oruc imprisoned for three years at the castle of Bodrum before Hizir launched a daring raid to rescue him.

Determined to avenge his brother, Oruc secured the support of the Ottoman governor of Antalya, who supplied him with a fleet of galleys to combat the Knights' marauding. In a series of attacks, he captured several enemy galleons, subsequently raiding Italy. Joining forces, from 1509 Oruc, Hizir and Ishak defeated a host of Spanish ships across the Mediterranean. In one such battle, in 1512, Oruc lost his left arm, earning the nickname Silver Arm after replacing it with a silver prosthetic limb.

Undeterred, the three brothers raided yet further off the Italian and Spanish coasts, in one month alone capturing a further twenty-three ships. They began producing their own gunpowder, and over the next four years raided, destroyed or captured a succession of ships, fortresses and cities. In 1516, they liberated Algiers from the Spaniards, Oruc declaring himself a sultan, though he relinquished the title the following year to the Ottoman sultan, who in return appointed him governor of Algiers and chief naval governor of the western Mediterranean – positions he held until 1518, when he and Ishak were killed by the troops of Charles I of Spain (later Emperor Charles V).

Hizir, the sole surviving brother and the man remembered today as Barbarossa, took on his brother's mantle. In 1519, he defended Algiers against a joint Spanish–Italian attack, striking back the same year by raiding Provence. Then, following numerous raids along the French and Spanish coasts, in 1522 he contributed to the Ottoman conquest of Rhodes that finally vanquished the Knights of St John. In 1525, he raided Sardinia, going on to recapture Algiers and take Tunis in 1529, launching further attacks from both.

In 1530, Emperor Charles V sought the help of Andrea Doria, the talented Genoese admiral, to challenge Barbarossa's dominance, but the following year Barbarossa trounced Doria, winning the personal gratitude of Sultan Suleiman the Magnificent, who made him Capudan Pasha – fleet admiral and chief governor of North Africa – and giving him the honorary name Barbarossa Hayreddin Pasha.

In 1538 – already a living legend among the Muslims for freeing African Muslim slaves from Spanish galleys and bringing glory to the Ottoman empire – Barbarossa scattered a combined Spanish, Maltese, Venetian and German fleet at the Battle of Preveza, thereby securing Turkish dominance of the eastern Mediterranean for nearly forty years. In September 1540, Charles offered him a huge bribe to switch sides, but Barbarossa refused outright, and in 1543, as his fleet lurked in the mouth of the River Tiber, he even threatened to advance on Rome, but was dissuaded by the French, with whom he had entered into a temporary alliance. By now the cities of the Italian coast, including the proud Genoese, had given up trying to defeat him, choosing instead to send huge payments in return for being spared from attack. Barbarossa was master of the Italian and Mediterranean coasts.

In 1545, undefeated and having ensured Ottoman dominance of the Mediterranean and North Africa, Barbarossa retired to a magnificent villa on the northern shore of the Bosphorus. Here he wrote his memoirs until he died from natural causes in 1546. He left his son, Hasan Pasha, as his successor as ruler of Algiers.

He had seized and enslaved as many as 50,000 people from the Italian and Spanish coasts, and was famous for his savage cruelty.

For the Ottomans, Barbarossa was a remarkable admiral. Christians saw him as a merciless pirate, perhaps the most terrifying that ever lived.

THE BORGIAS:
POPE ALEXANDER VI

1431–1503

AND HIS CHILDREN
CESARE & LUCREZIA

1475–1507   1480–1519

*Lucrezia was wanton in imagination, godless by nature, am-
bitious and designing ... she carried the head of a Raphael
Madonna and concealed the heart of a Messalina.*

Alexandre Dumas, *Celebrated Crimes* (1843)

Rodrigo Borgia, great-nephew of Pope Calixtus III, was a ruthless master of intrigue and power, an expertise that made him and his children legendary for debauch and murder. A cardinal at twenty-five, he had served as vice chancellor of the Holy See during the reigns of four popes, amassing a vast fortune in the process. By the time it was his turn to be pope, Borgia had the cash to buy the papacy with four mule loads of bullion. Whatever his sins, he was clever, witty, charming, experienced and conscientious in his attendance of the Curia and seductive both in politics and the bedroom: 'women were attracted to him like iron to a magnet', commented a witness. Two years after his election as pope – he called himself Alexander VI – Rome was attacked and seized by King Charles VIII of France but the pope managed to win over the French king, who soon marched on to Naples. Once the French had returned to their homeland, Alexander VI set about the full enjoyment of his papacy: he had already managed to install his eldest son Giovanni as duke of Gandia but in June 1497 the twenty-year-old vanished, only to be found in the Tiber with his throat cut and nine stab wounds. Alexander was heartbroken but he did not pursue the case because the chief suspect was his younger son Cesare, already a cardinal.

In 1498, Cesare persuaded his father to release him from his cardinalate and appoint him papal military commander. Now a layman again, Cesare had ambitions in France and as the architect of his father's new pro-French policies, he was rewarded with the French dukedom of Valentinois and allowed to marry the sister of the king of Navarre. The new Duke Cesare set about murdering or overthrowing all the rival lords in Italy who stood in the way of Borgia power. In the process Alexander and Cesare restored papal political power. But Cesare was hated: 'every night', wrote an ambassador in Rome, 'four or five men are discovered assassinated, bishops and others, so that all Rome trembles for fear of being murdered by the Duke'. By now Cesare Borgia was literally decaying, riddled and raddled by syphilis that was eating away his face so that he only appeared in public with a sinister gold mask.

For all his notoriety, Cesare Borgia was in his way utterly exceptional: he was tireless, scarcely slept and lived in a state of demented and boundless activity. Fearless and uninhibited, he also possessed his father's charm and intelligence. Cesare fathered at least eleven bastards and his orgies, often attended by his father and sister, were magnificent and brazen: at one famed banquet, the papal master of ceremonies recorded how 'fifty decent prostitutes in attendance, who danced naked' got onto their hands and knees to play a game of picking up chestnuts that were spread around the floor. 'Finally prizes were offered – silken doublets, pairs of shoes, hats – for those men who could perform the act most frequently with the prostitutes.' The orgy was not just attended by pope and duke but also Cesare's sister Lucrezia Borgia.

Lucrezia became infamous throughout Renaissance Italy for her corruption, carnality and viciousness. Her monstrosity was probably exaggerated, but contemporaries regarded her as the embodiment of evil, and whispered that she wore a hollow ring from which she would discreetly pour poison into the wine of all those who stood in her way.

Lucrezia, a pretty, captivating child, grew into a great beauty. She was described by a contemporary as 'of middle height and graceful of form ... her hair is golden, her eyes grey, her mouth rather large, the teeth brilliantly white, her bosom smooth and white and admirably proportioned'. Her father Pope Alexander arranged for the eighteen-year-old Lucrezia to marry Giovanni Sforza, lord of Pesaro, in order to build an alliance with the Sforzas – a powerful Milanese family – against the Aragonese of Naples.

The wedding, which took place at the Vatican, was a lavish affair, at which a scandalous play about pimps and mistresses was performed. Lucrezia spent two years in Pesaro, but was unhappy and returned to Rome. The Borgias, who already had a formidable reputation, suspected Giovanni of spying for Milan; when he visited his wife in Rome he became terrified when Lucrezia suddenly began to smile and show him signs of affection. Fearing for his life, he fled Rome in disguise. The alliance between Rome and Milan was no longer of use to the Borgias, who were now attempting to court Naples. Pope Alexander demanded that the Sforzas agree to a divorce, but the only legal way to do this was to force Giovanni to make a false confession that he was impotent and had therefore never consummated the marriage. Humiliated, he hit back with the allegation that Alexander had undermined the marriage in order that he could pursue a sexual interest in his own daughter.

In the midst of the divorce proceedings, Lucrezia – still claiming to be a virgin – retired to the Roman convent of San Sisto, where she was visited by a messenger from her father, the handsome courtier Pedro Calderon, with whom she soon began an affair. Within a year, a mysterious baby boy appeared among the Borgia clan, and shortly afterwards Calderon was found floating in the River Tiber, apparently murdered on the orders of a jealous Cesare. The historian Potigliotto speculated that either Cesare or Alexander had sired the boy.

In 1498, having had her claim to virginity upheld by the divorce court, Lucrezia was offered to the seventeen-year-old Alfonso, duke of Bisceglie, an illegitimate son of Alfonso II of Naples. However, it wasn't long before the Borgias fell out with Naples and moved closer to the French king, Louis XII. Lucrezia's young husband fled Rome in fear of his life, and when his bride convinced him to return, he was savagely attacked on the steps of St Peter's in Rome. It is possible that Lucrezia was complicit in the assault, although contemporaries believed that she genuinely loved her second husband, pointing out that she tended to his wounds and nursed him back to health. But the court of the Borgias was not a safe place to convalesce, and, on Cesare's orders, a month after the original attack, Alfonso was strangled while he lay in bed.

Lucrezia was said to be distraught at her young husband's death. Nonetheless, she soon resumed her part in Borgia power politics. In 1501, the year after Alfonso's murder, she married Alfonso d'Este, son of Ercole I, Duke of Ferrara.

In 1503, Alexander VI died of fever, aged seventy-two. His reputation is deserved but he was also successful in changing the papacy, improving its finances, administration and diplomatic influence. Cesare was left exposed. He was exiled to Spain where he was killed in battle aged thirty-one. His motto was 'Caesar or nothing.' In the end, it was nothing.

Lucrezia became a respected patron of the arts and literature in Ferrara, where she became duchess in 1505, while still finding time to have an affair with her bisexual brother-in-law and the humanist poet Pietro Bembo. She died in childbirth at the age of thirty-nine.

MAGELLAN

1480–1521

... the whole earth hangs in the air ... a thing so strange and seeming so far against nature and reason ... which is yet now found true by experience of them that have in less than two years sailed the world round about.

Thomas More, *Dialogue Concerning Heresies* (1529), referring to Magellan's 1519 voyage

Ferdinand Magellan was a fearless and determined sailor who achieved what Columbus had attempted: he sailed westwards from Europe and reached the East Indies, thus making the first recorded crossing of the Pacific Ocean. Although Magellan himself was killed in the Philippines, one ship from his fleet of five, after experiencing appalling hardships, finally returned to Spain – becoming the first to complete a circumnavigation of the entire globe.

Born to a noble Portuguese family, Magellan grew up around the royal court. In 1495 he entered the service of King Manuel I, 'the Fortunate', and enlisted as a volunteer on the first voyage to India planned by the Portuguese viceroy Francisco D'Almeida.

Magellan took part in a series of expeditions to the east, as Portugal sought to expand its trade routes and bring valuable spices back to Europe, becoming involved in skirmishes en route and achieving promotion to captain. In 1512 he returned to Portugal. He helped to take the Moroccan city of Azamor but was wounded during the fighting and walked with a limp for the rest of his life. Even worse, he was accused of trading with the Moors and subsequently fell from favour with King Manuel.

It was clear that Magellan's career in the service of the Portuguese crown was over. In 1513 he renounced his nationality and went to Spain. He proposed to Charles V that he could reach the Spice Islands of the east via the western passage that had eluded Christopher Columbus some twenty years earlier. With the aid of advances in navigation, diligent consultation with an astronomer and the sheer guts to suggest travelling at a latitude of up to 75° S, Magellan was in a good position to trump Columbus. So in September 1519, with five ships and 270 men, he embarked on his historic voyage.

Magellan sailed across the Atlantic, sighting South America in November 1519. He then headed south, wintering in Patagonia, where he had to crush a dangerous mutiny led by two of his captains. He set sail again in August 1520.

In October Magellan found a channel leading westwards between the South American mainland and the archipelago to the south, which enabled his fleet to avoid the stormy open seas south of Cape Horn. He called this passage All Saints' Channel, but it is now known as the Strait of Magellan after the great navigator. As the ships passed through, the sailors were overawed by the snowy mountains on either side. To the north was the southern tip of Patagonia, and to the south the islands they called the Land of Fire – *Tierra del Fuego* – because of the fires lit by the native people that burned on the shore. Once they had passed through the strait, they found themselves facing a vast expanse of open water. In honour of the steady, gentle wind that blew them across it, Magellan named the ocean the Pacific.

For ninety-eight days Magellan's crew sailed northwestwards across the open ocean, spotting only an occasional rocky, barren island. They had little water, and what they did have was bad. They ran out of supplies and were reduced to eating mouldy biscuit, rats and sawdust. But still Magellan pushed onwards, saying that he would rather eat the ships' leather than give up. And that was exactly what the crew did, chewing leather from the yardarms.

In March 1521 they reached the Philippines, which Magellan originally named after St Lazarus (they would later be renamed after King Phillip II of Spain). They took on supplies and reached the island of Cebu, where Magellan befriended the native king. By purporting to convert to Catholicism, the king managed to convince Magellan to become involved in his violent feuds with neighbouring islands, and it was in an attack on one of these on 27 April that Magellan was killed. The treacherous king then murdered two of Magellan's men before the crew could regroup and head home for Spain.

Only eighteen crewmen, four South American natives and one ship, the *Victoria*, made it around the Cape of Good Hope and back to Spain, plagued by contrary winds, harassment from the Portuguese, malnourishment and scurvy. Although Magellan was not among them, by the time of his death he had travelled well past the longitude of his original voyages to the east, when he had visited the Moluccas. He had also discovered the holy grail of navigators and traders: a passage to the eastern Spice Islands via the western ocean. This in turn helped to pave the way for Spanish and Portuguese dominance across the globe during the 16th century.

Great explorers like Columbus and Marco Polo may have discovered the hitherto unknown parts of the world, but it was Magellan who joined them all together.

BABUR AND THE MUGHALS

1483–1530

Wine makes a man act like an ass in a rich pasture.
Saying attributed to Babur

Babur was the nomad prince who emerged from a tiny Mongol kingdom to found India's Mughal empire. Babur's reign was brief, but he was a talented conqueror and intellectual, and his power over, and respect for, the myriad peoples whom he ruled created a vast empire of an incomparable cultural magnificence.

Claiming descent from Genghis Khan, the young Zahir-ud-din Muhammad was directly descended from the Turkic-Mongol conqueror Tamurlane (Timur). The family had lost much of Tamurlane's empire, so he was for much of his youth a king without a kingdom. Called Babur by tribesmen unable to pronounce his real name, he inherited the tiny central Asian state of Fergana at the age of twelve. Having fended off his uncles' attempts to unseat him, Babur set out to conquer neighbouring Samarkand. The fifteen-year-old prince miscalculated. In his absence rebellion at home robbed him of Fergana, and when he marched back to reclaim it, his troops deserted Samarkand, depriving him of that too. 'It came very hard on me,' Babur later recalled of his nomad years. 'I could not help crying a good deal.'

Defeat strengthened Babur's resolve. By 1504 the hardened warrior had secured himself the kingdom of Kabul in today's Afghanistan. From there he looked east into Hindustan's vast lands. After several attempts, Babur finally triumphed in 1526 at the Battle of Panipat, where his 12,000 men routed the sultan of Delhi's 100,000-strong army. Over the next three years he defeated the Rajputs, the Afghans and the sultan of Bengal, to become the unchallenged ruler of Hindustan – today's India. Thus did this descendant of Tamurlane carve out what was to become known as the Mughal empire, after the Persian word for Mongol.

Babur ascribed his astounding victories to 'the fountain of the favour and mercy of God'. Weaponry helped. Babur introduced to India the matchlock musket and the cannon, although initially they only earned him ridicule. As Babur's tally of victories attests, it soon became clear that with effective firepower his almost absurdly small armies could make huge inroads against opponents with a vast numerical superiority.

A supremely well-trained collection of Pashtuns, Persians, Arabs and Chaghatai Turks, Babur's men revered their consummate commander. He was a warrior of legendary strength – it was reported that he could run up slopes carrying a man on each shoulder, and that he had swum across every major river he had encountered, including the Ganges. The Mughal armies terrified their enemies and not without just cause, for vanquished combatants were beheaded and their heads strung up from parapets. Babur considered his son and heir Humayun's decision to have 100 prisoners of war shot at Panipat, rather than released or enslaved as was the custom, 'an excellent omen'.

In contrast, as a ruler, Babur was merciful. The Muslim emperor ruled over an array of peoples with immense tolerance and respect. He never forced their conversion or sought to alter their practices. Preach Islam 'by the sword of love and affection', he told Humayun, 'rather than the sword of tyranny and persecution'. His clarity of vision and his humanity allowed him to see that his vast empire could flourish in all its diversity: 'Look at the various characteristics of your people just as characteristics of various seasons,' he told his son. An advocate of justice regardless of race or religion, he hated hypocrisy, describing it as 'the lies and flattery of rogues and sycophants'.

Babur's respect for his conquered lands helped to forge an exquisite and unique culture. Babur brought to India his Timurid inheritance: the skills and practices of the jewel-city of Tamurlane's old capital, Samarkand. The resulting fusion produced centuries of breathtaking art and architecture, such as the monumental Taj Mahal. Himself a skilled author, calligrapher and composer, Babur initiated his dynasty's patronage of all these arts. He created magnificent formal gardens as a respite from India's ferocious heat. They were the first of their kind on the subcontinent, stocked with plants and fruits that he brought from his homelands to the northwest. Buried according to his wishes in the garden of Bagh-e-Babur in his beloved Kabul, the inscription on Babur's tomb reads: 'If there is a paradise on earth, it is this, it is this, it is this!'

Babur's flaw was his excess. He drank heavily and developed a notable fondness for marijuana. His extravagant generosity emptied his coffers. And when Humayun seemed mortally ill, Babur was said to have offered up his life in return for his son's. Babur's last words say much about the ruthlessness of the time and the humanity of the man: 'Do nothing against your brothers,' he told Humayun, 'even though they may deserve it.'

Babur's extraordinary story is recounted in his personal journal, the *Babur-nama*, charting his progress from Fergana's boy-king to Mughal emperor. It encompasses battles, intrigues, flora, fauna, geography, peoples, poetry, art, music, polo matches and feasts. It also gives the first documented mention of the priceless diamond the Koh-i-Noor. Encompassing even Babur's personal feelings, the *Babur-nama* is an astounding record of the era and a startling insight into the man.

HENRY VIII

1491–1547

He never spared a man in his anger, nor a woman in his lust.
Sir Robert Naunton, Fragmenta Regalia, 1641

Henry VIII was a golden and gifted boy who grew up to become a forceful, energetic and ambitious ruler – he was a majestic and ruthless monarch who created an 'imperial' monarchy by asserting English independence, defying Rome, breaking up the monasteries, promoting his realm's military and naval power and his own autocracy, all ultimately enabling the triumph of Protestantism. Yet he became a bloated, thin-skinned tyrant who ordered the killing – on faked evidence – of many, including two of his wives, because of his own wounded pride. He was, in his paranoid cruelty, the English Stalin.

Henry was second son of the shrewd, mean and pragmatic Henry VII who, as Henry Tudor, had seized the throne in 1485, reconciling the York and Lancaster factions after the Wars of the Roses, and established a new dynasty. The early death of his heir, Prince Arthur, in 1502, shortly after marrying Catherine of Aragon, highlighted the fragility of the parvenu Tudors, which explains much of Henry VIII's ruthlessness over the succession. Henry succeeded to the throne in 1509 and married his late brother's Spanish widow. He was handsome, strapping and vigorous but also highly educated: courtiers hailed the dawning of a golden age. He promoted his glory with the macho sporting entertainments of a Renaissance prince – hunting, jousting, dancing, feasting – and won popularity by executing his father's hated tax collectors, Empson and Dudley, on spurious charges. It set the pattern for how Henry would dispose of his ministers when expedient.

Henry longed to test his vigour in the lists of Europe, where Francis I of France and the Habsburg emperor, Charles V, were vying for dominance. He started to build a navy, including his huge battleship the *Mary Rose* (which later sank). At first, he backed the emperor against the French, leading an army to France and winning the Battle of Spurs in 1513, while defeating a Scottish invasion at Flodden. He made peace with France, meeting Francis at a magnificent summit, the Field of the Cloth of Gold, stage-managed by his able and hugely rich minister Cardinal Thomas Wolsey – a butcher's son who had risen to the scarlet – but after Francis was captured at Pavia in 1525, Henry again changed sides, aspiring to hold the balance of power in Europe.

Henry's queen, Catherine of Aragon, Emperor Charles V's aunt, had provided him with a girl, the future Queen Mary, rather than a male heir – an affront to Henry's pride and dynastic sensitivity, so he sought, via Wolsey, to have the marriage to his brother's widow annulled. The pope, under the influence of Emperor Charles, would not permit Catherine to be cast aside. 'The king's great matter' was not just a matter of personality but of Henry's insistence that his crown was 'imperial' – not subordinate to the pope or any other power. This became even more important when he fell in love with Anne Boleyn, one of Catherine's ladies-in-waiting, who – flirtatious, intelligent and ambitious – withheld her favours before marriage. The pope remained intransigent, so Henry turned on Wolsey. The cardinal would have faced the axe but died on his way to face charges of treason.

Henry now decided on a radical course, and in his Act of Supremacy and Treason Act of 1534 declared himself head of the

Church in England and independent of the pope. At last Henry's marriage to Catherine could be annulled, and in 1533 he married Anne Boleyn.

Henry, backed by his rising minister Thomas Cromwell, repressed anyone who questioned his religious policies: his former chancellor, Thomas More, was executed. A rebellion in the north, the Pilgrimage of Grace (1536), was defeated, then dispersed on Henry's word of honour, which he then broke, executing the rebels ruthlessly. Throughout his reign, Henry was pitiless in killing anyone who opposed him: after Dudley and Empson he went on to execute Edmund de la Pole, earl of Suffolk, in 1513, Edward Stafford, duke of Buckingham, in 1521, all the way to the young poet Henry Howard, earl of Surrey, in the last days of his life. His number of victims is hard to calculate – the historian Holinshed absurdly claimed 72,000 – but there were many.

Although Henry is sometimes credited with England's Protestant Reformation, doctrinally he remained a Catholic conservative. Nonetheless, his political revolution made a Protestant England possible. His lucrative dissolution of the monasteries – an act of vandalism on a massive scale – funded his reign and marked his new absolutism. Anne Boleyn delivered a child to Henry in 1533, but it was a girl, the future Elizabeth I. Henry turned against her, ordering Cromwell to concoct charges of adultery, incest and witchcraft, evidenced by her 'third nipple' used for suckling the Devil – actually a mole on her neck. Five men, including Boleyn's brother, were framed and executed. Anne was beheaded on 19 May 1536. Ten days later Henry married Jane Seymour, who delivered a son, the future Edward VI, but died in childbirth – the only wife Henry ever grieved for.

Cromwell, pushing a Protestant foreign policy and promoted to earl of Essex, persuaded Henry to marry Anne of Cleves. But Henry, himself now fat and prone to suppurating sores, was repelled by this 'Flanders Mare'. Cromwell was framed and executed in 1540, the very day Henry married the pretty Catherine Howard, aged just sixteen Henry ordered that Cromwell's beheading should be carried out by an inexperienced youth. The head was severed on the third attempt.

Each of the English wives was backed by an ambitious political-religious family faction. The Howards were pro-Catholic, but their teenage queen was a reckless and naïve flirt whose past mischief and present adulterous adventures allowed the Protestant faction to exploit the king's fragile sexual pride. In 1542, aged eighteen, she was beheaded. His sensible last wife, Catherine Parr, outlived him.

Henry determined to marry his young son Edward to the infant Mary Queen of Scots. But Scottish intractability was unmoved by the so-called Rough Wooing, during which Henry sent his armies over the Border to put 'man, woman and child to fire and sword without exception'. One of England's most majestic and formidable kings, yet a flawed tyrant and a statesman of very mixed achievements, Henry was both hero and monster, brutal egotist and effective politician. As the duke of Norfolk understood: 'The consequence of royal anger is death.' In 1544, he laid out the succession: the Protestant Edward, then Catholic Mary, followed by Protestant Elizabeth. Henry VIII was followed on the throne by his son, the fervent reformer Edward VI. He moved swiftly to firm up Protestantism's hold on England, outlawing the Latin mass and clerical celibacy and demanding that services be carried out in English. But he was sickly, and died at fifteen. His sister Mary I reversed Edward's reforms, fiercely enforcing Rome's return to English religious life. Many hundreds died at the stake, but despite her marriage to Philip II of Spain she remained childless and this bitter and increasingly deranged figure could not prevent the crown passing to her sister, Elizabeth, after her early death.

SULEIMAN THE MAGNIFICENT

1494–1566

I who am the sultan of sultans, the sovereign of sovereigns, the shadow of God on earth, sultan and emperor of the White Sea [Mediterranean] and the Black Sea . . .

Suleiman the Magnificent writing to the Holy Roman
Emperor, Charles V (1547)

Under the rule of Suleiman the Magnificent, the Ottoman empire, which stretched from the Middle East to North Africa, the Balkans and central Europe, reached its glorious peak. He expanded its borders, rooted out corruption, overhauled the laws, ruled with tolerance, patronized the arts and wrote fine poetry. His legacy was a vast, well-governed, culturally flourishing empire, which continued to thrive for a century after his death.

When Suleiman came to power as Ottoman sultan or *padishah* (emperor) in 1520, aged twenty-six, succeeding his father Selim the Grim, he inherited an empire centred on Turkey, which had been strengthened by his father's acquisitions of Syria, Palestine and Egypt, as well as the two holiest Islamic cities, Medina and Mecca. Suleiman saw himself as the universal emperor, successor to the Roman emperors but also as 'the second Solomon', his namesake – he determined to expand this empire in every direction.

His first target was Belgrade. In the summer of 1521 Suleiman captured the Serbian city from the king of Hungary, striking a heavy blow against Christendom and opening the path for further expansion into Europe. By 1526 Hungary had more or less succumbed to the Ottomans, and though it took another fifteen years for a formal partition of the kingdom to be realized, Suleiman now had a springboard from which to attack Vienna. The high-water mark of Suleiman's advance on central Europe came in 1529, when he tried unsuccessfully to capture Vienna. This failure contributed to establishing the limits of Ottoman hegemony in the 16th century. The struggle for Vienna was one of the most notable of those battles that saved Christian Europe from invaders – going all the way back to the defeat of Attila's Huns at Châlons in 451, the Frankish victory over the Moors at Tours in 732, and the repulsion of the Magyars by the Germans at Lechfeld in 955.

In 1526 Suleiman had defeated Louis II of Hungary at the Battle of Mohács, giving rise to a dispute over the Hungarian crown between the archduke of Austria, Ferdinand I, and Suleiman's own choice, the subservient Transylvanian noble John Zápolya.

Ferdinand was married to Louis II's sister and heiress, and he was also a member of the powerful Habsburg dynasty, headed by the Holy Roman Emperor, Charles V, ruler of Austria, Germany, the Low Countries and Spain. The battle for Hungary was thus a clash of two empires.

In spring 1529 Suleiman gathered an army of 120,000 men and marched them through Bulgaria. Bad weather caused the loss of numerous camels and bogged down the heavy cannon, but Suleiman managed to meet up with Zápolya and recapture several Hungarian fortresses, including the important city of Buda, before marching on Vienna.

Without support from Charles V, the archduke feared the worst. He left Vienna in the hands of the seventy-year-old Niklas Count Salm and fled to Bohemia. Salm, an experienced veteran, shored up the Viennese defences around St Stephen's Cathedral and waited.

When they arrived, Suleiman's troops tried to bombard the city's defences into submission. But the earthen reinforcements held firm. The Ottomans switched tactics and began digging trenches and mines to weaken the city walls. This, too, failed, and as a wet autumn approached, they attempted one final push.

Despite their superior numbers, the Ottoman besiegers were beaten back by the pikes of the Austrian defenders. Giving up hope, the Ottomans killed their prisoners and set off for home on 14 October, having to endure heavy snowfalls and skirmishing all the way.

Suleiman had missed his chance to advance into the heart of Europe. Charles V reinforced Vienna with 80,000 troops, and Suleiman had to be content with consolidating his territory in Hungary.

Meanwhile, in the Islamic world, Suleiman set his sights on the western frontiers of the Persian empire. The shah avoided a pitched battle, and in 1535 Suleiman entered Baghdad. The capture of the city, along with lower Mesopotamia and much territory around the Euphrates and Tigris rivers, meant that by the time a treaty was signed with the shah in 1554, Suleiman was indisputably the dominant force in the Near East.

The final thrust of Ottoman expansion under Suleiman secured Tripolitania (part of modern Libya), Tunisia and Algeria, a vast territorial gain that secured for the Ottomans a brief period of naval dominance in the western Mediterranean. Suleiman was now a key player in the battles between the kings Francis I of France and Charles V, the Habsburg emperor and king of Spain.

But territorial expansion was only one of Suleiman's ambitions. In the Muslim world his legal reforms earned him the title Suleiman the Lawgiver. In particular, he concentrated on the Sultanic *kanun* – a system of rules in cases that fall outside Islamic Shari'ah.

As well as being an energetic reformer, Suleiman was also

known as a scrupulously fair and even-handed ruler. He promoted his servants on the basis on their abilities, rather than of their personal wealth, their family background or their general popularity. He promoted tolerance of both Jews and Christians. He welcomed the wealthy, entrepreneurial and cultured Jews who had been expelled from Spain by Ferdinand and Isabella. Meanwhile he continued the policy of promoting Balkan Christian slave-boys, converted to Islam, to high positions.

Suleiman was devoted to the arts. Not only was he himself a talented poet (many of his own aphorisms have become Turkish proverbs), but he also enthusiastically promoted artistic societies within the empire. Artists and craftsmen were given career paths, leading from apprenticeship to official rank, with quarterly pay, and Istanbul became a centre of artistic excellence. Among the many fine mosques and other buildings commissioned by Suleiman is the Süleymaniye Mosque in Istanbul, which is Suleiman's final resting place. During his reign, numerous bridges were built throughout the empire, such as the Danube Bridge, the Bridge of Buda, and the great aqueducts that solved Istanbul's water shortage.

In Jerusalem, this 'Second Solomon' rebuilt the walls, creating famed gates such as the Damascus and Jaffa Gates, and embellished the Dome of the Rock. But he ruled with brutal inscrutability: like his father who had murdered his brothers and his other sons. Suleiman attended the strangulation of his own son and heir, Mustapha, and ordered the killing of his long-serving vizier and friend Ibrahim Pasha.

Suleiman was lean, slim and laconic, cultivating his own mystique. But he was capable of love. His favourite slave-girl was a Russian/Polish blonde nicknamed Roxelana who became his dominant wife; he renamed her Blossom of the Sultan – Hurrem Sulton. When he was away at war she wrote him passionate love letters and he wrote her love poems. She was a wily politician who managed to win their eldest son Selim II the Drunkard the crown. By the time he died of a stroke at the Battle of Szigetvar in 1566, his conquests had united most of the Muslim world, with all the major Islamic cities west of Persia – Medina, Mecca, Jerusalem, Damascus and Baghdad – under the same ruler. Eastern Europe, the Balkans and the southern Mediterranean were also dominated by the Ottomans. Known as the Lawgiver to his subjects, to Westerners he was always the Magnificent.

IVAN THE TERRIBLE

1530–84

You shut up the Kingdom of Russia . . . as in a fortress of hell.
Prince Kurbsky, letter to Ivan IV

Ivan IV of Russia, known as the Terrible, was a tragic but degenerate monster, terrorized and damaged as a child, who grew up to be a successful empire-builder and shrewd tyrant. Ultimately he deteriorated into a demented, homicidal sadist who killed many thousands in a frenzied terror, impaling and torturing his enemies personally. By murdering his son, he hastened the demise of his own dynasty.

Ivan was declared the Grand Prince of Muscovy when he was just three years old, after the early death of his father. Five years later his mother too died. With both parents gone, the task of caring for Ivan fell to the boyar Shuisky family – members of whom also served as regents for the remainder of the prince's minority. The boyars formed a closed aristocratic class of around 200 families; Ivan complained that they bullied him, terrorized him, neglected him and were attempting to usurp his birthright.

Ivan's coronation took place in January 1547, and the early years of his reign were characterized by reform and modernization. Changes to the law code were accompanied by the creation of a council of nobles and local-government reforms. Efforts were also made to open up Russia to European trade and commerce. Ivan oversaw the consolidation and expansion of Muscovite territory. In 1552 he defeated and annexed the Kazan khanate, and the storming of the city of Kazan itself was followed by the slaughter of over 100,000 defenders. More military successes followed, and further territories, including the Astrakhan khanate and parts of Siberia, were brought under Russian sway. He built the gaudy St Basil's Cathedral in Red Square to celebrate the conquest of Kazan.

After a near-fatal illness in 1553, Ivan's personality appeared to undergo a transformation, and from that point he became ever more erratic and prone to bouts of rage. In 1560 his wife, Anastasia Romanovna, died from an unknown disease, an event that appears to have caused Ivan to suffer a breakdown. He convinced himself that the boyars had conspired to poison him – and he may have been right. If so, the plot led to the death of his beloved wife. He decided that the boyars would have to be punished and their power eradicated. The defection of one of his grandees, Prince Kurbsky, intensified his insane paranoia.

The result, on the one hand, was further administrative reform, aimed at augmenting the power of locally elected officials at the expense of the nobility. Such moves appeared to point the way towards a more rational and more competent form of government. Yet at the same time Ivan unleashed a vengeful terror against the unsuspecting boyars, and a wave of arrests and executions followed. Ivan devised peculiarly horrible deaths for some of them: Prince Boris Telupa was impaled upon a stake and took fifteen agonizing hours to die, while his mother, according to one chronicler, 'was given to a hundred gunners, who defiled her to death'.

Worse was to come. In 1565 Ivan designated an area of Russia – dubbed the *Oprichnina* (meaning apart from) – within which the lands were to be directly ruled by the tsar. *Oprichniki* squads criss-crossed the territory to implement Ivan's will. Dressed in black cloaks that bore the insignia of a severed dog's head and a broom (on account of their role in 'sniffing out' treason and sweeping away Ivan's enemies), the *oprichniki* set about crushing all alternative sources of authority. The boyars were singled out for especially harsh treatment.

Ivan embarked on an orgy of sexual adventures – both heterosexual and homosexual – while destroying his imagined enemies. He personally killed and tortured many. Ivan's savagery was shockingly varied in nature: ribs were torn out, people burnt alive, impaled, beheaded, disembowelled, their genitals cut off. His 'sadistic refinement' in a public bout of torturing in 1570 outdid all that went before and most of what came after.

In 1570 the tsar's agents perpetrated a frenzied massacre in the city of Novgorod, after Ivan suspected that its citizens were about to betray him to the Poles. Some 1500 nobles were murdered – many by being drowned in the River Volkhov – and an equal number of commoners were officially recorded as dead, though the death toll may have been far higher. The archbishop of Novgorod was sewn up in the skin of a bear, and a pack of hounds was set loose on him.

As the harsh internal repression took its toll on Russia's people, Ivan's fortunes went into steep decline. During the 1570s the Tartars of the Crimean khanate devastated large tracts of Russia with seeming impunity – even managing to set fire to Moscow on one occasion. At the same time, the tsar's attempts at westward expansion across the Baltic Sea succeeded only in embroiling the country in the Livonian War against a coalition that included Denmark, Poland, Sweden and Lithuania.The conflict dragged on for almost a quarter of a century, with little tangible gain. And all the while the *oprichniki* continued to engage in their wild bouts of killing and destruction; their area of operation, once the richest region of Russia, was reduced to one of the poorest and most unstable.

In 1581 Ivan turned his destructive rage against his own family. Having previously assaulted his pregnant daughter-in-law, he got into an argument with his son and heir, also called Ivan, and killed him in a fit of blind rage. It was only after Ivan the Terrible's own death – possibly from poisoning – that Russia was finally put out of its long agony.

Ivan's second son, Fyodor, proved far less talented than the original heir apparent. In 1598 a former adviser to Ivan, Boris Godunov, seized control, and Ivan's bloodline was brought to an end.

The *oprichniki* inspired a later Russian tyrant, Josef Stalin, and served as a prototype for his secret police, the NKVD. His own terror was based on that of Ivan, whom he often called 'teacher'. 'Who now remembers the boyars wiped out by Ivan the Terrible?' he once said. 'His mistake was not to kill all the boyars'. Ultimately, Ivan the Terrible was mad as well as bad. As his best biographer, Isabel de Madariaga, wrote: 'Ivan was not like God, he tried to be God. His reign is a tragedy of Shakespearean proportions. His cruelty served no purpose … He is Lucifer, the star of the morning who wanted to be God and was expelled from the Heavens.'

ELIZABETH I

1533–1603

*I thank God that I am endowed with such qualities that if I were
turned out of my realm in my petticoat, I were able to live in any
place in Christendom.*

Elizabeth I, addressing Parliament (5 November 1566)

Elizabeth I, known as Gloriana, was England's greatest queen.
During her reign England began to emerge as a modern nation
and a seafaring power. She kept her country's religious divides
in check, presided over an unprecedented artistic flowering, and
inspired her people to resist the aggression of England's mightiest
enemy, Catholic Spain. And it was under Elizabeth that England's empire began to be built, with the New World's Virginia
being named after the redoubtable Virgin Queen.

Elizabeth had a difficult childhood. Her mother, Anne Boleyn,
had been sent to the executioner's block by her father, Henry VIII,
and she herself was declared a bastard. Henry had left the throne to
his only son, Edward VI, a determined youth during whose short
reign Protestantism was imposed on England. On Edward's pre-
mature death, Elizabeth's elder half-sister Mary took the throne,
and with considerable bloodshed restored the Catholic faith and
the pope's authority. Although Elizabeth clung to her Protestant
beliefs, she was careful to make a pretence of Catholic practice.
In the face of investigations by Mary's inquisitors, she learned the
valuable political lesson of keeping her own counsel.

When Elizabeth succeeded Mary as queen of England in

1558, she further showed her political good sense by making the extremely capable Sir William Cecil (later Lord Burghley) her chief minister, and he continued to serve her until his death in 1598. One of the first challenges Elizabeth faced as an attractive, young and highly eligible queen was whom she should marry. Through her reign she had a succession of male favourites, most notably Robert Dudley, earl of Leicester, but she never married. She herself claimed that she was wedded to her realm and could not give her love (or, indeed, obedience) to just one man. Whatever her inner feelings, it seems that she realized that marrying a foreign prince would threaten England with foreign domination, while marrying an English nobleman would sow dissension among the court factions and possibly plunge England back into the civil strife of the previous century, the time of the Wars of the Roses.

Elizabeth deployed a cautious approach to matters of religion. The Church of England that she created, although technically Protestant, blended both Protestant and Catholic elements. She expected people to conform outwardly, and to respect her position as head of the Church, but was not concerned about their inner beliefs: 'I would not open windows into men's souls,' she said.

Such tolerance was not on the agenda at the Vatican, and in 1570 Pope Pius V excommunicated Elizabeth, denying her right to sit upon the throne of England. For some Catholics, the rightful queen of England was Mary, Queen of Scots, Elizabeth's Catholic cousin, who had been ousted from the throne of Scotland and taken refuge in England, where she was effectively put under house arrest. Mary became the focus of numerous Catholic plots against Elizabeth's life. After years of conspiracies, and numerous warnings by her councillors as to the threat Mary represented, Elizabeth had finally had enough, and in 1587 Mary was tried and executed.

By now, religious tensions across western Europe were reaching boiling point. Outraged by the execution of Mary and by the raids of English privateers on Spanish ships and possessions in the New World – not to mention the support Elizabeth was lending to the Protestant rebels in the Spanish Netherlands – Philip II of Spain, the champion of Catholic Europe, sent a massive Armada against England. The plan was for the fleet of 130 ships to sail from Spain to the Spanish Netherlands, where they would pick up a Spanish army under the duke of Parma and head for England.

As the invasion fleet was spotted in the Channel in July 1588, beacon fires flared across England. The English navy, under the command of such men as Lord Howard of Effingham and Sir Francis Drake, made ready, while in Tilbury the queen herself addressed her troops with one of the most inspiring speeches in English history:

> *I am come amongst you all, as you see at this time, not for my recreation and disport, but being resolved, in the midst and heat of the battle, to live or die amongst you all; to lay down for my God, and for my kingdom, and for my people, my honour and my blood even in the dust. I know I have the body of a weak and feeble woman, but I have the heart and stomach of a king, and a king of England too. And think foul scorn that Parma or Spain, or any Prince of Europe, should dare to invade the borders of my realm!*

The English navy and the weather scattered the invasion fleet, to the eternal ignominy of Spain and the glory of Elizabeth.

A superb politician (and Latin scholar), Elizabeth ruled personally with astonishing intelligence, cunning, moderation and tolerance for forty-five years until her death, keeping absolute control except in her dotage, when she overindulged a vain young favourite, Robert, earl of Essex, who was executed for treason. No one except Winston Churchill so symbolizes the defiant, patriotic liberty of the English.

AKBAR THE GREAT

1542–1605

As in the wide expanse of the Divine compassion there is room
for all classes and the followers of all creeds, so in his domin-
ions, there was room for the professors of opposite religions, and
for beliefs good and bad, and the road to altercation was closed.
Sunnis and Shias met in one mosque, and Franks and Jews in
one church, and observed their own forms of worship.

Jahangir

Babur's grandson inherited a tottering throne when his good-natured but inept father Humayun died after falling off a ladder in his library. The family had lost many of Babur's Indian territories, but the boy-emperor was fortunate that his Turkoman minister-general managed at the Battle of Paniput to reconquer Delhi and Agra.

When he started to rule in his own right in 1560, Akbar soon emerged as a remarkably gifted and original emperor, soldier and visionary. He continued to conquer new provinces throughout his long reign, leaving an empire that included much but not all of modern India, Pakistan, Bangladesh, Afghanistan, from Kashmir to Ahmedabad, Kabul to Dacca.

Finding himself ruling a multi-faith, multinational, polyglot realm, he brilliantly adapted Islam to create a faith for all, consulting Muslims, Christians, Jews, Parsis and Hindus. The result borrowed from all these faiths and built around Akbar's authority, recognised by Islam juricts as 'infallible'. His creed was centred on the formula: 'There is One God and his Caliph is Akbar.'

He promoted talented men of all religions, banned slavery, abolished the Islamic tax on infidels, prohibited early marriage and allowed Hindu widows to refuse suttee and remarry.

This eccentric, tolerant and eclectic policy was made possible by Akbar's political-military success. This contemporary of Queen Elizabeth of England and the Ottoman Sultan Suleiman the Magnificent was probably the greatest ruler India has ever known; his prestige helped establish his Mughal Empire for the next two and a half centuries, its glories symbolized by his father's tomb and his descendant Shah Jahan's monumental Taj Mahal.

Tragically his successors failed to pursue his admirable tolerance, worsening the ethnic relations of India to this day. His dynasty ended less with a roar than a whimper with the deposition by the British of the tragic last Mughal in 1857.

TOKUGAWA IEYASU

1543–1616

The study of literature and the practice of the military arts must be pursued side by side.

Tokugawa Ieyasu, *Rules for the Military Houses* (1615)

The tenacity and patience of Tokugawa Ieyasu, Japan's ultimate shogun, laid the foundations for two and a half centuries of stable rule by his dynasty. Tokugawa transformed his family from an undistinguished warrior clan into the undisputed rulers of Japan, ending decades of anarchy and civil war. As capable a governor as he was a soldier, Ieyasu's flair for both administration and commerce ushered in a long period in which Japan could flourish in peace.

A legend tells how once Ieyasu was asked what he would do to a caged songbird that would not sing. 'I'd wait until it does,' the general replied. The story encapsulates Ieyasu's extraordinary patience, which was doubtless honed during his childhood years spent as the hostage of powerful neighbouring clans. He was well cared for, trained to be a soldier and a governor, and encouraged in his love of falconry. But he was powerless. He could only listen helplessly to the news of his father's murder and impotently look on as his family's fortunes disintegrated.

When the leader of the clan that held him captive was killed in battle, Ieyasu seized the chance to return home. Deftly exploiting Japan's precarious political balance, he restored order to his family and persuaded his former captors to release his wife and children. In his family's small domain, Ieyasu consolidated his rule, demonstrating the administrative and legislative skill that would later secure his grip over the whole of Japan.

Ieyasu's network of control spread outwards. His canny governance, disciplined armies and ability to spot the weaknesses of others made him one of Japan's most influential *daimyos* (feudal barons). He never overreached himself, however. Realizing after a few minor skirmishes that he was not yet strong enough to triumph on his own, he vowed fealty to Japan's dominant warlord, Toyotomi Hideyoshi. He also avoided involvement in the disastrous military expeditions to Korea that incapacitated so many of his rival *daimyos*.

Ieyasu's domain became the most prosperous in Japan. He encouraged artisans, businessmen and traders to come to Edo, the fishing village he chose as his base. Edo flourished, growing into the bustling town and port that was later to be renamed Tokyo.

Ieyasu's willingness to bide his time secured him an unassailable power base. Finally, in 1600, at the Battle of Sekigahara, Ieyasu emerged triumphant over his rivals as the undisputed master of

Japan. Three years later the imperial court appointed him shogun – the title borne since the 12th century by those warrior-governors who are the real power in Japan, the powerless emperors having only a ceremonial role as figureheads.

Ieyasu consolidated his clan's claim to the shogunate as diligently as he had consolidated his authority over his territory. After only two years as shogun he passed the title on to his son, thus establishing a hereditary claim that endured for 250 years. He made sure that no *daimyo* could become as powerful as he had by obliging all *daimyos* to spend long periods at court, thus undermining their ability to build up a local power base. When they were allowed to return to their own domains, Ieyasu kept their families as virtual hostages in Edo.

The small, stout Ieyasu trusted his maverick judgement to see him through. He appointed a falconer as a diplomat, and made an actor the director of mines. His enthusiasm for trading with the Europeans filled his vast warehouses with rice and gold. Will Adams, a Kentish shipbuilder who was shipwrecked by a typhoon on Japanese shores, became one of Ieyasu's most valued commercial advisers.

Ieyasu allowed nothing to threaten Japan's new-found unity and stability, and to this end in 1614 he suppressed Christianity and imprisoned all foreign missionaries. Long tolerant of Christianity, Ieyasu did not initiate the religious killings that his descendants practised – his motive was purely to prevent sectarian divisions among his countrymen. A stream of new laws established stringent control over every stratum of society, curtailing people's freedom of movement but ensuring a stability that Japan had not seen for a century. In 1615, in his most ruthless act, Ieyasu secured Tokugawa pre-eminence by destroying his family's last rivals to the shogunate, the Toyotomi. Among those put to death was his own grandson by marriage.

The shogun died a year later, from wounds sustained in the battle that finally extinguished the threat of the Toyotomi.

WALTER RALEIGH

c.1554–1618

Fain would I climb, yet fear I to fall.
Sir Walter Raleigh, line engraved on a window pane, according
to Thomas Fuller's History of the Worthies of England (1662).
Queen Elizabeth is said to have written beneath: 'If thy heart fails
thee, climb not at all.'

Walter Raleigh was the 'perfect man' of the Elizabethan age – not only a consummate courtier and a dashing soldier, but also a poet, a scholar and an entrepreneur. His charisma and chivalrousness made him a favourite of Queen Elizabeth herself, while his boldness and drive took him across the Atlantic to establish the first English colonies in the New World.

Raleigh was brought up in Devon and studied at Oxford, later going up to the Middle Temple to study law. As a young man he fought in the French Wars of Religion, and in 1580 he put down an Irish rebellion in Munster (with considerable brutality, it must be said). His service in Ireland brought him to the attention of the royal court, where his relationship with Queen Elizabeth blossomed.

The most famous story of Raleigh's early relationship with the queen is that he lay down his cloak to allow Elizabeth to walk unblemished across a muddy puddle. A further story tells of the pair scribbling lines of a couplet to one another on opposite sides of a glass window. Though these stories may be apocryphal, they attest to his reputation as a romantic courtier.

Having earned the queen's favour, Raleigh was showered with rewards. He was given vast territories in Ireland, valuable trade monopolies, control over the Cornish tin mines, political positions in Devon and Cornwall, and membership of the House of Commons.

At the same time, Raleigh turned his attentions to the New World. In 1583–4 he organized expeditions to Newfoundland and Virginia (which he had flatteringly named after Elizabeth, the Virgin Queen). In Virginia in 1585 he established the first English colony in America, on Roanoke Island, in modern-day North Carolina. Though conditions were unpleasant and the settlers soon took the chance to escape the misery of food shortages and attacks by the natives, Raleigh's vision had started the process of English colonization, which eventually led to British domination of North America.

In 1587 Raleigh dispatched another expedition to Roanoke Island, but this second settlement was even less successful than the first – ships that were meant to resupply the colonists were held up by the war with Spain, and when a ship eventually arrived in 1590, the settlers had vanished. This was hardly Raleigh's fault – the queen had commanded all ships to remain in port to defend the realm against the Spanish Armada.

Raleigh played no memorable part in the defeat of the Armada. He stayed on dry land, organizing the coastal defences and raising men, but the victory at sea of Howard and Drake meant that these preparations were unnecessary. Thereafter Raleigh's star went into something of a decline. He incurred the fury of the queen after he secretly married a lady-in-waiting, Elizabeth Throckmorton, without royal permission. The queen turned to a new favourite, Robert Devereux, Earl of Essex. Elizabeth never trusted Raleigh enough to award him ministerial office.

In 1595 Raleigh sailed to South America in search of the legendary golden city of El Dorado. Unfortunately, there was little support for his plan to colonize the gold-mining areas that were discovered in Venezuela. Raleigh's main import to England was the fashion of smoking tobacco – a phenomenon that so shocked one of his servants that he doused Raleigh in a pail of water, believing his master had burst into flames.

When Elizabeth died in 1603, the throne passed to her cousin James of Scotland, who arrived with fixed ideas about Raleigh. He was accused of plotting the king's downfall and imprisoned in the Tower. In 1616 he was released, though not pardoned, and set off once again for Venezuela. He had promised the king that he could open a gold mine without offending the Spanish, with whom he was extremely unpopular (he had been involved in an attack on Cadiz in 1596).The expedition was a disaster, and when he returned to England, James I invoked the suspended sentence of death that had been hanging over Raleigh since his initial arrest in 1603.

Raleigh was also, in keeping with his image as the perfect courtier, a writer of both verse and prose. Much of his poetry is addressed indirectly to Elizabeth, while his prose narratives relate his adventures in the New World. In his *History of the World*, written while he was imprisoned in the Tower, he details the divine and providential history of kings from the Creation. However, he had reached only the 2nd century BC when the sentence of death was carried out against him. It was a sad and inglorious end to such a dashing and dynamic career.

GALILEO

1564–1642

I do not feel obliged to believe that that same God who has endowed us with senses, reason and intellect has intended to forgo their use and by some other means to give us knowledge which we can attain by them.

Galileo Galilei, 'Letter to the Grand Duchess Christina' (1615)

Galileo Galilei helped to transform the way that people looked at the world – and the universe beyond. A physicist, mathematician and astronomer, Galileo made fundamental discoveries about the nature of motion and the movement of the planets. He realized the importance of experimentation and held that the physical world was best understood through mathematics. His insistence that the universe should be analysed via reason and evidence brought him into conflict with the Church, but his discoveries long outlasted the Inquisition that sought to suppress them.

Galileo's father was a musician, and the young man may well have helped with paternal experiments into the tension and pitch of strings. His formal education took place at Pisa University, where he matriculated in 1581, initially to study medicine. To his father's disapproval, Galileo spent most of his time on mathematics and left the university without a degree in 1585.

Galileo continued to study mathematics for the next four years, earning money through private tuition until he was appointed to a chair at the university in 1589. It was during this time that he supposedly demonstrated his theory of the speed of falling objects by dropping weights from Pisa's leaning tower.

His unorthodox views earned him the disapproval of the university authorities, and in 1592 Galileo was forced to move to Padua, where he taught until 1610. Crippled by his family's financial demands after his father died, Galileo earned extra money by selling home-made mathematical compasses and continuing to tutor private pupils.

In 1609 Galileo heard of a strange device invented in the Netherlands that could make distant objects appear close. It was the telescope, and Galileo immediately set about building his own. Within a year he was investigating the heavens with a device that provided 20x magnification. It was a turning point in his career.

With his telescope Galileo discovered Jupiter's four moons and noted that their phases indicated that they orbited Jupiter. This evidence dented the Church-approved Ptolemaic model of the universe, in which all heavenly bodies orbit the earth. Galileo also saw stars that were invisible to the naked eye. He immediately published his findings in a short book dedicated to one of his illustrious pupils, Cosimo II de Medici, grand duke of Florence. As a reward, Cosimo brought him back to Tuscany in triumph.

With greater financial freedom, Galileo was able to move his investigations on apace. He studied the rings of Saturn and discovered that Venus, like the moon, went through phases – an indication that it moved around the sun. These discoveries committed him to the theory – proposed by Nicolaus Copernicus a century before – that it was the sun, and not the earth, that was at the centre of the universe.

Copernicanism was a dangerous concept for Galileo to flirt with, and around 1613 it earned him the attention of the Inquisition. He travelled to Rome to defend Copernicus' heliocentric model but was silenced, and in 1616 he was warned explicitly not to promulgate such ideas any further.

By 1632 Galileo felt unable to keep silent on Copernicanism any longer and published his *Dialogue*, which drew together all of the major strands of thought about the nature of the universe and discussed them through the mouths of several fictitious characters.

When he was dragged to Rome the next year and asked to explain himself to the Inquisition, Galileo argued that he had obtained ecclesiastical permission to discuss Copernicanism in a hypothetical way. Unfortunately, he had not obtained permission to ridicule the papal attachment to older arguments, which he had done quite unashamedly. The Inquisition sentenced him to life imprisonment.

Fortunately for Galileo, his imprisonment amounted to little more than enforced internal exile to the Tuscan hills, where he was free to continue his work in a more muted form. Though he was going blind, he continued to study, concentrating on the nature and strength of materials and smuggling another book out of Italy to be published in the Netherlands in 1638. He died four years later, aged seventy-seven.

SHAKESPEARE

1564–1616

He was not of an age, but for all time!
Ben Jonson, 'To the Memory of My Beloved,
the Author, Mr William Shakespeare' (1623)

It is almost universally acknowledged – and not just in the English-speaking world – that William Shakespeare was the greatest writer ever to have lived. He was a peerless poet, playwright and storyteller, and his understanding of human emotions, and the complexities and ambivalences of the human condition, are unparalleled in literature.

Famously, little is known about Shakespeare's life. He was born in Stratford-upon-Avon in 1564, the son of John Shakespeare, a burgess of fluctuating fortunes, and his wife, Mary Arden. William attended the local grammar school, and at the age of eighteen he married Anne Hathaway, who was some years his senior and already pregnant. At some point in the ensuing decade, Shakespeare moved to London. He was probably a jobbing actor but began to make a mark as a poet and a playwright. By 1594 he was the established dramatist for the theatre company known as the Lord Chamberlain's Men (which renamed itself the King's Men after James I's accession).

For the next twenty years Shakespeare wrote play after dazzling play – comedies, tragedies, histories – which brought audiences flocking to the Globe Theatre on the south bank of the Thames. Shakespeare's fortunes flourished. He probably supported his father's application for a coat of arms and bought one of Stratford's largest houses, New Place. On his death in 1616, he was buried in the chancel of Stratford's parish church. There is little more that we know about Shakespeare's life.

But Shakespeare's works tell us all we need to know about the man. He has an extraordinary sympathy with men and women of all ages, from all strata of society, demonstrating a deep understanding of their faults and frailties, their kindnesses and cruelties, their loves and hates, their vanities and self-delusions. Joy and despair, anger and resignation, jealousy and lust, vigour and weakness are all depicted with searing honesty. There is the dangerous infatuation of first love in *Romeo and Juliet*, the destructiveness of middle-aged passion in *Antony and Cleopatra*, the heart-rending follies of old age in *King Lear*. Shakespeare also subjects the nature of power to his unflinching gaze: the burdens of kingship in *Henry IV*, the nature of tyranny in *Richard III*, the abuse of trust in *Measure for Measure*. At its heart, Shakespeare's work asks: what is a man? What makes a man? What makes a king?

Shakespeare's characters are multifaceted, complex, ambiguous. Hamlet, faced with his father's apparent murder, is beset by moral qualms and indecision as to whether he should take revenge. Macbeth and Lady Macbeth seize the throne by violence and then become mired in bloodshed, guilt and madness. In *Twelfth Night*, the jolly, roistering characters play a trick upon the pompous, puritanical steward Malvolio, but the trick goes beyond a joke and plunges into cruelty. In *The Tempest*, possibly Shakespeare's last play, Prospero, having used his magic powers to bring those who have wronged him into his power, decides 'the rarer action is / In virtue than in vengeance'. And then, in what is often taken to be an autobiographical touch on Shakespeare's part, Prospero, the magus, abandons his magical arts: 'deeper than did ever plummet sound / I'll drown my book'.

All this wealth of human experience Shakespeare embodies in language of astounding power and precision, from soaring passages of poetic intensity, through quick-fire witty dialogue, to the earthy prose of the common people who crowded into the pits of London's theatres. Shakespeare's richness of vocabulary is astonishing, drawing imagery from a range of fields and activities, from flora and fauna to warfare and heraldry, from astrology and astronomy to seafaring and horticulture. Puns and double entendres abound throughout his work, and virtually every line has layers of meanings. Not content with the vast vocabulary at his command, Shakespeare introduced many new words into English, from 'meditate' and 'tranquil' to 'alligator' and 'apostrophe'. He also gave us myriad phrases that have entered everyday speech: 'Discretion is the better part of valour', 'At one fell swoop', 'In one's heart of hearts', 'Seen better days', and many, many more.

As a master of dramatic art, Shakespeare has no peer. Many of his stories were not original – they were drawn, for example, from Boccaccio's fables, or folk tales, or Plutarch's *Lives*, or the Tudor chroniclers – but it is what he did with them that counts. He not only gave the two-dimensional figures in these tales fully rounded characters, he also knew how to build up tension, to create a mood of impending doom, and then to heighten that mood by interleaving an apparently incongruous comic scene (as he does, for example, in *Macbeth*). He was also a master of the *coup de théâtre*, such as the moment in *Much Ado About Nothing* when the hitherto lightweight, bantering world of the play is overthrown by Beatrice's sudden injunction to Benedict: 'Kill Claudio.' Thus none of Shakespeare's tragedies are unremittingly tragic, nor are his comedies filled with non-stop laughter. At the end of *Twelfth Night*, for example, although all the lovers are paired off happily, the action closes with a melancholy song from the Clown, bringing us back to the quotidian world where 'the rain it raineth every day'. Such simple, poignant touches are typical of Shakespeare and mark him out, just as much as his complexities, as a writer of genius.

But there are many who have argued that an undistinguished provincial who never went to university could not have written some of the finest plays known to humankind. Despite considerable evidence to the contrary, claims have been made that either 'William Shakespeare' was a fabricated pseudonym or his identity was simply used by someone else.

The instigator of the trend was an American schoolteacher who claimed descent from Sir Francis Bacon, the lawyer, statesman and philosopher. The Baconian Theory insists that Bacon co-authored the plays with a coterie of courtly writers such as Edmund Spenser and Sir Walter Raleigh. Unable to reveal their identities because of the controversial content of the plays, they left clues hidden among the texts.

Another candidate is the feisty and brilliant playwright Christopher Marlowe, a Cambridge-educated shoemaker's son who dabbled in espionage, and who was suspected of atheism and homosexuality. Conspiracy theorists insist that he did not die in a bar-room brawl in 1593, as is widely believed, but that he went underground to avoid the authorities and continued to write plays, using 'William Shakespeare' as a pseudonym.

A third candidate is the earl of Derby, whose aristocratic status precluded him from dabbling in the theatrical world as a professional. He had a company of actors, and among his papers were found several poems authored by a 'W.S.' His wedding may have been the first occasion on which *A Midsummer Night's Dream* was performed.

A final favourite in some quarters is the earl of Oxford, a poet, playwright (although no plays survive) and patron of an acting company. Oxford stopped producing poetry just before

Shakespeare first went into print with the dramatic poem *Venus and Adonis* in 1593 (although his first plays had already been produced). The case for Oxford is, however, handicapped by the fact that the earl died in 1604, before at least a dozen of Shakespeare's works were written. In 2011, Hollywood even produced a film – *Anonymous* – about the 'real' Shakespeare. It was not a hit.

Despite all these ingenious arguments, Shakespeare's contemporaries seemed in no doubt that he was the author of his works, and in 1623 his former colleagues compiled the First Folio edition of his plays 'to keep the memory of so worthy a friend and fellow alive as was our Shakespeare'. Modern textual analysis backs up the theory that all the poems and plays are by a single author whose name was William Shakespeare.

ABBAS THE GREAT

1571–1629

I preferred the dust from the shoe soles of the lowest Christian to the highest Ottoman personage.

Abbas the Great

Abbas was the most successful shah of Iran in the period between the great kings of the ancient world and the modern era. He extended the kingdom both eastwards and westwards but importantly for understanding Iran today, it was the triumphant Abbas the Great who consolidated the Twelver Shiism that is so distinctive now; he and family offered themselves as the divinely chosen representatives of the Hidden Imam; and reassembled Iran as a great power for the first time since the Arab conquests. All of this is very relevant to understanding Iran in the twenty-first century.

It was not Abbas who brought this form of Shiism to Iran: he was the descendant of a line of Shia sheikhs backed by a fanatical following of Turkoman tribesmen known as Qizilbash – 'red-heads' after their red bonnets: these featured twelve folds to symbolize the twelve Imams of the Shia. They believed that after Muhammad, God gave the guidance of humanity to a line of his descendants beginning with Ali and continuing with his son Husain. The line ended with the murder by the Sunnis of the eleventh imam in 874. His son, the twelfth imam, disappeared having been 'occulted' – hidden by God – ready to appear as the Madhi, the Chosen One, 'to bring justice to the world'.

In the meantime, other intermediaries – namely Abbas's Safavid family – touched by this divinity would rule until the twelfth imam reappeared. Abbas's great-grandfather Ismail had come to power in 1501, declaring himself shah and making this form of Shia the official religion. Ismail threatened the Ottoman sultans, who were Sunni, with his resurgent Shiite Iran, until Sultan Selim the Grim defeated Ismail in 1514. But this new Iran fell into disorder after Ismail's death, putting both its future and that of its distinctive Shiism into doubt. The Ottomans regained their dominance over the Caucasus and reconquered Iraq

Abbas was the grandson of the old reclusive Shah Tahmasp. Though his father was the eldest son, he was disqualified from the throne because he was blind. Abbas grew up amidst turbulence and vanished glory, dominated by powerful Qizilbash generals who behaved with unwise arrogance around the young prince. Abbas was lucky to survive the short and murderous reign of his demented uncle Ismail II, who actually ordered his execution but was found dead himself before it could be carried out. His mother was murdered by tribal rebels. Abbas' blind father was then placed on the throne in spite of his handicap, but the kingdom was cursed by marauding over-mighty Qizilbash warlords, Ottoman and Uzbek invasions, Portuguese imperialism, and family civil wars.

Abbas was the Shah's middle son, but he became heir after his elder brother was assassinated. In 1588, the blind shah abdicated and placed the crown on Abbas's head. Initially the seventeen-year-old found himself under the control of the Qizil-bash potentate Murshid Quli Khan to whom he owed the throne: after enduring many humiliations, Abbas had him assassinated and then set about ruling in his own right.

Abbas quickly showed his mettle: he reformed the army allowing him to defeat and diminish the powers of the Qizilbash tribes; then he re-conquered Khurasan, which had been lost to the Uzbeks, before turning on the Ottomans, defeating them in the Caucasus. In 1605 he decisively routed their army at Sufian near Tabriz then advanced into Azerbaijan and Georgia.

In order to undermine the Ottomans, he opened relations with Europe, especially the English, granting privileges to the East India Company, which he also used to back his campaign to reduce Portuguese influence in the Persian Gulf. His artistic masterpiece was his creation of a splendid new capital at Isfahan, where many of his beautiful creations still survive – particularly the Royal Square and Royal Mosque. Both an aesthete and a man of violence, Abbas was an exceptional political and military leader – colourful, highly intelligent, curious, a fine conversationalist with a sense of humour and theatre. Nevertheless he was ruthless in imposing royal power and punishing dissent, deploying a web of police spies to watch his enemies. Paranoiac and merciless, he had his own eldest son and heir Prince Safi murdered and blinded two of his other sons. Yet typically he regretted deeply his killing of Safi and sank into remorse and melancholy.

The Ottomans were the dominant power of the Near East and they had never accepted Abbas' resurgent Iran. In 1616, they again attacked him but the shah defeated them in 1618. A few years later, he used English backing to help defeat the Portuguese and take their island base of Hormuz. In 1622, he recaptured Kandahar in today's Afghanistan from the Mughal emperors of India. Taking advantage of court intrigues in Istanbul, Abbas was finally able in 1624 to retake Baghdad and Iraq, which had been lost to the Ottomans ten years earlier. At his death in 1629, this contemporary of James I of England left a vast and powerful Iran that included Afghanistan and Iraq and extended from the Caucasus to the borders of India, with Twelver Shiism established as its state religion. Iran remained stable and thriving for a century until the downfall of the dynasty in 1722. This was the work of Abbas.

WALLENSTEIN

1583–1634

The Duke of Friedland [Wallenstein] has up to now disgusted and offended to the utmost nearly every territorial ruler in the empire . . .

Anselm Casimir von Wambold, Elector of Mainz, in 1629

Albrecht von Wallenstein was a brutally ambitious mercenary captain who became so extraordinarily powerful and rich that he held emperors to ransom, mastered colossal estates, was raised to his own dukedom and principality, and almost joined the ranks of kings himself. But he overreached himself – his rise and fall was a tragedy of greed and megalomania.

Wallenstein was born in Hefimanice, Bohemia, into a family of minor Protestant aristocrats. His military career began in 1604 when he joined the forces of the Habsburg Holy Roman Emperor, Rudolph II. Two years later he converted to Catholicism – the religion of his new master – and this paved the way for his marriage in 1609 to an extremely wealthy widow from Moravia.

Wallenstein put the riches and estates he had gained by his marriage towards the furtherance of his own career in the service of the Habsburgs. In 1617 he came to the aid of the future emperor Ferdinand II by raising a force for the latter's war against Venice. When the Protestant nobles of Bohemia came out in revolt in 1618 at the start of the Thirty Years' War, and proceeded to confiscate Wallenstein's estates, the warlord raised a force to fight under the imperial standard. In the Thirty Years War, a vicious religious conflict between the Catholic emperor and the Protestant princes of Germany and central Europe, much of the continent was ravaged; vast numbers perished in battle and from famine – but amoral warlords like Wallenstein thrived on this tragedy. He went on to earn distinction on the battlefield, and not only reclaimed his estates but also took over the lands of the Protestant nobles he defeated. He went on to incorporate these into a new entity called Friedland, over which he was made count palatine and in 1625 a duke.

With the onset of the Danish War in 1625, Wallenstein raised an army of over 30,000 men to fight for the imperial Catholic League against the Protestant Northern League. A grateful Ferdinand – now emperor – immediately appointed him commander-in-chief. Wallenstein went on to achieve a series of brilliant victories, and Ferdinand rewarded him with the principality of Sagan and the duchy of Mecklenburg.

Power and success now seem to have gone to Wallenstein's head. He was no longer satisfied to remain the emperor's most dependable lieutenant; he wanted to be master of his own destiny. And to this end he opened negotiations with his erstwhile enemies – the Protestant Hanseatic ports of northern Germany. The growing cleavage between Wallenstein – who now styled himself Admiral of the North and the Baltic Seas – and the emperor was confirmed by the latter's Edict of Restitution in 1629. This declared that all Catholic lands that had, since 1552, fallen under Protestant control were to be restored to their former owners. For a man keen to build his own personal empire by means of deals with the Protestant nobles of northern Germany, the edict was a threat, and Wallenstein opted to disregard Ferdinand's orders. He had already aroused the jealousy of much of the imperial aristocracy, and they now took the opportunity to press for his dismissal – which came about in 1630. Wallenstein retired to Friedland and plotted his revenge.

With King Gustavus Adolphus of Sweden, a leading Protestant enemy of the emperor, Wallenstein hatched a plot that would have given him control of all Habsburg dominions. Ferdinand discovered Wallenstein's treachery, but his military reversals made him so desperate that he asked Wallenstein to return to his service – for a suitably high price – to help him fight the Swedes and their Saxon allies. Wallenstein agreed, and in 1632 gave battle to the Swedes at Lützen. Although Gustavus Adolphus was killed, the Swedes won the day.

Having revealed his military fallibility, Wallenstein was aware that his position was vulnerable. Determined to avoid a second dismissal, he refused to disband his army, and, worse, he did nothing to stop the Swedes securing further victories in Germany. At the same time, he attempted to negotiate with the emperor's enemies – Saxony, Sweden and France. Such double-dealing proved inconclusive, however, and Wallenstein resumed the offensive against these powers in late 1633.

But word of Wallenstein's latest treachery had reached the imperial court at Vienna. At this point Wallenstein resolved on one last throw of the dice, and in January 1634 prepared to come out in open revolt against the emperor. However, as he found the support of his subordinates ebbing away, he tried to cut one final deal: he would resign in return for a substantial pay-off. This offer was rejected, and Wallenstein fled to the Saxons and Swedes in a fresh effort to link up with them against the Habsburgs. That enterprise was doomed to failure, however, and in February 1634 Wallenstein was assassinated by troops from within his own army.

CROMWELL

1599–1658

A man of a great, robust, massive mind, and an honest, stout English heart.

Thomas Carlyle, describing Cromwell in his edition
Oliver Cromwell's Letters and Speeches (1845)

Oliver Cromwell took just twenty years to rise from obscure country gentleman to lord protector of England, Scotland and Ireland. His military genius was vital to Parliament's victory over Charles I in the Civil Wars. His political management – sometimes cajoling – of Parliament and the respect he engendered in the army helped to stabilize the fragile country after the king was beheaded. As head of state in the new Commonwealth, he enforced rigid puritanism, tempered with toleration for Jews and intolerance for Catholics: his foreign policy was successful and prestigious. He turned down the crown, but his burning commitment to God and the English people, rather than any personal ambition, marks him as the greatest king that England never had.

Cromwell was by birth a relatively lowly gentleman farmer from Huntingdon, now in Cambridgeshire. Both his own family and that of his wife were connected to various networks of puritans, and throughout his life he was deeply and sincerely devoted to carrying out the will of God as he saw it.

Cromwell first sat as an MP in the Parliament of 1628–9, making little impact. Charles I ruled without Parliament for the next 11 years, and Cromwell did not sit as an MP again until 1640. As tensions between Charles and the so-called Long Parliament began to build towards violent crisis, Cromwell's puritan and oppositionist credentials began to come to the fore. But he showed his real worth as the Civil War broke out, first captaining a troop of cavalry at the Battle of Edgehill (23 October 1642) and the next year forming his regiment of 'Ironsides', who were victorious at the Battle of Gainsborough (28 July 1643). His handling of the cavalry at the Parliamentary victory of Marston Moor (2 July 1644) secured his reputation nationally – though Cromwell was not interested in fame, regarding military success as an expression of God's will in the struggle for English liberties. By now he was leader of Parliament's Independent faction, determined not to compromise with the Royalists.

Cromwell and Parliament's supreme military leader Thomas Fairfax created a disciplined new force, the New Model Army, which in the mid-1640s changed the course of the war in Parliament's favour. The victorious Battle of Naseby (14 June 1645) determined the outcome of the First Civil War.

Cromwell's political centrality emerged in the years 1646–9, when he became power-broker between army, Parliament and the now-captive Charles in an attempt to restore a constitutional basis for government. But dealing with the slippery and inflexible Stuart monarch, who at root would brook no compromise to (as he saw it) his divinely inspired kingship, exhausted Cromwell. When Charles temporarily escaped in 1647 and sought to restart the war with the Scottish Presbyterians in support, Cromwell's attitude hardened. Defeating the Royalist, Welsh and Scottish rebels in 1648, he backed the trial for treason of the king, a show trial that ended, predictably enough, in the execution of Charles. On the cold morning of Tuesday 30 January 1649, after a last walk in St James's Park, King Charles I, wearing two shirts lest his shivering against the cold be misinterpreted as fear, mounted the scaffold erected outside the Banqueting Hall in Whitehall. He had been condemned to death as 'a tyrant, traitor, murderer and public enemy to the good of the nation'.

Charles, unrepentant and convinced that his death would make him a martyr for the Royalist cause, addressed the crowd. If his life was disastrous, his leaving it was heroic:

> I think it is my duty to God first and to my country for to clear myself both as an honest man and a good King, and a good Christian. I shall begin first with my innocence.
>
> In troth I think it not very needful for me to insist long upon this, for all the world knows that I never did begin a War with the two Houses of Parliament . . . they began upon me . . .
>
> I have forgiven all the world, and even those in particular that have been the chief causes of my death. Who they are, God knows, I do not desire to know, God forgive them . . .

After inspecting the axe, he said:

> I go from a corruptible, to an incorruptible Crown; where no disturbance can be, no disturbance in the World.

Having given the executioner his final instructions, the king knelt down, and his head was severed from his body with a single blow.

That night, Cromwell reputedly gazed at the royal body and murmured 'cruel necessity'.

Cromwell was now the most powerful man in England – head of the army and chairman of the council of state that ruled the new Commonwealth. But pro-Stuart Scotland and Ireland remained to be tamed.

Cromwell arrived in Ireland fearing that Charles I's son and heir, Charles, Prince of Wales, would attempt to launch an invasion of England from Ireland, whose Catholic population was sympathetic to the Royalist cause. He determined to conquer the country as soon as possible, fearful of running out of funds and alarmed by the prospect of further political instability back in England.

One of Cromwell's first targets in his campaign was the garrison town of Drogheda, to the north of Dublin. Commanding the garrison of just over 3000 English Royalist and Catholic Irish troops was an English Royalist, Sir Arthur Ashton. On 10 September 1649 Cromwell ordered Ashton to surrender, or the town would face the consequences.

After some negotiations Ashton rejected the terms offered to him. Cromwell, at the head of a 12,000-strong army and impatient for a quick success, launched his attack on 11 September. Speaking to his soldiers, he 'forbade them to spare any that were at arms in the town'. As his men broke into Drogheda, all of the defenders were put to the sword – even those who quickly surrendered. Hundreds of civilians were also murdered. Catholic priests were systematically targeted, and those who had sought refuge from the fighting in St Peter's Church were burnt alive when the besiegers torched the building. Of the Royalist troops, Cromwell stated, 'I do not think thirty of their number escaped with their lives.' Those who did were promptly sold into slavery in Barbados. One estimate put the total death toll at 3500, of whom 2800 were soldiers and the rest clergy and civilians.

Modern research shows that the massacres have been exaggerated but, nonetheless, there is no doubt they were war crimes. Cromwell later accounted for himself before the English Parliament. 'I am persuaded,' he said, 'that this is a righteous judgement of God upon these barbarous wretches, who have imbued their hands in so much innocent blood and that it will tend to prevent the effusion of blood for the future, which are satisfactory grounds for such actions, which otherwise cannot but work remorse and regret.'

In 1650–1 Cromwell led his armies to victory over the Scots at Dunbar and over Prince Charles's Anglo-Scottish adventure at Worcester (1651). The prince famously escaped to France, helped by disguise and a convenient oak tree, but his subsequent nine years of exile left Cromwell as king in all but name. In 1653, he chose to assume the traditional title of Lord Protector rather than seeking to become Oliver I.

The 1650s were remarkable for their diversity of opinions, religious and political, and it fell to Cromwell to try to rein in the forces that might split the country apart. To his enemies, then and now, he was a military dictator, the former upholder of parliamentary rights who himself happily dismissed parliaments when they became inconvenient. But Cromwell had to bridge the radical, almost socialist, views among the army ranks and the deeply held traditions of 17th-century middle England, at core Royalist and conservative.

It could have all gone disastrously wrong, and it is to Cromwell's credit that he produced serious achievements. He ensured political representation from Scotland and Ireland. In wars with the Dutch and Spanish, the navy, under Admiral Blake, achieved notable success. Cromwell negotiated for the Jews to be allowed back into England, a historic decision. And he remained devoted to social justice for the poor.

In 1657 Parliament offered Cromwell the crown – his chance, had he so wished, to revert to a type of government everyone understood and to beget a dynasty. He declined the crown, but on his death in 1658 his son Richard succeeded him as lord protector. The resulting power vacuum under Richard showed just how dependent Cromwellian England was on the talents, force and personality of the man himself.

Richard's rule was short: Tumbledown Dick lacked any of his father's acumen. General Monck – one of Cromwell's commanders – marched south and presided over the restoration of Charles II, receiving the dukedom of Albermarle as his reward. So ended the republican experiment, but not without marking Oliver Cromwell's place in history as a man of conscience, fearless leadership, military brilliance, piety and severity.

AURANGZEB

1618–1707

'I have sinned terribly, and I do not know what punishment awaits me.'

Aurangzeb's alleged death-bed confession

Aurangzeb, known as Alamgir (world-seizer), was the last of the great Mughal emperors of India, expanding his empire and ruling for almost half a century, but his cruelty to his father was shameful even by the standards of dynastic rivalries and his intolerant repression and imposition of Muslim orthodoxy undermined the admirably tolerant tradition of his great predecessors, the emperors Babur and Akbar the Great. He thus alienated his millions of

Hindu subjects, weakened his empire and started the rot that led to the British conquest.

The third son of Shah Jahan and Mumtaz Mahal, in the dynasty descended from Tamerlane, the Mongol conqueror, Aurangzeb was a pious Muslim from an early age. As a young man he proved himself a capable administrator and proficient soldier in his father's service, but resented the fact that Shah Jahan nominated his eldest and favourite son, Dara Shikoh, his heir, leaving Aurangzeb out of the line of succession. This led to a rift between father and son, and a growing rivalry between Aurangzeb and Dara Shikoh.

The rivalry between the two brothers became increasingly bitter after their father fell ill in 1657. Shah Jahan's second son, Shah Shuja, also claimed the imperial throne, as did a fourth brother, Murad Baksh. Yet the real struggle remained that between Aurangzeb and the original heir apparent. To this end, Aurangzeb allied himself with Murad against Dara Shikoh, whom he defeated in 1658. As Dara Shikoh fled, Aurangzeb had their father placed under house arrest. In a stunning act of betrayal, he then attacked and defeated Murad, and had him executed. Even as he did so, he attempted to buy off Shah Shuja by offering him a governorship. But it was not long before Aurangzeb made a move against the ill-prepared Shah Shuja, who was defeated, forced into exile and later disappeared – presumed murdered at the hands of Aurangzeb's agents. After once more defeating Dara Shikoh, Aurangzeb had his last surviving brother brought back to Delhi in chains. In 1659, against the backdrop of Aurangzeb's own coronation, Dara Shikoh was publicly executed and the head delivered to his grieving and shocked father in an act of grievous filial cruelty rarely matched in history.

With his brothers mercilessly disposed of, Aurangzeb set about expanding his dominions by means of military might, culminating three decades later with victories over the rulers of Bijapur and

Golconda, which brought the Mughal empire to its greatest extent. But the problems that would in the end fatally weaken this great empire began to emerge as soon as Aurangzeb assumed the throne. Immediately life at court became markedly more austere, in line with the more rigid and puritanical interpretation of Islam followed by the new emperor. Music was banned, while works of art – such as portraits and statues – that could be considered idolatrous were proscribed. Of greater consequence, the jizya tax on non-Muslims, which had been allowed to lapse under his predecessors, was now reinstituted, while non-Muslim worship was actively discouraged, and a large number of Hindu temples were destroyed.

Unsurprisingly, such measures provoked violent resistance. A Pashtun revolt erupted in 1672 and was only suppressed with difficulty. In 1675 Aurangzeb provoked a major Sikh rebellion after having the Sikh leader, Guru Tegh Bahadur, executed for refusing to convert to Islam. The guru's three closest aides had been executed with him: one was sawn in half, another was burnt alive and the third plunged into boiling water. As with the Pashtun revolt, this rebellion too was eventually contained.

Now the Marathas, a Hindu warrior caste from the Deccan area of western India, rebelled. Throughout his reign, Aurangzeb was obsessed with conquering the Deccan plateau, regardless of the cost (financial or human) or the practical impediments – such as the unwillingness of the Hindu peoples of the area to be subjugated. For a period in the late 1660s Mughal forces had appeared to bring much of the Deccan under control, and there was an opportunity for a peace deal with the Maratha overlord, Chatrapati Shivaji Maharaj. However, Aurangzeb proceeded to double-cross Shivaji, who then led an insurrection that successfully drove the Mughal armies out of the Deccan in the early 1670s. After Shivaji's death in 1680, his son and successor, Chatrapati Sambhaji Maharaj, continued to lead the resistance to Aurangzeb. At this time the emperor's own son, Akbar, left the Mughal court to fight alongside the Marathas against his father.

In 1689 Sambhaji was finally captured, publicly tortured and executed. Yet far from pacifying the area, this merely inflamed opposition. When the emperor died in 1707, the Mughal empire was convulsed by internal unrest.

By his death the empire was financially crippled, its people exhausted and restless. Aurangzeb's imposition of Islamic fundamentalism had obliterated the tolerant genius of his heroic forebears.

PEPYS

1633–1703

The greatness of his life was open, yet he longed to communicate its smallness also.

Robert Louis Stevenson,
Familiar Studies of Men and Books (1882)

Samuel Pepys was the author of one of the most vivid diaries ever written. For almost a decade Pepys – who held a senior position at the Admiralty – recorded his life and his world in engrossing detail, providing an extraordinary insight into what it was like to be alive in 17th-century London. Pepys himself comes over as a man of great curiosity, at once open-minded and sceptical, sensitive to both the comedy and the pathos of the human condition. He delights in the high life and the low and is unstintingly honest in depicting himself as a man with all-too-human needs and desires, yet beset by moral scruples and regrets.

Pepys's diaries are all the more remarkable because during his lifetime no one knew anything about them. To the world at large, Samuel Pepys, secretary to the Admiralty, Member of Parliament and president of the Royal Society, was a highly successful naval official who had risen from humble beginnings as a tailor's son. When he died in 1703 his contemporaries saw Pepys's legacy as the great library he bequeathed to his alma mater, Magdalene College, Cambridge. He was also admired for a lifetime of philanthropy towards educational establishments such as Christ's Hospital School, and for his achievements as a naval administrator who had tirelessly promoted meritocracy and efficiency. Pepys's most priceless legacy was only discovered over a century after his death, when the authorities at Magdalene employed an impoverished undergraduate to crack the diaries' seemingly impenetrable shorthand.

Pepys's descriptions of the disasters that befell England in the 1660s are some of the richest historical sources in existence. He charts day-to-day life during the Great Plague of 1665–6 and, from his perspective as an Admiralty insider, gives an invaluable insight into the Second Anglo-Dutch War of 1667. His almost hour-by-hour record of the Great Fire of London of 1666 is one of the finest pieces of reportage ever written.

Although Pepys largely owed his advancement at the Admiralty to royal favour, he never lets his diarist's eye be dazzled by the court. He can be as exasperated with the king as he is with his own servants, and more than once he vents his frustration that Charles II seems incapable of taking the duties of kingship seriously.

While most contemporary diarists were exclusively preoccupied with the spiritual or political sphere, Pepys's overwhelming interest is in more earthy matters. The diaries illuminate Pepys's fascination with the way humans behave, their greed, rivalries, ambitions, jealousies, and their fascination with scandal. The people he depicts might well be alive today, so vividly does he bring them to life.

What makes Pepys stand out above the average gossip monger is that he also turns his unflinchingly honest gaze upon himself. He never tries to show himself in the best light, nor does he conceal his flaws. This is no exercise in self-mortification or pious humility, however; rather, it reflects an all-consuming absorption in humanity, of which he is just the most familiar specimen. He records his own behaviour with almost scientific curiosity, including all the embarrassing, even mortifying, details that most diarists would leave out – for example, the occasion when his wife Elizabeth discovers him with his hand up her companion's skirt, or the combination of grief and guilty relief he feels at the death of a maverick brother. The diaries seethe with not just glimpses of the gorgeous underwear of Charles II's latest mistresses but of Pepy's sexual adventures too. Pepys's record of his tempestuous relationship with his wife, whom he married for love, remains one of literature's most candid portraits of the Gordian knot of marriage. He writes of the blazing rows, the tearful confrontations, the nose pulling and the insults. Then there are the reconciliations, the long lie-ins spent chatting, and the sympathy for each other when sick. Pepys omits nothing: the presents he buys Elizabeth to try to assuage his guilt after yet another episode of philandering; even the details of their sexual relations, rendered problematic by a 'pain in the lip of her chose'.

After almost ten years, fearing his eyesight was failing, Pepys stopped writing his diary. It was, he wrote, 'almost as much to see myself go into my grave'. Although his eyes recovered, he never kept another diary like it, and none of his subsequent writings ever equalled his diaries for brilliance. Pepys lived out the rest of his life as a worthy man, who, despite his personal misgivings, remained unceasingly loyal to his royal masters through the Revolution of 1688. Much in Pepys's public life was admirable – but it was his private, intimate work of outstanding literature and reportage, writing diaries of such immediacy, originality and searing honesty, that demands the admiration of posterity.

LOUIS XIV

1638–1715

The only King of France worthy of the name.

Napoleon I

Louis XIV was the greatest ruler of Europe in his day, the paragon of magnificence and absolutism, but his ambitions to dominate Europe with his vision of French monarchy plunged the continent into long and vicious wars that cost the lives of many. Yet he remains the Sun King, the very definition of royal glory and probably, with Napoleon Bonaparte, the greatest of French monarchs. He ruled for seventy-two years.

Louis was the son of King Louis XIII and his wife Anne of Austria: his birth came so late in their marriage that he was celebrated as a miraculous gift – Louis Godgiven. His father, who had ruled through his gifted chief minister, Cardinal Richelieu, had pursued a policy of strengthening the crown against the over-mighty interests of the old feudal aristocracy. However Louis XIII died leaving a child heir and his wife Anne of Austria as Regent. Richelieu was already dead but his chosen successor as chief royal adviser was another fascinating and able character, Jules Mazarin, born Mazarini, an Italian diplomatist and priest, later cardinal, whose political genius, vast fortune, art collecting and pursuit of pleasure impressed the boy king and alienated the aristocracy.

The result was the Frondes, a series of aristocratic rebellions supposedly in the name of Louis XIV and against Anne and Mazarin. The rebellions left the boy with a hatred of noble power and confirmed his faith in the divine right of Catholic monarchy that he believed he personified. This conviction was encouraged by Mazarin his tutor in all matters political. When Mazarin died in 1661, Louis started to govern in his own right and proved a formidably talented politician, and a man of astonishing, indeed prolific, energy whether in the council or the bed chambers, the battle or the hunting fields.

Controlled, disciplined, sensuous haughty, mysterious, magisterial and visionary, pious and debauched, Louis created the new Palace of Versailles and with it a complex court hierarchy and ritual designed to remove the nobles from their feudal ambitions and regional power centres and concentrate their interests in the person of the king. Versailles itself was designed not only to house the king, court and entire nobility, but also to represent Louis himself: 'I am Versailles,' he said, just as 'L'état, c'est moi.' The nobility competed for a glance, a word with the king: once when the king asked a noble when his baby was due, the nobleman answered, 'Whenever Your Majesty wishes it.'

The next twenty years were the height of the king's reign – he tamed the nobility, reformed his administration, improved his armies and France had become the dominant power on the continent.

Louis married Maria Theresa of Spain, with whom he had six children, only one of whom survived to adulthood. But the king, dark-skinned with full and sensual lips, was also an enthusiastic womanizer who enjoyed many mistresses, though there was usually a ruling *maitresse en titre* such as the famous Madame de Montespan, who often enjoyed considerable power. After the death of his queen, he quietly married his last mistress, Madame de

Maintenon, the pious and capable nanny of his children.

Meanwhile his vision of himself as the supreme Catholic monarch led to his revocation of the Edict of Nantes, increasing the persecution of Protestants in France. Abroad, his ambitions meant that he was constantly at war, whether with the Dutch, the Habsburg emperor, the Spanish or Swedes. His payment of vast bribes to King Charles II of England often neutralized English power. His military successes led to the creation of the League of Augsburg against him, but superb French commanders and armies delivered him continued success.

In 1700, the Spanish King Carlos II died, leaving the Spanish empire to Louis XIV's grandson Philippe of Anjou, a succession that, if accepted, would give the Sun King virtual dominion over not only much of Europe but of the Americas too. It was a step too far for Louis who – after decades of triumph and magnificence – was old, arrogant and perhaps exhausted. Certainly France was over-extended. Louis was faced with a difficult choice but ultimately he accepted the inheritance and his grandson became king of Spain. In 1702 William III of England along with his native Holland, the Habsburg emperor and others put together another Grand Alliance against Louis. His ambitions and absolutist Catholic vision cost France dear. As Louis aged, as his heirs died, as France suffered poverty and hunger, his armies were humiliated by the outstanding commanders the duke of Marlborough and Prince Eugene of Savoy in a trans-European conflict known as the War of the Spanish Succession. Louis lived too long: he saw France defeated and the deaths of his sons and grandsons. French invincibility was broken. In 1715, just as he had dined and dressed in public, so Louis died in public after telling his child-heir, 'I have delighted too much in war.' He was seventy-seven. His successor was his great-grandson, Louis XV, aged five.

NEWTON

1642–1727

Nature, and Nature's laws lay hid in night.
God said, 'Let Newton be!' and all was light.
Alexander Pope's famous 'Epitaph: Intended for Sir
Isaac Newton' (1730)

Sir Isaac Newton is arguably the greatest scientist of all time. Along with such figures as Copernicus, Kepler and Galileo, he is one of the giants of the scientific revolution. His most influential work, *Principia Mathematica*, fundamentally altered the way in which scientists observed and explained the natural world.

Newton's main legacy was the fusion of mathematics and natural science, but he was a polymath who made significant contributions to philosophy, astronomy, theology, history, alchemy and economics. Without Newton, our understanding of the world would be unimaginably different.

Newton was born on Christmas Day, 1642. From an early age he seems to have taken firmly against the company of others. He formed a few close friendships in his life, but his general tendency to vacillate between shunning other people and picking fights with them appears to have been a peculiar part of his genius. It allowed him to focus his mind entirely on the scientific puzzles of the day.

As an undergraduate at Trinity College, Cambridge, Newton paid little attention to the syllabus set for him, largely ignoring the study of Aristotle in favour of the bright new scientists of his own day. The works of men such as René Descartes, Robert Boyle and Thomas Hobbes gripped him, and as he made notes on his reading, he began to question the world around him in ever greater detail.

It was at the age of twenty-three that Newton's intellectual star really began to burn bright. He called 1665–6 his *annus mirabilis* – his wonder year. He focused on various mathematical problems concerning the orbits of the moon and planets, developing in the process the theorem of calculus – a powerful mathematical tool vital to modern physics and engineering. The name calculus was coined by the German scientist Gottfried Leibniz, who developed the theory independently; Newton called it the 'science of fluxions'. In later life the two men argued bitterly over who could lay claim to the discovery. In any case, it is clear that even as a young man in the 1660s Newton was already a mathematical pioneer.

Leaving Cambridge to escape the plague in 1666, Newton started to study natural mechanics. In old age he claimed to have first understood that it was gravity that controlled the orbit of the moon when he sat in his orchard and watched an apple fall from a tree. Apocryphal or not, the story soon became part of Newtonian folklore; perhaps its most felicitous appearance is in Byron's *Don Juan*, where Newton is recorded as 'the sole mortal who could grapple, Since Adam, with a fall, or with an apple'.

Back in Cambridge, Newton was swiftly appointed Lucasian professor of mathematics. He was free to pursue his own course of studies, and as he worked he corresponded with other leading scientists and mathematicians, including Boyle, Robert Hooke and Edmond Halley. During the 1670s he spent much time on theology, exploiting his formidable knowledge of the Bible and developing original and radical views on the Holy Trinity. He also became interested in alchemy – the science of turning base metals into gold – and began to build up a huge library of books on the subject. But it was the appearance of the so-called Great Comet of 1680–1 that lay at the root of Newton's finest work.

In 1684 Newton began work on the project that would eventually become his ground-breaking *Principia Mathematica*. It was a work that would change both his life and the entire face of science. At its core lie Newton's three fundamental laws of motion:

- an object in a state of rest or moving in a straight line will continue in such a state unless it is acted upon by an external force;
- the acceleration of a moving object is proportionate to and in the same direction as the force acting on it;
- for every action there is an equal and opposite reaction.

From these relatively straightforward laws Newton produced an astonishingly comprehensive analysis of the operation of the natural world. He explained everything from the behaviour of small bodies and particles to the orbits of comets, planets and the moon. He put mathematics at the heart of the physical explanation of the world, where it remains to this day.

Newton's brilliance rapidly made him one of the most eminent scientists in Europe. But he felt unable to continue working in the strictly conventional religious environment at Cambridge and was relieved to be appointed to a key role at the Royal Mint, which gave him a secure financial position for life. In 1703 he became president of the Royal Society, London's most prestigious scientific community, and in 1704 he published Opticks, which dealt with the behaviour of light and the forces that attract and repel particles and bodies. The following year he was knighted by Queen Anne, the first scientist ever to receive such an honour.

Amid all this achievement, Newton spent long periods of his

later life engaged in furious debates and personal feuds with other European scientists. Yet for all his personal foibles, there was no one then or since who could disagree with the epitaph on his monument in Westminster Abbey: 'Let Mortals rejoice That there has existed such and so great an Ornament to the Human Race.'

MARLBOROUGH

1650–1722

If I were young and handsome as I was, instead of old and faded as I am, and you could lay the empire of the world at my feet, you should never share the heart and hand that once belonged to John, Duke of Marlborough.

Sarah, duchess of Marlborough, quoted in W.S. Churchill,
Marlborough: His Life and Times (1938)

John Churchill, 1st duke of Marlborough, was Britain's most brilliant soldier-statesman. He won a string of glorious victories against the French and their allies in the War of the Spanish Succession that prevented Louis XIV and his Catholic absolutism dominating Europe in the opening years of the 18th century.

From early in his life, Churchill was a protégé of James, the Catholic duke of York, who later became the ill-starred James II. Churchill travelled with James when his brother, Charles II, sent the unpopular duke into exile in the 1670s. At this time James used Churchill as his skilled lobbyist at the royal court. Handsome, charming and clever, young Churchill was seduced by Charles II's voracious mistress Barbara, duchess of Castlemaine, and once had to leap from her window when the king arrived. He was already showing himself to be a particularly talented soldier; he fought under the legendary musketeer d'Artagnan in 1673 and performed with the utmost bravery, earning himself personal praise from his future enemy, the French king, Louis XIV.

In 1677 Churchill married Sarah Jennings, a strong-willed woman who proved politically astute. As his military career progressed, the couple spent long periods apart, but the marriage was nevertheless an enormously successful one. From 1683 Sarah was the best friend of, and favourite adviser to, Princess Anne – later Queen Anne, a connection vital to Marlborough's future favour and fortune.

Although he had been a close confidant of James II, Marlborough was at heart a Protestant. When his patron James II ascended the throne in 1685, Churchill was promoted in the army and raised to the peerage. But James proved a disastrous king, alienating the Protestant nobility, who rose against him to back the Dutch prince William and his wife Mary, Protestant daughter of the king himself. The defection of Churchill, now earl of Marlborough, played its part in James' downfall. Churchill had no difficulty in shifting his allegiance to William of Orange, who became joint monarch with his wife Mary II after the Glorious Revolution of 1688. He played an important role in the campaign against James's forces in Ireland in 1690, and though he was suspected for much of the 1690s of being a closet Jacobite (a supporter of James II), William trusted him enough to appoint him commander-in-chief of British forces in the Low Countries in 1701.

It was under Queen Anne, who came to the throne in 1702, that Marlborough's career really took off. He was elevated to a dukedom and appointed captain general of the armed forces, taking command of the first campaign of the War of the Spanish Succession. From the very beginning, Marlborough was able to out-think, out-march and outmanoeuvre the French. During his first campaigning season he succeeded in pushing the French into a highly disadvantageous position. But it was the campaign of 1704 that saw Britain's greatest success.

Thanks to the complex European dynastic politics of the early 18th century, in 1704 Marlborough found himself commanding a multinational coalition, a combined army of British, Dutch, Hanoverian, Hessian, Danish and Prussian soldiers, which he coordinated with his Austrian ally, Prince Eugene of Savoy, and the difficult, thin-skinned leaders of the Dutch Republic. Near the village of Blindheim (anglicized as Blenheim) on the River Danube in Bavaria, he came up against a force of French and Bavarian troops under the French commander Marshal Tallard. Tallard had more men and a stronger natural position on the battlefield, but he was no match for Marlborough. Throughout the battle of Blenheim, fought on 13 August 1704, Marlborough completely outmanoeuvred the Franco-Bavarian army, personally intervening at crucial points of the battle and ensuring that his enemies were never allowed to exploit any small advantage. More than 20,000 of Tallard's men were killed or wounded, and Tallard himself was captured.

It was a resounding victory for Marlborough. After the battle was over, he scrawled a note to his wife on a tavern bill: 'I have not time to say more, but to beg you will give my duty to the Queen and let her know her army has had a glorious victory.' From that moment, Marlborough's fame spread throughout Europe. In England, as a reward for his success, Marlborough was granted funds to build the magnificent Blenheim Palace, near Woodstock in Oxfordshire.

At home, Marlborough was also the political partner of the chief minister Earl Godolphin, making him a unique force in politics, in war and at court.

Other famous victories followed: Ramillies in 1706, Oudenarde in 1708 and Malplaquet in 1709. These were notably bloody affairs, but Marlborough's reputation soared. Throughout all of the campaigns between 1702 and 1710, Marlborough showed himself to be a shrewd tactician and a daring and confident commander, able to unify the forces of the disparate states of the Grand Alliance against the aggressively expansionist Louis XIV.

After 1710, royal intrigues and domestic politics started to undermine Marlborough. He and his wife lost favour at court when Sarah Marlborough haughtily argued with her former best friend, Queen Anne. Sarah Marlborough became a vicious and embittered enemy of the queen, whom she accused of lesbianism and whose reputation she ruined. The satirist Jonathan Swift aimed repeated barbs at the duke, accusing him of corruption. But, with the foresight of natural courtiers, the Marlboroughs simply aligned themselves with the elector of Hanover, who in 1714 became King George I and reappointed the duke as captain general.

However, by now Marlborough's powers were fading. He suffered two strokes in 1716 and was thereafter largely confined to Blenheim. In 1722 a final stroke killed him, and he was buried in Westminster Abbey. A century later the duke of Wellington declared, 'I can conceive of nothing greater than Marlborough at the head of an English army,' and since then military historians have largely agreed that Marlborough was the finest general England has ever produced.

Over three hundred years later, the Churchill family again produced an outstanding statesman who dominated his age: Winston Churchill.

PETER THE GREAT

1672–1725

> *I have conquered an empire but I have not been able to conquer myself.*

Peter I of Russia was a physical giant – 6 feet 8 inches tall – and dynamic ruler whose astonishing political acumen, colossal ambitions, ruthless methods and eccentric energy, transformed Russia into a European great power, vastly expanded his empire and founded the city of St Petersburg. He is often described as a pro-Western reformer but that is simplistic: he was certainly a reformer and advocate of Western technology but at heart he was a brutal autocrat, the ultimate personification of the hero-monster.

He grew up in a rough school: like other practitioners of political autocracy such as Tsar Ivan the Terrible and King Louis XIV, his early years were dangerous and uncertain, overshadowed by terrifying coups and intrigues. Peter was the son of the second tsar of a new dynasty – the Romanovs – and when his father Alexei died, his weak and sickly eldest brother Fyodor succeeded to the throne for a few years, but powerful boyar (noble) families effectively ruled in his stead. On Fyodor's death in 1682, the next two brothers in the family, Ivan V and Peter I succeeded jointly – Ivan too was unfit to rule and both were very young so Russia was ruled by their mother as regent. The revolt of Moscow's old court guardsmen, the streltsy, enabled Peter's formidable sister Sophia to seize power and rule in the boys' name.

Peter developed into an extraordinary figure – amazingly tall though with a somewhat small head, highly intelligent and indefatigable though sometimes affected by twitches and strange illnesses – he may have been epileptic. From an early age he was fascinated with all matters military, naval and technological, creating his own mini-army with regiments made up of his friends and cronies.

In 1689, Peter removed his sister and started to rule in his own right. He also married and had children. One of his first actions was attack the Ottomans and the Crimean Tartars to the south, hoping to capture Azov, but this enterprise failed and it was not until 1696 that he managed to take the city.

In 1697, he set off on his fact-finding adventure – the Grand Embassy – around western Europe, where he visited Holland and England amongst many other places and studied shipbuilding. The trip was bizarre – part technological research, part political investigation, part road trip and part hooliganish stagnight.

Peter was already a law unto himself: such was his supremacy as tsar in Russia that he often dressed as an ordinary sailor or soldier and liked in his inner circle to appoint other courtiers as 'mock-tsar' so that he could relax while his henchmen indulged in the wild orgies of drunkenness and debauch that literally killed some less energetic participants.

After eighteen months away in western Europe, the streltsy, the overmighty Kremlin guards, rebelled and Peter rushed home to organize their destruction – here was an opportunity to create his own army. Never shy of shedding blood with his own hands, he personally executed and tortured many in a public orgy of violence. But he also embarked on the famous reforms that were designed to update and empower Russia to take its place amongst the great powers of Europe: beards were banned, new army regiments trained, government reorganized and Peter probed northwards towards the Baltic, controlled by Sweden, southwards toward the Black Sea, under Ottoman rule, to find a port for Russia.

His Great Northern War, designed to win an outlet on the Baltic, and fought all around that sea and in Ukraine and Poland, was a mammoth, destructive and long struggle with the Swedish empire, in particular its brilliant warrior-king Charles XII. It began with a defeat at Narva, but Peter went ahead anyway and founded St Petersburg. Ultimately his sheer will and vision would make it Russia's capital city. The war raged for many years and culminated in Charles XII's invasion of Russia – a project that ranks with the invasions of Napoleon and Hitler in its scale, ambition and hubris. In one of the decisive battles of European history, Peter defeated the Swedes at Poltava in 1709. St Petersburg was safe but the war continued for another decade even after the death of Charles XII.

In 1710, Peter, always impatient and overambitious, attacked the Ottoman empire in the south, but his campaign very nearly ended in disaster when he and his army were surrounded by the Ottoman grand vizier and his army: he was lucky to escape.

Nonetheless his armies had conquered much of the Baltic shores and he concentrated on his reforms and new capital. His allies in these enterprises were often his own creations whom he raised to the highest wealth and aristocracy, such as his crony and friend, a former soldier and pie seller, Alexander Menshikov, whom he made into a prince and field marshal.

His great love was one of Menshikov's former mistresses, a young Livonian girl named Martha Scavronskaya – renamed Catherine by the tsar – who became Peter's most trusted ally, consolation and mother of more children including his daughter, the future empress Elizaveta. Much earlier, he had divorced his first wife Eudoxia with whom he had fathered his heir, Tsarevich Alexei. The boy represented the old Muscovite interests that Peter loathed and tensions between them represented political as well as personal rifts. Terrified, the prince took refuge with the Habsburg emperor in Vienna.

Furious, humiliated and threatened, Peter had him hunted down and lured home with promises of safety. Meanwhile, in Russia, anyone implicated in Alexei's escape was impaled, tortured and executed, often by the tsar himself. When Alexei arrived home, he was instantly arrested and tortured to death by his own father. Peter remained a dangerous and paranoid tyrant: when the brother of one of his former mistresses Anna Mons became too close to his wife Catherine, he was beheaded and his pickled head presented to her.

In 1721, he finally won his peace with Sweden and with it more territories around the Baltic. Peter was declared emperor of Russia, the first Russian monarch to add this title alongside the traditional honorific of tsar. Yet his murder of his son and his failure to appoint a male heir left an uncertain legacy. He was first succeeded by his peasant-born empress, who ruled as CatherineI, backed by Peter's friend Prince Menshikov. But her death brought Peter's young grandson, a child controlled by Muscovite conservatives, to the throne as Peter II. The unstable succession led to decades of palace coups and female rulers such as his daughter Elizaveta and, later, the wife of his grandson, Catherine the Great.

Probably Russia's greatest tsar, and the prototype of the ruthless yet revolutionary Russian ruler whose divergent characteristics could inspire figures as diverse as Catherine the Great, Stalin and Vladimir Putin, this remarkable life force died in 1725, aged only fifty-two.

NADER SHAH

1688–1747

Nader of Isfahan invaded [the Mughal Empire] with his troops resembling the waves of the sea, and put all the natives of the provinces of Kabul, the Punjab and Delhi at once to the sword.
Muhammad Muhsin Sadiki, *Jewel of Samsam* (c.1739)

Nader Shah of Iran was the self-made empire-builder who dominated his native country, defeated the Mughal emperors and Ottoman sultans, conquered vast new territories, stole the Peacock Throne for himself, and overthrew the Safavid dynasty to raise himself from enslaved orphan and freebooting bandit to the throne of King of Kings. But he sank into paranoid brutality, frenzied killing and finally the insanity that led to his murder. Known as the Second Alexander, he was the tragic and murderous Napoleon of Iran.

Nader was a member of a Turkmen tribe that inhabited a northern area of Iran. He began life in obscurity. His father died when he was young, and Nader and his mother were subsequently abducted and pressed into slavery by a band of raiding tribesmen. Nader, though, soon escaped and entered the military service of a local chieftain, a position in which he distinguished himself and rose rapidly through the ranks. But in due course the headstrong Nader abandoned the chieftain and embarked on a life of banditry. By the mid-1720s he could count on some 5000 followers.

This flouting of central authority was scarcely surprising; this was, after all, a time of deep unrest within Persia. Nader's home tribe had always given fealty to the Safavid shahs who had ruled the country for the previous two hundred years. Yet, by the early 18th century, the Safavid empire was in terminal decline. In 1719 it had been challenged by its former Afghan subjects who had invaded Persia proper, and within three years the shah, Soltan Hossein, had been deposed. In response, Nader had initially yielded to the Afghan conquerors, but he later opted for rebellion. He now allied himself with Tahmasp, the son of Soltan Hossein, who was attempting to regain his father's throne. Nader's military capabilities were soon recognized, and in 1726 he was appointed supreme commander of Tahmasp's forces.

By 1729 Nader had decisively defeated the Afghans and restored Tahmasp to the throne. He proceeded to attack the Ottoman Turks and reconquer the territory they had seized from Persia in Azerbaijan and Mesopotamia. Yet he was diverted by a domestic rebellion, and while he dealt with this, Shah Tahmasp attempted to bolster his own military credentials by launching a new assault on the Ottoman empire. It proved to be a disastrous move, and most of Nader's work was now undone. Incandescent with rage at Tahmasp's incompetence, in 1732 Nader deposed him and replaced him with his infant son, Abbas III – although Nader, as regent, wielded the real power.

By 1735 Nader had once more regained the territory lost to the Ottomans. But such battlefield accomplishments were no longer enough for Nader. In January 1736 he convened an assembly of Persia's most prominent political and religious figures and 'suggested' that the youthful shah be deposed and he, Nader, be appointed in his place. Unsurprisingly, the assembled notables gave their consent.

Nader now embarked on a spree of conquest that would earn him the epithet the Second Alexander. In 1738 he attacked Kandahar, the last redoubt of the Afghans. The city was levelled and a new town, Naderabad, named after the new shah, was built in its place. Nader also sent his navy across the Persian Gulf, where he subjugated Bahrain and Oman. Then in 1739 he launched the campaign for which he would become most infamous: his assault on the Mughal empire in India.

The main Mughal armies were obliterated at the Battle of Karnal in February 1739, leaving the way open to Delhi, the Mughal capital. On arriving at the city, Nader ordered a massacre of its inhabitants, resulting in the deaths in a single day of between 20,000 and 30,000 people. The city was then ransacked and all manner of treasures carried back to Persia – including the Peacock Throne, which would thereafter symbolize the shah's authority. But Nader's appetite for conquest was not yet satiated, and, as he pushed into central Asia, he took on Ottomans, Russians and Uzbeks.

In 1741 Nader survived an assassination attempt, after which he became ever more paranoid. Convinced that his eldest son, Reza Qoli Mirza, had been involved in the attempt on his life, he had him blinded, while the alleged fellow-conspirators were put to death. The growing severity of Nader's rule, far from crushing dissent, served only to provoke fresh bouts of unrest. These uprisings were met with ever more ferocious reprisals, and Nader was reputed to have had towers of skulls constructed as a demonstration of the price of disloyalty. At the same time, the ruthless discipline he imposed on his own soldiers grew increasingly harsh. This inclination towards cruelty was ultimately to prove fatal, for in 1747, whilst on his way to confront yet another rebellion, Nader was murdered by disgruntled troops.

Thousands died at his hands; his taxes and wars had ruined his own people and at his death, his empire fell to pieces. Yet his was an astonishing achievement. He was as brilliant as he was brutal: centuries later, Stalin studied Nader Shah as a man to admire for his flawed but pitiless grandeur.

VOLTAIRE

1694–1778

As long as people believe in absurdities, they will continue to commit atrocities.

Voltaire

The writer, philosopher, literary celebrity and friend of kings, François-Marie Arouet, better known by his pen name Voltaire, was the star of the Age of Enlightenment, one of the most influential men in Europe – and also one of the richest. His ridicule of the absurdities and atrocities of 18th-century Europe helped to give birth to the modern world – a world in which science and reason replaced superstition. Thanks to his indignation and energy, freedom of speech and of belief, and the even-handed administration of justice, came to be regarded as inalienable human rights.

Voltaire was famed even in his own time as a tireless multi-talented genius. He excelled as a playwright, a poet, a novelist, a satirist, a polemicist, a historian, a philosopher, a financial investor and a (sometimes sychophantic) courtier. Of his prodigious output of over 350 works, it is the slim satire *Candide* (1759) that most completely encapsulates his brilliance. Published, like most of Voltaire's work, to instant popular acclaim, it follows the hapless eponymous hero through a series of grim adventures as he clings to the conventional religio-philosophical piety that 'All is for the best in the best of all possible worlds' – despite increasingly conclusive evidence, as horror piles on horror, to the contrary. A devastatingly witty attack on everything from slavery to the professions, *Candide* exemplifies the power of Voltaire's razor-sharp pen to deflate pretension and hypocrisy.

Wiry, mischievous and wickedly brilliant, Voltaire was the changeling in an otherwise entirely conventional wealthy bourgeois family. He personally encouraged the rumours that his paternity lay elsewhere. By his late teens his acid wit – he once remarked of a rival poet's 'Ode to Posterity' that 'I fear it will not reach its mark' – had made him the pet of aristocratic society. Voltaire, the financial wizard, made a fortune from canny manipulation of the Paris lottery. Cirey, the Lorraine estate on which Voltaire spent ten years with his great love, the married and beautiful mathematics scholar the Marquise de Châtelet in the 1730s and 1740s, became a hothouse of intellectual debate and social mischief.

Voltaire's campaign against the monarchy's arbitrary practices was informed by first-hand experience: as a youth, his satirical pen had briefly landed him in the Bastille. A subsequent exile in London (1726–9) alerted Voltaire to the contrast between England's intellectual openness and the oppressive censorship of France. In his Philosophical Letters, published on his return to France in 1729, Voltaire embarked on a lifelong attack on the injustice and intolerance fostered by the Catholic Church and France's absolute monarchy. Thereafter, Voltaire and the French authorities existed in an uneasy truce. He briefly held a court appointment as royal historiographer in the 1740s, although his rooms – 'the most stinking shit hole in Versailles' – disappointed him. But having come to the conclusion that 'I am very fond of the truth, but not at all of martyrdom,' he spent most of his life away from the centre.

He based himself at Geneva from 1755, then, in 1759, settled at nearby Ferney in French territory, whose proximity to the Swiss border afforded him luxurious safety to exercise his pen. The pseudonyms he used were flimsy to say the least: he favoured the Archbishop of Paris for his most virulent attacks on the church. But they allowed him to disavow authorship, with wide-eyed innocence, while the outraged authorities banned and burned his books.

Voltaire's outstanding achievement was his campaign for civil rights, waged under his motto 'Écrasez l'infâme' ('Crush the infamy'). His calls for religious freedom and judicial fairness ushered in a new era. Leg braces, thumbscrews, the rack, sleep deprivation, pouring water on rags stuffed into the victim's throat to induce the sensation of drowning, hanging a victim by their arms with weights attached to their ankles – these were just some of the methods used in prisons across Europe in Voltaire's time to extract confessions from the 'guilty'.

Punishment could be still more gruesome. The execution in Paris, in 1757, of Robert Damiens, the man who tried to stab Louis XV, was incomparably grisly. First of all, as decreed by France's Parlement, the hand that had wielded the knife was burnt. The executioner then used pincers to tear away chunks of flesh, filling the wounds with molten lead. For over quarter of an hour, four horses, pulling in different directions, tried to dismember Damiens' broken body until finally his thighs and arms were severed with a knife. It was said that the would-be regicide was still just alive when his dismembered trunk was thrown on the fire.

Until the 18th century, torture was an accepted part of the judicial system. It was a means of wrenching the truth from the recalcitrant human will, a way of punishing the guilty in the most heinous way possible. The thinkers of the Enlightenment saw it otherwise – as a barbaric practice that had nothing to do with justice, one that risked punishing the innocent as well as the guilty.

Inflicting such intense pain on a man, argued the Italian Cesare Beccaria in 1764, in one of the age's most influential tracts, would only compel the victim to 'accuse himself of crimes of which he is innocent'. Hearing of the case of Jean Calas, a Huguenot (French Protestant) from Toulouse who in 1762 was accused of murdering his son, then tortured to obtain a confession and finally broken on the wheel, Voltaire raged against the superstitious barbarism of the Catholic Church and its excessive judicial influence.

During the latter half of the 18th century, Prussia, Sweden, France, Austria and Tuscany all abolished judicial torture. In 1801, under Tsar Paul, Russia decreed that 'the very name of torture, bringing shame and reproach on mankind, should be forever erased from the public memory'.

It was far from a distant memory; but now torture was a shameful secret rather than a commendable practice. And while the bloodbath of France's Terror has totally sullied its name, Dr Joseph-Ignace Guillotin's invention for swiftly and painlessly beheading the con- demned was meant to be a step away from the savage methods of the past. The deist Voltaire's Treatise on Tolerance (1763) expanded on his belief that reason should be government's abiding principle, and his assertion that religious freedom was not harmful to the state's well- being has become a fundamental principle of modern government. 'The right to persecute,' he declared, 'is absurd and barbaric.'

By now Voltaire's fame had spread across Europe: Frederick the Great and Catherine the Great, with whom he enjoyed a prolific correspondence, basked in his reflected glory, projecting them- selves as adherents of 'enlightened absolutism'. Both repeatedly invited him to visit and he duly stayed with Frederick (1750–53), but the realities of the Prussian court soured Voltaire's rapport with the man he now described as a 'likeable whore', and who once described him as a 'monkey'. He resisted Catherine's invitations, but it was he who flattered her by dubbing her 'the Great'. Lumi- naries from across the continent flocked to see Voltaire, and at Ferney he became the self-described 'innkeeper of Europe'. The brilliant schoolboy, described by his father-confessor as being 'devoured by a thirst for celebrity', had become 'King Voltaire', revered and reviled in equal measure across Europe as the scourge of authority, injustice and hypocrisy. As he lay dying in Paris in 1778, his rooms were crammed with crowds of people, all determined to catch a last glimpse of a legendary man.

The shrine to Voltaire erected by the French revolutionaries in the Panthéon acknowledges their debt to him. It bears the inscription: 'He taught us how to be free.' Voltaire had begun the process of translating the ideals of the Enlightenment into reality, and his words became the first bomb thrown against the *ancien régime*. He once told a friend, 'I have never made but one prayer to God, a very short one: "O Lord, make my enemies ridiculous." And God granted it.'

SAMUEL JOHNSON

1709–1784

> *Here lies Sam Johnson: – Reader, have a care,*
> *Tread lightly, lest you wake a sleeping bear:*
> *Religious, moral, generous, and humane*
> *He was: but self-sufficient, proud, and vain,*
> *Fond of, and overbearing in dispute,*
> *A Christian and a scholar – but a brute.*
>
> Soame Jenyns, suggested epitaph
> for Dr Johnson (1784)

Samuel Johnson was one of the most versatile, erudite and accomplished writers in the history of English literature. In addition to his remarkable and ground-breaking *Dictionary*, he also wrote copiously in a wide range of other genres: essays, literary criticism, travel writing, political sketches and satires, a tragedy, biography, poetry, translations, sermons, diaries, letters and pamphlets. He was a master conversationalist and a spiky, magnetic and brilliant figure in London society. Through the biography written by his disciple James Boswell, we can still appreciate one of the reigning personalities of literary history as though he were alive today.

Johnson's early years did not show much promise. As a child he suffered from both scrofula (tuberculosis of the lymph glands), which affected his sight, and smallpox, which disfigured his face, making him at best peculiar to look at. Throughout his life he was also prone to depression and had all manner of odd tics and twitches that now suggest Tourette's syndrome. Despite these disadvantages, the young Samuel was a bright boy and grew up in a family of booksellers in Lichfield. But poverty obliged him to leave Pembroke College, Oxford, after only a year, without taking a degree.

In 1735 he married Elizabeth Porter, a local widow twenty years his senior. Failing to obtain a teaching post, Johnson decamped to London in 1737 and began working for the *Gentleman's Magazine*, for which he wrote parliamentary sketches. He had already written a stage tragedy, Irene, and worked on satirical poems, biographies such as The Life of Mr Richard Savage, and a catalogue of the Harley collection of books and manuscripts.

It was in 1746 that Johnson began his *magnum opus*. He was commissioned to write a new English dictionary, and the project dominated the next nine years of his life. Nothing on such a scale had previously been undertaken, and the *Dictionary* proved to be a masterpiece of scholarship. It broke new ground in lexicography, encompassing a vast array of words from a gigantic pool of source material, and even made a good stab at discovering the etymology of many of the words that were included. The *Dictionary* was also a demonstration of Johnson's pithy and precise style. In a characteristic flash of witty self-deprecation, Johnson defines a lexicographer as 'a writer of dictionaries, a harmless drudge'.

The *Dictionary*, published in 1755, was immediately recognized as a work of brilliance, and Johnson was awarded with an honorary MA from Oxford before the book was even finished. In the meantime he had continued to write copiously in other genres. His essays in *The Rambler* dealt with matters as varied as capital punishment, good parenting and the emergence of the novel, and are replete with eminently quotable epigrams – such as 'No man is much pleased with a companion, who does not increase, in some respect, his fondness for himself.' Johnson had the same gift as Oscar Wilde for pointing out, with razor-like wit, the contradictions inherent in human nature.

Johnson lost his wife in 1752. He never married again, but his house was a refuge to friends from a variety of odd backgrounds. Ex-prostitutes, indebted unlicensed surgeons, female writers – a particular favourite with Johnson – all stayed under his roof. But Johnson was just as popular in the higher strata of society, receiving patronage from the Treasury and conversing with men like the American founding father, philosopher and inventor Benjamin Franklin. In 1763 Johnson met the young Boswell in a bookshop and took him on as a protégé. Boswell was a devoted fan, and his biography tells us much about Johnson's life and scintillating conversation which otherwise might have been lost.

As his fame grew Johnson turned out another pair of fine works: an admired edition of Shakespeare's plays in 1765 and *The Lives of the Poets*, which came out between 1779 and 1781. Johnson was often tart, if not harsh, on his contemporaries – when asked to pick the better of the two minor poets Smart and Derrick, he replied that there was 'no settling the point of precedency between a louse and a flea'. But despite this gruffness, he had a warm heart and a fond regard for his friends. He died in 1784 and was buried in Westminster Abbey, a sign of the esteem in which he was held by his contemporaries – an esteem that has not diminished over the succeeding centuries. 'I hate a fellow whom pride or cowardice or laziness drives into a corner, and who does nothing when he is there but sit and growl,' he once said. 'Let him come out as I do, and bark.'

FREDERICK THE GREAT

1712–1786

A man who gives battle as readily as he writes an opera . . . he has written more books than any of his contemporary princes has sired bastards; he has won more victories than he has written books.

Voltaire, 1772

The outstanding soldier-statesman of his age, the paragon of gifted kingship, Frederick the Great prefigured Napoleon. The most enlightened monarch of his day, Frederick was an aesthete and lover of the arts – an accomplished writer, composer, flautist and wit. Famed in his youth as a philosopher prince, on acceding to the throne in 1740, at the age of twenty-eight, this apparent milksop astonished Europe's crowned heads by becoming the most formidable ruler of the age.

With his typically wry wit, Frederick once declared that he had infected Europe with warfare just as a coquette infects her clients. Introspective and self-critical, Frederick's analysis and planning were always immaculate, his quick mind the first to seize the advantage on the battlefield. His martial qualities inspired in his formidably well-trained army the utmost respect and loyalty, despite the horrific privations his campaigns put them through. When Napoleon reached Berlin twenty years after Frederick's death, he paid homage at Frederick's tomb. As he entered, he declared to his men: 'Hats off, gentlemen! If he were alive, we would not be here!'

Frederick waged war to serve his state's interests, but he was never militaristic. He deplored war's effects and he abhorred hypocrisy. At other times he could be firmly pragmatic: 'If we can gain something by being honest, we will be it; and if we have to deceive, we will be cheats.'

In 1740 he boldly and ruthlessly invaded Austria's rich province of Silesia, unleashing almost twenty years of savage warfare across central Europe, but he kept the territory. Europe's hypocritical old guard was quick to share in the spoils when Frederick initiated the partition of the increasingly anarchic Poland. 'She weeps, but she takes,' Frederick wryly commented of Empress Maria Theresa when she took her slice of Poland.

The man who refused to wear spurs because he thought them cruel to horses abolished torture within days of coming to the throne. He banned serfdom in all his new territories, and in an age when capital punishment was decreed for stealing bread, the famously liberal Frederick signed only eight or ten death warrants a year. He once reprieved a father and daughter from the death sentence for committing incest on the grounds that one could not be absolutely sure about the girl's paternity. The atheist Frederick's religious tolerance extended to welcoming the Jesuits to Prussia – a sect that crowned heads all over Europe were trying to expel.

The first of Europe's enlightened despots, Frederick was tireless in fulfilling his self-designated role as the first servant of the state. Every day he forced himself to rise at 4 a.m., ordering his servants to throw a cold wet cloth in his face if he seemed reluctant. Even such an early start as this barely gave him time to do all he wanted. At his court, which he filled with artists, writers, musicians and philosophers, he practised the flute four times a day, held concerts after supper, conducted a vast correspondence with philosophers and statesmen, wrote poetry, and administered the affairs of state.

His endurance was as striking as his luck. He was prone to fits of depression and despair, but he never gave up. 'Fortune alone can deliver me from my present position,' he declared at one point during the Seven Years' War (1756–63). The timely death of his inveterate enemy Empress Elizaveta of Russia in 1762 brought about a volte-face in foreign policy as his ardent admirer Peter III came to the Russian throne. Having teetered on the brink of total annihilation early in the war, Prussia emerged triumphant from it.

Frederick's insecurity may well have been instilled in him by his miserable youth. His father Frederick William I's contempt for his son was famous. 'What goes on in that little head?' the austere, violent, volatile Frederick William would demand suspiciously of his 'effeminate' son, whose lifelong love for all things French directly contravened his father's orders. Matters came to a head when the eighteen-year-old Frederick tried to flee his wretched existence. After he was caught and imprisoned, his best friend (and some say lover) Hermann von Katte was executed outside the window of his cell.

Prussia may have grown in grandeur but Frederick did not. Towards the end of Frederick's life, a visiting dignitary encountered an elderly 'gardener' at the Sanssouci summer palace and had a friendly chat. Only later, when he was introduced to Prussia's king, did he realize who he had been talking to.

But he could turn nasty – in his wit, in his disciplining of his army, in his repudiation of his wife. His sexuality mystified contemporaries – there were allegations of affairs with male guardsmen. Certainly there were no mistresses. Perhaps he was asexual. He fell out spectacularly with his old correspondent Voltaire, who abused him in print as a miser and a tyrant. His pursuit of war to advance his country simultaneously exhausted its resources. His emphasis on the primacy of the state meant that his rule was never as enlightened as Voltaire had hoped.

Frederick's lifelong conservatism translated itself increasingly into rigidity with age. With typical self-deprecation, he frequently said that he had lived too long.

CASANOVA

1725–1798

Worthy or not, my life is my subject, and my subject is my life.
Giacomo Casanova

The name of Casanova or, to give his full name, Giovanni Giacomo Casanova de Seingalt, is synonymous with womanizing and wild living. Indeed, in his racy and scandalously frank memoirs, *Histoire de ma vie jusqu'à l'an 1787* (*The Story of My Life Until 1787*), this tall, dark and handsome self-appointed hero presents himself as 'the world's greatest lover', describing his many conquests, as well as his early life, adventures and travels, in salacious detail. It may therefore come as a surprise to find that the notorious philanderer, who sired many children out of wedlock and was himself, it was rumoured, the illegitimate son of a Venetian nobleman, was also a highly cultured man – and that is his real claim to fame. Whether they are mainly fact or boastful fiction, his memoirs are the greatest ever written.

Precociously intelligent, Casanova attended the University of Padua from the age of thirteen, obtained a doctorate in law at the age of sixteen (ironically, perhaps, his studies included moral philosophy), took holy orders, and also considered training as a doctor. 'The idea of settling down,' he wrote, 'was always repulsive to me.' The adventurous and talented Casanova was always on the move. He started out working in the church in Venice but was soon expelled under something of a cloud, due to his sexual appetites and dandified appearance. From there he had a short-lived career as a military officer, stationed in Corfu, then as a theatre violinist in Venice. He took a variety of jobs before leaving Venice in 1748, under suspicion of attempted rape (though he was later acquitted).

Born into a world of artists, con artists and courtesans, Casanova represented a sparkling conflation of two 18th-century social types – the society fraud and the man of letters. He was one of the fascinating mountebanks and charlatans who entertained, mesmerized and swindled the royal courts of the age, claiming variously to be noblemen, necromancers, alchemists (who could turn base metals into gold), Kabbalists, magi and hierophants. The first of them was the so-called Comte de Saint-Germain (1710–84), who claimed to be 2000 years old and able to remember the Crucifixion (his valet claimed to remember it too); Louis XV gave him 10,000 livres. The ultimate was Count Alessandro Cagliostro (1743–95), born Giuseppe Balsamo in Sicily, who made a fortune in courts across Europe claiming, among other feats, that he could convert urine into gold and offer eternal life. His seductive wife, born Lorenza in Sicily, accompanied him as Serafina, Princess di Santa Croce. After a rock-star-style tour of Europe, Count Cagliostro was finally embroiled in the Diamond Necklace Affair that so damaged Queen Marie-Antoinette, and he died in 1795 in an Italian prison.

But it was also a very literary age, when the fame of witty letter-writers, such as Casanova, spread throughout Europe. The greatest letter-writer of the era (along with Voltaire) was the genuine high aristocrat Charles-Joseph, Prince de Ligne (1735–1814), Belgian grandee, Austrian field marshal and international courtier, wit and socialite, who managed to be friends simultaneously with Emperor Joseph II, Catherine the Great of Russia, and King Frederick the Great. His hilarious letters were copied from court to court, and he finally died at the Congress of Vienna.

Passing himself off as the noble Chevalier de Seingalt, Casanova earned his living as the inventor of the Paris lottery, an agricultural adviser to the kings of Spain, an alchemist and a Kabbalist. He was repeatedly arrested for his debts and in 1755 for witchcraft and freemasonry – and then imprisoned for fifteen months in Venice's Piombi Prison, known as the Leads, from which it was supposedly impossible to escape. Escape he did, however, across the rooftops, stopping for a recuperative coffee in St Mark's Square before disappearing in a gondola.

He travelled widely, through Italy, Austria, Spain, England, Turkey and Russia, meeting Catherine the Great, George III of England and Pope Benedict XII, not to mention Rousseau and Voltaire. Most of his income came from the grandees who admired his intelligence and wit, or – in the case of the women – sought and often received his attentions. Never married, he was engaged frequently. His lovers included courtesans, peasants, heiresses, sisters, countesses and many nuns, sometimes together. In 1776, overcome by debt, he became a secret agent for the Venetian Tribunal of Inquisitors, using the name Antonio Pratiloni and snitching on heretics to the Catholic Church while living with a local seamstress.

Tales of derring-do and romantic trysts litter the memoirs, which are the main source of information about his chequered life. Heavily censored in earlier editions, they were not published in their full unexpurgated twelve-volume form until 1960; they paint a portrait of a lovable trans-European rogue and seducer. He wrote them as an old man looking back on an adventurous life, working as the librarian to the Bohemian Count Joseph Karl von Waldstein. Casanova was never one for letting the facts stand in the way of a good tale. Some of his dates simply do not fit: people are in the wrong places and die at the wrong times, and the pseudonyms he gives his various conquests make it impossible to be certain who was who. Unreliable, self-indulgent and shameless, the memoirs are nevertheless a literary classic, a real picture of an entire epoch.

'I have lived as a philosopher,' declared Casanova on his deathbed, 'and died as a Christian.' It was rather less straightforward, and rather more interesting, than that.

CAPTAIN COOK

1728–1779

The ablest and most renowned Navigator this or any country hath produced.
> Sir Hugh Palliser's monument to Captain Cook, erected at Chalfont St Giles, Buckinghamshire, after the news of Cook's death reached Europe

James Cook was responsible for exploring and charting boundless areas of the Pacific hitherto unknown to Europeans. A creative captain as well as a fine navigator, he devised a diet for his crews rich in vitamin C, thereby preventing the outbreaks of scurvy that usually afflicted those on long voyages. It was curiosity and ambition as well as science that drove Cook to fulfil his desire to voyage not only 'farther than any man before me, but as far as I think it is possible for a man to go'.

Cook's achievements were remarkable given his beginnings.

The son of a Yorkshire farm labourer, as a lad he was apprenticed to a grocer. This did not satisfy his restless spirit, and he set off for the port of Whitby. Here he signed on to serve on a merchantman and spent a number of years sailing on colliers up and down the east coast of England. Having acquired the rudiments of navigation, in 1755 he volunteered for the Royal Navy and rose swiftly through the ranks. During the Seven Years' War Cook achieved renown as a hydrographic surveyor, and his work charting the St Lawrence River and the coast of Canada was critical to subsequent British victories. His surveys and sailing directions concerning Newfoundland were used for well over a century.

Cook's observations of the solar eclipse of 1766 so impressed the Royal Society that, jointly with the Admiralty, it commissioned him to make a voyage to Tahiti to observe the transit of Venus – and also to explore and claim for Britain the undiscovered southern continent known as Terra Australis. The belief in the existence of such a continent – covering not only the South Pole but also extending far to the north into the Indian Ocean and the Pacific – had been held by geographers since the time of Aristotle. Cook's discoveries conclusively put the myth to rest: in circumnavigating New Zealand for the first time (1769), discovering Australia's east coast (1770) and sailing through the Torres Strait between Australia and New Guinea, Cook showed these lands to be separate entities. But the furtherance of science was only one of Cook's aims; he also claimed for King George III many of the lands he discovered – such as New South Wales and Hawaii (which he called the Sandwich Isles in honour of his patron, the Earl of Sandwich). During his second voyage (1772–5), he achieved the first circumnavigation of the Antarctic, and in so doing became the first person to cross the Antarctic Circle.

The scale of Cook's achievement owes much to his brilliant and fearless seamanship. Cook consistently continued his explorations when all others would have turned back. His navigation skills were considerable, and he also had the vision to draw on the knowledge of the two Tahitians he employed on his voyages. Boundlessly tenacious, Cook was never content with what he had achieved. He invariably extended his voyages, and his willingness to exceed the orders given to him by the Admiralty was rewarded by the discoveries he made.

Cook's maps and charts were often the first accurate depictions of the coasts he explored: he completed the outlines of Newfoundland, the northwest coast of North America, New Zealand and Australia. His use of the K1 chronometer, which by keeping time more precisely enabled him to measure longitude more accurately, was ground-breaking, and his results are remarkable for their accuracy, given the frequently adverse conditions in which he worked and the limitations of the instrumentation available to him.

Cook's pioneering work on the prevention of scurvy earned him a medal from the Royal Society, who were also impressed by the scientific achievements of his expeditions, in particular the records of new flora and fauna made by the scientists he took with him. Cook – praised in the House of Lords as 'the first navigator in Europe' – was elected a fellow of the Royal Society and awarded a captainship and honorary retirement by the Royal Navy. This last, however, he accepted only on the condition that he could still make further voyages. For, despite having a wife and a succession of children, Cook's life lay at sea.

In 1776 he set sail for the South Seas once again. During this voyage, Cook determined to make an attempt to break though the apparently impassable Arctic ice and find a route back to Europe to the north of Canada. While waiting for spring to arrive, Cook wintered in Hawaii, and here he became caught up in a disagreement with the islanders. In the resulting skirmish, Cook, who had initially been deified by the Hawaiians as the incarnation of their god, Lono, was killed. His body, according to custom, was stripped of flesh, which was then burnt – or possibly eaten. His bones were distributed among various chiefs and only handed back to Cook's men after protracted negotiations. His remains were buried at sea, as was only fitting, the sea having been his whole life. The map of the Pacific was his legacy.

CATHERINE THE GREAT

1729–1796

& POTEMKIN

1739–1791

Be gentle, humane, accessible, compassionate and open-handed; don't let your grandeur prevent you from mixing kindly with the humble and putting yourself in their shoes . . . I swear by Providence to stamp these words in my heart.

Catherine's private note to herself
on becoming empress (1762)

Catherine the Great was not only a successful politician, a triumphant empire-builder and a remarkable self-made woman of strong passions in a male-dominated age, she was also arguably the most humane ruler that Russia has ever produced. She ranks with Elizabeth I of England as one of history's outstanding female monarchs – though her achievements were even greater than Elizabeth's.

Catherine was certainly ruthless in her pursuit of power and admiration, self-indulgent in her famous love affairs and enormously extravagant in her enjoyment of arts and luxury – but she was also overwhelmingly benevolent, decent in her intentions, loyal to her friends, merciful to her enemies, tolerant of others, industrious, intellectual and enormously intelligent. Her success was against all the odds. She was not even Russian, had no claim to the throne and found herself, at the age of fourteen, thrown into a loveless marriage and the brutal bear pit of the Russian court.

She was not actually named Catherine, being born Sophie of Anhalt-Zerbst, a minor German princess in the patchwork of little principalities that was the Holy Roman Empire, which served as a sort of matchmaking agency for the monarchies of Europe. In 1746 the Empress Elizaveta of Russia summoned Princess Sophie to St Petersburg to marry her heir, Grand Duke Peter. She converted to the Orthodox Church, took the name Catherine and learned Russian – but found her husband disappointing. Puny, poxy, prejudiced, foolish and cowardly, Grand Duke Peter was out of his depth as the Russian heir – and as Catherine's husband. He also was German, but while Catherine embraced all Russian culture, he despised and feared Russia. She immediately charmed the empress, won friends and admirers among the courtiers and the Guards regiments, and proved adept at politics. It is uncertain if Peter even consummated the marriage, but it is certain that he did not satisfy the passionate Catherine.

When no child was forthcoming, the empress herself arranged for Catherine to take her first lover, Serge Saltykov. A son, Grand Duke Paul, was born. Catherine was not beautiful, but she was handsome, small and curvaceous, with bright blue eyes and thick auburn hair. She went on to take other lovers, though she only had a dozen in her entire lifetime – almost seventy years – which hardly justifies her reputation as a nymphomaniac. She was never promiscuous, more a serial dater. She enjoyed sex but was more of a romantic who longed to settle with one man.

Amid the vicious rivalries at the Russian court during the Seven Years' War, Catherine's intrigues almost destroyed her. But she used her cunning and charm to survive, shrewdly taking Grigory Orlov, a popular Guards officer, as her lover. When Elizaveta died and her husband succeeded to the throne, Peter III took only six months to alienate everyone. On 28 June 1762, dressed in male uniform, Catherine seized power. By the rules of the day, Peter had to be murdered to protect her dubious claim to the throne; the Orlovs strangled him – and she knew she would forever bear the blame.

Once in power, however, she ruled cautiously and sensibly. She set about expanding Russia south towards the Black Sea, seizing territory from the Ottoman Turks. She called a legislative commission to study the abolition of serfdom and the making of proper laws. She corresponded with the philosophes, including Voltaire, who hailed her as the Great. The huge peasant revolt of Pugachev and the realities of aristocratic rule meant that many of these ambitions ended in disappointment, but her rule was decent, sensible and orderly – she worked hard to make Russian law and society more merciful and humane.

When her long relationship with Orlov broke down, Catherine found the love of her life, who was also to be her partner in power. Grigory Potemkin was a dashing one-eyed cavalry general who was as politically brilliant as she was; but where he was wild and imaginative, she was sensible and diligent. The combination worked. Their fiery sexual affair started in late 1773, recorded in the most outrageous and romantic letters ever written by a monarch. She liked to say that they were 'twin souls', and they shared obsessional political ambition with heroic sexual appetites. They probably married, secretly, but when their affair ended, Potemkin, raised to prince, became her co-ruler and best friend and they each took younger lovers. Together they fought the Turks, annexed the Crimea, built cities, outwitted the English, constructed a Black Sea fleet, bought art collections. Following Potemkin's advice, Catherine found love with a series of ever-younger favourites, whom she enjoyed teaching about the classics, but who played no political role. These young men usually humiliated the old empress by running off with a girl their own age, leaving Potemkin to comfort her.

'The most extraordinary man I ever met,' wrote the Prince de Ligne about Potemkin, 'constantly reclining yet never sleeping, trembling for others, brave for himself, bored in the midst of pleasure, unhappy for being too lucky, a profound philosopher, able minister, sublime politician or like a ten-year-old child, embracing the feet of the Virgin, or the alabaster neck of his mistress. What is the secret of his magic? Genius, genius and more genius.' This one-eyed giant enchanted and scandalized Europe like a sultan in *The Arabian Nights*, even seducing one princess by serving plates of diamonds instead of pudding. Pushkin hailed the 'glory of his name', while Stalin reflected: 'What was Catherine the Great's achievement? To appoint talented men like Potemkin to rule Russia.'

Potemkin died in 1791 on an open Bessarabian steppe, weeping over Catherine's letters. When she heard the news she collapsed: 'There'll never be another Potemkin.' Theirs was one of the great love stories of history, in a league with that of Napoleon and Josephine or Antony and Cleopatra, but more romantic and much more successful than either of those. The ageing Catherine was heartbroken and allowed a talentless young lover, Platon Zubov, to replace Potemkin, leading to political mistakes, including the annexation of Poland and a bungled Swedish alliance.

Catherine's achievements – political, military and artistic – were colossal nevertheless. Her reign was a golden age, her vision of Russia essentially a liberal one, and her character exuded invincibility. Catherine the Great remains not only the paragon of Russian rulers, but history's most accomplished female potentate.

WASHINGTON

1732–1799

The time is now near at hand which must probably determine whether Americans are to be freemen or slaves ... The fate of unborn millions will now depend, under God, on the courage and conduct of this army.

George Washington, in his general orders to the Continental
Army (2 July 1776)

George Washington, the first president of the United States and commander of the American army in the War of Independence against Britain, remains the paragon of the decent, honest – and hugely gifted – leader. Covered in glory, blessed with all the talents, equipped for the highest office and command, he was a gentleman who combined virtue and modesty with ambition to serve. Legend has it that he turned down a crown, though in fact there was no sceptre to offer. He set the standards of probity and honesty for every president who followed him.

Born in Virginia in 1732 to a family of landowners who had emigrated from northern England in 1657, Washington started in public service as a brash young lieutenant colonel in the Virginia militia. In May 1754 he commanded a small force in – and perhaps initiated – the opening engagement of the French and Indian War (at the Battle of Jumonville Glen), which would eventually become the worldwide Anglo-French conflict known as the Seven Years' War. A few days later he built Fort Necessity on the Ohio River, though when it was besieged by a larger French force, he was eventually forced to capitulate – the only surrender of his career. The next year he again fought the French, under British general Edward Braddock.

His natural talents, military and administrative, earned his promotion to colonel and commander-in-chief of the Virginian troops in 1755, aged only twenty-three, and in 1758 he served under General John Forbes in the successful campaign to capture the French Fort Duquesne. Afterwards, Washington returned to his Mount Vernon estate, married a wealthy widow, Martha Curtis, and entered politics. In June 1774 he led the Virginia legislature's call for a continental congress to coordinate opposition to unpopular British colonial policies. In June 1775, after fighting had broken out, Congress unanimously elected him commander-in-chief of the Continental Army.

During the War of Independence, Washington managed to train the American army and to hold together all the different personalities and the differing characters of the states that made up the alliance, even in the face of defeat and adversity. Having forced the British to evacuate Boston in 1776, after a year-long siege, he committed mistakes in his defence of New York, losing the Battle of Long Island (the largest battle of the war) to General Howe and retreating, short of men and supplies, into Pennsylvania. Late in the year, however, he crossed back into New Jersey and took the British by surprise, defeating them at Trenton and Princeton.

But in 1777 his forces were defeated at the Brandywine in September and at Germantown in October, and Howe occupied Philadelphia. Washington led his army to Valley Forge in Pennsylvania, where the weakened forces encamped through the winter of 1777–8, perhaps the lowest ebb of the revolutionary cause. It was

Washington's personality above all that held together his broken army during that long winter. He used his almost dictatorial wartime powers with caution, tempered with bold action and skilled improvisation, common sense and respect for civil power. Aided by French entry into the war and the assistance of his brilliant aide Alexander Hamilton, in 1781 Washington commanded the superb Yorktown campaign against the British commander Cornwallis, whose army was besieged in the Virginia town which, after much bombardment, surrendered on 19 October 1781. This was to be the final major battle of the war.

After his victories, Washington retired to Mount Vernon. In 1787 he attended the Philadelphia Convention that discussed the creation of a new American government. Washington was elected president of the convention but refrained from joining the debate. The office of president of the United States was created to head the new government, and in 1788 Washington was elected to the post, winning re-election in 1792. As president, he attempted to maintain neutrality between the pro-French faction led by Secretary of State Thomas Jefferson and the pro-British faction of Treasury Secretary Alexander Hamilton, but he generally favoured the latter, angering those who supported the French revolutionary cause and wanted another war with Britain. One of the greatest of the Founding Fathers, a self-made bastard from the West Indies, Hamilton, backed by the president, effectively created the American state and its financial and tax systems. When Washington's second term ended, he refused to stand for a third, setting a precedent that held for 140 years before being enshrined in law by the Twenty-second Amendment in 1951.

His calm, dignified leadership was followed by a civilized return to private life at Mount Vernon, where this democratic hero of talent and decency, the founder of a future superpower, died of a throat infection in 1799.

JEFFERSON

1743–1826

I think this is the most extraordinary collection of talent and of human knowledge that has ever been gathered together at the White House – with the possible exception of when Thomas Jefferson dined alone.

J.F. Kennedy, welcoming forty-nine Nobel Prize winners to the White House in 1962

Thomas Jefferson was a radical polymath who put into words the principles of the American Revolution and then put those words into practice as a statesman. Private, intense and burning with ambition, Jefferson was a political visionary with astonishing foresight, a masterful politician with secret and well-hidden cunning who had the ability to coordinate conspiracies without leaving a clue of his involvement.

Jefferson's intellect was second to none. Heir to a slave-owning estate, the son of a wealthy Virginian planter, he could, at college and while studying law, as a close friend recalled, 'tear himself away from his dearest friends, to fly to his studies'. Gracious and charming in manner, he nonetheless had an intense dislike of oral debate and rarely spoke in public, careful never to give away his thoughts, except in his diaries and to a few trusted allies. But the intricate brilliance of the young politician was quickly noted in Virginia's colonial legislature.

Jefferson's power was in his pen. It is enshrined in the Declaration of Independence. As a delegate at the Second

Continental Congress in Philadelphia in 1776, Jefferson became the chief author of the document repudiating British sovereignty. In his exposition he championed universal liberty and equality. It was the first charter of civil rights, the founding document of freedom. The stamp of Jefferson's peerless mind, his determination to secure liberty and his immense generosity towards his fellow men are apparent in the declaration's every word.

Elected to the new Virginia House of Delegates, Jefferson was determined to translate his ideals into practice in Virginia's new constitution. He secured the abolition of primogeniture and entail. He tried in vain to introduce a scheme of universal education but later succeeded in founding the University of Virginia, which he considered among his greatest achievements. A deist himself, Jefferson pushed through a statute for religious freedom that established the complete separation of church and state, a division that lies at the very core of American democracy. Yet he was not physically brave: no hero of the War of Independence, he notoriously fled his post at the approach of the British when we was governor of Virginia. Nor was he above personal vendettas. Humiliated by the power of his rival Alexander Hamilton, the treasury secretary while Jefferson was secretary of state under Washington, he disapproved of Hamilton's conservative instincts as well as his brash grandiloquence, secretly coordinating a vicious campaign to blacken Hamilton's name and destroy his career. Retiring to his grand estate at Monticello, he awaited his moment to win the presidency. His Republican faction disapproved of Hamilton's state-building, which the radical Jefferson feared would lead to monarchy.

Jefferson's passionate belief in freedom at times made his liberalism somewhat anarchic. 'Was ever such a prize won with so little blood?' he asked during the early years of the French Revolution. He earned a reputation as a demagogic radical, but as the third president of the United States from 1801 Jefferson showed restraint and sensitivity in preventing the ideological schism that threatened to fracture the infant nation. 'We are all Republicans – we are all Federalists,' he declared at his inauguration.

The Republican Jefferson believed government's paramount duty was to protect the individual's right to 'life, and liberty, and the pursuit of happiness'. He deplored the Federalists' readiness to curtail civil rights in the supposed interests of the nation. But the presidency of the Federalist John Adams was disastrous and the Federalists disintegrated, allowing Jefferson to win the 1800 election. His rival Hamilton was later killed by vice president Aaron Burr in a duel.

As president, Jefferson played the ascetic citizen-leader while embracing the executive powers he had earlier denounced passionately. In one of the first acts of his presidency in 1801, Thomas Jefferson refused to pay the pirate state of Tripoli the extortionate tribute it demanded in return for safe passage of American ships on the high seas. In so doing, he sent America for the first time into combat against an Islamic power in the Middle East.

Nominally vassals of the Ottoman empire, but in reality independent states run by corsair dynasties, the regencies of Algiers, Tunis and Tripoli were known, along with the sultanate of Morocco, as the Barbary States. Unashamedly piratical, they existed very profitably on the revenue garnered from slave trading, looting, tribute and ransom.

The ships of the newly independent United States, now lacking British naval protection, were prime targets. Only substantial tributes could secure them some relief. By 1801 America was paying out 20 per cent of her annual federal revenue to the pirate states. When Jefferson assumed the presidency, he was determined to prove that war was preferable to tribute and ransom.

The Karamanli dynasty of Tripoli ruled what is now Libya. Pasha Yusuf Karamanli defied American power: 'I do not fear war, it is my trade.' Prospects initially looked bleak. In October 1803 the USS *Philadelphia* was shipwrecked and its crew taken captive by Tripoli. Infiltrating Tripoli harbour in February 1804, a daring young officer named Stephen Decatur set fire to the Philadelphia and thwarted the corsairs' hopes of turning the pride of the US fleet into a pirate ship. But his attempts to blow up Tripoli's fleet backfired, killing eleven US servicemen.

The erstwhile US consul to Tunis, William Eaton, managed almost single-handedly to reverse the fortunes of war. A maverick, educated at the elite Dartmouth College, fluent in Greek and Latin, a veteran of the Indian wars who could throw a knife with deadly precision from eighty feet, Eaton fulminated at the prospect of 'bartering our national glory for the forbearance of a Barbary pirate'. He proposed conquering Tunis with a force of 1000 marines. Then he suggested ways of enforcing regime change in Libya. The US secretary of state rejected both proposals.

Eaton acted unilaterally instead. He recruited a Karamanli prince, Hamet, in Egypt, and with nine marines and a mercenary force of 400 he led his motley troop of Arabs and Christians on a 500-mile desert march to launch a surprise attack on Tripoli's second-largest city, Derna (modern Darnah). In the fierce pitched battle that ensued, Eaton and Hamet emerged triumphant. But Eaton's plans to make good his coup and march on Tripoli were thwarted. The pasha hastily offered the USA a treaty, which US naval officials immediately negotiated. Hamet was sent back to Egypt. Deeply disappointed, Eaton returned to America – a renegade hero whose role in American history has never been fully acknowledged.

Jefferson's Louisiana Purchase of 1803 nearly doubled the size of the United States. This bold move, seizing on Napoleon's un-expected offer to sell French territory, was a decision taken (as Jefferson freely admitted) without constitutional authority. It was an act that secured America's stability and created what Jefferson called an 'empire for liberty'. It also earned him a landslide election to a second term as president.

The man who declared that 'all men are created equal' has been censured for his racial attitudes. Jefferson was an opponent of slavery in principle, yet he owned large numbers of slaves on his Virginian plantation. His only book, Notes on Virginia, revealed in its discussion of slavery a deep opposition to racial mixing and at times a surprising degree of racism.

Jefferson recognized his fundamental hypocrisy, based on an irreconcilable opposition between justice and self-preservation. 'We have the wolf by the ears,' he remarked of slavery to a friend, 'and we can neither hold him nor safely let him go.' Jefferson, who promoted his own Republican virtues, was no less anxious to shield his private life from posterity than from his contemporaries, but what we know of it shows the confusion of his attitudes. It has only recently been revealed that while ambassador to France (1785–9) Jefferson began a long relationship with his slave Sally Hemings (who was the half-sister of his beloved deceased wife Martha).

Jefferson's energy and creativity were phenomenal. He knew French, Italian, Spanish, Latin, Greek and Anglo-Saxon. At seventy-one he read Plato in the original (he thought it overrated). He collated Native American dialects. He was a keen archaeologist who pioneered new methods of excavation on the Indian burial mounds on his estate, and an oenophile who promoted the establishment of American vineyards. He smuggled back plants and seeds from his travels to enrich his new country. He invented a swivel chair and an early form of automatic door. He was a magnificent architect: his own constructions – the University of Virginia and his Virginian estate of Monticello – are now World Heritage Sites. His library, which he left to the American nation, became the Library of Congress.

At the White House President Jefferson greeted guests in his slippers. The 'sage of Monticello' welcomed visitors, only occasionally escaping to his retreat at Poplar Forest for the solitude he craved. All America wanted to sit at the feet of the republican radical who had proved himself America's greatest architect. He died on 4 July 1826, the fiftieth anniversary of the day the Declaration of Independence promulgated freedom across the world.

TOUSSAINT LOUVERTURE

c.1743–1803

The Spartacus ... whose destiny it was to avenge the wrongs committed on his race.

Comte de Lavaux, the French governor-general of
Saint-Domingue, describing Toussaint

Toussaint Louverture was the founding father of Haiti. A plantation slave himself, he won his own freedom and went on to help emancipate hundreds of thousands of others and to found the world's first black state. He was a skilful politician and general who led the Haitian revolution from the early 1790s and drove the mighty European powers of France, Spain and Britain out of Haiti. Though at times his enemies found him harsh and uncompromising, he left behind a nation free from slavery and transformed by his enlightened leadership.

Toussaint once said, 'I was born a slave, but nature gave me a soul of a free man.' His early years demonstrated this perfectly. He was born François Dominique Toussaint to a father who had been shipped by French slave traders to Saint-Domingue (the French colony, later called Haiti, occupying the western third of the island of Hispaniola). Toussaint rose swiftly through the ranks of service under his owner, the Comte de Bréda. Naturally intelligent and fortunate enough to acquire a basic education in French and Latin, he rejected the voodoo beliefs of many of his fellow slaves and remained an ardent Catholic all his life. By 1777 he had served as a livestock handler, healer and coachman, finally becoming Bréda's plantation steward, a post normally reserved for a white man.

Toussaint won his freedom at the age of thirty-four and there-after farmed a plot of fifteen acres with thirteen slaves of his own. The first uprising of the Haitian revolution broke out under the mulatto reformer Vincent Ogé in 1790, but Toussaint took no part. In August 1791 another revolt erupted as thousands of black slaves across Saint-Domingue rose in rebellion. Toussaint realized that this larger rising could not be ignored. After helping Bréda's family to escape and sending his own family to safety on the Spanish side of the island, he joined the rebel ranks.

There were more than half a million slaves on Saint-Domingue, compared to just 32,000 European colonists and 24,000 *affran-chis* (freed mulattoes and blacks). Although the black army was a ragtag and ill-equipped bunch, their superior numbers and Toussaint's brilliant drilling in guerrilla tactics soon told. He gained the surname Louverture in recognition of his brilliant generalship (*l'ouverture* being 'the opening' or, in military terms, 'the breakthrough').

In 1793 war broke out between France and Spain. By this time Toussaint was a major figure in the black Haitian army. His leadership was widely admired and he had attracted talented allies such as Jean-Jacques Dessalines and Henry Christophe, both future leaders of Haiti. Toussaint joined the Spanish and served with distinction in a series of engagements.

The following year the pressure told on the French and the

revolutionary government in Paris declared an end to slavery. In what has been seen by some as an underhand about-turn against his former allies, Toussaint abandoned the Spanish and declared his new allegiance to France. The French governor of Saint-Domingue, the Comte de Lavaux, appointed him lieutenant-governor and the Spanish were expelled.

By 1795 Toussaint was widely seen as a hero. The freed blacks adored him, while the whites and mulattoes respected his hard but fair line on the economy, in which he allowed the return of émigré planters and used military discipline to force idlers to work. Favouring racial reconciliation between blacks and whites, he held the firm belief that – despite their history of oppression, enslavement and persecution – his country's blacks could learn valuable lessons from white people. His personal popularity and political shrewdness allowed him to outlast a succession of French governors.

His political cunning was in evidence in 1798–9, when after a series of secret negotiations Toussaint negotiated a British withdrawal from Haiti. The political settlement allowed Toussaint to sell sugar and buy arms and goods. He undertook not to invade British territories such as Jamaica but rejected their offer of conferring on him the title king of Haiti – all his life he maintained that he was a true French citizen.

In 1801 Toussaint invaded the Spanish side of Hispaniola, over-running the entire island, freeing the Spanish slaves and surprising the defeated non-blacks with his magnanimity in victory. He declared himself governor-general and strove to convince Napoleon of his loyalty.

Napoleon, however, was not to be convinced. He considered Toussaint an obstacle to the profitability of Haiti and an affront to the honour of France. In December 1801 Napoleon sent a powerful invading force under his brother-in-law General Charles

Leclerc (accompanied by Napoleon's nymphomaniacal sister Pauline) to depose Toussaint.

Months of heavy fighting ended in May 1802, when Toussaint agreed to lay down his arms and retire to his farm. But he was not allowed to remain in his beloved country. He and his family were arrested and Toussaint was taken in a warship to France, where he was transferred in August to Fort-de-Joux in the Alps. Heartbroken and alone in a tiny dungeon, he wrote letters begging Napoleon for a fair trial. Napoleon never answered, and Toussaint died of pneumonia in 1803. It was a sad end to a great life, but his legacy – the Free Black Republic of Haiti – lived on.

JOHN PAUL JONES

1747–1792

I have drawn my sword in the . . . struggle for the rights of men . . . I am not in arms as an American, nor am I in pursuit of riches . . . I profess myself a citizen of the world.
John Paul Jones, 4 August 1785, as he restored to the Earl of Selkirk a silver plate he had taken in a raid on the Kirkcudbright-shire coast seven years previously

The founder of the US Navy and a maverick fighting admiral, John Paul Jones had the rambunctious, ruthless energy to change the course of a sea battle and emerge victorious. His successes during the American War of Independence may not have been strategically decisive, but they gave the Americans confidence in the strength of their own sea power and earned Jones his reputation as the first hero of the American navy.

John Paul (as he was born) spent his boyhood in Scotland. At the age of 13 he was apprenticed to a merchant ship and sailed across he Atlantic to the Caribbean and the eastern seaboard of North America a number of times, at least twice on board slavers. He was an able and tough seaman, and his toughness sometimes got him into trouble: in 1770 he was accused of flogging a sailor so severely that he later died, and in 1773 he killed the ringleader of a mutiny in self-defence. To evade the consequences he became a Freemason, moved to America and assumed the surname Jones.

In 1766, following the outbreak of the American War of Independence, Jones fought against the British first on board the USS *Alfred*, then as commander of the 21-gun sloop *Providence*, conveying men and supplies from New England to New York and Philadelphia. His success in this, and in capturing and burning British prizes, led to his promotion to captain. He was sent to Europe in command of the Ranger, to take the war to the enemy's home waters.

Throughout the spring of 1778 Jones and his men harassed the English coast. Moving north, they raided the peninsula in Kirkcudbright Bay known as St Mary's Isle, part of the estate of the Earl of Selkirk in southwest Scotland, near to his own birthplace. When his crew demanded plunder, Jones politely relieved the Countess of Selkirk of a silver plate with the family crest. Seven years later, when the opportunity arose, he returned it.

Following this episode, Jones sailed across the Irish Sea and captured the Royal Navy ship *Drake*, which he carried to France. Benjamin Franklin, the American diplomat stationed in Paris, rewarded him with com- mand of the *Bonhomme Richard*, a much larger ship than the *Ranger*. Accompanied by four smaller ships, the *Bonhomme Richard* sailed for Britain, and on 23 September 1779 the American squadron intercepted two Royal Navy ships guarding a merchant convoy off Flamborough Head.

It was a confusing and hair-raising battle, lasting three and a half hours. At one point during the fight, the American ensign on the *Bonhomme Richard* was shot away. The captain of the Royal Navy frigate Serapis asked whether the *Bonhomme Richard* had struck its colours as a sign of surrender, but was disabused when Jones, with legendary defiance, shouted 'I have not yet begun to fight!'

The *Bonhomme Richard* had its mainmast blown away and was holed below the waterline, but Jones managed to manoeuvre his battered ship alongside the Serapis, boarding and capturing it. Shortly afterwards his own ship sank. The other Royal Navy ship, the *Countess of Scarborough*, was also captured. Jones took his prizes back to the Netherlands and on to France, where he was hailed as a hero, awarded with the Ordre du mérite militaire and presented by Louis XVI with a gold-plated sword. Back in America, Congress passed a vote of thanks, and Jones took the only American ship of the line, the America, back to France.

The War of Independence over, Jones was engaged by the Russian empress, Catherine the Great, as a rear-admiral in the Russian navy to serve under her partner in love and power, Prince Potemkin, who in 1788 placed Jones in command of the ships-of-the-line squadron in his new Black Sea Russian fleet. Jones helped achieve a crushing vic- tory in which 15 Turkish vessels were destroyed and 4700 Turks killed or captured. Russian losses were minimal. Jones helped blockade the Turkish fortress at Ochakov, enabling Prince Potemkin to capture it. Despite the intrigues of jealous rivals and Potemkin's irritation, Jones was hailed as a hero and awarded the Order of St Anne by Catherine.

In 1789 Jones took advantage of a two-year leave of absence from the Russian navy to tour the major European cities, ending up in Paris in 1790. There he remained, in retirement, until his death two years later.

TALLEYRAND

1754–1838

It seems to me that one will do him no injustice in accepting him for what he claimed to be: the type, the representative, of the times in which he lived. But, good God! What times!

Baron de Vitrolles

Talleyrand was the undisputed grand master of diplomacy. Undeniably venal, sexually promiscuous, supposedly amoral in character and capable of ruthlessness in pursuit of his goals, but also charming and witty, Talleyrand was surprisingly consistent in his views. A champion of tolerance and liberalism, in government he advocated an English-style constitutional monarchy, in international affairs a balance of power and the rule of law. He remained all his life a dedicated enemy of power that was founded on conquest and force.

Born into an ancient noble family, Charles-Maurice de Talleyrand-Périgord was destined for the Church as a result of a 'dislocated foot', a disability that also prompted his parents to effectively disinherit him in favour of his younger brother. Talleyrand learned early on that charm and wiliness could more than compensate for his club foot.

Talleyrand seemed able to flourish in every circumstance. As the successful, if supremely decadent, bishop of Autun, during the last years of Louis XVI (1754–93), he argued vigorously for the Church's privileges yet became the revolutionary clergyman who equally enthusiastically dismantled them. He was always a moderate. Through a timely departure abroad on diplomatic affairs

(1792), he escaped the guillotine's worst excesses, living in England and America. On returning to a less bloodthirsty France in 1796, he managed to refute charges of counter-revolutionary behaviour, became foreign minister (1797) and struck up an alliance with the rising General Napoleon Bonaparte, organizing his seizure of power. As foreign minister, Talleyrand went on to help design Napoleon's rise to the position of emperor of the French, serving as his grand chamberlain and becoming prince of Benevento. He played his part in some of Napoleon's excesses – notably the kidnapping and execution of the duke of Enghien and the disastrous Spanish adventure – but he grasped quickly that Napoleon's ambitions had become despotic and self-serving. Talleyrand, humiliated by the emperor who described him as 'excrement in a silk stocking', now worked to undermine him.

Above all, in an age dominated by war, Talleyrand wanted to secure peace and stability in Europe, even if the means involved mendacity and secret intrigues. At the 1808 Congress of Erfurt he secretly persuaded Russia to oppose Napoleon's European designs and henceforth helped Tsar Alexander I to overthrow Napoleon. (Talleyrand was also acting as matchmaker for Napoleon, brokering his marriage to Marie-Louise of Austria and securing a religious settlement with the pope.) On Napoleon's fall in 1814, Talleyrand supervised the capitulation of Paris, welcoming the conquering Alexander into his house, fostering the restoration of the Bourbon King Louis XVIII and forming a liberal ministry as premier.

Talleyrand's most audacious diplomacy, though, resulted in the 1815 Treaty of Vienna. Roundly defeated, and viewed in Europe as hopelessly aggressive and regicidal, France faced partition by the victorious allies. Talleyrand managed to gain France a place at the table and then fracture the anti-French alliance. The resulting treaty restored France to her 1792 borders, with no reparations to pay, effectively still a great power.

After Napoleon's brief resurgence and defeat at Waterloo in 1815, Talleyrand, now a prince, again became prime minister, advocating a liberal monarchy on the English model. Forced out by ultra-royalists, he remained a respected grandee until another revolution overturned the stubborn Bourbons in 1830. He then returned in triumph under the July Monarchy of King Louis-Philippe to become ambassador to London in 1830, the glorious culmination of a diplomatic career of over forty years.

A survivor through several, radically different regimes, Talleyrand nevertheless remained in some ways a defiant symbol of a way of life that had disappeared. 'No one who has not lived under the Ancien Régime,' he once murmured, 'will know how sweet life can be.' But those living in the France of Napoleon and the restored Bourbons who attended Talleyrand's daily semi-public lever – the last of its kind – were given a startling glimpse of the extraordinary pomp and precision of this vanished world.

Talleyrand devoted the first two hours of every morning to his lever – the serious business of rising. Like the monarchs of pre-revolutionary France, permanently surrounded by a horde of courtiers and onlookers watching and assisting his every move, Talleyrand made getting dressed a public event. His rooms were open to all who wished to attend – provided they were amusing, or at least furnished with up-to-date news and gossip.

Talleyrand's lever was an incomparable opportunity for networking and the exchange of information and repartee. Statesmen and society ladies, doctors, academics, financiers, on occasion the tsar of Russia, all were regular visitors to the prince's apartments. As 11 o'clock approached and men and women of all ages intrigued and debated the events of the day, Talleyrand limped into the room swathed in white flannel and nightcap, a mummified figure who slept in a bed with a deep hollow because he was terrified of falling out of it.

The elderly Courtiade, the most famous valet of the age, directed proceedings. Two junior valets dressed Talleyrand's long grey hair as he sat in a chair by the fire. A sponge in a silver bowl was brought to him. After he had wiped his face, Talleyrand's hat was immediately set upon his pomade-drenched locks.

The man who kept the best table in France confined himself to a breakfast of a single cup of camomile tea, followed by two cups of warm water which he inhaled through his nostrils and expelled through his mouth.

Dressed from the neck up, the seated figure then had his legs unwrapped. The 'dislocated foot' about which Talleyrand was so sensitive was unashamedly revealed; his long, flat left foot and the stunted, gnarled right one were washed and dried. Pursued by his valets as he then meandered around the room, signing letters, listening to newspaper articles and issuing a stream of his famously understated bon mots, Talleyrand was unswaddled and helped into an array of clothes that were almost equally bulky.

Two hours after he had first limped into the room, Talleyrand, clad in a mass of cravats and waistcoats and several pairs of stockings, allowed his valets to add the finishing touch: his breeches. Fully dressed, his paperwork done, gossip exchanged, filled in on the news of the day, Talleyrand was ready to face the world.

Talleyrand lived lavishly, courted bribes (offending the rather more correct American diplomats) and was exuberantly promiscuous, fathering at least four illegitimate children. He married a disreputable courtesan, enjoyed many affairs with an army of beauteous mistresses and his last love was his own niece, the duchess of Dino. When asked if he believed in Platonic friendship with women, he replied 'After; but not before.' But his principles were consistent. A co-author of the Declaration of the Rights of Man, he was a son of the Enlightenment who had praised its ideals since his seminary youth. His faith in a constitutional monarchy drove him to support the candidate who seemed most likely to secure it. This necessitated chameleon-like changes of alliance in the turbulence of revolutionary France and brought accusations of opportunistic treachery. When Talleyrand called brie the 'king of cheeses', a contemporary remarked that it was the only king that he had never betrayed! But he was hardly unique in his dissimulation. 'Treason,' he said, 'is just a matter of dates.'

Diplomatic to the last, on his deathbed Talleyrand was reconciled with the Church and received the last sacraments.

MOZART

1756–1791

I cannot write about Mozart. I can only worship him.
Richard Strauss

Born in Salzburg, Austria, Wolfgang Amadeus Mozart was the epitome of genius, a child prodigy who went on to become one of the most brilliant composers in the history of Western classical music. Leaping from one musical genre to the next, in his short life Mozart composed some of the greatest and most melodic compositions of all time.

As a child virtuoso on the keyboard Mozart was the musical wonder of his age, touring Europe's capitals and courts with his sister Nannerl under the direction of their father, Leopold, himself a musician who was quick to recognize his children's precocious talents. As both a fond parent and an assiduous publicist, Leopold dressed his children in the latest fashions and airily reported that: 'We keep company only with aristocrats and other distinguished persons.' Wolfgang began composing at the age of five, was a seasoned performer at seven, and had written his first symphony by eight. Of Mozart's early compositions, Leopold wrote with satisfaction, 'Imagine the noise these sonatas will make in the world when it says on the title page that they are the work of a child of seven.'

Even the sceptics realized that no trickery lay behind the child's precocity. By the still tender age of thirteen, Wolfgang was an artist of unrivalled musical understanding, of whom Johann Hasse (1699–1783), one of the era's eminent composers, was said to have remarked that 'he has done things which for such an age are really incomprehensible; they would be astonishing in an adult'.

Mozart's versatility was astounding. He wrote chamber music, operas, symphonies, masses; he virtually invented the solo piano concerto, and his use of counterpoint was as revelatory as his limpid melodies and subtle harmonic shifts. He composed with legendary speed – his magnificent 'Jupiter' symphony, No. 41 in C Major, was written in a mere sixteen days, and he reportedly composed the overture to his opera *Don Giovanni* on the night before the work premiered. The range of his genius only increased over the years – from the exuberant violin concerti of his teens, dazzling operas such as *The Marriage of Figaro* and *The Magic Flute*, and masterpieces in late Classical style such as the Clarinet Quintet from 1789. His death at thirty-five left the musical world with the perpetual enigma of what might have been, had this sublimely talented composer lived to old age.

Fellow composers never wavered in their recognition of his genius. To Josef Haydn (1732–1809), the musical elder statesman of the time, he was 'the greatest composer ... either in person or by name', while the 'magic sounds of Mozart's music' left Franz Schubert (1797–1828) awestruck. The public response was more capricious. Some judged his last three symphonies 'difficult', and other works were criticized for being 'audacious' or too complex. But he was held in high regard at the time of his death, and today layman and professional alike recognize what one conductor has described as 'the seriousness in his charm, the loftiness in his beauty'.

Mozart's princely patrons were less deferential. Perennially short of money, Mozart's frustration at his lack of independence and his pitiful wages often led to stormy relations. From 1773 he was engaged to compose at the Salzburg court, but in 1781, summoned to produce music for Emperor Joseph II's court in Vienna, he was angry to find himself in the role of a servant, with a correspondingly meagre salary. He angrily demanded his release, which was – as he wrote in a letter of June that year – granted 'with a kick on my arse . . . by order of our worthy Prince Archbishop'.

Throughout his life, Mozart displayed the same mix of playfulness and seriousness that shines through his music. He was an affectionate child, and his difficult relationship with his domineering father led him to constantly seek approval: visiting Vienna, the six-year-old Mozart apparently jumped into Empress Maria Theresa's lap for a hug. The adult Mozart, always physically small, retained this childlike manner in his wilful extravagance, his open and sometimes crude sexuality and the distinctive, scatological humour that had led the teenage Mozart to write to his first love: 'Now I wish a good night, shit into your bed until it creaks.'

The composer for whom, as he put it, composing was the only 'joy and passion' was no solitary genius. While in later years his relationship with his father deteriorated, his love for his wife, Constanze, was abiding – despite Leopold's disapproval. Nevertheless, after Leopold's death in 1787 Mozart, now permanently in Vienna, went through a period when he composed less. Fearing poverty, he produced a stream of begging letters to patrons, acquaintances and his fellow Freemasons. While never destitute, Mozart had to rely on income from teaching and performances of his works. He lived beyond his means, having a weakness for fashionable clothes while also paying off debts to friends and publishers.

Mozart's last composition, the Requiem that became his own, is surrounded by mystery. Legend has it that Salieri, a jealous fellow composer, poisoned Mozart as he worked frantically on this composition, which had been anonymously commissioned by letter. But an acute attack of rheumatic fever (and a noble patron intent on passing off Mozart's compositions as his own) is probably nearer the truth. Even so, Mozart's modest burial – although not quite the pauper's of repute – sealed the myth of the neglected genius.

ROBESPIERRE

1758–1794

That man will go far, he believes everything he says.
Comte de Mirabeau on Robespierre at the outset of
the Revolution

Maxmilien Robespierre was the prototype for the modern European dictator: his sanctimonious vision of republican virtue and terror, and the brutal slaughter he unleashed in its name, were studied reverently by the Russian Bolsheviks and helped inspire the totalitarian mass killings of the 20th century. Known as the Sea-green Incorruptible, his name has become a byword for the fatal purity and degenerate corruption of the Reign of Terror which followed the French Revolution of 1789 and climaxed with the execution of King Louis XVI on 21 January 1793. The Terror illustrated not only the corrupt dangers of utopian monopolies of 'virtue', but how ultimately such witch hunts consume their own children.

Born in the Artois region of northern France, Robespierre's family was financially secure, but his childhood was not a happy one. His father was a drunk and his mother died when he was just six. Nonetheless, the young Maximilien won a place to study law at the prestigious Lycée Louis-le-Grand in Paris and soon made his name as a populist, defending the poor against the rich.

Like many of the other young professionals who were to drive the French Revolution – such as the fanatical lawyer Louis de Saint-Just (later nicknamed the angel of death) or the radical journalist Jean-Paul Marat – Robespierre eagerly absorbed the theories of the Swiss philosopher Jean-Jacques Rousseau, whose notion of a 'social contract' held that a government had to be based on the will of the people to be truly legitimate.

Although fussy about his appearance, often wearing the powdered wigs associated with the profligate aristocrats of *ancien régime* France, Robespierre – with his weak voice, small stature and pallid complexion – did not cut an imposing figure. But as the comte de Mirabeau said of him at the outset of the Revolution: 'That man will go far; he believes everything he says.'

In the wake of the storming of the Bastille in July 1789, the event that triggered the Revolution, Robespierre aligned himself politically with the far left. As the representative for Artois in the Constituent Assembly, set up in July 1789 to decide on a new constitution, he became closely involved with the radical faction called the Jacobins, rivals of the more moderate Girondins. His ideas gained a sympathetic hearing among the Parisian bourgeoisie, and he rose swiftly, in 1791 becoming public accuser (giving him the power of life and death over all citizens, without recourse to trial or appeal) and then first deputy for Paris a year later.

An implacable paranoia about potential enemies of the

Revolution haunted him and in December 1792, when Louis XVI was brought to trial, Robespierre – a fierce critic of the king – insisted that 'Louis must die, so that the country may live.'

Above all, it was as a leading member of the Committee of Public Safety that Robespierre forged his bloody reputation. Set up by the National Convention in April 1793, this was a revolutionary tribunal invested with unlimited dictatorial powers. Robespierre was elected a member in July 1793 and swiftly instigated the so-called Terror. Tens of thousands of 'traitors' – ostensibly those who had expressed sympathy with the monarchy or who thought the Jacobins had gone too far in their relentless pursuit of 'enemies of the people' – were rounded up without trial and lost their heads on the guillotine. In reality, anyone Robespierre counted an enemy was liquidated, the apparatus of the state ruthlessly employed to silence them. Robespierre himself personally ensured that his rivals Georges Danton and Camille Desmoulins were executed in April 1794.

Robespierre and his allies turned their attention to growing opposition to the Revolution in Lyon, Marseilles and the rural Vendée in western France. After more than 100,000 men, women and children had been systematically murdered on Robespierre's orders the revolutionary general François Joseph Westermann wrote in a letter to the Committee: 'There is no more Vendée. I crushed the children under the feet of the horses, massacred the women ... exterminated. The roads are sown with corpses.' For Robespierre, revolutionary virtue and the Terror went hand in hand. As he put it in February 1794: 'If the spring of popular government in time of peace is virtue, the springs of popular government in revolution are at once virtue and terror: virtue, without which terror is fatal; terror, without which virtue is powerless.'

Increasingly alienated by his tyranny, the National Convention turned decisively against him when he accused them of a conspiracy to oust him. A warrant was issued for his arrest and he retreated to his power base at the Hôtel de Ville in Paris. As troops entered the building to seize him, Robespierre, surrounded by his henchmen Georges Couthon, Louis de Saint-Just, Philippe Le Bas, and François Hanriot, tried to commit suicide but instead shot himself in the mouth, leaving his jaw hanging off. Bleeding heavily, and howling in agony, he was quickly taken away and finished off at the guillotine, suffering the fate of so many of his opponents before him.

Some see Robespierre as one of the founding fathers of social democracy, his revolutionary excesses occasioned by his championing the cause of the people. Many more though view him as a hypocritical despot whose terror was the precursor of the totalitarian butchery of Hitler and Stalin in modern times.

NELSON

1758–1805

Before this time tomorrow, I shall have gained a peerage, or Westminster Abbey.
Horatio Nelson, on the eve of the Battle of the Nile (1798)

Horatio Nelson was one of the most daring naval commanders in history, who, through a series of stunning victories, assured British supremacy at sea during the Revolutionary and Napoleonic Wars. He was adored in his own day, despite a complicated and very public love life, and has been celebrated ever since as the man who, by defeating the French and Spanish fleets off Cape Trafalgar in 1805, saved Britain from invasion. His death at the moment of victory wins him a special place in the pantheon of British military heroes.

When Nelson was thirteen, his uncle, a naval captain, took him to sea aboard the *Raisonnable*. For the next eight years Nelson learned the trade of a naval officer in the West Indies and on an expedition to the Arctic. He first saw action in the American War of Independence, and by the age of twenty-one he was captain of the frigate *Hinchinbrooke*. He was brave and often impatient; this endeared him to some but could make him unpopular.

When war broke out with Revolutionary France in 1793 Nelson was sent to the Mediterranean. He lost his right eye during the siege of Calvi in 1794, having been hit in the face by stones thrown up by enemy shot. In March 1795, as captain of the sixty-four-gun *Agamemnon*, he took a leading role in taking two French ships. The arrival of Sir John Jervis as commander-in-chief of the Mediterranean fleet was very useful to Nelson, for Jervis gave him free rein to exploit his natural abilities as a leader. During the Battle of Cape St Vincent, Nelson was at the head of the boarding party that took the Spanish ship *San Nicolas* and then the larger *San Josef*. It was unprecedented for an officer of Nelson's rank to throw himself into the heat of battle in such a manner, and he lapped up the public admiration that followed his success, along with the knighthood and promotion to rear admiral.

Despite Nelson's personal fame, morale amongst the ordinary seamen of the Royal Navy was low, and 1797 saw mutinies in British waters. Nelson was given command of the *Theseus* and once again led raiding parties from the front, dragging his crew's spirits up by sheer force of character – something that became known as the Nelson Touch. While attempting to storm the town of Santa Cruz, Tenerife, Nelson was seriously wounded, and his right arm had to be amputated. In 1798 he won a stunning victory over the French fleet at the Battle of the Nile. Although massively outgunned, the British fleet blew up the massive 120-gun *L'Orient* and took or sunk ten more ships of the line and two frigates. 'Victory is not enough to describe such a scene,' wrote Nelson, soon to be Baron Nelson of the Nile. All of Europe was watching, and the anti-French coalition was boosted immensely by the performance of the Royal Navy.

Between 1798 and 1800 Nelson spent much of his time in Sicily in the arms of Emma, Lady Hamilton, a liaison that caused great scandal, as the young Emma Hamilton was married to the elderly British envoy to Naples. Lady Hamilton bore Nelson a child in 1801, on the same day that Nelson learned he was to be posted as second-in-command of the British fleet off the coast of Denmark. In April the British demolished the Danish fleet at Copenhagen. During the battle, when his commander, Vice Admiral Parker, raised a flagged signal for a withdrawal, Nelson famously ignored the order by placing his telescope to his blind eye.

Nelson was made a viscount, and in 1803 he was sent back to the Mediterranean as commander-in-chief of the fleet there. Much of 1804 was spent chasing the French fleet back and forth across the Atlantic – a pursuit that captivated the British public. On his return to London, he was mobbed in the street wherever he went.

In 1805 Nelson achieved his apotheosis. On 21 October he engaged the combined French and Spanish fleets, under his archenemy Admiral Villeneuve, off Cape Trafalgar. He took twenty-seven ships to engage thirty-three enemy vessels, signalling by flag to his own men 'England expects that every man will do his duty.' Five hours of fighting began at noon, and, thanks to Nelson's bold and ingenious tactics, by 5 p.m. the British were comprehensively victorious. But early in the battle Nelson had been hit by a musket shot, which punctured his lung and lodged in his spine. He died at 4.30 p.m., allegedly whispering to a comrade officer, 'Kiss me, Hardy.'

WELLINGTON

1769–1852

Nothing except a battle lost can be half so melancholy as a battle won.

Duke of Wellington, in a dispatch from Waterloo (June 1815)

Arthur Wellesley, duke of Wellington, was one of the ablest generals of his age, and – with Oliver Cromwell, Admiral Nelson and the duke of Marlborough – stands among the greatest British military leaders of all time. His victory over Napoleon at the Battle of Waterloo, which he described as 'a damned nice thing – the closest run thing you ever saw', was a clash of the two most brilliant European generals of their day.

Wellesley, who was born in Dublin to an Anglo-Irish aristocrat, the earl of Mornington, was not an exceptional young man, intellectually or physically. He gave up his one striking talent, for playing the violin, in 1793, burning his instrument in a fit of melodrama. He entered the army and relied on the patronage of his more successful eldest brother to rise through the officer ranks to the position of lieutenant colonel and head of his regiment.

Wellesley went to India in 1797, studying books on war and military tactics during the long voyage. The effort paid off. In 1802 he confronted a force of 50,000 French-led Maratha soldiers at Assaye. Through an unconventional choice of field positions and brave leadership in a bloody battle, Wellesley won against imposing odds. He later called it the finest thing he had ever done in the fighting line.

Returning home in 1805, Wellesley was knighted, married the short-sighted, timid Kitty Pakenham (with whom he was never happy) and was sent for brief stints of duty in Denmark and Ireland, where he distinguished himself further. But it was his departure to fight the French on the Iberian Peninsula in 1808 that almost ended his career: frustrated by shared commands with inept generals, he rashly signed a treaty with the French without reading its foolish terms. He was hauled before an inquiry and criticized – but survived to advise the secretary of war, Viscount Castlereagh, on how he would wage cheap but effective war. Castlereagh gave him the job that marked the start of Wellesley's ascent to greatness.

Here, the British army had enough men to conduct defensive campaigns, and even to besiege large towns and castles, but insufficient strength to take advantage of these successes. He defeated the French at Talavera (for which he received a peerage, becoming Viscount Wellington), and managed to defend Lisbon from French attack by secretly building a network of fortifications. Despite a succession of British victories, at Vimeiro, Busaco, Almeida and elsewhere, Viscount Wellington was often frustrated in his ambitions to press on from Portugal into Spain.

By 1812 things had improved. Wellington fought his way to Madrid and persuaded the Spanish government to appoint him *generalissimo* of its own armies. By 1814 the French had been pushed back to their own border and he invaded Napoleon's own country. Wellington made sure his armies were better organized and better supplied than the French. He imposed superior discipline on his troops, and he did his best to respect the religion and property of the Spanish people, valuable lessons learned in India. He described his troops as 'the scum of the earth'. He had defeated Marshal Massena, perhaps the finest French general, but had never faced Napoleon himself and hoped he would never have to do so.

By now Wellington was the most famous man in England. He

had won a dukedom, the ambassadorship to France, and the role as British representative at the Congress of Vienna. He was the recipient of honours from governments of Europe. But in 1815 he was to face the ultimate test of his military mettle.

Napoleon, who had abdicated and then been exiled to Elba in 1814, had escaped and begun to rally troops around him. Wellington was the only man in Europe considered worthy enough to command the allied forces against the emperor as he plotted to attack the Low Countries. Wellington was unimpressed by his own combined forces, calling them 'an infamous army, very weak and ill equipped'. He also had little knowledge of Napoleon's plans for the battlefield and was taken aback when French troops began to move on 15 June 1815. 'Napoleon has humbugged me, by God!' he exclaimed; but when the two armies met on 18 June, Wellington had arranged his forces into a defensive formation that was to prove extremely resilient against the waves of bludgeoning French attacks that Napoleon launched.

Throughout the long, hard battle, Wellington remained calm, though his Prussian reinforcements, under Marshal Blücher, arrived late and virtually every man of his personal staff was killed or wounded. 'I never took so much trouble about any battle, and was never so near being beat,' he wrote afterwards. But this victory, his last, was resounding, and Wellington was lauded right across the continent.

As a commander, Wellington was distinguished by his acute intelligence, sangfroid, planning and flexibility but also by his loathing for the suffering of battle. As a man, he was sociable, enjoying close friendships with female friends and a long line of affairs with high-born ladies and low-born courtesans, including a notorious French actress whom he shared with Napoleon himself. When one such courtesan threatened him with exposure, he replied: 'Publish and be damned.'

After Waterloo, Wellington's prestige gave him great influence on government. By the 1820s he had been drawn into partisan politics, not his natural territory, although he was at heart a Tory and a reactionary. He served, with difficulty, as prime minister (1828–30), but he secured an agreement on Catholic emancipation – political representation for Catholics, especially important for Ireland. However, his opposition to the clamour for parliamentary reform led him to resign the premiership. He was briefly prime minister again in 1834, holding every secretaryship in the government. In 1842 he resumed his position as commander-in-chief of the British army, a post he held until his death.

A million and a half people turned out to see his funeral cortège make its way to St Paul's Cathedral in 1852. 'The last great Englishman is low', wrote the poet laureate Alfred Tennyson.

NAPOLEON I

1769–1821

Napoleon was a man! His life was the stride of a demi-god.
Johann Wolfgang von Goethe, *Conversations with Eckermann*
(1828)

Napoleon Bonaparte bestrode his era like a colossus. No one man had aspired to create an empire of such a magnitude since the days of Alexander the Great and Charlemagne. Napoleon's ambition stretched from Russia and Egypt in the east to Portugal and Britain in the west, and even though he did not succeed to quite this extent, his brilliant generalship brought Spain, the Low Countries, Switzerland, Italy and much of Germany under French domination – albeit at the cost of two decades of war and some 6 million dead. Although his enemies regarded him as a tyrant – and indeed much about his rule was oppressive – Napoleon introduced to mainland Europe many of the liberal and rational values of the Enlightenment, such as the metric system of weights and measures, religious toleration, the idea of national self-determination, and the Napoleonic Code of civil law. He was the quintessential autocrat but he was tolerant of all beliefs and ideas, provided he enjoyed political control. He did not – with a few exceptions – abuse his power. He lacked malice and he was certainly no mass-murdering sadistic dictator in the mode of the 20th century. Yet millions died for the sake of his personal ambition in the wars that he promoted.

After an unruly childhood, a youthful military education, and service in his native Corsica during the French Revolution, Napoleon rose to prominence as an artillery expert in the defence of the town of Toulon against the British in 1793. Two years later he was in Paris, taking command of the artillery against a counter-revolutionary uprising. He boasted that he cleared the streets with 'the whiff of grapeshot'.

In 1796 Napoleon led a French army into Italy, driving the Austrians out of Lombardy, annexing several of the Papal States, then pushing on into Austria, forcing her to sue for peace. The resulting treaty won France most of northern Italy, the Low Countries and the Rhineland. Napoleon followed this up by seizing Venice.

Napoleon was now regarded as the potential saviour of France, and he ensured that the republic was reliant on his personal power within the army. The government welcomed the respite when Napoleon sailed to Egypt to bolster French interests there at the expense of the British. In the campaign of 1798–9 he seized Malta, then defeated an Egyptian force four times as large as his own at the Battle of the Pyramids. Though the French navy lost control of the Mediterranean after Nelson's victory at the

Battle of the Nile, Napoleon pushed through Egypt into Syria, until his army succumbed to disease. The failure to take Acre marked the end of the war. In his advance and retreat, he showed his ruthless ambition: he massacred Ottoman prisoners and as he retreated, he ordered his doctors to kill some of his own wounded. Even though his dirty little Middle Eastern war had been a disaster, he abandoned his army and returned to France presenting the adventure as a success – indeed his tales of exotic glory now propelled him to power.

In 1799 Napoleon seized control of France in the Coup of 18 Brumaire. As first consul, he improved the road and sewerage systems and reformed education, taxes, banking and, most importantly, the law code. The Napoleonic Code unified and transformed the legal system of France, replacing old feudal customs with a systematized national structure and establishing the rule of law as fundamental to the state.

In 1804 Napoleon crowned himself Emperor of the French, ostensibly to prevent the Bourbon monarchy from ever being re-established. His plan to invade Britain – which was funding his European enemies – was thwarted by Nelson's destruction of Napoleon's navy at Trafalgar. However, on land Napoleon seemed invulnerable, defeating the Austrians, Russians and Prussians in a series of stunning victories at Ulm (1805), Austerlitz (1805) and Jena (1806), ending the alliance of these powers with Britain and establishing the Confederation of the Rhine as a French satellite in much of Germany. The emperors of Austria and Russia, the king of Prussia all bowed before his power: only Britain held out against him.

After this, Napoleon began to overreach himself. He made his brothers into kings, his marshals into princes. In 1808 he imposed his brother Joseph (who had first been king of Naples) as king of Spain, provoking the Spanish to revolt. The British sent troops to support the Spanish, and for the next few years many French troops were tied up on the Iberian Peninsula fighting the Spanish and a British army under Wellington

He had married Josephine de Beauharnais, the widow of a French aristocrat, for love – but she had failed to give him an heir. He divorced her and hoped to marry a sister of the Russian Tsar Alexander I – a match both prestigious and politic, since the security of his precarious empire depended on his personal friendship with the tsar, as agreed at Tilsit. But Alexander, initially dazzled by Napoleon, was no longer so impressed: Russia was turning against French dominance. Alexander refused the marriage – and Napoleon instead married Grand Duchess Marie-Louise, the Habsburg daughter of Austrian Emperor Francis. She gave him a son, Napoleon, the king of Rome. But the Russians began to withdraw from Napoleon's blockade of Britain.

In 1812 Napoleon amassed the *Grande Armée* of around 600,000 men to march on Russia. It was his moment of hubris. The Russians avoided engagement and retreated deep into the interior, implementing a scorched-earth policy as they went. When the Russians finally made a stand outside Moscow, at the Battle of Borodino, it was one of the bloodiest encounters in history. Though he took Moscow, Napoleon could not force the Russians to the negotiating table, and, with its lines of supply drastically over-extended, the Grande Armée was obliged to retreat through the bitter cold of the Russian winter. Only 40,000 men made it back to France.

Heartened by Napoleon's humiliation, the other European powers formed a new alliance against the French. The allies defeated Napoleon's forces in Spain and at Leipzig, taking Paris in 1814 and exiling Napoleon to the island of Elba.

But Napoleon was not done. Escaping from Elba in 1815, he made a triumphant progress north through France to Paris, telling the troops sent to stop him, 'If any man would shoot his emperor, he may do so now.' His old generals and their armies rallied round him, but the glorious Hundred Days of his restoration came to an end on 18 June 1815 near the little settlement of Waterloo in what is now Belgium. As the duke of Wellington, the British commander, conceded, it was 'the closest run thing'; but Napoleon's defeat was decisive.

The emperor was exiled to St Helena in the South Atlantic, dying of stomach cancer in 1821. Later, when Wellington was asked whom he reckoned to have been the best general ever, he answered: 'In this age, in past ages, in any age, Napoleon.'

BEETHOVEN

1770–1827

> *Sweet sounds, oh, beautiful music, do not cease!*
> *Reject me not into the world again.*
> *With you alone is excellence and peace,*
> *Mankind made plausible, his purpose plain.*
>
> Edna St Vincent Millay, 'On Hearing a
> Symphony of Beethoven' (1928)

Ludwig van Beethoven's music encompassed the transition between the Classical and Romantic styles, and his astounding contribution was all the more remarkable for being completed against the background of the encroaching deafness that plagued the last thirty years of his life. His nine symphonies raised the genre of orchestral music to a grand level, while his late-period string quartets and piano sonatas are some of the most transcendent achievements in classical music.

Born in Bonn, Germany, Beethoven was of Flemish descent. Both his father, Johann van Beethoven, and grandfather worked as court singers to the elector-archbishop of Bonn. Unfortunately, however, his father was also an alcoholic, who attempted to raise the family fortunes by touting his second son Ludwig as a child prodigy, somewhat unsuccessfully.

Unlike Mozart, Beethoven's genius took time to flower fully. Nevertheless, by the age of nine he was receiving composition lessons from Christian Gottlob Neefe, court organist at Bonn, becoming official assistant organist by the age of fourteen. Around this time Beethoven travelled to Vienna, and it is likely that he met Mozart and played to him. But his stay was interrupted by news of his mother's illness, and he was forced to return home to Bonn, where he found her dying of tuberculosis.

Beethoven now took charge of the family finances, largely because of his father's increasing incapacity. He began working as a musical tutor to the children of wealthy courtiers, as well as performing as a violinist in the court orchestra and the local theatre. His positions allowed him to meet many influential nobles, including the Viennese aristocrat Count Ferdinand Waldstein, a skilled musician who became a friend and patron. Possibly at Waldstein's arrangement, Beethoven went to Vienna to study with the composer Haydn, lessons paid for by the elector, his employer. He left Bonn in 1792 and never returned.

Impressing the Viennese salons and nobility with his virtuoso performances on the piano, Beethoven performed widely and was considered a superb improviser – even greater than Mozart. His compositions at this time included piano sonatas, variations and concerti, as well as his first two symphonies, all of which show the influence of his own heroes, Mozart and Haydn.

The following years, up until around 1802, are considered Beethoven's early period, during which he composed some significant piano works. Brilliant, fine compositions, they are not as innovative as the music of his later years. By now Beethoven's progressive deafness had become impossible for him to ignore. He was brought close to despair and, perhaps recognizing that his career as a virtuoso was over, began to focus on composition.

The story goes that when Beethoven oversaw the first performance of his Ninth Symphony at the Kärntnertor Theatre in 1824, the soloists in the orchestra had to point out that the audience was applauding his work. Turning to see the silent adulation, he began to weep. He was by now totally deaf and never heard the work that had just been performed to such acclaim.

Beethoven had noticed the first symptoms from 1796, when he had begun to experience tinnitus, a constant ringing in his ears that made it difficult to hear and appreciate music or to engage in conversation. By 1802 there was little doubt that his condition was serious, and worsening. For a composer there could be nothing so destructive. Fully realizing the depth of his affliction darkened his mood. In the summer of 1802, in a letter discovered only after his death and known as the 'Heiligenstadt Testament', he wrote:

> O ye men who think or say that I am malevolent, stubborn or misanthropic, how greatly do you wrong me. You do not know the cause of my seeming so . . . for six years I have been in a hopeless case, made worse by ignorant doctors, yearly betrayed in the hope of getting better, finally forced to face the prospect of a permanent malady whose cure will take years or even prove impossible.

All that kept him from suicide, he said, was his art, which made it 'unthinkable for me to leave the world forever before I had produced all that I felt called upon to produce'.

Although he could not hear the music he composed, Beethoven's gradual descent into deafness coincided with an increasing brilliance in his composition, with his middle-period works being characterized by themes of struggle and heroism, and those of his third period – the late period – a time of total deafness, displaying a powerful intellectual depth.

By 1817 Beethoven was completely deaf, and for the latter part of his life he was able to communicate with friends only through written conversations. The resulting notebooks are unique historical documents, recording his thoughts and opinions on his music and the way it should be interpreted, and there are also written notes in the scores of his works.

At Beethoven's autopsy he was diagnosed as having a 'distended inner ear', which had developed lesions over time. Since then, other explanations have been suggested, including syphilis, typhus, the physical damage caused by beatings from his father and the effects of immersing his head in cold water to stay awake.

Posthumous analysis of Beethoven's hair revealed dangerously high levels of lead, certainly damaging to health, the effects of which may have contributed to his unpredictable moods. We may never know the cause of his deafness for certain; but what is beyond doubt is Beethoven's heroism in defying his condition to create a musical world of such timeless resonance today.

Settled in Vienna, he produced a series of masterpieces. His Symphony No. 3, completed in 1803, was originally dedicated to Napoleon Bonaparte, whose revolutionary zeal made him a hero to Beethoven. When Napoleon declared himself emperor in May 1804, the disillusioned composer angrily removed the dedication. Nevertheless, this dramatic, powerful symphony remained a landmark in Beethoven's musical development and when published in 1806 was suitably re-entitled Sinfonia eroica.

Beethoven's middle period saw a rush of compositions that included the Waldstein and Appassionata piano sonatas, the Fourth

Piano Concerto, the Razumovsky Quartets and the Violin Concerto, and also his first and only opera, *Fidelio*. His Symphonies Nos. 4 and 5 also date from this period, with the Fifth, its opening theme recognizable the world over, being a landmark in musical originality. Just as original is his Symphony No. 6, known as the Pastoral, in which woodwind instruments imitate the birds of the local countryside. The Symphonies Nos. 7 and 8 mark the close of a period filled with orchestral masterpieces.

Composing less in his later years, as complete deafness claimed him, Beethoven's late-period works, from around 1815 onwards, are marked by increased intimacy and emotional power. His final piano sonatas, opuses 109, 110 and 111, are extraordinary virtuoso works, in which complexity is perfectly partnered with lyricism. On the other hand, his majestic Symphony No. 9, of 1824, explodes with the final movement's 'Ode to Joy', featuring a full choir and soloists – its soaring and exhilarating jubilance now used, somewhat absurdly, to drum up enthusiasm for the bureaucracy of the European Union. His last string quartets were completed in 1826, which coincided with the attempted suicide of Beethoven's nephew, to whom he was guardian. This, along with a bout of pneumonia and the onset of cirrhosis of the liver, probably contributed to his death in March 1827.

Prone to black moods and periods of emotional upheaval, Beethoven had difficulty maintaining relationships, and he never married – though a letter discovered after his death, addressed to his 'Immortal Beloved', has led many to speculate on the possibility of a secret, married lover. He was buried in great pomp, his funeral in Vienna befitting a composer who had become famous throughout Europe as one of the greatest of his, or any other, time.

JANE AUSTEN

1775–1817

Like Shakespeare, she took, as it were, the common dross of humanity, and by her wonderful power of literary alchemy, turned it into pure gold. Yet she was apparently unconscious of her strength, and in the long roll of writers who have adorned our noble literature there is probably not one so devoid of pedantry or affectation, so delightfully self-repressive, or so free from egotism, as Jane Austen.

George Barnett Smith, in *The Gentleman's Magazine*,
No. 258 (1895)

A parson's daughter who completed just six novels during her short life, Jane Austen emerged from deliberate anonymity to become English literature's best-loved female writer. Her gently ironic yet profound novels of love, manners and marriage transformed the art of writing fiction.

Acutely observed and subtly incisive, Austen's works are acknowledged as masterpieces. Her irony conceals a penetrating gaze, encapsulated in the famous opening line of *Pride and Prejudice* (1813): 'It is a truth universally acknowledged that a man in possession of a good fortune must be in want of a wife.' This was the world she chronicled: 'The Assemblies of Nottingham are, as in all other places, the resort of the young and the gay, who go to see and be seen; and also of those, who, having played their matrimonial cards well in early life, are now content to sit down to a game of sober whist or quadrille.' Thus, in 1814, was encapsulated the purpose of the endless round of entertainments that consumed the lives of England's gentry and aristocracy: to find matches for the new generation.

As the feminist writer Mary Wollstonecraft commented, a girl's 'coming out', at the age of fifteen or sixteen, was purely 'to bring to market a marriageable miss, whose person is taken from one place to another, richly caparisoned'. The market they chose was of paramount importance. One prudent clergyman advised his step-sisters not to move to rural Oxfordshire, on the grounds that the location 'is but an indifferent one for young ladies to shine in'. Ambitious young women – or those with ambitious parents – would head for London.

No one was under any illusions about where they stood in the pecking order. It was unlikely that a provincial parson's daughter, such as Jane Austen, with her modest portion and limited connections, would even meet, let alone marry, a son of the high aristocracy. The daughters of the elite, carrying substantial dowries, were rigorously protected against the adventurers who infiltrated London's society balls in the hopes of bagging themselves an heiress.

Parents and children alike were aware that choices were determined as much by financial considerations as by inclination. 'When poverty comes in at the door love flies out the window,' one gentlewoman reminded her daughter in 1801. The absolute minimum a gentleman could hope to scrape by on during this period was about £280 a year. But this would require a life, as one bride accepted, where 'we shall live in a quiet domestic manner and not see much company'.

Even an esquire on £450 a year would struggle to satisfy the social requirements of his class: a country household, lodgings in London, visits to the theatre and the opera, attendance at balls and pleasure gardens. One impecunious suitor complained to his beloved that: 'Every parent takes utmost care to marry his child [where there] is money, not considering inclination ... your papa no doubt may marry you to one [that] will make large settlements, keep an equipage and support you in all grandeur imaginable.' Prudence ruled as much as passion. The lurking spectre of spinsterhood propelled many young women towards a match offering little but financial security.

Austen's amused restraint was in marked contrast to the romantic melodrama in fashion at the time, and the historian Macaulay thought that her well-constructed comedies of manners were the closest to perfection that writing could ever hope to reach.

The seventh child of eight, Austen spent her life among a large and affectionate family in Hampshire and Bath. 'Her life passed calmly and smoothly, resembling some translucent stream which meanders through our English meadows, and is never lashed into anger by treacherous rocks or violent currents,' wrote George Barnett Smith in 1895. She wrote about ordinary lives, about the petty dramas of lively provincial society, about the preoccupations, the squabbles, the complexities and the exhausting difficulties of unexceptional people. Sir Walter Scott (1771–1832), the best-selling author of *Ivanhoe*, was one of the few to recognize the extent of Austen's genius at the time, writing that she had 'the exquisite touch which renders ordinary commonplace things and characters interesting'. She pastiched the fashionable Gothic melodrama in *Northanger Abbey*, and broke away from the prevailing tradition that literature should be about great figures, great events or great dramas. Austen showed that the small and the conversational could be just as compelling, and her witty depictions of the elaborate matrimonial dances of the English gentry are thinly disguised social commentary, displaying a shrewd understanding of human motivation and social necessity.

Along the way, Austen produced some of literature's most memorable characters, drawn with her typical precision and intricacy.

Aloof Mr Darcy, obsequious Mr Collins, flustered Mrs Bennet and her wry and long-suffering husband, Mr Bennet, populate *Pride and Prejudice*. Feisty, outspoken daughter Elizabeth Bennet is one of literature's most engaging heroines, closely followed by the flawed but well-intentioned Emma Woodhouse of *Emma* (1816), who finds her equilibrium with the sensible and honourable George Knightley.

Austen's novels may end happily, but not without revealing the situation of women of her class and era. Marriage determined a woman's fate. As Charlotte Lucas's marriage to the ridiculous Mr Collins so eloquently demonstrates, almost any kind of marriage was deemed better than being an old maid. Elizabeth Bennet's decision to challenge this convention is presented as admirable, but daring. Whereas we know that Elizabeth's wit and charm will win her a husband (and a well-deserved place in the aristocracy), we also know that scores of women like Charlotte will not be so lucky and will have to compromise. Under a calm surface, Austen illuminates the prejudices, the scandals, the sheer misfortune and misunderstanding that could leave women without a husband, and in the absence of a personal fortune, dependent entirely on the kindness of others for survival. Austen also suggested, through the successful social elevation of both male and female characters by means of marriage, that a stagnant but often snobbish aristocracy was in need of new blood.

The novelist who excelled in her treatment of love and marriage never herself married. She was, by all accounts, vivacious and attractive. The only surviving picture of her, a drawing done by her sister Cassandra, seems not to have done her justice. She had at least two semi-serious flirtations. At twenty-six she was briefly engaged to Harris Bigg-Withers, an heir five years her junior. Facing a lifetime with a man by all accounts as unfortunate as his name, Austen broke it off after less than a day. Rumours prevail of another, later attachment that was Austen's true love. Her beloved sister Cassandra, who also remained unmarried, destroyed much of her correspondence after her death.

Instead, Austen chose something her heroines never consider: a career. She had written since her childhood, producing stories, anecdotes and vignettes to amuse her family. In the upheaval after the family left her beloved childhood home, Austen stopped writing. Settling gratefully back in Hampshire with her mother and sister, Austen turned again to the works that she had begun a decade before. *Elinor and Marianne* became *Sense and Sensibility* (1811), and *First Impressions* became *Pride and Prejudice*. With the help of her brother Henry's negotiating skills, Austen's works were published under the authorship of simply 'a lady', with *Northanger Abbey* and *Persuasion* appearing posthumously in 1818. Famously private, Austen resisted attempts by the press and her proud family to make known the identity of this appealing writer, whose fans included the Prince Regent. Her authorship was made public only after her early death from, it is conjectured, Addison's disease.

In her short, uneventful life this extraordinary writer created works that resonate even more strongly today than they did in the early 19th century. The modern cult of Jane Austen continues apace, as fans try to discover more about the elusive novelist's life, and Hollywood films attempt to weave romantic tales out of the sketchy biographical details that exist. Many would agree, however, that her novels suffice. Discreet, ironic, witty and compassionate, Austen's masterful writing is the measure of the woman.

SIMÓN BOLÍVAR AND THE LIBERATION OF SOUTH AMERICA

1783–1830

'America is ungovernable. Those who have served the revolution have ploughed the sea.'

Simón Bolívar

Simón Bolívar was the Liberator – El Libertador – of Latin America: a dynamic, brilliant and swashbuckling soldier-statesman whose campaigns in the early 19th century not only defeated the Spanish empire but personally conquered a territory as large of Europe. Dashing and handsome, always slight and just five foot six inches tall but also haughty, obstinate, arrogant, egotistical and sensitive – like all great men – he was a superb writer and enlightened intellectual, an inspiring leader, a gifted general and tactician and a tireless campaigner of remarkable physical endurance. Partly a decadent dandy of the *ancien régime*, sometimes a romantic lover and often a compulsive womanizer, he was a man of liberal and constitutional instincts, as at home amongst rough cowboys of Spanish, Indian, mixed and black origins, as amongst the most delicate of European aristocracy. Indeed he not only liberated the territory but also the black and mixed-race slaves of the former Spanish empire, embracing views of racial equality that were almost a century ahead of their time.

Bolívar served as commander, president and dictator and

creator of many countries, trying to find a balance between traditional monarchy and capricious authoritarianism on one hand and chaotic democracy and chattering parliamentarianism on the other, favouring variously a middle road of a strong presidency for life tempered by elected assemblies and aristocratic rule. He was full of contradictions: while he despised monarchy, he was himself spoken of as a king; while purportedly never seeking the limelight or the trappings of power, he sought both all the time; and while usually gentle, loyal, generous and tolerant, he was capable of ruthless cruelty.

Born vastly rich, he gave his fortune to the revolution and died poor. In his mission to free America from the Spanish and to form his dream state of Greater Colombia, his political career ended in failure, but Bolívar, the greatest South American of all time, ranks with the most successful statesmen of history, alongside his contemporary Napoleon Bonaparte whose gifts he shared but whose overweening ambition he disdained. The modern states of Colombia, Venezuela, Panama, Ecuador, Peru, and Bolivia all owed their liberation to Bolívar personally and all of them were ruled by him at one time or another. He would be both the inspiration for Latin America's liberalism and democracy but also the prototype of its military dictators, the *caudillos*. He was driven as much by his love of liberty as by the drama of his own extraordinary life: 'My doctor has often told me,' he wrote, 'that for my flesh to be strong, my spirit needs to feed on danger. This is so true that when God brought me into this world, he brought a storm of revolutions for me to feed on . . . I am the genius of the storm.'

At a time when all of South and Central America was ruled by the Spanish Empire (with the exception of Brazil, which was Portuguese), Bolívar was born at the very apex of society, one of the richest families in Caracas, Venezuela, and he owned sugar estates, copper mines and many mansions. Society was a complicated hierarchy obsessed with race, ruled by Spanish aristocratic vice-roys and generals at the top, then a rich creole nobility (white Spaniarchs born in the colonies like the Bolívars), and then many degrees of mixed race in between, some part white-part Indian ('mestizos'), some part white-part black ('mulattos') and others 'sambos' (part Indian and black) and, at the bottom, a class of black slaves. But as with many such families, there were rumours of mixed race in the Bolívars' heritage.

Born on 24 July 1783, Bolívar lost both his parents at a young age and was raised by a combination of his black slave Hipolita and an array of often Enlightened professors, including the remarkable Simon Rodriguez who instructed him on a Rousseau-esque pro-gramme of swimming, riding and a love of nature along with the tenets of the French and American Revolutions. After Rodriguez had to flee for conspiring against the Spanish in the epoch of rev-olutionary foment, Bolívar attended military school and was then sent off to meet his uncles and relatives in Madrid, the imperial capital, where the teenage Bolívar mixed with the highest society of the royal Bourbon court, becoming the protégé of one of Queen Maria Luisa's lovers and famously playing with Prince Ferdinand, the future king. While in Madrid, he married the aristocratic Maria Teresa Rodriguez del Toro and took her back with him to Venezuela, where she died of yellow fever in January 1803. She was the love of his life and 'her death made me promise never to marry again ... If I were not widowed, my life would maybe have been different. I would not be the General Bolívar nor the Liberator.'

In 1804, heartbroken, Bolívar returned to Europe on a grand tour (and met up with his old tutor Simon Rodriguez), during which he saw Napoleon crowned emperor and himself sank into extravagant debauchery, enjoying passionate affairs with, amongst many others, a beautiful older Parisian lady. Those who met him during these years regarded him as a dissolute South American fop – they were soon to be proved wrong. In 1807, Bolívar returned to a South America that was now seething with revolutionary unrest, encouraged by centuries of Spanish incompetence, corruption and cruelty but also by the follies of the king and queen of Spain, the clueless Carlos IV and the nymphomaniacal Maria Luisa, whose misrule now allowed Emperor Napoleon to occupy Spain and appoint his brother Joseph Bonaparte as king. As war raged in Spain, the empire in Latin America started to fragment. In April 1810 a self-declared Supreme Junta seized power in Venezuela and declared independence. Bolívar was sent to London to invite the most famous advocate of a free Venezuela, Francisco de Miranda, who had served in the French Revolutionary army as a general and travelled the world, even flirting with Catherine the Great, to return to lead the nascent republic. Known to history as the Precursor to Bolívar's Liberator, Miranda returned and was elected president of the First Republic of Venezuela and then dictator and commander. But the old man proved weak, timid and inept: he was jealous of young Colonel Bolívar and lost his nerve. Bolívar himself, the leader of the younger Venezuelan officers, lost battles and strongholds until he retreated in depression to his estates.

When Miranda signed an agreement of capitulation with the Spanish, Bolívar, in one of history's great acts of betrayal, accused his former hero of treason, arrested Miranda and handed him over to the Spanish who imprisoned him: Miranda died in jail. For services rendered, the Spanish let Bolívar leave – one of their biggest mistakes. Meanwhile, other regions of Spanish America were rebelling and declaring independence and in 1813, Bolívar took up a military command in a rebel state of the United Provinces of New Granada (today's Colombia) in the so-called Admirable Campaign.

It was now that the great Bolívar began to emerge. When he took Merida in May 1813 and later Trujillo, he was nicknamed El Libertador, a title he embraced and enjoyed for the rest of his life. But the Spanish fought the rebels with astonishing cruelty which made them hard to resist until Bolívar decided, controversially, to fight barbarism with barbarism, issuing his notorious Decree of War to the Death, which permitted the killing of any Spaniard who did not back independence. While this tarnished his reputation, his tactics worked: in August he took Caracas and was officially declared El Libertador and president of the Second Republic. But the Spanish had now unleashed a race war against the Spanish-blooded elite of the rebels, arming the savage warlord Jose Tomas Bove whose *llaneros* (plainsmen) cavalry – known as the Legions of Hell for their psychotic taste for ingeniously ghastly killing – launched a campaign of unparalleled violence and torture, carrying all before them. Though the Spanish soon lost control of Bove and his *llaneros*, Bolívar's small forces were defeated and the republic collapsed as Bove took Caracas. Bolívar escaped back to New Grenada but he did not give up, taking command of the forces of the United Provinces there and capturing the capital Bogotá. But once again, the fissiparous feuds of the rebels, with their many rival warlords and fragmented and overlapping governments, and the savagery of the Spanish campaign, led to disaster. Bolívar escaped to Jamaica and then the new free republic of Haiti where he received aid from the president of the first modern black state, Alexandre Petion (heir to Toussaint Louverture) and Luis Brion, the Jewish merchant who provided his ships and became his first admiral.

On his first landing in Venezuela in June 1816, Bolívar declared the freeing of South America's slaves, but the expedition was a disaster and again he was lucky to escape, though he overcame his moments of despair: 'the art of victory is learned in failures.'

When he returned the next year, he defeated the Spanish and took Angostura but the talented Spanish commander Captain-General Morillo, deploying regular troops who had fought in the Napoleonic wars, again routed Bolívar's thinly spread forces. Nonetheless Bolívar opened a national congress that elected him president of Venezuela. Then he turned to liberate New Grenada (Colombia), winning the decisive battle of Boyacá on 7 August 1819, after which he returned to Venezuela where he decided to form a massive new state, Greater Colombia. But the Spanish still held Caracas and the highlands. After the Napoleonic Wars, Bolívar was able to hire British and Irish soldiers who formed his famed Albion Legion that helped him defeat Spanish troops – and indeed henceforth some of his closest adjutants were British. Now the newly restored King Ferdinand VII of Spain tried to rule as an absolute monarch and planned to send a new army to suppress Bolívar's revolution, but a mutiny forced him to recognize the liberal Cadiz Constitution. Morillo and the Spanish armies in Venezuela lost the will to fight on and recognized Bolívar as president. At a famous meeting, Morillo arrived with a huge guard in full regalia while Bolívar arrived with a tiny entourage: the two men were impressed by each other. But war soon returned and independence was finally secured at the Battle of Carabobo on 24 June 1821, Bolívar's great victory, aided by his favourite, a brilliant young commander named Antonio de Sucre, and his ruthless ally, the caudillo of the *llaneros* plainsmen, Jose Antonio Paez, the Centaur of the Plains. Bolívar triumphantly entered Caracas. On 7 September 1821, he was declared president of Greater Colombia.

A born showman, each of Bolívar's liberations of cities were marked by Roman-style triumphal processions during which he would be greeted by beautiful young girls wearing white who would crown him with the laurels of victory. Lithe and wiry, Bolívar loved dancing and he claimed its vigorous rhythm helped him to come up with his best ideas: 'There are men', he wrote in a typically melodramatic way, 'who need to be alone and far from the hubbub to be able to think ... I deliberated, reflected and mulled best when I was at the centre of the revelry amongst the pleasures and clamour of a ball.' He was as tireless at his victory balls as he was indefatigable in the saddle on his campaigns. And he adored women, usually taking the prettiest of these girls as his temporary mistresses, though none could really hold or tame El Libertador for long.

Bolívar now could have either retired or perhaps more wisely devoted himself to ruling his already-huge and unwieldy state, Greater Colombia. But instead, being Bolívar, he dreamed of conquering all of the continent, aware that as long as Spanish rule continued in Peru, the heart of the Spanish empire, his Greater Colombia would not be secure. Planning a new campaign, he divided the country between two of his generals: the pedantic and envious General Antonio Santander served as vice president and ruled New Grenada and Panama from Bogota while in Venezuela, Bolívar left the caudillo Paez in command. By backing these warlords instead of destroying them, Bolívar perhaps was mistaken, but he was convinced he would later return to forge his new state. First, in an astonishing campaign, Bolívar crossed vast distances and appalling terrain as he marched his army across the Andes to liberate Quito (today's Ecuador), winning the battles of Bombona and Pichincha, taking the city itself in June 1822. Here he met the most famous of his mistresses, Manuela Saenz, the illegitimate daughter of a Spanish nobleman, a convent-girl seduced by an officer, now the wife of a much older English merchant and long-time supporter of the revolution in Peru. Still in her early twenties, irrepressibly courageous, sensuous and dazzling in her beauty and wildly eccentric, she lived with Bolívar during his time in Quito and Peru.

Meanwhile, far to the south, Argentina and Chile had also thrown off Spanish rule, and their liberating hero, General Jose de San Martin, was approaching from the south, having freed some parts of Peru earning the title Protector of Peruvian Freedom. But Bolívar quickly annexed Quito to his own Greater Colombia. At a tense summit conference, the two greatest men of South American liberation met one another. San Martin, ascetic and awkward and far from his home bases, found himself outmanoeuvred by the flamboyant Bolívar who took over the liberation of Peru, land of the silver mines, ruled from the biggest and richest city of the Spanish empire, Lima. Appointed dictator of Peru, Bolívar and his beloved general Sucre defeated the Spanish at the battle of Junin and on 9 December 1824, Sucre won the decisive victory at Ayacuho. Out of Upper Peru, Bolívar formed what became the Republic of Bolivia. He now ruled a vast empire from Panama down to Bolivia and he embarked on a grand tour of his wide and remote lands. At his apogee, he said, 'a strong man delivers a single blow and an empire vanishes.' But in fact, Bolívar had overreached himself: at home, Greater Colombia was falling apart and its elites, encouraged by the disloyal Santander and Paez, were tired of Bolívar's expensive and grandiose wars far away.

Leaving his Grand Marshal Sucre to become (at various moments) president of Peru and Bolivia, Bolívar returned finally to Caracas and then Bogotá. Planning to leave his ideal constitution in place in Bolivia, Bolívar drafted various new ideas and decrees for his perfect government. His constitution for Bolivia envisaged a president-for-life restrained by a tricameral legislature (with the classical Roman names of Senate, Chamber of Tribunes and Chamber of Censors) and a very limited and wealthy electorate. Fearing the chaos, civil wars and murder he had seen in the liberation struggle and glimpsing the impossible racial, economical and geographical differences between Lima and Quito, Caracas and Bogotá, Bolívar rejected both traditional monarchy and a federal republic like that of the United States, and proposed a strong ruler for life, backed by an oligarchical elite. Delegates in Greater Colombia failed to agree on a constitution but, exhausted by his campaigns and the petty rivalries and parochial instincts of Santander and Paez, Bolívar at first tried to compromise with his effective deputies and then decided to seize power and become dictator.

On 24 June 1828 he entered Bogotá to a euphoric welcome and two months later in an Organic Decree he was declared president-liberator – though typically he took power diffidently saying, 'Under a dictatorship how can we talk of liberty? On this let us agree: pity the nation that obeys one man as we should pity the man who holds all power.' The people were delighted but many of his supporters were shocked and he was accused of tyranny – rumours unfairly accused him of seeking a royal crown. Bolívar was joined in Bogotá by his fiery and exuberant mistress Manuela, who scandalized the elite by dressing in military uniforms, having affairs with her black servants and taking lovers at random. On 25 September a group of officers, backed secretly by Santander himself (who had been sent off to be an ambassador abroad), tried to assassinate Bolívar by bursting into his mansion and fighting their way towards his bedroom. Manuela helped him escape from a window and he then hid under a bridge as the conspirators broke down the door and beat the brave Manuela to the ground.

Once the conspirators had been defeated and executed (except Santander, who was sent into exile), Bolívar emerged, shaken by his own unpopularity and weakening from illness. Bolívar hailed Manuela as the *Libertadora del Libertador* – Liberatrix of the Liberator – but as rebellions broke out across the republic, Bolívar governed as his vision gradually fell apart. Ecuador declared its independence, and Peru invaded and was defeated by Sucre, while

Paez ruled Venezuela as effective dictator. Desperately ill with tuberculosis and spectrally thin, Bolívar warned his people on 20 January 1830 in a tragic and defensive speech: 'Today I cease to govern you ... Fearing I may be regarded as an obstacle to establishing the Republic, I personally have cast down the supreme position of leadership ... I have been the victim of ignominious suspicions ... Never I swear to you, has it crossed my mind to aspire to a kingship ... I beg you to remain united lest you become the assassins of the country and your own executioners.' Resigning from the presidency on 27 April 1830, his dream had already fallen apart and he was despairing: 'America is ungovernable; he who serves the revolution ploughs the sea; the country is bound to fall into unimaginable chaos after which it will pass into the hands of tyrants ... and a frenzy of violence.' He planned to leave for Europe from the port of Cartagena. As he left Bogotá to convalesce, his closest disciple Marshal Sucre rushed to say goodbye but missed him. The rumours, probably true, that Bolívar planned to promote Sucre as a successor may have doomed the marshal. In June 1830 Sucre was murdered; Bolívar was inconsolable. He was dying, but he even turned that into a world-historical drama: 'If my death can heal and fortify the nation, I go to my tomb in peace.' On 17 December 1830, abandoned by all but a tiny entourage as Greater Colombia broke up into different states, the Liberator died aged just forty-seven.

SHAKA

1787–1828

It became known to us that Shaka had ordered that a man standing near us should be put to death for what crime we could not learn: but we soon found it to be one of the common occurrences in the course of the day.

Recollections of a surgeon visiting Shaka in 1824

Shaka was the founder of the Zulu empire and the creator of the Zulu nation but he was also a vicious, paranoid, vindictive, cruel and self-destructive tyrant.

Shaka was raised with an absent father and a strong, devoted and wronged mother in an atmosphere of instability, violence and fear. His father, Senzangakona, was chief of the Zulu tribe, but, unusually, opted to marry a lower-class woman from the neighbouring eLangeni clan. The marriage broke up when the young Shaka was six, and his mother took him back to the eLangeni; however, she was ostracized there because of her marriage. Not only did the future leader spend the rest of his youth without a father, he also had to deal with the social stigma that resulted from a marriage that brought disgrace upon his mother. Unable to cope, his mother went into exile, eventually finding a home with the Mtetwa clan in 1802.

Shaka's fortunes began to change when, at twenty-three – already tall, muscular and striking – he was called up to perform military service by Dingiswayo, a chief of the Mtetwa. As a warrior Shaka soon achieved a reputation for brilliance and bravery, and he helped the Mtetwa establish their dominance over many smaller clans, including the Zulus. He also witnessed, at first hand, Dingiswayo's efforts to reform the organization and attitude of the armed forces – lessons he did not forget.

In 1816 news arrived that Shaka's father had died. Dingiswayo now released him from his service so that he might return and claim his birthright as Zulu chief. Although the Zulu were, at that time, one of the smaller clans on the east coast of southern Africa, Shaka had big plans for the future.

On his return, he immediately crushed internal opposition to his rule. He then set about remodelling the Zulu into a warrior people. The army was re-equipped and reorganized, embracing the horned buffalo battle formation that would become its trademark. When deployed, the objective of this formation was always the same: the annihilation of the enemy's troops.

At a time when most battles were little more than skirmishes, with no real sense of strategic direction, Shaka's disciplined and ruthless approach constituted a revolution in clan warfare. His armies quickly established a terrifying reputation, and Shaka began to use them to redraw the map of southern Africa.

The first to feel his wrath were those clans closest to the Zulu along the eastern seaboard, including the eLangeni. Shaka brought down a terrible vengeance on those who had inflicted misery on his mother when he had been a boy, impaling the clan's leaders on wooden stakes cut from their own fences.

Other victories followed, and after each one Shaka incorporated the men of the vanquished clans into his own armies. Within a year he had quadrupled the size of the forces at his command. When in 1817 Dingiswayo – still Shaka's nominal overlord – was murdered by a rival, Chief Zwinde of the Ndwandwe clan, the way was clear for untrammelled Zulu expansion.

Thereafter, one clan after another was conquered and their

lands devastated. Those who lay within Shaka's path faced a stark choice: submit, flee or die. The major clans in the area, including the Ndwandwe, were overwhelmed, as were numerous smaller clans to the south of the Zulu. By 1823 Shaka had devastated much of southeastern Africa.

It was not just those who came into immediate contact with Shaka and his forces who were affected. The flight inland of thousands who feared Shaka's marauding armies tore up the established clan structure and social framework of the African interior. In the Mfecane (crushing) that followed, as many as 2 million people may have died as this internal 'scramble for Africa' spiralled out of control.

The worst was yet to come. In 1827 Shaka's mother died, and the warrior-chief abandoned all sense of restraint. He was no longer concerned with establishing a huge Zulu empire, but instead sought to inflict the pain he himself felt at his mother's death on as many others as possible. In the first phase of this public mourning process, some 7000 Zulus were slaughtered. Pregnant women were killed, along with their husbands, whilst even cattle were butchered by the agents of Shaka's rage.

Death and destruction now became the only phenomena that gave meaning to Shaka's life, and he unleashed his armies to carry fire and slaughter far and wide. The violence only ended when Shaka was assassinated by his half-brothers Dingane and Mhlangana in 1828. A life that had promised so much ended in dishonour: stabbed to death with spears, the once great chief was buried without ceremony in a pit.

At time of his death, Shaka governed over 250,000 people and could raise an army of 50,000. He had built a huge kingdom out of almost nothing, but the price paid by ordinary Africans was vast. Millions had died as a consequence of Shaka's unbridled ambition.

Prior to his death, Shaka had established friendly relations with the British, but not with the Afrikaners (Boers), and under his half-brother successor, Dingane, the first armed clashes occurred with Boer settlers in Natal. After an initial victory, a Zulu force of several thousand suffered a decisive defeat at the hands of a much smaller contingent of Boers at the Battle of Blood River in December 1838 – an event that triggered a Zulu civil war with Mpande – another of Shaka's half-brothers – who formed an alliance with the Boers and succeeded in overthrowing Dingane. Over the following couple of years, much of the Zulu empire fell under Boer control, but Britain's formal annexation of Natal in 1843 led to the restoration of these lands to the Zulus.

Thereafter, until the second half of the 19th century, the British made no concerted effort to confront the Zulus. Indeed, government policy was to safeguard the integrity of the Zulu empire from Boer expansionism. All this changed, however, in January 1879 when, to placate the Akrikaners after the annexation of the Transvaal two years earlier, the British instigated the Zulu War, aiming to seize Zululand as an area ripe for Afrikaner settlement. They ordered the Zulu king Cetshwayo – Mpande's son – to disband his army within thirty days; when he failed to comply, hostilities began.

By September 1879, Cetshwayo had been captured and the territory brought under British control (though not before the British had suffered a famous defeat at the Battle of Isandhlwana and been pinned down at the siege of Rorke's Drift – an incident forever commemorated in the 1964 film Zulu). Though unrest continued in the years that followed, prospects for an independent Zulu homeland had suffered fatal damage. In 1887, Zululand was formally annexed to the crown – a move that signalled the permanent dissolution of the Zulu empire.

BYRON

1788–1824

A variety of powers almost boundless, and a pride no less vast in displaying them, – a susceptibility of new impressions and impulses, even beyond the usual allotment of genius, and an uncontrolled impetuosity in yielding to them...

Byron, as described by his friend and biographer Thomas
Moore in his *Life of Lord Byron* (1835)

Lord Byron, the dashing, brooding poet, was the quintessence of the romantic hero. Women lost themselves trying to save him; society looked on in fascinated outrage as the aristocratic outsider defied their conventions. Shadowed by a permanent aura of depravity, irresistible in his vulnerability, mocking, witty, flamboyant and bold, Byron gave birth to a new image of the hero. Yet it is the incandescent, exuberant genius of the poetry that makes him immortal

George Gordon, Lord Byron, was, as he wrote in his unfinished masterpiece *Don Juan*, 'the Grand Napoleon of the realms of rhyme'. The poet who could dash off sixty to eighty stanzas after a hearty dinner hit the English literary landscape like a hurricane. When the first two cantos of his *Childe Harold* were published in 1812, they sold out immediately. 'I awoke one morning,' noted the twenty-year-old poet, 'and found myself famous.'

Byron was the poster boy of the Romantic generation. The melancholic disillusionment of *Childe Harold* and the mordant, mocking irony of *Don Juan* satirized the hypocrisies and pretensions of society and mourned the failure of reality to live up to lofty ideals. Driven forward in searing, pounding rhythms, Byron's poetry embodied the spirit of the age:

I live not in myself, but I become
Portion of that around me; and to me,
High mountains are a feeling, but the hum
Of human cities torture

Everyone assumed that Byron was the lost and disenchanted eponymous hero of *Childe Harold*, restlessly wandering across the continent. The poet's history was indeed romantic enough. Son of the profligate, charming Captain John 'Mad Jack' Byron, the boy was brought up in penury in Aberdeen by his widowed mother until the death of his great-uncle transformed his fortunes. Brought back to England, the wild, club-footed ten-year-old inherited the magnificent ruins of Newstead Abbey and the title of Lord Byron.

Sitting in a corner, staring moodily into space, the slight, pale, beautiful Byron was a magnet for society's women. 'He is really the only topic almost of every conversation – the men jealous of him, the women of each other,' commented the political hostess Georgiana, duchess of Devonshire. With his innumerable conquests, Byron cut a swathe through society – from Lady Caroline Lamb, who was so mad about the poet that when he was attending a party to which she was not invited, she would wait outside in the street for him, to Lady Oxford, the middle-aged hostess who encouraged her young lover's radicalism.

'Mad, bad and dangerous to know,' as Lady Caroline Lamb famously described him, the poet had no qualms about scandalizing society. 'It may be now and then voluptuous – I can't help that' was Byron's insouciant response to claims that *Don Juan* was a 'eulogy of vice'. Byron, living (by his own admission) in 'an abyss of sensuality', was infamous for his aura of tortured depravity and for the drinking orgies held with his friends, garbed in monks' habits, amid the Gothic ruins of Newstead Abbey. 'There never existed a more worthless set', was the verdict of the war hero the duke of Wellington.

A domineering mother and a childhood of sexual abuse by his nurse May Gray had thwarted his capacity for relationships; he constantly thirsted for new sensations and new lovers, whether male or female. He fell passionately in love and became equally swiftly disillusioned. Augusta Leigh, whose own daughter was probably Byron's, was the great love of his life, but she was also his half-sister. To all other women he could be monstrously cruel. He had an anguished relationship with his great friend Shelley's sister-in-law, Claire Clairmont, whom he made pregnant and then rejected. The much-loved daughter of this affair Byron placed in an Italian convent, where she died aged five. Byron's marriage to the humourless Annabella Milbanke was a disaster. It broke down irretrievably after less than a year amid talk of Byron's marital violence, incestuous relationships and bisexuality – rumours so scandalous that they forced him in 1816 to leave England and the baby daughter of this marriage, Augusta Ada, never to return.

In Venice Byron swam home at night along the Grand Canal, pushing a board with a candle on it to light his way. The man who had kept a bear in his rooms at Cambridge lived in a palazzo that was a veritable menagerie. Shelley once listed the members of the household: 'ten horses, eight enormous dogs, three monkeys, five cats, an eagle, a crow, a falcon . . . [and] I have just met on the grand staircase five peacocks, two guinea hens and an Egyptian crane'.

Visitors flocked to see the poet. Some found him grown fat and grey, but his vigour was restored by a passionate affair with a radical young Italian countess. Restless once again, Byron launched him-self into yet another campaign: the fight for Greek independence from the Turks. He poured his money and his soul into the project. But at Missolonghi in Greece, weakened by a life of dissipation and excess, Byron caught a fever and died. Such was the end, at the age of just thirty-six, of the poet whose magnificent defiance of petty convention had outraged and enraptured Europe for a generation.

BALZAC

1799–1850

I find people very impertinent when they say I am deep and then try to get to know me in five minutes. Between you and me, I am not deep but very wide, and it takes time to walk around me.
Balzac, in a letter to Countess Maffei (1837)

Honoré de Balzac was one of the most prolific of literary giants. His masterpiece, *La Comédie humaine*, is made up of nearly 100 works which contain more than 2000 characters and together create an alternative reality that extends from Paris to the provincial backwaters of France. Balzac's works transformed the novel into a great art form capable of representing life in all its detail and colour, so paving the way for the ambitious works of writers such as Proust and Zola. Balzac, the plump, amiable, workaholic genius, was in many respects the father of the modern novel.

As the unremarkable child of a beautiful but unpleasant mother and a self-indulgent father, Balzac did not seem marked for greatness. After school he worked as a legal clerk, but this did not excite a young man with grand ambition but little direction in which to channel it, and around the age of nineteen he decided to become a writer. He went to Paris, determined to adopt a lifestyle appropriate to his new calling. He ran up great debts cultivating the image of a literary man about town, frequently dodging his creditors and flirting with bankruptcy.

One important thing was lacking: success. Balzac's first work, *Cromwell*, a verse tragedy about the leader of the English Commonwealth, was a failure that made his family despair. By 1822 he had written several more, equally unsuccessful, works. His output throughout the 1820s consisted of slushy or sensational potboilers and historical romances in the style of Sir Walter Scott. Some were published under pseudonyms, others under no name at all. None gave any indication that Balzac was about to become a literary titan.

But around 1830 Balzac began to form a new and revolutionary concept of fiction. A few writers had toyed with the idea of placing characters across more than one book, but no one had applied the idea to their life's work. Balzac leapt at the concept, realizing that he could create a self-contained world that stretched across all his novels. When the idea came to him, he is said to have run all the way to his sister Laure's house on the right bank of the Seine, shouting, 'Hats off! I am about to become a genius!'

With a focus for his efforts, Balzac swiftly began to produce work of real significance. He was a phenomenally energetic writer, routinely working for eighteen hours at a stretch, fuelled by up to fifty cups of coffee a day. He described himself as a 'galley slave of pen and ink'; others called him a Napoleon of letters. One story, *The Illustrious Gaudissart*, was produced in a single sitting – 14,000 words in a night. He was a furious amender of proofs from his publishers, revising and reworking his stories through six or seven drafts.

The tales that made up *La Comédie* humaine are characterized by Balzac's superb gift for storytelling, his rich sense of humour, and his delicate description of characters, scenes and places. In *Le Père Goriot* (1835), the tale of a penniless young provincial and the old man who gives up everything for his daughters, Balzac brings Paris to life almost as a character in its own right:

> *Left alone, Rastignac walked a few steps to the highest part of the cemetery, and saw Paris spread out below on both banks of the winding Seine. Lights were beginning to twinkle here and there. His gaze fixed almost avidly upon the space that lay between the column of the Place Vendôme and the dome of the Invalides; there lay the splendid world that he wished to conquer.*

His imaginative gift and powers of description set the tone for the development of the 19th-century realist novel. As Oscar Wilde said, Balzac 'created life, he did not copy it'. The world of *La Comédie humaine* stretched from Paris to the French countryside, and its rich cast included sensitive portraits not only of young provincial men on the make in Paris, such as Rastignac, but also of young and old women, bureaucrats, politicians, courtesans, spinsters, nobles, peasants, actors and innkeepers – in his words, 'scenes of private life, Parisian life, political life, military life'. He also created the most unforgettable villain, the bisexual criminal mastermind turned police chief Vautrin, who was based on the real criminal-turned-police-chief Vidocq. It was Balzac who reflected that 'behind every great fortune lies a great crime'. The greatest works in this vast body of stories include *Eugénie Grandet* (1833), *Le Père Goriot, Lost Illusions* (1837), *La Cousine Bette* (1846) and *A Harlot High and Low* (1838–47).

From the age of twenty-three, when he fell for the forty-five-year-old mother of some children he was tutoring, Balzac was in search of the ideal woman. He eventually found her in a Polish countess, Evelina Ha´nska, whom he married after a romantic correspondence that lasted fifteen years. By the time he married her, in March 1850, Balzac had no more than five months to live. He died in August, killed by the strain of his punishingly indulgent working habits. At his funeral, the writer Victor Hugo remembered Balzac as 'among the brightest stars of his native land'.

PUSHKIN

1799–1837

The poet is dead: a slave to honour
Felled, by slanderous rumour
With a bullet in his breast, and thirsting for revenge
His proud head now bowed down.
The poet's spirit could not bear
The shame of petty calumnies . . .

Mikhail Lermontov, from his homage to
Pushkin, circulated secretly a few days after the
great poet's death

Alexander Pushkin is the heroic ideal of the romantic poet. A genius of exuberance, versatility, wit, poignancy and originality, a passionate and promiscuous lover of women, a victim of tyranny who remained true to his art – he personifies the triumph of creativity over the dead hand of bureaucracy. He helped create modern Russia – its culture, its language, its very image of itself. He also wrote history and short stories.

Pushkin is generally considered to be Russia's greatest poet. Translation cannot do justice to the extraordinary way in which he moulded the Russian language to his art, mixing archaic with modern, vernacular with formal, and readily inventing new words when old ones did not suffice. The profound simplicity of Pushkin's poetry transformed the way that Russians – writers and ordinary people – use language.

The precocious son of an old noble family, Pushkin became renowned when, as a fourteen-year-old schoolboy, his first poetry was published. His romantic narrative poem *Ruslan and Ludmilla*, written six years later, broke every literary convention of its day and was a runaway success. The leader of Russian poetry's old guard, Vasily Zhukovsky, gave Pushkin a portrait of himself inscribed: 'To the victorious pupil from the defeated master.' Barely out of his teens, Pushkin was already recognized as Russia's pre-eminent poet.

Pushkin's astounding energy and drive transformed Russian literature. He cast off the stifling blanket of religion and censorship, creating works of extraordinary originality that laid the foundations of the modern Russian literary tradition. *Eugene Onegin* (1825– 32) his great novel in verse, is considered by many to be the finest Russian novel ever written. Set in a Russian landscape with Russian characters, it was a decisive step away from the allegorical tradition and towards the realism later employed by Tolstoy, Dostoyevsky, Nabokov and Bulgakov. This is the story of the doomed love between Tatiana, provincial beauty, and Onegin, cynical nobleman and foppish, bored intellectual. He flirts with her; she falls in love; he rejects her and kills her sister's fiancé in a duel (foreshadowing Pushkin's own death). Many years later, Onegin meets her again. She is now a St Petersburg *grande dame,* a society beauty, a princess married to an aristocrat. He realizes he loves her – but she replies, 'I love you but I am now another's wife.' Onegin is heartbroken – he 'stood seared as if by heaven's fire. How deep his stricken heart is shaken. With what a tempest of desire.' The characters remain eternal but nothing is so timeless as the tragic sadness of Onegin's love for the married Tatiana – and her undying love for him, loves that cannot ever be.

The poet-revolutionary was the image of the romantic hero. He was a sympathetic and social, rather than active, conspiratorial member of the aristocratic set later known as the Decembrists, who conspired to reform the oppressive autocracy of the tsars. The group's members were famed for their drinking, gambling and womanizing as much as for their liberal views.

Pushkin's work revolutionized the way Russians thought about their history and their drama, and especially the way they thought about their writers. Never one to play down his own achievements, Pushkin was one of the first Russian writers to make a collected edition of his various writings. Within a year of his death, a critic was able to declare: 'Every educated Russian must have a complete Pushkin, otherwise he has no right to be considered either educated or Russian.'

Russia's oppressive autocrats tried to break the will of the fiery radical. Pushkin was, in his own words, 'persecuted six years in a row, stained by expulsion from the service, exiled to an out-of-the-way village for two lines in an intercepted letter'. It was not all bad: he adored the exotic romance of Odessa, Moldavia and the Caucasus, which inspired him. He also managed many affairs, keeping lists, sketches and poems to record his conquests, who included Princess Lise Vorontsov, wife of the viceroy of New Russia, Prince Michael Vorontsov and a great-niece of Catherine the Great's minister Prince Potemkin. They probably had a child together (brought up as Vorontsov) and he wrote a poem to her called *The Talisman*.

But Pushkin was keenly aware of the oppressive hand of censorship and surveillance – and its potential to get worse. During the abortive Decembrist uprising of 1825, he could only look on helplessly as his generation's dreams of liberty were ruthlessly smashed by the dreary martinet Tsar Nicholas I. Finally, beaten down by almost a decade of censorship and exile, Pushkin was wooed into Nicholas's service with the illusory promise of reform. The tsar appointed himself as Pushkin's personal censor.

Imperial favour broke Pushkin even more effectively than imperial displeasure. Personally censored by the tsar, Pushkin was rendered almost speechless. The volatile radical poet fell increasingly out of favour at court, but, despite his increasingly desperate pleas to retire to a life of literary seclusion, he was not allowed to leave. His popularity meant he was still viewed as a loose cannon. Besides, half the court, including the tsar, were infatuated with Pushkin's beautiful wife Natalya. His misery, drinking and gambling increased.

Pushkin's romantic death, the result of a simmering romantic crisis, turned the hero into a legend. In February 1837 the creepy and sleazy French social climber Georges d'Anthès, having been frustrated by Natalya's decisive rejection of his approaches, publicly insulted her and challenged her husband to a duel. Pushkin, who had been itching to fight for months, accepted with alacrity. In the ensuing duel, Pushkin was fatally wounded, dying two days later at the age of thirty-eight.

The volatile, charismatic poet-radical who fought for liberty and died for love is revered in Russia almost as a god. His statue stands in Moscow's Pushkin Square, decked out with flowers even in deep winter. Pushkin had decreed in his great poem 'Monument' that 'My verses will be sung throughout all Russia's vastness / My ashes will outlive and know no pale decay . . . ' In this he proved a prophet too.

ALEXANDRE DUMAS
PÈRE & FILS

1802–1870   1824–1895

His successes . . . resound like a fanfare. The name of Alexandre Dumas is more than French, it is European; it is more than European, it is universal . . . Alexandre Dumas is one of those men who can be called the sowers of civilization.

Victor Hugo

Alexandre Dumas's soaring imagination holds us spellbound. As vividly drawn in life as one of his own characters, this master storyteller scorned literary pretension. Irrepressible to the end, he swaggered through a life that might have sprung straight from the pages of his books.

Dumas's rip-roaring historical novels are crammed with romance, adventure, courage and daring. At one moment comical and poignant, the next mysterious and terrifying, they induce every emotion except boredom. In *The Count of Monte Cristo, The Three Musketeers* and *The Man in the Iron Mask*, Dumas created some of the most thrilling stories ever written. He wove together history and fantasy, using scraps gleaned from old books to embroider timeless characters and gripping plots. His fecund imagination has rendered the names d'Artagnan and Dantès as familiar as Louis XIV and Richelieu.

He was the son of a swashbuckling creole general (himself the illegitimate son of a marquis) and an innkeeper's daughter. Given his ancestry, it is hardly surprising that Alexandre Dumas *père* specialized in tales of romance, derring-do, betrayal and intrigue. The fatherless boy who grew up in the small French town of Villers-Cotterêts was the son of the 'Black Count', a flamboyant and eccentric Napoleonic general whose integrity brought him only disgrace and provoked an early death.

Thomas-Alexandre Davy de la Pailleterie was the creole son of a black slave girl and a minor Norman marquis. Born in French Saint-Domingue in 1762 and raised by his mother's family after she died when he was twelve, at eighteen Thomas-Alexandre was taken by his father to France to be educated as befitted a nobleman. But when he joined the army as an ordinary soldier in 1786, he assumed his mother's surname Dumas in order to avoid embarrassing his father's family.

As the French Revolution overturned the strict hierarchy of France's *ancien régime*, he rose up the army ranks. Dumas's daring and skill in campaigns in the Vendée, in Italy and in Egypt had earned him the rank of general by the age of thirty-one. But in 1802 he was ordered to put down the slave rebellion in Saint-Domingue, and when he refused, Napoleon made his displeasure all too clear.

Politically disgraced, Dumas retired to the countryside, to the wife he had first met when he was billeted at her father's inn in Villers-Cotterêts in 1789. Dogged by poverty and ill health, in 1806 the giant of a man died, leaving behind a widow and a small son and daughter.

The Black Count died in his forties, leaving his indigent widow to bring up two children on her own. When Dumas finally made his way to Paris, the mixed-race, rambunctious provincial was mocked for his frizzy blond curls and his antiquated dress. His father's erstwhile friends evaded his pleas for patronage. Only a stroke of luck prevented an ignominious return to the countryside. Dumas's beautiful penmanship secured him a position as a clerk in the office of the Duc d'Orléans (later King Louis-Philippe, 1830–48). It gave him enough money and plenty of time to pursue the writing that he believed would make his fortune. His faith was vindicated. In 1829 his play *Henry III and his Court* made him famous overnight.

The self-styled 'king of the world of Romance' provided his audiences with a magical form of escapism. He was the champion of romanticism, seeing the theatre as 'above all a thing of the imagination'and rejecting the cold orations and philosophical monologues of traditional French drama. His characters fought, wept, made love and died on stage with passion, the triumphant climaxes of his plays rendering his audiences delirious. When Dumas started writing novels, his imagination enraptured Paris. As *The Three Musketeers and The Count of Monte Cristo* appeared simultaneously, their daily instalments of action and melodrama were instant talking points. Despite their tendency to melodrama, his characters were so exuberant that they still pulse with life today – the musketeers Aramis, Porthos, Athos and D'Artagnan (with their motto 'One for all, and all for one'), the sinisterly beautiful Milady de Winter, and Edmond Dantès, the count of Monte Cristo himself.

In *The Three Musketeers*, D'Artagnan, the cocky but charming provincial Gascon swordsman, joins the experienced king's men to fight the sinister intrigues of Cardinal Richelieu and others. In *The Count of Monte Cristo*, an innocent man, Dantès, is imprisoned forever in the Château d'If island prison, where an old prisoner helps him escape – 'Death is the escape from the Château d'If'– to claim a buried fortune and mysterious title. Dantès – now Monte Cristo – returns to seek justice in the classic tale of revenge.

At the height of his success Dumas was Paris' literary star. His image was on medallions and etchings. His workrooms were strewn with flowers and bursting with visitors. Extravagant, exuberantly dressed in capes and sporting flashy canes, with a menagerie of outlandish pets and an endless stream of still more glamorous mistresses, Dumas was the perfect subject for caricature. It was not always kind and it was often racist. But his generosity, his child-like sensitivities and his bombastic naivety earned him as much love as ridicule.

The critics sneered at Dumas's popularity, at his readability, at his prodigious and varied output. He was never elected to the bastion of France's artistic establishment, the Académie française. He was attacked in print for being no more than the foreman of a 'novel factory' because he used collaborators. Assistants did indeed research and draft his work, but it was he who brought about the literary alchemy. Furiously scribbling away in his shirtsleeves, he injected the romance, suspense and humour that gave his work its magic. Dumas had no time for academic introspection. The self-styled popularizer wrote to entertain, to enchant and consume, to dispel the mundaneness of life. He succeeded. 'It fertilizes the soul, the mind, the intelligence,' wrote Victor Hugo, one of France's other titanic men of letters. Dumas 'creates a thirst for reading'.

Dumas was always blithely unconcerned by the sniping of others less successful than himself. He abandoned his tenuous claim to the title of marquis; his name was title enough. He had his motto – 'I love those who love me' – carved in huge letters on Monte Cristo, the opulent château he built to celebrate his success.

His lifestyle was precarious. Debts forced him to sell Monte Cristo. On his deathbed he remarked wryly: 'I came to Paris with twenty-four francs. That is exactly the sum with which I die.' His action-packed cape-and-sword romances became less fashionable as literary styles changed. But he was undaunted by his oscillating fortunes. Irrepressible and indefatigable, he continued to write. He founded magazines and he lectured. He even participated in Garibaldi's campaign to unify Italy.

When Dumas died, at the home of his devoted son at Puys near Dieppe, it was, in the words of one young journalist, 'as though we had all lost a friend'. The 'affectionate and much-loved soul' was also the 'splendid magician' who created works that gave 'passage into unknown worlds'.

Dumas had a son who would also make his name in literature. In 1822, when he was twenty, Alexandre Dumas had moved to Paris to make his fortune and quickly took up with the first of many mistresses, Marie-Catherine Labay, a dressmaker who lived in the rooms opposite him. Young Alexandre, the child of this affair, was six years old before his father formally recognized him and won custody of him in a vicious legal battle. (Father and son, both Alexandre and both writers, are distinguished as *père* and *fils*.) His father cherished him and gave him the most expensive education possible (although he could not prevent his son's classmates from taunting him for his mixed-race heritage). But his mother's distress at losing her son was an experience that the adult Dumas *fils* would revisit in his work.

The son adored his father but was different from him in almost every way. Dumas fils, a member of the Académie française, wrote moralizing novels and plays that made him the darling of the French literary establishment. His love affair as a youth with the young courtesan Marie Duplessis, one of the celebrated beauties of her time, inspired his best-known work, *La Dame aux camélias* (1848), in which a young man falls in love with a beautiful girl of pleasure. His father ends it and she dies of tuberculosis. Verdi made it into the opera *La Traviata* (1853), and there have been eight film versions starring actresses from Sarah Bernhardt to Greta Garbo and Isabelle Huppert.

Father and son both produced great works, but *The Three Musketeers* and *The Count of Monte Cristo* – the father's masterpieces – remain not just timeless but universal, still bestsellers and the subjects of innumerable movies. In 2002, President Jacques Chirac of France presided as Republican Guards dressed as the Musketeers moved Dumas's body to rest in the Panthéon. 'With you,' said the president, '*we were* D'Artagnan and Monte Cristo!'

DISRAELI

1804–1881

Mr Disraeli . . . has always behaved extremely well to me, and has all the right feelings for a minister towards the sovereign . . . He is full of poetry, romance and chivalry. When he knelt down to kiss my hand, which he took in both of his, he said 'in loving loyalty and faith'.
Queen Victoria, letter to her daughter Crown Princess Victoria of Prussia (4 March 1868)

The greatest showman of British leaders, the most literary, and one of the wittiest, Benjamin Disraeli – known appropriately by everyone, even his wife, as Dizzy – matured from an adventurer into a heroic statesman, superb parliamentarian and virtuoso orator. Under him, the Conservative Party developed its guiding ideology, one that was to endure for over a century: fervent support for the monarchy, the empire and the Church of England, but also a commitment to achieving national unity (One Nation) by social reform. And although baptized a Christian in 1817, he remains the only British prime minister to have come from a Jewish background (let alone a Sephardic Moroccan one), a source of pride throughout his career. 'I'm the empty page between the Old and New Testaments', he told Queen Victoria. When he faced anti-Semitic taunts in Parliament, he proudly replied, 'Yes I am a

Jew and when the ancestors of the Rt Hon. Gentleman were living as savages in an unknown island, mine were priests in the Temple of Solomon.'

Most of Disraeli's political achievements came late in life. The son of the writer Isaac d'Israeli, he was best known in his early years as a rakish literary figure, Byronic poseur and financial speculator. (Indeed, he and Winston Churchill remain the only outstanding literary figures among British leaders.) 'When I want to read a book, I write one,' he once said; his books included romantic and political novels – the most famous being *Coningsby* – which often earned him substantial sums of money. He travelled the Ottoman empire and visited Jerusalem, where he rediscovered and reinvented his exotic persona as a Jewish Tory. He was famed for his extravagant dress sense and bumptiousness, which made him as many enemies as friends. His financial life was rackety, his sex life was shocking and, at one point, he lived in a *ménage à trois* with the lord chancellor Lord Lyndhurst and their joint mistress, the married Lady Henrietta Sykes. It was all a far cry from the sobriety of his arch-opponent, the Liberal leader W.E. Gladstone, with whom he had a fiery, combative relationship. He married late – childlessly but happily.

Disraeli entered Parliament in 1837, his maiden speech a disaster as the bumptious dandy (in green velvet) was booed: 'You will hear me,' he said as he sat down. Before long he was recognized as a brilliant speaker and a tricky character. In 1846 he was instrumental in splitting the Conservative Party, by opposing the repeal of the Corn Laws in defiance of his leader, Robert Peel. When the Conservative Party formed a minority government in 1852, the earl of Derby appointed Disraeli chancellor of the exchequer. But his first budget was rejected by Parliament, and Derby's government resigned after just ten months. Disraeli served twice more as chancellor under Derby, in 1858–9 and 1866–8.

It was in 1867 that Disraeli – now in his sixties – made his first great contribution to posterity, when he and Derby vigorously pushed through the 1867 Reform Act. This nearly doubled the number of people entitled to vote (although it did not enfranchise any women) and had the effect of underpinning the two-party system in England, lining up Conservatives against Liberals. When Derby became so ill that he had to resign the premiership in 1868, Disraeli was the natural choice to lead the Conservatives and the government. But his premiership was short. Gladstone's Liberals returned to power at the end of the year.

After another six years of opposition, Disraeli was prime minister once more (1874–80). 'I have climbed to the top of the greasy pole,' he said. This time the Conservatives had a majority. Queen Victoria adored him – in contrast to Gladstone, whom she loathed. He joked that with royalty it was necessary to 'lay on the flattery with a trowel'. He flattered Victoria as 'we authors, ma'am'. In 1876 Disraeli gave the queen the title of empress of India, and he was created earl of Beaconsfield, describing his presence in the House of Lords as 'dead – but in the Elysian Fields!' In foreign affairs he successfully impressed upon Europe and the world that Britain was indeed 'Great'. He protected British shipping interests and the route to India by arranging the purchase of a controlling stake in the Suez Canal. In European politics he played a canny hand to contain Russia's ambitions as the Ottoman Empire, the so-called 'sick man of Europe', declined.

One of Disraeli's most influential achievements was in creating an imperial ethos for the British empire. He sang the virtues of *imperium et libertas* (empire and liberty), and he saw Britain's mission as not just to trade and establish colonial settlements, but also to bring British civilization and values to the diverse peoples of its ever expanding dominions. He was convinced of Britain's unique and pre-eminent position in international politics, and to an extent his belief was vindicated at the Congress of Berlin in 1878, where his cunning and flamboyance dominated the attempts to solve the Russo-Turkish problem and the nationalist aspirations in the Balkans, securing peace and resisting Russian territorial ambitions. He also brought Cyprus under the British flag. 'The old Jew is *the* man,' said the German Chancellor, Bismarck. The 'old wizard' Disraeli received a hero's welcome following the congress.

Throughout his political career, Disraeli maintained an intense feud with Gladstone, whom he called 'that unprincipled maniac ... [an] extraordinary mixture of envy, vindictiveness, hypocrisy and superstition'. The feeling was mutual. Gladstone compared Disraeli's defeat in 1880 to 'the vanishing of some vast magnificent castle in an Italian romance'. Disraeli brooded on his defeat but finished off a new novel, *Endymion*, published soon afterwards. He died not long after that – having lived a life like one of his own novels.

GARIBALDI

1807–1882

Anyone who wants to carry on the war against the outsiders, come with me. I can offer you neither honours nor wages; I offer you hunger, thirst, forced marches, battles and death. Anyone who loves his country, follow me.

Garibaldi to his followers when fleeing Rome, as described
by Giuseppe Guerzoni, in *Garibaldi* (Vol. 1, 1882)

Maverick general of irregular troops and irrepressible liberator of peoples, Garibaldi led an almost incredible life of battle and adventure. But his cause was as heroic as his exploits: the liberation of the long-subdued disparate states of Italy from the shackles of corrupt tyrants and hidebound empires. In this process, known as the Risorgimento, Garibaldi led his Redshirt followers to decisive victories over the Spanish Bourbon and Austrian Habsburg dynasties that still ruled much of Italy.

Garibaldi was born in Nice, which from 1814 to 1860 was part of the Italian kingdom of Piedmont-Sardinia. He ran away from home in order to avoid a clerical education but was then reunited with his father in the coastal trade, becoming a sea captain in his early twenties. In his mid-twenties he joined the Young Italy movement, influenced by the nationalist republicanism of Giuseppe Mazzini, conspiring in an anti-monarchical uprising in Genoa in 1834. The plot was discovered; Garibaldi fled, but, drawn to other liberation causes, he travelled to South America.

There he fought for the rebellious state of Rio Grande do Sul, which was trying to secede from Brazil. He lived a life of hardship and danger. During one campaign he met his beloved creole partner Anna Maria Ribeiro da Silva (Anita), later mother of three of his children. She followed him when he received command of an Italian legion fighting for Uruguay against Argentina. Leading these first Redshirts, he won a reputation as a masterly guerrilla commander.

In 1848, as Europe caught fire with revolution, Garibaldi returned to Italy to offer his services in the struggle against Austrian hegemony. Spurned by Piedmont (he was, after all, still a wanted man there), he took part in a republican experiment in Rome that saw Pope Pius IX flee the city, and he organized the brave, but hopelessly outnumbered, resistance to the French and Neapolitan forces that restored the pope in 1849.

Garibaldi and several thousand followers retreated across central Italy, evading French and Austrian forces but suffering many losses – including his beloved Anita. Garibaldi himself made it to the coast of Tuscany, going into five years of exile as a trading skipper in New York and Peru.

Finally, in 1854, Garibaldi was able to return to his Piedmontese homeland, where he planned a united Italian monarchy (instead of a republic) with King Victor Emmanuel II and his powerful prime minister Cavour. Napoleon III of France backed the plan. In 1859 Garibaldi, now a Piedmontese major general, led Alpine troops into action against the Austrian Habsburgs in northern Italy, capturing Varese and Como. Austria ceded Lombardy to Piedmont.

In early 1860 Piedmont angered Garibaldi by returning Nice and the Savoy region to the French, in return gaining the sovereignty of the central Italian states. Garibaldi's thoughts turned to the south, the so-called Kingdom of the Two Sicilies, backward, impoverished and ruled by the Bourbons. With a mere 1146 of his Redshirts, and tacitly supported by Emmanuel and Cavour, he landed in Marsala, Sicily in May 1860 and soon captured Palermo. He forced 20,000 Neapolitan soldiers to surrender and declared himself a very popular dictator. He then crossed the Straits of Messina, entered victoriously into Naples and forced King Francis II to flee. Garibaldi handed over his conquests to Victor Emmanuel, recognizing him as king of Italy. He had nearly achieved his vision of a united Italy; only the French-defended Papal States and Austrian-ruled Venetia remained outside the new kingdom.

Two ostensibly private campaigns by Garibaldi to take the Papal States, in 1862 and 1867, came to nothing, the first leaving him injured at the Battle of Aspromante, ironically by troops sent by Victor Emmanuel to intercept him. (In contrast, the 1867 campaign was secretly funded by the king.) But more success came in the north, when Garibaldi led Italian forces – allied to the Prussians in a wider war – against the Austrians at Bezzecca (21 July 1866). By complex treaty negotiations, Venetia was ceded to the nascent Italian kingdom.

The Papal States finally surrendered to Italian government troops in September 1871, the last piece of the Italian jigsaw, but Garibaldi played no part. His last adventure was in support of the French against the Prussians in 1870–1. Retiring to Caprera, the island he had acquired in the 1850s, he lived peacefully – as politician, memoirist, novel-writer, but always a living legend who, on his death in June 1882, plunged Italy into mourning.

Mazzini had the philosophies, Cavour the strategies and Victor Emmanuel the crown, but it was Garibaldi, the swashbuckling patriot, who created a nation.

NAPOLEON III

1808–1873

Hegel remarks somewhere that all great world-historical facts and personages appear, so to speak, twice. He forgot to add: the first time as tragedy, the second time as farce.

Karl Marx on Napoleon III

Napoleon III's reign ended in disaster but for twenty years he enjoyed astonishing success, restoring order in France and then restoring France's position in Europe, winning the Crimean War in alliance with Britain, defeating Austria, helping to unite Italy, rebuilding Paris. Described by Bismarck as a 'sphinx without a riddle' and by Victor Hugo as 'Napoleon the Little' in comparison to his uncle Napoleon the Great, he was nonetheless a statesman of talent, and along with his nemesis Bismarck, one of the pioneers of modern politics and electioneering – the quest for the support of the middle classes and the centre.

His career was based on the fame of his uncle, Napoleon I. Louis-Napoleon Bonaparte was the son of Louis Bonaparte and Hortense de Beauharnais, king and queen of Holland, his father being a younger brother of the emperor, his mother a daughter of the Empress Josephine. On the death of the emperor in 1821, his heir was his son, the king of Rome, known as Napoleon II to Bonapartists or the duke of Reichstadt to everyone else, but he died young and never reigned. During the 1820s, Louis-Napoleon became the Bonapartist pretender, a romantic drifting figure whose quixotic attempts to seize power in France, invariably funded by his mistresses and backed by a crew of desperate and inept adventurers, ended in comical disaster. It was probably the comedy that saved his life, for he avoided severe penalties and was instead imprisoned for a while in the fortress of Ham – from which he famously escaped. Even early in his career, the young man showed drive and courage however unsuccessful he may have been.

His prospects remained hopeless until 1848 when the revolutions that shook Europe overthrew the July Monarchy of King Louis Philippe of France. Suddenly Louis-Napoleon Bonaparte, a romantic if inscrutable figure and bearer of the magical name, was on everyone's lips. When presidential elections were held, Louis-Napoleon, who was still relatively unknown in France, was able to appear to be all things to all people and played the election campaign with considerable skill and shrewdness, winning a landslide to become the first president of France. But he wanted more, calling himself the Prince-president. In a *coup d'état* in December 1851, he ruthlessly seized power, arresting his enemies and shooting down opposition, to become effective dictator of France. A year later, promising that the empire meant peace, he was crowned Emperor Napoleon III.

For his first decade in power, he ruled with authoritarian flamboyance, crushing any dissent but enjoying considerable success in his plans to restore France to a position of pre-eminence amongst the powers of Europe and to secure his own empire. He used tensions over the holy sites in Jerusalem to push the Ottoman sultan for more French influence in competition with Nicholas I of Russia. When the tsar used military force to invade Ottoman territory with a view to overthrowing the Sultanate, Napoleon allied with Britain to declare war: the Crimean War revealed both French and British military incompetence on a vast scale but ended in victory for the allies – and the acceptance of Napoleon III as a legitimate monarch by Queen Victoria, who hosted the emperor at Windsor and found him charming.

Napoleon married a Spanish aristocrat named Eugenie de Montejo who gave him a legitimate heir, the prince imperial. He backed Italian independence and unity, defeating Austria at the Battle of Solferino, thereby helping to expel the Habsburgs from Italy. During the 1860s, he changed his policies at home, fostering the liberal empire, a more constitutional monarchy that allowed greater parliamentary debate. France enjoyed a raging stock market boom, an orgy of new consumerism and ostentatious spending while Napoleon ordered the rebuilding of a glorious new Paris by Baron Haussman.

But the urban poor were discontented by rising prices, and the difference between rich and poor as well as uninhibited corruption, personified by the new property millionaires and the rise of sexual celebrities, the *grande horizontales*, courtesans. In many ways, the modern world – stock market and property boom and bust, consumerism, celebrity, electioneering, tycoons – started with Napoleon III.

Napoleon himself was notorious for his womanizing: his early career had been funded by an English courtesan called Harriet Howard and he remained an enthusiastic keeper of mistresses: indeed members of his cabinet travelling on the imperial train were once treated to the sight of the emperor in flagrante when his apartment door slid open. His affair with the gorgeous Contessa di Castaglione, a spy-temptress-adventuress who was the cousin of the Italian leader Cavour, was said to have encouraged his embrace of Italian liberation. But he was already committed to Italian freedom – her perfect figure displayed beneath her notorious see-through dresses was irresistible in its own right. For all his fame and flamboyance, Napoleon remained strangely unknowable and mysterious. With his waxed moustaches and short legs he was hardly a heroic figure – power exhausted him and ill health undermined his decision-making. His lack of judgement in 1869 allowed him to be manipulated by Bismarck into a declaration of war that proved catastrophic.

The ailing emperor was out of his depth as warlord or even war leader. Defeat at Sedan led to his abdication and exile in England: France's last monarch died abroad. His son the prince imperial was killed serving in British forces against the Zulus.

The downfall of his glittering, pleasure-loving, modern empire in the defeat, revolution and massacre of the Paris Commune, was best described by Emile Zola in his novel Nana in which the empire is symbolized by a shallow, greedy, wanton courtesan who dies in her hotel room as the crowds overthrow the regime, her beautiful body consumed by worms. Marx described how history repeated itself in the Napoleons: Napoleon I as a 'tragedy', Napoleon III as a 'farce'.

LINCOLN

1809–1865

We here highly resolve that the dead shall not have died in vain, that this nation, under God, shall have a new birth of freedom; and that government of the people, by the people, and for the people, shall not perish from the earth.

From Lincoln's address at the dedication of the National Cemetery at Gettysburg (19 November 1863)

'Honest Abe', the president who saved the Union and freed the slaves, is a legend of American history. Truly good as well as truly great, this gaunt, austere figure, who rose from the Kentucky backwoods to lead his nation, evinced a humble charm that has made him loved as much as he is admired.

Though he received almost no formal education – off-and-on schooling 'by littles', as he put it – he educated himself and could quote swathes of the Bible and Shakespeare, becoming a master of the English language. Abraham Lincoln's journey from the one-room Kentucky log cabin of his birth to the White House is the blueprint for the American Dream. His father and much-loved stepmother were almost illiterate. The lowly one-time rail-splitter taught himself law, established a flourishing Illinois practice, and – defending his well-known non-attendance at church – entered politics. First a Whig, then a founding member of the Republican Party, in 1860 Lincoln became the 16th president of the United States.

Lincoln's leadership may in the end have kept the states united, but his election was the catalyst for their split. In 1858 Lincoln famously declared: 'A house divided against itself cannot stand. I believe the government cannot endure permanently half-slave and half-free.' Lincoln's preference for freedom was well known, and even before he took office in 1861, seven Southern states declared themselves a new nation – the Confederate States of America. Respecting the Constitution, Lincoln would not open hostilities – it was the Confederates who initiated civil war when they fired on Fort Sumter – but refusing to countenance permanent secession, he was firm in his resolve: the Union would not be broken.

Lincoln wanted to save the Union both for its own sake and to preserve an ideal of democratic self-government that he saw as an exemplar for the world. In his 1863 Gettysburg Address, Lincoln bound the nation 'conceived in liberty and dedicated to the proposition that all men are created equal' to the principles of democracy and equality on which it had been founded in 1776: 'this nation,' he proclaimed, 'shall have a new birth of freedom; and ... government of the people, by the people, and for the people, shall not perish from the earth'. Lincoln reaffirmed a vision of the nation and its identity that endures to this day.

Lincoln's wartime leadership ensured the Union's victory. The struggle demanded extreme measures. Using emergency wartime powers, Lincoln suspended habeas corpus, blockaded southern ports and imprisoned without trial thousands of suspected Confederate sympathizers. His opponents, including the Copperheads lobbying for peace within the Union, criticized him violently, but, given the time and the circumstances, his methods were relatively humane. His innate magnanimity is clear in his treatment of the defeated Confederates: 'Let 'em up easy,' he told his generals.

As the Union army's commander-in-chief, the former lawyer displayed an instinct for strategy that belied his lack of military training. After several false starts, in Ulysses S. Grant he found a commander who instinctively understood his vision of how the war should be pursued: 'I cannot spare this man,' was Lincoln's reported response to criticism of Grant. 'He fights.'

While Grant pursued the conflict with aggressive and highly successful campaigns, Lincoln travelled around the country inspiring fighters and followers alike. The eloquence and integrity of his addresses reached a climax at Gettysburg, where he dedicated the nation's future to those who had died in its name.

Lincoln had been 'naturally anti-slavery' since his youth, and it had been the issue that made him leave the law and re-enter politics in 1854. It was the Civil War that turned Lincoln into an outright abolitionist. His 1862 Emancipation Proclamation used his wartime powers to free all slaves in the rebel states. Bringing black support and enlisting soldiers for the Union cause, it was a decision as politically justifiable as it was morally sound. For Lincoln it was a triumph: 'I never, in my life,' he said, 'felt more certain that I was doing right, than I do in signing this paper.' Anxious to prevent a peacetime revocation of his emergency decree, Lincoln secured in 1865 the Thirteenth Amendment that enshrined in America's Constitution the freedom of all its people.

Shot in the back of the head by the southern radical John Wilkes Booth as he attended the theatre with his wife Mary on 14 April 1865, Lincoln became America's first president to be assassinated in office. Some confusion surrounds the words spoken by John Stanton, the secretary of war, as Lincoln breathed his last. But truly Lincoln belongs both 'to the angels' and 'to the ages'.

JACK THE RIPPER

Active 1888–1891

More murders at Whitechapel, strange and horrible. The newspapers reek with blood.

Lord Cranbrook, Cabinet minister, 2 October 1888

Jack the Ripper stalked the dingiest areas of Victorian London, preying on the most vulnerable and ostracized members of society: prostitutes. In a frenzied bout of blood lust, he murdered at least five women from August to November 1888. The Ripper, also known as the Whitechapel murderer or the leather apron, remains the most infamous murderer never to be caught and the first serial killer to achieve an international profile. 'Horror ran through the land,' reads one account from the period. 'Men spoke of it with bated breath, and pale-lipped women shuddered as they read the dreadful details.'

All of the Ripper's murders took place in or around the poverty-stricken Whitechapel area of east London. His victims were street prostitutes. Although they were not raped, in nearly every case their throat was cut and lower torso mutilated in such a way as to suggest a depraved sexual motive for the murder and an obsession with wombs. Such was the precision with which the bodies were maimed that police felt the killer must have had at least some knowledge of either anatomy or butchery.

On 7 August 1888, Martha Tabram was stabbed thirty-nine times in the stairwell of a block of flats in Whitechapel, and left with her lower body exposed. Whether the Ripper was responsible is disputed, but he was unquestionably behind the murder of Mary Ann Nichols, found in a cobbled alleyway in Whitechapel on 31 August, strangled and then repeatedly stabbed in the throat, stomach and genitalia. Detective Inspectors Frederick George Abberline, Henry Moore and Walter Andrews were brought in to assist local inquiries (later supplemented by the City police under Detective Inspector James McWilliam) and separate suspects were questioned concerning both murders, but nothing came of their investigations. Then, on 8 September, a pattern began to emerge, as the body of Annie Chapman was found in Spitalfields, with her throat cut and some of her organs ripped from her body.

The killer clearly thrived on the fear he was creating. On 30 September, after killing his next victim, Elizabeth Stride, outside the International Working Men's Club in Dutfield's Yard, he boldly walked eastwards to Aldgate, probably passing the police patrols that were passing every fifteen minutes, where he accosted Catherine Eddowes near a warehouse. Just discharged from a local police station for being intoxicated, she was found lying on her back with her throat cut, stomach opened and organs removed. The last victim of the Ripper was Mary Jane Kelly, another local prostitute, murdered in her room in Spitalfields and chopped into tiny pieces on 9 November.

On 27 September, midway through the killings, the Central

News Agency received a poorly written confession, in red ink, signed 'Jack the Ripper'. Although this may have been a hoax, on 16 October a local committee set up to keep vigil in the area was sent what appeared to be half a human kidney, apparently from one of the murder victims. As news of a serial killer stalking the streets appeared in the press, so fear escalated into hysteria, and the London police commissioner, Sir Charles Warren, was forced to resign.

Who was the Ripper? Wilder speculation has alleged political motives on his part. Was he a social reformer – perhaps even Thomas Barnardo – eager to bring the squalid conditions of areas such as Whitechapel to public attention? Could he have been a twisted Irish nationalist: perhaps their leader in the House of Commons, Charles Stewart Parnell, who, known to walk the streets of Whitechapel, was followed for a time by police before being ruled out as a suspect? The writer George Bernard Shaw seemed to give some credence to the idea when he wrote, in September 1888: '[while] we conventional Social Democrats were wasting our time . . . some independent genius has taken the matter in hand . . . by simply disembowelling four women'.

The most controversial suggestion was that Prince Albert Victor, the duke of Clarence and eldest son of the prince of Wales, was involved in the killings, and that the government and royal family covered up the crimes to prevent a scandal. The idea has intrigued conspiracy theorists in particular, not least because the prince was known for his dissipated lifestyle, but the weight of evidence suggests he was elsewhere when several of the murders were committed.

Suspicion fell for a time on the sizeable Jewish community in east London, as old prejudices flared up during the killings, with rumours of ritual religious murder. The Ripper had left some body parts after the double murder of 30 September, and chalked a message in a stairwell claiming that 'The Juwes are men that will not be blamed for nothing.' Aaron Kosminski – a Polish Jew who worked as a hairdresser in London before being committed to a lunatic asylum in 1891 – was later named chief suspect by Assistant Chief Constable Sir Melville Macnaghten, but no charges were ever brought, despite Robert Anderson (head of CID) and Chief Inspector Donald Swanson (whom he temporarily entrusted with the case) also considering Kosminski the chief suspect. Others, though, claim the cryptic message on the wall points to a Masonic connection, the Juwes representing Jubela, Jubelo and Jubelum, ritually killed, according to Masonic tradition, for murdering Grand Master Hiram Abif.

Macnaghten also named three other possible suspects: Montague Druitt, a barrister and teacher with an interest in surgery, who was believed to be insane and later found dead; Michael Ostrog, a Russian-born thief and con man who was detained in asylums on several occasions; and Francis Tumblety, a physician who fled the country under suspicion for the Kelly murder. Other suggestions have included Jacob Isenschmid, an insane Swiss pork butcher, and Severin Klowoski, a Polish surgeon who poisoned three wives. According to crime novelist Patricia Cornwell, however, the most likely candidate was in fact a German-born artist named Walter Richard Sickert, whose paintings included numerous misogynistic images of violent assaults on women, though criminologists had previously dismissed Sickert as a credible suspect.

Why did the Ripper murders suddenly stop? Was the perpetrator consigned to a mental institution and thus prevented from continuing his killing spree. Did he die from syphilis or perhaps even commit suicide? Could it be that, having made his grotesque point, he was content to retire again into the shadows? Did he move elsewhere when the police presence in London became too much to handle? Or did he not stop at all but simply change his modus operandi, being guilty of not just five but eleven murders in

Whitechapel between 3 April 1888 and 13 February 1891. No one can say for sure, but the slaughter ended as abruptly as it had begun.

The Ripper has been portrayed, based on a few alleged sightings, as a tall man, wearing an apron and carrying a black doctor's bag full of surgical knives, but the *Star* newspaper, reporting at the time, captures far more powerfully the awfulness of his crimes and the sheer terror he provoked. 'A nameless reprobate – half beast, half man – is at large,' it wrote. 'Hideous malice, deadly cunning, insatiable thirst for blood – all these are the marks of the mad homicide. The ghoul-like creature, stalking down his victim like a Pawnee Indian, is simply drunk with blood, and he will have more.'

DARWIN

1809–1882

The more one knew of him, the more he seemed the incorporated ideal of a man of science.

T.H. Huxley, in Nature (1882)

Along with Copernicus, Newton and Einstein, Charles Darwin stands as one of a small handful of scientists who have brought about a fundamental revolution in our ways of thinking. Before Darwin, the account of creation as described in the Bible was almost universally believed. After Darwin, a vast, chilling wedge of doubt was hammered into the claims of religion to explain the universe and our place in it. He altered radically the way we think about ourselves.

As a boy, Darwin was quiet and unassuming, with a keen interest in collecting minerals, coins and birds' eggs. After an unexceptional schooling he was sent to university in Edinburgh to study medicine. He found the dissection of dead bodies repellent and left without taking a degree, but his interest in natural history and geology had blossomed and it continued when he went on to study at Cambridge.

After Darwin graduated in 1831, his professor of botany recommended him to the Admiralty for the position of unpaid ship's naturalist on board HMS *Beagle* as it made a five-year surveying voyage around the world. The *Beagle* took Darwin around the coasts of South America, across the Pacific to the Antipodes, then on to South Africa, before returning to England. The experience opened his eyes to the wondrous variety of life forms around the planet – and the differences and similarities between them.

During the voyage Darwin read Charles Lyell's revolutionary *Principles of Geology*, which argued that geological features were the result of slow, gradual processes occurring over vast aeons of time. This 'uniformitarianism' was at odds with the orthodox 'catastrophism', which argued that such features were the result of sudden, violent upheavals over a relatively short timescale – and so conformed with the Church's view that the earth was of very recent creation, as described in Genesis. On his travels Darwin collected more evidence in favour of Lyell's theory, such as fossil shells in bands of rock at a height of 12,000ft (3660m).

By the time Darwin reached the Galapagos Islands, a remote archipelago off the west coast of South America, his mind was open to new ways of thinking about the natural world. He had already noticed how the rheas – the large flightless birds of the South American pampas – looked like the ostriches of Africa, and yet were clearly different species. In the Galapagos he collected specimens of finches from the different islands, which were similar to each other yet also subtly different. Back home, closer study made it clear that the finches from the different islands were actually different species. Darwin realized they must all have had a common ancestor, but over time they had undergone a process of transmutation.

Ideas of evolution were not new, although they were not widely accepted. Darwin's own grandfather, Erasmus, had held the view – shared with the French scientist Jean-Baptiste Lamarck (1744–1829) – that species evolved over time by inheriting acquired characteristics. What Darwin himself came to realize was that animals (and plants), in order to survive, adapt over time to changes in their natural habitat, and if they are geographically isolated for long enough these adaptations will become so pronounced that the rhea of South America, for example, emerges as a different species from its cousin, the African ostrich.

Darwin's big breakthrough followed his reading in 1838 of Thomas Malthus's *Principles of Population*, which argued that human population growth is always checked by limits in the food supply, or by disease or war. Darwin realized that the variations or adaptations he saw in animals resulted from the 'struggle for existence', in which those individuals who possessed or inherited a characteristic that better fitted them to survive in their environment were more likely to breed and pass on this favourable characteristic. He called this process natural selection.

It was an idea of great simplicity, and yet of enormous explanatory power. Through the 1830s, 1840s and 1850s Darwin continued to amass evidence, reluctant to put his theory before the public, aware as he was of the devastating impact it would have on religious belief and the comforting notion of a moral and purposeful world.

Darwin agonized and prevaricated, suffering more and more

from the psychosomatic, but nevertheless painful, illnesses that were to plague him for the rest of his life. Then in 1858 he received a letter from a young naturalist, Alfred Russell Wallace, who had, it was clear, independently come up with the idea of natural selection. On 1 July 1859 the two presented a joint paper at the Linnaean Society in London. And in November of that year Darwin published *On the Origin of Species by Means of Natural Selection*.

It was a knockout blow to the old, comfortable certainties. Any reasonable, thinking person found it almost impossible to dissent, such was the compelling nature of the argument and the overwhelming volume of the evidence. The big guns of the Church of England were wheeled out to mount a counteroffensive, but to no avail. In place of 'All things bright and beautiful, all creatures great and small' came, as Tennyson had foreseen, 'Nature, red in tooth and claw'.

The implication that man and the apes must share a common ancestor was obvious. Darwin made this explicit when, in 1871, he eventually published the long-awaited sequel *The Descent of Man*. No longer did humanity possess some special status as God's appointed steward on earth, separate from and superior to the other animals. Man was now just one beast among many. It was a bleaker world view that Darwin bequeathed to us, but it was also more intellectually honest and showed us that there was still as much – or more – wonder and mystery in a Darwinian universe.

DICKENS

1812–1870

*In literary matters my dividing line is: do you like Dickens or do
you not? If you do not, I am sorry for you, and that is the end of
the matter.*

Stanley Baldwin

Charles Dickens was the English writer of his age. Rambunctious,
touching, tragic and comic by turns, his novels captured the
public's imagination like no others before or since. He transmuted
the realities he saw into an enthralling and encyclopedic social
panorama of hypnotic power. His works effectively constitute
a world, such that even those who have read little of the author
know what is meant by the term Dickensian.

The master storyteller wrote a canon of classics. His books
weave together darkness and light, romance and melodrama, the
terrifying and the tender; one moment they are gruesome and
fantastical, the next tear-inducingly funny. From the debtors'
prison of *Little Dorrit* (1855–7) to the workhouse and thieves' dens
of *Oliver Twist* (1837–8), to the machinations of the Chancery
Court in *Bleak House* (1852–3), Dickens created a vision of London
as a pulsating, living organism, which even today dominates our
conceptions of the Victorian metropolis. From the moment his
first major work, *The Pickwick Papers*, was serialized (1836), and a
print run of 400 mushroomed to 40,000, he was established as the
writer who understood the English better than anyone else.

Dickens's rudimentary schooling was cut short at fifteen by the profligacy of his father, an erstwhile naval clerk. The boy who had wanted since childhood to be an actor and who was remembered by his schoolfellows for his 'animation and animal spirits' became instead a reluctant legal clerk. In spring of 1833 Dickens, by now a journalist (a more exciting but 'wearily uncertain' career), got an audition at Covent Garden Theatre but failed to keep the appointment on account of illness. An accident of fate, perhaps, because that summer he began to write. By the following year, under the pen-name Boz, Dickens was winning in print the fame that he had previously hoped for on the stage. His love of the theatre clearly influenced his work. Later he would adapt classics such as *A Christmas Carol* (1843) for the stage. But he never renewed his application to Covent Garden.

The colourful names of Dickens' characters were of paramount importance to him. He could not begin a new book until he had them right. He kept lists of those with special potential and scribbled down myriad variations. Martin Chuzzlewit was nearly Martin Sweezlewag. With age his work grew darker and more serious, but comedy was never far off. Frequently seized by hysterical mirth at the most inappropriate times, Dickens was always quick to see the ridiculous side of things.

Dickens researched carefully and many of his characters were based on fact, such as Fagin in *Oliver Twist*. In 1849 the journalist Henry Mayhew, founder of *Punch* magazine, began a series of articles for the *Morning Chronicle*. They would eventually become the mammoth four-volume *London Labour and the London Poor*, a work that shocked his middle-class readership with its unflinching picture of the realities of London's slums and which influenced radicals, reformers and writers, among them Charles Dickens.

Mayhew revealed the dark underside of the city, a world of crime, filth and depravity. Interviewing chimney sweeps and flower girls, beggars and street entertainers, pickpockets and prostitutes, Mayhew depicted a world, as the writer Thackeray described it, 'of terror and wonder'. He spoke of the 'pure-finders', who gathered dog faeces to sell to tanners. He introduced his readers to the 'mud-larks', children who made their living scavenging around the banks of the cholera-infested, sewage-filled Thames for coins and wood or for coal dropped from the barges.

Mayhew let his subjects speak in their own words and reported his findings with a humanist's eye. He told of Jack, a West End crossing-sweep, 'a good-looking lad with a pair of large, mild eyes'; of his friend Gander, who earned extra money with his acrobatic 'catenwheeling'. He described their room in the lodging house that was as clean as it could be and the old woman who cared for them as well as she was able. He told the story of the drunken prostitute China Emma, the 'shrivelled and famine-stricken' woman lying in 'a hole . . . more like a beast in his lair than a human being in her home'.

It was in this world that the model for *Oliver Twist*'s Fagin lived. One of London's most notorious pawnbrokers and fences (receivers of stolen goods), Ikey Solomon became famous for his farcical escape from Newgate Prison. After he was arrested in 1827 for theft and receiving, the hackney coach that was intended to carry him to jail was in fact driven by his father-in-law. As the coach took a detour through Petticoat Lane, a gang of Solomon's friends overpowered the guards and set Ikey free.

Solomon fled to New York, but, in lieu of the notorious criminal, the authorities transported his wife and children to Tasmania. 'Determined to brave it all for the sake of my dear wife and children', Solomon sailed to join them. For want of a warrant, it was a year before Tasmanian officials could arrest him and send him back to England.

Solomon's trial at the Old Bailey was one of the sensations of the day. But unlike Fagin, Solomon did not hang. Found guilty on two counts of theft, he was sentenced to fourteen years' transportation and promptly sent back to Tasmania. Solomon lived out the rest of his days there. The man said at one point to be worth £30,000 died in his sixties, estranged from his family and leaving an estate of just £70.

But as well as drawing on the accounts of other peoples' lives for inspiration, Dickens knew from his own experience how quickly a man could slide into degradation. At the same age at which Oliver Twist is confronted with the terrifying darkness of the world, Dickens had become a child labourer. His time in a blacking factory, necessitated by his father's bankruptcy, was brief. When the family's fortunes recovered some months later, Dickens returned to school. His parents never spoke of it again. He himself kept it a close secret, though the memory never left him. He wanted always, he said, 'to present [the poor] in a favourable light to the rich'. His enduring fear of a return to poverty compelled him to work ever harder.

Dickens-mania gripped rich and poor alike. Instalments of his works were read out to crowds of the urban poor, who had clubbed together to hire the latest episode from the circulating library. Dickens made the public laugh and he made them cry. His characters were as real to them as life. At New York Harbour, crowds pressed around disembarking passengers to ask about the fate of *The Old Curiosity Shop*'s Little Nell. Her death inspired hysteria; the Irish nationalist Daniel O'Connell was allegedly so enraged that he threw the book out of a train carriage window.

'I have great faith in the poor,' Dickens wrote to a friend in 1844. 'I shall never cease, I hope, until I die, to advocate their being made as happy and as wise as the circumstances ... may admit.' In his fantastical exaggerations the radical philanthropist showed the bleakness that faced so many. For some readers, it was an illustration of their lives; it made others realize how wretched such lives could be. One American reviewer considered Dickens' works a force for reform far more effective than anything the 'open assaults of Radicalism or Chartism' could achieve.

Dickens was renowned for his wit and his marvellous talent for mimicry. He developed an extraordinarily successful second career giving public readings of his works. His mammoth tours across England and America sold out in every city. He turned his flock of offspring into an amateur theatrical troupe, performing plays in which he generally took the starring role. In the course of these ventures he met Ellen Ternan, the young actress who was the great love of his later life.

He had a reputation for oddity. He was obsessed with light, filling his brightly painted room with mirrors. When Dickens was a child, his father pointed out to him a house that, he said, would demonstrate a man's having made it in life. So in 1856 the adult Dickens bought it – Gad's Hill Place in Higham, Kent. He was a demanding father, while his total repudiation of his wife Catherine after over twenty years of marriage was undeniably cruel.

Dickens' masterpiece was *A Tale of Two Cities* (1859). Set in the French Revolution, it ends with Sydney Carton, rogue-turned-saviour, giving his life for that of a better man, saying 'It is a far, far better thing that I do now, than I have ever done; it is a far, far better rest that I go to, than I have ever known.'

BISMARCK

1815–1898

*Politics is the art of the possible, the attainable – the art of the
next best.*

Otto von Bismarck

Otto von Bismarck, son of a Junker landowner, was the Iron
Chancellor who united Germany, won three wars, created a
hybrid authoritarian-democratic German empire and dominated
European affairs for almost thirty years. A bundle of contradictions, he was both a militarist ultra-conservative and the bringer
of a welfare state and universal suffrage to Germany, a modernizer
whose German constitution left real power in the hands of emperor and army, a brutally ruthless and vindictive politician who
was also a neurotic hypochondriac and near hysteric, an insomniac
who could not stop eating, a Christian believer whose methods
were utterly amoral. At home and abroad, he used the threat of
democracy to force kings and princes to do his bidding and in the
process he created a Germany that was the most dynamic power in
Europe, but his creation was utterly flawed and unworkable, partly
because he had designed it around himself as ruling chancellor.

As a flamboyantly ambitious and eccentric student, he paid
court to two English girls but then fell in love with a graceful
and fascinating girl called Marie von Thadden who had recently
married one of his friends. Under her influence he embraced the
fashionable pietist evangelical Lutheranism, though this never
restrained his political intrigues. Ultimately he married the plain,

399

humourless and religious Joanna von Puttkamer with whom he had a successful but probably boring and unhappy marriage blessed with many children.

During the 1848 Revolutions, Bismarck was outraged at the liberal rebellion and planned to lead his peasants to Berlin to back the king. He projected himself as a diehard authoritarian praising the divine right of kings in a series of provocative speeches designed to win him attention. His regular memoranda of advice to the regent and later king of Prussia, the conservative Wilhelm I, a bluff if emotional Prussian soldier, made clear that he wanted to serve as chief minister but would demand total control over foreign affairs. Instead he was appointed ambassador to the diet of the German Confederation in Frankfurt, then to St Petersburg and lastly to Paris. During these postings and a visit to London, he met the statesmen of the time, including Napoleon III of France and Benjamin Disraeli. He openly and with astonishing foresight told Disraeli exactly how he would manipulate the German princes, France and Austria, using war and the threat of democracy to reunite Germany. Within a few years he had precisely fulfilled his promises.

In 1862, King Wilhelm's crisis over the Prussian military budget led him to appoint Bismarck minister-president and foreign minister of Prussia. Bismarck almost ruined his job at once with an unwise and notorious speech that threatened 'blood and iron' – war – as the only way for Prussia to find its destiny in Europe. Nonetheless in partnership with War Minister Roon and Chief of Staff von Moltke, Bismarck set about doing exactly that. Prussia's rival for leadership of the many German principalities was the Habsburg empire of Austria–Hungary ruled by Emperor Franz-Joseph. First Bismarck exploited the crisis of the succession of the duchies of Schleswig-Holstein to defeat the hapless king of Denmark and then exclude Austria from German affairs.

In 1866 he manipulated Austria into a war in which Emperor

Franz-Josef was defeated at the Battle of Königgrätz, ending once and for all Austrian pretensions to a role in Germany. Prussia was able to then annex several German kingdoms, including Hanover.

Bismarck was raised to count. Thoughout all this, he depended solely on the king of Prussia for his power – in effect he had no party, but Wilhelm had in turn become dependent on Bismarck. Crises were solved by Bismarck's weeping, hypochondria or threats of resignation, but he took enormous trouble to retain royal support, despite being hated by Queen Augusta as well as Crown Prince Frederick and his wife Vicky, Queen Victoria's liberal daughter. 'It is not easy to be king under Bismarck,' said King Wilhelm.

In 1869, when Spain offered its throne to a Hohenzollern prince, a kinsman of the king of Prussia, Napoleon III insisted that the offer be refused – quite reasonably – since the French feared Prussian power on both sides of their borders. But French arrogance played into Bismarck's hands: he doctored the text of a French telegram to make it insulting to King Wilhelm, who was outraged. The French declared war but were totally defeated at the Battle of Sedan by the Prussians. Emperor Napoleon III abdicated, a prisoner.

Bismarck's victory allowed him to unite Germany into a new Empire with Wilhelm I as emperor (*Kaiser* in German) and himself as chancellor. He was made a prince. In Germany, he combined a façade of universal suffrage, parliamentary democracy, and a modern industrial economy, with the reality of secretive authoritarian military rule by the kaiser, Junker-aristocratic army officers and of course Bismarck himself. Real power remained with the kaiser, but it was a complex system that only Bismarck with his unique prestige and political genius could manage and control.

Despite confessing 'I am bored', he ruled for almost two more decades after creating the German empire, running a cultural campaign to attack Catholic power, at times allying with socialists, at others pushing conservative policies, creating a welfare state, promoting foreign alliances with Austria and Russia while aiming to keep the balance of power in Europe, fearing that 'one day the great European war will come out of some damned foolish thing in the Balkans.'

Ultimately his power tottered as he aged and his patron Wilhelm died in 1888. Wilhelm was succeeded as kaiser by Crown Prince Frederick who was already tragically dying of cancer. After a short reign his place was taken on the throne by the young, impetuous and unbalanced Kaiser Wilhelm II, who in 1890 demanded the Chancellor's resignation. Bismarck was seventy-five but he was infuriated at his downfall. He had created Germany, and a new Europe but his successors – particularly Kaiser Wilhelm II – could not control his creation.

FLORENCE NIGHTINGALE

1820–1910

What a comfort it was to see her pass. She would speak to one, and nod and smile to as many more . . . we lay there by the hundreds, but we could kiss her shadow as it fell and lay our heads on the pillow again content.

An anonymous soldier in the Crimean War

The Lady of the Lamp overcame obstacles and obduracy to transform the state of medical care in the British army and to establish nursing as a trained and respectable profession for women: she improved the lives of millions.

Named after her Italian birthplace, Florence Nightingale was raised in England and educated at home by her father to a standard well above that considered advisable for women of her era. By the time the bright and bookish Nightingale reached her teens, she was well aware that marriage and a life in society – the usual prospects for a girl of her class – held little appeal for her.

When, at sixteen, she heard God's voice informing her that she had a mission, Nightingale set about escaping from the family fold into a life of her own. But it was several years before her parents allowed her to enter the socially disreputable profession of nursing. She became an expert on public health and hospitals until finally, at almost thirty, she persuaded her parents to let her go to Germany to one of the few institutions that provided training for nurses.

When the Crimean War broke out and newspapers began reporting graphically the terrible condition of the wounded British soldiers, Nightingale, by now the superintendent of the Institution for the Care of Sick Gentlewomen in London, was one of the first to respond. Sidney Herbert, an old friend and secretary of state for war, asked her to lead a party of nurses and to direct nursing in the British military hospitals in Turkey. In November 1854 Nightingale and her party arrived at the Barrack Hospital in Scutari, near Istanbul.

Battling against filthy conditions and a chronic shortage of supplies, faced with insubordinate nurses who were frequently drunk and intransigent doctors reluctant to acknowledge the authority of a woman, Nightingale transformed the military hospitals. She personally attended almost every patient, administering comfort and advice as she made her nightly rounds. The mortality rate of wounded soldiers when she arrived was 50 per cent; by the time she left, it was just 2 per cent.

Nightingale constantly set herself new and ever more ambitious goals. Within a year of taking up her first London post she was longing to escape 'this little molehill'. After nursing the sick in Turkey for a while, she set her sights on the greater goal of transforming the welfare of the British army as a whole. It was a task to which she dedicated the rest of her life. She pushed for the establishment of royal commissions on the matter and produced reports that were instrumental in the foundation of the Army Medical School. When she turned her attention to army health in India, she became so supreme an authority on the subject that successive viceroys sought her advice before taking up their posts.

'The very essence of Truth seemed to emanate from her,' wrote one contemporary, awed by 'her perfect fearlessness in telling it'. Undaunted by resistance, Nightingale triumphed over the Scutari doctor who initially refused to allow nurses into the wards; the inspector-general of hospitals who tried to argue that her authority did not extend to the Crimea; the government officials who were tepid about her mission to improve the health and well-being of the British soldier.

The woman appointed general superintendent of female nursing in the military hospitals abroad transformed nursing into a respected profession. On her return to England she promoted training for midwives and for nurses in workhouses, and in 1860 she established the world's first school for nurses, at St Thomas' Hospital in London.

Austere to the point of asceticism, Nightingale rejected her status as heroine, refusing official transport home from the Crimea and rebuffing all suggestions of public receptions. Back in England, she sequestered herself, rarely leaving her house. The invalidism of the world's most famous nurse is considered to have been largely psychosomatic. Nevertheless, attended by a constant stream of important visitors, Nightingale was able to devote herself tirelessly to an extensive network of causes.

Her single-mindedness bred a certain ruthlessness. Driven by a sense of divine mission, Nightingale was impatient with those whom she considered to lack the necessary zeal. When the dying Herbert had to curtail his involvement in some or other charitable cause, she cut him off. But it was this tenacity that enabled her to bring about such extraordinary changes in the nursing profession. In 1910 the ninety-year-old Nightingale, blind for a decade, died in London.

PASTEUR

1822–1895

There are not two sciences: there is science and the application of science; these two are linked as the fruit is to the tree.

Louis Pasteur

The French microbiologist Louis Pasteur was a scientist whose varied and innovative studies made a massive contribution to the battle against disease in humans and animals. He did much pioneering work in the field of immunology, most importantly producing the first vaccine against rabies. His investigations into the micro-organisms that cause food to go bad were of vital importance to French and British industry, while the process of pasteurization he developed is still extremely important in preserving food and preventing illness.

Pasteur came from a family of tanners. As a child he was a keen artist, but it was clear to his teachers that he was academically very able. In 1843 he was admitted to the fine Parisian training college the École Normale Supérieure. He became a master of science in 1845, and in 1847 he presented a thesis on crystallography which earned him a doctorate.

With such a prestigious academic background and some ground-breaking research into physical chemistry behind him, Pasteur gained a professorship in the science faculty at the University of Strasbourg. Here he met Marie Laurent, the daughter of the university rector; they were married in 1849 and had five children together, two of whom survived childhood.

After six years in Strasbourg, Pasteur moved on to Lille. He held the firm view that the theoretical and practical aspects of science should work hand in hand, so he began teaching evening classes to young working men in Lille and taking his regular students around nearby factories. He also began to study the process of fermentation; one of his early achievements, in 1857, was to show that yeast could reproduce in the absence of oxygen. This became known as the Pasteur effect.

By 1857 Pasteur was back at the École Normale Supérieure. Here he continued his research into fermentation and demonstrated with unusual experimental rigour that the process was driven by the activity of minute organisms. In 1867 the French emperor Napoleon III relieved Pasteur of his teaching duties and granted him a research laboratory. With a new freedom of study, Pasteur set about resolving, once and for all, the great scientific debate over spontaneous generation – the question of whether germs and micro-organisms could simply 'appear' from nowhere. He found that germs were in fact transported in air and that food decomposed because it was exposed to them.

In 1862 Pasteur first tested the process, now known as pasteurization, by which milk and other liquids are heated to remove bacteria. In time this process would revolutionize the way food was prepared, stored and sold, and so save many people from infection. Pasteur also applied his theoretical work to the French vinegar and wine industries and the British beer industry, allowing the businesses concerned to produce goods that did not perish so quickly. It was as a result of a suggestion from Pasteur that the British surgeon Joseph Lister began in the 1860s to adopt antiseptic methods during operations.

In 1865 Pasteur saved the French silk industry by helping to identify and eradicate a parasite that was killing silkworms. By 1881 he had developed techniques to protect sheep from anthrax and chickens from cholera. He observed that creating a weakened form of a germ and vaccinating animals with it gave them effective immunity. It was an important development of Jenner's earlier use of cowpox germs to vaccinate against smallpox.

The most important vaccination Pasteur produced was against rabies. By manipulating the dried nervous systems of rabid rabbits, he created a weakened form of the terrible disease and managed to inoculate dogs against it. He had treated only eleven dogs in 1885 when he took dramatic action to save the life of a nine-year-old boy who had been bitten by a rabid dog. It was extremely risky but totally successful. Pasteur remained a hero of the medical establishment until his death, after a series of strokes, in 1895. He was buried in Notre Dame Cathedral in Paris, then reinterred in a crypt at the Pasteur Institute.

Pasteur was one of many scientists who have performed medical miracles that have done so much to alleviate human suffering. Edward Jenner was one of the first, immunizing a child against smallpox in 1796. From the 1860s Joseph Lister (1827–1912) began his pioneering work on asepsis in surgery, using carbolic acid as an antiseptic to reduce the risk of infection. Operations had already been rendered far safer in the preceding decades by the physician John Snow (1813–58), who had introduced the use of anaesthesia to enable pain-free operations. Snow was also responsible for reducing the incidence of cholera by tracing its cause to contaminated water supplies.

In 1895 the German physicist Wilhelm Röntgen (1845–1923) discovered X-rays, thereby paving the way for vast improvements in the treatment of internal injuries. In 1928 Alexander Fleming (1881–1955) discovered penicillin, the first antibiotic, when he noticed that the mould in a dirty lab dish prevented bacteria from growing. In the 1950s the work of the French immunologist Jean Dausset (b.1916) led to great advances in our understanding of how the body fights disease. In 1953, Francis Crick (1916–2004) and James Watson (b.1928) discovered the double-helix shape of DNA. All those who worked on these projects deserve to be remembered as heroes of medicine.

TOLSTOY

1828–1910

When literature possesses a Tolstoy, it is easy and pleasant to be a writer; even when you know you have achieved nothing yourself . . . this is not as terrible as it might otherwise be, because Tolstoy achieves for everyone. What he does serves to justify all the hopes and aspirations invested in literature.

Anton Chekhov

Leo Tolstoy is, in the opinion of many, the greatest novelist of all time. His two masterpieces, *War and Peace* and *Anna Karenina*, certainly rank among the finest novels ever written. He was also a skilful writer of short stories and essays, a powerful historian and a mystical philosopher who developed unusual yet influential Christian ideas about the human condition and moral improvement.

The essence of Tolstoy's greatness is his masterful grasp of human behaviour and motivation, which he combined with a natural gift for storytelling and an astonishing breadth and universality of vision. Though he was a deeply complex man, tormented by his failure to live up to his own standards, he had one of the sharpest and most original minds in the history of literature.

Count Leo Tolstoy was born into a prominent aristocratic family on his ancestral estate, Yasnaya Polyana, some 100 miles south of Moscow. His childhood was upset by the early deaths of both his parents, yet he still remembered it in idyllic terms. He was educated at home by tutors, but when he enrolled at the University of Kazan in 1844, it became apparent that he was neither a willing nor a diligent student, preferring to drink, gamble, womanize and socialize, and he left in 1847 without taking a degree.

He returned to Yasnaya Polyana with the intention of educating himself and improving the lot of his serfs, but his resolve soon weakened. In 1851 he went to the Caucasus, joined the army and used his experiences to write stories such as 'Hadji Murat', his best shorter work. It is a story of nobility, courage and betrayal in the life of a daring Chechen fighter during the thirty-year Russian war to defeat the legendary Chechen/Dagestani commander Imam Shamyl and conquer the northern Caucasus. Tolstoy also served during the combined Anglo-French-Italian siege of the chief Russian naval base in the Crimea, Sebastopol. An eleven-month campaign of appalling slaughter and incompetence ended in 1856 with the Russians sinking their ships, blowing up the garrison and evacuating. The experience was the basis for three literary sketches in which Tolstoy refined his technique of minutely analysing thoughts and feelings. 'The hero of my tale,' the author wrote, 'whom I love with all the power of my soul ... is Truth.' In 1862 he married Sofia Andreyevna Behrs and again returned to his estate, this time with a plan to teach and learn from the simple peasant children.

Tolstoy's most productive period came between 1863 and 1877. From 1865 he was working on *War and Peace*, which he finished in 1869. This vast work is both domestic and political. It consists of three main strands: the monumental struggle of Russia and France, Alexander I versus Napoleon, between 1805 and 1812, particularly the French invasion and retreat from Moscow; the interlinked tales of two aristocratic Russian families, the Rostovs and the Bolkonskys; and lengthy essays on history. It is clear that Tolstoy identified himself with the curious, diffident and doubting, but kind, direct and moral character of Pierre Bezukhov.

Tolstoy has an original view of the wars he describes. He portrays Napoleon as a bungling egomaniac, the Russian tsar Alexander I as a man of fine words, obsessed with his own legacy, and the maligned Russian commander Mikhail Kutuzov as a wily old man of war. Combat itself is seen as chaos, without any overall connection or intrinsic structure. The fictional characters all to some extent see life in the same way and find solace only through what would become Tolstoy's main philosophy: salvation through devotion to family and the tasks of everyday life.

War and Peace, with its acute understanding of individual motivation and action, may have redefined the novel, but Tolstoy's next major project, *Anna Karenina*, was no less influential. Written between 1875 and 1877, it applied the principles of *War and Peace* to family life. 'All happy families resemble each other,' he wrote; 'each unhappy family is unhappy in its own way'. At the centre of the story lies the tragic affair of Anna with Count Alexei Vronsky, an army officer. In vivid detail Tolstoy paints Anna's mental contortions under the pressure of society's hypocrisies and her inner struggles (ultimately in vain) to rationalize her own behaviour.

Like *War and Peace, Anna Karenina* was a vehicle for Tolstoy's moral convictions. From 1877 he became more and more obsessed with the spiritual side of his life and suffered various crises of faith. He was excommunicated from the Orthodox Church in 1901 for his distinctive reinterpretation of Christianity, in which he emphasized pacifist resistance to evil, love for one's enemies, extreme asceticism and avoidance of anger and lust. He soon had a growing band of disciples across the world.

Tolstoy continued to write, using the profits from his third major novel, *Resurrection* (1899), to help the persecuted Doukhobor Christian sect to emigrate to Canada.

Deeply unhappy in his marriage and his divided court of disciples, the ailing Tolstoy escaped from home with one of his daughters and a doctor but collapsed and died in the winter of 1910 in a railway station, refusing to see his wife. He had a simple burial on his family estate. Though frequently preposterous, his moral, ethical and spiritual ideas became highly influential; Gandhi, for one, was impressed by his doctrine of non-violent resistance. But it is his contribution to literature that towers above all else.

CIXI

1835–1908

After this notice is issued to instruct you villagers . . . if there are any Christian converts, you ought to get rid of them quickly. The churches which belong to them should be unreservedly burned down. Everyone who intends to spare someone, or to disobey our order by concealing Christian converts, will be punished according to the regulation . . . and he will be burned to death to prevent his impeding our programme.

Boxer poster, 1900

Beautiful, cunning and cruel, Empress Dowager Cixi was the archetypal dragon lady. She rose from obscurity to become the effective ruler of China for forty-seven years, during which time she presided over a humiliating decline in the country's fortunes. In the second half of the 19th century, the Qing dynasty that had ruled China for more than 250 years struggled to cope with the challenges posed by modernization and increasing pressure from the European powers. Having suffered military defeats at the hands of its foreign rivals, and faced with growing internal unrest, China's last imperial dynasty finally fell in 1911. No one had contributed more to this collapse than the empress dowager herself.

When she entered Emperor Xianfeng's household as his concubine in 1851, the future empress dowager was known as Lady Yehenara, daughter of Huizheng. She was renamed Yi soon after, and then Noble Consort Yi following the birth of her son Zaichun in 1856. When the emperor died in 1861, Zaichun assumed the throne, and to reflect her new position as Divine Mother Empress Dowager, Yi was given the title Cixi, meaning motherly and auspicious.

Before his death, Xianfeng had charged eight 'regent ministers' to govern during his son's minority, but a palace coup saw power pass instead to the late emperor's consort, Mother Empress Dowager Ci'an, and the Divine Mother Empress Dowager Cixi. Aided by the ambitious Prince Gong, they were to enjoy a twelve-year period of shared rule, exercising power 'from behind the curtain'.

Zaichun, renamed Tongzhi (meaning collective rule), was belatedly allowed to begin his 'reign' in 1873, but the two matriarchs, having gained a taste for power, had no intention of quietly slipping into retirement. Cixi in particular continued to dominate the young emperor, cowing him into accepting her authority.

After just two years, Tongzhi died, but the accession of Cixi's four-year-old cousin, Emperor Guangxu, saw the two women restored as regents. Six years later, in 1881, Empress Ci'an died suddenly, leading to rumours that Cixi had poisoned her. Ci'an's death opened the way for Cixi to exercise unfettered power, reinforced in 1885 when she stripped Prince Gong of his offices.

By this time the empress dowager had accumulated a huge personal fortune. At a time of growing financial crisis for China, she built a string of extravagant palaces and gardens, and a lavish tomb for herself. Meanwhile, she stifled all efforts at reform and modernization. In 1881, she banned Chinese nationals from studying abroad because of the possible influx of liberal ideas. When proposals were brought forward for a vast new railway that would open up much of China, she vetoed the plans, claiming it would be 'too loud' and would 'disturb the emperors' tombs'.

The young Emperor Guangxu was due to assume the reins of power in 1887. At her instigation, various accommodating court officials begged her to prolong her rule, due to the emperor's youth. 'Reluctantly' she agreed, and a new law was passed that allowed her to continue 'advising' the emperor indefinitely.

Even after she finally handed over power in 1889 – retiring to the massive Summer Palace she had built for herself – Cixi continued to overshadow the imperial court. She forced the new emperor to marry his niece, Jingfen, against his will. When he later snubbed his wife to spend more time with Consort Zhen – known as the Pearl Concubine – Cixi had Zhen flogged.

In the mid-1890s the empress dowager insisted on diverting funds from the Chinese navy to pay for extensive refurbishments to her Summer Palace for the celebration of her sixtieth birthday. When Japan launched a war against China in 1894, the latter's armed forces were defeated. The reformers won the confidence of Emperor Guangxu, and in 1898 he launched his 'first hundred days' of measures.

The empress dowager was unwilling to cede an inch. In September 1898 she organized a military coup that effectively removed Guangxu from power. He nominally continued as emperor until 1908, but was declared not fit to rule the country in an edict she herself authored.

Cixi's undoing proved to be the Boxer Rebellion of 1900.

In 1900, a clandestine group, the Righteous and Harmonious Fists (the Boxers), which taught its members martial arts (and even claimed it could train them to be immune from bullets) led an uprising in Shandong province and gained a following among the rural poor. It produced mass propaganda accusing Catholic missionaries of acts of sexual abuse and Western immigrants of trying to undermine China. Violent attacks against both became commonplace.

Believing the movement might help her retain power, Cixi endorsed the rebellion as an expression of Chinese popular culture. Thereafter, anti-Western riots and the destruction of foreign property escalated and in the summer of 1900 a Boxer 'army' laid siege to Western embassies in Beijing. The Chinese imperial army was complicit in the assault, doing little to relieve the defenders. It took the arrival of international troops to lift the siege (after which the city was looted), and several more months for the rising itself to be quelled.

Ironically, the rebellion increased foreign interference in China. The Boxer Protocol of 1901 not only forced the Chinese government to accede to a huge reparations bill, but also gained Western countries major trade concessions and allowed them to station forces permanently in Beijing – a further insult to the sense of wounded national pride upon which the abortive rebellion had been predicated. Her announcement of support for the Boxer movement, which she saw as a bulwark of traditional Chinese values against Western and liberal influences, prompted the Western powers to march on Beijing and seize the Forbidden City. Cixi was forced to flee, and imperial authority was only restored after the emperor signed a humiliating treaty. Cixi died in November 1908, leaving Puyi as emperor, aged two. Overthrown by the Revolution of 1911, briefly reinstated in 1917, set up as puppet emperor of Manchukuo by the Japanese from 1932 until 1945, he was China's last monarch. Cixi had proved the gravedigger of the Chinese empire.

LEOPOLD II: THE RAPE OF CONGO

1835–1909

Many were shot, some had their ears cut off; others were tied up
with ropes round their necks and bodies and taken away.
Roger Casement, reporting to the British foreign
secretary on the treatment of the natives in Leopold's
Congo Free State

Leopold II, king of the Belgians, was the colonist who developed the vast and lucrative central African colony of the Congo at a terrible human cost. He carved himself a colossal personal empire, exploiting and killing millions, to build his fortune – turning the heart of Africa into Joseph Conrad's Heart of Darkness.

Leopold succeeded his father, Leopold I, in 1865. He avoided involving Belgium in the Franco-Prussian War of 1870–1, realizing that his small country had no influence in the power politics of Europe. But European neutrality did not amount to high-mindedness; instead, Leopold's ambitions extended beyond Europe, and in 1876 he confided in his ambassador in London: 'I do not want to miss a good chance of getting us a slice of this magnificent African cake.'

Leopold set his sights on the untapped natural resources of the river basin of the Congo, covered in dense rainforest and eighty times the size of Belgium. In 1876 he formed the Association Internationale Africaine to promote the exploration and colonization of Africa, and two years later commissioned the British-American explorer Henry Morton Stanley to explore the Congo region. By buying off local tribes for a pittance and duping them into signing away their lands to European control, Stanley requisitioned massive portions of the Congo for Leopold. Thus was created the Congo Free State, for which Leopold gained international recognition at the Conference of Berlin of 1884–5.

The Congo Free State was free only in name. It was not even a Belgian colony, but rather Leopold's personal property, from which he squeezed profits as he plundered the area's rich natural resources, notably rubber and ivory. Leopold never visited the Congo, preferring to govern it through a series of agents, whose own profits were gleaned from commission.

Order in the Congo Free State was maintained by the Force Publique, a notoriously cruel mercenary army of 20,000 men, officered by Europeans but relying on badly paid Africans as foot soldiers. The Force Publique was charged with the collection of the rubber tax, an oppressive levy that effectively required forced labour. Arriving in tribal villages, Leopold's agents seized the women and children and refused to release them until the men went into the rainforest and brought back the requisite quantity of rubber, which was then sold on, all the time swelling Leopold's coffers.

In order to stop them wasting ammunition on hunting wild animals, the Force Publique were ordered to account for every bullet they fired by bringing back the right hand of their victim. The hands of thousands of innocent Congolese were cut off by the mercenaries, whether they were dead or alive. Villages were burned down, inhabitants tortured and some reports even suggested that members of the Force Publique engaged in cannibalism. The headquarters of Leon Rom, the barbaric Belgian soldier in charge of the Force Publique, was surrounded by hundreds of severed heads.

These atrocities caused the death of an estimated 10 million people, half the population of the Congo, either at the hands of the Force Publique or through hunger and deprivation. Meanwhile, Leopold presented himself to the rest of Europe as a humanitarian, determined to liberate the area from the scourge of the Arab slave trade, and spreading European 'civilization'. But the Christian missionaries who penetrated into the heart of the Congo told a very different story, and reports of awful abuses began to filter back to Europe.

In the first decade of the 20th century there were a number of tribal rebellions. These were brutally suppressed, but they did serve to provoke further scrutiny into conditions in the Congo Free State. In 1900 Edmund Dene Morel, an English trader, began to campaign against the horrific conditions in the territory, and in 1903 the British Foreign Office commissioned the diplomat Roger Casement to go to the Congo to find out what was going on. Casement's detailed eyewitness report did much to stir up international outrage, and writers such as Arthur Conan Doyle, Joseph Conrad and Mark Twain joined in the campaign. In 1908 the Belgian Parliament finally voted to annex the Congo from their own king, ending his control of the region.

It was not until 1960 that Congo achieved full independence, but the brutal legacy of Leopold II still continues to haunt the country, which has suffered from years of civil war in which millions have been killed. Leopold died on 17 December 1909, a shamed and hated figure, who justified his behaviour in the Congo to the very end of his life. Mark Twain wrote that the ageing king was a 'greedy, grasping, avaricious, cynical, bloodthirsty old goat', while for Arthur Conan Doyle the rape of the Congo was simply 'the greatest crime in history'.

TCHAIKOVSKY

1840–1893

Truly there would be reason to go mad were it not for music.
Tchaikovsky, on the fundamental importance of music
to his existence

Pyotr Ilyich Tchaikovsky is one of the most enduringly popular composers in the Western tradition, whose symphonies and concertos have been recorded more often than those of any other composer, and whose ballet scores are among the most famous in the world.

While weathering the strains of an intensely difficult personal life, Tchaikovsky rejected the folk-based styles of other Russian composers of his age to create soaring, sweeping and heart-breakingly poignant romantic works that contrast vividly with the brilliant but bleak operas of Wagner or the impassioned restraint of Brahms. From the 'Romeo and Juliet' Overture and *Swan Lake* to the '1812' Overture and his great opera *Eugene Onegin,* Tchaikovsky's music is as widely loved today as when it was written.

Like Beethoven and Mozart, Tchaikovsky showed early musical talent. He played the piano from the age of five and composed songs for his siblings, as well as reading and writing in French and German. His father was a mining engineer – comfortable but not wealthy – and the young Tchaikovsky was marked down for a career in law, attending the St Petersburg Imperial School of Jurisprudence from the ages of twelve to nineteen, then going straight into a civil service job at the ministry of justice. As he grew older, his talent for music grew ever more evident. He enrolled at the new St Petersburg Conservatory of Music in 1862 (resigning his job the next year) and, after maturing astonishingly quickly, left in 1865, already a fully developed musical personality. The following year he moved to Moscow, where he taught musical theory at the Russian Musical Society.

By 1870 Tchaikovsky had produced his first great work, the concert overture 'Romeo and Juliet'. It passed almost unnoticed when it premiered in Moscow but had more success in an 1872 revised version in St Petersburg. It was an abstract orchestral work that nevertheless told a story – one perfectly suited to Tchaikovsky's tragic and passionate temperament. His life had been affected by tragedy since 1854, when his beloved mother had died of cholera. He later wrote, 'I have attempted with love to express both the agony and also the bliss.'

In love lay Tchaikovsky's personal agony. From the late 1860s he was passionately involved with several young male students, and one of his favourites, Edouard Zak, killed himself in 1873. This had a profound effect on Tchaikovsky. A few years later, perhaps in an attempt to purge himself of homosexual tendencies but more likely to avoid gossip and scandal, he married an obsessive ex-student, Antonina Miliukova. She had plagued him with letters and threatened to kill herself if he did not return her affection. Despite clear warning signs that it was a completely inappropriate match, Tchaikovsky proposed to her in May 1877 and wed her in July that year. By September the marriage was over in all but name.

Despite this tumultuous period in his romantic life, Tchaikovsky was in fluent composing vein. He produced the ballet score *Swan Lake* in 1875–6. In 1877–8 he composed his outstanding Fourth Symphony and his greatest opera, *Eugene Onegin*, a musical interpretation of Pushkin's famous verse story. At first *Onegin* was not well received, but as time passed it came to be recognized as an operatic masterpiece – and when the piano score was published it sold in hatfuls. A lifelong Francophile, Tchaikovsky's music shows the clarity and lightness of French models rather than the more sombre and introverted tones of his German contemporaries.

With his marriage over, Tchaikovsky entered another important phase of his life: his relationship with the wealthy philanthropist Nadezhda von Meck. Though the pair never properly met, she bankrolled his career with an annual salary of 6000 roubles. This allowed him to quit his job and devote his life to composing. Meck supported him from 1876 until her abrupt severance of links in 1890, the period when Tchaikovsky composed some of his most famous works. In 1880 he wrote his overture '1812', with its bombastic finale that includes sixteen cannon and the ringing of church bells. It premiered in Moscow two years later. By this time Tchaikovsky's fame was beginning to peak. He was commissioned to write the Coronation March for Tsar Alexander III in 1883, and his presence as a conductor was sought across Europe.

He wrote his Fifth Symphony in 1888 and followed this with two ballets – *The Sleeping Beauty*, completed in 1889, and *The Nutcracker*, completed in 1892. He also composed an opera, *The Queen of Spades*, unveiled in Moscow in 1890. All these works benefited from a more stable emotional environment, the lack of financial worries, and a strict work regime. By this time his fame had spread to America, where he was asked to conduct his Coronation March at the opening concert in New York's Carnegie Hall.

Like his mother, Tchaikovsky most probably died from cholera, contracted from drinking contaminated water in a St Petersburg restaurant in October 1893. It was just days after the premiere of perhaps his most outstanding and tragic work, the Sixth Symphony, the 'Pathétique'. Requiem services and tributes were held throughout Russia in his memory. He created a passionate, highly charged, intensely emotional musical world, which still has an immediate appeal to listeners everywhere.

CLEMENCEAU

1841–1929

We present ourselves before you with the single thought of total war.

Georges Clemenceau

Georges Clemenceau was France's greatest war leader during the First World War. Clemenceau's bullishness, his lifelong tenacity and his insistence on a punitive settlement with Germany earned him his nickname the Tiger.

Clemenceau was born in a village in the Vendée, in western France, in 1841. He grew up among peasants and received his political education from his father, who shaped his republican views. In 1861 he went to Paris to study medicine, where he became involved in radical republican politics and journalism, critical of the regime of Emperor Napoleon III, and thus attracted the attention of the police.

In 1870–1 France lost the Franco-Prussian War. Clemenceau was involved in the overthrow of Napoleon III and elected to the provisional government. He vehemently but unsuccessfully opposed the imposition on France of a harsh treaty, by which France lost the provinces of Alsace and Lorraine to the new German empire. In May 1871 Clemenceau tried, but failed, to mediate between the government and the rebels of the Paris Commune.

Throughout the 1880s and 1890s Clemenceau continued to serve in both politics and journalism. One of his triumphs was his support between 1894 and 1906 of the young Jewish army officer

Alfred Dreyfus, a victim of anti-Semitism in the government, army and press, who was wrongly accused of being a German spy. Clemenceau's newspapers exposed the corruption and injustice in that notorious case. In 1902 he was elected as a senator.

Clemenceau served as prime minister in 1906–9. In the lead-up to the First World War he argued for rearmament against Germany, and after war broke out he became a vociferous critic of successive governments and of the military high command, hurling accusations of ineptitude, defeatism and closet pacifism.

In November 1917, at the age of seventy-six, Clemenceau accepted the invitation to become prime minister. Ruthless and belligerent, he forced through his belief in 'war until the end' and dealt severely with those he regarded as traitors and defeatists. He insisted on a unified Allied command under General Foch as the only way to win the war. By November 1918 his views had been proven right.

At the Paris Peace Conference of 1919, Clemenceau remembered the events of 1870–1, and in negotiations with British Prime Minister David Lloyd George and President Woodrow Wilson he insisted on Germany being disarmed, accepting 'war guilt' and agreeing to pay massive reparations. He made sure that the treaty was signed in the Hall of Mirrors at Versailles, the very place where Wilhelm I, having humiliated France, had declared himself German emperor in 1871. Clemenceau's force of character and decency made him a fighter for justice and a superb war leader, but his vindictive demands at Versailles were a mistake.

Clemenceau lost the presidential election of 1920 and retired. Before he died, nine years later, he published his memoirs, in which he predicted another war with Germany, some time around 1940.

SARAH BERNHARDT

1844–1923

There are five kinds of actresses: bad actresses, fair actresses, good actresses, great actresses – and then there is Sarah Bernhardt.

Mark Twain

Born in Paris, the actress famed across the world as the Divine Sarah was as tempestuous in life as she was on stage. With bound-less resilience – possibly a result of her insecure childhood as the illegitimate child of a Dutch courtesan – she was first a successful actress in France, before storming the London stage in 1876. Even the loss of her leg in later life posed no major obstacle to her flamboyant acting. And as soon as she had recovered from the amputation, she made a morale-boosting tour of the First World War front, conveyed about in a litter chair. She entertained no thoughts of retirement but just made sure that henceforth her parts could be played sitting down.

Convent-educated but in fact Jewish, as a young girl Bern-hardt toyed with the idea of becoming a nun. But her mother's influential lover, Charles, Duc de Morny (1811–65), apparently decided otherwise. A brilliant French statesman, now undeserv-edly forgotten, he was the son of Queen Hortense of Holland and Emperor Napoleon III's half-brother, as well as a natural grandson of Prince Talleyrand. A financier, racehorse owner and aesthete, not to mention an enthusiastic lover, he married a Russian prin-cess. He was the mastermind of Napoleon III's coup and regime, and president of the Corps Legislatif, but his early death helped doom the Second Empire. It was entirely appropriate that this personification of French power, worldliness and style should have launched (and possibly fathered) the most famous French actress until the era of film.

Morny secured Bernhardt a place at the Paris Conservatoire and a job at the Comédie Française, where she made her debut in 1862, having already won student prizes. Gripped by stage fright, Bernhardt might have seemed better qualified as courtesan than actress. After six years of hard slog, she made her breakthrough and was acclaimed for her roles as Cordelia in a French translation of King Lear and the minstrel Zanetto in Le Passant, a verse play by François Coppée. Her success in the latter was such that she was commanded to reprise her performance in the presence of Napoleon III.

Audiences clamoured to experience her inimitable stage style, suffused with stormy outbursts of wild emotion, tears and grief. For many it became unimaginable that her most famous roles, Marguerite in Dumas's La Dame aux camélias and the title roles in Racine's Phèdre and Scribe's Adrienne Lecouvreur, could be played by anyone else.

Victor Hugo, in whose tragedies she starred, was entranced by her 'golden voice', while Sigmund Freud marvelled that 'every inch of that little figure lives and bewitches'. Yet Bernhardt was denounced by priests, not only for the risqué content of the plays she herself produced but also for her many lovers and unabashed sexuality. She lived life on her own terms, claiming to be 'one of the great lovers of my time'. Her promiscuity was notorious: 'My dear, when one has sat on a rose bush and pricked oneself, one cannot say which thorn was responsible,' was the response of her lover the Prince de Ligne (descendant of the 18th-century grandee and courtier) when Bernhardt revealed that she was pregnant with his child. Other lovers included Hugo and Gustave Doré.

Her middle-aged marriage to the young actor Jacques Damala ended when he ran up extensive debts and deserted her to join the French Foreign Legion. Perhaps her beloved son Maurice was the only man who never let her down.

In the early 1880s she left Paris to begin long international tours through Europe and America, where she not only took the leading female roles in productions of both the classics and modern French plays, but also acted male parts, her slight build making her convincing as Hamlet, for example. A brilliant self-promoter, she conquered Paris, then the world, and was 'too American not to succeed in America', as the writer Henry James wryly commented. Bernhardt was the first international star of the pre-cinematic age – and did star in several early silent movies, among them *Queen Elizabeth* and *La Dame aux camélias*, from 1912.

The multi-talented Bernhardt was also a gifted writer and sculptor, a skilful editor and translator of many plays. She herself became an actor-manager, organizing her own profitable tours. When her histrionic style went out of fashion, she simply directed her own theatre company, renting the Théâtre des Nations in 1898 (later renamed the Théâtre Sarah Bernhardt).

Bernhardt mythologized everything, constantly changing the story of her paternity, and she was probably the healthiest 'consumptive' ever to have lived (on at least one occasion, coughing 'blood' that was actually red liquid from a concealed bladder). But she was unremittingly loyal. Hearing that her runaway husband was now living in drug-addicted squalor, she personally rescued him, paying for private nursing. She was a fervent French patriot and mesmerized audiences to the very end.

MAUPASSANT

1850–1893

Monsieur de Maupassant . . . possesses the three essential qualities
of the French writer: clarity, clarity and clarity. He exhibits the
spirit of balance and order that is the mark of our race.

Anatole France, in La vie littéraire (1888)

Maupassant was the French writer who almost single-handedly made the short story an art form. A famous hedonist and sportsman, he shocked many with his 'immoral' literature. His work recognized the appeal of sensuality and human nature's ambivalence towards it. It is this sensitivity, combined with prose of exquisite clarity, that makes him a writer of greatness.

In 1880 Émile Zola decided to publish a collection of stories inspired by the recent Franco-Prussian War. Maupassant's contribution, 'Boule de Suif', was a masterpiece in miniature that ensured its author overnight success. It was typical of his style and originality, a tale of how a prostitute is exploited and betrayed by the hypocritical middle class in wartime. Many regarded such writing as little more than padding for newspaper columns, but Maupassant went on to develop the short story as a distinctive genre that was taken up by a series of later writers from James Joyce to Ernest Hemingway, and from Anton Chekhov to Somerset Maugham.

Born of impoverished Norman nobility, Maupassant gave up his unrewarding post in the civil service to embrace life as a writer. His genius was to reveal, in simple narrative, fundamental human truths with a skill that rivalled – and sometimes even surpassed – that of the finest novelists. The concision, elegance and humanity of the 300-plus short stories he produced over the ensuing decade demonstrate his mastery of the form.

Maupassant sought to present not 'a banal, photographic view of life . . . but a vision more complete, more gripping, more searching than reality itself'. In this, he owed much to the tutelage of the great novelist Gustave Flaubert (1821–80). Flaubert, a friend of Maupassant's mother, took the young man under his wing when he returned to Paris after serving in the Franco-Prussian War of 1870–1.

Flaubert introduced him to the leading writers of the day, saying, 'He's my disciple and I love him like a son.' In turn Flaubert was a surrogate father (some murmured a real one) to Maupassant, whose own parents had separated when he was eleven and whose father was always a remote figure. Maupassant's style was honed under Flaubert to such an extent that the Russian master Tolstoy was moved to praise his searing insight and his disciplined, beautiful prose as the marks of genius.

At the same time Tolstoy deplored Maupassant's immorality. He was perverse and witty: one story told of a hungry gentleman in a stranded train on a very hot day who finally availed himself of the milk of a breast-feeding peasant. Another tells of a respectable upper-class lady who, looking out of her window, is mistaken for a call-girl by a good-looking young blade and afterwards seeks forgiveness by buying her husband a present with the proceeds. His work was often set in brothels or boudoirs; yet he was equally fascinated by war, by the shrewd peasants of his native Normandy, by finance and journalism, and by the strange twists of fate. The writer's fascination with sex (one critic described him as a 'complete erotomaniac') reflected a phenomenal promiscuity in life. Indeed, his boating trips with hedonistic Parisian girls inspired his short story 'Mouche', and his literary success financed the maintenance of several mistresses. Maupassant's best-selling novel *Bel-Ami* (1885) is a masterpiece, probably the best account ever written of that very modern world where journalism and politics meet, and the author went on to name his yacht after it.

Maupassant believed that the artist's duty was not to be a moral arbiter but to present society with its own reflection and leave people to draw their own conclusions. He declared, 'for a writer there can be no halfway house: he must either tell what he believes to be the truth, or tell lies'. The resulting incisiveness of his writing highlights the contrast between appearance and reality, illustrating how vanity and pride lead to self-deception and falsehood. Maupassant wrote of betrayal and seduction; of fortune favouring the ruthless and the selfish; of societies based on collective hypocrisy; and of madness. He did not shy away from the deep ambiguities hidden within ourselves, while his writing has the power to dispel society's myths.

Maupassant himself was living proof of such ambiguities. On the one hand, he was a man of action, a passionate oarsman who could comfortably row fifty miles in a day and once saved the English poet Swinburne from drowning. His military service and his love of the sea influenced many of the narratives and settings of his work. On the other hand, he was prone to anxiety and morbid thoughts and was increasingly gripped by the depression from which his mother had also suffered.

In his early twenties Maupassant discovered he had syphilis but refused to have it treated. Mentally he became increasingly unstable, as his frantic existence accelerated his physical deterioration. In 1892, a year after his brother (also suffering from syphilis) died insane, Maupassant attempted suicide. He was committed to a nursing home, where he died less than a year later – aged just forty-three.

In just over a decade as a writer, Maupassant produced some 300 short stories, six novels, three travel books and a volume of verse. His frenetic life and work matched each other. Yet whilst his life was short, his stories live for ever.

OSCAR WILDE

1854–1900

From the beginning Wilde performed his life and continued to do so even after fate had taken the plot out of his hands.

W.H. Auden, in the *New Yorker* (9 March 1963)

Oscar Wilde – poet, playwright, aphorist, novelist and writer of childrens' stories, aesthete, victim of prejudice and hypocrisy, and insouciant, irrepressible wit – treated his own life as a work of art; he was its hero – and should remain ours. A lover of paradox and a connoisseur of life's absurdities, he effortlessly skewered the pretensions, prejudices and hypocrisies of his age. His destruction by the society that had lionized him was a tragic echo of the themes he explored with such charm and forensic skill in his own work.

Wilde's plays, such as *A Woman of No Importance* and *The Importance of Being Earnest*, are rarely off the stage. His dazzling wit is enduringly quotable: 'I take my diary everywhere I go. One must always have something sensational to read on the train,' declares Gwendolyn to Cicely in *The Importance of Being Earnest*, a play that is said to be the most perfect comedy ever written. More than any other writer of the time, his satire deconstructs the pompous edifice of late Victorian society and does so with considerable *élan*. But under the glittering surface lies the potential for tragedy, and much of his work shimmers on the edge of darkness. *The Picture of Dorian Gray*, the novel Wilde published in 1889, pushed the limits of respectability with its themes of decay, cruelty and illicit love, causing Wilde's wife, Constance, to remark that 'since Oscar wrote that book no one invites us anywhere any more'. Yet it is a timelessly sensitive and affecting evocation of our fears of death and ageing. Even his fairy tales, *The Happy Prince* and *The Selfish Giant*, do not shy away from the unpalatable reality of cruelty going unpunished and heroism unrewarded.

Wilde was born in Dublin of Anglo-Irish parents, but his desire to be centre stage prompted him to pursue an education and a life in England. The archetype of a *fin de siècle* aesthete, Wilde cultivated a flamboyant appearance and a quick and cutting way with words, turning himself into a celebrity long before his writing confirmed that he was worth all the attention. 'The only thing worse than being talked about is not being talked about,' he said. By his early twenties the tall, drawling Oxford graduate, got up in a velvet suit with Regency-style knee-breeches, was notorious. Even the prince of Wales demanded an introduction, declaring: 'Not to know Mr Wilde is to be not known in society.' From celebrity came a career: caricatures of the dandy who declared art to be the highest form of action began to appear on the London stage. When an enterprising producer took one of these plays on an American tour, he decided to take Wilde on a parallel lecture tour on the subject of aestheticism. Wilde – who reportedly arrived at US Customs with the comment 'I have nothing to declare except my genius' – became as famous across the Atlantic as he was in England. It was only in the half decade before his fall that Wilde fully became the writer he had always planned to be.

Wilde's homosexuality has become as famous as his work. He was a butterfly broken on a wheel. His provocative effeteness had prompted rumours about his sexuality for years, but Wilde was a married father who only became actively homosexual in his thirties after his marriage hit a bad patch. 'The only way to get rid of temptation is to yield to it,' said Wilde famously. He described his sexual adventures as 'feasting with panthers'. Caught up in a vendetta between his preposterously vain and destructive lover Lord Alfred (Bosie) Douglas and Douglas' father, the lunatic martinet the marquess of Queensberry, Wilde found himself the subject of a sustained campaign of childish abuse. Queensberry sent him phallic bouquets of vegetables, and the note he left at Wilde's club in February 1895 accusing him of being a 'posing somdomite' [sic] was the final straw. Urged on by Bosie, Wilde sued for libel.

It was a terrible mistake. Under cross-examination Wilde was as flippantly witty as ever, playing to his new audience, the occupants of the court's public gallery. But even his eloquent defence of immorality in his work could not cancel out details of his dalliances. The establishment could not tolerate such revelations. Wilde lost the case and was immediately tried and sentenced to two years' hard labour for gross indecency. Cries of 'Shame' filled the galleries. Queensberry called the bailiffs in to repossess Wilde's house in lieu of costs. His son, who had fled to the Continent to escape indictment, publicly bemoaned his suffering, at a safe distance.

While Wilde was serving out his time in Reading Gaol, a fellow inmate, Trooper Charles Thomas Wooldridge, convicted of murdering his wife by cutting her throat with a razor, was hanged. It was to 'C.T.W.' that Wilde dedicated his last great work, the elegiac *Ballad of Reading Gaol*, written in exile in France after his release in 1897. The poem had to be published under a pseudonym, 'C.3.3' (his prison number), due to the notoriety of his own name. Intermingling light and shade, the poem expresses a longing for innocence, beauty and redemption even in the mire of despair, and at the same time calls for forgiveness and understanding.

I never saw a man who looked
With such a wistful eye
Upon that little tent of blue
Which prisoners call the sky,
And at every drifting cloud that went
With sails of silver by.

The poem concludes:

And all men kill the thing they love,
By all let this be heard,
Some do it with a bitter look,
Some with a flattering word,
The coward does it with a kiss,
The brave man with a sword!

Whilst in prison Wilde wrote *De Profundis*, a bitterly brilliant 50,000-word letter to Bosie, a testament to his destruction by his great love. He never recovered, physically or psychologically, from his incarceration. Ostracized by society, unable to see his beloved sons, he spent his final years wandering the Continent. His wit was undiminished to the last: 'I am dying, as I live,' he declared, 'beyond my means.' Shortly before his death, as he lay in a dreary room in Paris, he is said to have murmured, 'Either that wallpaper goes, or I do.'

WILHELM II

1859–1941

Ruthlessness and weakness will start the most terrifying war of the world, whose purpose is to destroy Germany. Because there can no longer be any doubts, England, France and Russia have conspired them selves together to fight an annihilation war against us.

The last emperor of Germany – known to the British simply as the Kaiser – was an inconsistent, bombastic, tactless, preposterous, perhaps even mentally deranged, absolutist monarch who managed to use the empire's constitution to gain control of German military and foreign policy yet who ultimately proved unable to govern or sustain his own power. However, for twenty years, Wilhelm II was the vociferous and dynamic ruler of the most modern and powerful country in Europe and his personality dominated international affairs. He came to symbolize the brutal militaristic expansionism of the rising new German empire but his unbalanced personality represented its dangerous insecurity, its inferiority complex and political flaws. He certainly contributed to the growing instability of Europe and the acceleration of the arms race with Britain. He must take much blame, along with the German military-bureaucratic elite, for the humanitarian catastrophe of the First World War – though it is simplistic to place the entire weight of guilt on his shoulders.

Son of the liberal Crown Prince Frederick of Prussia and his wife the English princess Vicky, daughter of Queen Victoria, Wilhelm's left arm was damaged at birth and remained shorter than the other throughout his life, often causing him embarrassment and discomfort. As he grew up, he worshipped the swagger, machismo and discipline of the Prussian military caste, becoming a self-conscious parody of the Prussian officer with his waxed moustaches, shining boots, batons, ever more flamboyant aquiline helmets and self-designed dandyish uniforms. Despite, or perhaps because of his damaged arm, his frail figure and health, his white feminine skin and camp taste for uniforms, his embrace of Prussian militarism was obsessional.

At first he worshipped the magnificent Machiavellian power of the Iron Chancellor Bismarck, but his real hero was his grandfather Wilhelm I the first kaiser – or emperor – of the new German empire, who personified the austere, unflashy, patriotic service of the perfect Junker officer. Simultaneously he came to despise the Anglophile liberalism of his own father and mother. He combined the old and the new in his personality for he was convinced that he would be a German absolutist monarch backed by divine right, yet he was also a keen proponent of the new technologies – somehow managing to see himself as both medieval knight and modern technocrat. His opinions were, from the very beginning whimsical, for he combined rabid anti-Semitism with support for the new business class, obsessional militarism with a liking for architecture and art, and absolutist authoritarianism with pretensions to supporting the working class and liberalising labour laws.

In 1888, Wilhelm's grandfather died and his father became emperor, but tragically the new kaiser was already dying of throat cancer and Bismarck remained in total control. On his father's death a few months into his reign, Wilhelm succeeded to the throne. Bismarck had already had to spend time paying off Wilhelm's mistresses and buying back the young emperor's love letters after his sexually perverse early adventures. Worse, from now on, Bismarck had to hide and suppress Wilhelm's often insane and tactless comments on official documents, but soon the emperor's speeches – which varied from boasting how German troops would massacre Chinese with the brutality of the Huns to proposing the shooting of German strikers by troops – were embarrassing the German elite.

By 1890, Wilhelm was determined to rid himself of the ancient Bismarck using his own pro-labour policies to procure his resignation. He replaced him first with a worthy officer, General von Caprivi, and then with the antique Prince von Hohenlohe, but it was clear that Wilhelm was set on ruling himself. Bismarck had created the hybrid constitution of the German empire with all the trappings of democracy, but beneath them the royal Prussian prerogative was intact and absolute: this had suited Bismarck because his chancellorship depended on the favour of the kaiser. But now Bismarck was gone, the kaiser was determined to seize it himself, and over the next few years, Wilhelm, displaying some political skill, took control of German policy, particularly basing his power on his right to run the military through his personal military cabinets and to appoint the chancellor and ministers.

The kaiser was advised during this successful new course of German politics by his unlikely best friend Prince Philip von Eulenberg, who was his ambassador to Vienna, an aesthete, musician, writer and believer in divine right, kaiserine power, social conservatism, German imperialism and psychic seances. Thanks to Eulenberg's intrigues and plans, the kaiser managed to find and promote a candidate for chancellor, Bernard von Bulow, who saw himself as an imperial courtier instead of independent statesman. In 1900, Wilhelm appointed Bulow to the post, henceforth dominating policy. At the same time, the kaiser promoted the creation of the German Imperial Navy, launching an arms race with the British. His outbursts – his support for the Boers against the British, his disastrous visit to Morocco which outraged France, then his notorious *Daily Telegraph* interview in which he offended all the powers of Europe, particularly the British – exposed his emotional immaturity and mental instability yet also destabilized European politics.

Although he now found himself dominant as home, he was undermined by a series of embarrassing political scandals that again revealed his own personal flaws: it emerged that he was surrounded by a secret homosexual clique and that his best friend Eulenberg led a homosexual double life. At one point, an old general, the chief of his military cabinet, died of a heart attack while dancing for the kaiser dressed in a ballet tutu. The kaiser never spoke to Eulenberg again – but the rising scandals in his court circle, homosexual and heterosexual alike – bewildered him and undermined his prestige. His interventions in German policy were often ill conceived and inconsistent but his foreign policies only contributed to a worsening international tension.

In 1914, faced with the assassination of the Austrian grand duke Franz Ferdinand by Serbian terrorists, Wilhelm's overexcited manouverings helped guide Germany to the policy of encouraging and indeed guaranteeing the Austrian right to attack Serbia. Despite his personal pleas to Tsar Nicholas II for peace, he backed the plans to attack France through the Low Countries and was eager for war against Russia, even though all this implied a war on two fronts.

Once war had started, Wilhelm again pushed for the alliance with the Ottomans, and backed submarine warfare (which ultimately pulled America into the war) as well as the brutal colonization of Russia. For Allied troops, the kaiser, nicknamed Kaiser Bill, was the ultimate enemy. His entire life had been a preparation for his role as Germanic warlord but when the war came, he was listless and depressive, overexcited and irrational in equal parts, proving totally incapable of political, military or strategic planning, let alone administration. His ministers and generals regarded him with contempt and he was intimidated by the real rulers of Germany from 1916, Field Marshal von Hindenburg and General Ludendorff. When defeat came in 1918, Wilhelm was hopelessly associated with the catastrophic militarism and imperial corruption that had brought Germany to defeat. He abdicated and went into Dutch exile where he fulminated against Jews and liberals, dying in 1941.

LLOYD GEORGE

1863–1945

How can I convey to the reader any just impression of this extraordinary figure of our time, this siren, this goat-footed bard, this half-human visitor to our age from the hag-ridden magic and enchanted woods of Celtic antiquity.

John Maynard Keynes, quoted in R.F. Harrod, *The Life of John Maynard Keynes* (1951)

Much of the fabric of modern British society rests on the achievements of David Lloyd George. Known as the Welsh Wizard for his oratory, and as the Goat for his womanizing, he was a passionate Welshman of radical politics and modest beginnings. As chancellor of the exchequer, he established the foundations of the welfare state, and as prime minister during the First World War he led the country to victory.

Lloyd George often found – and cast – himself an outsider in Westminster politics. One of his first causes, during the 1890s, was that of Welsh freedom. Yet with his great powers of oratory he rose fast through the Liberal Party. From 1899 he fiercely opposed the Second Anglo-Boer War.

In 1905 Lloyd George was appointed to the Cabinet as president of the board of trade, and in 1908 he was promoted to chancellor under the new prime minister, H.H. Asquith. As chancellor, he proved to be a bold reformer with a strong social conscience, pushing through legislation introducing old-age pensions.

In 1909 he went even further and announced the 'People's Budget', which he intended to 'wage implacable warfare against poverty'. The aim was to introduce a tax on land and higher-rate taxes on higher incomes to fund pensions, public works such as road-building, and new battleships to face the perceived threat from Germany. The House of Lords hated Lloyd George's proposals, and their rejection of the budget led to a constitutional crisis and ultimately the 1911 Parliament Act, which abolished the Lords' right of veto. Lloyd George extended the welfare state with the National Insurance Act of 1911, which introduced a way for working people to insure against future unemployment and to provide for their health care. Though unpopular with some at first, it made Lloyd George a hero to many.

During the First World War, Asquith's sleepy, passive conduct of the conflict contrasted with the tireless dynamism and the driving charisma of 'LG'. As minister of munitions and then as secretary for war, Lloyd George mobilized almost the entire population in the war effort, drafting women to take over factory work traditionally reserved for men, who were now away fighting. As a result of this and other measures, there was a great leap in productivity. But Lloyd George became increasingly critical of Asquith's handling of the war, and in December 1916 he allied himself with the Conservatives and some members of his own party to replace Asquith as prime minister, thereby splitting the Liberal Party.

Lloyd George led the war effort by sheer force of personality, but he was unable to overcome the rigidity and stupidity of the generals. He never had the power to prevent the colossal human losses of trench warfare. He agreed with his French counterpart, Clemenceau, that the Allies desperately needed a unified command, which came about in April 1918. By November 1918, Germany having exhausted itself in its final offensives in the spring and summer of that year, the war was won. In the subsequent peace negotiations, Lloyd George attempted to find a compromise between the idealistic, conciliatory Americans and the vengeful French.

Following the war, Lloyd George – long a believer in female emancipation – extended voting rights to women. He went on to help bring an end to the war of independence in Ireland, which had broken out in January 1919. In 1921 he negotiated a treaty allowing twenty-six southern counties to form the Irish Free State. But six northern counties remained part of the United Kingdom as Northern Ireland, with violent consequences for another eighty years.

Despite these achievements, Lloyd George found himself in political difficulties. His reputation was marred by scandals surrounding the sale of peerages, and the Conservatives in his coalition government opposed his plans to increase public expenditure on housing and social services, forcing him to resign in October 1922. Although he became reconciled with the main bulk of the Liberal Party and returned as their leader in 1926, the Liberals were now a spent force, eclipsed by the rise of the Labour Party.

After 1922 Lloyd George's vanity and folly undermined him. His visit to Hitler handed the Nazis a propaganda coup, though he later came to oppose appeasement and called for rearmament. He had resigned as leader of the Liberals in 1931 because of ill health, but continued to sit as an MP, declining Churchill's offer of a cabinet position during the Second World War on the grounds of his age. Long married to Margaret Owen, he had many mistresses, above all his secretary Frances Stevenson, whom he married in 1943. In that year he also voted for the last time in Parliament, in support of the Beveridge Report, which outlined the cradle-to-grave extension of the welfare state that Lloyd George had done so much to create. It was a fitting farewell to politics. Early in 1945 he was raised to the peerage, but he died before he could take his seat in the House of Lords.

TOULOUSE-LAUTREC

1864–1901

He did not overturn reality to discover truth, where there was nothing. He contented himself with looking. He did not see, as many do, what we seem to be, but what we are. Then, with a sureness of hand and a boldness at once sensitive and firm, he revealed us to ourselves.

From Toulouse-Lautrec's obituary in the Journal de Paris

Vicomte Henri de Toulouse-Lautrec, the iconic chronicler of Parisian nightlife, confronted society with a vibrant celebration of humanity in all its distortions. He is world-famous today principally for his posters, but while these are undeniably superb, they have obscured his brilliance as a painter and portraitist who brought poignant sensitivity to his studies of the women of the *demi-monde*. In truth he was the Rembrandt of the night.

Toulouse-Lautrec's art illuminates Paris's artistic quarter in all its glory, immortalizing the chorus girls and entertainers who crowded its streets, cabarets and cafés. It was a ground-breaking departure in art. His work caused outrage, but he did not do it to shock. Rather, he wanted to 'depict the true and not the ideal'. In so doing, he humanized his subjects because they were people he knew so well, giving them a nobility that society had always denied them.

Toulouse-Lautrec's style – clear, economical lines, bright colours and vigorous, often ironic representations – was as revelatory as his subjects. After he decided to become an artist, his wealthy aristocratic family arranged for him to be tutored by a family friend and society painter. Toulouse-Lautrec developed his distinctive style almost in spite of his training. Notwithstanding his eagerness to please, he found himself unable to copy a model exactly. 'In spite of himself,' a friend recalled, 'he exaggerated certain details, sometimes the general character, so that he distorted without trying or even wanting to.' A subsequent tutor found this freedom of expression 'atrocious'. Aged nineteen, he was given an allowance to set up his own studio, whereupon he moved to Montmartre and began to paint his friends.

Toulouse-Lautrec soon became famous for his lithographs. Bold and clear, their elegant style anticipates art nouveau. They showed that art did not have to consist solely of oil on canvas, and as posters they turned advertising into an art form. The vast audience this gave him transformed his career. 'My poster is pasted today on the walls of Paris,' he declared proudly of his first lithograph in 1891. His lithographs showed the great singing, dancing and circus stars of the Parisian night, especially the Moulin Rouge: *Aristide Bruant dans son cabaret* or *Moulin Rouge – La Goulue* and *Jane Avril sortant du Moulin Rouge* are now pasted on walls across the world. His paintings are remarkable for their humanity: his debonair boulevardier Louis Pascal shows that he could render men masterfully too, while his study for *The Medical Inspection* catches the pathos of whores queuing up in the surgery. Some of his most beautiful paintings show these women relaxing together or alone, such as *Abandon*, the

Two Friends or the touching *Red Haired Woman Washing*. Both the stars and the ordinary girls were his friends and lovers.

Like the rest of his family, Toulouse-Lautrec was enthusiastically sporty, but at the age of thirteen he broke his left thigh bone and a year later his right. Despite a long convalescence and numerous painful treatments, his legs never grew again. With a man's torso on dwarfish legs, he never exceeded 5 feet in height. The cause was a bone disease, probably of genetic origin.

There is a clear irony in the contrast between the energy and physicality of Lautrec's paintings and his own atrophied state. He was never reconciled to his condition. His compositions often hide the legs of his figures. Surrounded by unusually tall friends, 'he often refers to short men,' commented one acquaintance, 'as if to say "I'm not as short as all that!"' But the 'tiny blacksmith with a pince-nez' was under no illusions about himself: 'I will always be a thoroughbred hitched to a rubbish cart' was just one of a litany of self-deprecating remarks.

Even in the raffish, boozy world of Montmartre, Lautrec's alcohol consumption was legendary. He helped to popularize the cocktail. The earthquake – four parts absinthe, two parts red wine and a splash of cognac – was a particular favourite. Syphilis accelerated his physical and mental decline, and when his beloved mother left Paris suddenly in 1899, it precipitated a total mental collapse. He was sent to a sanatorium, where he produced one of his greatest series of drawings, *At the Circus*. But after a brief spell he returned to Paris.

Toulouse-Lautrec degenerated into a haze of alcohol, the earthquake giving way to an esoteric diet of 'eggs, which Monsieur eats raw mixed with rum'. Removed to one of his family's châteaux, he was reduced to dragging himself along by his arms as his useless legs failed to work. Almost paralysed and nearly totally deaf, Toulouse-Lautrec was just thirty-six when he died.

'He would have liked the elegant, active life of all healthy sports-loving persons,' wrote his father after his death. His son achieved in art all the vitality missing from his life.

GANDHI

1869–1948

I know of no other man in our time, or indeed in recent history, who so convincingly demonstrated the power of the spirit over things material.

Sir Stafford Cripps, British Labour politician, speech at the Commonwealth Prime Ministers' Conference, London (1 October 1948)

Mohandas Karamchand Gandhi was the father of the Indian Nation, whose use of peaceful protest to achieve political independence has served as an inspiration for generations of political leaders seeking an end to oppression. The embodiment of man's capacity for true humanity, Gandhi came to be known by the name of Mahatma, meaning Great Soul.

Gandhi never had a clearly defined role in Indian politics. But Indian independence was as much his achievement as it was of the politicians in the Indian National Congress. Gandhi's leadership forged a national identity among the Indian people. The tools of his protests – boycotts and non-cooperation – could be taken up by all. From spinning and weaving one's own cloth in preference to buying British textiles, to 250-mile (400-km) mass marches protesting against monopolies, Gandhi's methods of political involvement transcended the boundaries of age, gender, caste and religion.

No longer was political activism confined to the literate elite. Inspired by this small, frail figure dressed in homespun cloth, millions participated in the peaceful protests which reached their zenith in the Quit India campaign of 1942. As the British authorities arrested hundreds of thousands of protesters, it became apparent that their rule was increasingly untenable. Some contemporaries criticized Gandhi's methods of protest as 'passive' – incapable of achieving anything of real import. The achievement of Indian independence in 1947, and the triumph of countless civil rights movements since, proved them wrong.

Gandhi's fragile appearance belied his iron will. Although he came from a distinguished family – his father served as prime minister in several princely states – as a youth Gandhi displayed little promise in any sphere. His politicization began in earnest when he was a young lawyer working in South Africa. Here Gandhi experienced discrimination at first hand when he was thrown off a train after a white traveller complained about the presence of an Indian in her carriage. Gandhi set about campaigning for Indian rights and in so doing developed the philosophy of protest that came to define him. *Satyagraha*, the 'truth force', was an all-consuming discipline that involved non-violent resistance to an oppressive authority. It required vast inner strength that could only be achieved by extreme self-control. Gandhi pursued it in every aspect of his life. Despite being happily married he adopted celibacy – and then tested his control by sleeping naked with attractive disciples. As a law student in London he had become an ardent practitioner of vegetarianism, and fasting became a frequent practice of his, which he used for both spiritual advancement and to attain political goals. Setting up ashrams, where he lived with his wife and followers, he abandoned his worldly goods and reduced his dress to the homespun *dhoti* – a type of loincloth. One of the few possessions that Gandhi left at his death was a spinning wheel.

Gandhi's campaigns against discrimination and injustice were many and varied. He fearlessly challenged social, religious and political practices in the pursuit of justice for the oppressed, be they women, peasants or nations. Visiting London in 1931 for a conference on constitutional reform, Gandhi chose to stay with the poor of the East End. A devout Hindu, he was nonetheless steadfast in his calls for a reform of the caste system and an end to the practice by which certain groups of people, by virtue of their birth, were stigmatized as untouchable. For Gandhi there was 'no such thing as religion overriding morality', and his deep religious belief never closed his mind to the merits of the beliefs of others: he considered himself not just a Hindu but 'also a Christian, a Muslim, a Buddhist and a Jew'. The bungled partition of the subcontinent into India and Pakistan on religious lines and the descent into sectarian massacres deeply distressed him, and one of his last actions was a personal fast during the Indo-Pakistan war of 1947.

Gandhi always displayed remarkable personal courage. He endured imprisonment by the British government several times, and he demonstrated more than once his willingness to risk death to secure the future of the Indian nation. As Hindu–Muslim violence threatened to consume India, Gandhi made an unarmed and unprotected pilgrimage through the heart of the unrest in Bengal in an effort to quell it. His assassination in 1948 by a Hindu extremist who resented his conciliatory stance towards Pakistan so shocked his people that it helped stop the slide into mayhem and restore order: he therefore died both a martyr and a peacemaker. 'My service to my people,' he once said, 'is part of the discipline to which I subject myself in order to free my soul from the bonds of the flesh ... For me the path of salvation leads through the unceasing tribulation in the service of my fellow countrymen and humanity.'

LENIN

1870–1924

One out of ten of those guilty of parasitism will be shot on the spot ... We must spur on the energy of the terror ... shoot and deport ... launch merciless mass terror against kulaks, priests, and white guards ...

Lenin in 1918

Vladimir Ilyich Lenin was the gifted, ruthless, fanatical, yet pragmatic Marxist politician who created the blood-soaked Soviet experiment that was based from the very start on random killing and flint-hearted repression, and which led to the murders of many millions of innocent people. Lenin was long revered in communist propaganda and in naïve Western liberal circles as the kind-hearted and decent father of the Soviet peoples, but the newly opened Soviet archives reveal that he relished the use of terror and bloodletting and was as frenziedly brutal as he was intelligent and cultured. He was, however, one of the political titans of the 20th century, and without his personal will there would have been no Bolshevik Revolution in 1917.

Unimpressive in appearance but exceptional in personality, Vladimir Ilych Ulyanov, known as Lenin, was small and stocky, prematurely bald, and had a bulging, intense forehead and piercing, slanted eyes. He was a genial man – his laughter was infectious – but his life was ruled by his fanatical dedication to Marxist revolution, to which he devoted his intelligence, pitiless pragmatism and aggressive political will.

Lenin was raised in a loving family, and was descended from nobility on both sides. His father was the inspector of schools in Simbirsk, while his mother was the daughter of a wealthy doctor and landowner; further back his antecedents included Jews, Swedes and Tartar Kalmyks (to whom he owed his slanting eyes). Lenin possessed the domineering confidence of a nobleman, and as a young man he had even sued peasants for damaging his estates. This helps to explain Lenin's contempt for old Russia: 'Russian idiots' was a favourite curse. When criticized for his noble birth, he replied: 'What about me? I am the scion of landed gentry ... I still haven't forgotten the pleasant aspects of life on our estate ... So go on, put me to death! Am I unworthy to be a revolutionary?' He was certainly never embarrassed about living off the income from his estates.

The rustic idyll on the family estate ended in 1887 when his elder brother Alexander was executed for conspiring against the tsar. This changed everything. Lenin qualified as a lawyer at Kazan University, where he read Chernychevsky and Nechaev, imbibing the discipline of Russian revolutionary terrorists even before he embraced Marx and became active in the Russian Socialist Workers' Party. After arrests and Siberian exile, Lenin moved to western Europe, living at various times in London, Cracow and Zurich. In 1902 he wrote *What Is to Be Done?* which defined a new vanguard of professional and ruthless revolutionaries and led to the break-up of the party into the so-called majority faction – the Bolsheviks under Lenin – and the more moderate Menshevik minority.

'Trash', 'bastards', 'filth', 'prostitutes', 'Russian fools', 'cretins' and 'silly old maids' were just some of the insults Lenin heaped on his enemies. He had enormous contempt for his own liberal sympathizers, whom he called 'useful idiots', and mocked his own gentler comrades as 'tea-drinkers'. Revelling in the fight, he existed in an obsessional frenzy of political vibration, driven by an intense rage and a compulsion to dominate allies – and to smash opposition.

Lenin cared little for the arts or personal romance: his wife, the stern, bug-eyed Nadya Krupskaya, was more manager and amanuensis than lover, but he did engage in a passionate affair with the wealthy, liberated beauty Inessa Armand. Once in power, Lenin indulged in little flings with his secretaries – at least according to Stalin, who claimed Krupskaya complained about them to the Politburo. But politics was everything to Lenin.

During the 1905 Revolution, Lenin returned to Russia; but the Bolshevik uprising in Moscow was suppressed by Tsar Nicholas II and Lenin had to escape back into exile. Desperately short of money and always pursuing factional ideological feuds that split the party further, Lenin used bank robberies and violence to fund his small group. During these escapades, Stalin caught Lenin's eye and he consistently promoted him even when other comrades warned him of Stalin's violent propensities: 'That's exactly the sort of person I need!' he replied. By 1914 the Bolsheviks had almost been crushed by the tsarist secret police, and most were in exile or prison: as late as 1917 Lenin – who spent the war in Cracow, then Switzerland – was wondering if the Revolution would happen in his own lifetime.

But in February 1917 spontaneous riots brought down the tsar. Lenin rushed back to Petrograd (St Petersburg), invigorated the Bolsheviks into an energetic radicalism, and through his own personal will created a programme that promised peace and bread, and so popularized his party. Despite huge opposition from his own comrades, Lenin – backed by two gifted radicals, Trotsky and Stalin – forced the Bolsheviks to launch the October coup that seized power in Russia and changed history.

From the moment Lenin took power as premier – or chairman

of the Council of People's Commissars – the new Soviet Republic was threatened on all sides by civil war and foreign intervention. Lenin made peace with Germany at Brest-Litovsk and introduced the New Economic Policy to encourage some un-Marxist free enterprise, but pursued victory in the Russian Civil War with war communism, brutal repression and deliberate terror. 'A revolution without firing squads is meaningless,' he said. In 1918 he founded the Cheka, the Soviet secret police, and encouraged pitiless brutality. Between 280,000 and 300,000 people were murdered under his orders; this only came to light when the archives were opened in 1991. 'We must ... put down all resistance with such brutality that they will not forget it for several decades,' he wrote.

After Lenin himself was shot and almost killed in an assassination attempt in August 1918, the Red Terror against all those considered enemies of the people – such as the kulaks (wealthy peasants), was intensified. His most energetic and talented protégés, Stalin and Trotsky, were also the most brutal. When the peasantry opposed his policies and millions perished in famines, Lenin said, 'Let the peasantry starve.'

The following order, issued in 1918, is typical:

> Comrades! The insurrection of five kulak districts should be pitilessly suppressed.
> The interests of the whole revolution require this because the last decisive battle with the kulaks is now under way everywhere. An example must be demonstrated.
> 1. Hang (and make sure that the hanging takes place in full view of the people) no fewer than one hundred known kulaks, rich men, bloodsuckers.
> 2. Publish their names.
> 3. Seize all their grain from them.

*4. Designate hostages in accordance with yesterday's telegram.
Do it in such a fashion that for hundreds of kilometres around
the people might see, tremble, know, shout: they are strangling
and will strangle to death the bloodsucking kulaks.
Telegraph receipt and implementation.
Yours, Lenin.*

PS: Find some truly hard people.

By 1920 the Soviet Revolution was safe, but Lenin himself was
exhausted, and he never really recovered from the bullet wounds
he had received in 1918. In 1922 he promoted Stalin to general
secretary of the party, but when Stalin insulted other comrades
and then Lenin's own wife, Lenin tried to remove him from his
position. It was too late. Lenin was felled by a series of strokes,
but managed to record a testament in which he attacked all his
potential successors, including Trotsky and especially Stalin, whom
he said was 'too rude' for high office. But his health collapsed and
he died in 1924. He was embalmed, displayed in a mausoleum in
Red Square, and worshipped like a Marxist saint.

In the Soviet Union, Leninism and Stalinism were one and
same: a utopian totalitarian creed, founded on repression, bloodletting and the destruction of personal freedom. Thanks to Lenin,
this ideology took the lives of over 100 million innocent people in
the 20th century.

PROUST

1871–1922

And suddenly the memory revealed itself. The taste was of the little piece of madeleine . . .

> Marcel Proust, *Du côté de chez Swann* (*Swann's Way*, vol. 1, 1913), translated by C.K. Scott-Moncrieff and S. Hudson, revised by T. Kilmartin

It is said that Marcel Proust spent the first half of his life living it, and the second half writing about it. The result was *À la recherche du temps perdu*, a semi-autobiographical novel sequence that is perhaps the most complete evocation of a living world ever written, and also a meditation on the nature of time, the self, memory, love, sexuality, society and experience. Proust's work was originally translated under the title *Remembrance of Things Past* (a quotation from Shakespeare), but a more recent translation, published in 1992, is more accurately entitled *In Search of Lost Time*.

In 1909 Marcel Proust, the dilettante son of a wealthy Jewish bourgeois family, ate a madeleine (a type of small sponge cake) dipped in tea and was instantly transported back to his grandfather's house in the country, where he had spent much of his childhood. Overwhelmed by the completeness of the memory, by its sights and smells, Proust found a purpose to the writing that he had dabbled in since he was a youth. At the age of 38, Proust began the work that was to become *À la recherche du temps perdu*.

As Proust embarked upon his re-creation of a world long gone, he withdrew completely from the world of the present. In his youth he had used his childhood asthma as an excuse to avoid any kind of career other than that of avid socialite. But when he began *À la recherche*, he shut himself off from society, sealing himself up in a cork-lined room. He became an obsessive invalid, his deteriorating health exacerbated by hypochondria. He insisted that his morning post be steamed in disinfectant, and he ingested nothing but handfuls of opiates and barbiturates.

Proust's approach baffled some: one publisher rejected his first volume, believing that an author did not need thirty pages to describe turning over in bed before going to sleep again. Discarding the notion of a plot-driven work, Proust takes his reader on an almost stream-of-consciousness journey back through his life. He digresses, for pages at a time, on some aspect of philosophy, or history, or art, in a manner that is yet incandescently beautiful, poetical and tragic but also hilarious, outrageous and frivolous. The mundane – drinking a cup of tea, lying awake at night – is just as important as the dramatic. Proust hypnotizes his readers, immersing them in a world as real as their own.

As his writing gathered pace, the neurasthenic, eccentric Proust adopted an exclusively night-time existence. His staff had to maintain complete silence as he slept during daylight hours. He would pay calls on friends well after midnight or expect them to accompany him on early-morning visits to the cathedral of Notre Dame, dressed in a fur coat over his nightshirt.

Proust had an almost hysterical need to be the focus of attention. His invalidism was just one way of securing the attention of his mother; later on his self-enforced seclusion ensured the same concern from his friends. The desperation of the child when his mother goes out for the night in *À la recherche* vividly evokes Proust's almost Oedipal love for his mother. He tried to buy affection, employing his male lovers as staff, but he drove them away with his obsessive attentions.

A brilliant conversationalist and mimic, Proust was completely without malice. His extravagance was legendary: he financed a male brothel and once hired out the entire floor of a hotel in his compulsive search for silence. His long-suffering staff were extremely well paid, and handsome waiters handsomely tipped. Even after he had sequestered himself away, he still sent food parcels to the soldiers at the front in the First World War.

Proust was, in his youth, a terrible snob. But the desperate need of this Jewish homosexual to be accepted in Parisian high society did not prevent him from demonstrating real courage in the face of that society's virulent anti-Semitism. At the time of the Dreyfus Affair, Proust stood up as a prominent supporter of the Jewish army officer wrongfully convicted of treason – a move that risked social ostracism. And while he was always afraid in life of being rejected for his sexuality, he was not afraid to approach it in his writing, asserting that he needed to be as precise about Baron Charlus' sexual forays as the Duchesse de Guermantes' red shoes.

He achieved his goal. Proust's delicate, life-like descriptions are astoundingly complete. His fascination with the shifting nature of perception produced some of the most exquisite characterizations ever committed to the page. Over two thousand characters, in all their life-like ambiguity, people *À la recherche*. And they are described in some of the most beautiful prose ever written: every one of the novel sequence's 8 million words seems to have been precisely chosen.

Proust was still correcting manuscripts a few hours before his death. Otherworldly in life, in death 'he was totally absent', commented one friend. But the notebooks into which Proust had poured his memory, his health and his soul seemed, to the writer Jean Cocteau, 'alive, like a wristwatch still ticking on a dead soldier'.

SHACKLETON, SCOTT & AMUNDSEN

1874–1922 & 1868–1912 & 1872–1928

Difficulties are just things to overcome, after all.
Shackleton, in the journal of his South Polar journey
(11 December 1908)

Sir Ernest Shackleton, Robert Scott and Roald Amundsen were the three most inspirational Arctic explorers of the early 20th century.

Shackleton was born to Irish parents who settled in England, and at the age of sixteen he joined the merchant navy. His voyages took him all around the world, until in 1901 he was appointed to serve on board the *Discovery*, a steam vessel specially built for work in the ice, which was carrying Commander Robert Falcon Scott to Antarctica. Scott chose Shackleton to accompany him and Edward Wilson on a dog- and man-hauled sled journey towards the South Pole.

On the journey – during which temperatures dipped below –80°C – all three men eventually became ill with scurvy, but Shackleton, coughing up blood, seemed worst affected. Although he was invalided home, where he briefly tinkered with politics, he never gave up the dream of a further attempt on the South Pole. In 1907 he returned to Antarctica, this time as leader. He had bought a ship, raised funds and engaged a crew of seamen and scientists. The expedition broke new ground. One party reached the South Magnetic Pole, another made the first ascent of Mount Erebus, an active volcano. In late 1908 Shackleton led another, heroic sled journey towards the geographic South Pole. Despite bitter conditions, in January 1909 the party came within 100 miles of their destination – further south than any man had ever been before, although his party did not quite make it to the Pole. On his return to Britain, Shackleton was lauded as a hero and knighted by the king.

Ernest Shackleton's gallant attempt on the South Pole in 1908–9 narrowly preceded the battle between his former comrade Robert Falcon Scott and the Norwegian Roald Amundsen, which would become one of the most famous races of discovery in history.

Scott joined the Royal Navy in 1880, when he was just twelve years old. By 1897 he had become a first lieutenant. He led the 1901–4 mission to Antarctica and was recognized as a dedicated scientific investigator and navigator. When he returned to England he was promoted to captain.

By 1910, having seen Shackleton overtake him in the bid to journey ever deeper south, Scott – still a national figure – raised the funds for a private expedition of scientific and geographical discovery, with the ultimate aim of reaching the South Pole.

At the same time, Amundsen had established his name as commander of the first vessel to sail through the sought-after Northwest Passage – a route joining the Atlantic and Pacific oceans across the top of North America – and was also intent on reaching the North Pole. When he heard in 1909 that others had claimed the North Pole, he decided to turn south.

During his time in the Arctic Amundsen had learned a lot from the indigenous people about survival in the harsh cold, and he had become expert in using dogs to pull sledges. This, combined with careful planning, meant that when his party set out for the South Pole in October 1911, even severe conditions and the choice of a new, untrodden route could not prevent them reaching their destination on 14 December. Amundsen left behind a tent, with a note for Scott to confirm that he had been there. The Norwegian was a brilliant planner and student of Arctic life but also showed heroic endurance – and he should be celebrated just as much as Scott.

Scott's party was less skilled in polar travel, and they reached the Pole more than a month after the Norwegian. Despite physical fortitude, Scott's return journey was hampered by some of the severest Antarctic weather ever known, injuries to members of the party, and ill-placed food depots.

It became clear in mid-March 1912 that their party was doomed. One man had already died of an infection. Then, on 17 March, a second man, Captain Oates, left the tent, saying 'I am just going outside and may be some time,' a comment of classic English understatement, and crawled into a blizzard, hoping that his certain death would increase his companions' chances of survival.

But Oates's sacrifice was not enough. The group was pinned to their tent by blizzards and they froze to death just eleven miles from the next food depot. All the while, Scott kept recording his moving journal of events. 'Had I lived, I should have had a tale to tell of the hardihood, endurance and courage of my companions which would have stirred the heart of every Englishman,' he wrote in his final entry. 'These rough notes and our dead bodies must tell the tale.'

In 1914 Shackleton set out in charge of the British Imperial Trans-Antarctic expedition. His aim was to cross Antarctica from the Weddell Sea to McMurdo Sound, via the South Pole. However, the voyage of the *Endurance* was overtaken by misfortune. The enormous rafts of floating ice in the Weddell Sea closed in on the ship, and after ten months of drifting with the pack ice the Endurance was crushed, without even having reached the expedition's jumping-off point on the coast. All of the men aboard were forced onto the surrounding ice floes, where they camped for another five months as they drifted north with the ice. In April 1916 they made their way to the northern edge of the ice floe and embarked in three small boats; after six days they reached Elephant Island in the South Shetlands.

From there, Shackleton and a handful of colleagues decided to head to the island of South Georgia, 800 miles away. They completed the hazardous journey across the stormy Southern Ocean in a tiny boat, reaching the island's south coast in seventeen days. Even then, they had to climb an uncharted mountain range in the middle of the island to reach a Norwegian whaling station on its northern coast. In a single push over two days, Shackleton and two companions made it. From there, Shackleton organized the rescue of the rest of his men on Elephant Island, reaching them at the fourth attempt. Incredibly, not a single life had been lost.

When Shackleton returned to England, he was too old to be conscripted to fight in the First World War, but he volunteered anyway. A diplomatic mission to try to woo Chile and Argentina to the Allied war effort was a failure, as was a covert mission to establish a British presence in Norwegian territory. Shackleton returned to England in 1919 to lecture and write. In 1921 he set out on a voyage to circumnavigate Antarctica but died of a heart attack on board his ship, the *Quest*, in 1922, at South Georgia.

The polar historian Apsley Cherry-Garrard wrote, 'for a joint scientific and geographical piece of organization, give me Scott . . . for a dash to the pole and nothing else, Amundsen; and if I am in the devil of a hole and want to get out of it, give me Shackleton every time'.

CHURCHILL

1874–1965

He mobilized the English language and sent it into battle.
President John F. Kennedy, conferring honorary US
citizenship on Winston Churchill (9 April 1963)

Sir Winston Churchill was one of the most remarkable men ever to lead the British people. This extraordinary leader rallied Britain in her dark hour, when Europe was dominated by Hitlerite Germany, and he inspired and organized the British conduct of the war, against all odds, until victory was achieved. After a meteoric career spanning the first half of the 20th century as self-promoting adventurer, bumptious young politician, mature minister and then lone prophet of Nazi danger, serving in almost every major government position, he emerged from isolation and proved as superb a warlord as he was a writer, historian and orator. Perhaps even more so than Nelson, he is regarded as Britain's national hero.

Churchill's father scolded him when he was a schoolboy for idling away his time at Harrow and Sandhurst, and warned him of an impending career as a 'mere social wastrel, one of the hundreds of public-school failures'. He need not have worried. As a young soldier in the Sudan and as a war correspondent in southern Africa during the Anglo-Boer War, Churchill devoted himself to swashbuckling charges and escapes, journalism and self-promotion, but he also devoured the great British historians of the past, such as Macaulay and Gibbon, and adopted their elegant – sometimes portentous – style as his own.

As a young man, Churchill rode in the cavalry charge – the last of its kind by the British military – at the Battle of Omdurman in 1898, a heroic action by the 21st Lancers that earned three men the Victoria Cross and the regiment a royal cipher.

The Battle of Omdurman ended a long conflict in Sudan. In 1881 Muhammad Ahmed, who styled himself al-Mahdi, the prophesied saviour of Islam, led a rebellion against British rule. The Mahdi and his successor, the Khalifa, and their army of fanatical dervishes repeatedly defeated the British forces. London sent out the ultimate Victorian Christian-military ascetic, General Charles Gordon, who became an imperial hero-martyr, killed when the Mahdi took Khartoum in 1885. This almost brought down Gladstone's government. In 1898 Lord Salisbury dispatched an army led by the gifted but strange General Herbert Kitchener to avenge Gordon, who was Kitchener's own hero. Kitchener, who spoke Arabic and had made his name on espionage missions into the desert dressed as a Bedouin, was an inscrutably severe soldier and a superb planner, nicknamed the Sudan Machine; he was also a connoisseur of interior decoration and an avid porcelain collector.

Churchill wrote a vivid account of the resulting battle, and the famous cavalry charge:

The trumpet jerked out a shrill note, heard faintly above the trampling of the horses and the noise of the rides. On the instant all the sixteen troops swung round and locked up into a long galloping line, and the 21st Lancers were committed to their first charge in war.

The pace was fast and the distance short. Yet, before it was half covered, the whole aspect of the affair changed. A deep crease in the ground – a dry watercourse, a khor – appeared where all had seemed smooth, level plain; and from it there sprang, with the suddenness of a pantomime effect and a high-pitched yell, a dense white mass of men nearly as long as our front and about twelve deep . . .

The Dervishes fought manfully. They tried to hamstring the horses. They fired their rifles, pressing the muzzles into the very bodies of their opponents. They cut reins and stirrup-leathers. They flung their throwing-spears with great dexterity. They tried every device of cool, determined men practised in war and familiar with cavalry; and, besides, they swung sharp, heavy swords which bit deep . . . Then the horses got into their stride again, the pace increased, and the Lancers drew out from among their antagonists. Within two minutes of the collision every living man was clear of the Dervish mass.

Churchill's next adventure was in the Boer War when captured by the Boers. His escape from his captors was another piece of derring-do, immortalized by Churchill's own account.

After moving into politics Churchill was elected a Conservative MP, but in 1904 he scandalized his party by crossing the floor to join the Liberals. He also married his wife Clementine that year, and for the rest of his long life she was to provide him with unwavering support – and frank criticism when she felt it was necessary. Churchill became home secretary in 1910 and First Lord of the Admiralty the following year. During the First World War, Churchill ensured the fleet was ready but took the blame for the failure of the Gallipoli campaign, which cost the lives of 46,000 Allied troops. He resigned to serve at the Western Front, returning to become Lloyd George's minister of munitions in 1917.

In 1919–21 Churchill was secretary of state for war and air, then, switching allegiance to rejoin the Conservatives, chancellor of the exchequer in 1924–9. In the 1930s he was out of office again, almost in political exile, but from the backbenches he foresaw the dangers of Hitler and German rearmament. His warnings were ignored by the appeasing government of Neville Chamberlain and much of the press. It was not until the Second World War broke out that he returned to favour and was brought into the War Cabinet, returning to his old position as First Lord of the Admiralty in 1939: 'Winston's back!', the Admiralty signalled to the fleet.

When, in May 1940, Chamberlain resigned in the face of the Nazi onslaught on western Europe, there was a political feeling that Britain should make peace with Hitler. In one of the clearest cases of how one man can change history and save not just a nation but a way of life, Churchill insisted on defiance, and he became prime minister. He rose to the occasion. Just after becoming prime minister he addressed Parliament:

I say to the House as I said to ministers who have joined this government, I have nothing to offer but blood, toil, tears, and sweat . . . What is our policy? . . . to wage war against a monstrous tyranny, never surpassed in the dark, lamentable catalogue of human crime. . . . What is our aim? . . . Victory, victory at all costs, victory in spite of all terror; victory, however er long and hard the road may be; for without victory, there is no survival.

With British troops evacuated from Dunkirk and a German invasion of the homeland apparently inevitable, Churchill told the House of Commons: 'We shall fight on the landing grounds, we shall fight in the fields and in the streets, we shall fight in the hills; we shall never surrender.' Two weeks later, as he announced the fall of France, he again addressed the House: 'Let us therefore brace ourselves to our duties, and so bear ourselves that, if the British Empire and its Commonwealth last for a thousand years, men will still say, "This was their finest hour."'

He kept his nerve as the RAF defeated the Luftwaffe in the Battle of Britain, making a Nazi invasion impossible. In the Cabinet war rooms, Churchill directed the war with energy and imagination, whether travelling abroad to visit troops and foreign leaders or holding meetings from his bed in the morning and pushing his exhausted officials until 3 or 4 a.m., drinking large volumes of champagne and brandy as he worked. He worked hard to develop a good relationship with President Roosevelt, and he engaged positively with Stalin, despite his innate dislike of communism. At a series of summit conferences, he agreed with both leaders not only the strategy against Hitler but also the shape of the postwar world.

In the election held in July 1945 after the defeat of Germany, Churchill and the Conservatives lost power. The following year he described, presciently, the 'Iron Curtain' now descending across a Cold War Europe. He returned as prime minister from 1951 to 1955. He turned down the offer of a dukedom but the 'greatest living Englishman' remained an Edwardian romantic imperialist with an Augustan style and vision, although he never lost his impish wit. When his grandson once asked him if he was the greatest man in the world, he replied, 'Yes! Now bugger off!' When accused of drinking too much, he responded, 'I've taken more out of alcohol than alcohol has taken out of me.' His writing was as fine as his leadership; he was the only political leader in history to have won the Nobel Prize for Literature. On his death in January 1965, Churchill received a state funeral, an honour rarely accorded those outside the royal family.

IBN SAUD

1876–1953

His personal ambition is boundless, but is tempered by great discretion and caution. He is a relentless enemy while opposition lasts, but in the hour of victory is one of the most humane Arabs in history. As for his system of rule . . . he keeps his own counsel even among his relatives, and essentially his rule is absolute.

Eldon Rutter

Abdul Aziz al Saud – known to Westerners as Ibn Saud – was a self-made king, a shrewd statesman, masterful diplomatist, tribal politician, religious ascetic and an athletic desert warrior. Over six foot four inches tall, he was famous for his prowess in battlefield, on camel-back and in the bedroom and created the new kingdom of Saudi Arabia, still a medieval dynastic autocracy well into the 21st century. Saudi Arabia remains a key player in the Middle East yet there is a contradiction at its heart: this ally of America is an Islamic autocracy in which opposition is repressed, women have few rights and the country is ruled by a strictly puritanical and anti-Western form of Islam – Wahhabism – which the Saudis export along with their oil riches.

Ibn Saud's achievement was not the first blossoming of his dynasty but the third. In the 18th century a puritanical Islamic preacher named Muhammad al-Wahhab had attacked the superstitions and shrines of traditional Islam in Arabia, demanding a return to the fundamentalist asceticism that he claimed was the original way of the Prophet. Wahab allied himself with a local sheikh around Riyadh in the Najd region of Arabia named Muhammad ibn Saud. They formed a political and religious alliance cemented by dynastic marriages between the families. Wahhabism proved a powerful force and Arabians flocked to join Saud's armies. The Ottoman empire nominally ruled Arabia, with the sultan-caliph in Istanbul serving as guardian of the Holy Places, Mecca and Medina. But the Ottoman empire was in crisis, struggling to control its heartlands, let alone the remote provinces of Arabia. Taking advantage of this, Saud and Wahhab founded a Saudi state around 1744 that terrorized more moderate Muslims, destroyed their shrines, conquered much of Arabia, raided up into the Ottoman provinces of Iraq and ultimately conquered Mecca and Medina, where they imposed their new puritanism. The Ottoman sultan repeatedly sent armies to destroy the Saudis but in vain until, in the early 19th century, Istanbul asked the semi-independent Pasha of Egypt, Mehmet Ali, to restore order. In 1818, Mehmet Ali and his son, Ibrahim Pasha, completed the defeat of the Saudis, the Saudi sheikh was sent to be beheaded in Istanbul and the sultan was back in charge. A few years later, the Saudis reestablished a small state in the Najd but it was not until Ibn Saud that the family restored its fortunes fully. In the meantime, Arabia was dominated by the al Rashid family that drove out the Sauds while the Ottomans appointed the sherifs of Mecca from the traditional Hashemite family.

As a child, Ibn Saud had to escape by night from the family seat in Riyadh to avoid the triumphant Rashid family, living with his father in Kuwaiti exile. But young Ibn Saud was determined to changed the family fortunes: backed by his elder ally Muburak al Sabah and the Sabahs, the ruling family of Kuwait, he pulled off a remarkable coup with a tiny army of Bedouins and tribesman when he seized Riyadh in 1902.

It was the beginning of a remarkable career of military

adventure and diplomatic intrigue. Ibn Saud won victories against the Rashid and other rivals but the battles were small, the armies scarcely larger than a thousand fighters at a time. But the young prince was able to resucitate and harness the vigorous fanaticism of the Wahhabis whom he mobilized into a new military-religious legion – the Ikhwan or the Brothers – who became the heart of his desert army. He built up a relationship with the British, and when the Ottomans and British started to bid for his favour during the First World War, Saud played them off against one another. But he was less aggressive in his promises than Sherif Hussain, the Hashemite amir of Mecca, who offered the British an Arab revolt from Arabia to Syria against the Ottoman sultan. Hussain was Saud's sworn enemy and the two increasingly vied for control of the whole of Arabia. Declaring himself king of the Arabs, Sherif Hussain, backed by his sons Abdullah and Faisal, launched their attack against the Ottomans, funded by vast British financial grants. But their actions never delivered a mass Arab revolt and scarcely defeated the Ottomans, even around Mecca.

Ibn Saud meanwhile waited out the war, and when the Ottoman empire collapsed in 1918, the Hashemites proved no match for him and his Ikhwan fighters. In a series of clashes, Hussain's ambitious eldest son Prince Abdullah (the future king of Jordan) was defeated by the Saudi forces. Britain was alarmed at the collapse of its ally. Saud had his own problems: the Ikhwan were hard to control and started to raid into Iraq (controlled by Britain), where they especially loathed the Shiites whom they regarded as heretics. In response, the British army and RAF attacked the Ikhwan. Ultimately Ibn Saud managed to suppress the over-mighty leaders of the Ikhwan and then defeated King Hussain's son King Ali of Hejaz, taking control of all of Arabia and Mecca and Medina in 1924 before finally overcoming the Ikhwan in battle, the last time he commanded in person. Ibn Saud declared himself king of Hejaz and in 1932 he became king of Saudi Arabia. (The Hashemites went on to amass precarious thrones outside Arabia: Faisal was first king of Syria, then Iraq where, his family ruled until 1958. Abdullah's great-grandson Abdullah II became king of Jordan in 1999).

Ibn Saud had always prided himself on his prowess as a fighter and a lover: he was usually married to three wives, divorcing earlier ones as he married the new. It was said he kept a harem of seventy odalisques and he left around seventy children including forty sons.

The kingdom he created was an absolutist dynastic monarchy combined with a Wahhabi theocracy in which the Saudi king acted as a guarantor of religious purity. The discovery of oil empowered the kingdom, giving it vast wealth, a process that began in 1933. On his death in 1953, Ibn Saud was succeeded by his feckless, inept and inconsistent son Saud, who was deposed by the princes in 1958. He kept the title but handed over power to Faisal who succeeded as king on Saud's death. Faisal was experienced and shrewd but was assassinated in 1975. The succession then went to Ibn Saud's sons, King Khalid and then King Fahd. In 1979 fanatics seized the shrine of Mecca, challenging the corruption of the Saudis: as many as 1,000 were killed when Saudi forces stormed the complex and restored order. The real contradiction of Saudi rule was exposed by the 9/11 attack on America: the al-Qaeda terrorists were overwhelmingly Saudis, most notably their leader Osama bin Laden. Well into the 21st century Saudi Arabia was still ruled by Ibn Saud's octogenarian sons but power has gradually passed to the younger generation.

STALIN

1878–1953

He sought to strike, not at the ideas of his opponent, but at his skull.
Leon Trotsky, 1936

Stalin was the Soviet dictator who defeated Hitlerite Germany in the Second World War, expanded the Russian empire to its greatest extent, industrialized the USSR and made it a nuclear superpower. During a reign of terror lasting thirty years, this mass murderer was responsible for the annihilation of more than 25 million of his own innocent citizens, and confined 18 million to slave-labour camps.

Josef Vissarionovich Djugashvili was born in Gori, a small town in Georgia in the Caucasus, the son of an alcoholic cobbler called Beso and his clever, forceful wife, Keke. Poor, unsure of his real paternity, with a pockmarked face, webbed feet and one shorter arm, young Soso (as he was known) grew up to be a highly intelligent, super-sensitive, emotionally stunted child possessed of both an inferiority complex and an overweening arrogance. His mother managed to win him a place at the seminary in Tiflis, where he studied for the priesthood, learned Russian, studied the classics and published romantic poetry. But after his conversion to Marxism, he became a fanatical and pitiless revolutionary and joined Lenin's Bolshevik Party. He was a born conspirator who dominated his comrades, undermined and betrayed his rivals, murdered suspected police spies, always pushing towards the extremes. He was repeatedly arrested but repeatedly escaped, returning from exile in

Siberia for the 1905 Revolution. He became the leading financier of the Bolsheviks through bank robberies and extortion.

After the crushing of the 1905 Revolution, Stalin created his own outfit of gangsters and hit men who killed police agents and raised cash for Lenin in a series of outrageous, bloody bank robberies, protection rackets, train heists and piratical hold-ups on the Black Sea and the Caspian. Stalin's career as an outlaw culminated in the Tiflis bank robbery in June 1907, in which his gangsters killed fifty people and got away with 300,000 roubles. Stalin then moved his outfit to oil-rich Baku, always on the run, always spreading violence and fear.

At this time Stalin was married to Kato Svanidze, with whom he had a son, Yakov, but Kato died in 1907. Contemptuous of a settled existence, he enjoyed affairs with many women, became engaged to many of them, fathered illegitimate children – and abandoned all of them heartlessly. He married again in 1918, but failed to make his new wife, Nadya Alliluyeva, any happier than his other women. She committed suicide in 1932, leaving Stalin two legitimate children, Vasily and Svetlana.

He lived under many aliases – but in the end he called himself Stalin – man of steel. His violent escapades having drawn the attention of Lenin, Stalin was elected to the Party's Central Committee. Lenin realized Stalin combined two vital political talents – he was practical and capable of organizing violence, but he could also edit, write and work on theory. 'He's exactly the type I need,' he said. Stalin was arrested for the last time in 1912 and exiled to the Arctic Circle, where he spent most of the First World War. When the tsar was unexpectedly overthrown in March 1917, Stalin returned to Petrograd, where he was later joined by Lenin. After his seizure of power in the October Revolution, Lenin recognized that the brilliant, showy Leon Trotsky and the morose, ruthless Stalin were his two most competent henchmen, and promoted them to his ruling executive committee, the Politburo.

With the outbreak of the Civil War, Lenin maintained power by terror, deploying Stalin as a brutal troubleshooter. But Stalin proved to be unimpressive as a military leader compared with Trotsky, whom Stalin constantly tried to undermine.

In 1922 Lenin, keen to balance Trotsky's prestige, promoted Stalin to the post of the party's general secretary. Before long, however, Lenin became outraged by his protégé's arrogance and tried to sack him – but it was too late. After Lenin suffered a fatal stroke in 1924, Stalin allied himself with Lev Kamenev and Grigory Zinoviev against Trotsky, who was defeated by 1925, sent into exile in 1929 and assassinated by one of Stalin's hit men in 1940. After Trotsky's exile, Stalin swung rightwards, allying himself with Nikolai Bukharin to defeat Kamenev and Zinoviev.

In 1929 Stalin was hailed as Lenin's successor, the *Vozhd* – the Leader – and thenceforth became the subject of a frenzied cult of personality. Jettisoning Bukharin, Stalin embarked on a ruthless push to industrialize the backward USSR and collectivize the peasantry. When the peasantry resisted, Stalin launched a quasi-war against the better-off peasants, known as kulaks, shooting many, exiling more, and continuing to sell grain abroad even as 10 million were shot or died in a famine he himself had created. It was one of Stalin's greatest crimes.

In 1934, despite a triumphant party congress, there was a plot to replace Stalin with his young henchman, Sergei Kirov, who was later assassinated in Leningrad. Stalin may or may not have ordered the killing, but he certainly used it to launch the Great Terror to regain control and crush any dissent. With the aid of the NKVD secret police, Stalin subjected those he regarded as his leading political enemies to a series of show trials, extracting false confessions by torture. Zinoviev, Kamenev and Bukharin were all found guilty of fabricated crimes and shot, as were two successive leaders of the NKVD, Yagoda and Yezhov. But the show trials were just the tip of the iceberg: in 1937–8 Stalin drew up secret orders to arrest and shoot thousands of 'enemies of the people' by city and regional quotas. The politburo and central committee were purged; 40,000 army officers were shot, including three of the five marshals. Even Stalin's closest friends were not immune: he signed death lists of 40,000 names. Soviet society was terrorized and poisoned. In those years approximately one million were shot, while many millions more were arrested, tortured and exiled to the labour camps of Siberia, where many died. 'You can't make an omelette without cracking eggs,' he said.

In 1939, faced with a resurgent Nazi Germany and distrusting the Western democracies, Stalin put aside his anti-fascism and signed the Non-Aggression Pact with Hitler. Poland was partitioned between Germany and the USSR, and 28,000 Polish officers were murdered in the Katyn Forest on Stalin's orders. Stalin also seized and terrorized the Baltic States, and launched a disastrous war against Finland.

Stalin ignored constant warnings that Hitler was planning to attack the USSR. The invasion came in June 1941, and within days the Soviet armies were retreating. Stalin's inept interference in military matters led to colossal losses – some 6 million soldiers – in the first year of war. But by late 1942 he had finally learned to take advice, and his generals scored a decisive victory over the Germans at Stalingrad. This was the turning point in the war, and by the time Berlin fell to the Red Army in May 1945, the Soviets controlled all of eastern Europe – and were to maintain a steely grip on it for the next forty-five years. Stalin was indifferent to the cost of victory: some 27 million Soviet citizens – both soldiers and civilians – perished during the war, during the course of which Stalin had ordered the deportation of entire peoples to Siberia, including a million Chechens, of whom half died in the process.

During the war, Stalin built personal relationships with the Allied war leaders, Franklin Roosevelt and Winston Churchill, charming and manipulating both in a series of summit meetings of the Big Three at Tehran, Yalta and Potsdam. He proved an adept diplomat.

Just when he was at his apogee in 1945, President Harry Truman (Roosevelt's successor) revealed that America had the atomic bomb, which they went on to use against Japan. Faced with rising US power, Stalin successfully threw all his resources into a secret project to create a Soviet A-bomb, which was achieved by 1949.

Stalin's last years were spent in glorious, paranoid isolation. Soon after the end of the war he relaunched his reign of terror. In 1949 two of his own chosen heirs were shot in the Leningrad case, along with many others. In 1952, apparently convinced that all Jews in the USSR were in alliance with America, he planned to execute his veteran comrades, implicating them in the fabricated Doctors' Plot, alleging that Jewish doctors were conspiring to assassinate the Soviet leadership. Stalin died after a stroke in March 1953.

A master of brutal repression, subtle conspiracy and political manipulation, this cobbler's son became both the supreme pontiff of international Marxism and the most successful Russian tsar in history. Stalin and the Bolsheviks, along with his great foes Hitler and the Nazis, brought more misery and tragedy to more people than anyone else in history.

Tiny in stature, with inscrutable features, honey-coloured eyes that turned yellow in anger, Stalin was gifted but joyless, paranoid to the point of insanity, utterly cynical and ruthless, yet a fanatical Marxist. A terrible husband and father who poisoned every love relationship in his life, he believed that human life was always expendable and physical annihilation was the essential tool of politics. 'One death,' he told Churchill with characteristic gallows humour, 'is a tragedy; a million is a statistic.' Stalin had no illusions about his brutality: 'The advantage of the Soviet model,' he said, 'is that it solves problems quickly – by shedding blood.' Ten to 20 million died at his hands and 18 million passed through his Gulag concentration camps.

One of history's most pitiless monsters, he nonetheless remains a hero to many: a textbook prefaced by President Vladimir Putin himself in 2008 hailed him as 'the most successful Russian leader of the 20th century'.

EINSTEIN

1879–1955

To raise new questions, new possibilities, to regard old problems from a new angle requires creative imagination and marks real advances in science.

Einstein on the essence of scientific creativity

It is no coincidence that Albert Einstein's name has become all but synonymous with genius. He was the most important physicist of the 20th century – some would say of any century. His discoveries, both building on and supplanting the classical mechanics of Newton, marked a paradigm shift that radically transformed our understanding of the universe.

Einstein's theory of relativity may be one of the most famous and fruitful scientific insights of all time, but the man behind it was far more than just a scientist. Throughout his life Einstein was committed to social issues and pacifism, speaking out against tyranny and persecution and despairing at the creation of the atomic bomb. Fifty years after his death, he remains an instantly recognizable figure, his face famously etched with wit and good humour.

Born into a family of secular middle-class Jews, Albert Einstein was brought up in Germany. As a child he was slow to develop (he was nicknamed der Depperte – the dopey one), but a magnetic compass given to him when he was five and a book on geometry he received when he was twelve pricked his intellectual curiosity in a way that the rigid German school system could not. Sent to boarding school in Munich, at the age of fifteen the boy ran away from both school and impending military service and joined his parents, who had moved to Italy in search of work.

Unimpressed by the arrival of their dissolute, draft-dodging son, the Einsteins welcomed Albert's enrolment at university in Zurich, where he spent some of his happiest years. Here he met his first wife, Mileva Maric, a Serbian and fellow physicist whom he married in 1903. The same year he ended a long search for employment with an appointment to the patent office in Berne.

Analysing patents was undemanding work that left Einstein time to apply his mind to mathematical and scientific problems. He was struck in particular by the apparent incompatibility of Newton's laws of motion and James Clerk Maxwell's equations describing the behaviour of light. In 1905 he published a momentous series of scientific papers dealing with the movement and behaviour of light, water and molecules. The most important proposal was the special theory of relativity, which has been described as the towering intellectual achievement of the 20th century, one that changed the way people understood the laws that govern the universe. According to this theory, nothing can move faster than light, the speed of which is constant throughout the universe. It also showed, via the famous equation $E = mc2$, that energy (E) and mass (m) are equivalent and bound together in their relationship by the speed of light (c). Special relativity does away with the idea of absolute time;

it proposes instead that time is relative, its measurement dependent on the motion of the observer. Space and time are all part of the same thing, a single continuum known as space–time.

What special relativity did not account for was the effect of gravity upon space–time. In 1915, in a series of lectures at the University of Göttingen, he finally resolved this problem by outlining his general theory of relativity.

According to this theory, the presence of objects of mass curves or warps space–time. Like a bowling ball placed in the middle of a trampoline, a large object such as a planet or star causes other objects to move through space–time towards it. So the earth, for instance, is not 'pulled' towards the sun; rather, it follows the curve in space–time caused by the sun and is prevented from falling into it only by its own speed.

Einstein's prediction that light from a star passing close to the sun's gravitational field would be deflected, causing the star's apparent position in the sky to change, was confirmed by observations during a solar eclipse in 1919. Another peculiar effect predicted by Einstein and later confirmed by observation is time dilation: the idea that time is not absolute but slows down at speeds approaching the speed of light. One upshot of time dilation is the bizarre twins paradox. If one of a pair of twins stays on earth while the other travels at close to the speed of light on a round trip to a distant star, the latter will have aged less than the stay-at-home sibling.

In this and numerous other ways, the theory of relativity continues to confound our common-sense ways of looking at and understanding the world around us. Nevertheless, it is today firmly established as the fundamental conceptual platform on which the physical sciences are built.

Few people noticed Einstein's revolutionary theories until Max Planck, the German scientist and father of quantum theory, helped to publicize them. By 1913 Einstein had risen in the academic world to become director of the Institute of Physics at the University of Berlin.

While Einstein's fame rocketed during this period, his personal life was in turmoil. After a lengthy separation he finally divorced Mileva in 1919 and promptly married his cousin Elsa Löwenthal. Einstein was now the most famous scientist in the world. He met and corresponded with many of the world's leading scientists and artists, including Sigmund Freud, the Indian mystic Rabindranath Tagore and Charlie Chaplin. 'The people applaud me,' Chaplin once told Einstein, 'because everybody understands me; they applaud you because no one understands you.'

Though he was far from religiously orthodox and his theories seemed to cast doubt on religions, Einstein always believed in some form of higher principle or spirit. 'The scientist is possessed by the sense of universal causation,' he wrote. 'His religious feeling takes the form of a rapturous amazement at the harmony of natural law, which reveals an intelligence of such superiority that, compared with it, all the systematic thinking and acting of human beings is an utterly insignificant reflection.' He maintained a belief in what he called *der Alte* – the Old Man.

In 1931 the rising Nazi Party attacked Einstein and his 'Jewish physics'. He left Germany for ever the following year, realizing his life was in danger. He settled in the USA at the University of Princeton. His pacifism – which had led to his open opposition to the First World War – weakened in the face of Nazi tyranny. He supported rearmament against Hitler, and in 1939 he co-wrote a letter to President Franklin D. Roosevelt in which the dangers of the development of nuclear weapons by the Nazis were pointed out. This prompted the Allied powers to collaborate in the Manhattan Project in order to produce the first atomic bomb themselves.

When the Second World War ended in 1945 with the destruction of Hiroshima and Nagasaki, Einstein turned sharply and publicly against further nuclear development and favoured international restrictions. He was even monitored by the FBI for his pacifist views. In 1952 he was offered the presidency of Israel; though he was a lifelong Zionist, he respectfully declined. When he died in 1955, Einstein had not achieved his long-term goal of finding a unified theory that would provide a comprehensive explanation of the fundamental forces governing the universe and so offer (as he figuratively put it) an insight into the mind of God. Such a goal has continued to elude succeeding generations of scientists, whose work has nevertheless been revolutionized by Einstein – a colossus of science and the most humane of men.

ENVER, TALAT & JEMAL: THE THREE PASHAS

1881–1922 & 1881–1922 & 1872–1922

What on earth do you want? The question is settled. There are no more Armenians.
Talat Pasha responding to questioning about the Armenians from the German ambassador, 1918

The Three Pashas were the aggressive Turkish nationalists who emerged from the Young Turk movement and seized power in the Ottoman empire in 1913, led it into a disastrous war and ordered the massacre of a million Armenians during World War One.

All three hailed from the Macedonian provinces and therefore felt the need to prove themselves true Turks and compensate for their parochial origins. Ismail Enver was the war minister and the leader of the regime, a nationalistic military officer who regarded himself as the Ottoman Napoleon: young and brave, he was also vain, deluded and reckless. He made his name fighting Italy in Libya, and Bulgaria in the Balkans, but as a general he was inept and amateurish. Nonetheless by the age of at thirty-one he had seized power, married in to the Ottoman royal family, moved into a palace and received the title of vice-generalissimo. His colleague Ahmet Jemal, was the most flamboyant of the three: a tiny, energetic showman, bon viveur and army officer, capable of the dirty work in Istanbul, organizing killings of opponents. Yet he was also intelligent, flexible and charming, with an array of beautiful Jewish mistresses and friendships with foreigners. He became navy minister and effective viceroy of the Arab provinces of the empire. The third pasha was Talat, a civil servant in the post office until he was sacked for his membership of the Young Turks – officially the Committee of Union and Progress (CUP) – and became the interior minister of the regime.

The three men had all joined the Young Turks, espousing its early and liberal ideas. They fought to achieve the revolution of 1908, and the restoration of Parliament

After the assassination of Prime Minister Mahmud Sevket Pasha in July 1913, and then the shooting (by Enver himself) of the war minister Talat, Enver and Jemal became the 'Three Pashas', the junta of triumvirs who led the empire into World War One after Enver had personally shot the war minister. Their early liberal ideas soon proved illusionary as they embraced a militant and racist Turkish nationalism, increasingly inspired by the belief that only war and violence could restore the vigour of the Ottomans. The most notable example of this was their treatment of the Empire's Armenian minority.

At the beginning of the 19th century, the predominantly

Christian Armenians had still been referred to as the Millet-i Sadika – the loyal community. However, Russian expansion into the Caucasus helped stimulate Armenian nationalism. The Ottoman empire contained far fewer Christians after the 1878 Congress of Berlin, exposing the Armenians to Muslim resentment as outsiders and traitors; ordinary Turks envied Armenian mercantile wealth. Many Turks came to see the rise of Armenian nationalism as a threat to the very existence of the Ottoman state.

Already, in the final years of the 19th century, Sultan Abdul Hamid II and others had acquiesced in a series of pogroms against Armenians: possibly hundreds of thousands died in 1895–6, while the Adana massacre of 1909 cost an estimated 30,000 lives.

In 1914/15, Enver took command of the offensive against Russia in the Caucasus. The endeavour was to end in total failure. However, Russia armed Armenian insurgents. When Russian/Armenian forces took Van in mid-May 1915, setting up an Armenian mini-state, the Three Pashas immediately laid the blame at the door of the supposedly disloyal Armenians. Talat prepared the state's revenge.

On 24 April 1915, the security forces rounded up over 250 Armenian intellectuals and community leaders in Istanbul, deported them to the east and then murdered them. After the initial deportations in April, the programme was soon extended to the entire Armenian community. Men, women and children were sent on forced marches – without food or water – to the provinces of Syria and Mesopotamia. On 27 May, the Three Pashas passed the Deportation Law, confirmed by act of Parliament. The Special Organization, a paramilitary security force, was allegedly set up under Enver and Talat to carry out deportations and massacres.

During the deportations, men were routinely separated from the rest of the population and executed. Women and children were obliged to march on, and subjected to intermittent beatings and massacres. Those who survived the journey were herded into concentration camps. Conditions there were appalling. Many prisoners were tortured, made the subject of gruesome medical experiments or slaughtered. Many more died from hunger and thirst. Some of the worst excesses in the camps were recorded by the American ambassador, Henry Morgenthau, who reported how the guards would 'apply red-hot irons to his [an Armenian's] breast, tear off his flesh with red-hot pincers, and then pour boiled butter into the wounds. In some cases the gendarmes would nail hands and feet to pieces of wood – evidently in imitation of the Crucifixion, and then, while the sufferer writhed in agony, they would cry: "Now let your Christ come and help you!"'

Talat Pasha was reported to have told an official at the German embassy in 1915 that the Ottoman government was 'taking advantage of the war in order to thoroughly liquidate its internal enemies, the indigenous Christians . . . without being disturbed by foreign intervention'. Between 1 and 1.5 million Armenians, out of a population of just under 2.5 million, perished in this period, whether this was an officially ordered genocide or a disorderly series of massacres.

Meanwhile in the Middle East, Jemal, facing an Arab revolt under British patronage, was launching a reign of terror in Damascus, Beirut and Jerusalem against Arab nationalists. The Ottomans achieved some surprising successes, destroying a British army at Kut in Iraq and routing the British forces in the Dardanelles. Nonetheless, Jemal failed to take Egypt and the British offensive was soon advancing on Jerusalem as the Russians pushed across the Caucasus.

Talat then focused more of his attention on the deteriorating military position, and in 1917 was appointed grand vizier of the Sublime Porte (Ottoman prime minister). But he failed to stem the tide of military defeats, and resigned in October 1918, fleeing Turkey aboard a German submarine. The other two of the Three Pashas fled. In 1919, the world's first war crimes trials were held under Allied auspices. The CUP leadership was found guilty and Talat, as the mastermind of the massacres, was sentenced to death. The Turks appealed to Germany for his extradition, but before this could happen Talat was murdered in Berlin in March 1921. His assassin was a survivor of the massacres who had seen his sisters raped and murdered by Turkish troops. Jemal was assasinated too, while Enver died in battle charging the Bolsheviks in central Asia.

The persecution of the Armenians that Talat initiated provided the inspiration that others would draw on later in the century. Thus, as he contemplated his slaughter of the Jews, Hitler remarked, 'Who, after all, speaks today of the annihilation of the Armenians?' Even to this day, to mention the Armenian massacres in Turkey is interpreted as the crime of 'insulting Turkishness', and is punishable by imprisonment.

ATATÜRK

1881–1938

We shall attempt to raise our national culture above the level of contemporary civilization. Therefore, we think and shall continue to think not according to the lethargic mentality of past centuries, but according to the concepts of speed and action of our century.
Atatürk, speaking at the 10th anniversary of the
Turkish Republic (29 October 1933)

Atatürk – the name adopted in 1934 by Mustafa Kemal – means Father of the Turks. He was a leader of immense vision, who created a new Islamic secularism, led Turkey out of the ruins of the moribund Ottoman empire and transformed it into a modern, Westernized republic. He became a military hero in the First World War and subsequently led the Turks to victory over an invading Greek army, sometimes with ruthlessness. He went on to become Turkey's first president, leading the country until his death in 1938. He was by far the greatest of the strongmen of the inter-war period. In our own time of challenge from Islamist fanaticism, Atatürk's vision has never been more important or relevant, yet his methods were harsh and the massacre of Smyrna was at least partly his responsibility.

Atatürk was born in what is now the Greek city of Thessaloniki. He was an academically gifted child and attended military schools from the age of twelve. Once he had been commissioned as an army officer, he joined the group known as the Young Turks, who were critical of the Ottoman regime and eager for reform and progress. Atatürk was one of those leaders who was as gifted a politician as he was a military commander. During the First World War, he was the victor of Gallipoli, defeating the Allied attack there. He also served in the Caucasus, Sinai and Palestine. He demonstrated a talent for winning the ultimate loyalty of his troops. 'I don't order you to attack,' he told them, 'I order you to die.'

At the end of the war Atatürk found himself on the losing side. As many of the Arab lands once ruled by the Ottomans were distributed among the victorious Allies, he became involved with a national movement to create a modern nation out of the Turkish heartland of the defunct empire. British prime minister David Lloyd George and the Allies believed in a classically inspired Greek empire, assigned much of Anatolia (the Asian part of modern Turkey) to the Greeks, and encouraged its premier, Eleftherios Venizelos, to invade, thus launching a recklessly unnecessary war. Atatürk resisted ruthlessly and brilliantly, culminating in victory at the Battle of Dumlupinar in 1922 – and the appalling atrocity of the Great Fire of Smyrna, in which Turkish troops were re-sponsible for conflagration, rapine and murder, destroying one of Europe's most cosmopolitan cities and killing 100,000 people. Commander-in-Chief Atatürk must bear some responsibility. Turkish independence was assured, however – confirmed in 1923 by the Treaty of Lausanne.

With the military struggle over, another challenge arose: to secure the modernization of a new secular Turkish state. In October 1923 the Republic of Turkey was declared, and Atatürk became president. As a nationalist, one of his first aims was to purge the country of foreign influence. As a progressive, his next priority was to separate the Islamic religion from the state.

The last Ottoman sultan had been deposed in 1922, and in 1924 Atatürk abolished the caliphate – the institution by which successive sultans had claimed rule over all Muslims. In place of an autocratic theocracy, Atatürk embraced, at least in theory, the principles of democracy and a legal code based on European models. Although Turkey remained a single-party state virtually without respite throughout the 1920s and 1930s, Atatürk tried to operate as an 'enlightened authoritarian' – ruling without opposi-tion but with a progressive and reforming agenda.

Economically, Turkey lagged behind much of the Western world in the 1920s. Atatürk set up state-owned factories and industries, built an extensive and efficient rail service, and established nation-al banks to fund development. Despite the ravages of the Great Depression after 1929, Turkey resisted the moves towards fascist or communist totalitarianism that took hold elsewhere.

Atatürk declared that Turkey 'deserves to become and will become civilized and progressive'. A major part of that drive was in the cultural and social field. The restrictions of Islamic custom and law were lifted. Women were emancipated – Mustafa Kemal's adopted daughter became the world's first female combat pilot

– and Western dress was strongly encouraged, at times by official rules. Panamas and European hats replaced the traditional fez, which was banned by law. Education was transformed in towns and rural areas alike, and a new Turkish alphabet (a variant on the Roman alphabet) was introduced. Literacy levels rose from 20 per cent to 90 per cent.

Atatürk encouraged the study of earlier civilizations connected with the heritage of the Turkish nation. Art, sculpture, music, modern architecture, opera and ballet all flourished. In every area of Turkish life, Atatürk pressed forward his modernizing, nationalistic mission, and a new culture began to emerge. In the process he rode roughshod over non-Turkish minority groups, suppressing the Kurds, among others.

Dramatically good-looking, Atatürk was an eccentric leader, a vigorous womanizer and a heavy drinker. His Herculean workload combined with these prodigious appetites to bring about a collapse in his health, and in 1938 he died of cirrhosis of the liver. He was only fifty-seven. He was loved by his people for his charisma, his energy and his personable style, and his funeral brought forth a massive wave of grief across the country. His memory is still revered; today in Turkey there are portraits and sculptures of him everywhere, and it remains a crime to insult the visionary father of the nation, yet during the early 21st century, his fiercely secular order was challenged by the autocratic rule of Recep Tayyip Erdogan.

PICASSO

1881–1973

Painting is not made to decorate apartments. It's an offensive and defensive weapon.

Art today would not be the same without the genius of the Spanish painter Pablo Picasso. In a career spanning nearly eighty years, Picasso – ever vigorous, ever full of *joie de vivre* – showed himself to be the most versatile and inventive artist not just of the 20th century but perhaps of all time, a master of painting and drawing as well as other media, such as collage, set design, pottery and sculpture. But his talent was not simply aesthetic. His most famous painting, *Guernica*, captured the total horror of war, while in his simple etching of the dove of peace he pointed the way for a happier future.

Picasso was born in Malaga to an artistic but conventional family. Inspired by his father, he showed exceptional talent for painting from a very young age. By the age of fourteen he had his own studio and was already exhibiting in public and receiving praise from the critics. Before he was out of his teens, he was in Paris, mixing with the European avant-garde.

In 1901 Picasso embarked on a phase known as his Blue Period, in which his paintings – still relatively naturalistic – were dominated by shades of blue. The paintings from this time are mainly melancholy, lonely portraits, often depicting extreme poverty. Much of Picasso's dark mood was influenced by the suicide of a close friend, Casagemas. In a brilliant but gloomy self-portrait from this period, Picasso looks haggard and intense, far older than his twenty years. Soon, though, the mood lifted and Picasso moved into his Rose Period, in which his subjects – often circus people or acrobats – were depicted mainly in shades of pink.

In 1907 Picasso struck out in a bold new direction, influenced by Cézanne and African masks, and produced one of the first masterpieces of modernism, *Les Demoiselles d'Avignon*. It is a striking and wildly angular and distorted depiction of five aggressively sexual women in a brothel. Thus, along with George Braque, who was producing strikingly original compositions of his own, Picasso gave birth to cubism, a completely new mode of capturing the essence of the subject on the canvas. Traditional perspective is abandoned in favour of multiple perspectives, as if the subject is seen from a number of different angles simultaneously. It was a revolutionary way of seeing. 'I paint objects as I think them,' Picasso said, 'not as I see them.'

After his cubist phase, Picasso moved on to a neo-classical period, in which he painted monumental human figures in Mediterranean settings, influenced in part by Ingres and Renoir, and then, in the 1920s and 1930s, he became loosely associated with the surrealist movement, experimenting further with distortions of the human face and figure, exploring the depiction of sexuality, and letting his imagination conjure up strange monsters.

Despite his excursions into surrealist painting, Picasso remained very engaged with the world around him He supported the Republicans during the Spanish Civil War, his painting *Guernica* expressing his outrage at the violence of fascism. *Guernica* is Picasso's best-known work, created in the aftermath of the horrific bombing of the Spanish town of the same name in 1937 by forces acting on behalf of Franco's Nationalist forces. The vast canvas presents a twisted mass of dark colours, contorted bodies, screaming heads and terrified animals – a vision of wartime apocalypse. The masterpiece is both a memorial to the helpless people killed in this action during the brutal Spanish Civil War (1936–9) and a warning of the wider horrors that war brings, then and now.

Picasso remained so enraged with Franco's regime that he refused to allow the painting to be taken to Spain while the dictator was still alive. It finally reached Madrid in 1981, where it remains, too fragile to be removed to the Guggenheim Museum in Bilbao, despite Basque requests.

In 1944 he joined the French Communist Party. Around this time he wrote: 'What do you think an artist is? An imbecile that only has eyes, if he is a painter; ears, if he is a musician; or a lyre in the deepest strata of his heart, if he is a poet? Quite the opposite, he is at the same time a political being.' In 1949 he somewhat absurdly contributed his famous design of the dove of peace to the communist-sponsored World Peace Congress held in Stalinist Poland. Picasso always had sympathy with the sufferings of the oppressed, even if his flirtations with Stalinist tyranny were misguided.

In the decades that followed, Picasso continued to produce large quantities of work in a great variety of media, often exploring and reinventing great works of art from the past, such as Velasquez's *Las Meninas* or Delacroix's *Women of Algiers*. By now he was the most famous living artist in the world, his pictures purchased for large sums by galleries and rich private collectors. Sometimes Picasso would pay for an expensive meal in a restaurant by drawing a few lines on a napkin.

Throughout his long career Picasso had a ravenous appetite for life and all its pleasures. Over the years he had a succession of wives and mistresses, sometimes overlapping each other, and in his later works he often depicts himself as some kind of satyr, or

Olympian god, enjoying wine, women and *la vie* en rose beside his beloved Mediterranean.

ROOSEVELT

1882–1945

His life must . . . be regarded as one of the commanding events in human destiny.

Winston Churchill, following the death of Roosevelt

Franklin Delano Roosevelt, in his unparalleled four terms as US president, pulled the country out of the depths of the Depression, commanded the American military effort in the Second World War and helped create the 'American century', with his colossal, rich nation as the arsenal of freedom. A charming, shrewd and enigmatic man of tolerant liberal convictions, immense personal courage and ruthless political cunning, Roosevelt's determination to secure democracy at home and abroad makes him one of the greatest leaders in history.

Roosevelt was first elected president in 1932 by a country in the grip of a terrible economic slump, with 30 million out of work. As soon as he took office, he set about implementing the New Deal he had promised the American people, setting them back on the path to economic prosperity. Unprecedented levels of government intervention in agriculture, trade and industry allowed capitalism to recover from the blows dealt it by the Wall Street Crash.

Roosevelt's administrations took on unheard of levels of responsibility for the people's welfare. In the face of bitter opposition from free marketeers, he introduced social security, protected workers' rights to organize trade unions, and regulated working hours and wages. At the same time, through the 1930s, he oversaw the restoration of America's economic strength, so re-establishing the faith of Americans in their political system and their way of life – and giving the country the muscle to face the trials of global war that were to come.

Roosevelt wanted his country to be 'the good neighbour' to the world and sought for the United States a new role as a guarantor of freedom around the world. He recognized early the barbaric evil of Nazi Germany and knew that neutrality in the Second World War would, in the long term, damage US interests, but such was the strength of isolationist feeling that he was obliged to fight the 1940 presidential election on the promise of keeping America out of the war.

At the same time, Roosevelt did everything he could to support the Allies, instituting the Lend-Lease programme of economic and military support that helped Britain to fight on alone against the Nazis after the fall of France. In January 1941 he enunciated the Four Freedoms for which he stated America would be willing to fight: freedom of expression, freedom of worship, freedom from want and freedom from fear. In August 1941 he met Churchill and the two issued the Atlantic Charter, which asserted the universal right to national self-determination and security and laid down the principles of what was to become the United Nations.

The Japanese attack on Pearl Harbor in December 1941 ended US isolation. For Roosevelt, it was not enough to defeat Germany and Japan: 'It is useless to win battles if the cause for which we fight the battles is lost,' he declared. 'It is useless to win a war unless it stays won.' His duplicity and shrewdness in statecraft whether in war or peace was best summed up in his own words, 'You know I am a juggler and I never let my right hand know what my left hand does. I may have one policy for Europe and one diametrically

opposite for North and South America. I may be entirely inconsistent, and furthermore I'm perfectly willing to mislead and tell
untruths if it will help the war.'

During the conflict, Roosevelt not only laid the foundations of
the United Nations, but also, with Churchill and Soviet dictator
Stalin, became an architect of the postwar world. He prided himself
on charming Stalin and building a personal relationship with the
Soviet leader, often by baiting his close ally Churchill.

He has been criticized for yielding too much of eastern Europe
to Stalin during these discussions, but since Soviet forces were in
occupation there already, it is probable that only another war would
have liberated them.

Roosevelt's belief that the weak should be defended against the
predations of the rich and powerful had been drummed into him
since childhood. Although he had had a privileged upbringing
in the patrician society of the East Coast, an inspirational headmaster had instilled in him a deep sense of social responsibility.
This was later enhanced by his marriage to his distant cousin
Eleanor. A bluestocking of progressive social ideals, she was an
indefatigable campaigner on behalf of the disadvantaged right
up until her death in 1962.

Roosevelt's genius lay in his handling of people. To the millions
of Americans who listened as he outlined his policies on the radio
in his avuncular 'fireside chats', it seemed as though he was personally guaranteeing their well-being. 'We have nothing to fear
but fear itself,' he reassured them. Roosevelt's relationship with
Churchill, his ally in the darkest war years, was one of genuine
affinity; he once ended a long and serious cable by telling the
British prime minister: 'It is fun being in the same decade as you.'

After the Big Three Allied leaders met at Yalta in February 1945,
Roosevelt appeared to the press in a wheelchair, apologizing for
his 'unusual posture' but saying it was 'a lot easier' than carrying

'ten pounds of steel around the bottom of my legs'. It was his first public acknowledgement of the paralytic effects of the polio that he had contracted at the age of thirty-nine, and which he had battled and concealed by wearing leg braces and by other means. This was both a defence against public perceptions of weakness and a truly heroic personal refusal to let a debilitating ailment wreck his determination to carry out his presidential tasks.

Roosevelt's sudden death from a massive cerebral haemorrhage in April 1945, just before the first meeting of the UN, stunned the world.

MUSSOLINI

1883–1945

> . . . the Fascist conception of the State is all embracing; outside of it
> no human or spiritual values can exist, much less have value.
>
> Mussolini, *The Doctrine of Fascism*, 1932

Benito Mussolini, the dictator of Italy from 1922 to 1943, was the father of fascism – a domineering autocrat whose totalitarian politics paved the way for Nazism. Ruthlessly suppressing any form of dissent at home, he was also an avaricious colonialist with Roman imperial delusions, directly responsible for the death of over 30,000 Ethiopians in his infamous Abyssinian campaign as well as complicit, through his alliance with Adolf Hitler, in the atrocities of Nazi Germany.

Benito Amilcare Andrea Mussolini was born on 29 July 1883 in Predappio, central northern Italy. His father was a blacksmith and his mother a schoolteacher, a profession he took up but then swiftly abandoned. After an unsuccessful year trying to find employment in Switzerland in 1902 – during which he was imprisoned for vagrancy – he was expelled and sent back to Italy for military service.

In his twenties, following in the footsteps of his father, Mussolini was a committed socialist, editing a newspaper called *La Lotta di Classe* (*The Class Struggle*) before, in 1910, becoming secretary of the local socialist party in Forli, for which he edited the paper *Avanti!* (*Forward!*). He also wrote an unsuccessful novel called *The Cardinal's Mistress*. Increasingly known to the authorities for inciting disorder, he was imprisoned in 1911 for producing pacifist propaganda after Italy declared war on Turkey. Unsurprisingly, he initially opposed Italy's entry into the First World War, but – perhaps believing a major conflict would precipitate the overthrow of capitalism – he changed his mind, a decision that saw him expelled from the socialist party. He swiftly became captivated by militarism, founding a new paper, *Il Popolo d'Italia*, as well as the pro-war group Fasci d'Azione Rivoluzionaria, although his own military service was cut short in 1917 following injuries sustained after a grenade explosion in training.

Mussolini was now a confirmed anti-socialist, convinced that only authoritarian government could overcome the economic and social problems endemic in postwar Italy, as violent street gangs (including his own) battled for supremacy. To describe his decisive, personality-driven politics, he coined the term *fascismo* – from the Italian word fascio, meaning union, and the Latin *fasces*, the ancient Roman symbol of a bundle of rods tied around an axe, denoting strength through unity. In March 1919, the first fascist movement in Europe crystallized under his leadership to form the Fasci di Combattimento. His black-shirted supporters, in stark contrast to the flailing liberal governments of the period, successfully broke up industrial strikes and dispersed socialists from the streets. Though

Mussolini was defeated in the 1919 elections, he was elected to Parliament in 1921, along with thirty-four other fascists, forming the National Fascist Party later that year. In October 1922, after hostility between left- and right-wing groups had escalated into near anarchy, Mussolini – with thousands of his Blackshirts – staged the so-called March on Rome (in fact he caught the train) but he presented himself as the only man who could restore order. In desperation, King Victor Emmanuel III fatefully asked him to form a government.

The new regime was built on fear. On 10 June 1924, Giacomo Matteotti, a leading socialist party deputy, was kidnapped and murdered by Mussolini's supporters after criticizing that year's elections, which saw fascists take 64 per cent of the vote. By 1926, Mussolini (calling himself Il Duce – the leader – and initially supported by the liberals) had dismantled parliamentary democracy and stamped his personal authority on every aspect of government, introducing strict censorship and a slick propaganda machine in which newspaper editors were personally handpicked. Two years later, when he placed executive power in the hands of the Fascist Grand Council, the country had effectively become a one-party police state.

In 1935, seeking to realize his dreams of Mediterranean domination and a North African empire, Mussolini ordered the invasion of Ethiopia. In October of that year Mussolini invaded Abyssinia (modern-day Ethiopia), using air power and chemical weapons (mustard gas) in a barbaric campaign that lasted seven months and involved the systematic murder of captured prisoners, either on public gallows or thrown from aircraft mid-flight. The campaign resulted in the annexation of Ethiopia into Italian East Africa, along with Eritrea and Somaliland.

Mussolini had dreams of empire but the campaign was also to avenge Italy's humiliation of March 1896, when Ethiopia had defeated an Italian army at Adowa. The 1935 invasion – for which the Italians used a border dispute as a specious pretext – pitted Italian tanks, artillery and aircraft against Emperor Haile Selassie's ill-equipped and poorly trained army.

Making steady progress towards the Ethiopian capital, the Italians looted the Obelisk of Axum, an ancient monument, and firebombed the city of Harar, eventually taking the capital Addis Ababa on 5 May 1936, forcing Haile Selassie to flee the country. Mussolini's victorious commander Marshal Badoglio was absurdly named the duke of Addis Ababa. Along the way, in a flagrant violation of the Geneva Protocol of 1925, the Italians dropped between 300 and 500 tonnes of mustard gas, even gassing the ambulances of the Red Cross.

Meanwhile, from the safety of Rome, Mussolini ordered that 'all rebel prisoners must be killed', instructing his troops to 'systematically conduct a politics of terror and extermination of the rebels and the complicit population'. In February 1936, after a failed assassination attempt on the colonial governor, Italian troops went on the rampage for three days.

The Italian military establishment had warned Mussolini that a challenge to British and French influence in Africa and the Middle East might provoke Britain into a war that 'would reduce us to Balkan level', but Britain – under Neville Chamberlain – and France were pursuing a policy of appeasement in this period, and Mussolini correctly calculated they would not act decisively, which encouraged Hitler. However, Italy's Ethiopian empire was short-lived, liberated by Britain in 1941. Haile Selassie reigned until 1974 – and it was Badoglio who replaced Mussolini in 1943 and made peace with the Allies. Mussolini's Abyssinian atrocities led the League of Nations to impose sanctions on Italy. Increasingly isolated, he left the League and allied himself with Hitler in 1937 – the same year in which he granted asylum and support to the brutal Croatian fascist Ante Pavelic´ – emulating the Führer in pushing through a raft of anti-Semitic laws. It soon became clear, however, that Mussolini was the minor partner in the relationship, Hitler failing to consult him on almost all military decisions.

After Hitler invaded Czechoslovakia in March 1939, putting paid to hopes of peace sparked by the Munich Agreement of the previous year, Mussolini ordered the invasion of neighbouring Albania, his troops brushing aside the tiny army of King Zog. In May, Hitler and Mussolini declared a Pact of Steel, pledging to support the other in the event of war – a move that sent shudders of fear across Europe.

Italy did not enter the Second World War until the fall of France in June 1940, when it looked like Germany was on course for a quick victory, but the Italian war – beginning with a botched assault on Greece in October, then humiliating routs in North Africa – was an unmitigated disaster. For all the puffed-up militarism of his regime, Mussolini's army was disastrously un-prepared for a war on this scale, haemorrhaging troops in the Balkans and Africa. Following the Anglo-American arrival on the shores of Sicily in June 1943, Mussolini's fascist followers aban-doned him and had him arrested, only for German commandos to rescue him from imprisonment and place him at the head of a puppet protectorate in the north of Italy. On 27 April 1945, as the Allies closed in, Mussolini – disguised as a German soldier – was captured by Italian partisans at the village of Dongo, near Lake Como. He was shot the following day, along with his mis-tress. Their bodies were taken to Milan and hung upside down from meat hooks in Piazza Loreto.

TOJO: THE RISE AND FALL OF THE JAPANESE EMPIRE

1884–1948

The Greater East Asian War was justified and righteous.
Hideki Tojo, after his failed suicide attempt
in September 1945

General Hideki Tojo, nicknamed the Razor, was prime minister of Japan during much of the Second World War, the architect of its imperial aggressions, and the force behind its appalling policy of aggrandizement and brutality that cost the lives of millions and destroyed his own country. Yet it is futile to lay the blame for Japan's atrocities and aggression on one man: Tojo was merely the representative of a prevalent mindset and conduct amongst a Japanese nobility, bureaucracy and military, supported enthusiastically by the public. New research has shown that the Emperor Hirohito was himself fully involved in the commands that led directly to the murder of so many.

Tojo, the son of a general, embarked on a military career at a young age, serving as an infantry officer, a military attaché and an instructor at the military staff college. By 1933 he was a major general. Prior to this Tojo had become a member of a hard-right militaristic group that expounded fanatical ultra-nationalism. However, during the attempted coup by ultra-nationalists on 26 February 1936 Tojo remained loyal to

Emperor Hirohito and assisted in its suppression.

Tojo's loyalty was rewarded in 1937 when he was named chief of staff of the Kwantung Army in Manchuria. In this position he played an important role in launching the Second Sino-Japanese War – an eight-year conflict that would leave millions dead as the Japanese military ignored both human decency and the laws of war in pursuit of imperial conquest in China. Non-combatants – men, women and children – were deliberately targeted, resulting in such atrocities as the so-called Rape of Nanking, in which, between December 1937 and March 1938, Japanese troops butchered between 250,000 and 350,000 Chinese civilians.

As the war in China progressed, the Japanese army tightened its control over the civilian government, and Tojo became more deeply immersed in politics. In May 1938 he was appointed deputy minister of war in the government of Prince Fumimaro Konoe. In that role he was one of the more vocal advocates of a pact with Nazi Germany and Fascist Italy, and also pushed for a preventive strike against the Soviet Union.

In July 1940 Tojo became minister of war, and proceeded to oversee Japan's formal entry into the Axis alliance with Germany and Italy. By July 1941 Tojo had convinced Vichy France to endorse Japanese occupation of several key bases in Indo-China – a move that paved the way for US sanctions against Japan and increased tensions between the two countries. When Fumimaro Konoe was finally pushed into retirement in October 1941, Tojo, while holding on to his portfolio as minister of war, stepped up to replace him as prime minister. He immediately declared his commitment to the creation of a New Order in Asia. Initially, he supported the efforts of his diplomats to bring this about through agreement with the United States. But as it became clear that no deal was possible with the USA on the terms desired, he authorized the attack on the American naval base at Pearl Harbor on 7 December 1941 that unleashed the war in the Pacific.

Victorious Japan overran Singapore, Malaysia, much of China, the Philippines, Indonesia and a vast swathe of the Pacific, pushing towards India through Burma, but the US Navy destroyed the Japanese fleet at the Battle of Midway in June 1942 and thereafter gradually retook the Pacific under General MacArthur. Tojo assumed almost dictatorial powers, but in the aftermath of the American capture of the Marianas in July 1944 he resigned.

Tojo bore responsibility for the Japanese conduct of the war, which was almost as barbaric as that of the Nazis in Europe. The Japanese archives show that Emperor Hirohito was not the pawn of the militarists but enthusiastically supported and directed them. Hirohito must share some of the responsibility shouldered by Tojo for Japan's war crimes. During the Sook Ching massacre of February–March 1942, for instance, up to 50,000 ethnic Chinese were systematically executed by Japanese forces in Singapore. At the same time, the Japanese embarked on the Three Alls policy in China – by which Japanese troops were ordered to 'Kill all, burn all and loot all' in order to pacify the country, resulting in the killing of 2.7 million civilians. Another example of the brutal effects of Japanese militarism was the infamous Bataan Death March. After a three-month struggle for the Bataan Peninsula in the Philippines, some 75,000 Allied troops (comprising around 64,000 American and 11,000 Filipino troops) formally surrendered to Japanese forces on 9 April 1942. They were then forced to undertake a march to a prison camp sixty miles away. On the journey, many were executed – stopping without permission was taken as a sign of insubordination and met with instant retribution. Many more died from the conditions they endured. Here is the testimony of one POW, Lester Tenney, who experienced the Death March and lived to tell the tale:

The Japanese soldiers arrived in our area at 6:00 a.m. on April 10, 1942, and after a few minutes of hollering and seeking cigarettes, they herded us together and forced us to walk to the main road on Bataan and we took with us only those possessions we had on our bodies at that time. Many had no canteen and no head covering. So we marched for the first four days without food or water . . . We walked from sun up to sun down. No lunch break, no dinner, and sleeping was in a large warehouse that could easily hold 500 men but was crowded with 1200 men who had little if any space to lay down. And when you had to remove your body waste you were forced to do it on the floor where you slept . . . I saw with my own eyes a POW being killed with a bayonet into his back because he stopped at a free flowing artesian well for a cup of water. Killed for a drink of water. And what about the Caribou wallows that lined every road in the Philippines where the animals sat during the hot days. The water in those wallows was filthy, and contained among other things, animal dung. But when you are thirsty and without water for days on end, a desire for water takes over your sense of right and wrong and you leap from the line of marchers and push the scum on top of the water away so you could get a drink of this so-called water. Dysentery was the end result, and death followed closely behind.

Even after Tojo had stepped down, the barbaric rules that he had helped create, in which human life was deemed valueless, endured – resulting in such atrocities as the Manila massacre of February 1945, in which 100,000 Filipino civilians were slaughtered.

Alongside the killing, the Japanese carried out hideous medical experiments on captured prisoners and subject populations. Biological and chemical weapons were tested on selected victims; others were operated on without anaesthetic, or exposed to the elements to see how their bodies reacted. International conventions on the treatment of prisoners of war were disregarded, and POWs were forced to work in appalling conditions, deprived of food and medicine, and tortured and executed without restraint.

Japan resisted defeat with brutality and suicidal determination. As American forces approached Japan itself and Soviet troops attacked Japanese Manchuria, US nuclear bombs were dropped on Hiroshima and Nagasaki, bringing surrender.

To this day, the character and scale of what took place remains difficult to comprehend. In the wake of Japan's unconditional surrender in August 1945 Tojo tried to commit suicide. However, in April 1946, he was placed on trial for war crimes. He was found guilty, and hanged on 23 December 1948. The Americans embraced the Emperor Hirohito as the ideal, much-loved national figure to become the constitutional monarch of a new democratic Japan. Hirohito ruled for a long time – but he was lucky not to be executed with General Tojo.

BEN-GURION

1886–1973

In Israel, to be a realist you must believe in miracles.
David Ben-Gurion, in an interview (1956)

David Ben-Gurion was the architect and defender of the fledgling state of Israel, and its first prime minister. A fiery but highly pragmatic visionary, Ben-Gurion transformed the political map of the Middle East, creating the first land for the Jewish people for two thousand years. Not only did he manage to build up and defend this precarious homeland against attacks of overwhelmingly superior force from every side, but he also created the only liberal democracy in the entire Middle East, an achievement that still stands today. The sheer force of Ben-Gurion's vitality was evident in every aspect of his life. As well as devoting himself to the building of a nation, he had a voracious desire for knowledge, teaching himself Ancient Greek to read Plato, and Spanish to read Cervantes.

Already a committed Zionist and socialist when he arrived in Ottoman-controlled Palestine from Poland in 1906 as an impoverished youth of twenty, David Gruen soon adopted the Hebrew version of his name: Ben-Gurion. Under this name, the ascetic, ambitious, secular idealist rose from a position as a promising political activist challenging Turkish rule to head of the Zionist Executive in British Palestine. Ultimately, with his declaration of Israel's independence on 15 May 1948, Ben-Gurion became prime minister of the new Jewish state – a position he was to hold, save for a two-year interlude in the 1950s, for the next fifteen years. His drive undiminished by age, he remained in Parliament until three years before his death in 1973.

Ben-Gurion united a historically disparate and divided people in a state of their own. As the Second World War broke out in Europe, he masterminded the smuggling of thousands of Jewish refugees into Palestine, while the nations of the world closed their doors to them. His directive to Palestinian Jews to join the British army to help fight the Nazis, at the same time as the British tried to bar Jewish immigration into Palestine, inspired international sympathy for the Zionist cause.

During the period of British rule, Ben-Gurion helped to create institutions – trade unions, agricultural associations, military forces – that would provide the skeleton of an independent Israel. He effectively created a shadow Jewish state within British Palestine, ready to assume power at a moment's notice. Without this structure in place, it is hard to imagine that Israel would have been able to combat the simultaneous attacks of five Arab nations that took place within hours of the new state's declaration of independence.

Ben-Gurion's leadership during the post-independence years shows his great skill as a statesman. Even in the most heightened of crises Ben-Gurion – who was by nature something of an autocrat – refused to implement emergency measures that might undermine Israel's commitment to democracy. The settlement of the Negev, once a desert but now one of Israel's most prosperous regions, was instigated on his initiative. Having begun his life in Palestine as a farmhand, Ben-Gurion always believed that Zionism involved the conquest of land by Jewish labour, and when he retired he went to live on the kibbutz that he had helped to pioneer as a younger man.

Bold, mercurial, but unswerving in the courage of his Zionist and democratic convictions, Ben-Gurion's decisions – not least his declaration of Israel's independence – often seemed impossible or were in defiance of international pressure. He was a political moderate willing to be ruthless to secure the survival of the state. His secret agreement in 1956, by which Israel would invade Sinai to give Britain and France a pretext for seizing the Suez Canal, met with international condemnation. But Ben-Gurion defended the validity of his actions, and, in the event, it secured for Israel another eleven years of peace.

Ben-Gurion's vision did not blind him to political reality, nor did his single-mindedness preclude empathy with Israel's enemies. He was one of the first to recognize the validity of Arab objections to Zionism, and he consistently tried to accommodate the Arabs, despite accusations of treachery and opportunism from both sides of the Israeli political spectrum. After the Six Days' War, he was a lone voice, wisely arguing that Israel should renounce its vast territorial gains, apart from a united Jerusalem and the Golan Heights.

Ben-Gurion sought to create a state that would be 'A Light unto the Nations', and, despite the difficulties presented by the demands of politics and security, he never abandoned a desire to abide by the highest moral standards. The role that this stubborn, fervently optimistic, resolute Zionist played in securing and defending a homeland for the Jewish people cannot be underestimated. Israel's existence and democracy are a tribute to the tenacity of David Ben-Gurion.

Yet he also contributed to its flaws – its proportional representation, backed by Ben-Gurion, means that Israel's destiny is at the mercy of tiny ultra-religious and nationalist parties, and its governments may never be strong enough to make the peace deals the country desperately needs.

HITLER

1889–1945

If one day the German nation is no longer sufficiently strong or sufficiently ready for sacrifice to stake its blood for its existence, then let it perish and be annihilated by some other stronger power . . .

Adolf Hitler, 27 November 1941

Adolf Hitler is the embodiment of the historical monster, the personification of evil and the organizer of the greatest crimes of mass-murder ever committed, responsible for a world war in which more than 70 million died, including 6 million in the Holocaust. No other name has earned such opprobrium or come to typify the depths to which humanity can sink. Amidst the horrors of history, the crimes of the Nazi Führer continue to occupy a unique place.

Born in Braunau am Inn in Austria, Hitler left school at sixteen without any qualifications. He suffered disappointment when his application to study to be an artist in Vienna was twice rejected. He struggled to survive in Vienna on the strength of his painting, imbibing nationalism and anti-Semitism.

In 1913 Hitler moved to Munich, and in August 1914 joined the German army, subsequently fighting on the Western Front and reaching the rank of corporal. When in November 1918 the German government agreed to an armistice, Hitler – and many other nationalistic Germans – believed that the undefeated German army had been 'stabbed in the back'. He was appalled by the Treaty of Versailles, under which Germany lost much territory and most of its armed forces.

After the war, Hitler joined the German Workers' Party (DAP), impressed by its fusion of nationalism, anti-Semitism and anti-Bolshevism. Before long he won a reputation as a rabble-rousing orator, and in 1921 he became leader of the National Socialist German Workers' Party (NSDAP) – the Nazi Party, evolving a cult of power worship, cleansing violence and wanton killing, racial superiority, eugenics and brutal leadership. He created a para-military wing, the SA (*Sturmabteilung* or Storm Division), headed by Ernst Röhm.

Inspired by Mussolini's example in Italy, Hitler resolved to seize power, and in November 1923 in Munich launched an attempted putsch against the democratic Weimar Republic. This failed and he was arrested and sentenced to five years in prison – but served only a few months, during which period he wrote *Mein Kampf* (My Struggle), which exuded rampant anti-Semitism, anti-communism and militant nationalism. He also changed tactics, deciding to seek power through the ballot box – and then to replace democracy with an autocratic state.

Hitler's opportunity came with the arrival of the Great Depression. In subsequent elections, as the economy deteriorated, the Nazi Party increased its vote, becoming the largest party in the Reichstag (German Parliament) in July 1932, a position confirmed by elections in November. On 30 January 1933 Hitler was sworn in as chancellor.

After the burning down of the Reichstag in February 1933, Hitler suspended civil liberties and passed an enabling act, which allowed him to rule as dictator. Opposition was crushed. Hitler even turned the repression inwards: the Night of the Long Knives in June 1934 saw the murder of Röhm and the SA leadership by the SS (*Schutzstaffel* or Protection Squad). Two months later Hitler, backed by henchmen such as Hermann Goering and Joseph Goebbels, achieved absolute civil and military power when he became Führer (leader) and head of state.

The Nazis initiated an economic recovery, reducing unemployment and introducing ambitious new schemes such as the building of the brand-new *autobahn* (motorway) network. Many of Hitler's erstwhile opponents were prepared to give him the benefit of the doubt. Yet the economic miracle was largely achieved via a huge rearmament drive, in violation of the Treaty of Versailles – the first phase in Hitler's broader determination to launch a deliberately barbaric European and racial war.

In March 1936 Hitler reoccupied the demilitarized zone in the Rhineland. He carefully noted the response of the international community – nothing. This encouraged him. In March 1938 he annexed Austria; in September he secured the German-speaking Sudeten area of Czechoslovakia; and in March 1939 he occupied the remainder of Czechoslovakia. In each instance, he experienced little resistance from the other European powers. He had fulfilled his core pledge: Versailles had been reduced to nothing more than a 'scrap of paper'.

Hitler signed the Molotov–Ribbentrop Pact with the Soviet dictator Josef Stalin which partitioned eastern Europe between these two brutal tyrants. In September 1939 Hitler conquered Poland, a move that triggered British and French declarations of war. But in the spring of 1940 the German armies turned west, conquering Norway, Denmark, the Low Countries and France in a lightning campaign. In 1941 both Yugoslavia and Greece fell, and only Britain remained undefeated. Hitler now dominated his barbaric continental empire and appeared impregnable.

In June 1941, Hitler launched a surprise attack on Stalinist Russia in Operation Barbarossa, the largest and most brutal conflict in human history in which 26 million Soviets alone died. He moved east to command his greatest enterprise from military headquarters in eastern Poland (the Wolf's Lair). German forces won a series of astonishing victories at the start of the Barbarossa campaign, almost taking Moscow, the Soviet capital, and capturing some 6 million prisoners.

Meanwhile another even more horrific project was gathering steam within Nazi-occupied Europe. *Mein Kampf* had spoken darkly of Hitler's intentions towards the Jews, and the Nuremberg Laws of 1935–6, which deprived Jews of their civil rights in Germany, had hinted at worse to come. As the war clouds gathered towards the end of the decade there were more ominous signs: *Kristallnacht* (Night of Broken Glass) in November 1938 had brought a wave of attacks on Jewish homes and properties across Germany.

Hitler was initially content to enslave and starve the Slavs and drive the Jews out of German lands; they were interned in ghettoes and concentration camps across occupied Poland. But he now ordered a policy of extermination, using *Einsatzgruppen* (task forces) to shoot a million Jews. Barbarossa served as the trigger and excuse for the 'Final Solution of the Jewish Question'. Under Hitler's orders to SS Reichsführer Heinrich Himmler, Jews were dispatched to extermination camps to be slaughtered in gas chambers on an industrial scale. The Holocaust, as it became known, claimed 6 million Jewish lives, as well as the lives of many more minorities hated by the Nazis, including Gypsies, Slavs and homosexuals. It remains a crime of unparalleled magnitude.

But the Soviets defeated the Germans at Stalingrad in 1942–3. After their victory at Kursk in the summer of 1943, the Soviets slowly but inexorably destroyed Hitler's empire, advancing all the way to Berlin. In June 1944, the Allies invaded northern France in the D-Day landings and started to fight their way to meet the Soviets in Germany itself. Yet an ever more deluded, brutal Hitler refused to countenance reality, demanding that his soldiers fight to the last man. As Germany was slowly crushed between the Red Army in the east and the British and Americans in the west, Hitler fled to the *Führerbunker* in Berlin on 16 January 1945, along with support staff and, later, Eva Braun and the Goebbels family. On 16 April the Red Army launched the Battle of Berlin, attacking in a pincer movement that swiftly smashed into the city.

Hitler spent his time ordering non-existent armies to launch non-existent offensives, denouncing his potential successors Goering and Himmler as traitors, and holding twee tea parties with his devoted female secretaries. Elsewhere in the bunker, his SS guards and female staff held wild drunken orgies. On 28 April, hearing of Himmler's attempt to broker peace, Hitler furiously had SS officer Hermann Fegelein (Eva Braun's brother-in-law and Himmler's golden boy) shot in the Chancellery garden.

On 29 April Hitler married Eva Braun in a civil ceremony in the *Führerbunker*. The next day, Braun and Hitler swallowed cyanide capsules – previously tested on his dog, Blondi – and Hitler shot himself in the right temple. Scotching rumours that he escaped to South America, eyewitness claims that his body was burned were substantiated when officers of SMERSH (the Red Army counter-intelligence unit) discovered remains near the bunker, confirmed by dental records as Braun's and Hitler's. His skeleton was buried under the Magdeburg Soviet airbase in East Germany, then dug up and incinerated in 1970 on the orders of KGB chief Yuri Andropov. In 2000 part of the skull was put on display by the Federal Archives Service in Moscow.

NEHRU

1889–1964

A moment comes, which comes but rarely in history, when we step out from the old to the new; when an age ends; and when the soul of a nation long suppressed finds utterance.

Jawahalarl Nehru, fondly nicknamed Pandit-ji, was the first prime minister of India, which he ruled for almost twenty years, and the father of the greatest democracy on earth. Yet he was also an often-flawed politician whose socialistic planning policies held back the Indian economy, whose centralising tendencies exacer-bated the tragedy of Partition and whose foreign policies played into the hands of the Soviets. However his legacy is not just the success of democratic India but also the most successful political dynasty of modern democracy: in east Asia and the Middle East, dynasty is central to power. India was dominated by Nehru and his family and remains so well into the 21st century.

The descendant of lawyers to the East India Company, Nehru

was the son of Motilal Nehru, a successful and wealthy lawyer, anglicized and sophisticated, who was one of the leaders of the Indian Congress Party, at times its president. Nehru was given the best English education, studying at Harrow School, which had been attended by that long-time foe of Indian independence Winston Churchill himself – and then Trinity College, Cambridge. But Nehru – who at Harrow and Cambridge was sometimes known as Joe Nehru – was involved with his father and Gandhi in the independence movement from an early age. At times he and his father were arrested together and Nehru, despite conflicts with Gandhi during the 1930s, had emerged as a leader in his own right by the start of the war. Nehru spent much of the time in and out of British jails as the British government wrestled with the challenge of whether to keep India or give it independence. There were rumours of Nehru's schisms with Gandhi but the latter recognized him as his protégé and heir in 1941.

By the end of the war it was clear that Britain would indeed yield to Indian demands for independence: in 1946 the British prime minister Clement Attlee dispatched a Cabinet mission to decide how to proceed. Consulting with the two leading parties, Nehru's Congress representing the Hindus and the All-India Muslim League under Muhammad Ali Jinnah, the British proposed a decentralized India with some self-government for Muslim and Hindu provinces. Leader of the largest party in the newly elected Constituent Assembly, Nehru became the prime minister of a provisional government. Attlee sent Lord Louis Mountbatten out to India as the last viceroy with orders to grant independence no later than 1948. But Mountbatten himself made the fateful decision to accelerate events in 1947. Mountbatten was faced with opposition to dividing India from the Hindu elite and opposition from the Muslims to centralizing India under a Hindu elite. Under this mounting pressure, Mountbatten finally agreed to a hurried and ill-conceived partition of the Raj into two countries, India and Pakistan, that would result in the massacre of a million people – and a vast migration. Mountbatten was frustrated by Jinnah and the Muslims but became close to Nehru; it is likely that Nehru had an affair, or at least a romantic relationship with the formidable vicereine, Lady Edwina Mountbatten.

On 15 August 1947, Nehru declared Indian independence with the famous words:

Long years ago we made a tryst with destiny, and now the time comes when we shall redeem our pledge, not wholly or in full measure, but very substantially. At the stroke of the midnight hour, when the world sleeps, India will awake to life and freedom. A moment comes, which comes but rarely in history, when we step out from the old to the new, when an age ends, and when the soul of a nation, long suppressed, finds utterance. It is fitting that at this solemn moment we take the pledge of dedication to the service of India and her people and to the still larger cause of humanity.

Winning the first full elections and subsequent polls, Nehru became the first prime minister of an independent India and remained in office for the next sixteen years. He established democracy and stability in India, a colossal achievement, but many of his other policies were counterproductive.

A Fabian socialist, he practised state planning on a scale that paralysed and crippled the economy for decades. In foreign policy, his non-aligned movement, claiming neutrality between the USA and USSR, played into Soviet hands, bringing India far too close to the Soviets, who remained major funders of the Nehru/Congress family well into the 1970s: their KGB station in Delhi was the largest in the world.

In 1962 Nehru's forward policy on the Chinese border led to a short but dangerous war Sino-Indian war. He died in office, but apart from democracy, his chief legacies were his family and the Congress Party political machine.

From the earliest days of independence, his chief of staff and hostess had been his ambitious and ruthless only child, Indira, who had married Ferouz Gandhi (no relation to Mahatma) in 1941. By the 1960s, there were tensions between the old prime minister and his fiery daughter, whom he suspected of brazen ambition.

After the short premiership of Shashri, Indira Gandhi, despite being mocked by her rivals as 'Dumb Doll', won election as prime minister in 1966. In 1971, when East Pakistan tried to secede from Pakistan, Indira Gandhi backed the rebels and fought Pakistan in a short war, resulting in an independent Bangladesh. Victory over Pakistan made her overconfident. She won the 1971 election aided by her Eradicate Poverty campaign. But when she was indicted by the courts for electoral corruption and misuse of funds, she defied the resulting protests, refused to resign and declared a state of emergency, ruling by fiat, supported by her ambitious younger son and chosen heir, Sanjay. She imposed her powers ruthlessly, arresting thousands of opposition supporters. When she finally called elections in 1977, she and her son lost their seats and the new government arrested them and put them on trial.

However in 1980, Indira won a landslide election and returned to power until her assassination by her own Sikh bodyguards in 1984. As prime minister, she was succeeded by her diffident and gentle eldest son, Rajiv, a pilot (Sanjay had been killed in a flying accident in 1980), who governed until 1989 when his corruption-tainted government lost the elections. He was assassinated by Tamil Tigers in 1991 but his Italian-born widow Sonia assumed leadership of the Congress Party, which won the election of 2004. Refusing to become premier herself, she appointed Manoman Singh as PM but in 2014 the dynasty was decisively defeated by the Hindu nationalists, the BJP, in elections – losing power and signalling the end of an era.

FRANCO

1892–1975

I am responsible only to God and history.

General Franco

General Francisco Franco, the generalissimo of Spain from 1939 to 1975, is in some ways the forgotten tyrant, his deeds overshadowed by Adolf Hitler and Josef Stalin, yet he was truly one of history's monsters. In the 1930s, this fascistic warlord won power with brutality and terror in a savage civil war, aided by his ally Hitler, and proceeded to terrorize the civilian population of Spain for twenty-five years. As democracy thrived in the rest of western Europe following the Second World War, his brutal military dictatorship continued to crush dissent, and to shoot and torture his supposed enemies.

Franco was born in northwest Spain in 1892, in the naval city of Ferrol. His mother was a pious and conservative upper-middle-class Catholic; his father a difficult and eccentric man who expected his son to follow him into the navy. Due to naval cutbacks, however, at just fourteen years old, Franco entered the army instead. Fiercely professional, he soon carved out his reputation as a brave and driven soldier, becoming a captain in 1916 and the youngest general in Spain in 1926, aged thirty-four.

Although staunchly loyal to the monarchy, Franco was not overtly involved in politics until 1931, when the Spanish king abdicated, leaving the government in the hands of left-wing republicans. When the conservatives won power back two years later, they identified Franco as a powerful potential ally and promoted him to major general, instructing him to suppress an uprising by Asturian miners in October 1934. Election victory for the left-wing Popular Front in 1936, however, saw Franco effectively demoted and sent to the Canary Islands, but just months later the right-wing Spanish nationalist bloc called on the army to join them in rebellion against the government, which had failed to stabilize the country. The Spanish Civil War had begun.

In a radio broadcast from the Canary Islands in July 1936, Franco declared he would join the rebels with immediate effect and, after mixed fortunes for Nationalist forces in Morocco and Madrid, he was declared generalissimo, effectively the leader of the Nationalist cause during the three years of war that followed.

Franco's wartime campaign was notorious for his indiscriminate brutalizing of civilian populations, aided on occasions by German and Italian fascist governments. Franco organized a White Terror in which 200,000 people were murdered. The most infamous atrocity was the 1937 market-day bombing of the Basque town of Guernica by the German Condor Legion. Though it was not a military target and had no air defences, the Luftwaffe pounded the town throughout the day and swooped over outgoing roads to mow down fleeing civilians as the town was engulfed in a fireball. An estimated 1654 people were slaughtered.

As Generalissimo Francisco Franco signed his deathlists, he would place E for execute for those to die, C for those spared and, most macabre and revealing of all, GARROTE Y PRENSA (Garrotte with press coverage) next to the names of certain well-known people. Nothing so sums up the miserable wickedness of the victors of the Spanish Civil War. Franco resembled the 19th-century Spanish general who on his deathbed was asked if he forgave his enemies. 'I have none.' he replied, 'I had them all shot.'

For a generation of left-wing intellectuals, the struggle of Republican Spain to defend itself against Franco's Nationalists epitomized the struggle between socialist progress and fascist reaction. Idealistic intellectuals such as George Orwell, Ernest Hemingway and the French novelist André Malraux flocked to Spain to fight for the Republican cause. In total, about 32,000 foreign volunteers from Europe and America fought in the campaign, while Nazi Germany and Fascist Italy pumped money and troops into Franco's army – and dropped bombs on the civilian populations in Republican-dominated areas.

In support of the Republic, Stalin's USSR supplied 331 tanks and 600 planes, together with a large number of pilots, in return for Spanish gold reserves. The Red Terror in Spain, according to recent historical research, accounted for the deaths of somewhere between 40,000 and 100,000 people. Precise figures are unknown.

During the bloody summer of 1936, 8000 suspected Nationalists were massacred in Madrid, and another 8000 in Catalonia – both Republican-controlled areas. Wealthy farmers, industrialists and those associated with the Catholic Church received particularly brutal treatment at the hands of the various Republican factions. Nearly 7000 clerics, including nearly 300 nuns, were killed, despite being non-combatants.

Some Republicans defended these massacres on the grounds that the other side was worse. Others tried to stand back. Commenting on the atrocities committed by his own side, the anarchist intellectual Federica Montseny noted 'a lust for blood inconceivable in honest men' before the war.

One of the ironies of history is that while the Stalinist terror within the Republicans is as notorious as the Red Terror that slaughtered supposed rightists, Franco and the Nationalists killed many, many more: some 200,000 were murdered by Franco in his White Terror during the war, while another half million remained in his torture chambers and camps afterwards. Franco really delivered on his associate General Queipo's promise: 'For every person you kill, we will kill ten.'

Victory, when it finally came, was not enough for Franco. 'The war is over,' he declared in 1939, 'but the enemy is not dead.' He had drawn up lists of reds during the conflict: alleged communists to be arrested. Now in control of the state, he set about rounding up and liquidating his enemies. Hundreds of thousands of Republicans fled the country as, between 1939 and 1943, anything between 100,000 and 200,000 non-combatants or surrendering troops were summarily and systematically executed.

Repression characterized every aspect of Franco's regime. He nominally re-established the monarchy – without appointing a king – but retained all executive powers in his own hands. Democracy was abandoned, criticism regarded as treason, imprisonment and abuse of opponents rife, Parliament a mere puppet to the executive, rival political parties and strikes banned, the Catholic Church given a free rein over social policy and education, the media muzzled, creative talent strangled by strict censorship and any dissent ruthlessly suppressed by his secret police, who practised widespread torture and murder right up to Franco's death in 1975. Dismissive of international criticism, Franco himself insisted on personally signing all death warrants until his death while his family married into the aristocracy and amassed colossal wealth.

A true mark of the regime was Franco's shameful decision to grant asylum to Ante Pavelic´, the fascist dictator of Croatia during the Second World War – a man thought to be responsible for over 600,000 deaths. Franco also during that time repaid Hitler and Mussolini's support during the Civil War by sending troops – albeit limited in number – to assist the Nazis in their fight against the Soviets. But he survived by resisting Hitler's request for him to join the war and then posing as an anti-communist after 1945.

The ghost of Franco has yet to be completely exorcized from Spanish politics, as recently as 2004 a commission having been set up to compensate his victims and oversee the exhumation of the mass graves.

MAO ZEDONG

1893–1976

I look at Mao, I see Stalin, a perfect copy.
Nikita Khrushchev

Chairman Mao, revolutionary, poet and guerrilla commander, was the communist dictator of China whose brutality, egotism, utopian radicalism, total disdain for human life and suffering, and insanely grandiose schemes led to the murder of 70 million of his own citizens. A born manipulator and ruthless pursuer of power, this monster was happy to torment and murder his own comrades, to execute millions, permit millions more to starve and even risk nuclear war, in order to promote his Marxist-Stalinist-Maoist vision of a superpower China under his own semi-divine cult of personality.

Mao was born in the village of Shaoshan in Hunan province on 26 December 1893. Forced to work on the family farm in his early teens, he rebelled against his father – a successful grain dealer – and left home to seek an education at the provincial capital, Changsa, where he participated in the revolt against the Manchu dynasty in 1911. He flirted with various careers, but never committed to anything until he subsequently joined the recently formed Chinese Communist Party in 1921. He married Yang Kaihui in 1920, by whom he had two sons (later marrying He Zizhen in 1928 and well-known actress Lan Ping – real name Jiang Qing – in 1939). At twenty-four, he recorded his amoral philosophy: 'People like me only have a duty to ourselves . . .' He worshipped 'power like a hurricane arising from a deep gorge, like a sex-maniac on the heat . . . We adore times of war . . . We love sailing the sea of upheavals . . . The country must be destroyed then reformed . . . People like me long for its destruction.' In 1923, the communists entered an alliance with the Kuomintang (Nationalist Party). Sent back to Hunan to promote the Kuomintang, he continued to foment revolutionary activity, predicting that Chinese peasants would 'rise like a tornado or tempest – a force so extraordinarily swift and violent that no power, however great, will be able to suppress it'.

In 1926, the Kuomintang leader Chiang Kai-shek – the toothless military strongman whose vicious, corrupt and utterly inept gangster-backed regime would enable Mao and the communists ultimately to triumph and conquer China – ordered the so-called Northern Expedition to consolidate fragmented government power. In April 1927, having defeated over thirty warlords, he slaughtered the communists in Shanghai, being named generalissimo the following year, with all China under his rule. Mao, meanwhile, had retired to a base in the Jinggang Mountains, from where, emerging as a red leader, he embarked on a guerrilla campaign. 'Political power grows from the barrel of a gun,' he said.

In 1931, Mao became chairman of the Chinese Soviet Republic in Jiangxi. Happy to murder, blackmail and poison his rivals – killing 700,000 in a terror 1931–5 – he displayed the same political gifts as Stalin: a will for power, ruthlessness, an addiction to turmoil and an astonishing ability to manipulate. Like Stalin also, he destroyed his wives and mistresses, ignored his children and poisoned everyone whose lives he touched: many went insane.

In 1933, after several defeats, Chiang launched a new war of attrition resulting in a dramatic turnaround that prompted the communists to sideline Mao and, on the advice of Soviet agent Otto Braun, launch a disastrous counter-attack, leading in 1936 to a full-scale retreat that became known as the Long March. By the late 1930s, using gullible Western writers like Edgar Snow and Han Suyin, Mao had created his myth as a peasant leader, poet and guerrilla-maestro, the march portrayed as an epic journey in which he heroically saved the Red Army from Nationalist attack. In fact, much was invented to conceal military ineptitude and his deliberate wastage of armies to discredit communist rivals.

In 1937, Japan launched a full-scale invasion of China. Chiang was forced by Zhang Xueliang, the Young Marshal who kidnapped the generalissimo, to combine forces with Mao. Secretly Mao strove to undermine Chiang's war effort, even briefly cooperating with Japanese intelligence. By 1943, he had achieved supremacy in the Communist Party, poisoning and purging rivals and critics with brutal efficiency. He continued to court Soviet support for the communists, whose future was assured when Stalin helped defeat Japan in 1945.

Chiang's militarily incompetent kleptocracy, heavily backed by America, collapsed as Mao, backed by massive Soviet aid and advice from Stalin, gradually drove the Kuomintang off the mainland. In 1949, Mao declared the People's Republic of China, embarking on an imperial reign of wilful caprice, ideological radicalism, messianic egotism, massive incompetence and mass-murder: 'We must kill. We say it's good to kill,' ordered this 'man without limits'. Three million people were murdered that year.

In 1951–2, Mao subjected China to his so-called Three-Anti

and Five-Anti campaigns to eliminate China's bourgeoisie. Spies infiltrated everywhere, informing on supposed transgressors, who were heavily fined, sent to labour camps or executed. Mao ruled like a red emperor, paranoid about his security, always on the move, shrewdly manipulating his henchmen and pitilessly sacrificing old comrades to maintain power at all costs. He constantly declared: 'Too lenient, not killing enough.' While he lived like an emperor on fifty private estates using military dancing girls as 'imperial concubines', he drove China to become a superpower, deploying Chinese troops against America in the Korean War as a way of persuading Stalin to give him military, especially nuclear, technology. It would not matter, he mused, 'if half the Chinese were to die' in a nuclear holocaust.

Mao continued to wage war on his people throughout the 1950s. The 1958–9 Anti-Rightist Campaign – through which over half a million people were labelled rightists – saw hundreds of thousands consigned to years of hard labour or execution. The Great Leap Forward of 1958–62, a massive drive to increase steel production, encouraged villagers to create useless little forges, coupled with a move to collectivize China's peasantry into rural communes. Emulating Stalin with his manmade 1932–3 famine, Mao sold food to buy arms even though China starved in the the greatest famine in history: 38 million died. When defence minister Marshal Peng Dehuai criticized his policies, Mao purged him but his anointed successor, President Liu Shaoqi, managed to claw back some power from Mao in 1962.

Denouncing Liu, who was destroyed and allowed to die in poverty, Mao avenged himself by getting control of the army and state through his chosen successor, the talented, neurotic Marshal Lin Biao and supple chief factotum Premier Zhou Enlai. He masterminded another terror, the Cultural Revolution, in which he asserted his total domination of China by attacking the party and state, ordering gangs of students, secret policemen and thugs to humiliate, murder and destroy lives and culture. Three million were killed between 1966 and 1976; millions more were deported or tortured.

From 1966, Mao used his wife Jiang Qing to promote his purges. An only child and the daughter of a concubine, Jiang had become an actress after leaving university, acquiring an enduring belief in the importance of the arts. She had married Mao in 1939. Her call for radical forms of expression, instilled with 'ideologically correct' subject matter, escalated into an all-out assault on the existing artistic and intellectual elites. Renowned for her inflammatory rhetoric, she manipulated mass-communication techniques to whip young Red Guards into a frenzy before sending them out to attack – verbally and physically – anything 'bourgeois' or 'reactionary'. In an orgy of denunciation, terror and murder, the Communist Party, including moderates like President Liu Shaoqi and General Secretary Deng Xiaoping, was purged. Mao personally directed both the individual persecutions of his closest comrades, using Jiang Qing, whom he hated, and the vast chaotic violence aimed at restoring his absolute tyranny.

The ageing Mao fell out with Lin Biao, creator of the *Little Red Book*, who died in a plane crash while fleeing in 1971. This left Mao in the hands of the grotesque Jiang Qing and the Maoist radicals known as the Gang of Four.

Having fallen out with Moscow, Mao pulled off one last coup: US President Richard Nixon's visit to China in 1972. Dying, Mao restored, then again purged, the formidable pragmatist Deng Xiaoping. Mao disdained Jiang Qing but she and the Gang of Four remained powerful. Mao died in 1976.

Deng arrested Madame Mao in a palace coup. In 1981 Jiang was found guilty of 'counter-revolutionary' crimes. Her death sentence was commuted to life imprisonment but she committed suicide in 1991. A hated figure, she was described by one biographer as a 'vicious woman who helped dispose of many people'; the 'white-boned demon' who, in her own words (when on trial), was 'Chairman Mao's dog. Whomever he asked me to bite, I bit.'

In the 21st century, Mao's China has been tempered by capitalism but he remains its Great Helmsman, his mummy still worshipped in its tomb, his Communist Party still in absolute control, his secret police still brutally repressing political, cultural and personal freedom. Mao remains the most formative and powerful Chinese statesman of the last few centuries.

ISAAC BABEL

1894–1940

I am innocent. I have never been a spy. I never allowed any action against the Soviet Union. I accused myself falsely. I was forced to make false accusations against myself and others . . . I am asking for only one thing - let me finish my work.

Isaac Babel

The Soviet author Isaac Babel ranks alongside the Frenchman Maupassant (indeed he wrote a story called 'Guy de Maupassant') as one of the most gifted short-story writers of all – and his fate was even more tragic. Babel's passionate, tender, original, sensual, violent and witty stories exemplify the beauty and power of the genre. His gift as a writer is encapsulated in the comment of his friend the poet Osip Mandelstam: 'It is not often that one sees such undisguised curiosity in the eyes of a grown-up.'

Babel was born in the Jewish streets of the cosmopolitan port of Odessa in the Ukraine. The Jewish underworld of gangsters, whores and rabbis he observed there is vividly depicted in his *Tales of Odessa*. Babel's life was spent defying persecution. As a child, he had seen Odessa's Jews murdered in a pogrom. When he moved to St Petersburg to study literature – a city where Jews were banned along with 'traitors, malcontents and whiners' – he had to assume a false name.

Babel fought briefly on the Romanian front during the First World War, but he was injured and discharged. It was his experiences as a correspondent for the Red Army's savage and primitive Red Cossacks during Lenin's 1920 war to spread revolution into Poland that inspired his greatest collection of short stories, *Red Cavalry*. These tales of the brutality of war made Babel, in the words of his daughter, 'famous almost overnight'. However, various Soviet commanders close to Stalin were disgusted by the frank and rambunctious portrayal of the Red Cossacks and became dangerous enemies.

Babel flourished in the relative liberality of the 1920s, but as Stalin's Terror intensified, he ceased to write as a sort of protest: 'I have invented a new genre,' Babel told the Union of Soviet Writers in 1934, 'the genre of silence.' In the 1920s his wife and daughter had moved to France, his mother and sister to Brussels; but despite increasing repression and censorship Babel kept faith with Russia's revolution and chose to remain. He was a raconteur and bon viveur. He was also fatally fascinated by the Terror and rashly but characteristically set about writing a novel about the secret police. Babel had had a long affair with the flirtatious wife of Nikolai Yezhov, Stalin's secret-police boss at the height of the Terror. When Yezhov fell from power, his wife was driven to suicide and all her lovers, including Babel, were dragged into the case and destroyed.

In 1939 the Soviet secret service arrested Babel at his cottage in the writers' colony of Peredelkino, leaving behind his new wife and baby. Interrogated and tortured, he confessed to a long-held association with Trotskyites and to anti-Soviet activity. Tried in prison, he was shot on Stalin's orders for espionage in January 1940. His family was told that he had died in a Siberian prison camp. In 1954 Babel was posthumously cleared of all charges. His reputation as a great writer has risen steadily ever since.

YEZHOV: THE GREAT TERROR

1895–1940

If during this operation, an extra thousand people are shot, that's not such a big deal.

Nikolai Yezhov, 1937

Nikolai Ivanovich Yezhov was the dwarfish Soviet secret police-man who organized and coordinated Stalin's Great Terror, during which a million innocent victims were shot and millions more exiled to concentration camps. Such was the frenzy of arrest, tor-ture and killing under Yezhov's sometimes meticulous, sometimes drunken control that this murderous witch-hunt was known as the Meatgrinder.

Born in a small Lithuanian town to a forest warden (who also ran a brothel) and a maid, Yezhov only had a few years' schooling before going to work in a factory. He joined the Red Army after the Revolution and served during the Civil War. He was a shrewd, able, tactful and ambitious party administrator and personnel expert. By the early 1930s, he was close to Stalin, in charge of all party personnel appointments and a central committee secretary. A colleague noted that 'I don't know a more ideal worker. After entrusting him with a job, he'll do it. But he doesn't know when to stop.' But this suited Stalin, who called his new favourite 'my blackberry' – a play on the word yezhevika.

In 1934 the assassination of Stalin's closest henchman, Sergei Kirov, allowed him to unleash the Great Terror against 'enemies of the people', real and imagined. In 1935 Stalin gave Yezhov special responsibility for supervising the NKVD, the secret police. The chief of the NKVD, Genrikh Yagoda, was out of favour; Yezhov aimed to destroy him and take his place. But Yezhov's first task was to take over the case against Stalin's former allies, Zinoviev and Kamenev. Yezhov supervised their interrogations, threatening to kill their families, turning up the heating in their cells in mid-summer – but also promising them their lives if they confessed to absurd crimes at the first show trial. They finally agreed. The show trial, staged in 1936, was a success, but despite Yezhov's promises, Zinoviev and Kamenev were shot in his presence. Yagoda had the bullets dug out of their brains so he could keep them in his desk; later Yezhov found the bullets, and kept them in his own drawer. In September 1936 Stalin sacked Yagoda and promoted Yezhov to people's commissar of internal affairs (NKVD).

As Yezhov supervised the spread of the Terror, arresting ever-larger circles of suspects to be tortured into confessing imaginary crimes, the Soviet press worked the population up into a frenzy of witch-hunting against Trotskyite spies and terrorists. Yezhov claimed that Yagoda had tried to kill him by spraying his curtains with cyanide. He then arrested most of Yagoda's officers and had them shot. Then he arrested Yagoda himself. 'Better that ten innocent men should suffer than one spy get away,' Yezhov announced. 'When you chop wood, chips fly!'

On Stalin's orders, in May 1937 Yezhov arrested Marshal Mikhail Tukhachevsky, the most talented Red Army officer, together with many other top generals. The idea was to break the independent power of the army, but the generals had to confess to convince the other Soviet leaders that they were guilty of crimes against the state. Yezhov personally supervised their savage torture: when Tukhachevsky's confession was found in the archives in the 1990s it was covered in a brown spray that was found to be the blood spatter of a human body in motion. The generals were all shot in Yezhov's presence. Stalin, who never attended torture sessions or executions, questioned him on their conduct at the final moment. In all, some 40,000 officers were shot.

Yezhov now expanded the Terror in a bizarre way, clearly on Stalin's orders, by initiating random killing by numbers, giving each city and region a quota of two categories: category one was to be shot and category two to be exiled. These quotas constantly expanded, until approximately a million were shot and many millions more deported to hellish labour camps in Siberia. Wives of the more prominent victims were arrested and usually shot too. Children aged between one and three were to be confined to orphanages, but children older than that could be shot. 'Beat, destroy without sorting out,' Yezhov ordered, adding, 'Better too far than not far enough.'

By 1938 the Soviet Union was in a turmoil of fear and killing, all supervised by Yezhov. Stalin kept a low profile, but Yezhov was now everywhere, hailed as the hero-avenger of a society in which enemies were omnipresent. He was now almost as powerful as Stalin, worshipped in poems and songs, with towns named in his honour. Yezhov devised special execution chambers at Moscow's notorious Lubyanka Prison and elsewhere; the chambers had a sloping concrete floor like an abattoir, wooden walls to absorb bullets and hoses to wash away the blood.

But by now Yezhov was cracking up and losing control. He constantly toured the country arresting and killing; he worked all night, torturing suspects and drinking heavily; he was becoming more and more paranoid, fearing that at any moment Stalin would turn against him. He had many of his close friends, ex-girlfriends and his own godfather shot. The stress ate at him: he boasted drunkenly that he ruled the country, he could arrest Stalin. As the third show trial starring Bukharin and Yagoda opened in Moscow, even Stalin became alarmed by the uncontrolled nature of the Terror he had unleashed. It had served its purpose, and now he needed a scapegoat. Stalin was hearing about Yezhov's excesses, drunkenness, debauchery and boasting. He ordered Yezhov to kill his top lieutenants, including his deputy, who was chloroformed in Yezhov's own office and then injected with poison. As he felt Stalin's disapproval, Yezhov started to kill anyone who could incriminate him – a thousand were killed in five days without Stalin's permission.

'I may be small in stature,' Yezhov once said, 'but my hands are strong – Stalin's hands!' Yezhov was so tiny – just 5 feet (151 cm) tall – that as a young man he had been rejected by the tsarist army. He was also unstable, sickly, sexually confused, frail and skinny, but at the same time jovial, hard-drinking and possessed of a puerile sense of humour (including a taste for farting competitions). With his handsome face, blue eyes and thick dark hair, and his fondness for dancing, singing and playing the guitar, he was a popular figure, especially with women – although, unusually for the Soviet leadership, he was promiscuously bisexual.

His first wife was a party comrade called Antonina, whom he divorced to marry a glamorous and promiscuous Jewish woman named Yevgenia, who held a salon for writers and film stars. At the time of Yezhov's downfall, his successor Beria began to investigate Yevgenia's sexually adventurous antics. Yezhov tried to divorce her in time, probably to save her and their adopted daughter Natasha, but possibly to save himself too. All her lovers, including the brilliant writer Isaac Babel, were arrested and shot. Yevgenia committed suicide.

In the autumn of 1938 Stalin promoted another protégé, Lavrenti Beria, to become Yezhov's deputy. In October the politburo denounced the management of the NKVD.

In November Yezhov appeared for the last time for the annual parade on Lenin's Mausoleum. He was sacked from the NKVD on 23 November, though he remained officially commissar of water transport. But he barely turned up for work, instead losing himself in a series of drunken homosexual orgies, waiting for the knock on the door. When it came, and the inevitable trial and death sentence followed, Yezhov collapsed. On the way to the execution chamber he himself had designed, he wept, got hiccups and fell to the floor. He had to be dragged to his death.

Yezhov was a typical half-educated but diligently ambitious Soviet bureaucrat, but finding himself with an almost absolute fiat over life and death, empowered by Stalin himself, he revelled in the hunt, the details of administering murder and the slaughter itself, and personally spent nights torturing his victims. Stalin's 'Bloody Dwarf' became the second most powerful man in the Soviet Union, but the stress almost drove him mad, and he ended a victim of his own meatgrinder. A degenerate monster, a slavish bureaucrat, a slick administrator, a sadistic torturer yet also a broken reed, Yezhov pioneered a new sort of mass-production totalitarian slaughter for the mid-20th century. 'Tell Stalin,' he announced at his trial, 'I shall die with his name on my lips.'

ZHUKOV

1896–1974

If we come to a minefield, our infantry attacks exactly as if it was not there.

Georgi Zhukov to Dwight Eisenhower

The Soviet general Georgi Zhukov is much less famous in the West than generals such as Eisenhower and Montgomery, but he was undoubtedly the greatest commander of the Second World War, turning the tide against the Nazi invaders at Moscow, Leningrad and Stalingrad, and then leading the Red Army in its bloody counteroffensive all the way to Berlin. Without the heroic Soviet effort, with its sacrifice of 26 million lives, the war might have ended very differently. Zhukov was a communist and a ruthless Stalinist general, who placed results far above his concern for individuals and casualties and used summary executions at the front to enforce discipline. Yet he was also a gifted leader, who represents not the cruelty of his master, Soviet dictator Stalin, but the heroism of the Russian people.

Military service dominated Zhukov's life. Conscripted as a private in the First World War, this son of peasants was decorated and promoted. He then fought for the Bolsheviks in the Russian Civil War of 1918–21. Further promotions followed in the 1920s, and Zhukov became known both as a strict disciplinarian and as a diligent planner. When Stalin slaughtered the officers of the Red Army in the 1937 Terror, Zhukov survived and was promoted.

In 1939 Zhukov commanded the Soviet army against the

Japanese on the Khalkin-Gol River. His daring use of tanks led to the defeat of the Japanese within three days. The invaders lost as many as 61,000 of their 80,000 men, and the shock put them off attacking Russia ever again. Zhukov earned the title of Hero of the Soviet Union and in 1940 was appointed chief of staff, but staff work did not suit him: he was a fighting general. When Hitler invaded the Soviet Union in June 1941, Zhukov formed a tempestuous, but ultimately successful, partnership with Stalin. The Soviet dictator recognized Zhukov's brilliance and professionalism, accepting him as his military mentor and making him deputy supreme commander-in-chief.

Stalin used Zhukov as a troubleshooter, as the Germans thrust deep into Russia, taking millions of prisoners. When Minsk fell and Stalin almost lost his nerve, Zhukov – the toughest general in Russia – burst into tears. In July, after a row with Stalin, Zhukov was sacked as chief of staff. But he went on to command and save Moscow and Leningrad. In the latter, he bolstered the besieged city's defences so that the city did not fall. In Moscow, he took over the defences as the Germans advanced. With the loss of one quarter of the 400,000 men at his disposal, Zhukov managed to halt the German blitzkrieg in the freezing winter of 1941, just saving the capital and driving the Germans back 200 miles (320km). It was a vital victory.

The next task was to organize the Soviet counter-attack in the most dreadful battle of the war – Stalingrad. Zhukov, along with Marshal Vasilevsky and Stalin himself, conceived of the plan to lure German forces into Stalingrad. With a million men, more than 13,000 guns, 1400 tanks and 1115 planes, Zhukov oversaw the encirclement of the German Sixth Army. The average life expectancy of a Soviet soldier brought into the long battle was little more than twenty-four hours, and around a million men from both sides were killed. But Stalingrad turned the tide of the war.

Promoted to marshal, Zhukov next led the Red Army to victory in the greatest tank battle ever fought, at Kursk in 1943. The Red Army pushed ever westward, into Poland and then into Germany itself, where the last great battle of the European war was fought through the streets of Berlin. Stalin typically took overall command of the Battle of Berlin himself, forcing the two commanders, Zhukov and Marshal Konev, to compete in the race to the Reichstag. In the early hours of 1 May 1945 Zhukov telephoned Stalin to inform him that Hitler was dead. The next day the city surrendered.

When the war was over, Zhukov was a national and international hero. The Soviet military rank and file idolized him, and Western generals thought extremely highly of him. Ironically, all this made him a political threat: Stalin had him accused of Bonapartist tendencies and demoted him, but he ensured Zhukov was not arrested.

After Stalin's death in 1953, Zhukov was brought back to the centre of Soviet politics as defence minister. He helped Nikita Khrushchev become Stalin's heir by arresting Lavrenti Beria, the head of Stalin's secret police, but he was independent and had a fractious relationship with the new leader. In 1957 he again supported Khrushchev, helping to defeat the old Stalinists, but afterwards he was sacked, once more accused of Bonapartism.

Zhukov, who died in 1974, was tough and brutal and sometimes made costly mistakes. He believed in Stalinist methods and was arrogant about his own ability. But as Eisenhower was to put it, 'no one did more to achieve victory in Europe than Marshal Zhukov' – he was undoubtedly the outstanding general of the Second World War. As his colleague Marshal Timoshenko noted, 'Zhukov was the only person who feared no one. He was not afraid even of Stalin.' Ultimately, he represents native Russian military genius and now his statue on horseback stands just outside the Kremlin near Red Square.

CAPONE

1899–1947

*You can get much further with a kind word and a gun than you can
with a kind word alone.*

Al Capone

Al 'Scarface' Capone epitomized the murderous American Mafia
mobsters who ran their rackets with impunity during the Prohibition era. Ironically, despite his deep involvement in organized
crime and murder, the only charge he was ever convicted of was
income-tax evasion.

Born in Brooklyn, New York, Alphonse 'Al' Capone was the son
of Gabriele Capone, an Italian barber who had arrived in America
with his wife Teresina in 1894. Al embarked on his career in organized crime when he left school aged just fourteen, and fell under
the influence of a gangster boss, Johnny 'the Fox' Torrio. From
there he graduated to the Five Points Gang in Manhattan. It was
during this period that he was slashed in the face after a bar-room
brawl, leaving him with the scar by which he would later be known.
He was also suspected of involvement in two killings, though
witnesses refused to come forward and nothing was ever proven.

Capone's mentor Torrio had left New York for Chicago in 1909
to run a brothel racket. Ten years later he sent for his protégé,
and it was probably Capone who was responsible for the murder
in 1920 of Torrio's boss, 'Big Jim' Colosimo, with whom Torrio
had fallen out. Torrio subsequently emerged as the undisputed
kingpin of crime in the Windy City.

The introduction of Prohibition in 1920 endowed America's gangsters with a gold mine of opportunities. Trade in smuggled alcohol became big business, and speakeasies where bootlegged liquor was readily available became the defining image of the era. But behind the relaxed jollity of the speakeasy and the gangster glamour lay violence, wanton sadism and psychopathic brutality.

In 1923 a reform-minded mayor, William E. Dever, was elected in Chicago on a platform of reining in the mobsters. As a result, Torrio and Capone opted to relocate much of their business to the satellite town of Cicero. The following year, with council elections scheduled for Cicero, Capone was determined to ensure that his candidates won, by whatever means. In the resulting violence, his brother Frank was killed and an election official was murdered, amid a wave of kidnappings, ballot-box theft and general intimidation. When it was all over Capone had won in Cicero, in one of the most dishonest elections ever seen.

Within weeks Capone, apparently believing himself impregnable, shot dead a small-time gangster called Joe Howard who had insulted a friend of his in a bar. The crime made Capone a target for William McSwiggen – the 'hanging prosecutor' – and though he failed to pin any charges on Capone, McSwiggen did succeed in putting the gangster firmly in the public spotlight, setting Capone on the road to becoming America's public enemy number one.

In 1925 Torrio retired after an attempt on his life by a rival concern, the North Side Gang run by Dean O'Banion, George 'Bugs' Moran and Earl 'Hymie' Weiss. Capone now took over from Torrio as the leading figure in the Chicago underworld. Thereafter, he developed an increasingly public persona, ostentatiously attending major sporting occasions, such as baseball games, and even the opera, presenting himself as an honest, successful businessman, with a flair for the common touch. In truth everyone knew the real source of Capone's wealth.

Protection rackets, illegal gambling, bootlegging and prostitution – wherever there was a quick buck to be made, Capone had a hand in it. His eye for profit was combined with a ruthless approach to dealing with possible rivals – and the greatest threat to his hegemony, in Capone's view, was the North Side Gang, the hoodlums who had earlier attacked Johnny Torrio.

The result was the 1929 St Valentine's Day Massacre. Disguising his men as policemen, Capone sent them to Moran's warehouse at 2122 North Clark Street, where they lined seven of the North Siders up against a wall and machine-gunned them in cold blood. Several of the victims were also blasted with a shotgun in the face. The gang leader, Moran, escaped, but with his key lieutenants dead his operation went into steep decline. Capone was left as Chicago's undisputed Mr Big.

But outrage over the killings generated pressure for more action on the part of the authorities against Capone. It was this that led the FBI to launch its ingenious bid to pursue Capone for income-tax offences. Aware that he was unlikely ever to be indicted for any of his more violent activities (both because of the distance he now kept between himself and specific actions and because of the fear of reprisals that kept any potential witnesses from testifying), the federal government appointed a Treasury agent, Eliot Ness, and a hand-picked team of agents – the Untouchables – to go after Capone.

As a strategy it proved to be a stunning success. In June 1931 Capone was formally charged with income-tax evasion, and that October he was found guilty and sentenced to eleven years in prison. Initially sent to Atlanta penitentiary, in 1934 he was transferred to the maximum-security facility at Alcatraz. In 1939 he was released early, owing to ill health. But he was never able to regain control over his criminal empire. A shadow of his former self, Capone retreated into obscurity – finally dying of syphilis in 1947, a forgotten figure.

BERIA

1899–1953

*Let me have one night with him and I'll have him confessing he is the
King of England.*

Lavrenti Beria

Lavrenti Pavlovich Beria was a sinister Soviet secret policeman,
psychopathic rapist and enthusiastic sadist who ordered the deaths
of many and took a personal delight in the torture of his victims.
The personification of the criminal monstrosity of the Soviet state,
he was a coarse, cynical intriguer, a vindictive cut-throat, a deft
courtier and a perverted thug. Yet he was also a highly intelligent,
enormously competent and indefatigable administrator with the
vision ultimately to reject Marxism and propose the sort of liberal
programme that Mikhail Gorbachev brought to fruition years later.

Beria was born in Georgia in 1899 to a very religious mother
but of uncertain paternity – he was probably the illegitimate son
of an Abkhazian nobleman. In Baku during the Russian Civil War
he worked as a double agent, serving both the anti-Bolshevik
regime and the Bolsheviks. Once Baku was retaken by the Bolsheviks, he proved a shrewd politician, and in 1921 he joined the
new secret police, the Cheka, rising quickly to become head of the
Georgian branch. He first met Stalin, a fellow Georgian, in 1926,
and always behaved towards him not like a Bolshevik comrade
(as was then the fashion) but like a medieval liege to his king.
Stalin decided to use him against the old Georgians who ran the
Caucasus, promoting him against their protests to first secretary

of Georgia, and then of the entire Caucasus. When Stalin made his courtiers garden with him, Beria used an axe and told Stalin he would use it to tear out any weeds that he was ordered to extract. Beria understood Stalin's vanity and produced a book on the history of the communists in the Caucasus that inflated Stalin's importance before the Revolution.

Stalin's local ally in the Caucasus was Abkhazian boss Nestor Lakoba, who had helped to promote Beria. But now Lakoba and Beria clashed, and in 1936 Stalin allowed Beria to destroy his old friend which he did by poisoning Lakoba after an evening at the opera in Tiflis. Then, in what was to become a typical pattern, Beria set about destroying the entire Lakoba family, killing his brothers, young children and friends. When the Great Terror really started, Beria killed and tortured his way through the Caucasus, murdering far more victims than his quota.

In late 1938 Stalin brought Beria to Moscow and promoted him to 'assist Yezhov', the head of the NKVD, the secret police. Beria had been friendly with Yezhov, but now his role was to destroy him. On 25 November he was made boss of the NKVD in Yezhov's place, and set about restoring order to the frenzied chaos of Yezhov's killing machine. The Terror was officially over – but it never ended, it simply became secret, as Beria set about purging more Soviet leaders and generals. He liked to torture them himself, and beat one victim so hard that he knocked out one of his eyes. Stalin and Beria enjoyed coming up with imaginatively lurid ways of destroying their enemies. When Beria found out that Lakoba's wife feared snakes above anything else, he drove her to insanity by placing snakes in her cell. He kidnapped and murdered his comrades' wives and killed other comrades in faked car crashes.

After Stalin signed the Non-Aggression Pact with Hitler in 1939, allowing him to annex eastern Poland, the Baltic States and Moldavia, Beria supervised the brutal killing and deportation of hundreds of thousands of innocent people suspected of anti-Soviet tendencies. In 1940 Beria, on Stalin's orders, presided over the execution of 28,000 Polish officers in the Katyn Forest. Following Hitler's invasion of the Soviet Union in 1941, Beria became ever more powerful. Promoted to commissar-general of security and made a marshal of the Soviet Union, he was one of the key administrators on the new state defence committee through which Stalin ran the war. Running the vast Gulag camp system as well as much of the country's industrial production, Beria continued to run the secret police and terrorize the generals on Stalin's behalf. In 1941 Beria proposed the deportation of the Volga Germans, and later, in 1944, the deportation of the Chechens, Karachai, Kalmyks, Balkars and Crimean Tartars. Hundreds of thousands were killed or perished en route. In 1945 Beria accompanied Stalin to Yalta, where President Roosevelt, spotting Beria at a dinner, asked his identity: 'That's Beria,' replied Stalin. 'My Himmler.'

Beria's wife Nina was pretty and elegant, and his son Sergo was his pride and joy. He loved his family, but spent nearly all his time in the office, day and night, and the rest of his energy was devoted to a priapic addiction to sex. He always had mistresses – his last one was a fourteen-year-old beauty – and he was also addicted to rape.

The stories of his degeneracy circulated by his enemies after his fall are true. He would send out his bodyguards to kidnap and deliver young girls whom he had spotted from his cruising limousine, invite them to dinner, propose a toast to Stalin, and slip sleeping pills into their wine. He would then force himself on them. Afterwards, his chauffeur would take them home, and present them with a bouquet of flowers. Even during the Second World War, when he was virtually running the country, and afterwards when he was in charge of the nuclear project, Beria still found time for these squalid escapades, and caught venereal diseases several times. When Berias's crimes were reported to Stalin, the dictator tolerated him – commenting that Beria was a busy man under great stress.

During the Potsdam Conference, President Truman informed Stalin about America's new nuclear weapons. Stalin immediately placed Beria in charge of over 400,000 workers, including many brilliant scientists, tasked with developing a Soviet atom bomb. In 1946 Beria became a full member of the Politburo. But Stalin had started to distrust him, sensing his cynicism about Marxism itself and his increasing dislike of his master. Stalin removed him from the ministry of internal affairs in 1946, purged his protégés and promoted Abakumov, another ruthless thug, to be minister of state security, independent of Beria. Yet Beria still managed to wield considerable influence. In 1949, to Stalin's delight, Beria delivered the Soviet atom bomb. In the same year, Beria managed to turn Stalin against two of his chosen heirs, and both were shot in the Leningrad Case.

By the early 1950s Stalin was in decline, forgetful, more and more paranoid, and never more dangerous. He now loathed 'Snake-eyes' Beria, who, in turn, hated Stalin and his system, even though he himself was one of its monsters. When Stalin died in March 1953, Beria emerged from the deathbed as the strongman of the new regime. Although his title was first deputy premier, he dominated the nominal premier, the weak Malenkov, and took charge of the ministry of internal affairs. He disdained the coarse, clumsy but shrewd Khrushchev, whom he fatally underestimated. Freed of the hated Stalin, Beria overconfidently proposed the freeing of millions of prisoners, liberalization of the economy and the loosening of Soviet hegemony over eastern Europe and the ethnic republics. Yet at the same time he was still arresting his personal enemies and intimidating his rivals. No one trusted him everyone feared him. Three months after Stalin's death, Khrushchev orchestrated a palace coup backed by Marshal Zhukov and the Soviet military. Beria was arrested, and secretly confined in a military bunker. Here he begged for his life, writing pathetic letters to his ex-comrades, but to no avail: at his trial he was sentenced to death. On the day he was due to die, he cried and collapsed until his executioner, a Soviet general, stuffed a towel in his mouth and shot him through the forehead.

Short, squat, bald and increasingly fat, Beria had a flat face with large fleshy lips, greeny-grey skin, and, behind his glinting pince-nez, grey, colourless eyes. At the same time, he was energetic, witty, quick, curious and an avid reader of history. 'He was enormously clever with inhuman energy,' said Stalin's deputy Molotov. 'He could work for a week with one night's sleep.' According to one of his henchmen, 'Beria would think nothing of killing his best friend.' Several of his colleagues observed that if he had been born in America, he would have been head of General Motors. Yet – with his love of intrigue, poison, torture and killing – he would also have flourished at the court of the Borgias.

HEMINGWAY

1899–1961

Man is not made for defeat. A man can be destroyed but not defeated.

The essence of man's – and Hemingway's – indomitable
spirit captured in *The Old Man and the Sea* (1952)

Ernest Hemingway was arguably the most important American writer of the 20th century. His novels and short stories, rejecting the stuffy 19th-century values he saw in his own family and in the world around him, introduced a new and powerful style of writing: sparse, economical, tough, masculine prose that captures the horrors of war and the trials of love, and advocates a strong moral code for conducting life in a complex world of pain and betrayal. Hemingway could be unpredictable, violent, bad-tempered, vainglorious, ridiculous and drunken, but these were all aspects of a troubled yet brilliant mind. He was awarded the Nobel Prize in recognition of his work and his distinctive and unique contribution to literature.

Hemingway grew up in a Chicago suburb. His father, physician Dr Clarence Hemingway, urged him towards manly outdoor activities like hunting, shooting and fishing. His mother, Grace, instilled in him a familiarity with literature. He used to claim that the first words he said as a baby were 'Afraid of nothing! Afraid of nothing!' probably untrue but typical of his famed machismo. As a young man Hemingway went to Italy to serve in the First World War. He was blown up by a mortar in 1918, but, despite being injured by shrapnel and coming under machine-gun fire, he managed to carry two comrades to safety.

Though he later embellished this experience, it was an outstanding act of bravery for which the Italian government awarded him the Silver Medal of Honour. While recuperating, Hemingway fell in love with a Red Cross nurse, Agnes von Kurowsky, who declined to marry him. He never forgot the experience.

When he returned to America, his mother reprimanded him for his 'lazy loafing and pleasure seeking', accusing him of 'trading on his handsome face' and 'neglecting his duties to God'. Hemingway had always despised his mother's written style, her sermonizing and her religion, which he saw as running counter to human happiness. Now he began to despise her wholesale. The breach with his family was never reconciled, and when in 1921 Hemingway took a job as foreign correspondent on the *Toronto Star*, based in Paris, he cut himself free and became his own man.

In Paris Hemingway fell in with prominent literary figures such as Gertrude Stein, Ezra Pound, and his friend F. Scott Fitzgerald, author of *The Great Gatsby* and the other American literary genius of the time. In 1924–5 Hemingway published his short-story cycle *In Our Time*, and in 1926 the successful novel *The Sun Also Rises*, which dealt with the lives of the aimless socialites of America's postwar 'Lost Generation', who decadently drifted around Europe without purpose.

Hemingway's first masterpiece was *A Farewell to Arms*, published in 1929. It was heavily autobiographical, telling a love story set in the First World War. A young ambulance man, Frederic Henry, falls in love with Catherine Barkley, an English nurse tending to his recuperation. After Henry deserts his post, the couple flee to Switzerland, but Catherine and her baby die in childbirth, leaving Henry desolate.

Spain played a dominant part in Hemingway's life and works. He wrote a sensitive study of bullfighting, *Death in the Afternoon*, in 1932, and when the Spanish Civil War broke out in 1936, he became deeply involved in the Republican cause, raising money to assist the struggle against General Franco's Nazi-backed Nationalists. His experience was the basis for his second masterpiece, *For Whom the Bell Tolls*, published in 1940. Set during the Civil War, this tells the story of an American volunteer guerrilla, Robert Jordan, who is sent to blow up a railway line in support of a Republican attack. Jordan's love for a Spanish girl, Maria, develops in a narrative that skilfully explores the Spanish character and the brutality of war.

Hemingway covered the Second World War as a journalist, flying several missions with the Royal Air Force, seeing action on D-Day and taking part in the liberation of Paris. After the war he spent most of his time working at Finca Vigía, his home in Cuba. The jewel of this final period was *The Old Man and the Sea* (1952), the tale of an elderly fisherman and his struggles to land an enormous marlin. This short book won Hemingway the Pulitzer Prize in 1953 and the Nobel Prize the following year.

Alcohol, age and various serious accidents, including two plane crashes, took their toll on Hemingway. During the 1950s he spiralled into depression, and the more unpleasant aspects of his nature – he could be sour, quarrelsome, prone to violence – all came to the fore. Forced from Cuba in 1960 by Fidel Castro's revolution, Hemingway settled in Ketchum, Idaho. Aware that his creative powers were in terminal decline, and realizing that the electric-shock therapy he was receiving for depression was useless, he killed himself with a shotgun in 1961. He was sixty-two years old.

Hemingway may have been a troubled and troublesome character, but he was also a figure of enormous energy and dynamism who left an indelible mark not just on modern literature but on language too.

HIMMLER & HEYDRICH:

1900–1945   1904–1942

THE HOLOCAUST

I also want to mention a very difficult subject before you here, completely openly. It should be discussed amongst us, and yet, nevertheless, we will never speak about it in public. I am talking about the Jewish evacuation: the extermination of the Jewish people.

Heinrich Himmler, 4 October 1943

Heinrich Himmler was the chief organizer of the greatest crime in human history – the industrialized murder of 6 million Jews by execution squads and gas chambers, the dead consumed by crematoria. Under his master Adolf Hitler, Himmler was the second most powerful man in the Third Reich, amassing huge powers as Reichsführer-SS, police chief and interior minister, and masterminding not just the Holocaust but also the massacre of Gypsies and homosexuals and the brutal enslavement of Slavs and other *Untermenschen* – subhumans.

Reinhard Heydrich was Himmler's chief assistant in these diabolical projects and both men were the highly educated, upper-middle-class children of cultured intellectuals – the very opposite of the thuggish Nazi streetfighters.

Himmler was born in Munich to Gebhard Himmler, a respectable headmaster and tutor of the Wittelsbach royal family of Bavaria, and his wife Anna Maria. Himmler's godfather was a Wittelsbach Bavarian prince, the king of Bavaria's uncle. Slightly built and preferring chess and stamp-collecting to the sports field, he was the antithesis of the Aryan ideal. He did eventually marry following a chance meeting with divorcée Margarete Siegroth in a hotel lobby. The couple had one daughter, Gudrun.

Himmler met future Nazis in the right-wing paramilitary Freikorps after the First World War. Supporting Hitler from the start and joining the Nazi Party in 1925, his unflinching loyalty, coupled with his administrative abilities and utter ruthlessness, led to his appointment in 1928 as Reichsführer-SS, head of the *Schutzstaffel* (SS). After Hitler became chancellor of Germany in 1933, Himmler created the non-uniformed intelligence service, the SD (*Sicherheitsdienst*), and the following year he organized the Night of the Long Knives in which Ernst Röhm and the leadership of the SA – *Sturmabteiling* (Stormtroops) – were murdered. By 1936, he controlled the plainclothes political police, the dreaded secret police, the Gestapo, and all uniformed police.

The outbreak of war in 1939 saw Himmler appointed commissioner for the consolidation of the German race, charged with eliminating 'inferior' people from the Reich, and he set about expanding his concentration camps to detain opponents, Slavs and Jews. In September, Reinhard Heydrich – his talented protégé, head of both the SD intelligence service and Gestapo – ordered the forcible eviction of Jews from across the Reich into ghettos in Poland, where thousands were executed, starved or died from disease.

Tall, slim, athletic, blue-eyed and blond, though with broad feminine hips, Heydrich became Himmler's chief organizer of the secret but colossal slaughter of Europe's Jews. He specialized in clandestine intrigues, running a brothel to bug well-known patrons and using concentration-camp prisoners, murdered with injections, to provide the pretext for Hitler's invasion of Poland.

Heydrich was born of musical parents in the city of Halle, near Leipzig, in 1904. His father was a Wagnerian opera singer and the respected headmaster of the Halle Musical Conservatory while his mother, who was extremely strict and regularly beat her son, was a talented pianist. Young Heydrich was never popular among his peers, who nicknamed him Moses because of (untrue) rumours that he had Jewish ancestry.

Deeply sensitive about these rumours, in his teens Heydrich came to believe in the supposed inherent superiority of the Germanic people, but he was totally uninvolved in politics until a social-professional scandal ended his naval career. After the First World War, Heydrich joined the navy where the ambitious but sensitive officer who played violin beautifully was teased for his supposed Jewish origins. He had just become engaged to Lina Von Osten when he was cashiered from the navy for a simultaneous sexual relationship with another woman. In 1931, aged twenty-seven, he joined the SS, impressing Heinrich Himmler during his interview with his knowledge of secret police techniques derived from his obessional reading of American detective novels and police procedures. In 1933 he was promoted to brigadier general and given the responsibility of setting up the SD, the SS security service, where he identified the administrative talents of Adolf Eichmann, who became the Jewish expert of the SS.

In 1939 Heydrich was put in charge of the Reich Main Security Office, and after the invasion of Poland formed five SS *Einsatzgruppen* (task forces) to murder in cold blood – and bury in mass graves – political enemies, dissidents, aristocrats and Jews in the occupied territory.

Himmler now proposed plans – put together with Heydrich – to Hitler to rid Europe of all Jews through 'forced evacuation to the east' – their euphemism for physical extermination – the 'final solution to the Jewish problem'. Hitler approved. In June 1941, following the invasion of the Soviet Union, Himmler – delegated to carry out 'special tasks' – dispatched his SS *Einsatzgruppen*, who murdered 1,300,000 Jews, Gypsies and communists. Himmler and Heydrich personally toured the areas behind the front, encouraging and organizing more murders of men, but also increasingly women and children. Himmler himself personally witnessed executions, and when, in August 1941, brains from one of the victims spattered his SS uniform, he demanded that concentration camps be equipped with gas chambers as a more efficient way of killing, more humane for the executioner.

On 20 January 1942 Heydrich convened a meeting of the fifteen leading Nazi bureaucrats, many of them lawyers and eight of them possessing doctorates, in a large house in an affluent suburb of Berlin, near a picturesque lake called the Wannsee.

Over a million Jews had already been murdered by the mobile *Einsatzgruppen*, but the work was considered too slow and demoralizing. The purpose at Wannsee was to convey directives from the Führer regarding the final solution of the Jewish question and create an administrative and legalistic framework for mass murder. 'Europe was to be combed of Jews from east to west,' and those present were charged with the capture, transportation and industrial extermination of the estimated 11 million European Jews.

'Another possible solution of the problem has now taken the place of emigration, i.e. the evacuation of the Jews to the East,' said Heydrich. The notes, kept by Adolf Eichmann, carefully avoid direct reference to extermination but 'evacuation' was the accepted euphemism for slaughter, as Heydrich made clear:

Under proper guidance, in the course of the final solution the Jews are to be allocated for appropriate labour in the East. Able-bodied Jews, separated according to sex, will be taken in large work columns to these areas for work on roads, in the course of which action doubtless a large portion will be eliminated by natural causes. The possible final remnant will, since it will undoubtedly consist of the most resistant portion, have to be treated accordingly, because it is the product of natural selection and would, if released, act as the seed of a new Jewish revival.

Numerous such camps – including Bergen-Belsen, Auschwitz-Birkenau, Belzec and Treblinka – were hastily constructed. Bergen-Belsen held over 60,000 Jews, of whom over 35,000 died of starvation, overwork, disease and medical experiments. Dachau – built in March 1933 to house political prisoners – served as a labour camp and centre for horrific medical experiments, those too sick to work being summarily executed or sent to the nearby Hartheim killing centre. Meanwhile, 3 million Russian prisoners of war were deliberately starved to death on Hitler/Himmler's orders.

Most notorious of the death camps was Auschwitz-Birkenau, established by Himmler in May 1940, and by 1942 equipped with seven gas chambers in which an estimated 2.5 million were murdered, roughly 2 million of whom were Jews, Poles, Gypsies and Soviet POWs. Only about 200,000 people survived, the rest cremated or piled into mass graves.

Himmler and Heydrich had very different styles: Himmler considered himself a soldier, but his real gift was as a bureaucratic intriguer and Hitlerite courtier. He devoted much time to devising pedantic and preposterous rules for his new SS order. Himmler spent his rare leisure with his assistant, who became his mistress. Heydrich was a gifted sportsman and musician. In between his many duties, he trained as a pilot, flying daring missions in Norway and Russia, where he crashed and had to be rescued. He had many love affairs and sexual adventures. He was chilling but never banal. Himmler was terrifying but always blandy pedantic.

In addition to his already vast responsibilities, in September 1941 Heydrich was appointed Reichsprotektor of Bohemia and Moravia (formerly part of Czechoslovakia), where he instituted repressive measures and became known as Der Henker (the Hangman). On 27 May 1942, as he rode without an escort in an open-top green Mercedes, he was ambushed by two British-trained Free Czech fighters and died later of his wounds. In retaliation, the Nazis wiped out the entire Czech village of Lidice.

In June 1942, Himmler ordered the deportation of 100,000 Jews from France and approved plans to move 30 million Slavs from eastern Europe to Siberia. The following month he ordered the 'total cleansing' of Jews from the Polish General Government – 6000 a day from Warsaw alone were transported to the death camps.

In 1943, Himmler was appointed minister of the interior. The following year Hitler disbanded the military intelligence service (the *Abwehr*) and made Himmler's SD Nazi Germany's sole intelligence service. In 1944, as the Allies advanced from the west,

Himmler failed completely as military commander of Army Group Vistula.

Recognizing defeat was inevitable, Himmler desperately attempted to destroy evidence of the death camps, then attempted to seek peace with Britain and America. Hitler ordered his arrest. Himmler fled in disguise but was arrested in Bremen, after which he swallowed a cyanide capsule.

A chinless, bespectacled ex-chicken-farmer who suffered from nervous ailments, he built a second family with his mistress, the ex-secretary whom he called Bunny – but the attic of their house contained furniture and books made from the bones and skins of his Jewish victims. He was a meticulous administrator who organized the systematic extermination of 6 million Jews (two-thirds of the Jewish population of Europe), 3 million Russians, 3 million non-Jewish Poles, 750,000 Slavs, 500,000 Gypsies, 100,000 of the mentally ill, 100,000 Freemasons, 15,000 homosexuals and 5000 Jehovah's Witnesses – murder on a scale never before imagined.

KHOMEINI

1902–1989

I shall kick their teeth in. I am appointing the government. I am appointing the government by the support of this nation!

The Grand Ayatollah Khomeini led the 1979 revolution that overthrew the last shah of Iran and became the supreme leader of a theocracy, the Islamic Republic of Iran, that has become an often disruptive power across the Near East. This aged, white-bearded Shiite cleric proved to be a dynamic, shrewd and unforgiving revolutionary leader who created a totally new system with his own power protected in a constitution that has proved surprisingly enduring, thanks to the brutal suppression of any opposition. Today's resurgent, bold Iran, pursuing a nuclear arsenal and regional hegemony, threatening war against the 'Great Satan' America and annihilation of the 'Little Satan' Israel, backing the Hamas and Hezbollah militias in Gaza and Lebanon, murdering and terrorizing its own people, is the Iran of Khomeini.

Khomeini, whose family had spent much time in India under the British Raj and who used the nom de plume Hindi for some of his own poetry, studied the Koran and in particular Iran's Twelver Shiism at madrassas in Arak and the holy city of Qom. The Iranian clergy were challenged and almost broken by the rule of Reza Shah, who made himself king of Iran during the 1920s, in a campaign to modernize and secularize the country like his hero Ataturk had done in Turkey.

Reza Shah was forced to abdicate the throne to his young son Muhammad Reza Pahlavi, who at first proved adept at managing the powerful Shiite ayatollahs. Khomeini, not yet a cleric of the top rank, still accepted the idea of a limited constitutional monarchy but gradually he became repulsed by the secular and modernizing instincts of the new shah.

Khomeini was already in his sixties when the deaths of the leading ayatollahs enabled him to emerge as a clerical leader. In 1963, Muhammad Reza Pahlavi announced his White Revolution, a revolution of land ownership, liberation and education of women, and modernization imposed from above by the monarch himself. It was anathema to Khomeini who, calling a meeting of the top *ulema* (clergy), denounced the shah, whom he called a 'wretched miserable man', a decadent tyrant like Muawiya's son, Caliph Yazid of history.

The shah responded by attacking the clergy in Qom itself. As the tension rose, Khomeini was arrested. When the Shah's prime minister demanded Khomeini apologize, supposedly slapping the cleric's face, Khomeini refused. He was already in contact with an expanding network of Islamic schools and charities with political and violent programmes: days later the shah's prime minister was assassinated. Vast crowds protested against the shah and backed the ayatollahs.

In the face of this rising tension the shah gave his new prime minister powers to use the military to repress the rebellion. Four hundred protesters were shot by the army and the shah regained the initiative. Khomeini was forced into exile, for a period in Turkey but mainly in Najab in Iraq, the only other country with a huge Shiite population.

The shah had now emerged as a regional military potentate, a trusted ally of America and recipient of billions of dollars as the oil prices rose. But his White Revolution was gradually destroying itself: thousands of Iranians embraced the new possibilities of education, joining the middle class just as millions of poor Iranians, excited by new industry, new education, new housing, new wealth, had left their villages for Teheran only to discover a new listless poverty and disappointment in slums. Here they were left adrift under the corrupt and distant magnificence of the increasingly autocratic shah and his court of technocrats and cronies, a rule enforced by increasingly bombastic splendour and the regime's brutal SAVAK secret police. President Saddam Hussein of Iraq frequently suggested to the shah that he liquidate Khomeini but the shah always demurred.

Meanwhile in Najab and later in French exile near Paris, Khomeini recorded cassettes of his preaching that were smuggled into Iran where they found a growing audience. He had embraced his new concept of divine sovereignty – veleyet e faqih – the guardianship of the religious expert over the people. Traditionally the Shia believed that the leadership of the Prophet descended through his direct descendants – the Twelve Imams – until the last, the twelfth, who had vanished but would one day return to lead them. Khomeini was now increasingly revered as 'the Imam', more than just an ayatollah, but a mystical national-religious leader in his own right.

In 1978, the shah's regime was paralysed by a series of strikes and growing protests just as the inept President Jimmy Carter weakened his regime by criticising its human rights abuses. The shah proved curiously incapable of reacting, turning to the US and British ambassadors but refusing to empower a military strongman to repress the growing tide of protest. Few knew that the shah, having concentrated all power in his own hands, was secretly suffering from cancer.

Meanwhile Khomeini proved himself an adept manipulator of Iranian and Western opinion, concealing his theocratic views while posing as a democratic populist, surrounding himself with democrats and Westernized liberals who convinced foreigners that he would oversee a new, free Iran. In fact his cassettes were open in their fanatical and violent language against the shah, America and Jews. When the shah left Iran 'on vacation', millions celebrated. On 1 February 1979, Khomeini returned and overthrew the provisional government – 'I shall kick their teeth in; I appoint the government,' he declared – and appointed his own new government under a moderate democrat, Mehdi Barzagan: 'he shall be obeyed because I appointed God's government'. In the absence of the Twelfth Imam, Khomeini immediately assumed near absolute powers, overseeing a terror that executed or murdered thousands of the shah's supporters and soon any of his own supporters who questioned his style of rule. His new constitution for an Islamic government was approved by a vast majority and while he created a semi-democratic façade – with an elected president and parliament – the real power lay with himself, now the supreme leader, chosen by a committee of expert clergymen, who controlled the entire state. Swiftly the state became a far more ruthless and repressive dictatorship than it had ever been under the hapless shah.

When America gave the dying shah medical treatment, Iranian students seized US diplomats as hostages; American military intervention failed disastrously; and Khomeini revelled in the humiliation of the Great Satan. Meanwhile in 1980, the Iraqi Saddam Hussein invaded Iran but Khomeini, using the war to consolidate his power, counter-attacked and regained the initial losses. When Iraq offered a truce, Khomeini refused, sending thousands of conscripts in human waves at the Iraqi lines. The war lasted six years and was a disaster for Iran and Iraq – 500,000 to one million died. In 1989, Khomeini reacted to the publication of the book the *Satanic Verses* by the British author Salman Rushdie by issuing a *fatwa* (religious decree) sentencing him to death.

When Khomeini died in 1989, his nominated successor, Ayatollah Ali Khamenei, was duly chosen as supreme leader, though he lacked Khomeini's unique authority. Nonetheless, the Iranian Islamic Republic has been highly successful in projecting Shiite and Iranian power, seeking nuclear weapons, using militias such as Hezbollah and Hamas, and involving itself in the wars in Iraq and Syria. It is an aggressive, oppressive theocracy yet its hybrid semi-democracy, with elected presidents and parliaments, has given it the flexibility to survive and to build power unprecedented since the days of the Persian empire.

ORWELL

1903–1950

In Burma and Paris and London and on the road to Wigan pier,
and in Spain, being shot at, and eventually wounded, by fascists
– he had invested blood, pain and hard labour to earn his anger.
                                                    The novelist Thomas Pynchon

Of all the writers of the 20th century, none did more to shape the way ordinary people think and speak than George Orwell. His novels Animal Farm and *Nineteen Eighty-Four* not only offer stark warnings of the dangers of tyranny and state control; they shifted political perceptions and enriched the English language itself. He was also the greatest English-language essayist of his century, always original, penetrating and eloquent. Orwell's politics were consistently left-wing, but he scathingly cut through the rigid conventions of leftist sympathy for Stalinist mass murder. His principled criticism of the horrors of totalitarianism marked him out as an intellectual icon for people of any political hue. Even the word Orwellian has become part of the English language.

George Orwell was the pen name of Eric Arthur Blair. He was born in 1903 to an English family posted in Bengal, where his father was an officer working in the opium department of the Indian Civil Service. Although Orwell moved back to England while still an infant, the experience of imperialism left a deep impression that is visible in much of his work.

In 1922 Orwell joined the Indian Imperial Police and was posted to Burma. His time there was the basis for brilliantly observed essays such as 'A Hanging' and 'Shooting an Elephant', as well as the poignant and gripping novel Burmese Days (1934). His strong sense of conscience led him to resign in 1927, and he came back to England highly disillusioned with the realities of imperial power.

It was in such a state of mind that Orwell set about turning himself into a writer. In the late 1920s and early 1930s he took a number of grim menial jobs in Paris, often as a *plongeur* (dishwasher) in hotel kitchens, then returned to London and 'went native', living as a tramp in hostels and boarding houses. The lice, dirt, greasy pan-scrubbing and toerags were all condensed into his first narrative, *Down and Out in Paris and London* (1932). It laid bare the misery of the very poor in Europe and started a lifelong obsession with the living conditions of the working classes.

His next book, *The Road to Wigan Pier* (1937), gave a vivid and powerful account of the everyday living conditions of miners in the urban heartlands of northwest England, with telling insights into the hardships of unemployment and poor housing. It also includes a personal account of Orwell's own progress towards socialism. Even before the book was published, Orwell decided to put actions before words and set off for Spain in 1936 to join the Republicans in the struggle against Franco's right-wing National-ists. The experience of fighting in the Spanish Civil War provided the raw material for an account of his involvement, written in the first person – *Homage to Catalonia* (1938).

During his time in Spain, Orwell was shot in the neck, after which he returned to England. During the Second World War he took a job making BBC propaganda for the Far East, but he soon quit and concentrated his energies on writing *Animal Farm* (1945), an allegorical, anti-Stalinist tale of a farmyard where the pigs take over from the humans, before gradually slipping into tyrannical and corrupt ways. The pigs' slogan – 'All animals are equal, but some animals are more equal than others' – is among the most famous lines of 20th-century literature.

Orwell's greatest contributions to the English language are found in his powerful political novel *Nineteen Eighty-Four* (1948). In this chilling warning against the perils of state control, which reveals an astonishingly truthful understanding of the cruelty and wickedness of how communism really worked, he introduced a plethora of suggestive concepts, including the Thought Police, Room 101, Big Brother, Doublespeak and Groupthink. The novel was completed shortly before Orwell died of tuberculosis at the age of forty-six, having suffered ill health for most of his adult life.

At the same time as writing his novels and other books, Orwell was producing an uninterrupted flow of columns, essays and book reviews. He dealt with all manner of topics. One of his finest essays, 'Politics and the English Language', was an extraordinary argument in which he linked lazy use of words with political oppression. But these complex ideas were always expressed in the most elegant, laconic phrases. Every essay he wrote, even when he was impassioned and angry, was delicately phrased and accessible to every reader.

Orwell left a huge body of work. His books have never been out of print since his death and collections of his essays continue to be published. Many of the ideas expressed in his novels are still as fresh today as ever. His bitter criticisms of the Soviet Union and the repressive nature of communism were fully vindicated by the collapse of the Soviet Union from the late 1980s. Orwell's astonishing clarity of vision, combined with an unerring ability to convey challenging ideas in ways that are accessible to all, has ensured that his standing as a great writer of and for the people is uncontested.

DENG XIAOPING

1904–1997

It doesn't matter if a cat is black or white, so long as it catches mice.

Deng Xiaoping

Deng was the paramount leader of China who transformed Mao Zedong's revolutionary communist state into today's resurgent superpower, ruled harshly by the communist oligarchy but empowered by a free-market economy. Deng's new China was soon strong enough to challenge America itself. Gritty, practical and sardonic, Deng was both a brutal Maoist enforcer and a survivor who endured wars, purges and palace coups to emerge as the ruler who has set the path of the world's most populous country. His nicknames describe him perfectly: the Steel Factory and the Needle Inside the Ball of Cotton.

In many ways, his reputation is underestimated: while Soviet President Mikhail Gorbachev oversaw the peaceful end of Soviet communist rule and the dismembering of the Soviet empire, he had wanted to keep the Soviet Union in place and reform it. Instead it fell apart; communism lost power – and Russia endured a decade of instability until prestige and order was restored by the authoritarian sovereignty of Vladimir Putin. Perhaps the most influential political titan of the late 20th century, Deng succeeded in guiding China towards his vision where his fellow communist leaders failed.

Born in Szechuan province in 1904, Deng was converted to Marxism as a young man: leaving home at sixteen, he studied in

France and after the Bolshevik Revolution in Russia, in Moscow. Returning to China in the late 1920s just as the right-wing Kuomintang (KMT) under Chiang Kai-shek turned on its communist allies in 1927, Deng threw in his lot with the communists – and Mao Zedong personally, a loyalty from which he never wavered. When the KMT embarked on its campaigns to destroy the communists, Deng endured the Long March under Chairman Mao Zedong.

For decades, Mao and his fellow communists lived a life of constant warfare with external enemies, internal purging and feuding – it was a rough school. Deng, who served as commissar and often effectively as commander of many Red Army units, was one of the veteran communist leaders along with his friend and patron Chou Enlai who gradually came to accept the total power that Mao, that master of manipulation, mercilessly and cunningly imposed with secret police terror and constant murderous purges. Mao himself liked and trusted few and tormented even his closest allies, but it seems that he respected Deng's evident competence and toughness.

After the Second World War and the civil war between the KMT and the communists during which he distinguished himself as a commander/commissar, Deng was one of the leaders of the communists who watched Mao declare the new People's Republic in 1949. He ran his home province Sichuan for several years, overseeing the killings and beatings of tens of thousands of so-called landlords – usually smallholding farmers. When 10 million in the province died during Mao's merciless Great Leap Forward, he praised its management.

Mao brought Deng to the capital as a vice-premier, promoting him as the general secretary of the Communist Party in 1957: he sent half a million intellectuals to labour camps.

But as Mao came under attack for his dangerously radical policies in the late 1950s, Deng was allied with President Liu

Shaochi, who appeared to challenge Maoist supremacy. Deng was never anything else but a Marxist and an extremely ruthless communist potentate but he was also pragmatic, a manager. It was in 1961 that he famously said in a speech that 'I don't care if a cat is black or white. It is a good mouse if it catches mice.'

In 1965, Mao launched his vicious, vindictive and destructive purge of China, the Cultural Revolution, designed to restore his own personal dictatorship, communist radicalism and liquidate the new party elite who had dared to challenge his absolute power. President Liu and many others were destroyed in this terrifying purge that threw China into chaos, supervised by Mao himself. Premier Chou Enlai managed to survive by cravenly agreeing to all Mao's brutal measures. Deng was fortunate: though he was sacked and sent to work in a factory as an ordinary worker, and his son was thrown by Red Guards out of a window and rendered paraplegic, Deng was not tortured or humiliated, a decision that had to come from Mao himself.

Mao's chosen successor was his chief ally in the Cultural Revolution, the talented but neurotic and vain Marshal Lin Biao, the vice-chairman, who, in an attempted coup, was killed flying towards Russia. As the old chairman, now ageing, ailing and senile, but still omnipotent, called a halt to the Cultural Revolution, he recognized that the country needed stable management. Lin Biao was dead; Chou was dying of cancer so Mao looked to Deng.

In 1974, Deng was brought back as first vice-premier and effective ruler of the country. But as Mao deteriorated, his wife Jiang Qing along with the rest of the radical faction she led – better known as the Gang of Four – realized that Deng represented a real danger to their plans to take power after the chairman's death.

Once again, Deng was purged. His old ally Premier Chou Enlai succumbed to cancer and Mao himself died, succeeded to everyone's surprise by a little-known provincial boss Hua Guofeng.

Deng, the leader of the political and military veterans, trusted by both Party and Red Army, led an effective coup against the Gang of Four, who were arrested, tried and imprisoned.

Henceforth he quickly emerged as the leader of China, effortlessly pushing Hua aside. Though he never felt the need for a full Maoist cult of personality nor for the full list of titles such as president, chairman or premier, it was soon clear that Deng was in charge, rechanneling the revolution to preserve absolute one-party communist control but freeing up the economy: 'To get rich is glorious!' he supposedly declared. Backed by his protégés such as General Secretary Zhao Ziyang and others, Deng, semi-retired, guided China from behind the scenes, enjoying only his position running the country's chess federation – and the chairmanship of the Party Military Commission which commanded the army. Under his guidance, China negotiated the return of Hong Kong and Macao and emerged as a new military, almost imperial, superpower as its economy boomed. But in 1989, the Soviet Union tottered; eastern Europe regained its freedom; the Iron Curtain was raised. When communist rule was challenged by thousands of students in Tiananmen Square, Deng faced the end of the party's monopoly on power and it was ultimately the decision of the paramount leader to crush the protests with total ruthlessness. The China of today – a harsh police state under a communist Party monopoly with an increasingly international imperialistic and economic reach – is Deng's China.

SCHINDLER

1908–1974

I hated the brutality, the sadism, and the insanity of Nazism. I just couldn't stand by and see people destroyed. I did what I could, what I had to do, what my conscience told me to do. That's all there is to it. Really, nothing more.

Oskar Schindler

A womanizing, heavy-drinking war profiteer, Oskar Schindler was responsible for one of history's greatest acts of selfless heroism. His decision to save over 1000 Jewish slave labourers from death at the hands of the Nazis has been immortalized in literature and film – an act of individual nobility that epitomizes the triumph of humanity over evil. Like Dickens's sinner-hero Sydney Carton in *A Tale of Two Cities*, Schindler demonstrates that real heroes are often not pious and conventional but worldly rogues, eccentrics and outsiders.

Oskar Schindler was an extravagant and genial businessman from Moravia, in what is now the Czech Republic. He was born into a wealthy family, but his various enterprises were destroyed by the Great Depression that spread through Europe in the 1930s. A wheeler-dealer who excelled at bribery and manipulation, Schindler became one of the first to profit from the Aryanization of German-occupied Poland. In 1939 he took over a Kraków factory from a Jewish industrialist and filled it with Jewish slave labour.

In the late 1930s, sensing which way the political wind was blowing, Schindler had worked for German intelligence – an action that had seen him briefly imprisoned in his native country. When the Germans invaded Czechoslovakia in 1938, Schindler, now set free, joined the Nazi Party. His boozy bonhomie earned him a swift rise. But after watching yet another Nazi raid on the Kraków Ghetto, which adjoined his factory, he decided to use his considerable influence to counteract his party's anti-Semitic policy and to save as many Jews as he could.

The very qualities that made Schindler a successful profiteer enabled him to save his workforce of over 1000 Jews. A consummate actor, Schindler used his charm to deflect his fellow Nazis from sending his Jews to the extermination camps. Gestapo officers arriving at his factory, demanding that he hand over workers with forged papers, would reel drunkenly out of his office three hours later without either workers or their papers. He was arrested twice for procuring black-market supplies for his Jews, but his bribes and his easy manner secured his release. 'Whatever it took to save a life, he did,' his lawyer later said. 'He worked the system extraordinarily well.'

When 300 of his female workers were sent by administrative error to Auschwitz, Schindler secured their release with a hefty bribe. He forbade anyone, including officials, to enter his factory without his express permission. He spent every night in his office, ready to intervene in case the Gestapo came. As the Nazis retreated and the 25,000-strong population of the nearby labour camp at Plaszów was sent to Auschwitz, Schindler pulled every string to have his factory and all his workers moved to Moravia. Even though he was now himself in danger, he stayed with his Jews until the Russians arrived in May 1945 and he knew that they were safe.

Schindler rarely talked about his motivation. As a child, his best friends had been the sons of a rabbi who lived nearby. 'It didn't mean anything to me that they were Jewish,' he said later when asked why he acted against Nazi policy, 'to me they were just human beings.' When pressed to explain his apparent volte-face, his reasoning was astounding in its simplicity: 'I believed that the Germans were doing wrong . . . when they started killing innocent people . . . I decided I am going to work against them and I am going to save as many as I can.' 'I knew the people who worked for me,' he told another. 'When you know people, you have to behave towards them like human beings.'

Many are still confounded by why this unlikely hero would sacrifice everything to save these people. But for Schindler, who began saving Jews long before the tide of war had turned, it was simply a matter of conscience. In the words of another man he saved: 'I don't know what his motives were, even though I knew him very well. I asked him and I never got a clear answer . . . but I don't give a damn. What's important is that he saved our lives.'

The opportunistic Schindler ended the war penniless. He spent his vast fortune to protect lives, even selling off his wife's jewels. His marriage to the long-suffering Emilie finally broke down in 1957. 'He gave his Jews everything,' she later said. 'And me nothing.' He was shunned in Germany after the war, his actions a constant challenge to the collective self-deception that nothing could have been done. His postwar business ventures flopped. The Jews whom Schindler had saved came to the support of their erstwhile benefactor. A Jewish organization funded his brief, unsuccessful stint as a farmer in Argentina and his short-lived German cement factory. From all over the world the Schindler Jews sent money. He died of liver failure in 1974. He is buried, according to his wishes, in Jerusalem, 'because my children are here'.

KIM IL SUNG, KIM JONG IL &

1912–1994   1941–2011

KIM JONG UN

1984–

The oppressed peoples can liberate themselves only through struggle. This is a simple and clear truth confirmed by history.

Kim Il Sung

Brutal, murderous, repressive and deluded by his own propaganda, Kim Il Sung was the self-styled 'Great Leader' and long-time dictator of North Korea. He led his country on a path to war, international isolation and economic collapse, and during his half-century in power North Korea became arguably the most totalitarian and surreal regime in the world. Indeed, long after his death he remains eternally the president – and the third generation of this hereditary dynasty continued to rule this bizarre and hellish state well into the 21st century.

Kim Il Sung was born Kim Sung Ju, the eldest of three sons of a Christian father. Japan had invaded Korea in 1910 and Kim grew up under Japanese rule until, in the 1920s, his family moved to Manchuria in northeast China, where he learnt Chinese and became interested in communism. After the Japanese invaded first Manchuria and then the rest of China, Kim joined the anti-Japanese resistance movement. During the Second World War he fled to the Soviet Union, where he underwent further military training and political indoctrination.

After Japan's defeat in 1945, Korea was divided into two zones of occupation, with the Soviets in the north and the Americans in the south. In 1946 the Soviets set up a satellite communist state in the north, with Kim as its head. While the south of the country proceeded with free elections, Kim immediately began imposing a repressive Stalinist totalitarian system; this included the creation of an all-powerful secret police, concentration camps, the redistribution of property, suppression of religion and killing of 'class enemies'.

In June 1950 – despite warnings from Stalin urging patience – Kim ordered his troops to invade South Korea in order to reunite the country, thereby triggering the Korean War. North Korea received logistical, financial and military support from China and the Soviet Union, while the South received backing from the UN, who sent an international force, mainly composed of US troops. Despite initial successes, the North Korean troops were soon beaten back. Kim was only rescued by massive Chinese intervention. After three years the conflict – which cost between 2 and 3 million lives – ended in a stalemate.

At home, Kim tightened his grip, banishing outside influence and liquidating internal enemies. An attempted coup by eleven party members in 1953 – the first of a number of such attempts – ended in a Stalinist show trial of the participants, who were swiftly executed. A purge of the party followed, and tens of thousands of Koreans were sent to labour camps – still a feature in North Korea.

Kim promoted an all-pervasive cult of personality centred around the *Juche* (or Kim Il Sungism), a political philosophy based on his own supposedly god-like qualities. According to the state media, Kim was the flawless Eternal Leader or Supreme Leader.

Meanwhile, with military spending taking up nearly a quarter of the country's budget, poverty became rife. In the 1990s food shortages led to famine, in which as many as 2 million people may have perished. The country maintained its utter isolation. Korea came to be seen as a rogue state and a sponsor of terrorism, particularly against its southern neighbour: North Korea was responsible for the assassination in 1983 of seventeen South Korean officials who had been on an official visit to Burma, and for the downing in 1987 of a South Korean commercial jet, resulting in the deaths of 115 people. North Korea went on to develop its own nuclear arsenal.

The ailing Kim Il Sung was already training one of his sons, Kim Jong Il to succeed him in a Marxist version of a hereditary monarchy. The younger Kim started to wield power in the Agitprop Department of the Central Committee at the end of the 1960s.

In 1980, he finally emerged as a Politburo member and his father named him as his heir apparent. By this time he had become a major influence, and had liquidated any hint of opposition, organizing terrorism abroad in the form of bombings and assassinations, as well as kidnappings. It was he who devised the South Korean jet bombing and the killings of South Korean ministers in Burma, and it was on his orders that Japanese citizens were kidnapped.

His own life was recast as a heroic story, in which he was the Son of God. His birth, in a log cabin in a revolutionary camp on holy Mount Paektu was portrayed as a sacred event foretold by a swallow, a double rainbow and a new star. In fact he had been born in 1942 in the Soviet Union. By 1991, he was already the real ruler of North Korea, having been promoted to supreme commander of the armed forces. In 1994, his father, the Great Leader, finally died aged eighty-two and Kim, hailed as Dear Father and Dear Leader, succeeded him as general secretary of the party (not the presidency, for Kim Il sung remained eternal immortal president).

Kim became the object of a preposterous cult – it was said

he could change the weather, melt snow and bring sunshine. He was, it was alleged, the author of no less than 1,500 books and six operas; he was the Glorious General from Heaven, and the Guiding Star of the 20th Century.

In reality, he was just 5 foot 2 inches tall and had a paunch that was accentuated by his ever-present green zip-up Mao tunic. He wore wrap-around dark glasses and platform shoes, and sported a bouffant quiff. Kim dined extravagantly on shark's-fin soup and sashimi sliced off living fish, drank Scotch whisky and always travelled on the armoured train given to his father by Stalin. He loved movies, especially *Godzilla*, and wrote a book *On the Art of Cinema*. Kim even went so far as to kidnap a director and some actors from South Korea to star in his movies.

His policies of *Juche* – self-reliance (actually isolation) – coupled with *Songun* – Military First (which meant maintaining a million soldiers, a nuclear programme and engaging in brinksmanship through murderous military skirmishes with South Korea) – led to famine amongst his people in the 1990s: one million, or 5 per cent, died. He ruled by brutal repression and terror. One in twenty of his people have been incarcerated in concentration camps, while 200,000 toiled within them at any given time.

Yet he was no buffoon, rather a skilful and ruthless manipulator. His acquisition of a nuclear device in 2006 allowed him to force the Americans into negotiations for food aid in order to save his regime. He ended the talks when he had extracted maximum concessions and supplies from his enemy, only to restart them again later when his authority looked to be under threat.

By 2004, the dictator started to suffer strokes or coronaries and in 2010 he chose his youngest son Kim Jong Un as heir apparent. In December 2011, the Dear Leader died of a heart attack on his train. He was hailed as Great Saint Born of Heaven and his son, aged just twenty-seven and with no political experience, was chosen as the Great Successor and appointed Supreme Commander and Chairman of the Party – and he is often referred to as the Marshal.

At the time of his succession, Kim Jong Un was the world's youngest head of state. A menace to the world, he has conducted ruthless purges against his own government and family, killing an uncle and ministers by firing anti-aircraft cannons at them, and poisoning his own half-brother in Kuala Lumpur airport. He has also procured nuclear weapons and intercontinental missiles to deliver them. Plump and awkward, the boy-king of North Korea promoted in equestrian statuary with his father and grandfather is a sadistic tyrant, a latter-day Nero, but also a cunning politician, determined to preserve his state, his clan and his own power – whatever the cost.

JFK

1917–1963

Democracy is a difficult kind of government. It requires the highest qualities of self-discipline, restraint, a willingness to make commitments and sacrifices for the general interest . . .

John F. Kennedy, speech in Dublin (28 June 1963)

The 35th president of the United States was a gifted and charismatic man, the youngest – after Teddy Roosevelt – to reach the White House, and the only Roman Catholic to do so. In the three short years of his presidency he gave America and the world a vision of a peaceful and prosperous future. His assassination in 1963 was met with grief across the globe.

John F. Kennedy was the son of Joe Kennedy, a ruthless self-made business tycoon who had made fortunes in whiskey during the Prohibition era and in movies and real estate afterwards. As President Roosevelt's ambassador to London, he was discredited by becoming a shameless appeaser of Nazi Germany. But his children overcame this stain on the family's reputation to become almost American royalty. His son John (Jack) Kennedy joined the US Navy in September 1941, shortly before the USA joined the war, and went on to serve in the Pacific theatre. He was decorated with the Navy and Marine Corps Medal for saving the crew of his PT (patrol torpedo) boat after it was rammed by a Japanese destroyer off the Solomon Islands.

Not long after leaving the navy, Kennedy entered politics, serving as a Democratic Party congressman between 1946 and 1952, when he was elected to the Senate. In 1960 he defeated Senator Lyndon B. Johnson of Texas to become the Democratic candidate for the presidency. Running with Johnson as his vice-presidential candidate, Kennedy beat the Republican Richard Nixon, partly as a result of his superior gift for public speaking and his ability to look good on TV. When he was inaugurated as president in 1961, he gave an inspirational speech: 'Ask not what your country can do for you,' he told his fellow Americans. 'Ask what you can do for your country.'

Kennedy's presidency was a glamorous one, full of youthful idealism, in which the White House played host to many artists and cultural figures. Kennedy himself was an obsessional, indeed priapic, lothario, having affairs with the film star Marilyn Monroe, society women and Mafia molls: he told British Prime Minister Harold Macmillan that if he did not have a woman every day, he suffered from headaches. None of this was known or revealed at the time; he and his elegant first lady Jackie created an American 'court' such that it came to be known as Camelot. Politically

Kennedy's presidency was dominated by the Cold War, the global struggle for supremacy between the democratic free world, led by America, and the communist dictatorships of the Soviet Union and its allies. In 1961 Kennedy authorized the CIA-led invasion of Cuba at the Bay of Pigs, a fiasco in which Cuban exiles unsuccessfully tried to overthrow Fidel Castro.

Matters escalated in 1962 with the Cuban Missile Crisis, in which Kennedy became involved in a nuclear stand-off with the Soviet leader, Nikita Khrushchev, spelling acute danger not only for America but also for the world.

Since the 1959 revolution Cuba had been ruled by Fidel Castro, a Soviet ally. Nikita Khrushchev, the Soviet leader, felt Russia was losing the arms race, so he recklessly bet his foreign policy on changing the balance of power. He had decided to place nuclear warheads in Cuba, which America traditionally considered part of its backyard.

On 14 October 1962 an American U-2 spy plane overflew Cuba, taking aerial photographs. The courage of a CIA spy in the Russian military, Colonel Oleg Penkovsky, who was later exposed and shot in 1963, enabled American analysts to identify medium-range ballistic missiles near San Cristóbal, only 90 miles (145km) from the coast of Florida.

President Kennedy was briefed on 16 October. The next day American military units began to move southeast. Meanwhile, a second U-2 mission identified further construction sites and between sixteen and thirty-two missiles already on Cuba. On 18 October, without revealing that he knew about the missiles, Kennedy warned the Soviet foreign minister, Andrei Gromyko, of the 'gravest consequences' should the Soviet Union introduce significant offensive weapons to the island.

Four days later, having ruled out an air strike against the missile sites, Kennedy went on national television to reveal the discovery of the Soviet missiles and announce a naval 'quarantine' (block-ade) of Cuba, which was only to be lifted when the weapons were removed. On 24 October American ships moved into position. Though Khrushchev declared the blockade illegal, Soviet freighters heading for Cuba stopped dead in the water.

In an exchange of telegrams between Kennedy and Khrushchev that evening, neither side gave ground. But American military defences were moved, for the only time in history, to DEFCON 2, a heightened state of readiness for imminent attack.

On 25 October the United Nations called for a cooling-off period between America and the Soviet Union. Kennedy firmly refused. The next day Khrushchev offered to remove the missiles in exchange for American assurances not to invade Cuba.

On 27 October Khrushchev made another offer: removal of Soviet missiles from Cuba in exchange for the removal of Ameri-can missiles from Turkey, which bordered the Soviet Union. Then, around noon, a U-2 spy plane was shot down over Cuba by a Soviet missile, and the pilot killed. At a meeting with his military advisers, Kennedy agreed to hold back from an immediate mili-tary response and to offer terms in accordance with Khrushchev's initial suggestion. But there was no expectation that Khrushchev would now accept. Kennedy warned America's NATO allies to expect war the next day.

However, when the next day dawned, Khrushchev announced that the Soviet Union would remove its weapons from Cuba. Ken-nedy had negotiated a deal whereby the US missiles in Turkey would be removed in secret. Though few in Moscow, Washington, Cuba or Turkey were entirely satisfied with the outcome, the crisis was over.

Kennedy emerged from the crisis with immense credit. He had been tough but not rash and had called Khrushchev's bluff. The Soviet leader, by contrast, was criticized for his recklessness and lost face: in 1964 he was overthrown in a Kremlin coup by Leonid

Brezhnev. The rest of the world was simply relieved that the greatest nuclear crisis in history had somehow been averted.

Khrushchev backed down over Cuba, but in 1963 there were still great tensions in Germany, where Western and Soviet forces faced each other on either side of the divided country. Kennedy gave one of the great speeches of modern times in Berlin, where the Soviets had recently built the infamous wall to prevent East Germans escaping to the West. 'Freedom has many difficulties and democracy is not perfect, but we have never had to put up a wall to keep our people in,' he said. In the same speech, he used the famous phrase '*Ich bin ein Berliner*,' calling for solidarity across the Western world.

As well as being involved in a military stand-off, the USA and the Soviet Union were in competition in the space race. In 1961 Kennedy persuaded Congress to vote $22 billion to put an American on the moon before the end of the 1960s. When Neil Armstrong and Buzz Aldrin landed on the moon in 1969, it was testament to Kennedy's far-sighted commitment to space exploration. Less far-sighted was his commitment to increasing amounts of military support for South Vietnam in its battle with the communist North, a policy that was to mire America in a decade-long conflict that in the end it had to abandon. However, there is some evidence that Kennedy, had he lived, planned to withdraw from Vietnam after the 1964 election.

On the home front, Kennedy was initially slow to give his complete backing to the civil rights movement. But in 1962 he sent 3000 troops to the University of Mississippi to allow a black student, James Meredith, to enrol for classes. By 1963 he had thrown his whole weight behind civil rights and gave a stirring speech on national television. After his death, the Civil Rights Act of 1964, which he had proposed, became law.

Kennedy's assassination in Dallas, Texas, in 1963 was a moment that stopped the world in its tracks. He was gunned down while being driven through the city in an open-topped car, probably by Lee Harvey Oswald, who was himself murdered days later by Jack Ruby, a dubious nightclub operator. The wealth of conspiracy theories provoked by Kennedy's death is testament to the glamorous and optimistic effect that this young and charismatic president had on the world he helped save from annihilation.

NASSER

1918–70

I have been a conspirator for so long that I mistrust all around me.

Gamal Abdul Nasser

Gamal Abdul Nasser was the most influential Middle Eastern leader of the mid-twentieth century, the dictator of Egypt, the region's most powerful country, and perhaps the most popular Arab potentate since Saladin. Yet his career ended in defeat and disappointment and the failure of his secular pan-Arabism opened the door to a new Islamic fundamentalism. Nevertheless for almost twenty years he was for many Arabs *El Rais* – the Boss.

Born in a village near Cairo, Nasser was the son of a post office worker. He was educated in Alexandria, where he lived with his grandmother and joined the army in 1937. Egypt was then ruled by the Albanian dynasty of kings descended from Mehmet Ali, the Ottoman warlord and pasha who seized control of the county after Napoleon Bonaparte's invasion, becoming first khedives then sultans and finally kings of Egypt. The country was actually run by a hybrid elite of Ottomans and Albanians as well as Egyptians

– but even this was under the domination of Britain, which had controlled Egypt since 1882. Reading widely everything from the Koran to Dickens, Nasser was political from an early age, loathing the control of the British over Egyptian life.

Studying at the military academy, he met his political ally Abdul Hakim Amer, a genial, vain, bombastic and flamboyant fellow officer with whom he served in Sudan. Hoping for a Nazi victory to overthrow British rule in Egypt, he and Amer worked to put together a group of like-minded officers. Faced with the UN plan to partition Palestine between Jewish and Arab states, Nasser was tempted to fight on the Arab side and finally got his chance when King Farouk of Egypt, obese, incompetent and debauched, joined the other countries of the Arab League in an attack on the nascent Jewish state of Israel. The Egyptians, including Nasser, advanced fast into the Negev but the young officer witnessed the ineptitude of the king and his officers as well as the lack of equipment and absence of proper preparation.

By August 1948, Nasser was the deputy commander of Egyptian units surrounded by the Israelis in the so-called Falluja Pocket. It was a formative experience: Nasser was humiliated by the disastrous war effort and on his return he formed with his friend Amer and others the Association of Free Officers. Nasser consulted with the Muslim Brotherhood, but concluded early on that their Islamic programme clashed with his own Arab nationalism. The Free Officers selected General Muhammad Neguib to be their front man.

When Nasser heard in May 1952 that Farouk was planning to arrest the Free Officers, he launched an almost bloodless *coup d'état*, allowing the king to depart from Alexandria in his yacht with full honours. The revolutionaries were unsure whether to create a democracy or a military regime. Since Nasser was only a lieutenant colonel, Neguib became president of the new Egyptian

Republic, but real power was in the hands of the Revolutionary Command Council, which was effectively controlled by Nasser in his role as deputy chairman.

In 1954, as Nasser pushed land reforms and demanded that the alarmed British should leave the Suez Canal, he clashed with the more moderate Neguib. But he asserted his confidence by taking real power as prime minister. Nasser's passionate and elegant oratory was already captivating Egyptian audiences. In October, as Nasser addressed a huge crowd in Alexandria, a young Muslim Brother tried to assassinate him but Nasser defiantly and courageously continued his speech:

My countrymen, my blood spills for you and for Egypt. I will live for your sake and die for the sake of your freedom and honor. Let them kill me; it does not concern me so long as I have instilled pride, honour and freedom in you. If Gamal Abdel Nasser should die, each of you shall be Gamal Abdel Nasser . . . Gamal Abdel Nasser is of you and from you and he is willing to sacrifice his life for the nation.

On his return to Cairo, Neguib was deposed; Nasser became the unrivalled president, a position he retained for the next fifteen turbulent years. He appointed his crony Amer commander-in-chief of the army before launching a massive crackdown on communists and, above all, the Muslim Brotherhood. He arrested 20,000 of their members and had their leader and ideologue Sayyid Qutb executed.

Henceforth Nasser, with his tall good looks and superb oratory, was immensely popular, but it was his embrace of pan-Arabist nationalism that excited not just Egyptians but the entire Arab world, which was emerging from a century of foreign domination. Nonetheless he ruled an effective one-party state with the aid of a growing and brutal secret police, backed by an ever more corrupt and oligarchical military junta who swiftly became rich (though he himself had no interest in material matters).

Nasser committed himself to the non-aligned movement, emerging as its leader alongside Marshal Tito of Yugoslavia and Nehru of India. In 1956 Nasser announced the nationalisation of the Suez Canal, outraging British Prime Minister Anthony Eden who, facing the decline of British imperial power, now saw Nasser as a new Hitler. The British responded by putting together a secret deal with the French and the Israelis to attack and destroy Nasser. The Israelis would invade Sinai; the Anglo-French would then 'intervene'. The Israelis succeded in a dazzling campaign to take Sinai but the British intervention was a disaster and US President Eisenhower condemned it. The Israelis were forced to withdraw and it marked the end of British imperial influence in the Middle East.

Nasser's prestige was at its height: his speeches and radio stations beamed out anti-imperialist, anti-Zionist propaganda promising the Arabs pride and grandeur at last. His pan-Arabist ideas excited the Arab people across the region and inspired nationalist officers in most Arab countries. In Jordan, Iraq, Syria, Yemen and even in Saudi Arabia, the regimes were shaken by Nasserist infiltration. In 1958, sympathetic officers in Iraq massacred King Faisal II and his family and created an Iraqi republic on the Nasserist model. In Jordan, King Hussein scarcely clung on to power as Nasserist officers dominated the army. King Saud of Arabia ordered Nasser's assassination, but the plot was exposed and he was deposed, replaced by his brother Faisal.

Syria and Egypt formed a United Arab Republic under Nasser as president – though it soon fell apart. Nasser flew to Moscow to meet Soviet leader Nikita Khrushchev, alarming the Americans: he was anti-communist and persecuted Egyptian Marxists, but despite his non-aligned leadership, he leant clearly towards the Soviets. A coup in North Yemen by Nasserist officers led to Nasser sending Egyptian troops to fight royalist forces backed by the Saudis.

In Egypt, Nasser – omnipotent, isolated and ill – came to understand that his regime had become a corrupt dictatorship with its rich army elite and its secret police. Above all he realized that Field Marshal Amer – powerful, hedonistic, and a drug addict – had failed to create a strong army. In 1967, Syrian clashes with Israel challenged Nasser, the most powerful Arab leader of the greatest Arab country, to live up to his years of bombast. Soviet leaders warned that Israel planned an attack on Syria – but this was utterly false.

Nasser probably hoped to raise the tension and demonstrate Egyptian power without actually fighting Israel. He expelled UN peacekeepers from Sinai and closed the Straits of Tiran, promising a victorious war and the massacre of the Jews of Israel. At the same time, he allowed Amer to move Egyptian forces up into Sinai and prepare an attack while his officers assumed control of the Syrian and Jordanian armies. At the last moment, he panicked and ordered Amer to desist but the damage was done: Israelis were in a state of existential terror, convinced a second Holocaust was upon them. The prime minister Levi Eshkol was dithering; the chief of staff General Yitzak Rabin had a breakdown. Finally Eshkol brought Moshe Dayan, former general and now politician, famous for his cool intelligence and his trademark black eye- patch into the government as defence minister. Faced with an apparently imminent Egyptian attack coordinated with Syria and Jordan, Dayan launched a pre-emptive strike, wiping out the Egyptian air force in minutes and defeating Egyptian troops on the ground. Syrian and Jordanian forces attacked Israel, which defeated both in turn – while Egypt under Nasser and Amer still claimed victory. In fact Nasser's clumsy brinkmanship and bullying domination of the other Arab countries, combined with Amer's incompetence, had brought about a defeat even greater than that suffered by King Farouk.

Nasser offered to resign but vast crowds in Cairo insisted he remain president. However he was a broken man, dying of a massive heart attack in 1970, succeeded by his vice president, Anwar Sadat, who avenged Nasser's defeat in his Yom Kippur War against Israel in 1973. This allowed Sadat to make peace with Israel – a brave act which he paid for with his life, assassinated in 1981. His successor, air force general Hosni Mubarak, was overthrown in the Arab Spring of 2011 which led to the election of a Muslim Brotherhood president. But in the tradition of Nasser, the army commander Abdel Fattah al-Sisi seized power. Nasser remains the prototype for the ideal ruler in the greatest Arab nation.

MANDELA

1918–2013

I have fought against white domination, and I have fought against black domination. I have cherished the idea of a democratic and free society in which all persons live together in harmony and with equal opportunities. It is an ideal which I hope to live for and to achieve. But if needs be it is an ideal for which I am prepared to die.

Nelson Mandela, defending himself at the
Rivonia Trial (1964)

In his fight for freedom against South Africa's apartheid system Nelson Mandela inspired millions across the world with his courage, endurance and nobility of spirit. The transfer of South Africa from apartheid to black rule could have led to vindictive massacres, similar to the slaughter when India became independent, but, thanks to one politician, this revolution was essentially tolerant, peaceful, orderly and bloodless. This is the towering achievement of a man who embodies South Africa's journey towards democracy and racial equality.

On 11 February 1990 Nelson Mandela walked out of the gates of the Victor Verster Prison in the Dwars Valley near Cape Town. It was the first time that he had been free for twenty-seven years, a triumph of hope that signified the beginning of a new era for a country riven by apartheid since 1948. It was Mandela who in 1994 became South Africa's first democratically elected president.

The privileged son of a Tembu chieftain of royal descent, Mandela grew up in rural Transkei and had a boarding-school education that exposed him to little of the discrimination that most of South Africa's black population faced. Before Mandela fled his home to avoid an arranged marriage, his most significant experience of oppression had been his naming as Nelson by a primary-school teacher who found his African name too difficult to pronounce.

But on arrival in Johannesburg the young lawyer began to live up to his birth name: Rolihlahla or troublemaker. Mandela became one of the first freedom fighters for the African National Congress (ANC). He was repeatedly arrested and imprisoned for his non-violent protests throughout the 1950s. When the ANC was outlawed, Mandela – the 'Black Pimpernel' – went on the run, drumming up overseas support and military training for the organization. In 1961 he became the leader of the ANC terrorist wing, Umkhonto we Sizwe (Spear of the Nation), planning violence against military/government targets. He regarded terror as a last resort to be used only when peaceful methods seemed hopeless, but he later confessed that the increasingly violent ANC terror and guerrilla campaigns also abused human rights. After being arrested and jailed in 1962 for leaving the country, in the Rivonia Trial of 1964 Mandela was sentenced to life imprisonment.

Mandela's speech from the dock echoed through the townships from the Cape to the Paarl. It helped to politicize a people who had had every opportunity for education, advancement and independence taken away from them by the apartheid policies of the Afrikaner Nationalist government, which had crushed their rights and dignity. His words gave them hope.

Mandela was a man of awesome obduracy. Sentenced to hard labour in a stone quarry on Robben Island, Mandela transformed his prison camp into the 'Island University', assigning instructors to educate the teams of inmates as they toiled at their back-breaking work. He put on plays and distributed books to fill the hours. After twenty-seven years' waiting, Mandela delayed his final departure from prison by one more day: 'They are going to release me the way I want to be released,' he explained, 'not the way they want me to be released.'

As Mandela's stature grew across the world, the apartheid government, under hardliners like P.W. Botha, tried to do deals with this prisoner who had become their Achilles heel. They offered to release him if he would denounce the ANC; Mandela refused: 'Until my people are free, I can never be free.' Peace takes men of vision and courage on both sides, and in 1989 the new South African president, F.W. de Klerk, was courageous enough to take the necessary risks. In 1990 he lifted the ban on the ANC just days before he released Mandela. And once free, Mandela almost immediately renounced violent action, thus making the vow he had refused to undertake while imprisoned.

Mandela has never indulged in racism. At his trial he called for freedom regardless of colour, and on his release he refused to stir up racial tensions. As president (1994–9) he included representatives of all ethnic groups in his multi-party government. He established the Truth and Reconciliation Commission to investigate human rights abuses. The Madiba – the honorific tribal name by which South Africans know him – shared the 1993 Nobel Peace Prize with de Klerk. His one embarrassment was the violent gangsterism of his wife Winnie, whom he divorced. He later married the widow of President Machel of Mozambique and retired to his home village, revered by all.

'My life is the struggle,' said Mandela – but in a continent cursed by murderous dictators he was sadly unique, and in South Africa itself, his inept and corrupt successors have corroded the legacy of his achievements.

THE SHAH OF IRAN

1919–1980

My advisers built a wall between myself and my people. I didn't realize what was happening. When I woke up, I had lost my people.
                                                            Muhammad Reza Pahlavi

Always known simply as the shah, or king, Muhammad Reza Pahlavi was for almost forty years the ruler of Iran, the nation that, along with Egypt, is usually the most important country in the Near East. A Western ally, an Iranian nationalist, an absolutist king, a revolutionary modernizer, he gradually emerged as the key potentate in the region as he became the effective dictator of a country made vastly rich by oil revenues. He enjoyed great successes in his reforms and modernization, his intentions were admirable – yet he was a flawed authoritarian, limited by his personality, and by the corruption and repression of his regime. His achievements were overshadowed by his downfall.

His family had risen from literally nothing to the imperial throne itself. Muhammad was the eldest son of Reza Shah, a low-born Persian army officer who climbed to the rank of general in a Cossack regiment trained for the Qajar shahs of Iran by Russian officers. The father was ramrod straight, tall, harsh and ambitious but scarcely educated. However the last shahs of the Qajar dynasty of kings had lost control of their country, which was dominated by court intrigues, tribal rebellions, economic chaos, rampant warlordism, ethnic strife, democratic revolutions, Communism, separatism and foreign interference – especially by Britain and Russia, the two dominant imperial powers. Finally in 1921, the general marched his Cossacks into Teheran and seized power, first as minister of war. By 1923 he was ruling Iran and in 1925, as the last Qajar shah left for exile, the Cossack general raised himself to shah of the Imperial State of Iran, founding the Pahlavi dynasty.

An admirer of Atatürk, Reza Shah ruled harshly and energetically, modernizing the country, persecuting any opposition, reuniting the separatist provinces and diminishing the power of Shiite clergy whenever possible. The crown prince was educated at La Rosey in Switzerland, where he embraced Western culture and skiing. But in 1941, as he tried to chart a course between Nazi Germany and the Allies, Britain and Soviet Russia, Reza Shah disastrously miscalculated the security of his own position. The Allies could not risk the loss of Iran and its oil to Nazi Germany so they invaded the country, partitioned it and sent Reza Shah into exile in South Africa, where he died. However, unsure what regime to install, they allowed Reza to abdicate in favour of his young son Muhammad, whose reign would last for thirty-seven years.

During the war, the young Shah had little choice but to bow before Russian and British interests but from the very beginning he started to try to impose his own will on government. When the Allies finally withdrew from Iran after the war, he became to assert himself politically. Throughout his long career, he faced Western intervention based on oil interests, Soviet Russian intrigue, communist subversion, and the threat of the Shiite clergy. Growing up paranoid and trusting very few, the shah generally feared Anglo-American intrigue and the communist threat more than the Shiite Ayatollahs. He faced repeated coup attempts from all sides, his prime ministers and ministers were assassinated and he himself survived several attempts to take his life with great courage.

Overall, despite the catastrophic end of his career, his ability to survive and constantly increase his power and influence were signs of not just persistence but also political cunning. Yet his personality was a strange mixture of timidity and shyness, overweening arrogance and delusion, ruthless realpolitik, driving ambition and sensual hedonism. His judgement of personalities was often dire, his protection of corrupt relations and aides notorious, and his methods of clandestine espionage and secret police repression ultimately counterproductive. His will to power was strong, yet at times of crisis, he was often timid and indecisive, lacking confidence.

Faced with powerful prime ministers often imposed by foreign powers, the shah patiently bided his time, waiting for the chance to destroy these overmighty rivals. He carefully husbanded his powers to dismiss ministers and to command the army. By the late 1940s, he faced a new challenge from his prime minister, Dr Muhammad Mossadeq, a wealthy and aged feudal landowner, famous for wearing pyjamas during the day, a habit that shocked Western leaders, and for his demagogic nationalism that demanded the nationalization of Western oil interests. The shah hated Mossadeq, who was also alarming Britain and America. In 1952, the shah planned to dismiss Mossadeq and appoint a new prime minister, General Fazlolah Zahedi, but the coup, backed by the British and American secret services, particularly CIA operative Kermit Roosevelt, initially stalled. The shah fled to Iraq and then Italy, returning once General Zahedi had overthrown Mossadeq.

Now the shah worked to rid himself of Zahedi too. By the late 1950s, the shah had become totally dominant in Iran, a dominance that became an enlightened royal dictatorship. American President J.F. Kennedy was sceptical of the shah, regarding him as a dictator but gradually US leaders came to see him as an ally. The shah never lost his paranoia about American and British troublemaking, always maintaining good relations with the Soviets as a threat and insurance policy.

He now launched his White Revolution, a modernizing programme of high technology, land reform, female rights and suffrage, diminishing of Shiite clerical control, education, and industrialization. When the Shiite ayotollahs resisted this programme in a series of riots between 1961 and 1962, the shah appointed his closest ally Asodollah Alam prime minister and allowed him to use the army to suppress the rebellion. This success over the clergy gave the shah and his top aides the illusion that they had triumphed over the ayatollahs.

Meanwhile he built up a formidible military machine, funded by America, to become the self-appointed guardian of the Gulf and a Near Eastern military great power. At home, he used his secret police, SAVAK, to keep the communists, nationalists and the clergy under control but human rights abuse and routine torture, made the regime unpopular. Worse, the rise in the oil price had given the shah endless revenues to pursue grandiose schemes and buy more American arms, even starting a nuclear

programme. The oil riches brought rampant corruption and os-
tantatious decadence. The Shah himself dominated every decision
and every part of Iranian life but the imperial family were notorious for their corruption.

As a young man he had married Princess Fawzia, sister of
Farouk, last king of Egypt, but this had ended in divorce. He then
married a young Iranian-German girl named Soraya who was
perhaps the true love of his life but she was unable to have children. Thirdly and happily the Shah married Farah Diba, a pretty
Iranian student with whom he had a son and heir as well as several
daughters. But his own secret love life became notorious. As the
diaries of his minister of court (and sometime prime minister)
Alam reveal, he regarded his sexual adventures as essential to his
well-being under great stress: he was never without an array of
mistresses and the beautiful courtesans of the Madame Claude
agency of Paris were regularly flown in for his pleasure.

But the Alam diaries also reveal his increasing megaloma-
niacal delusions as he was spoilt by international successs,
domestic flattery and oil wealth. In 1971, in a £100 million folly
of imperial hubris and French catering, he chose to celebrate
not the Persian relationship with Islam but the 2500th anniversary of the Iranian empire founded by Cyrus the Great: these
Persepolis parties damaged his reputation further. However
the shah – now at the point of his greatest power and success –
was actually secretly suffering from cancer. Furthermore, the
very success of his reforms – in education, in the economy,
in land reform – had planted the seeds of his destruction: a
poverty-stricken middle class with educational pretensions but
resentment of imperial cronies and their corruption; students and
liberals tortured by SAVAK; thousands of ex-peasants who had
moved to Teheran to enjoy the new boom only to be forgotten
in vast slums, where they were co-opted and cared for by Islamic

preachers and organizations; and a determined and organized movement of Islamic Shiite fundamentalism under the control of the exiled Ayatollah Khomeini. The inept Jimmy Carter undermined the shah further with his comments on human rights in Iran. When the riots and protests intensified in late 1978, the Shah was oddly listless and distracted, lacking the will to order a full crackdown: he simply did not wish to shed any more blood. In early 1979, as he lost control of the streets, the shah flew away 'on holiday', never to return. Pursued by the new Iranian regime, betrayed by the Americans and forced to move from country to country as he died of cancer, his end was a Shakespearean tragedy.

POL POT: CAMBODIA'S KILLING FIELDS

1925–1998

Pol Pot does not believe in God, but he thinks that heaven, destiny, wants him to guide Cambodia the way he thinks it the best for Cambodia . . . Pol Pot is mad . . . like Hitler.

Prince Norodom Sihanouk, former ruler of Cambodia

Pol Pot, the communist Khmer Rouge leader who created the democidal hell known as Democratic Kampuchea, only ruled Cambodia for four years, but in that short time he murdered millions of innocent people – half the population – impoverished the country, killed all intellectuals, even people who wore spectacles, and tried to restart time at a diabolic Year Zero.

Born as Saloth Sar, Pol Pot (a revolutionary name he adopted in

1963) was the son of a wealthy farmer. His family were courtiers to the Cambodian royal family and in 1931, as a child of six, he moved to the capital city, Phnom Penh, to live with his brother, an official at the royal palace, and was educated at Catholic and French schools. In 1949 he went to Paris on a scholarship to study electronics, and became involved with the French Communist Party and with other left-wing Cambodian students studying in Paris. Pol Pot was never academically inclined and was forced to return home after failing his exams.

After a spell as a teacher, in 1963 Pol Pot began to devote all his energy to revolutionary activities. That same year he was appointed head of the Workers' Party of Kampuchea – effectively the Cambodian communist party, also referred to as the Khmer Rouge, which strongly opposed the existing government of Prince Norodom Sihanouk. The prince – and sometime king – had led the country with irresponsible self-indulgence since independence from France in 1953. Pol Pot forged links with North Vietnam and China, which he visited in 1966. He was impressed with Chairman Mao's Cultural Revolution. Indeed Mao was to be his main patron and hero. The following year he spent time with a hill tribe in northeastern Cambodia, and was impressed by the simplicity of peasant life, uncorrupted by the city.

In 1968 the Khmer Rouge launched an insurrection, seizing the mountainous region on the border with Vietnam. The United States, embroiled in the Vietnam War and fearing that North Vietnamese troops were using Cambodia as a safe haven, began a bombing campaign, which radicalized Cambodia in Pol Pot's favour. In 1970, Prince Sihanouk was overthrown in a right-wing coup by former defence minister Lon Nol. The Khmer Rouge's shadowy army of guerrillas in black pyjamas soon controlled the countryside.

On 17 April 1975 the capital finally fell to the Khmer Rouge.

Pol Pot – ruling with a tiny clique of comrades such as Ieng Sary and Khieu Samphan under the anonymous cover of the Organization – declared that 1975 was 'Year Zero' and started to purge Cambodia of all non-communist influences. All foreigners were expelled, newspapers were outlawed and large numbers of people with the merest taint of association with the old regime – including all religious leaders, whether Buddhist, Christian or Muslim – were executed. There were even reports of people being killed because they wore spectacles – a sign of 'bourgeois intellectuals'.

Pol Pot – now known as Brother Number One – then embarked on an insane and doomed attempt to turn Cambodia into an agrarian utopia. The cities were cleared of their inhabitants, who were forced to live in agricultural communes in the countryside. In terrible conditions, with food shortages and crippling hard labour, these communes soon became known as the Killing Fields, where several million innocent Cambodians were executed. Despite a massive shortfall in the harvest of 1977 and rising famine, the regime arrogantly rejected the offer of outside aid.

The capital, Phnom Penh, once a vibrant city of 2 million people, became a ghost town. Following Chairman Mao's dictum that the peasant was the true proletarian, Pol Pot believed that the city was a corrupting entity, a haven for the bourgeoisie, capitalists and foreign influences.

City dwellers were marched at gunpoint to the countryside as part of the plans of the new regime to abolish cash payments and turn Cambodia into a self-sufficient communist society, where everyone worked the soil. The regime made a distinction between those with 'full rights' (who had originally lived off the land) and 'depositees' taken from the city, many of whom were massacred outright. Those depositees – capitalists, intellectuals and people who had regular contact with the outside world – who could not be 're-educated' in the ways of the revolution, were tortured and killed at a number of concentration camps, such as the S-21 prison camp (also known as Strychnine Hill), or taken straight to the Killing Fields, where their rations were so small that they could not survive. Thousands were forced to dig their own graves before Khmer Rouge soldiers beat their weary bodies with iron bars, axes and hammers until they died. The soldiers had been instructed not to waste bullets.

Those who were spared immediate execution became slave labourers in the programme of agrarian collectivization. Hundreds of thousands of civilians – often uprooted and separated from their families – were worked to death, or starved because of a lack of rations. Many more were executed in the fields for the most minor indiscretions – such as engaging in sexual relations, complaining about conditions, stealing food or espousing religious beliefs.

Some of the Killing Fields containing mass graves have now been preserved as a testimony to the genocide perpetrated by Pol Pot and his followers. The most infamous of them is Choeung Ek, where 8895 bodies were discovered after the fall of the regime.

The country was now riddled with spies and informers, and even children were encouraged to inform on their parents. Pol Pot went on to conduct purges within the Khmer Rouge itself, leading to the execution of more than 200,000 members.

External enemies proved more difficult to suppress, however. With only China maintaining support for the regime, Cambodia become embroiled in a conflict with Vietnam, whose forces invaded and captured Phnom Penh on 7 January 1979, forcing Pol Pot and the Khmer Rouge to flee to the western regions and over the border into Thailand. The new Vietnamese-controlled regime tried Pol Pot in absentia for genocide and sentenced him to death. Undeterred, Pol Pot directed an aggressive guerrilla war against the new regime, and kept an iron grip on the Khmer Rouge. As late as 1997 he ordered the execution of his colleague Song Sen, along with his family, on suspicion of collaborating with Cambodian government forces. Shortly afterwards he himself was arrested by another senior Khmer Rouge figure, and sentenced to life imprisonment, dying in April 1998 of heart failure.

In his murderous, almost psychotic, schemes for a communist utopia, Pol Pot, Brother Number One, outran anything in George Orwell's imagination. During a reign of just under four years, he oversaw the deaths of between two and five million men, women and children – over a third of the entire population of Cambodia.

THATCHER

1925–2013

I am extraordinarily patient, provided I get my own way in the end.

Margaret Thatcher

Margaret Thatcher first entered Parliament in 1959, making her maiden speech a year later. Interviewed in 1970, by that time education secretary, she said, 'It will be years before a woman either leads the Conservative Party or becomes prime minister. I don't see it happening in my time.' Nine years later she succeeded Labour's James Callaghan as prime minister and went on to spend eleven years and 209 days at 10 Downing Street, during which time she transformed the British political, economic and social landscape. She was the longest-serving prime minister for more than 150 years and the first woman to hold the post in Britain.

Born Margaret Roberts in 1925, daughter of a Grantham shopkeeper who was also a Methodist lay preacher and a town alderman, she was grammar-school educated and middle class. After a scholarship to Oxford and a brief career as a research chemist (during which she helped to develop the first soft ice cream), she trained as a barrister. She took the Conservative seat of Finchley in the 1959 election, encouraged by Denis, her shrewd, wealthy businessman husband, who steadfastly supported her career. The very qualities for which the company ICI had criticized her in a post-university interview, reporting that 'this woman is headstrong, obstinate and dangerously self-opinionated', surely aided her swift ascent at Westminster.

Emerging to lead the party in 1975, as the dark horse challenger to the then leader Edward Heath, she was at first conciliatory but gradually moved towards radical free-market policies in opposition, as the country under the Labour government succumbed to waves of industrial strikes, culminating in the so-called Winter of Discontent. This was enough to win the conservatives the general election of 1979, and Margaret Thatcher became prime minister. Britain then was rotten and enfeebled, the sick man of Europe, but she rejuvenated the country.

With the Labour Party beset by extremism and in disarray, Thatcher's brand of non-paternalistic conservatism appealed to aspirational working-class voters, and she would win two more elections.

'The lady's not for turning,' she declared famously at her party conference in October 1980, when all around her were encouraging compromise. She unhesitatingly broke with what she saw as political defeatism in the years since 1945, and successfully injected a new Churchillian pride and vigour into national life. She privatized badly run state industries, trying to roll back state involvement in the economy and people's lives. Her declaration that 'there is no such thing as society' is frequently taken out of context. But, none-theless, she staunchly believed that the individual should bear the burden of responsibility for his or her welfare.

When the Argentine military junta invaded the Falkland Islands in 1982, it seemed impossible that Britain could launch a war across 8000 miles of ocean; but Thatcher ordered the creation of a task force, inspired the nation to defeat tyrannical aggression, and reconquered the Falklands.

Her political partner abroad was Ronald Reagan, US president 1981–9, a genial unintellectual ex-actor, much mocked in Europe, though he was a superb orator. Ironically, with his clear, big ideals and gentle charm, and despite the folly of the Iran Contra scandal, he turned out to be one of the greatest modern presidents, his hatred of Soviet totalitarianism – the 'Evil Empire' – leading to the arms race that won the Cold War and in turn to the dissolution of the Soviet Empire. Reagan died in 2004, but his diaries attest to his close partnership with Thatcher. She shared Reagan's anti-Sovietism, earning the nickname the Iron Lady from the Soviet press, which she relished. (French President François Mitterrand once described her as having the 'eyes of Caligula and the mouth of Marilyn Monroe', a unique mixture of aggression and femininity that was frequently caricatured by satirists.) Reagan and Thatcher engaged with the new Soviet leader, Mikhail Gorbachev, whom she called 'someone we can do business with', encouraging his reforms and retreat from oppression and empire.

In 1984–5 she was faced with the miners' strike, launched in response to plans to close many pits. This strike, which she regarded as an attempt to topple her government, was quelled by wearing the miners down, breaking the grip of trade unionism, and mobilizing police and army to control rioting strikers. It was a test of her leadership but also the final attempt by undemocratic trade unions to dominate the British government using strikes as blackmail.

But later her new Community Charge (dubbed the Poll Tax) caused riots. Her opposition to closer cooperation within the European Community undermined her credibility at a point when her chancellor had already resigned. When her deputy, Geoffrey Howe, resigned, his speech triggered a 1990 Conservative leadership election. She was overthrown by a palace coup, abandoned by almost all of her cabinet, and left Downing Street in tears. Baroness Thatcher took her seat in the House of Lords two years later, her husband receiving a baronetcy.

With President Reagan, Thatcher was instrumental in engineering the triumph of capitalist democracies over communism in the Cold War; she helped to draw back the Iron Curtain and gave freedom to millions. She won a seemingly impossible war, transformed sclerotic Britain into a healthy and reinvigorated country, made London Europe's financial centre, broke the power of the unions, and became a global political star. There was no one else like her. Labour prime minister Tony Blair admitted he was, in many ways, her heir. No British prime minister of modern times provokes such strong views: she is still hated by the Left. But if you live in Britain today, the society around you is in no small part a creation of Margaret Thatcher, the greatest British leader since Churchill.

ANNE FRANK

1929–1945

I hear the ever approaching thunder, which will destroy us too,
I can feel the suffering of millions and yet, if I look up into the
heavens, I think that it will all come right, that this cruelty too
will end, and that peace and tranquillity will return again.

Anne Frank (15 July 1944)

The diary of a Jewish girl in hiding during the Second World War has become a totemic symbol of the Holocaust, a monument to the 6 million Jews killed and a talisman for victims of persecution across the world. But Anne Frank was far more than a symbol. She was a teenager whose refusal to be broken by fear or despair in the face of the blackest persecution is a triumph of humanity, the mark of a truly heroic soul. She also became, in spite of her youth, a great writer, an observer and recorder of the terrible events of her dark time and her family's struggle to survive. Hers was not the only such diary to emerge, but it was the finest – an immortal classic.

On 6 July 1942 Anne Frank, her parents Otto and Edith, and her elder sister Margot left their house on the Merwedplein in Amsterdam. Wearing layers of clothes and carrying no suitcases to avoid arousing suspicion, they made their way to Otto Frank's office building on the Prinsengracht. At the top of the stairs there was a door, later concealed behind a false bookcase. It led to what Anne named the Secret Annexe – four rooms where the Franks, with another family, the van Pels, and a dentist called Fritz Pfeffer, would hide for the next two years.

The Franks were German Jews who had emigrated to the Netherlands a decade earlier, following Hitler's rise to power. A lively and vivacious girl, Anne was given a red-checked cloth-bound book on her thirteenth birthday. Addressing her first entry 'to Kitty', she hoped that 'I shall be able to confide in you completely, as I have never been able to do in anyone before, and I hope that you will be a great comfort and support to me.'

The German occupation of the Netherlands was two years old when Anne began her diary. By 1942 Jews were subject to a curfew and made to wear yellow stars on their clothing. They were forbidden to take the tram, to ride bicycles or to take pictures. On 5 July 1942 sixteen-year-old Margot received papers ordering her to report for transportation to a work camp. At 7.30 the following morning the Franks left their house.

The Annexe's occupants had prepared themselves for a long stay. Anne's parents had been making secret trips to the hiding place for months. But nothing could have prepared them for the oppressive reality of hiding away from the world. Their survival was dependent on their 'helpers', four loyal employees of Otto Frank who risked their lives to bring them food, clothes, books and news. Absolute silence had to be maintained during the day to avoid arousing the suspicions of the workers in the store downstairs. 'We are as quiet as baby mice,' wrote Anne in October 1942. 'Who, three months ago, would have guessed that quicksilver Anne would have to sit still for hours – and what's more, could?'

Anne was a talented writer, funny, quick and possessed of a somewhat caustic eye. But her diary is also the work of a normal teenager – bright, impetuous, moody and impatient. She struggled between the 'good Anne' she would like to be and the 'bad Anne' she felt she more often was. She was insightful, unstintingly honest and, increasingly, wise.

'There is no way of killing time,' she wrote in 1943. But she refused to give up hope. 'It's really a wonder that I haven't dropped all my ideals, because they seem so absurd and impossible to carry out,' she wrote on 15 July 1944. 'Yet I keep them, because in spite of everything I still believe that people are really good at heart.'

Three weeks later the German police stormed the Secret Annexe. It is still unknown who betrayed them. The Annexe's inhabitants were sent to Westerbork, then to Auschwitz. In October Anne and Margot were transferred to Bergen-Belsen. They died of typhus within days of each other in March 1945, just a few weeks before the British liberated the camp.

Otto Frank was the only one of the Annexe's inhabitants to survive. When he returned to Amsterdam after the war, Miep Gies, one of their loyal helpers, gave him the diary that she had found scattered on the Annexe's floor. Asked later for his response on first reading his daughter's diary, Otto replied: 'I never knew my little Anne was so deep.'

While she was in hiding, Anne became convinced that she wanted to be a writer. Anne was not the only Jewish child diarist of the Holocaust. Probably there were many. A gifted Czech boy, Peter Ginz, kept a witty diary in Prague during 1941–2: 'When I go to school,' he wrote, 'I counted 9 "sheriffs"' – referring to Jews made to wear the yellow star. He was gassed in Auschwitz in 1944. These gifted diarists were not the only ones to turn hell into literature: *Night* by Elie Wiesel (b.1928) and *If This is a Man* by Primo Levi (1919–87) are the two masterpieces of this European dark age.

A year before she died, Anne Frank wrote of her desire 'to be useful or give pleasure to people around me who yet don't really know me. I want to go on living even after my death!'

GORBACHEV & YELTSIN:

THE CREATION OF MODERN RUSSIA

We are not abandoning our convictions, our philosophy or traditions, nor do we urge anyone to abandon theirs.

Mikhail Gorbachev

The fall of communism, the break-up of the Soviet empire, the liberation of eastern Europe from Soviet oppresssion and the emergence of a new Russia were the achievements of two rival Russian leaders, both of whom had decent intentions that were ruined by the pressures of real politics. Neither of them intended things to turn out as they did. Both of their careers ended in failure – and both actually produced effects that were the very opposite of their intentions. Indeed the achievements of each were counterproductive – and yet world changing.

A communist believer during his entire active career and indeed a believer in one-party rule, Mikhail Gorbachev, son of a combine harvester driver from Stavropol in south Russia, swiftly entered the top stream of Soviet leadership: he qualified in law and then climbed the Communist Party hierachy to become first secretary of Stavropol in 1970. Early on in his life he married Raisa, who was to be his partner and adviser in power: both of their families had experienced Stalin's Terror in their own families – yet neither lost their faith in the party.

By the 1970s, the reign of Leonid Brezhnev had produced economic stagnation, political sclerosis and falling prestige for the communist regime. In a party ruled by octogenarian Stalinist bureaucrats, the dynamic, cheerful and highly intelligent Gorbachev was noticed: in 1979 he was promoted to the Politburo in Moscow and placed in charge of agriculture under the wing of the KGB Chairman Yuri Andropov, probably the most capable politician in the leadership during the last decades of Soviet rule.

After Brezhnev's death Andropov succeeded to the top post but was too old to reform the USSR. On his death in 1984, Gorbachev did not push for the leadership: the senile and exhausted Konstantin Chernenko assumed power and survived just a few months. With this death it was clear that a new and young leader was needed: Gorbachev became first secretary and took control.

Swiftly he changed both the tone and facts of Soviet rule: he declared *perestroika* – restructuring – and *glasnost* – openness; but as a devout communist committed to the dictatorship of the proletariat and the party on which his power depended, he was no Western liberal democrat. He simply hoped to reform, consolidate and strengthen the Soviet dictatorship but instead unleashed forces he could not control. His economic mismanagement undermined his own achievements: his ban on alcohol deprived a desperate budget of key funds. Gorbachov's tinkering with the command economy produced instant shortages and discontent – he did not understand how capitalism worked.

But he did gradually open up a semi-free press and allowed limited free elections – though he did not risk any kind of vote on his own role, relying on the party for his legitimacy. To Russians, he came to stand for a dangerous experiment, his tone – so charming to Westerners – sounded pompous and lecturing to his own people.

Abroad his achievements were truly revolutionary and titanic: he overturned the Brezhnev Doctrine of intervention in eastern European satellites: in partnership with his Georgian foreign minister, Eduard Shevardnadze, he negotiated arms control agreements with US President Ronald Reagan; more amazingly he offered to free countries like Poland after decades of tyranny. In 1989, he withdrew Soviet troops from their catastrophic war in Afghanistan and allowed eastern Europeans to grasp freedom: Soviet client regimes fell in every country. In Germany, he allowed the Berlin Wall to be brought down – and Germany to be reunited. Reagan had confronted the Soviet Union with powerful democratic rhetoric and rising American defence spending – both of which certainly played a part in the fall of the Soviet imperium – but the achievement of this was overwhelmingly thanks to Gorbachev's conviction that this could be done peacefully. At home Gorbachev was determined to promote communist rule and the coherence of the Soviet Union but his own actions had undermined both fatally: the elections of leaders in the separate republics had produced a more legitimate leadership than that of the party.

When he came to power in 1985, Gorbachev had promoted a tall, energetic but reckless new leader named Boris Yeltsin to Moscow party chief and Politburo member. Almost the same age as Gorbachev,Yeltsin was the son of a builder who had been repressed by Stalin. Growing up in Sverdlovsk, he rose to local party secretary by1976. Yeltsin was the opposite of Gorbachev: while the latter was contemplative, legalistic, sometimes verbose, often witty, and brave, Yeltsin was bombastic, emotional, courageous – and an alcoholic. The two soon clashed and Gorbachev sacked Yeltsin in 1987, giving him a public dressing-down. But, both opportunistic and idealistic, Yeltsin was ahead of Gorbachev in realizing that the Soviet Union and communism itself would and should soon fall.Yeltsin embraced liberal democracy – yet it also suited him. He was elected president of the Russian Republic in 1989, giving him potential legitimacy unavailable to Gorbachev. In July 1990 he dramatically resigned from the Communist Party.

In the following months, the strain started to show as ethnic turmoil and bloodshed intensified in the Caucusus and Soviet security forces seemed to be out of control, killing protesters in Lithuania. The Politburo and security service, the KGB, plotted to overthrow Gorbachev: in August 1991, a committee of incompetent drunken communist leaders and Chekists arrested Gorbachev on his Black Sea holiday and sent tanks into Moscow, but crowds defended the White House offices of Yeltsin. Yeltsin bravely climbed onto a tank outside to defiantly address the crowds. The coup fell apart but its real victim was Gorbachev, who had lost his prestige.

When Gorbachev tried to regain the momentum, Yeltsin ended the monopoly of the Communist Party and then conspired with the elected presidents of the other Soviet republics to end the Soviet Union. Gorbachev resigned on Christmas Day 1991, thus ending the Soviet Union, which broke up into its independent republics. Gorbachev realised that communist oligarchy was wrong and after his fall he sincerely embraced liberal democracy but it was too late.

Yeltsin dominated Russia in the 1990s and, initially, his enthusiasm and openness were refreshing. Almost for the first time in its history, Russia enjoyed totally free elections, a totally free press, a free economy, a free investigation of history and of state crimes – and all these were Yeltsin's achievements. But he was fatally flawed: alcoholic, inconsistent and capricious, he ruled like a tsar through cronies and henchmen such as his sinister bodyguard General Korzhakov and his billionaire financial adviser Boris Berezovsky. Yeltsin's privatisation of the Russian economy was hopelessly mismanaged, making billionaires of the so-called Oligarchs, over-powerful businessmen like Berezovsky.

In 1993, communist hardliners in Parliament threatened the entire democratic project with an armed revolt which Yeltisn defeated by ordering the storming by special forces of the White House in Moscow. The following year, faced with rebellion and the assertion of independence by Chechnya, Yeltsin invaded the little republic. As they committed atrocities on a vast scale, killing thousands of innocent civilians and utterly destroying cities such as Grozny, Russian forces were humiliated by dynamic Chechen fighters. Yeltsin was forced to retreat, withdraw Russian forces from Chechnya and infamously recognise Chechen independence – an unprecedented Russian humiliation. The decay of financial corruption, Kremlin intrigue, economic chaos, mafia disorder and resurgent repression unleashed by the Chechen war discredited his real achievements.

By 1996, Yeltsin, ill and isolated, faced a new election which he seemed likely to lose: his billionaire cronies, the Oligarchs, mobilized their fortunes to help him win re-election but now even democracy was tainted. The next three years saw economic meltdown and Yeltsin's personal decline as he sacked prime ministers with imperial whimsy and embarrassed his country with acts of drunken bufoonery.

In 1999 he chose a young, ambitious and severe ex-KGB officer and cabinet minister named Vladimir Putin to be his successor, dramatically resigning the presidency. Putin proved more than equal to the task: he restored the power of the state and the prestige of Russia as a great power, crushed mafia corruption and broke the influence of the Oligarchs. At the same time he demonstrated his discipline and vigour by again attacking Chechnya with brutal and bloody competence, crushing the rebellion at the cost of hundreds of thousands of civilian lives. Putin promoted his colleagues from the security services who dominated Russian government and business, diminished democracy and press freedom, ended the election of local governors and personified a new Russian form of authoritarian government that he called sovereign democracy. Putin utterly dominated Russia in a way Gorbachev and Yeltsin had never done, probably the dominant Russian leader of the early 21st century.

ELVIS

1935–1977

The coloured folks been singing it and playing it just like I'm doin' now, man, for more years than I know . . . They played it like that in their shanties and in their juke joints and nobody paid it no mind 'til I goosed it up.

Elvis Presley, in an early interview

Elvis, the King. Thus the United States, that most republican of nations, dubbed its favourite musical son, ensuring that his pre-eminence would remain inviolate. He didn't invent rock 'n' roll, he didn't write many songs, he never toured abroad, and he has since been eclipsed in almost every bald statistic of popular-music success. But all that is irrelevant. His sublimity of voice – startling in its reach from raunch and rebellion to the angelically tender – his devastating good looks, and the pulsating charisma of the performer entranced millions. He was a global star, and, by carrying the black music of blues and gospel to a white audience in a way that was unthinkable before, he enabled the musical synthesis that remains the bedrock of popular music today.

Elvis Aaron Presley had a poor Southern upbringing and was much closer to his lively and impressive mother than his shirking, petty-criminal father. He was a shy teenager, often bullied for being a mother's boy. When he left school, he started driving lorries, just as his father did. But it was not long before his remarkable voice came to the attention of the record producer Sam Philips. Philips was looking for a white man to sing 'Negro' songs, and when he heard Presley's self-funded singles, recorded in 1953 as a birthday present for his mother, Philips felt he had found his man.

In 1954 Presley recorded 'That's All Right', a blues song. Radio stations in Tennessee immediately began playing it, and Presley went on a tour of the Southern states. He came up against the ingrained prejudice of many white Americans opposed to seeing blacks and whites mixing together or sharing culture. But even this generations-old legacy of separateness could not compete with the adoration from the young and more colour-blind fans that Presley began to attract. By 1956 pressure from white teenagers had forced radio stations nationwide to play Elvis' singles – hits such as 'Heartbreak Hotel' (1956), 'Love Me Tender' (1956) and the title song to the film *Jailhouse Rock* (1957) – and he remained completely frank about his musical influences. In some quarters black critics accused him of stealing their music; in contrast, Little Richard called Elvis 'a blessing', who 'opened the door' for black music. What was undeniable was that his momentum was unstoppable.

Elvis signed a management deal with 'Colonel' Tom Parker, to whom he turned over all of his business affairs. Parker was a shadowy character, but he was a master merchandiser and turned Elvis into the greatest musical brand the world had ever seen. Under his guidance, Elvis found that he could draw crowds and audiences on a phenomenal scale. He broke records for sales of singles and albums, and he could attract 80 per cent of the American television audience for his TV appearances. Young men wanted to be him, young women wanted him, and older generations were scared and shocked. In the city of Liverpool, John Lennon recruited

Paul McCartney to the band that had Elvis as its lodestar and that wanted to be 'bigger than Elvis'.

Back home, as Elvis' music and high-energy stage act grew ever more popular, conservative America became more disgusted and worried that its offspring were being irrevocably corrupted. His habits of shaking his legs, rolling his tightly leather-clad hips, thrusting and throwing himself about in front of the microphone were considered the height of obscenity. As a result, there were many who saw Elvis' draft into the US Army, and subsequent posting to Germany in 1958, as something of a relief. When he returned to America in 1960, he was a more subdued character, and during the 1960s, as the era of the pop groups burgeoned, he chose to concentrate on a lacklustre film career rather than return to music. But he reinvented himself for a musical comeback in 1968, adopting some of the influences of the Beatles and the Rolling Stones, the very stars who had re-interpreted his kind of music and sold it back to America.

Elvis's popularity remained huge throughout the 1970s, and he sold out enormous venues across the United States, particularly in Las Vegas, albeit in a new persona where he was now encased in the outré outfits of the cabaret scene. He still made it into the charts, for example with 'Always on My Mind' (1973). But his health and state of mind declined alarmingly. He grew fat, gorging himself on fast food. He also became addicted to prescription drugs. He slept for most of the day and cut a bloated figure on stage – although that voice remained mesmerising.

Elvis died on 16 August 1977. He suffered heart failure at Graceland, his mansion in Memphis, Tennessee. His funeral was a massive event, watched by millions. He ranks with the American singers Frank Sinatra, Bob Dylan and Michael Jackson, those English bands the Beatles and the Rolling Stones, and the French singer Edith Piaf as musical giants who have moved beyond the realm of music into the conscious identity of nations.

SADDAM HUSSEIN

1937–2006

What has befallen us of defeat, shame and humiliation, Saddam, is the result of your follies, your miscalculations and your irresponsible actions.

> Shia Iraqi army commander in 1991, inaugurating the uprising against Saddam's rule that was subsequently crushed by the dictator's forces

Saddam Hussein, the dictator of Iraq, aspired to be an Arab hero and conqueror, but his long reign of ruthless oppression, sadistic cruelty, gangsterish corruption, unnecessary wars, mass murder and a ludicrous personality cult led to a series of political miscalculations that brought about the destruction of his regime and his own death on the scaffold. This crude despot appears here because the campaign to overthrow him was the greatest Western foreign policy catastrophe of modern times, discrediting and diminishing American and British military and moral power for a generation, unleashing terrorism, mayhem and apocalyptic war while removing the will to stop it.

Saddam was born in a small Sunni village close to the town of Tikrit. His father died before he was born so he was brought up in his stepfather's house – repeatedly beaten and spending much of his youth as a street kid. In 1947 he went to live with his mother's brother, from whom, at the age of ten, he received his first schooling.

In the early 1950s Saddam moved with his uncle to

Baghdad and tried to get into military college but failed the exams. Meanwhile, he imbibed from his uncle a hatred of British influence in the kingdom of Iraq, became a regular participant in anti-government demonstrations, and formed his own street gang to attack political opponents. In time he became drawn towards the Ba'ath Party, which combined socialism with anti-Western, pan-Arab nationalism, and in 1958 he participated in the army coup led by Brigadier Abdel Karim Kassem that overthrew and murdered King Faisal II. Many, especially the Ba'athists, were disappointed that Kassem failed to lead Iraq into a union with neighbouring Arab countries, and in 1959 Saddam was involved in a failed attempt to assassinate Kassem, after which he went into exile in Syria and Egypt.

A Ba'athist-dominated coup in 1963 induced Saddam to return, but the new ruler of Iraq, Abdul Salam Arif, soon fell out with his Ba'athist allies, and Saddam was imprisoned for several years before escaping in 1967. He went on to become the right-hand man of the Ba'ath Party leader, Ahmad Hassan al-Bakr, and after the party seized power in 1968, he emerged as the strong man of the regime, becoming vice-president, as well as head of Iraq's security apparatus and general secretary of the Ba'ath Party. He deliberately fashioned his regime on that of Stalin, whom he studied.

From his new position Saddam oversaw the nationalization of the Western-owned Iraqi Petroleum Company, using the funds accrued to develop the country's welfare state (especially its health system). He also initiated a major drive against illiteracy, made improvements to Iraqi infrastructure and generally sought to encourage modernization and industrialization. At the same time, however, he also worked assiduously to accumulate power to himself, moving loyal lieutenants into key positions, building up a brutal secret police and strengthening his grip on levers of state.

In mid-1979 Saddam pressured the ailing al-Bakr to resign, and assumed the presidency himself. He immediately summoned the Revolutionary Council, comprising the senior Ba'ath Party leadership, and announced that 'Zionism and the forces of darkness' were engaged in a conspiracy against Iraq. Then, to the horror of his audience, he announced that those involved were present in the room. While Saddam sat smoking a huge cigar, a series of names were read out, and, one by one, sixty-six people were led away. Subsequently twenty-two of these men were found guilty, and Saddam personally supervised their killing, requiring senior figures in the Iraqi leadership to carry out the death sentences.

Saddam set about transforming Iraq into what one dissident labelled the 'Republic of Fear'. His notorious secret police, the Mukhabarat, together with the state internal security department the Amn, established a fierce grip over the entire country. Regular massacres were carried out of Jews, Freemasons, communists, economic saboteurs or merely people who crossed Saddam or his greedy, pitiless family, all of whom served in his government. Purge followed upon purge, attended by show trials and televised confessions. Over the subsequent two decades Saddam Hussein killed at least 400,000 Iraqis – many of whom endured all manner of torture. His psychopathic sons, particularly the sadistic, demented heir apparent Uday, conducted their own struggles for power and brutal reigns of terror, personally torturing their enemies. At one point, Saddam's two sons-in-law, fearing murder by Uday, fled to Jordan, but were tricked into returning and then slaughtered by Uday.

Not content with dominating Iraq, Saddam was also determined to assert regional hegemony. He invaded Iran in 1980, using Iran's Islamic revolution of 1979 as a pretext to seize Iran's oilfields, and thus sparked a disastrous eight-year war that ended in stalemate and cost over a million lives. Adept at playing off the great powers against one another, he was significantly aided by the West, which regarded Iran as the greater of two evils.

During the war, Iran had encouraged the Iraqi Kurds to mount an uprising against Ba'athist rule. Saddam responded in merciless fashion, deploying mustard and nerve gas against the civilian population – most notoriously at the town of Halabja, where some 5000 Kurds died in a single attack in March 1988. Four thousand villages were destroyed and 100,000 Kurds slaughtered.

The end of the Iranian war left Iraq exhausted despite huge oil revenues. In August 1990 Saddam invaded and occupied Kuwait. It proved to be a catastrophic miscalculation. The United Nations authorized a massive US-led military coalition to drive the Iraqis out of Kuwait, which they swiftly achieved in 1991. Iraqi Kurds and Shiites – encouraged by the coalition – rebelled against Saddam, but without Western military support they were brutally put down.

By the terms of the ceasefire agreement, Iraq had agreed to abandon nuclear, chemical and biological weapons. Yet Saddam failed to cooperate with UN weapons inspectors, barred them entirely from 1998, and engaged in constant military brinkmanship and diplomatic chicanery.

Saddam's situation was transformed by the al-Qaeda terrorist attacks on America on 11 September 2001. President George W. Bush – confident after overthrowing Al-Qaeda's backers, the Taliban, in Afghanistan – advocated 'regime change' in Iraq and the creation of Iraqi democracy to encourage freedom in the Arab world, citing as justification Saddam's dictatorship, continued pursuit of weapons of mass destruction and support for terrorist groups. Ironically, there were no weapons of mass destruction. But fearing that the truth might expose his regime's weakness to Iran, Saddam let the world believe he was rebuilding his nuclear arsenal. He miscalculated (for the second time) that America would not dare invade. In March 2003, US-led coalition forces invaded and overthrew Saddam, who was finally captured, tried and sentenced to death. His execution was bungled, as Shiites insulted and attacked him. Nonetheless the sentence was richly deserved.

MUHAMMAD ALI

1942–2016

I'm the greatest thing that ever lived. I'm so great I don't have a mark on my face. I shook up the world.

> Cassius Clay, soon to become Muhammad Ali, after
> defeating Sonny Liston in 1964

Muhammad Ali was not just the greatest boxer of his generation, he was one of the greatest sportsmen of all time. As a fighter, he displayed a prodigious, sublime talent, but he also transcended the world of sport. Deep-felt conviction, outspoken politics, courage, wit, style, sheer chutzpah, all combined to create a legend. Even in retirement, Ali triumphed as an iconic figure who lit the torch at the 1996 Atlanta Olympics and spoke poignantly about non-violent Islam in the post-9/11 world.

Cassius Clay, as Ali was named at birth, took up boxing as a twelve-year-old. He had an exceptional amateur career, winning 134 bouts and losing only seven. He went to the Rome Olympics in 1960 and won a gold medal at light heavyweight, impressing with his speed and lightning reflexes. The Miami boxing trainer Angelo Dundee took Clay on as a young professional and had little to do to improve his brazen style. He kept a low guard, relying on his speed to dance around opponents. Early in life he would proclaim himself 'the greatest'. When he destroyed the great heavyweight Sonny Liston in two fights – the second a severe pounding in May 1965 – it seemed that he was set to fulfil his own prophecy.

Outside the ring, Clay was undergoing a transformation that would shape the rest of his life. He became involved with Malcolm X and the Nation of Islam – a radical black Islamic movement. It appealed to Clay because of the racism he had experienced growing up in the Southern states of the USA. Soon the outspoken young man had changed his name to Muhammad Ali. By the time of the rematch against Liston and a subsequent savaging of another big-name heavyweight, Floyd Patterson, Ali was as divisive outside the ring as he was brilliant in it.

The combination of Ali's extravagant fighting style, his forthright talk and his refusal to join the US Army in 1966 ('Man, I ain't got no quarrel with them Vietcong,' he explained at the time) rapidly made him a hate figure for white America. He declared himself a conscientious objector, and in 1967 he was stripped of his world title and banned from fighting in America for three years. Undeterred, Ali delivered more than 200 anti-war speeches condemning the actions of the USA in east Asia.

When Ali returned to the ring, he took part in three of the most famous fights of all time: the Fight of the Century (1971), which he lost to Joe Frazier; the Rumble in the Jungle (1974), in which he reclaimed the heavyweight crown then held by George Foreman; and the Thriller in Manila (1975), which represented redemption against Frazier. In the Foreman fight, held in Zaire (now the Democratic Republic of the Congo), Ali used his 'rope-a-dope' tactics, hanging back for seven rounds and allowing Foreman to punch himself out, then countering in the eighth to knock out his younger opponent.

The Thriller in Manila is probably the most celebrated of all Ali's fights. In the build-up to the contest he taunted Frazier with various slurs and poems. The two men battered one another for fourteen rounds, until finally Frazier's corner threw in the towel.

Afterwards Ali said of his own heroic efforts: 'That must be what death feels like.' He had thrown everything into an incredible victory, and – history having vindicated his stance on Vietnam – he had earned redemption in the eyes of the world.

Ali fought on until the early 1980s, by which time his powers had visibly declined. However, in spite of the sad end to his career, he is rightly remembered as one of history's greatest ever sportsmen. Only the footballer Pelé and a very few others can be said to have dominated their sports in the same manner. World champion three times, he was the quintessence of glamour and glory in his sport, thanks to his skill and guile in the ring and his psychological mastery of his opponents.

But Ali was more than just a superb sportsman. He was a principled man who stuck by his beliefs even when threatened. Though his pronouncements on race were not always well judged and he could be cruel to his opponents, Ali transcended such indiscretions and won over almost all his critics with his bravery and charisma.

Since his diagnosis in 1984, Ali was progressively affected by the symptoms of Parkinson's disease. The sight of his quavering hand lighting the Olympic torch in Atlanta in 1996 touched the world; the transition from angry young man to symbol of world unity was complete. In 1999 he was voted Sports Personality of the Century. Despite his frailty, he travelled the world supporting a range of humanitarian causes for as long as he was able before his death in 2016.

ESCOBAR

1949–1993

The ingeniousness of my brother was extraordinary.
Roberto Escobar

The most powerful, wealthy and murderous criminal of the 20th century, Pablo Escobar was the paramount Colombian drug lord who became the mastermind and kingpin of the international cocaine trade. He accrued billions of dollars, and in the process was responsible for hundreds of kidnappings and murders. A godfather figure of unrivalled magnitude, and a law unto himself, Escobar threatened the very integrity of the state of Colombia.

Escobar was the son of a peasant and a schoolteacher, and grew up in a suburb of Medellín. He became involved in criminal activities from an early age, stealing cars and even, it was said, gravestones, which he sandblasted before selling them as new. He graduated to minor fraud, selling contraband cigarettes and forged lottery tickets, and then in the late 1960s, as demand for cannabis and cocaine multiplied, he saw an opening in the drug trade.

During the first half of the 1970s Escobar became increasingly prominent in the Medellín Cartel, in which a number of crime syndicates cooperated to control much of Colombia's drug-trafficking industry. In 1975, a leading Medellín crime lord, Fabio Restrepo, was assassinated, and Escobar soon took over his operation.

In May of the following year, Escobar was charged with organizing a drug run to Ecuador. He tried to bribe the judges who were presiding over his case, but when that failed he murdered two officers who had arrested him and the chief witnesses, thereby ending the proceedings. This became part of an established pattern, a strategy called plata o plomo (silver plate or lead bullet – i.e. accept a bribe or face assassination). He killed many thousands, on his orders or personally, often with astonishing savagery.

Escobar was a savvy political operator, aware of the need to grease the palms of local politicians. In Medellín he was also a Robin Hood populist, contributing small but significant portions of his personal fortune to local building projects or struggling football clubs, gaining him some popularity among the people of the city. He briefly ran his own newspaper, and in 1982 he became a deputy for the Liberal Party in the Colombian Congress.

By the early 1980s Escobar's cartel monopolized the South American drug trade, and was responsible for an estimated 80 per cent of cocaine and cannabis shipped to the United States, Mexico, Puerto Rico and the Dominican Republic. His operation involved purchasing coca paste in Bolivia and Peru, processing it in drug factories dotted across Colombia, and then smuggling thousands of tons every week out of the country and into the United States, by sea, air and road.

In 1989 *Forbes* magazine listed Escobar as the seventh richest man in the world, with an estimated fortune of $24 billion. He owned many beautiful homes, a private zoo, numerous yachts and helicopters, a fleet of private aeroplanes and even two submarines; he also kept a private army of bodyguards and assassins on the payroll. He was utterly unforgiving to those who threatened his position, even in the smallest possible way: after catching a servant stealing silver from one of his palatial homes, he had the unfortunate man tied up and thrown into the swimming pool, leaving him to drown.

It was not long before Escobar began to be targeted by the United States authorities. In 1979 the USA and Colombia had signed an extradition treaty, as part of a tougher approach to the drug trade. Escobar hated this treaty and began a campaign of assassination against anyone who supported it or who called for stronger policies against the drug cartels. He was widely believed to have been behind the storming in 1985 of the Colombian Supreme Court by left-wing guerrillas, which left eleven judges dead. Four years later Escobar ordered the murder of three presidential candidates, as well as the downing of an airliner, which killed 107 people, and the bombing of the national-security building in Bogotá, killing fifty-two. The same year two of his henchmen were arrested in Miami, trying to buy missiles.

In 1991, as the net seemed to be closing in around him, Escobar offered a deal to the Colombian authorities: in order to avoid extradition he would accept five years' imprisonment. As part of the deal, Escobar was allowed to build his own 'prison', which naturally turned out to be another luxurious palace, from where he could direct his drugs empire by telephone. He was allowed to leave to attend the occasional football match or party, and was also permitted to receive visitors, including prostitutes (the younger the better) and business associates, two of whom were murdered on his premises – he liked to torture his victims personally.

On 22 July 1992, as he was being transferred to a tougher prison, Escobar managed to escape. The Colombian authorities launched a massive manhunt, with help from the USA, and also from Escobar's enemies, including Los Pepes (People Persecuted by Pablo Escobar), a paramilitary group composed of his victims and members of the rival Cali Cartel. During the sixteen-month search, hundreds of people – both policemen and Escobar's henchmen – were killed. Escobar was eventually tracked down to a safe house in Medellín and shot in the leg, torso and head as he attempted a daring rooftop escape; he died instantly. It was 2 December 1993, the day after his 44th birthday.

Escobar's supporters regarded him as a hero and a champion of the poor, but in reality he was a monster and an outlaw of unrivalled greed and sadism. His token gestures of philanthropy did not disguise his scant regard for human life, and at the height of its influence his cartel was responsible for an average of twenty murders every month.

OSAMA BIN LADEN &

1957–2011

ABU BAKR AL-BAGHDADI: THE JIHADIS

1971–?

The pieces of the bodies of infidels were flying like dust particles. If you would have seen it with your own eyes, you would have been very pleased, and your heart would have been filled with joy.
Osama bin Laden, at the wedding of his son following the murder of seventeen US soldiers in the suicide bombing of the USS *Cole*, 12 October 2000

The rise of radical Islamic terrorism – jihadism – in the 21st century was the result of the decay of the old Arab dictatorships, the failure of the Arab states created by British and French ministers after the First World War, the outbreak of civil wars, and the simultaneous sense of Arab powerlessness in the face of American omnipotence – just as Western power lost its confidence and control over the Middle East. Jihadism was personified by two men.

Osama bin Laden was the fanatical mastermind of the murderously spectacular 9/11 plane-bomb attacks against the Twin Towers and Pentagon that killed thousands of innocent people in the name of an intolerant and dogmatic distortion of the Islamic faith. Promoting a jihadi ideology that glories in killing and endorses a nihilistic cult of suicide, he aimed to eliminate American and Western power, wipe out Israel and restore a caliphate over any part of the world ever ruled by Islam. But his only real practical policy was terrorizing innocent people and assaulting tolerant democratic societies, using impressionable youths as living bombs against victims chosen solely because they are citizens of the free, democratic West.

Bin Laden was born in Riyadh in 1957, the son of Muhammad Awad bin Laden – who acquired huge wealth after his construction company secured exclusive rights from the Saudi royal family to religious building projects within the country – and his tenth wife, Hamida al-Attas, subsequently divorced. The only son of that marriage, though with numerous siblings on his father's side, Osama – after his mother's remarriage to Muhammad al-Attas – was raised as a Sunni Muslim, displaying uncompromising piety from an early age. He studied at an elite school and then King Abdulaziz University, marrying his first wife, Najwa Ghanem, in 1974. He has had another four wives, divorcing two, and has fathered between twelve and twenty-four children.

In 1979, bin Laden, together with thousands of other devout jihadists – known collectively as the mujahedeen – travelled to Afghanistan to repel the Soviet Union's invasion of the country. He joined fellow militant Abdullah Azzam and established Maktab al-Khadamat, a paramilitary organization devoted to fighting what he saw as jihad. The war was also backed and funded by the United States, ever fearful of Soviet expansion, and when bin Laden returned to Saudi Arabia in 1990, he was widely feted for having resisted the forces of communism. Already, though, he was making plans for a new organization to further his goal of driving America ('the Great Satan') out of the Muslim world. It would become known as Al-Qaeda (the Base).

Following the Gulf War of 1991, bin Laden denounced the Saudi royal family for allowing US troops to be stationed in the country, upon which, in 1992, they expelled him. He moved to Sudan, from where, working with the Egyptian Islamic Jihad (EIJ), he masterminded the 29 December 1992 attack on Aden in which two people were killed. Following an unsuccessful assassination attempt, however, on President Mubarak of Egypt in 1995, the EIJ were expelled from Sudan, prompting bin Laden to return to Afghanistan, where he allied himself with the Taliban, bankrolling training camps for thousands of jihadists.

In 1997, he sponsored the infamous Luxor massacre of 17 November, which killed sixty-two civilians, and the following year Al-Qaeda bombed US embassies in Kenya and Tanzania, killing nearly 300 people. A more sinister trend emerged in October 2000 when, once more in Aden, a suicide bomber attacked the US Navy ship USS *Cole*, killing seventeen. Such bombing swiftly became Al-Qaeda's weapon of choice, militant young Muslims being indoctrinated to seek martyrdom. Later the same year, bin Laden, with his lieutenant Dr Ayman al-Zawahiri – whom he had first met during the Afghan war – co-signed a *fatwa* declaring that Muslims had a duty to kill Americans and their allies.

Bin Laden and al-Zawahiri subsequently concocted their most ambitious plan yet. Early on the morning of 11 September 2001, two teams of jihadis boarded four passenger jets at airports in Washington DC, Boston and Newark. Authorities learned shortly afterwards that the planes had been hijacked by nineteen Middle Eastern men. At 8.46 a.m. local time, American Airlines Flight 11 flew into the north of the Twin Towers in New York, the biggest buildings in Manhattan. Then, as television cameras were trained on the unfolding disaster, United Airlines Flight 175 slammed at 9.02 a.m. into the south tower. Thirty-five minutes later, news filtered through that American Airlines Flight 77 had crashed into the Pentagon in Virginia, and at 10.03 a.m. United Airlines Flight 93, destined for the White House, was brought down over Pennsylvania by heroic passengers who had heard the fate of the other planes as they frantically called their relatives on onboard telephones.

Apocalyptic scenes followed in New York. The Twin Towers, both of which had been fatally weakened by the impact of the jets and ensuing fires, collapsed to the ground – the south at 9.59 a.m. and the north at 10.28 a.m. – killing thousands of victims still trapped inside, and sending out a cloud of dust that engulfed the south side of Manhattan. Excluding the hijackers, nearly 3000 people died that day – 246 on the jets, 125 in the Pentagon and 2603 in the Twin Towers (including 341 heroic firefighters and 2 paramedics).

Committing itself to a war on terror, America vowed to hunt down bin Laden, who already topped the FBI's most wanted list. Allied forces soon toppled the Taliban regime in Afghanistan, where Al-Qaeda had been allowed to operate for years, but bin Laden fled to the mountains bordering Afghanistan and Pakistan. A chance to capture him there was missed in late 2001 when advancing troops failed to search the Tora Bora caves where he was almost certainly hiding. When the caves were subsequently raided in August 2007, he was gone.

Since 9/11, radicalized Muslims, led by bin Laden's twisted message of hate and violence, have relentlessly continued Al-Qaeda's murderous campaign. In Iraq, through a ruthless campaign of bombing, Al-Qaeda focused on fomenting sectarian slaughter between Sunni and Shia Muslims to foil American plans for Iraqi democracy. On 2 May 2011, after the biggest manhunt in history, US Navy SEAL commandos, watched by President Barack Obama in the White House Situation Room in real time, raided a house in Abbottabad, the town in Pakistan that houses Pakistan's military academy, and killed bin Laden. His body was buried at sea.

But Al-Qaeda had already been eclipsed by a new manifestation of jihadism: the Islamic State. On bin Laden's death, the Iraqi branch of Al-Qaeda led by a certain Abu Bakr al-Baghdadi threatened vengeance, continuing a campaign of bombings in Iraq. But al-Baghdadi was different: he was planning to exploit Sunni disaffection with the corrupt, Shiite-dominated government in Iraq to create something new – a jihadi army and state.

No one is quite sure of his identity, but he was probably the Iraqi-born Ibrahim al-Badri who for many years quietly studied Islam until the American invasion of 2003, which inspired him to found a small militant group which later merged into the Islamic State of Iraq in 2006. Using his new nom de guerre, al-Baghdadi was already a powerful terrorist when he was arrested by the US army and imprisoned in 2004. Prison was his university: he befriended a variety of detainees, both jihadists and secular ex-henchmen and soldiers of Saddam Hussein. When the Americans foolishly released him, al-Baghdadi put his plans into operation, first infiltrating Syria where a brutal civil war between the president, Bashir al-Assad, and various opposition groups had created an opportunity. Al-Baghdadi took control of some of these factions, improved their training, inspired them with a new and utterly devastating vision of warfare, and set up a new so-called Islamic State in Raqqa, funded by donations and oil trading. Crossing into Iraq, his fighters routed the Iraqi army to take the major city of Mosul, suddenly ruling a huge new state straddling Iraq and Syria.

Rich in oil cash, recruiting thousands of Western jihadis from countries like France and Belgium who were attracted by the success of his black-bannered armies, al-Baghdadi declared a caliphate with himself as Caliph Ibrahim. Publicly beheading Western and Arab hostages on television and the internet, massacring innocent sects of non-Sunni Muslims and other ethnic groups such as the Yazidis, the caliphate offered its fighters a full state inspired by an apocalyptic–messianic vision, the benefits of slave girls stolen as the spoils of war, and a successful military entity with a deliberate policy of spectacular savagery. The world was horrified and the Iraqi army, aided by a Western coalition, finally started to destroy the leadership, economy and military of Islamic State in 2014. But as al-Baghdadi's cities and lands fell, his terrorist cells and independent sympathizers in the West launched vicious terror attacks on civilians using bombs and guns, but often just trucks and knives.

IS's military defeat was inevitable – and indeed al-Baghdadi's death has been reported many times: he was possibly killed by a Russian airstrike in May 2017 – but the end of this mysterious figure may never be know, perhaps vanishing in the apocalyptic desert dust of his collapsing, short-lived realm. However, the threat of terror will last much longer, as the genie of death-cult jihadism continues to shapeshift to exploit the opportunities of our times.

THE UNKNOWN TITAN

On 5 June 1989, as the Chinese Communist Party brutally crushed the Tiananmen Square student uprising, a column of tanks was held up by a solitary young man as it attempted to drive out of the square. Again and again he prevented the tanks from moving on, until finally they turned off their engines. He then jumped up onto the leading tank to scold the commander for shedding so much innocent blood.

Dubbed 'Tank Man' or the 'Unknown Rebel', the young man's real name was never discovered, nor his fate. Some said he was executed, others that he is still alive in China. Captured on film and broadcast around the world, the image of the man's astonishing courage summed up the tragedy of Tiananmen Square – the brutal suppression of the democratic student protesters and the reckless killing of thousands of innocents.

Tank Man's protest and the uprising as a whole failed to change China's destiny. Nevertheless, *Time* magazine named him one of the 100 most influential people of the 20th century. This anonymous figure came to symbolize the heroism of the simple impulsive acts of ordinary people.

The Tiananmen Square protests were a popular uprising aimed at changing the course of communist China. Soon after the death of Chinese dictator Mao Zedong in 1976, the tough pragmatist Deng Xiaoping – himself a victim of the orchestrated upheaval of Mao's Cultural Revolution (1966–1975) – emerged as China's 'Paramount Leader'. Deng followed a policy of economic liberalization combined with absolute political control by the Communist Party. The party's general secretary, Hu Yaobang, pressed for greater reforms but was sacked by Deng after student protests in 1987.

On 15 April 1989 Hu's death sparked student more protests, which were at first small-scale but soon became widespread. This was the era of Mikhail Gorbachev's glasnost and liberalization in Russia, so Deng and the Chinese leadership were already nervous. Students and teachers were soon joined by workers. The protests became focused on Tiananmen Square in Beijing, which before long was occupied by vast numbers of protesters.

On 19 May General Secretary Zhao Ziyang addressed the seething student crowds on the square in a conciliatory spirit (but with a tone of warning too), telling them: 'Students! You talk about us, criticize us, it is all necessary. You are still young . . . you must live healthily . . . We are already old, it doesn't matter to us anymore . . .'. On 30 May a statue of the Goddess of Democracy was erected. By now the elders of the Communist Party, led by Deng, still chairman of the Central Military Commission, and President Marshal Yang Shangkun, were convinced that stability and Party control were threatened and ordered its suppression. Hardline premier Li Peng declared martial law. The 27th and 28th Armies entered the city, and the assault started at 10.30 p.m. on 3 June.

There was indiscriminate fire; it is believed that about 2600 were killed and 30,000 injured. Journalist Jan Wong, watching from the Beijing Hotel on 5 June as the Unknown Rebel stopped the tanks, recalled: 'So the tank is turning, then the young man jumps in front of the tank, and then the tank turns the other way and the young man jumps down that side. They did this a couple of times. Then the tank turned off its motor. The young man climbed up onto the tank and seemed to be talking to the person inside. After a while, the young man jumps down, the tank turns on its motor and the young man blocks it again . . .' He reportedly told the tank commander: 'Why are you here? You have caused nothing but misery.' Just then, two people on the sidelines pulled him into the crowd – perhaps to a life in hiding, perhaps to face a firing squad.

The following year President Jiang Zemin claimed that 'the young man was never, never killed'. Tank Man remains an inspiration: the unknown hero who represents all the other unknown heroes.

Simon Sebag Montefiore

'When history is written this way, one can never have too much'
The Times

THE ROMANOVS
The intimate story of Russia's imperial dynasty
'Epic history on the grandest scale'
Financial Times

9781474600873 • £12.99 • Paperback
9781474600279 • £12.99 • Ebook
9781409161035 • £25.00 • Audio

JERUSALEM: THE BIOGRAPHY
The epic 3,000-year history of the city at the centre of the world.
'Utterly compelling from start to finish'
Sunday Times

9781780220253 • £12.99 • Paperback
9780297858645 • £9.99 • Ebook
9781409113799 • £25.00 • Audio

YOUNG STALIN
The dramatic early life of one of history's most dangerous and enigmatic men.
'A masterpiece'
The Times

9780753823798 • £9.99 • Paperback
9780297863847 • £9.99 • Ebook
9780752888927 • £16.99 • Audio

STALIN: THE COURT OF THE RED TSAR
The thrilling biography of Stalin and his entourage in the terrifying decades of his supreme power.
'The most civilised and elegant chronicle of brutality and ruthlessness I have ever read'
Daily Telegraph

9781780228358 • £12.99 • Paperback
9780297863854 • £12.99 • Ebook
9780752884691 • £19.99 • Audio

CATHERINE THE GREAT AND POTEMKIN: THE IMPERIAL LOVE AFFAIR
A sweeping tale of passion, power, conquest and extravagance on a magnificent Russian scale.
'One of the great love stories of history'
Economist

9781780228341 • £14.99 • Paperback
9780297866237 • £14.99 • Ebook

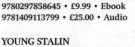

W&N
www.simonsebagmontefiore.com